Lecture Notes in Computer

1186

Edited by G. Goos, J. Hartmanis and J

Advisory Board: W. Brauer   D. Gri

Springer
Berlin
Heidelberg
New York
Barcelona
Budapest
Hong Kong
London
Milan
Paris
Santa Clara
Singapore
Tokyo

Foto Afrati
Phokion Kolaitis   (Eds.)

Database Theory – ICDT '97

6th International Conference
Delphi, Greece, January 8-10, 1997
Proceedings

 Springer

Series Editors

Gerhard Goos, Karlsruhe University, Germany

Juris Hartmanis, Cornell University, NY, USA

Jan van Leeuwen, Utrecht University, The Netherlands

Volume Editors

Foto Afrati
National Technical University of Athens
Department of Electrical and Computer Engineering
1577 73 Zographou, Athens, Greece
E-mail: afrati@softlab.ece.ntua.gr

Phokion Kolaitis
University of California, Department of Computer Science
Santa Cruz, CA 95064, USA
E-mail: kolaitis@cse.ucsc.edu

Cataloging-in-Publication data applied for

Die Deutsche Bibliothek - CIP-Einheitsaufnahme

Database theory : 6th international conference ; proceedings /
ICDT '97, Delphi, Greece, January 8 - 10, 1997. Foto Afrati ;
Phokion Kolaitis (ed.). - Berlin ; Heidelberg ; New York ;
Barcelona ; Budapest ; Hong Kong ; London ; Milan ; Paris ;
Santa Clara ; Singapore ; Tokyo : Springer, 1997
  (Lecture notes in computer science ; Vol. 1186)
  ISBN 3-540-62222-5
NE: Afrati, Foto N. [Hrsg.]; ICDT <6, 1997, Delphoi>; GT

CR Subject Classification (1991): H.2, F.1.3, F.4.1, I.2.1, H.4

ISSN 0302-9743
ISBN 3-540-62222-5 Springer-Verlag Berlin Heidelberg New York

© Springer-Verlag Berlin Heidelberg 1997
Printed in Germany

Typesetting: Camera-ready by author
SPIN 10549959   06/3142 – 5 4 3 2 1 0   Printed on acid-free paper

Στη μνήμη του Παρι Κ. Κανελλακη

To the memory of Paris C. Kanellakis

Foreword

Database research is a field of computer science where theory meets applications. Several database concepts and methods that were formerly regarded as issues of more theoretical interest are fundamental parts of today's implemented systems. Examples abound in the fields of database design, query languages, query optimization, concurrency control, statistical databases, and many others.

The papers contained in this volume were presented at ICDT'97, the 6th International Conference on Database Theory, in Delphi, Greece, January 8–10, 1997. ICDT is an international forum for research on the principles of database systems. It is organized every two years and has a tradition of being held in beautiful European sites, Rome in 1986, Bruges in 1988, Paris in 1990, Berlin in 1992, and Prague in 1995. From 1992 on, ICDT has been merged with another series of conferences on theoretical aspects of database systems, known as the Symposium on Mathematical Fundamentals of Database Systems (MFDBS). MFDBS was initiated in Dresden in 1987, and continued in Visegrad (1989) and Rostock (1991). ICDT aims to enhance the exchange of ideas and cooperation within a unified Europe and between Europe and the other continents.

ICDT'97 was organized in cooperation with:
    ACM Computer Society;
    IEEE Computer Society.

ICDT'97 was sponsored by
    National Technical University of Athens (NTUA);
    Department of Electrical and Computer Engineering of NTUA;
    Institute of Communication and Computer Systems, NTUA;
    Hellenic Telecommunications Organization (OTE);
    Greek Computer Society;
    INTRACOM Hellenic Telecommunications and Electronics Industry;
    AmeriData Global Greece Inc., a GE Capital Service Company;
    EDBT Foundation.

This volume contains 29 technical papers selected from 118 submissions. Several excellent submissions were authored solely by students. The ICDT'97 Best Student Paper Award, sponsored by the EDBT Foundation, was awarded to C. Chekuri and A. Rajaraman for their paper *Conjunctive Query Containment Revisited*. In addition to the technical papers, the conference featured the following two invited presentations: *Querying Semi-Structured Data* by Serge Abiteboul and *Information Integration Using Logical Views* by Jeff Ullman. The conference also featured a state-of-the-art tutorial on *Methods of Data Mining* by Heikki Mannila.

The members of the program committee were:

External reviews were provided by:

Silvio Salza   Francesco Scarcello   Andrea Schaerf
Marco Schaerf   Michael Schrefl   Luc Segoufin
Timos Sellis   Seppo Sippu   Kengatharan Sivalingam
Hua Nam Son   Thomas Steyvers   Markus Stumptner
Dan Suciu   Dimitri Theodoratos Matti Tikkanen
Pál Tőke   Francesca Toni   Riccardo Torlone
Markus Tresch   Heikki Tuuri   Jari Veijalainen
Helmut Veith   Scott Weinstein   Mathias Weske
Peter Widmayer Tatu Ylonen

Conference Organization Committee

Foto N. Afrati (co-chair)   Theodoros Andronikos
Isambo Karali   Theodoros Kavalieros
Ioannis Milis   Theodoros Mitakos
Kostas Petropoulos   Francesca Toni
Theodora Varvarigou (co-chair)

We wish to sincerely thank all the authors who submitted papers for consideration. We are truly grateful to all program committee members and to all external referees for their care in evaluating the submitted papers. We also wish to thank the members of the organizing committee for their efforts with the local organization of the conference. Finally, we wish to express our appreciation and gratitude to the sponsoring organizations for their assistance and support.

Originally, the ICDT'97 program committee included Paris C. Kanellakis as a member. Paris had a strong presence and involvement in previous ICDT conferences, since he had been an invited speaker, program co-chair, program committee member, and steering committee member. His tragic and untimely death in December 1995 has inflicted a great loss on our community. This volume is dedicated to his memory.

Delphi, January 1997   Foto N. Afrati and Phokion G. Kolaitis
                                        Program Co-Chairs

Table of Contents

Session 4: New Applications

Session 5: Logic and Databases II

Session 6: Concurrency Control

Session 7: Unstructured Data

Session 8: Object-Oriented Databases

Session 9: Access Methods

Session 10: Spatial Data and Bulk Data

Querying Semi-Structured Data

Serge Abiteboul*

INRIA-Rocquencourt
Serge.Abiteboul@inria.fr

1 Introduction

The amount of data of all kinds available electronically has increased dramatically in recent years. The data resides in different forms, ranging from unstructured data in file systems to highly structured in relational database systems. Data is accessible through a variety of interfaces including Web browsers, database query languages, application-specific interfaces, or data exchange formats. Some of this data is *raw* data, e.g., images or sound. Some of it has structure even if the structure is often implicit, and not as rigid or regular as that found in standard database systems. Sometimes the structure exists but has to be extracted from the data. Sometimes also it exists but we prefer to ignore it for certain purposes such as browsing. We call here *semi-structured data* this data that is (from a particular viewpoint) neither raw data nor strictly typed, i.e., not table-oriented as in a relational model or sorted-graph as in object databases.

As will seen later when the notion of semi-structured data is more precisely defined, the need for semi-structured data arises naturally in the context of data integration, even when the data sources are themselves well-structured. Although data integration is an old topic, the need to integrate a wider variety of dataformats (e.g., SGML or ASN.1 data) and data found on the Web has brought the topic of semi-structured data to the forefront of research.

The main purpose of the paper is to isolate the essential aspects of semi-structured data. We also survey some proposals of models and query languages for semi-structured data. In particular, we consider recent works at Stanford U. and U. Penn on semi-structured data. In both cases, the motivation is found in the integration of heterogeneous data. The "lightweight" data models they use (based on labelled graphs) are very similar.

As we shall see, the topic of semi-structured data has no precise boundary. Furthermore, a theory of semi-structured data is still missing. We will try to highlight some important issues in this context.

The paper is organized as follows. In Section 2, we discuss the particularities of semi-structured data. In Section 3, we consider the issue of the data structure and in Section 4, the issue of the query language.

---

* Currently visiting the Computer Science Dept., Stanford U. Work supported in part by CESDIS, NASA Goddard Space Flight Center; by the Air Force Wright Laboratory Aeronautical Systems Center under ARPA Contract F33615-93-1-1339, and by the Air Force Rome Laboratories under ARPA Contract F30602-95-C-0119.

2 Semi-Structured Data

In this section, we make more precise what we mean by semi-structured data, how such data arises, and emphasize its main aspects.

Roughly speaking, semi-structured data is data that is neither raw data, nor very strictly typed as in conventional database systems. Clearly, this definition is imprecise. For instance, would a BibTex file be considered structured or semi-structured? Indeed, the same piece of information may be viewed as unstructured at some early processing stage, but later become very structured after some analysis has been performed. In this section, we give examples of semi-structured data, make more precise this notion and describe important issues in this context.

2.1 Examples

We will often discuss in this paper BibTex files [Lam94] that present the advantage of being more familiar to researchers than other well-accepted formats such as SGML [ISO86] or ASN.1 [ISO87]. Data in BibTex files closely resembles relational data. Such a file is composed of records. But, the structure is not as regular. Some fields may be missing. (Indeed, it is customary to even find compulsory fields missing.) Other fields have some meaningful structure, e.g., author. There are complex features such as abbreviations or cross references that are not easy to describe in some database systems.

The Web also provides numerous popular examples of semi-structured data. In the Web, data consists of files in a particular format, HTML, with some structuring primitives such as tags and anchors. A typical example is a data source about restaurants in the Bay Area (from the Palo Alto Weekly newspaper), that we will call Guide. It consists of an HTML file with one entry per restaurant and provides some information on prices, addresses, styles of restaurants and reviews. Data in Guide resides in files of text with some implicit structure. One can write a parser to extract the underlying structure. However, there is a large degree of irregularity in the structure since (i) restaurants are not all treated in a uniform manner (e.g., much less information is given for fast-food joints) and (ii) information is entered as plain text by human beings that do not present the standard rigidity of your favorite data loader. Therefore, the parser will have to be tolerant and accept to fail parsing portions of text that will remain as plain text.

Also, semi-structured data arises often when integrating several (possibly structured) sources. Data integration of independent sources has been a popular topic of research since the very early days of databases. (Surveys can be found in [SL90, LMR90, Bre90], and more recent work on the integration of heterogeneous sources in e.g., [LRO96, QRS+95, C+95].) It has gained a new vigor with the recent popularity of the Web. Consider the integration of car retailer databases. Some retailers will represent addresses as strings and others as tuples. Retailers will probably use different conventions for representing dates, prices, invoices, etc. We should expect some information to be missing from some sources. (E.g., some retailers may not record whether non-automatic transmission is available).

More generally, a wide heterogeneity in the organization of data should be expected from the car retailer data sources and not all can be resolved by the integration software.

Semi-structured data arises under a variety of forms for a wide range of applications such as genome databases, scientific databases, libraries of programs and more generally, digital libraries, on-line documentations, electronic commerce. It is thus essential to better understand the issue of querying semi-structured data.

2.2 Main aspects

The structure is irregular:
This must be clear from the previous discussion. In many of these applications, the large collections that are maintained often consist of heterogeneous elements. Some elements may be incomplete. On the other hand, other elements may record extra information, e.g., annotations. Different types may be used for the same kind of information, e.g., prices may be in dollars in portions of the database and in francs in others. The same piece of information. e.g., an address, may be structured in some places as a string and in others as a tuple.

Modelling and querying such irregular structures are essential issues.

The structure is implicit:
In many applications, although a precise structuring exists, it is given implicitly. For instance, electronic documents consist often of a text and a grammar (e.g., a DTD in SGML). The parsing of the document then allows one to isolate pieces of information and detect relationships between them. However, the interpretation of these relationships (e.g., SGML exceptions) may be beyond the capabilities of standard database models and are left to the particular applications and specific tools. We view this structure as implicit (although specified explicitly by tags) since (i) some computation is required to obtain it (e.g., parsing) and (ii) the correspondence between the parse-tree and the logical representation of the data is not always immediate.

It is also sometimes the case, in particular for the Web, that the documents come as plain text. Some ad-hoc analysis is then needed to extract the structure. For instance, in the Guide data source, the description of restaurant is in plain text. Now, clearly, it is possible to develop some analysis tools to recognize prices, addresses, etc. and then extract the structure of the file. The issue of extracting the structure of some text (e.g., HTML) is a challenging issue.

The structure is partial:
To completely structure the data often remains an elusive goal. Parts of the data may lack structure (e.g., bitmaps); other parts may only unveil some very sketchy structure (e.g., unstructured text). Information retrieval tools may provide a limited form of structure, e.g., by computing occurrences of particular words or group of words and by classifying documents based on their content.

An application may also decide to leave large quantities of data outside the database. This data then remains unstructured from a database viewpoint. The loading of this external data, its analysis, and its integration to the database have to be performed efficiently. We may want to also use optimization techniques to only load selective portions of this data, in the style of [ACM93]. In general, the management and access of this *external data* and its interoperability with the data from the database is an important issue.

Indicative structure vs. constraining structure:
In standard database applications, a strict typing policy is enforced to protect data. We are concerned here with applications where such strict policy is often viewed as too constraining. Consider for instance the Web. A person developing a personal Web site would be reluctant to accept strict typing restrictions.

In the context of the Lore Project at Stanford, the term *data guide* was adopted to emphasize non-conventional approaches to typing found in most semi-structured data applications. A *schema* (as in conventional databases) describes a strict type that is adhered to by all data managed by the system. An update not conforming is simply rejected. On the other hand, a *data guide* provides some information about the current type of the data. It does not have to be the most accurate. (Accuracy may be traded in for simplicity.) All new data is accepted, eventually at the cost of modifying the data guide.

A-priori schema vs. a-posteriori data guide:
Traditional database systems are based on the hypothesis of a fixed schema that has to be defined prior to introducing any data. This is not the case for semi-structured data where the notion of schema is often posterior to the existence of data.

Continuing with the Web example, when all the members of an organization have a Web page, there is usually some pressure to unify the style of these home-pages, or at least agree on some minimal structure to facilitate the design of global entry-points. Indeed, it is a general pattern for large Web sources to start with a very loose structure and then acquire some structure when the need for it is felt.

Further on, we will briefly mention issues concerning data guides.

The schema is very large:
Often as a consequence of heterogeneity, the schema would typically be quite large. This is in contrast with relational databases where the schema was expected to be orders of magnitude smaller than the data. For instance, suppose that we are interested in Californian Impressionist Painters. We may find some data about these painters in many heterogeneous information sources on the Web, so the schema is probably quite large. But the data itself is not so large.

Note that as a consequence, the user is not expected to know all the details of the schema. Thus, queries over the schema are as important as standard queries over the data. Indeed, one cannot separate anymore these two aspects of queries.

The schema is ignored:
Typically, it is useful to ignore the schema for some queries that have more of a discovery nature. Such queries may consist in simply browsing through the data or searching for some string or pattern without any precise indication on where it may occur. Such searching or browsing are typically not possible with SQL-like languages. They pose new challenges: (i) the extension of the query languages; and (ii) the integration of new optimization techniques such as full-text indexing [ACC+96] or evaluation of generalized path expressions [CCM96].

The schema is rapidly evolving:
In standard database systems, the schema is viewed as almost immutable, schema updates as rare, and it is well-accepted that schema updates are very expensive.

Now, in contrast, consider the case of genome data [DOB95]. The schema is expected to change quite rapidly, at the same speed as experimental techniques are improved or novel techniques introduced. As a consequence, expressive formats such as ASN.1 or ACeDB [TMD92] were preferred to a relational or object database system approach. Indeed, the fact that schema evolves very rapidly is often given as the reason for not using database systems in applications that are managing large quantities of data. (Other reasons include the cost of database systems and the interoperability with other systems, e.g., Fortran libraries.)

In the context of semi-structured data, we have to assume that the schema is very flexible and can be updated as easily as data which poses serious challenges to database technology.

The type of data elements is eclectic:
Another aspect of semi-structured data is that the structure of a data element may depend on a point of view or on a particular phase in the data acquisition process. So, the type of a piece of information has to be more eclectic as, say in standard database systems where the structure of a record or that of an object is very precise. For instance, an object can be first a file. It may become a BibTex file after classification using a tool in the style of [TPL95]. It may then obtain *owner, creation-date*, and other fields after some information extraction phase. Finally, it could become a collection of reference objects (with complex structures) once it has been parsed. In that respect also, the notion of type is much more flexible.

This is an issue of objects with multiple roles, e.g., [ABGO93] and objects in views, e.g., [dSAD94].

The distinction between schema and data is blurred:
In standard database applications, a basic principle is the distinction between the schema (that describes the structure of the database) and data (the database instance). We already saw that many differences between schema and data disappear in the context of semi-structured data: schema updates are frequent, schema laws can be violated, the schema may be very large, the same queries/updates may address both the data and schema. Furthermore, in the context of semi-structured data, this distinction may even logically make little sense. For instance, the same classification information, e.g., the sex of a person, may be kept as data in one source (a boolean with *true* for male and *false* for female) and as type in the other (the object is of class *Male* or *Female*). We are touching here issues that dramatically complicate database design and data restructuring.

2.3 Some issues

To conclude this section, we consider a little more precisely important issues in the context of semi-structured data.

Model and languages for semi-structured data:
Which model should be used to describe semi-structured data and to manipulate this data? By languages, we mean here languages to query semi-structured data but also languages to restructure such data since restructuring is essential for instance to integrate data coming from several sources. There are two main difficulties (i) we have only a partial knowledge of the structure; and (ii) the structure is potentially "deeply nested" or even cyclic. This second point in particular defeats calculi and algebras developed in the standard database context (e.g., relational, complex value algebra) by requiring recursion. It seems that languages such as Datalog (see [Ull89, AHV94]) although they provide some form of recursion, are not completely satisfactory.

These issues will be dealt with in more details in the next two sections.

Extracting and using structure:
The general idea is, starting with data with little explicit structure, to extract structuring information and organize the data to improve performance. To continue with the bibliography example, suppose we have a number of files containing bibliography references in BibTex and other formats. We may want to extract (in a data warehousing style) the titles of the papers, lists of authors and keywords, i.e., the most frequently accessed data that can be found in every format for references, and store them in a relational database. Note that this extraction phase may be difficult if some files are structured according to formats ignored by our system. Also, issues such as duplicate elimination have to be faced. In general, the issue of recognizing an object in a particular state or within a sequence of states (for temporal data) is a challenging issue.

The relational database then contains links to pieces of information in the files, so that all data remains accessible. Such a structured layer on top of a irregular and less controlled layer of files, can provide important gains in answering the most common queries.

In general, we need tools to extract information from files including classifiers, parsers, but also software to extract cross references (e.g., within a set of HTML documents), information retrieval packages to obtain statistics on words (or groups of words) occurrences and statistics for relevance ranking and relevance feedback. More generally, one could envision the use of general purpose data mining tools to extract structuring information.

One can then use the information extracted from the files to build a structured layer above the layer of more unformed data. This structured layer references the lower data layer and yields a flexible and efficient access to the information in the lower layer to provide the benefits of standard database access methods. A similar concept is called *structured map* in [DMRA96].

More ways to use structure: the data guide
We saw that many differences with standard databases come from a very different approach to typing. We used the term *data guide* to stress the differences. A similar notion is considered in [BDFS97]. Now, since there is no schema to view as a constraint on the data, one may question the need for any kind of typing information, and for a data guide in particular. A data guide provides a computed loose description of the structure of data. For instance, in a particular

application, the data guide may say that *persons* possibly have ougoing edges labelled *name, address, hobby* and *friend,* that an *address* is either a string, but that it may have outgoing edges labelled *street,* and *zipcode.* This should be viewed as more or less accurate indications on the kind of data that is in the database at the moment.

It turns out that there are many reasons for using a data guide:

1. *graphical query language*: Graphical interfaces use the schema in very essential ways. For instance, QBE [Zlo77] would present a query frame that consists of the names of relations and their attributes. In the context of semi-structured data, one can view the data guide as an "encompassing type" that would serve the role of a type in helping the user graphically express queries or browse through the data.

2. *cooperative answer*: Consider for instance the mistyping of a label. This will probably result in a type error in a traditional database system, but not here since strict type enforcement is abandoned. Using a data guide, the system may still explain why the answer is empty (because such label is absent from the database.

3. *query optimization*: Typing information is very useful for query optimization. Even when the structure is not rigid, some knowledge about the type (e.g., presence/absence of some attributes) can prove to be essential. For instance, if the query asks for the Latex sources of some documents and the data guides indicate that some sources do not provide Latex sources, then a call to these sources can be avoided. This is also a place where the system has to show some flexibility. One of the sources may be a very structured database (e.g., relational), and the system should take advantage of that structure.

The notion of the *data guide associated to* some particular data with various degrees of accuracy, its use for expressing and evaluating queries, and its maintenance, are important directions of research.

System issues:

Although this is not the main focus of the paper, we would like to briefly list some system issues. We already mentioned the need for new query optimization techniques, and for the integration of optimization techniques from various fields (e.g., database indexes and full text indexes). Some standard database system issues such as transaction management, concurrency control or error recovery have to be reconsidered, in particular, because the notion of "data item" becomes less clear: the same piece of data may have several representations in various parts of the system, some atomic, some complex. Physical design (in particular clustering) is seriously altered in this context. Finally, it should be observed that, by nature, a lot of the data will reside outside the database. The optimization of external data access (in particular, the efficient and selective loading of file data) and the interoperability with other systems are therefore key issues.

3 Modeling Semi-Structured Data

A first fundamental issue is the choice of a model: should it be very rich and complex, or on the contrary, simple and lightweight? We will argue here that it should be *both*.

Why a lightweight model? Consider accessing data over the Internet. If we obtain new data using the Web protocol, the data will be rather unstructured at first. (Some protocols such as CORBA [OMG92] may provide a-priori more structured data.) Furthermore, if the data originates from a new source that we just discovered, it is very likely that it is structured in ways that are still unknown to our particular systems. This is because (i) the number of semantic constructs developers and researchers may possibly invent is extremely large and (ii) the standardization of a complex data model that will encompass the needs of all applications seems beyond reach.

For such novel structures discovered over the network, a *lightweight* data model is preferable. Any data can be mapped to this *exchange* model, and becomes therefore accessible without the use of specific pieces of software.

Why also a heavyweight data model? Using a lightweight model does not preclude the use of a compatible, richer model that allows the system to take advantage of particular structuring information. For instance, traditional relations with indexes will be often imported. When using such an indexed relation, ignoring the fact that this particular data is a relation and that it is indexed would be suicidal for performance.

As we mentioned in the previous section, the types of objects evolve based on our current knowledge possibly from totally unstructured to very structured, and a piece of information will often move from a very rich structure (in the system where it is maintained); to a lightweight structure when exchanged over the network; to a (possibly different) very rich structure when it has been analyzed and integrated to other pieces of information. It is thus important to dispose of a flexible model allowing both a very light and a very rich structuring of data.

In this section, we first briefly consider some components of a rich model for semi-structured data. This should be viewed as an indicative, non-exhaustive list of candidate features. In our opinion, specific models for specific application domains (e.g., Web databases or genome databases) are probably more feasible than an all-purpose model for semi-structured data. Then, we present in more details the Object Exchange Model that is pursuing a minimalist approach.

3.1 A maximalist approach

We next describe primitives that seem to be required from a semantic model to allow the description of semi-structured data. Our presentation is rather sketchy and assumes knowledge of the ODMG model. The following primitives should be considered:

1. The ODMG model: the notions of objects, classes and class hierarchy; and structuring constructs such as set, list, bag, array seem all needed in our context.
2. Null values: these are given lip service in the relational and the ODMG models and more is needed here.
3. Heterogeneous collections: collections need often to be heterogeneous in the semi-structured setting. So, there is the need for some union types as found for instance in [AH87] or [AK89].
4. Text with references: text is an important component for semi-structured information. Two important issues are (i) references to portions of a text (references and citations in LaTex), and (ii) references from the text (HTML anchors).
5. Eclectic types: the same piece of information may be viewed with various alternative structures.
6. Version and time: it is clear that we are often more concerned by querying the recent changes in some data source that in examining the entire source.

No matter how rich a model we choose, it is likely that some weird features of a given application or a particular data exchange format will not be covered (e.g., SGML exceptions). This motivates the use of an underlying minimalist data format.

3.2 A minimalist approach

In this section, we present the Object Exchange Model (OEM) [AQM+96], a data model particularly useful for representing semi-structured data.

The model consists of graph with labels on the edges. (In an early version of the model [PGMW95], labels were attached to vertices which leads to minor differences in the description of information and in the corresponding query languages.) A very similar model was independently proposed in [BDHS96]. This seems to indicate that this model indeed achieves the goals to be simple enough, and yet flexible and powerful enough to allow describing semi-structured data found in common data sources over the net. A subtle difference is that OEM is based on the notion of objects with object identity whereas [BDHS96] uses tree markers and *bisimulation*. We will ignore this distinction here.

Data represented in OEM can be thought of as a graph, with objects as the vertices and labels on the edges. Entities are represented by *objects*. Each object has a unique *object identifier* (oid) from the type oid. Some objects are atomic and contain a value from one of the disjoint basic atomic types, e.g., integer, real, string, gif, html, audio, java, etc. All other objects are complex; their value is a set of *object references*, denoted as a set of (*label, oid*) pairs. The labels are taken from the atomic type string. Figure 1 provides an example of an OEM graph.

OEM can easily model relational data, and, as in the ODMG model, hierarchical and graph data. (Although the structure in Figure 1 is *almost* a tree, there is a cycle via objects &19 and &35.) To model semi-structured information sources, we do not insist that data is as strongly structured as in standard database models. Observe that, for example, (i) restaurants have zero, one or more addresses; (ii) an address is sometimes a string and sometimes a complex structure; (iii) a zipcode may be a string or an integer; (iv) the zipcode occurs in the address for some and directly under restaurant for others; and (v) price information is sometimes given and sometimes missing.

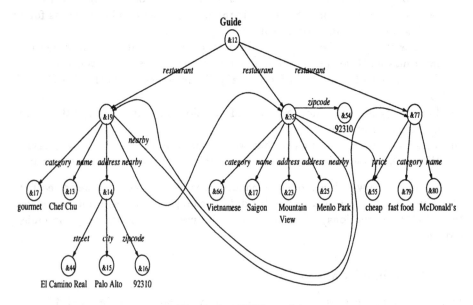

Fig. 1. An OEM graph

We conclude this section with two observations relating OEM to the relational and ODMG models:

OEM vs. relational: One can view an OEM database as a relational structure with a binary relation *VAL(oid, atomic_value)* for specifying the values of atomic objects and a ternary relation *MEMBER(oid, label, oid)* to specify the values of complex objects. This simple viewpoint seems to defeat a large part of the research on semi-structured data. However, (i) such a representation is possible *only* because of the presence of object identifiers, so we are already out of the relational model; (ii) we have to add integrity constraints to the relational structure (e.g., to prohibit dangling references); and (iii) it is often the case that we want to recover an object together with its subcomponents and this recursively, which is certainly a feature that is out of relational calculus.

OEM vs. ODMG: In the object exchange model, all objects have the same type, namely OEM. Intuitively, this type is a tuple with one field per possible label containing a set of OEM's. Based on this, it is rather straightforward to have a type system that would incorporate the ODMG types and the

OEM type (see [AQM$^+$96]). This is a first step towards a model that would integrate the minimalist and maximalist approaches.

4 Querying and Restructuring

In the context of semi-structured data, the query language has to be more flexible than in conventional database systems. Typing should be more liberal since by nature data is less regular. What should we expect from a query language?

1. standard database-style query primitives;
2. navigation in the style of hypertext or Web-style browsing;
3. searching for pattern in an information-retrieval-style [Rie79];
4. temporal queries, including querying versions or querying changes (an issue that we will ignore further on);
5. querying both the data and the type/schema in the same query as in [KL89].

Also, the language should have sound theoretical foundations, possibly a logic in the style of relational calculus. So, there is a need for more works on calculi for semi-structured data and algebraizations of these calculi.

All this requires not only revisiting the languages but also database optimization techniques, and in particular, integrating these techniques with optimization techniques from information retrieval (e.g., full text indexing) and new techniques for dealing with path expressions and more general hypertext features.

There has been a very important body of literature on query languages from various perspectives, calculus, algebra, functional, and deductive (see [Ull89, AHV94]), concerning very structured data. A number of more recent proposals concern directly semi-structured data. These are most notably Lorel [AQM$^+$96] for the OEM model and UnQL [BDHS96] for a very similar model. Although developed with different motivations, languages to query documents satisfy some of the needs of querying semi-structured data. For instance, query languages for structured documents such as OQL-doc [CACS94] and integration with information retrieval tools [ACC$^+$96, CM95] share many goals with the issues that we are considering. The work on query languages for hypertext structures, e.g., [MW95, BK90, CM89b, MW93] and query languages for the Web are relevant. In particular, query languages for the Web have attracted a lot of attention recently, e.g., W3QL [KS95] that focuses on extensibility, WebSQL [MMM96] that provides a formal semantics and introduce a notion of locality, or WebLog [LSS96] that is based on a Datalog-like syntax. A theory of queries of the Web is proposed in [AV97].

W3QL is typical from this line of works. It notably allows the use of Perl regular expressions and calls to Unix programs from the where clause of an SQL-like query, and even calls to Web browsers. This is the basis of a system that provides bridges between the database and the Web technology.

We do not provide here an extensive survey of that literature. We more modestly focus on some concepts that we believe are essential to query semi-structured data. This is considered next. Finally, we mention the issue of data restructuring.

4.1 Primitives for querying semi-structured data

In this section, we mention some recent proposals for querying semi-structured data.

Using an object approach: The notion of objects and the flexibility brought by an object approach turn out to be essential. Objects allow to focus on the portion of the structure that is relevant to the query and ignore portions of it that we (want to) ignore.

To see that, consider first the relational representation of OEM that was described in Section 3.2 and relational query languages. We can express simple queries such as *what is the address of Toto?* even when we ignore the exact structure of *person* objects, or even if all persons do not have the same structure:

```
select unique V'.2
from    persons P, MEMBER N, MEMBER A, VAL V, VAL V'
where   P = N.1 and P = A.1 and
        N.2 = "name" and N.3 = V.1 and V.2 = "Toto" and
        A.2 = "address" and A.3 = V'.1
```

assuming a unary relation *persons* contains the oid's of all persons. Observe that this is only assuming that persons have names and addresses.

In this manner, we can query semi-structured data with almost no knowledge on the underlying structure using the standard relational model. However, the expression of the query is rather awkward. Furthermore, this representation of the data results in losing the "logical clustering" of data. The description of an object (a tuple or a collection) is split into pieces, one triplet for each component. A more natural way to express the same query is:

```
Q1    select A  from persons P, P.address A
      where   "Toto" = P.name
```

This is actually the correct OQL syntax; but OQL would require *persons* to be an homogeneous set of objects, fitting the ODMG model. On the other hand, Lorel (based on OEM) would impose no restriction on the types of objects in the *persons* set and Q1 is also a correct Lorel query. In OEM, *persons* object will be allowed to have zero, one or more names and addresses. Of course, the Lorel query Q1 will retrieve only persons with a name and an address. Lorel achieves this by an extensive use of coercion.

Using coercion: A simple example of coercion is found with atomic values. Some source may record a distance in kilometers and some in miles. The system can still perform comparison using coercion from one measure to the other. For instance, a comparison $X < Y$ where X is in kilometer and Y in miles is coerced into $X < mile\_to\_km(Y)$.

The same idea of coercion can be used for structure as well. Since we can neither assume regularity nor precise knowledge of the structure, the name or address of a person may be atomic in some source, a set in other sources, and not be recorded by a third. Lorel allows one to use Q1 even in such cases. This is done by first assuming that all properties are set-valued. The empty set (denoting the absence of this property) and the singleton set (denoting a functional property) are simply special cases. The query Q1 is then transformed by coercing the equality in $P.Name = "Toto"$ into a set membership $"Toto"$ in $P.Name$.

So, the principle is to use a data model where all objects have the same interface and allow a lot of flexibility in queries. Indeed, in Lorel, all objects have the same type, OEM.

Path expressions and Patterns: The simplest use of path expressions is to concatenate attribute names as in "Guide.restaurant.address.zipcode". If Guide is a tuple, with a restaurant field that has an address field, that has a zipcode field, this is pure field extraction. But if some properties are set-valued (or all are set-valued as for OEM), we are in fact doing much more. We are traversing collections and flattening them. This is providing a powerful form of navigation in the database graph. Note that now such a path expression can be interpreted in two ways: (i) as the set of objects at the end of the paths; and (ii) as the paths themselves. Languages such as OQL-doc [CACS94] consider paths as first class citizen and even allow the use of path variables that range over concrete paths in the data graph.

Such simple path expressions can be viewed as a form of browsing. Alternatively, they can be viewed as specifying certain line patterns that have to be found in the data graph. One could also consider non-line patterns such as person { name , ss# }, possibly with variables in the style of the psi-terms [AKP93].

Extended path expressions: The notion of path expression takes its full power when we start using it in conjunction with wild cards or path variables. Intuitively, a sequence of labels describes a directed path in the data graph, or a collection of paths (because of set-valued properties). If we consider a regular expression of the alphabet of labels, it describes a (possibly infinite) set of words, so again a set of paths, i.e., the union of the paths described by each word. Indeed, this provides an alternative (much more powerful way) of describing paths.

Furthermore, recall that labels are string, so they are themselves sequences of characters. So we can use also regular expressions to describe labels. This is posing some minor syntactic problems since we need to distinguish between the regular expressions for the sequence of labels and for the sequence of characters for each label. The approach taken in Lorel is based on "wild cards". We briefly discuss it next.

To take again an example from Lorel, suppose we want to find the names and zipcodes of all "cheap" restaurants. Suppose we don't know whether the zipcode occurs as part of an address or directly as subobject of restaurants. Also, we do not know if the string "cheap" will be part of a category, price, description, or other subobject. We are still able to ask the query as follows:

```
select R.name,  R(.address)?.zipcode
from    Guide.restaurant R
where   R.% grep "cheap"
```

The "?" after *.address* means that the address is optional in the path expression. The wild-card "%" will match any label leading a subobject of restaurant. The comparison operator grep will return true if the string "cheap" appears anywhere in that subobject value. There is no equivalent query in SQL or OQL, since neither allow regular expressions or wild-cards.

This last example seems again amenable to a relational calculus translation although the use of a number of % wildcards may lead to some very intricate relational calculus equivalent, and so would the introduction of disjunction. Note that the Kleene closure in label sequences built in path expressions in [AQM+96] and OQL-doc [CACS94] takes immediately out of first order. For instance, consider the following Lorel query:

```
select t  from MyReport.#.title t
```

where "#" is a shorthand for for a sequence of arbitrary many labels. This returns the title of my report, but also the titles of the section, subsections, etc., no matter how deeply nested.

The notion of path expression is found first in [MBW80] and more recently, for instance, in [KKS92, CACS94, AQM+96]. Extended path expressions is a very powerful primitive construct that changes the languages in essential ways. The study of path expressions and their expressive power (e.g., compared to Datalog-like languages) is one of the main theoretical issues in the context of semi-structured data. The optimization of the evaluation of extended path expressions initiated in [CCM96] is also a challenging problem.

Gluing information and rest variables: As mentioned above, a difficulty for languages for semi-structured data is that collections are heterogeneous and that often the structure of their components is unknown. Returning to the *persons* example, we might want to say that we are concerned only with *persons* having a name, an address, and possibly other fields. MSL [PGMW95] uses the notion of *rest* variables to mention "possibly other fields" as for instance in:

```
res(name:X, address:Y; REST1) :- r(name:X, address:Y; REST1),
                                 Y = (city:"Palo Alto"; REST2)
```

Here r is an collection of heterogeneous tuples. The first literal in the body of the rule will unify with any tuple with a *name* and *address*. The *REST*1 variable will unify with the remaining part of the tuple. Observe that this allows filtering the tuples in r without having to specify precisely their internal structure.

This approach is in the spirit of some works in the functional programming community to allow dealing with heterogeneous records, e.g, [Wan89, CM89a, Rem91]. One of the main features is the use of extensible records that are the basis of inheritance for objects as records. However, the situation turns out to be much simpler in MSL since: (i) there is much less emphasis on typing; and

(ii) in particular, it is not assumed that a tuple has at most one *l*-component for a given label *l*.

Object identity is also used in MSL [PAGM96] to glue information coming from possibly heterogeneous various objects. For instance, the following two rules allow to merge the data from two sources using *name* as a surrogate:

```
&person(X) ( name:X, ATT:Y ) :- r1 ( name:X, ATT:Y )
&person(X) ( name:X, ATT:Y ) :- r2 ( name:X, ATT:Y )
```

Here &*person(X)* is an object identifier and *ATT* is a variable. Intuitively, for each tuple in *r1* (or *r2*) with a name field *X*, and some *ATT* field *Y*, the object &*person*(*X*) will have an *ATT* field with value *Y*. Observe the use of object identity as a substitute for specifying too precisely the structure. Because of object identity, we do not need to use a notion such as *REST* variable to capture in one rule instantiation all the necessary information.

We should observe again that these can be viewed as Datalog extensions that were introduced for practical motivations. Theoretical result in this area are still missing.

4.2 Views and restructuring

Database languages are traditionally used for *extracting* data from a database. They also serve to specify *views*. The notion of view is particularly important here since we often want to consider the same object from various perspectives or with various precisions in its structure (e.g., for the integration of heterogeneous data). We need to specify complex restructuring operations. The view technology developed for object databases can be considered here, e.g., [dSAD94]. But we dispose of much less structure to start with when defining the view and again, arbitrarily deep nesting and cycles pose new challenges.

Declarative specification of a view: Following [dSAD94], a view can be defined by specifying the following: (i) how the object population is modified by hiding some objects and creating virtual objects; and how the relationship between objects is modified by hiding and adding edges between objects, or modifying edge labels.

A simple approach consists of adding hide/create vertices/edges primitives to the language and using the core query language to specify the vertices/edges to hide and create. This would yield a syntax in the style of:

```
define view Salary with
        hide select P.salary from persons P
            where P.salary > 100K
        virtual add P.salary := "high" from persons P
            where P.salary > 100K
```

For vertex creation one could use a Skolem-based object naming [KKS92].

The declarative specification of data restructuring for semi-structured data is also studied in [ACM97].

A more procedural approach A different approach is followed in [BDHS96] in the languages UnQL and UnCAL. A first layer of UnQL allows one to ask queries and is in the style of other proposals such as OQL-doc or Lorel, e.g., it uses wild cards. The language is based on a comprehension syntax. Parts of UnQL are of a declarative flavor. On the other hand, we view the restructuring part as more procedural in essence. This opinion is clearly debatable.

A particular aspect of the language is that it allows some form of restructuring even for cyclic structures. A *traverse* construct allows one to transform a database graph while traversing it, e.g., by replacing all labels A by the label A'. This powerful operation combines tree rewriting techniques with some control obtained by a guided traversal of the graph. For instance, one could specify that the replacement occurs only if particular edge, say B, is encountered on the way from the root.

A lambda calculus for semi-structured data, called UnCAL, is also presented in [BDHS96] and the equivalence with UnQL is proven. This yields a framework for an (optimized) evaluation of UnQL queries. In particular, it is important to be able to restructure a graph by local transformations (e.g., if the graph is distributed as it is the case in the Web). The locality of some restructuring operations is exploited in [Suc96].

Acknowledgements This paper has been quite influenced by discussions on semi-structured data with many people and more particularly with Peter Buneman, Sophie Cluet, Susan Davidson, Tova Milo, Dallan Quass, Yannis Papakonstantinou, Victor Vianu and Jennifer Widom.

References

[ABGO93] A. Albano, R. Bergamini, G. Ghelli, and R. Orsini. An object data model with roles. In *VLDB*, 1993.

[ACC+96] S. Abiteboul, S. Cluet, V. Christophides, T. Milo, G. Moerkotte, and Jerome Simeon. Querying documents in object databases. Technical report, INRIA, 1996.

[ACM93] S. Abiteboul, S. Cluet, and T. Milo. Querying and updating the file. In *Proc. VLDB*, 1993.

[ACM97] S. Abiteboul, S. Cluet, and T. Milo. Correspondence and translation for heterogeneous data. In *Proc. ICDT*, 1997.

[AH87] S. Abiteboul and R. Hull. IFO: A formal semantic database model. *ACM Trans. on Database Systems*, 12:4:525–565, 1987.

[AHV94] S. Abiteboul, R. Hull, and V. Vianu. *Foundations of Databases*. Addison-Wesley, Reading-Massachusetts, 1994.

[AK89] S. Abiteboul and P. C. Kanellakis. Object identity as a query language primitive. In *Proc. ACM SIGMOD Symp. on the Management of Data*, pages 159–173, 1989. to appear in *J. ACM*.

[AKP93] Hassan Ait-Kaci and Andreas Podelski. Towards a meaning of Life. *Journal of Logic Programming*, 16(3-4), 1993.

[AQM+96] S. Abiteboul, D. Quass, J. McHugh, J. Widom, and J. Wiener. The lorel query language for semistructured data, 1996. ftp://db.stanford.edu//pub/papers/lorel96.ps.

[AV97] S. Abiteboul and V. Vianu. Querying the web. In *Proc. ICDT*, 1997.

[BDFS97] P. Buneman, S. Davidson, M. Fernandez, and D. Suciu. Adding structure to unstructured data. In *Proc. ICDT*, 1997.

[BDHS96] P. Buneman, S. Davidson, G. Hillebrand, and D. Suciu. A query language and optimization techniques for unstructured data. In *SIGMOD*, San Diego, 1996.

[BK90] C. Beeri and Y. Kornatski. A logical query language for hypertext systems. In *VLDB*, 1990.

[Bre90] Y. Breitbart. Multidatabase interoperability. *Sigmod Record*, 19(3), 1990.

[C+95] M.J. Carey et al. Towards heterogeneous multimedia information systems: The Garlic approach. In *Proc. RIDE-DOM Workshop*, 1995.

[CACS94] V. Christophides, S. Abiteboul, S. Cluet, and M. Scholl. From structured documents to novel query facilities. In *SIGMOD'94*. ACM, 1994.

[CCM96] V. Christophides, S. Cluet, and G. Moerkotte. Evaluating queries with generalized path expressions. In *SIGMOD*, Canada, June 1996.

[CM89a] Luca Cardelli and John C. Mitchell. Operations on records. In *Proceedings of the Fifth Conference on the Mathematical Foundations of Programming Semantics*. Springer Verlag, 1989.

[CM89b] Mariano P. Consens and Alberto O. Mendelzon. Expressing structural hypertext queries in graphlog. In *Proc. 2nd. ACM Conference on Hypertext*, Pittsburgh, 1989.

[CM95] M. Consens and T. Milo. Algebras for querying text regions. In *Proc. on Principles of Database Systems*, 1995.

[DMRA96] L.M.L. Delcambre, D. Maier, R. Reddy, and L. Anderson. Structured maps: Modelling explicit semantics over a universe of information, 1996. unpublished.

[DOB95] S.B. Davidson, C. Overton, and P. Buneman. Challenges in integrating biological data sources. *J. Computational Biology 2*, 1995.

[dSAD94] C. Souza dos Santos, S. Abiteboul, and C. Delobel. Virtual schemas and bases. In *Intern. Conference on Extending Database Technology*, Cambridge, 1994.

[ISO86] ISO 8879. Information processing—text and office systems—Standard Generalized Markup Language (SGML), 1986.

[ISO87] ISO. Specification of astraction syntax notation one (asn.1), 1987. Standard 8824, Information Processing System.

[KKS92] M. Kifer, W. Kim, and Y. Sagiv. Querying object-oriented databases. In *SIGMOD*, 1992.

[KL89] M. Kifer and G. Lausen. F-logic: A higher-order language for reasoning about objects. In *sigmod*, 1989.

[KS95] D. Konopnicki and O. Shmueli. W3QS: A query system for the World Wide Web. In *VLDB*, 1995.

[Lam94] L. Lamport. *Latex*. Addison-Wesley, 1994.

[LMR90] W. Litwin, L. Mark, and N. Roussopoulos. Interoperability of multiple autonomous databases. *Computing Surveys*, 22(3), 1990.

[LRO96] A. Levy, A. Rajaraman, and J.J. Ordille. Querying heterogeneous information sources using source descriptions. In *Proc. VLDB*, 1996.

[LSS96] Laks V. S. Lakshmanan, Fereidoon Sadri, and Iyer N. Subramanian. A declarative language for querying and restructuring the Web. In *RIDE*, New Orleans, February 1996. In press.

[MBW80] J. Mylopoulos, P. Bernstein, and H. Wong. A language facility for designing database-intensive applications. *ACM Trans. on Database Sys.*, 5(2), June 1980.

[MMM96] A. Mendelzohn, G. A. Mihaila, and T. Milo. Querying the world wide web, 1996. draft, available by ftp: milo@math.tau.ac.il.

[MW93] T. Minohara and R. Watanabe. Queries on structure in hypertext. In *Foundations of Data Organization and Algorithms, FODO '93*. Springer, 1993.

[MW95] A. O. Mendelzon and P. T. Wood. Finding regular simple paths in graph databases. *SIAM J. Comp.*, 24(6), 1995.

[OMG92] OMG ORBTF. *Common Object Request Broker Architecture*. Object Management Group, Framingham, MA, 1992.

[PAGM96] Y. Papakonstantinou, S. Abiteboul, and H. Garcia-Molina. Object fusion in mediator systems. In *VLDB*, Bombay, 1996.

[PGMW95] Y. Papakonstantinou, H. Garcia-Molina, and J. Widom. Object exchange across heterogeneous information sources. In *Data Engineering*, Taipei, Taiwan, 1995.

[QRS+95] D. Quass, A. Rajaraman, Y. Sagiv, J. Ullman, and J. Widom. Querying semistructured heterogeneous information. Technical report, Stanford University, December 1995. Available by anonymous ftp from db.stanford.edu.

[Rem91] D. Remy. Type inference for records in a natural extension of ml. Technical report, INRIA, 1991.

[Rie79] C.J. Van Riejsbergen. *Information retrieval*. Butterworths, London, 1979.

[SL90] A. Sheth and J. Larson. Federated database systems for managing distributed, heterogeneous, and autonomous databases. *Computing Surveys*, 22(3), 1990.

[Suc96] D. Suciu. Query decomposition and view maintenance for query languages for unstructured data. In *Proc. VLDB*, 1996.

[TMD92] J. Thierry-Mieg and R. Durbin. Syntactic definitions for the acedb data base manager. Technical report, MRC Laboratory for Molecular Biology, Cambridge, CB2 2QH, UK, 1992.

[TPL95] M. Tresch, N. Palmer, and A. Luniewski. Type classification of semistructured data. In *Proc. of Intl. Conf. on Very Large Data Bases*, 1995.

[Ull89] J.D. Ullman. *Principles of Database and Knowledge Base Systems, Volume I,II*. Computer Science Press, 1989.

[Wan89] M. Wand. Complete type inference for simple objects. In *Proceedings of Symp. on Logic in Computer Science*, 1989.

[Zlo77] M. Zloof. Query-by-example: A data base language. *IBM Systems Journal*, 16:324–343, 1977.

Information Integration Using Logical Views*

Jeffrey D. Ullman

Stanford University

Abstract. A number of ideas concerning information-integration tools can be thought of as constructing answers to queries using views that represent the capabilities of information sources. We review the formal basis of these techniques, which are closely related to containment algorithms for conjunctive queries and/or Datalog programs. Then we compare the approaches taken by AT&T Labs' "Information Manifold" and the Stanford "Tsimmis" project in these terms.

1 Theoretical Background

Before addressing information-integration issues, let us review some of the basic ideas concerning conjunctive queries, Datalog programs, and their containment. To begin, we use the logical rule notation from [Ull88].

Example 1. The following:

```
p(X,Z) :- a(X,Y) & a(Y,Z).
```

is a rule that talks about a, an *EDB predicate* ("Extensional DataBase," or stored relation), and p, an *IDB predicate* ("Intensional DataBase," or predicate whose relation is constructed by rules). In this and several other examples, it is useful to think of a as an "arc" predicate defining a graph, while other predicates define certain structures that might exist in the graph. That is, $a(X,Y)$ means there is an arc from node X to node Y. In this case, the rule says "$p(X,Z)$ is true if there is an arc from node X to node Y and also an arc from Y to Z." That is, p represents paths of length 2.

In general, there is one atom, the *head*, on the left of the "if" sign, :- and zero of more atoms, called *subgoals*, on the right side (the *body*). The head always has an IDB predicate; the subgoals can have IDB or EDB predicates. Thus, here $p(X, Z)$ is the head, while $a(X, Y)$ and $a(Y, Z)$ are subgoals.

We assume that each variable appearing in the head also appears somewhere in the body. This "safety" requirement assures that when we use a rule, we are not left with undefined variables in the head when we try to infer a fact about the head's predicate.

We also assume that atoms consist of a predicate and zero or more arguments. An argument can be either a variable or a constant. However, we exclude function symbols from arguments.

---

* This work was supported by NSF grant IRI–96–31952, ARO grant DAAH04-95-1-0192, and Air Force contract F33615-93-1-1339.

1.1 Conjunctive Queries

A *conjunctive query* (CQ) is a rule with subgoals that are assumed to have EDB predicates. A CQ is *applied* to the EDB relations by considering all possible substitutions of values for the variables in the body. If a substitution makes all the subgoals true, then the same substitution, applied to the head, is an inferred fact about the head's predicate.

Example 2. Consider Example 1, whose rule is a CQ. If $a(X, Y)$ is true exactly when there is an arc $X \rightarrow Y$ in a graph G, then a substitution for X, Y, and Z will make both subgoals true when there are arcs $X \rightarrow Y \rightarrow Z$. Thus, $p(X, Z)$ will be inferred exactly when there is a path of length 2 from X to Z in G.

A crucial question about CQ's is whether one is *contained* in another. If Q_1 and Q_2 are CQ's, we say $Q_1 \subseteq Q_2$ if for all databases (truth assignments to the EDB predicates) D, the result of applying Q_1 to D [written $Q_1(D)$] is a subset of $Q_2(D)$. Two CQ's are *equivalent* if and only if each is contained in the other. It turns out that in almost all cases, the only approach known for testing equivalence is by testing containment in both directions. Moreover, in information-integration applications, containment appears to be more fundamental than equivalence, so from here we shall concentrate on the containment test.

Conjunctive queries and their containment were first studied by Chandra and Merlin ([CM77]). Here, we shall give another test, following the approach of [R*89], because this test extends more naturally to the generalizations of the CQ-containment problem that we shall discuss. To test whether $Q_1 \subseteq Q_2$:

1. *freeze* the body of Q_1 by turning each of its subgoals into facts in the database. That is, replace each variable in the body by a distinct constant, and treat the resulting subgoals as the only tuples in the database.
2. Apply Q_2 to this *canonical* database.
3. If the frozen head of Q_1 is derived by Q_2, then $Q_1 \subseteq Q_2$. Otherwise, not; in fact the canonical database is a counterexample to the containment, since surely Q_1 derives its own frozen head from this database.

Example 3. Consider the following two CQ's:

$$Q_1: \mathtt{p(X,Z)} \; \mathtt{:-} \; \mathtt{a(X,Y)} \; \& \; \mathtt{a(Y,Z)}.$$
$$Q_2: \mathtt{p(X,Z)} \; \mathtt{:-} \; \mathtt{a(X,U)} \; \& \; \mathtt{a(V,Z)}.$$

Informally, Q_1 looks for paths of length 2, while Q_2 looks only for nodes X and Z such that X has an arc out to somewhere, and Z has an arc in from somewhere. Intuitively, we expect, $Q_1 \subseteq Q_2$, and that is indeed the case.

In this and other examples, we shall use integers starting at 0 as the constants that "freeze" the CQ, although obviously the choice of constants is irrelevant. Thus, the canonical database D constructed from Q_1 consists of the two tuples $a(0, 1)$ and $a(1, 2)$ and nothing else. The frozen head of Q_1 is $p(0, 2)$.

If we apply Q_2 to D, the substitution $X \rightarrow 0$, $U \rightarrow 1$, $V \rightarrow 1$, and $Z \rightarrow 2$ yields $p(0, 2)$ in the head of Q_2. Since this fact is the frozen head of Q_1, we have verified $Q_1 \subseteq Q_2$.

Incidentally, for this containment test and the more general tests of following subsections, the argument that it works is, in brief:

- If the test is negative, then the constructed database is a counterexample to the containment.
- If the test is positive, then there is an implied homomorphism μ from the variables of Q_2 to the variables of Q_1. We obtain μ by seeing what constant each variable X of Q_2 was mapped to in the successful application of Q_2 to the canonical database. $\mu(X)$ is the variable of Q_1 that corresponds to this constant. If we now apply Q_1 to any database D and yield a particular fact for the head, let the homomorphism from the variables of Q_1 to the database symbols that we use in this application be ν. Then μ followed by ν is a homomorphism from the variables of Q_2 to the database symbols that shows how Q_2 will yield the same head fact. This argument proves $Q_1 \subseteq Q_2$.

Containment of CQ's is NP-complete ([CM77]), although [Sar91] shows that in the common case where no predicate appears more than twice in the body, then there is a linear-time algorithm for containment.

1.2 CQ's With Negation

An important extension of CQ's is to allow negated subgoals in the body. The effect of applying a CQ to a database is as before, but now when we make a substitution of constants for variables the atoms in the negated subgoals must be false, rather than true (i.e., the negated subgoal itself must be true).

Now, the containment test is slightly more complex; it is complete for the class Π_2^p, problems that can be expressed as $\{w | (\forall x)(\exists y)\phi(w, x, y)\}$, where strings x and y are of length bounded by a polynomial function of the length of w, and ϕ is a function that can be computed in polynomial time. This test, due to Levy and Sagiv ([LS93]), involves exploring an exponential number of "canonical" databases, any one of which can provide a counterexample to the containment. Suppose we wish to test $Q_1 \subseteq Q_2$. We do the following:

1. Consider each substitution of constants for variables in the body of Q_1, allowing the same constant to be substituted for two or more variables. More precisely, consider all partitions of the variables of Q_1 and assign for each block of the partition a unique constant. Thus, we obtain a number of canonical databases $D_1, D_2, \ldots, D_k$, where k is the number of partitions of integer n, and n is the number of variables in the body of Q_1. Each D_i consists of the frozen positive subgoals of Q_1 only, not the negated subgoals.
2. For each D_i consider whether D_i makes all the subgoals of Q_1 true. Note that because the atom in a negated subgoal may happen to be in D_i, it is possible that D_i makes the body of Q_1 false.
3. For those D_i that make the body of Q_1 true, test whether any $Q_2(D_i')$ includes the frozen head of Q_1, where D_i' is any database that is a superset of D_i formed by adding other tuples that use the same set of symbols as D_i. However, D_i' may not include any tuple that is a frozen negative subgoal of Q_1. When determining what the frozen head of Q_1 is, we make the same substitution of constants for variables that yielded D_i.

4. If every D_i either makes the body of Q_1 false or yields the frozen head of Q_1 when Q_2 is applied, then $Q_1 \subseteq Q_2$. Otherwise, not.

Example 4. Let us consider the following two conjunctive queries:

$$Q_1\colon \text{p(X,Z)} \colon\text{-} \text{ a(X,Y) \& a(Y,Z) \& NOT a(X,Z).}$$
$$Q_2\colon \text{p(A,C)} \colon\text{-} \text{ a(A,B) \& a(B,C) \& NOT a(A,D).}$$

Intuitively, Q_1 looks for paths of length 2 that are not "short-circuited" by a single arc from beginning to end. Q_2 looks for paths of length 2 that start from a node A that is not a "universal source"; i.e., there is at least one node D not reachable from A by an arc.

To show $Q_1 \subseteq Q_2$ we need to consider all partitions of $\{X, Y, Z\}$. There are five of them: one that keeps all three variables separate, one that groups them all, and three that group one pair of variables. The table in Fig. 1 shows the five cases and their outcomes.

	Partition	Canonical Database	Outcome
1)	$\{X\}\{Y\}\{Z\}$	$\{a(0,1), a(1,2)\}$	both yield head $p(0,2)$
2)	$\{X, Y\}\{Z\}$	$\{a(0,0), a(0,1)\}$	Q_1 body false
3)	$\{X\}\{Y, Z\}$	$\{a(0,1), a(1,1)\}$	Q_1 body false
4)	$\{X, Z\}\{Y\}$	$\{a(0,1), a(1,0)\}$	both yield head $p(0,0)$
5)	$\{X, Y, Z\}$	$\{a(0,0)\}$	Q_1 body false

Fig. 1. The five canonical databases and their outcomes

For instance, in case (1), where all three variables are distinct, and we have arbitrarily chosen the constants 0, 1, and 2 for X, Y, and Z, respectively, the canonical database D_1 is the two positive subgoals, frozen to be $a(0,1)$ and $a(1,2)$. The frozen negative subgoal NOT $a(0,2)$ is true in this case, since $a(0,2)$ is not in D_1. Thus, Q_1 yields its own head, $p(0,2)$, and we must test that Q_2 does likewise on any database consisting of symbols 0, 1, and 2, that includes the two tuples of D_1 and does not include the tuple $a(0,2)$, the frozen negative subgoal of Q_1. If we use the substitution $A \to 0$, $B \to 1$, $C \to 2$, and $D \to 2$, then the positive subgoals become true for any such superset of D_1. The negative subgoal becomes NOT $a(0,2)$, and we have explicitly excluded $a(0,2)$ from any of these databases. We conclude that the Levy-Sagiv test holds for case (1).

Now consider case (2), where X and Y are equated and Z is different. We have chosen to use 0 for X and Y; 1 for Z. Then the canonical database for this case is D_2, consisting of the frozen positive subgoals $a(0,0)$ and $a(0,1)$. For this substitution, the negative subgoal of Q_1 becomes NOT $a(0,1)$. Since $a(0,1)$ is in D_2, this subgoal is false. Thus, for this substitution of constants for variables in Q_1, we do not even derive the head of Q_1. We need check no further in this case; the test is satisfied.

The three remaining cases must be checked as well. However, as indicated in Fig. 1, in each case either both CQ's yield the frozen head of Q_1 or Q_1 does not yield its own frozen head. Thus, the test is completely satisfied, and we conclude $Q_1 \subseteq Q_2$.

1.3   CQ's With Arithmetic Comparisons

Another important extension of CQ-containment theory is the inclusion of arithmetic comparisons as subgoals. In this regard we must consider the set of values in the database as belonging to a totally ordered set, e.g., the integers or reals. When we consider possible assignments of integer constants to the variables of conjunctive query Q_1, we may use consecutive integers, starting at 0, but now we must consider not only partitions of variables into sets of equal value, but among the blocks of the partition, we must consider the relative order of their values. The canonical database is constructed from those subgoals that have nonnegated, uninterpreted predicates only, not those with a negation or a comparison operator.

If there are negated subgoals, then we must also consider certain supersets of the canonical databases, as we did in Section 1.2. But if there are no negated subgoals, then the canonical databases alone suffice.

Example 5. Now consider the following two conjunctive queries, each of which refers to a graph in which nodes are assumed to be integers.

$$Q_1: \mathtt{p(X,Z)} \ \text{:- } \mathtt{a(X,Y)} \ \& \ \mathtt{a(Y,Z)} \ \& \ \mathtt{X<Y}.$$
$$Q_2: \mathtt{p(A,C)} \ \text{:- } \mathtt{a(A,B)} \ \& \ \mathtt{a(B,C)} \ \& \ \mathtt{A<C}.$$

Both ask for paths of length 2. But Q_1 requires that the first node be numerically less than the second, while Q_2 requires that the first node be numerically less than the third.

The number of different canonical databases is 13. We must consider the five different partitions of $\{X, Y, Z\}$, as we did in Fig. 1. However, we also have to order the blocks of each partition. For partition (1) of Fig. 1, where each variable is separate, we have 6 possible orders of the blocks. For partitions (2) through (4), where there are only two blocks, we have 2 different orders. Finally, for partition (5), with only one block, there is one order.

In this example, the containment test fails. We have only to find one of the 13 cases to show failure. For instance, consider $X = Z = 0$ and $Y = 1$. The canonical database D for this case is $\{a(0,1), a(1,0)\}$, and since $X < Y$, the body of Q_1 is true. Thus, $Q_2(D)$ must include the frozen head of Q_1, $p(0,0)$. However, no assignment of values to A, B, and C makes all three subgoals of Q_2 true, when D is the database. That is, in order to make subgoals $a(A, B)$ and $a(B, C)$ both true for D, we surely must use 0 or 1 for all of A, B, and C. Then to make $A < C$ true, we must have $A = 0$ and $C = 1$. But then, whether B is 0 or 1 we shall have in Q_2 a subgoal $a(0,0)$ or $a(1,1)$, neither of which is in D. Thus, D is a counterexample to $Q_1 \subseteq Q_2$.

The containment test for CQ's with arithmetic is from [Klug88], and [vdM92] shows that the problem of testing containment for CQ's with arithmetic comparisons is complete for Π_2^p, at least in the case of a dense domain such as the reals. [LS93] actually includes arithmetic comparisons in their work on negation, and we should note that the above technique works even if there are negated subgoals as well as arithmetic comparisons. There is a more general approach that works for any interpreted predicates, not just a predicate like $<$ or $\leq$ that forms a total order; it appears in [ZO93]. However, this technique does not include CQ's with negated subgoals.

1.4   Datalog Programs

Let us now return to the original model of rules, excluding negated subgoals and arithmetic comparisons. However, we shall now consider collections of rules, which we call a *Datalog program*. Such collections of rules have a natural, least-fixedpoint interpretation, where we start by assuming the IDB predicates have empty relations. We then use the rules to infer new IDB facts, until no more facts can be inferred. More on the semantics of Datalog, including efficient algorithms for evaluating the IDB predicates, can be found in [Ull88], [Ull89]. While we shall not discuss Datalog with negated subgoals here, because the meaning is debatable in some cases, the principal ideas are surveyed in [Ull94]. Here is an example of a Datalog program and its semantics.

Example 6. Consider the three rules:

```
1)   p(X,Z) :- q(X,Y) & b(Y,Z).
2)   q(X,Y) :- a(X,Y).
3)   q(X,Z) :- a(X,Y) & p(Y,Z).
```

Intuitively, think of a graph with two kinds of arcs: "a-arcs" and "b-arcs." Then p and q represent certain kinds of paths. Rule (1) says that a q-path followed by a b-arc is a p-path. Rule (2) says that a single a-arc is a q-path, while rule (3) says that a-arcs followed by p-paths are also q-paths. It may not be obvious what is going on, but one can prove by an easy induction that the p-paths consist of some number $n \geq 1$ of a-arcs followed by an equal number of b-arcs. A q-path is the same, except it has one fewer b-arc.

To get a feel for why this claim holds, consider a particular graph G described by the a and b EDB predicates. Then rule (2) says all the paths a are in the relation for q. We can therefore use rule (1) to infer that any path of the form ab is in the relation for p; more precisely, if there is a path from node X to node Z that follows an a-arc and then a b-arc, $p(X, Z)$ is true. Next, rule (3) tells us that any path of the form aab is a q-path; rule (1) says paths of the form $aabb$ are p-paths, and so on.

Containment questions involving Datalog programs are often harder than for CQ's. [Shm87] shows that containment of Datalog programs is undecidable, while [CV92] shows that containment of a Datalog program in a CQ is doubly exponential. However, the important case for purposes of information integration is the containment of a CQ in a Datalog program, and this question turns out to be no more complex than containment of CQ's ([R*89]).

To test whether CQ Q is contained in Datalog program P, we "freeze" the body of Q, just as we did in Section 1.1, to make a canonical database D. We then see if $P(D)$ contains the frozen head of Q. The only significant difference between containment in a CQ and containment in a Datalog program is that in the latter case we must keep applying the rules until either the head is derived, on no more IDB facts can be inferred.

Example 7. Consider the Datalog program from Example 6, which we shall call P, and the CQ Q:

```
p(A,C) :- a(A,B) & b(B,C).
```

Freezing the body of Q, we obtain the canonical database

$$D = \{a(0,1), b(1,2)\}.$$

Now, we apply P to D. Rule (2) lets us infer $q(0,1)$ from $a(0,1)$. Then, rule (1) lets us infer $p(0,2)$ from $q(0,1)$ and $b(1,2)$. Since $p(0,2)$ is the frozen head of Q, our test has concluded positively; $Q \subseteq P$.

2   Synthesizing Queries From Views

Query containment algorithms connect to information integration via a concept called "synthesizing queries from views." The idea, originally studied by [YL87] and [C*95], is suggested in Fig. 2. There are a number of "EDB" predicates, for which we use p's in Fig. 2. These predicates, which are not truly EDB predicates since they usually don't exist as physically stored relations, can be thought of as representing the basic concepts used in queries. There are also *views*, denoted by v's in Fig. 2, that represent resources that the integrator uses internally to help answer queries. Each view has a definition in terms of the EDB predicates, and we suppose here that these definitions are conjunctive queries.

2.1   Solving Queries by Views

A query Q is expressed in terms of the EDB predicates, the p's. Our problem is to find a "solution" S for the query Q. A *solution* is an expression (also a CQ in the figure) in terms of the views. In order to be a valid solution, when we replace the views in S by their definitions, we get an *expansion* query E, which must be equivalent to the original query Q. An alternative formulation of the query-synthesis problem is to ask for all solutions S whose expansion E is contained in Q (perhaps properly contained). "The solution" for Q is then the union of all these partial solutions.

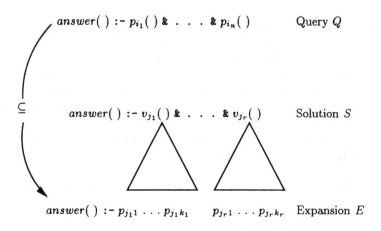

$$answer(\ ) :- p_{i_1}(\ )\ \&\ .\ .\ .\ \&\ p_{i_n}(\ ) \qquad \text{Query } Q$$

$$answer(\ ) :- v_{j_1}(\ )\ \&\ .\ .\ .\ \&\ v_{j_r}(\ ) \qquad \text{Solution } S$$

$$answer(\ ) :- p_{j_1 1} \ldots p_{j_1 k_1} \qquad p_{j_r 1} \ldots p_{j_r k_r} \qquad \text{Expansion } E$$

Fig. 2. Constructing a query from views

Example 8. We shall consider an example that illustrates some technical points, but suffers in realism for the sake of these points. Let us suppose that there is a single EDB predicate $p(X, Y)$ which we interpret to mean that Y is a parent of X. Let there be two views, defined as follows:

```
v1(Y,Z) :- p(X,Y) & p(Y,Z).
v2(X,Z) :- p(X,Y) & p(Y,Z).
```

Note that the views have the same body but different heads. The first view, v_1, actually produces a subset of the relation for p: those child-parent pairs (Y, Z) such that the child is also a parent of some individual X. The second view, v_2, produces a straightforward grandparent relation from the parent relation.

Suppose that we want to query this information system for the great grandparents of a particular individual, whom we denote by the constant 0. This query is expressed in terms of the EDB predicate p by

```
q(C) :- p(0,A) & p(A,B) & p(B,C).
```

Our problem is to find a CQ whose subgoals use only the predicates v_1 and v_2 and whose expansion is equivalent to the query above. A bit of thought tells us that

```
s1(C) :- v2(0,D) & v1(D,C).
```

is a solution. That is, if we replace each of the subgoals of s_1 by the definition of the views (being careful to use unique variables in place of those variables that appear in the bodies of the view definitions but not in the heads of those definitions), we get the expansion:

```
e1(C) :- p(0,E) & p(E,D) & p(F,D) & p(D,C).
```

We can use the CQ containment test in both directions to prove that $e_1 \equiv q$. Intuitively, the subgoal $p(F, D)$ in e_1 is superfluous, since every time there is binding for E and D that makes $p(E, D)$ true, we can bind F to the same value as E and make $p(F, D)$ true.

There are other solutions that, when expanded, are contained within q, but are not equivalent to it. Some examples are:

```
s2(C) :- v1(0,D) & v2(D,C).
s3(C) :- v1(0,D) & v1(D,E) & v1(E,C).
s4(C) :- v2(0,D) & v1(D,C) & v2(C,E).
```

Solution s_2 is equivalent to q if individual 0 has a child in the database. Otherwise, 0 cannot appear as a first component in the relation for v_1, and the result of s_2 is empty. Thus, $s_2 \subseteq q$, but not conversely. Solution s_3 is actually equivalent to s_2, while s_4 gives those great grandparents of individual 0 who are themselves grandchildren.

2.2 Minimal-Solution Theorems

It might appear from Example 8 that one can only guess potential solutions for a query and test them via CQ-containment tests. However, there are theorems that limit the search and show that the problem of expressing a query in terms of views, while NP-complete, is no worse than that. As discussed in Section 1.1, we expect that queries will be short, so NP-complete problems are unlikely to be a major bottleneck in practice.

The principal idea is that any view used in a solution must serve some function in the query; a view without a function may be deleted from the solution. For example, every subgoal of the query must be covered by some view. The question of when a view covers a query subgoal is a bit subtle, because two or more views may cover the same subgoal. For instance, consider Example 8, where both $p(E, D)$ and $p(F, D)$ from expansion e_1 "cover" $p(A, B)$ from the query. More precisely, A, E, and F may each represent a parent of individual 0, while B and D represent a parent of that parent. Note that $p(E, D)$ and $p(F, D)$ come from the expansion of $v_2(0, D)$ and $v_1(D, C)$, respectively, in solution s_1, so these two subgoals from different views each play the same role in the expansion.

Let us define a solution S for a query Q to be *minimal* if

1. $S \subseteq Q$.
2. There is no solution T for Q such that
   (a) $S \subseteq T \subseteq Q$, and
   (b) T has fewer subgoals than S.

Theorem 1. ([L*95]) *If queries are CQ's without negation, arithmetic comparisons, or constants in the body, then every minimal conjunctive-query solution for a query Q has no more subgoals (uses of views) than Q has subgoals.*

Theorem 2. ([RSU95]) *If queries are CQ's without negation or arithmetic comparisons (but with constants in the body permitted, as in Example 8), then every minimal CQ-solution for a query Q has no more subgoals than the sum of the number of subgoals and number of variables in Q.*

Both Theorems [L*95] and [RSU95] offer nondeterministic polynomial-time algorithms to find either

1. A single solution equivalent to the query Q, or
2. A set of solutions whose union is contained in Q and that contains any other solution that is contained in Q.

In each case, one searches "only" an exponential number (as a function of the length of Q) of minimal queries. If we are looking for one solution equivalent to Q, then we may stop if we find one, and we conclude there is none if we have searched all solutions of length up to the bound and found none. If we want all solutions contained in the query, then we search all up to the bound, taking those that are contained in Q.

3   Information-Integration Systems

Information integration has long been recognized as a central problem of modern database systems. While early databases were self-contained, it is now generally realized that there is great value in taking information from various sources and making them work together as a whole. Yet there are several difficult problems to be faced:

- "Legacy" databases cannot be altered just because we wish to support a new, integrating application above them.
- Databases that ostensibly deal with the same concepts may have different shades of meaning for the same term, or use different terms for the same concept.
- Information sources, such as those on the "web," may have no fixed schema or a time-varying schema.

A common integration architecture is shown in Fig. 3. Several sources are *wrapped* by software that translates between the source's local language, model, and concepts and the global concepts shared by some or all of the sources. System components, here called *mediators* ([Wie92]), obtain information from one or more components below them, which may be wrapped sources or other mediators. Mediators also provide information to components above them and to external users of the system.

In a sense, a mediator is a view of the data found in one or more sources. Data does not exist at the mediator, but one may query the mediator as if it were stored data; it is the job of the mediator to go to its sources and find the answer to the query.

Today, the components labeled "mediator" in Fig. 3 are unlikely to be true mediators, but rather *data warehouses*. If a mediator is like a view, then a warehouse is like a materialized view. That is, the warehouse holds data that is constructed from the data at the sources. The warehouse is queried directly, with

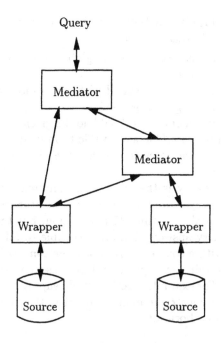

Fig. 3. Common integration architecture

no involvement by the sources. There are numerous problems associated with the design and implementation of warehouses (see [Wid95], e.g.), not the least of which is that it is difficult and/or expensive to keep the warehouse up-to-date, as the underlying data changes.

There are, however, several research projects developing true mediator capabilities, and in this section we shall introduce two of them:

1. *Information Manifold* ([K*95], [L*96a], [L*96b]), a project of AT&T Laboratories.
2. *Tsimmis* ([T96], [P96], [P*95a], [GM*95], [P*95b]), a project at Stanford University.

Both systems use logic-based technology, and while neither is based on Datalog *per se*, the operation of each can be translated into Datalog.

3.1 Information Manifold

Information Manifold (*IM*) is based on a dialect of *description logic* called CARIN ([LR96]). Description logic is a fragment of first-order logic that can almost be thought of as nonrecursive Datalog with IDB predicates restricted to be unary, although there are certain capabilities of description logic that are beyond what Datalog provides ([Bor96]). Here, we shall use Datalog in examples of the architecture of IM.

The architecture of IM is essentially that described in Section 2. The following points characterize IM in these terms:

- An IM application has a collection of "global" predicates in terms of which all queries are expressed.
- Each information source is associated with one or more views. Views are also defined in terms of the global predicates.
- However, the definition of a view should not be given the usual interpretation of "this source provides *all* facts derivable from its definition and the global predicates." Rather, the intension is that the view provides *some* of those facts.
- The solution to a query is the union of all minimal CQ's (over the views) contained in the query. Note that there could be other solutions to the query in sources not available to this IM application, but the minimal solutions provide all the query answers that are accessible to IM.
- Also associated with a source are zero or more *constraints*. A constraint is a guarantee that certain facts that might be present in the view will in truth *not* appear there. For example, a source might supply a parent-child predicate as its view, and a constraint might state that the only pairs supplied will have female children born after 1970.

Example 9. Let us consider an integrated information system about employees of a company. This example too is somewhat contrived for the sake of some technical points. In this system, the global predicates are:

1. $emp(E)$, meaning E is an employee.
2. $phone(E, P)$, meaning P is E's phone.
3. $office(E, O)$, meaning O is E's office.
4. $mgr(E, M)$, meaning M is E's manager.
5. $dept(E, D)$, meaning D is E's department.

There are three sources, each of which provides one view. The definitions of the views are:

```
v1(E,P,M) :- emp(E) & phone(E,P) & mgr(E,M).
v2(E,O,D) :- emp(E) & office(E,O) & dept(E,D).
v3(E,P)   :- emp(E) & phone(E,P) & dept(E,toy).
```

That is, the first source, which supports view v_1, gives information about employees, their phones and managers. The second source supports view v_2 and gives information about the offices and departments of employees. The third source supports view v_3 and provides the phones of employees, but only for employees in the Toy Department. Notice that the constraint department = "Toy" is enforced by the subgoal $dept(E, toy)$ in the definition of v_3. This constraint would be important if we asked a query about employees known not to be in the Toy Department; then we would know that v_3 does not appear in any minimal solution.

Also note that there is no reason to believe the phone information provided by v_1 and v_3 is consistent. Further, it is entirely possible that the information is *incomplete*; only one of these sources provides phone information, even though the employee is in the Toy Department. In fact, perhaps neither source tells us Sally's phone, even though she has a phone.

Suppose this system is asked a query: "what are Sally's phone and office?" We can express this query in terms of the global predicates as:

```
q1(P,O) :- phone(sally,P) & office(sally,O).
```

There are two minimal solutions to this query. Both use v_2 to get Sally's office, while the two solutions differ on whether v_1 or v_3 is used to get the phone. That is, the full answer to query q_1 is the union of the CQ's:

```
answer(P,O) :- v1(sally,P,M) & v2(sally,O,D).
answer(P,O) :- v3(sally,P) & v2(sally,O,D).
```

Note that the expansions of these solutions:

```
answer(P,O) :- emp(sally) & phone(sally,P) & mgr(sally,M) &
               emp(sally) & office(sally,O) & dept(sally,D).
answer(P,O) :- emp(sally) & phone(sally,P) & dept(sally,toy) &
               emp(sally) & office(sally,O) & dept(sally,D).
```

are not equivalent to q_1; they are the CQ's that come closest to q_1 while still being contained in q_1.

3.2 Tsimmis

Tsimmis, which stands for "The Stanford-IBM Manager of Multiple Information Sources," is a DARPA-funded, joint project of the Stanford database group and the IBM/Almaden database research group, although the IBM contingent has recently begun work on their own information integration project called *Garlic* ([G96]). Tsimmis follows the mediator architecture of Fig. 3, allowing us to create a hierarchy of wrappers and mediators that talk to one another. Tsimmis components talk among themselves using a data model called OEM (*Object-Exchange Model*) and a query language called MSL (*Mediator Specification Language*). MSL is also used to describe mediators and wrappers at a high level, and these components can be generated automatically from the MSL specification.

OEM. The OEM model ([P*95a]) is "object-oriented," and data is assumed to be organized into objects. An *OEM object* consists of:

1. A *label*, roughly the name of the object's class.
2. A *type* for the value of the object. The type is either an atomic type: integer, string, Java script, and so on, or it is the type "set of OEM objects."
3. A *value*, either an actual value if the object is atomic, or a set of OEM objects.

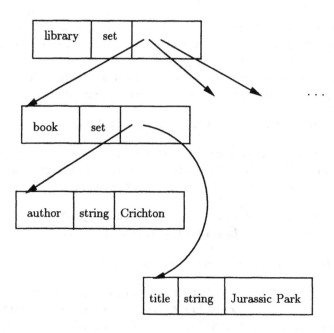

Fig. 4. An OEM object

4. An (optional) object-ID.

Example 10. Figure 4 suggests an OEM object with label **library**, whose value is a set of objects representing the documents in the library. We also see one member object, with label **book**. The value of this object is a set, and we have shown two members of that set. Both are atomic objects, one labeled **title** and having value **Jurassic Park**, and the other labeled **author** with value **Crichton**.

MSL. MSL statements are logical rules, but the rules are not exactly Datalog. Rather, MSL uses a form of object-logic, in which

- Labels and values are connected using triangular brackets, <...>.
- It is also possible to include an object-ID inside triangular brackets as an optional first component.
- Object-ID's may be constructed using function symbols, as in HiLog ([C*89]).
- Some (not necessarily all) members of a set of objects may be described by enclosing them in curly braces {...}.

Example 11. Let us reconsider Example 9, where we had three sources. Source 1 produces employee-phone-manager information, Source 2 produces employee-office-department information, and Source 3 produces employee-phone information for members of the Toy Department. Each of these sources will be assumed to export appropriate OEM objects. For example, Source 1 exports objects with atomic subobjects labeled **name**, **phone**, and **mgr**. We wish to describe, using

MSL rules, a mediator named **med** that uses these three sources and exports two types of objects:

- Employee-phone-office objects with label **epo**.
- Employee-department-manager objects with label **edm**.

Each object of these types will have subobjects with the appropriate labels. Figure 5 shows the MSL rules that describe these objects exported by **med**.

```
1)  <f(E) epo {<name E> <phone P>}>@med :-
                  <emp {<name E> <phone P>}>@source1
2)  <f(E) epo {<name E> <phone P>}>@med :-
                  <emp {<name E> <phone P>}>@source3
3)  <f(E) epo {<name E> <office O>}>@med :-
                  <emp {<name E> <office O>}>@source2

4)  <edm {<name E> <dept D> <mgr M>}>@med :-
                  <emp {<name E> <mgr M>}>@source1 AND
                  <emp {<name E> <dept D>}>@source2
```

Fig. 5. An MSL mediator-description

In this example, we have made the (unrealistic) assumption that employee names are unique. Thus, as we assemble **epo** objects for an employee named E, we use the object-ID $f(E)$, expecting that this ID is unique. Rule (1) says that whenever there is an **emp** object at Source 1 with a **name** subobject having value E and a **phone** subobject with value P, we "create" at the mediator **med** an object whose ID is $f(E)$ and whose label is **epo**. This object has a subobject with label **name** and value E and a second subobject with label **phone** and value P. Rules (2) and (3) are similar; rule (2) takes employee/phone information from Source 3, while rule (3) takes employee/office information from Source 2. Three important points are:

- Because the object-ID is specified in rules (1) through (3), whenever information about the same employee E is found in two or more sources, the subobjects implied by the heads of these rules will be combined into the value of the same object — the one with ID $f(E)$. Thus, it will be typical that employee objects will have three subobjects, with labels **name**, **phone**, and **office**. They could even have more than three subobjects. For example, Sources 1 and 3 could give different phones, so two subobjects labeled **phone** would appear. A single source could also have several phones or offices for employee E, and all of these would appear as subobjects at the mediator.
- The fact that rule (1) only mentions **name** and **phone** subobjects at Source 1 doesn't mean it will fail if there are more subobjects, e.g., a **manager** subobject. MSL only mentions subobjects it needs, allowing any other subobjects

to be present. There is even a way (the *rest-variable*) to refer to "whatever other subobjects are present."

- There is no assumption that variables like E or P are atomic. They might turn out to have sets of objects as values, and in fact different objects at the sources may have different types for values having the same label. For instance, some employees may have strings for names, while others have objects with first- and last-name subobjects.

Rule (4) in Fig. 5 follows a somewhat different philosophy in constructing the **edm** objects at **med**. Here, an object is produced only if we are successful in finding, for employee E, a department at Source 2 and a manager at Source 1. If either is missing, then there is no object for employee E at **med**. In contrast, rules (1) through (3) allow there to be an **epo** object for E if any one of the three sources mentions E. Note also that the object-ID component in the constructed sources is optional, and in rule (4) there is no need to specify an ID. Thus, the head of rule (4) has only label and value components, while the other rules have 3-component heads.

Converting MSL to Datalog. There is a way to convert MSL into completely equivalent Datalog ([P96]). We shall not go into this process, but rather give a simplification that will help us compare IM and Tsimmis.

Example 12. The following rules capture much of the content of the MSL rules in Fig. 5:

```
epo(E,P,O) :- v1(E,P,M) & v2(E,O,D).
epo(E,P,O) :- v3(E,P) & v2(E,O,D).

edm(E,D,M) :- v1(E,P,M) & v2(E,O,D).
```

Recall that v_1, v_2, and v_3 are the three views that we introduced in Example 9. They correspond to the sources 1, 2, and 3 in Example 11.

There is one important way that the rules above differ from the MSL rules in Fig. 5. We only get *epo* facts for employees such that among the three views we find both a phone and office for that employee. In contrast, as we mentioned in Example 11, the MSL rules can yield a phone without an office or vice-versa. This capability of MSL is an essential contribution to dealing with heterogeneous, often incomplete information sources.

Querying Tsimmis Mediators. When we query an MSL mediator, we are effectively querying the objects exported by the mediator. There is no notion of "global" predicates as there is in IM. Rather, we must refer to the labels (equivalent to predicates) that the mediator exports. Completion of our running example will illustrate the distinction between the Tsimmis and IM approaches.

Example 13. Again let us ask "what are Sally's phone and office?" This time, however, we ask it of the mediator **med**, whose exported objects we have represented in Datalog by the rules of Example 12. The appropriate query is thus:

```
answer(P,O) :- epo(sally,P.O).
```

MSL-generated mediators answer their queries by expanding the rules by which the mediator is defined, in order to get the same query in terms of information at the sources. In our simple example, we would replace the *epo* subgoal in the query by the bodies of the two rules that define *epo* at **med**, thus obtaining:

```
answer(P,O) :- v1(sally,P,M) & v2(sally,O,D).
answer(P,O) :- v3(sally,P) & v2(sally,O,D).
```

Notice that this expansion is identical to what IM obtained for the same query.

3.3 Comparing the IM and Tsimmis Query Processors

We should not suppose from Example 13 that the result of "equivalent" IM and Tsimmis queries are always the same, even after accounting for the difference in the underlying logics. The processes of query translation are rather different.

- IM uses the query synthesis strategy outlined in Section 2.
- IM queries are in terms of global predicates, which are translated into views.
- Tsimmis queries are in terms of predicates synthesized at a mediator. These concepts, in turn, are built from views in the IM sense, exported by the sources.
- Tsimmis uses a strategy of rule expansion to answer queries. Although the expansion can result in an exponential number of terms, the flavor of the search is different from IM's. In Tsimmis we can expand each subgoal of the query independently, using every rule whose head unifies with the subgoal.

Example 14. The following is an example of how the two systems can differ. In this example, Tsimmis appears to flounder, but we should emphasize that it is an atypical example, contrived for the sake of illustration.

Suppose we wanted to know Sally's office and department. That is:

```
q2(O,D) :- office(sally,O) & dept(sally,D).
```

Using the views of Example 9, IM would find that the only minimal solution to the query q_2 is

```
answer(O,D) :- v2(sally,O,D).
```

However, using the Tsimmis mediator **med** of Example 11, we can only express our query as:

```
q3(O,D) :- epo(sally,P,O) & edm(sally,D,M).
```

The reason for this awkwardness is that each mediator exports a specific collection of objects. We do not have the freedom to penetrate, in our query, to the terms used by the mediator's sources.

The mediator **med** would process query q_3 by expanding each subgoal. The result would be the pair of rules:

```
answer(O,D) :- v1(sally,P1,M1) & v2(sally,O,D) &
                v1(sally,P2,M2) & v2(sally,O,D).
answer(O,D) :- v3(sally,P1) & v2(sally,O,D) &
                v1(sally,P2,M) & v2(sally,O,D).
```

Of course, the MSL optimizer will eliminate redundant terms and simplify this solution. However, it cannot completely eliminate the subgoals using the irrelevant views v_1 and v_3. As a result, it produces an empty answer in the case that we do not know a phone or manager for Sally.

Let us again emphasize that the apparent failure of Tsimmis in Example 14 is due only to the fact that we contrived the mediator to export inconvenient objects. The motivation for the design of Tsimmis is that the mediators it creates may perform some very complex processing of source data to produce its exported objects. It may not be feasible to define or create objects for every conceivable query. In comparison, IM is limited in the way it can combine its sources, since it must rely on the particular search algorithm of Section 2 to combine sources.

3.4   Further Comparisons of IM and Tsimmis

In addition to the differences in query processing discussed in Section 3.3, there are a number of other ways in which IM and Tsimmis differ.

Levels of Mediation. IM is designed to have two levels: the sources and the "global mediator." In contrast, Tsimmis assumes that there is an indefinite number of levels, as the output of one mediator can be a source for a higher-level mediator. Of course, it would in principle be possible for one IM application to be a source for another. However, then we would have to wrap the first application, defining for it a fixed set of views that it exported. We thus might face the same sort of awkwardness that we explored in Example 14 in the context of Tsimmis.

Adding Sources. IM makes it quite convenient to add new sources. One must write a wrapper for the sources and define its views and constraints in terms of the global concepts. However, no change to the query-processing algorithm is needed. The new views will be used whenever they are appropriate for the query. In contrast, new Tsimmis sources not only must be wrapped, but the mediators that use them have to be redefined and their MSL definitions recompiled. The administrator of the system must figure out whether and how to use the new sources.

Semistructured Data. As we have mentioned, Tsimmis supports the notion that data does not have a fixed or uniform schema; we call such data *semistructured*. Objects with the same label, say **employee**, may have different sets of information available, and even the same information may appear with different structures in different objects. For example, some employees may be retired and have no salary subobject. Others may have an integer salary. Others may have a structured salary including base, weekly commissions, and so on. The MSL language has been designed to allow the mediator-implementor to deal with the lack of schema. The reader will find more on the important issue of handling semistructured data in [A97].

Constraints. Only IM has an explicit mechanism for describing special properties of the information that a particular source will supply and using that information in its query-processing algorithm.

Automatic Generation of Components. Tsimmis has stressed the automatic generation of both wrappers ([P*95b]) and mediators ([P96]). In a sense, IM has no need for automatic generation of mediators, since each application has one "mediator" and the query-processing algorithm it uses is the same as that of any other IM application. Tsimmis wrapper-generation technology could be used to wrap IM sources, although the difference in the models and languages (OEM/MSL versus Description Logic) makes direct adaptation impossible.

3.5 Extensions of the Query/View Model of Mediation

Both IM and Tsimmis have concentrated on conjunctive queries as the principal model of both queries and views. However, there has been some exploration in both projects of the possibility of using more powerful languages for defining views. The natural "next step" is to use recursive Datalog programs to generate infinite families of views. While describing a simple source by a finite set of views or rules is adequate, sources that support a rich query language (e.g., an SQL database) are better described by infinite families of queries.

Example 15. Suppose the source is an on-line bibliography that allows queries in which one or more properties are specified. We might describe the source by the recursive program of Fig. 6.

```
answer(X) :- book(X) and QUALS(X).

QUALS(X) :- QUALS(X) & Q(X).
QUALS(X) :- Q(X).

Q(X) :- property(X, $pname, $value).
```

Fig. 6. A recursive program generating views

There are several things we must understand about the notation in Fig. 6. First, predicates *QUALS* and *Q* are expected to be expanded in all possible ways, generating an infinite set of conjunctive queries, each of the form

```
answer(X) :- book(X) & property() &
               property() & ... & property()
```

That is, each query asks for books X that satisfy certain properties.

The variables $pname and $value are parameters that are intended to be filled in for each property, allowing the CQ to match queries in which particular properties are required to have specific values. A typical query is:

```
query(X) :- book(X) & property(X, author, crichton) &
              property(X, subject, dinosaurs).
```

The idea has been explored in the context of Tsimmis in [P*95b]. It also has been proposed as an extension to IM in [LRU96]. In each case the satisfactory incorporation of recursively generated, infinite view sets requires extending the previously known algorithms for containment of conjunctive queries and Datalog programs.

4 Conclusions

Both IM and Tsimmis offer interesting approaches to the difficult problems of information integration. Moreover, they both draw upon similar, fairly ancient ideas from database logic, such as conjunctive query containment, as well as new ideas in database theory. They differ in a number of ways, including the underlying logic, the approach to semistructured data, and the query processing algorithm. Each represents an exciting direction for further research in database systems and for the creation of a new class of information-processing tools.

Acknowledgements

Comments by Pierre Huyn, Phokion Kolaitis, Alon Levy, Yannis Papakonstantinou, Anand Rajaraman, and Shuky Sagiv are greatly appreciated.

References

[A97]   Abiteboul, S. Querying semistructured data. These proceedings.

[Bor96] Borgida, A. On the relative expressiveness of description logics and predicate logics. *Artificial Intelligence* **82**, pp. 353–367, 1996.

[CM77]   Chandra, A. K. and P. M. Merlin. Optimal implementation of conjunctive queries in relational databases. *Proc. Ninth Annual ACM Symposium on the Theory of Computing*, pp. 77–90, 1977.

[C*95]   Chaudhuri, S., R. Krishnamurthy, S. Potamianos, and K. Shim. Optimizing queries with materialized views. *Intl. Conf. on Data Engineering*, 1995.

[CV92]   Chaudhuri, S. and M. Y. Vardi. On the equivalence of datalog programs. *Proc. Eleventh ACM Symposium on Principles of Database Systems*, pp. 55–66, 1992.

[C*89]   Chen, W., M. Kifer, and D. S. Warren. HiLog: a first order semantics for higher order programming constructs. in *Second Intl. Workshop on Database Programming Languages*, Morgan-Kaufmann, San Francisco, 1989.

[GM*95]   Garcia-Molina, H., Y. Papakonstantinou, D. Quass, A. Rajaraman, Y. Sagiv, J. Ullman, and J. Widom. The TSIMMIS approach to mediation: data models and languages. Second Workshop on Next-Generation Information Technologies and Systems, Naharia, Israel, June, 1995.

[G96]   http://www-i.almaden.ibm.com/cs/showtell/garlic/Initpage.html

[K*95]   Kirk, T., A. Y. Levy, Y. Sagiv, and D. Srivastava. The Information Manifold. *AAAI Spring Symp. on Information Gathering*, 1995.

[Klug88]   Klug, A. On conjunctive queries containing inequalities. *J. ACM* **35**:1, pp. 146–160, 1988.

[L*95]   Levy, A., A. Mendelzon, Y. Sagiv, and D. Srivastava. Answering queries using views. *Proc. Fourteenth ACM Symposium on Principles of Database Systems*, pp. 113–124, 1995.

[L*96a]   Levy, A. Y., A. Rajaraman, and J. J. Ordille. Querying heterogeneous information sources using source descriptions. *Intl. Conf. on Very Large Databases*, Sept., 1996.

[L*96b]   Levy, A. Y., A. Rajaraman, and J. J. Ordille. Query answering algorithms for information agents. *13th Natl. Conf. on AI*, Aug., 1996.

[LRU96]   Levy, A. Y., A. Rajaraman, and J. D. Ullman. Answering queries using limited external processors. *Proc. Fifteenth ACM Symposium on Principles of Database Systems*, pp. 227–237, 1996.

[LR96]   Levy, A. Y. and M.-C. Rousset. CARIN: A representation language combining Horn rules and description logics. *13th European Conf. on AI*, Budapest, Aug., 1996.

[LS93]   Levy, A. Y. and Y. Sagiv. Queries independent of update. *Proc. International Conference on Very Large Data Bases*, pp. 171–181, 1993.

[P96]   Papakonstantinou, Y. Query processing in heterogeneous information sources. PhD thesis, Dept. of CS, Stanford University, 1996.

[P*95a]   Papakonstantinou Y., H. Garcia-Molina, and J. Widom. Object exchange across heterogeneous information sources. *Intl. Conf. on Data Engineering*, March, 1995.

[P*95b]   Papakonstantinou, Y., A. Gupta, H. Garcia-Molina, and J. D. Ullman. A query translation scheme for rapid implementation of wrappers. Fourth *DOOD*, Singapore, Dec., 1995.

[RSU95]   Rajaraman, A., Y. Sagiv, and J. D. Ullman. Answering queries using templates with binding patterns. *Proc. Fourteenth ACM Symposium on Principles of Database Systems*, pp. 105–112, 1995..

[R*89]   Ramakrishnan, R., Y. Sagiv, J. D. Ullman, and M. Y. Vardi. Proof tree transformation theorems and their applications. *Proc. Eighth ACM Symposium on Principles of Database Systems*, pp. 172–181, 1989.

[Sar91]   Saraiya, Y. Subtree elimination algorithms in deductive databases. Doctoral Thesis, Dept. of CS, Stanford Univ., Jan., 1991.

[Shm87]   Shmueli, O. Decidability and expressiveness aspects of logic queries. *Proc. Sixth ACM Symposium on Principles of Database Systems*, pp. 237–249, 1987.

[T96]   http://db.stanford.edu/tsimmis

[Ull88]   Ullman, J. D. *Principles of Database and Knowledge-Base Systems, Vol. I.*
           Computer Science Press, New York.

[Ull89]   Ullman, J. D. *Principles of Database and Knowledge-Base Systems, Vol. II.*
           Computer Science Press, New York.

[Ull94]   Ullman, J. D. Assigning an appropriate meaning to database logic with
           negation. in *Computers as Our Better Partners* (H. Yamada, Y. Kambayashi,
           and S. Ohta, eds.), pp. 216–225, World Scientific Press.

[vdM92]   van der Meyden, R. The complexity of querying indefinite data about linearly
           ordered domains. *Proc. Eleventh ACM Symposium on Principles of Database
           Systems*, pp. 331–345, 1992.

[Wid95]   Widom, J. Research problems in data warehousing. *Fourth Intl. Conf. on
           Information and Knowledge Management*, pp. 25–30, 1995.

[Wie92]   Wiederhold, G. Mediators in the architecture of future information systems.
           IEEE Computer **25**:3, pp. 38–49, 1992.

[YL87]   Yang, H. Z. and P. A. Larson. Query transformation for PSJ queries. *Proc.
           International Conference on Very Large Data Bases*, pp. 245–254, 1987.

[ZO93]   Zhang, X. and M. Z. Ozsoyoglu. On efficient reasoning with implication
           constraints. *Proc. Third DOOD Conference*, pp. 236–252.

Methods and Problems in Data Mining

Heikki Mannila*

Department of Computer Science
University of Helsinki,
FIN-00014 Helsinki, Finland
E-mail: `Heikki.Mannila@cs.helsinki.fi`
URL: `http://www.cs.helsinki.fi/~mannila/`

Abstract. *Knowledge discovery in databases* and *data mining* aim at semiautomatic tools for the analysis of large data sets. We consider some methods used in data mining, concentrating on levelwise search for all frequently occurring patterns. We show how this technique can be used in various applications. We also discuss possibilities for compiling data mining queries into algorithms, and look at the use of sampling in data mining. We conclude by listing several open research problems in data mining and knowledge discovery.

1 Introduction

Knowledge discovery in databases (KDD), often called data mining, aims at the discovery of useful information from large collections of data. The discovered knowledge can be rules describing properties of the data, frequently occurring patterns, clusterings of the objects in the database, etc. Current technology makes it fairly easy to collect data, but data analysis tends to be slow and expensive. There is a suspicion that there might be nuggets of useful information hiding in the masses of unanalyzed or underanalyzed data, and therefore semiautomatic methods for locating interesting information from data would be useful. Data mining has in the 1990's emerged as visible research and development area; see [11] for a recent overview of the area.

This tutorial describes some methods of data mining and also lists a variety of open problems, both in the theory of data mining and in the systems side of it. We start in Section 2 by briefly discussing the KDD process, basic data mining techniques, and listing some prominent applications.

Section 3 moves to a generic data mining algorithm, and discusses some of the architectural issues in data mining systems. Section 4 considers the specific problems of finding association rules, episodes, or keys from large data sets.

In Section 5 we consider the possibilities of specifying KDD tasks in a high level language and compiling these specifications to efficient discovery algorithms.

---

* Part of this work was done while the author was visiting the Max Planck Institut für Informatik in Saarbrücken, Germany. Work supported by the Academy of Finland and by the Alexander von Humboldt Stiftung.

Section 6 studies the use of sampling in data mining, and Section 7 considers the possibilities of representing large data sets by smaller condensed representations, Section 8 gives a list of open problems in data mining.

Before starting on the KDD process, I digress briefly to other some topics not treated in this paper. An important issue in data mining is its relationship with machine learning and statistics. I refer to [11, 31] for some discussions on this. *Visualization* of data is an important technique for obtaining useful information from large masses of data. The area is large; see [25] for an overview. Visualization can also be useful for making the discovered patterns easier to understand.

Clustering is obviously a central technique in analyzing large data collections. The literature on the area is huge, and too wide to even scratch here.

Similarity searches are often needed in data mining applications: how does one find objects that are roughly similar to the a query point. Again, the literature is vast, and we provide only two recent pointers: [4, 49].

2   The KDD process

The goal of knowledge discovery is to obtain useful knowledge from large collections of data. Such a task is inherently interactive and iterative: one cannot expect to obtain useful knowledge simply by pushing a lot of data to a black box. The user of a KDD system has to have a solid understanding of the domain in order to select the right subsets of data, suitable classes of patterns, and good criteria for interestingness of the patterns. Thus KDD systems should be seen as interactive tools, not as automatic analysis systems.

Discovering knowledge from data should therefore be seen as a process containing several steps:

1. understanding the domain,
2. preparing the data set,
3. discovering patterns (data mining),
4. postprocessing of discovered patterns, and
5. putting the results into use.

See [10] for a slightly different process model and excellent discussion.

The KDD process is necessarily iterative: the results of a data mining step can show that some changes should be made to the data set formation step, postprocessing of patterns can cause the user to look for some slightly modified types of patterns, etc. Efficient support for such iteration is one important development topic in KDD.

Prominent applications of KDD include health care data, financial applications, and scientific data [39, 30]. One of the more spectacular applications is the SKICAT system [9], which operates on 3 terabytes of image data, producing a classification of approximately 2 billion sky objects into a few classes. The task is obviously impossible to do manually. Using example classifications provided by the users, the system learns classification rules that are able to do the categorization accurately and fast.

In industry, the success of KDD is partly related to the rise of the concepts of data warehousing and on-line analytical processing (OLAP). These strategies for the storage and processing of the accumulated data in an organization have become popular in recent years. KDD and data mining can be viewed as ways of realizing some of the goals of data warehousing and OLAP.

3 A generic data mining algorithm and architecture

A fairly large class of data mining tasks can be described as the search for interesting and frequently occurring patterns from the data. That is, we are given a class $\mathcal{P}$ of patterns or sentences that describe properties of the data, and we can specify whether a pattern $p \in \mathcal{P}$ occurs frequently enough and is otherwise interesting. That is, the generic data mining task is to find the set

$$PI(d, \mathcal{P}) = \{p \in \mathcal{P} \mid p \text{ occurs sufficiently often in } d$$
$$\text{and } p \text{ is interesting}\}.$$

An alternative formalism would be to consider a language $\mathcal{L}$ of sentences and view data mining as the problem of finding the sentences in $\mathcal{L}$ that are "sufficiently true" in the data and furthermore fulfill the user's other criteria for interestingness. This point of view has either implicitly or explicitly been used in discovering integrity constraints from databases, in inductive logic programming, and in machine learning [6, 7, 26, 30, 32]; some theoretical results can be found in [37], and a suggested logical formalism in [23].

While the frequency of occurrence of a pattern or the truth of a sentence can defined rigorously, the interestingness of patterns or sentences seems much harder to specify and measure.

A general algorithm for finding $PI(d, \mathcal{P})$ is to first compute all frequent patterns by the following algorithm *Find-frequent-patterns*, and then select the interesting ones from the output.

Algorithm 1 FFP: Finding all frequent patterns. Assume that there is an ordering $<$ defined between the patterns of $\mathcal{P}$.

1. $\mathcal{C} := \{p \in \mathcal{P} \mid \text{for no } q \in \mathcal{P} \text{ we have } q < p\}$;
           $- \mathcal{C}$ contains the initial patterns from $\mathcal{P}$;
2.   **while** $\mathcal{C} \neq \emptyset$ **do**
3.   **for** each $p \in \mathcal{C}$
4.   find the number of occurrences of p in d;
5. $\mathcal{F} := \mathcal{F} \cup \{p \in \mathcal{C} \mid p \text{ is sufficiently frequent in } d\}$;
6. $\mathcal{C} := \{p \in \mathcal{P} \mid \text{all } q \in \mathcal{P} \text{ with } q < p \text{ have been considered already}$
                              $\text{and it is possible that } p \text{ is frequent}\}$;
7.   **od**;
8.   output $\mathcal{F}$.

The algorithm proceeds by first investigating the initial patterns with no predecessors in the ordering $<$. Then, the information about frequent patterns is used to generate new candidates, i.e., patterns that could be frequent on the basis of the current knowledge.

In the next section we show how this algorithm can be used to solve several data mining problems. If line 6 is instantiated differently, hill-climbing searches for best descriptions [19, 30] can also be fitted into this framework. In hill-climbing, the set C will contain only the neighbors of the current "most interesting" pattern.

The generic algorithm suggests a data mining system architecture consisting of a discovery module and a database management system. The discovery module sends queries to the database, and the database answers. The queries are typically of the form "How many objects in the database match p", where p is a possibly interesting pattern; the database answers by giving the count.

If implemented naively, this architecture leads to slow operations. To achieve anything resembling the efficiency of tailored solutions, the database management system should be able to utilize the strong similarities between the queries generated by the discovery module.

The view of data mining as locating frequently occurring and interesting patterns from data suggests that data mining can benefit from the extensive research done in the area of *combinatorial pattern matching* (CPM); see, e.g., [14]. One can even state the following *CPM principle of data mining*:

> *It is better to use complicated primitive patterns and simple logical combinations than simple primitive patterns and complex logical form.*

4 Examples

In this section we discuss three data mining problems where instantiations of the above algorithm can be used.

4.1 Association rules

Given a schema $R = \{A_1, \ldots, A_p\}$ of attributes with domain $\{0, 1\}$, and a relation r over R, an *association rule* [1] about r is an expression of the form $X \Rightarrow B$, where $X \subseteq R$ and $B \in R \setminus X$. The intuitive meaning of the rule is that if a row of the matrix r has a 1 in each column of X, then the row tends to have a 1 also in column B.

Examples of data where association rules might be applicable include the following.

- A student database at a university: rows correspond to students, columns to courses, and a 1 in entry (s, c) indicates that the student s has taken course c.
- Data collected from bar-code readers in supermarkets: columns correspond to products, and each row corresponds to the set of items purchased at one time.

- A database of publications: the rows and columns both correspond to publications, and $(p, p') = 1$ means that publication p refers to publication p'.
- A set of measurements about the behavior a system, say exchanges in a telephone network. The columns correspond to the presence or absence of certain conditions, and each row correspond to a measurement: if entry (m, c) is 1, then at measurement m condition c was present.

Given $W \subseteq R$, we denote by $s(W, r)$ the *frequency* of W in r: the fraction of rows of r that have a 1 in each column of W. The *frequency* of the rule $X \Rightarrow B$ in r is defined to be $s(X \cup \{B\}, r)$, and the *confidence* of the rule is $s(X \cup \{B\}, r)/s(X, r)$.

In the discovery of association rules, the task is to find all rules $X \Rightarrow B$ such that the frequency of the rule is at least a given threshold σ and the confidence of the rule is at least another threshold θ. In large retailing applications the number of rows might be 10^6 or even 10^8, and the number of columns around 5000. The frequency threshold σ typically is around $10^{-2} - 10^{-4}$. The confidence threshold θ can be anything from 0 to 1. From such a database one might obtain thousands or hundreds of thousands of association rules. (Of course, one has to be careful in assigning any statistical significance to findings obtained from such methods.)

Note that there is no predefined limit on the number of attributes of the left-hand side X of an association rule $X \Rightarrow B$, and B is not fixed, either; this is important so that unexpected associations are not ruled out before the processing starts. It also means that the search space of the rules has exponential size in the number of attributes of the input relation. Handling this requires some care for the algorithms, but there is a simple way of pruning the search space.

We call a subset $X \subseteq R$ *frequent* in r, if $s(X, r) \geq \sigma$. Once all frequent sets of r are known, finding the association rules is easy. Namely, for each frequent set X and each $B \in X$ verify whether the rule $X \setminus \{B\} \Rightarrow B$ has sufficiently high confidence.

How can one find all frequent sets X? This can be done in a multitude of ways [1, 2, 16, 18, 43, 48]. A typical approach [2] is to use that fact that all subsets of a frequent set are also frequent. A way of applying the framework of Algorithm *Find-frequent-patterns* is as follows.

First find all frequent sets of size 1 by reading the data once and recording the number of times each attribute A occurs. Then form *candidate* sets of size 2 by taking all pairs $\{B, C\}$ of attributes such that $\{B\}$ and $\{C\}$ both are frequent. The frequency of the candidate sets is again evaluated against the database. Once frequent sets of size 2 are known, candidate sets of size 3 can be formed; these are sets $\{B, C, D\}$ such that $\{B, C\}$, $\{B, D\}$, and $\{C, D\}$ are all frequent. This process is continued until no more candidate sets can be formed.

As an algorithm, the process is as follows.

Algorithm 2 Finding frequent sets.

1. $C := \{\{A\} \mid A \in R\}$;
2. $\mathcal{F} := \emptyset$;
3. $i := 1$;

4.   **while** $C \neq \emptyset$ **do**
5. $\mathcal{F}' :=$ the sets $X \in C$ that are frequent;
6.   add $\mathcal{F}'$ to $\mathcal{F}$;
7. $C :=$ sets Y of size $i + 1$ such that
8.   each subset W of Y of size i is frequent;
9. $i := i+1$;
10 . **od**;

The algorithm has to read the database at most $K + 1$ times, where K is the size of the largest frequent set. In the applications, K is small, typically at most 10, so the number of passes through the data is reasonable.

A modification of the above method is obtained by computing for each frequent set X the subrelation $r_X \subseteq r$ consisting of those rows $t \in r$ such that $t[A] = 1$ for all $A \in X$. Then it is easy to see that for example $r_{\{A,B,C\}} = r_{\{A,B\}} \cap r_{\{B,C\}}$. Thus the relation r_X for a set X of size k can be obtained from the relations $r_{X'}$ and $r_{X''}$, where $X' = X \setminus \{A\}$ and $X'' = X \setminus \{B\}$ for some $A, B \in X$ with $A \neq B$. This method has the advantage that rows that do not contribute to any frequent set will not be inspected more than once. For comparisons of the two approaches, see [2, 18, 43].

The algorithms described above work quite nicely on large input relations. Their running time is approximately $O(NF)$, where $N = np$ is the size of the input and F is the sum of the sizes of the sets in the candidate collection C during the operation of the algorithm [37]. This is nearly linear, and the algorithms seem to scale nicely to tens of millions of examples. Typically the only case when they fail is when the output is too large, i.e., there are too many frequent sets.

The methods for finding frequent sets are simple: they are based on one nice but simple observation (subsets of frequent sets must be frequent), and use straightforward implementation techniques.

A naive implementation of the algorithms on top of a relational database system would be easy: we need to pose to the database management system queries of the form "What is $s(\{A_1, \ldots, A_k\}, r)$?", or in SQL

    select count(*) from r t
    where $t[A_1] = 1$ and $\cdots$ and $t[A_k] = 1$

The number of such queries can be large: if there are thousands of frequent sets, there will be thousands of queries. The overhead in performing the queries on an ordinary DBMS would probably be prohibitive.

The customized algorithms described above are able to evaluate masses of such queries reasonably efficiently, for several reasons. First, all the queries are very simple, and have the same general form; thus there is no need to compile each query individually. Second, the algorithms that make repeated passes through the data evaluate a large collection of queries during a single pass. Third, the algorithm that build the relations r_X for frequent sets X use the results of previous queries to avoid looking at the whole data for each query.

Association rules are a simple formalism and they produce nice results for binary data. The basic restriction is that the relation should be sparse in the sense that there are no frequent sets that contain more than about 15 attributes. Namely, the framework of finding all association rules generates typically at least as many rules as there are frequent sets, and if there is a frequent set of size K, there will be at least 2^K frequent sets.

The information about the frequent sets can actually be used to approximate fairly accurately the confidences and supports of a far wider set of rules, including negation and disjunction [36].

4.2 Finding episodes from sequences

The basic ideas of the algorithm for finding association rules are fairly widely applicable. In this section we describe an application of the same ideas to the problem of finding repeated *episodes* in sequences of events.

Consider a sequence of events (e, t), where e is the type of the event and t is the time when the event occurred. Such data is routinely collected in, e.g., telecommunication networks, process monitoring, quality control, user interface studies, and epidemiology. There is an extensive statistical literature on how such data can be analyzed, but most methods are suited only for small numbers of event types.

For example, a telecommunications network alarm database is used to collect all the notifications about abnormal situations in the network. The number of event types is around 200, and there are 1000-10000 alarms per day [17].

As a first step in analyzing such data, one can try to find which event types occur frequently close together. Denoting by E the set of all event types, an *episode* φ is a partially ordered set of elements from E. An episode might, e.g., state that events of type A and B occur (in either order) before an event of type C.

Given an alarm sequence $r = (e_1, t_1), \ldots, (e_n, t_n)$, a *slice* r_t of r of width W consists of those events (e_i, t_i) of r such that $t \le t_i \le t + W$. An episode φ *occurs* in r_t, if there are events in r_t corresponding to the event types of φ and they occur in an order respecting the partial order of φ. An episode is *frequent*, if it occurs in sufficiently many slices of the original sequence.

How to find all episodes from a long sequence of events? Using the same idea as before, we first locate frequent episodes of size 1, then use these to generate candidate episodes of size 2, verify these against the data, generate candidate episodes of size 3, etc. The algorithm can be further improved by using incremental recognition of episodes; see [38] for details, and [35] for extensions with logical variables etc. The results are good: the algorithms are efficient, and using them one can find easily comprehensible results about the combinations of event types that occur together. See also [42] for a temporal logic approach to this area.

4.3 Finding keys or functional dependencies

The key finding problem is: given a relation r, find all minimal keys of r. It is a special case of the problem of finding the functional dependencies that hold in a given relation. Applications of the key finding problem include database design, semantic query optimization [24, 44, 46]; one can also argue that finding functional dependencies is a necessary step in some types of structure learning.

The size of an instance of the key finding problem is given by two parameters: the number of rows, and the number of columns. In the typical database applications the n, the number of rows, can be thousands or millions. The number of attributes p is typically somewhere from 5 to 50. However, for some data mining applications, p could easily be 1000.

While the problem of finding the keys of a relation is simple to state, its algorithmic properties turn out to be surprising complex. See [33, 34] for a variety of results, and Section 8 for theoretically intriguing open problems.

The algorithm for finding $PI(d, p)$ in Section 3 can straightforwardly be applied to finding the keys of a relation. The patterns are sets of attributes. A pattern $X \subseteq R$ is frequent, if X is a superkey, and the relation $<$ between patterns is the converse of set inclusion.

In the first two examples in this section algorithm *Find-frequent-patterns* produced good results. However, for finding keys this method is not particularly suitable, since the part of the pattern space that has to be inspected can be huge, as a key can be very far from the starting point in the ordering $<$. Several suggested algorithms try to jump in the subset lattice to avoid looking at all superkeys.

5   KDD queries and their compilation

Viewing data mining as computing $PI(d, p)$ is based on the methodological idea of first generating lots of rules or patterns, and then letting the user select the truly interesting ones from these. The advantage of this approach is that one does not have to go back to the data every time the user finds a new topic of interest. The disadvantage is that if the user is interested in only a very tightly specified set of rules or patterns, finding a far wider set of rules can be quite wasteful.

To make the idea of generating rules and selecting interesting ones from them work, one has to provide the user methods and tools for selecting, ordering, and grouping of rules. See [29, 30] for some work along these lines. Many data mining systems try to do the pruning of uninteresting rules while the rules are located; it seems to me that the user's needs are so hard to predict that an automatic selection of interesting patterns is not easy. Still, if the user has a fixed set of interesting attributes in mind, or otherwise has some specific knowledge of the patterns that are needed, it would be wasteful to avoid using this information.

Currently, data mining research and development consists mainly of isolated applications. One can even argue that data mining is today at the same state as data management was in the 1960's [20, 21]: then all data management applications were *ad hoc*; only the advent of the relational model and powerful query languages made it possible to develop applications fast. Consequently, data mining would need a similar theoretical framework.

The approach of computing $PI(d, \mathcal{P})$ presented in the previous section provides one possible framework. A data mining task could be given by specifying the class $\mathcal{P}$ and the interestingness predicate. That is, the user of a KDD system makes a *pattern query*. Mimicking the behavior of an ordinary DBMS, the KDD system compiles and optimizes the pattern query, and executes it by searching for the patterns that satisfy the user's specifications and have sufficient frequency in the data.

As an example, consider the simple case of mining for association rules in a course enrollment database. The user might say that he/she is interested only in rules that have the "Data Management" course on the left-hand side. This restriction can be utilized in the algorithm for finding frequent sets: only candidate sets that contain "Data Management" need to be considered.

Developing methods for such pattern queries and their optimization is currently one of the most interesting research topics in data mining. So far, even the simple techniques such as the above have not been sufficiently studied. It is not clear how far one can get by using such methods, but the possible payoff is large.

Such queries have some similarities with the strategies adopted in OLAP. The difference is mainly that OLAP is verification-driven, in the sense that the questions are fairly well fixed in advance. Data mining, on the other hand, is discovery-driven: one does not want to specify in advance what exactly is searched for.

In addition to developing query processing strategies for data mining applications, changes in the underlying storage model can also have a strong effect on the performance. A very interesting experiment in this direction is the work on the Monet database server developed at CWI in the Netherlands by Martin Kersten and others [5, 19]. The Monet system is based on the vertical partitioning of the relations: a relation with k attributes is decomposed into k relations, each with two attributes: the OID and one of the original attributes. The system is built on the extensive use of main memory, has an extensible set of basic operations, and supports shared-memory parallelism. Experiments with Monet on data mining applications have produced quite good results [18, 19].

6 Sampling

Data mining is often difficult for at least two reasons: first, there are lots of data, and second, the data is multidimensional. The hypothesis or pattern space is in most cases exponential in the number of attributes, so the multidimensionality can actually be the harder problem.

A simple way of alleviating the problems caused by the volume of data (i.e., the number of rows) is to use sampling. Even small samples can give quite good approximation to the association rules [2, 48] or functional dependencies [28] that hold in a relation. See [27] for a general analysis on the relationship between the logical form of the discovered knowledge and the sample sizes needed for discovering it.

The problem with using sampling is that the results can be wrong, with a small probability. A possibility is to first use a sample and then verify (and, if necessary, correct) the results against the whole data set. For instances of this scheme, see [28, 48]; also the generic algorithm can be modified to correspond to this approach. We give the sample-and-correct algorithm for finding functional dependencies.

Algorithm 3 Finding the keys of a relation by sampling and correcting.
Input. A relation r over schema R.
Output. The set of keys of r.
Method.

1. $s :=$ a sample of r;
2. $\mathcal{K} := keys(s)$;
3.   **while** there is a set $X \in \mathcal{K}$ such that X is not a key of r **do**
4.   add some rows $u, v \in r$ with $u[X] = v[X]$ to s;
5. $\mathcal{K} := keys(s)$;
6.   **od**;
7.   output $\mathcal{K}$.

7   Condensed representations

We remarked in Section 2 that KDD is an iterative process. Once a data mining algorithm has been used to discover potentially interesting patterns, the user often wants to view these patterns in different ways, have a look at the actual data, visualize the patterns, etc. A typical phenomenon is also that some pattern p looks interesting, and the user wants to evaluate other patterns that closely resemble p. In implementing such queries, caching of previous results is obviously useful. Still, having to go back to the original data each time the user wants some more information seems somewhat wasteful. Similarly, in the generic data mining algorithm presented in Section 3 the frequency and interestingness of each pattern are verified against the database. It would be faster to look at some sort of short representation of the data.

Given a data collection $d \in \mathcal{D}$, and a class of patterns $\mathcal{P}$, a *condensed representation* for d and $\mathcal{P}$ is a data structure that makes it possible to answer queries of the form "How many times does $p \in \mathcal{P}$ occur in d" approximately correctly and more efficiently than by looking at d itself.

A simple example of a condensed representation is obtained by taking a sample from the data: by counting the occurrences of the pattern in the sample, one gets an approximation of the number of occurrences in the original data. Another, less obvious example is given by the collection of frequent sets of a 0-1 valued relation [36]: the collection of frequent sets can be used to give approximate answers to arbitrary boolean queries about the data, even though the frequent sets represent only conjunctive concepts. The data cube [15] can also be viewed as a condensed representation for a class of queries. Similarly, in computational geometry the notion of an ε-approximation [41] is closely related.

Developing condensed representations for various classes of patterns seems a promising way of improving the effectiveness of data mining algorithms. Whether this approach is generally useful is still open.

8 Open problems

Data mining is an applied field, and research in the area seems to succeed best when done in cooperation with the appliers. Hence I am a little hesitant to offer a list of research questions or open problems; on the other hand, it seems to me that such a list gives a reasonable sample of the research issues in the area.

Thus, this section contains a list of research topics in data mining that I consider interesting or important. The problems are very varying, from architectural issues to specific algorithmic questions. For brevity, the descriptions are quite succinct, and I also provide only a couple of references.

Framework and general theory

1. Develop a general theory of data mining. Possible starting points are [6, 7, 23, 26, 30, 37]. (One might call this *the theory of inductive databases.*)
2. What is the relationship between the logical form of sentences to be discovered and the computational complexity of the discovery task? (The issue of logical form vs. sample size is considered in [27].)
3. Prove or disprove the CPM principle (Section 3).
4. What can be said about the performance of Algorithm 3 and its analogues for other problems?
5. How useful is the concept of condensed representation? [36]

System and language issues

6. What is a good architecture of a data mining system? How should a database management system and the search modules be connected? [19, 3]
7. Develop a language for expressing KDD queries and techniques for optimizing such queries. Some suggestions are given in [22, 45, 40].
8. A subproblem of the previous one: how can caching strategies help in processing sequences of related queries? [19]
9. Extend the association rule framework to handle attributes with continuous values. (Some partial solutions to this problem are given in [12, 13, 47].)
10. Investigate the usefulness of temporal databases in the mining of event sequence data.
11. Develop tools for selecting, grouping, and visualizing discovered knowledge [29, 30]. How can background knowledge be used?

Algorithmic open problems

12. Design an algorithm for the key finding problem that works in polynomial time with respect to the size of the output and the number of attributes, and in subquadratic time in the number of rows. Solutions to the two following problems would imply considerable progress for this problem.

13. Finding the keys of a relation contains as a subproblem the problem of finding transversals of hypergraphs [33, 8, 36]. Given a hypergraph $\mathcal{H}$, can the set $Tr(\mathcal{H})$ of its transversals be computed in time polynomial in $|\mathcal{H}|$ and $|Tr(\mathcal{H})|$?

14. When one reduces the problem of finding keys to transversals of hypergraphs, one has to solve the following preliminary problem. Given a relation r over schema R and two rows $u, v \in r$, denote $ag(u, v) = \{A \in R \mid u[A] = v[A]\}$, and let $disag(u, v) = R \backslash ag(u, v)$. Denote $ag(r) = \{ag(u, v) \mid u, v \in r, u \neq v\}$, and $disag(r) = \{disag(u, v) \mid u, v \in r, u \neq v\}$. Further, let $maxag(r)$ be the collection of maximal elements of $ag(r)$ and $mindisag(r)$ the collection of minimal elements of $disag(r)$. Given a relation r, compute $mindisag(r)$ in time $O(q(|mindisag(r)|)f(|r|))$, where q is a polynomial and $f = o(|r|^2)$.

15. In the analysis of event sequences, patterns are typically subsequences. Given a sequence $s = a_1 \cdots a_n$, a pattern $p = b_1 \cdots b_k$ and a window width W, decide in $o(nk)$ time whether p occurs as a subsequence in s within a window of width W, i.e., whether there are indices $1 \leq i_1 < i_2 < \cdots < i_k \leq n$ such that $i_k - i_1 \leq W$ and for all $j = 1, \ldots, k$ we have $a_{i_j} = b_j$. [38, 35] (The solution should work for very large alphabets.)

Acknowledgements

Comments from Dimitrios Gunopulos and Hannu Toivonen are gratefully acknowledged.

References

1. R. Agrawal, T. Imielinski, and A. Swami. Mining association rules between sets of items in large databases. In *Proceedings of ACM SIGMOD Conference on Management of Data (SIGMOD'93)*, pages 207 – 216, May 1993.

2. R. Agrawal, H. Mannila, R. Srikant, H. Toivonen, and A. I. Verkamo. Fast discovery of association rules. In U. M. Fayyad, G. Piatetsky-Shapiro, P. Smyth, and R. Uthurusamy, editors, *Advances in Knowledge Discovery and Data Mining*, pages 307 – 328. AAAI Press, Menlo Park, CA, 1996.

3. R. Agrawal and K. Shim. Developing tightly-coupled data mining applications on a relational database system. In *Proc. of the 2nd Int'l Conference on Knowledge Discovery in Databases and Data Mining*, pages 287–290, 1996.

4. S. Berchtold, D. A. Keim, and H. P. Kriegel. The X-tree: An index structure for high-dimensional data. In *Proceedings of the 22nd International Conference on Very Large Data Bases (VLDB'96)*, pages 28–29, Mumbay, India, 1996. Morgan Kaufmann.

5. P. A. Boncz, W. Quak, and M. L. Kersten. Monet and its geographical extensions: a novel approach to high-performance GIS processing. In P. M. G. Apers, M. Bouzeghoub, and G. Gardarin, editors, *Advances in Database Technology - EDBT'96*, pages 147–166, 1996.

6. L. De Raedt and M. Bruynooghe. A theory of clausal discovery. In *Proceedings of the Thirteenth International Joint Conference on Artificial Intelligence (IJCAI-93)*, pages 1058 – 1053, Chambéry, France, 1993. Morgan Kaufmann.

7. L. De Raedt and S. Džeroski. First-order *jk*-clausal theories are PAC-learnable. *Artificial Intelligence*, 70:375 – 392, 1994.

8. T. Eiter and G. Gottlob. Identifying the minimal transversals of a hypergraph and related problems. *SIAM Journal on Computing*, 24(6):1278 – 1304, Dec. 1995.

9. U. M. Fayyad, S. G. Djorgovski, and N. Weir. Automating the analysis and cataloging of sky surveys. In U. M. Fayyad, G. Piatetsky-Shapiro, P. Smyth, and R. Uthurusamy, editors, *Advances in Knowledge Discovery and Data Mining*, pages 471 – 494. AAAI Press, Menlo Park, CA, 1996.

10. U. M. Fayyad, G. Piatetsky-Shapiro, and P. Smyth. From data mining to knowledge discovery: An overview. In U. M. Fayyad, G. Piatetsky-Shapiro, P. Smyth, and R. Uthurusamy, editors, *Advances in Knowledge Discovery and Data Mining*, pages 1 –34. AAAI Press, Menlo Park, CA, 1996.

11. U. M. Fayyad, G. Piatetsky-Shapiro, P. Smyth, and R. Uthurusamy, editors. *Advances in Knowledge Discovery and Data Mining*. AAAI Press, Menlo Park, CA, 1996.

12. T. Fukuda et al. Data mining using two-dimensional optimized association rules: Scheme, algorithms, visualization. In *Proceedings of ACM SIGMOD Conference on Management of Data (SIGMOD'96)*, pages 13–23, 1996.

13. T. Fukuda et al. Mining optimized association rules for numeric attributes. In *Proceedings of the Fifteenth ACM SIGACT-SIGMOD-SIGART Symposium on Principles of Database Systems (PODS'96)*, 1996.

14. Z. Galil and E. Ukkonen, editors. *6th Annual Symposium on Combinatorial Pattern Matching (CPM 95)*, volume 937 of *Lecture Notes in Computer Science*, Berlin, 1995. Springer.

15. J. Gray, A. Bosworth, A. Layman, and H. Pirahesh. Data Cube: A relational aggregation operator generalizing group-by, cross-tab, and sub-totals. In *12th International Conference on Data Engineering (ICDE'96)*, pages 152 – 159, New Orleans, Louisiana, Feb. 1996.

16. J. Han and Y. Fu. Discovery of multiple-level association rules from large databases. In *Proceedings of the 21st International Conference on Very Large Data Bases (VLDB'95)*, pages 420 – 431, Zurich, Swizerland, 1995.

17. K. Hätönen, M. Klemettinen, H. Mannila, P. Ronkainen, and H. Toivonen. Knowledge discovery from telecommunication network alarm databases. In *12th International Conference on Data Engineering (ICDE'96)*, pages 115 – 122, New Orleans, Louisiana, Feb. 1996.

18. M. Holsheimer, M. Kersten, H. Mannila, and H. Toivonen. A perspective on databases and data mining. In *Proceedings of the First International Conference on Knowledge Discovery and Data Mining (KDD'95)*, pages 150 – 155, Montreal, Canada, Aug. 1995.

19. M. Holsheimer, M. Kersten, and A. Siebes. Data surveyor: Searching the nuggets in parallel. In U. M. Fayyad, G. Piatetsky-Shapiro, P. Smyth, and R. Uthurusamy, editors, *Advances in Knowledge Discovery and Data Mining*, pages 447 – 467. AAAI Press, Menlo Park, CA, 1996.

20. T. Imielinski. A database view on data mining. Invited talk at the KDD'95 conference.

21. T. Imielinski and H. Mannila. Database mining: a new frontier. *Communications of the ACM*, 1996. To appear.

22. T. Imielinski and A. Virmani. M-sql: Query language for database mining. Technical report, Rutgers University, January 1996.

23. M. Jaeger, H. Mannila, and E. Weydert. Data mining as selective theory extraction in probabilistic logic. In R. Ng, editor, *SIGMOD'96 Data Mining Workshop, The University of British Columbia, Department of Computer Science, TR 96-08*, pages 41–46, 1996.

24. M. Kantola, H. Mannila, K.-J. Räihä, and H. Siirtola. Discovering functional and inclusion dependencies in relational databases. *International Journal of Intelligent Systems*, 7(7):591 – 607, Sept. 1992.

25. D. Keim and H. Kriegel. Visualization techniques for mining large databases: A comparison. *IEEE Transactions on Knowledge and Data Engineering*, 1996. to appear.

26. J.-U. Kietz and S. Wrobel. Controlling the complexity of learning in logic through syntactic and task-oriented models. In S. Muggleton, editor, *Inductive Logic Programming*, pages 335 – 359. Academic Press, London, 1992.

27. J. Kivinen and H. Mannila. The power of sampling in knowledge discovery. In *Proceedings of the Thirteenth ACM SIGACT-SIGMOD-SIGART Symposium on Principles of Database Systems (PODS'94)*, pages 77 – 85, Minneapolis, MN, May 1994.

28. J. Kivinen and H. Mannila. Approximate dependency inference from relations. *Theoretical Computer Science*, 149(1):129 – 149, 1995.

29. M. Klemettinen, H. Mannila, P. Ronkainen, H. Toivonen, and A. I. Verkamo. Finding interesting rules from large sets of discovered association rules. In *Proceedings of the Third International Conference on Information and Knowledge Management (CIKM'94)*, pages 401 – 407, Gaithersburg, MD, Nov. 1994. ACM.

30. W. Kloesgen. Efficient discovery of interesting statements in databases. *Journal of Intelligent Information Systems*, 4(1):53 – 69, 1995.

31. H. Mannila. Data mining: machine learning, statistics, and databases. In *Proceedings of the 8th International Conference on Scientific and Statistical Database Management, Stockholm*, pages 1–6, 1996.

32. H. Mannila and K.-J. Räihä. Design by example: An application of Armstrong relations. *Journal of Computer and System Sciences*, 33(2):126 – 141, 1986.

33. H. Mannila and K.-J. Räihä. *Design of Relational Databases*. Addison-Wesley Publishing Company, Wokingham, UK, 1992.

34. H. Mannila and K.-J. Räihä. On the complexity of dependency inference. *Discrete Applied Mathematics*, 40:237 – 243, 1992.

35. H. Mannila and H. Toivonen. Discovering generalized episodes using minimal occurrences. In *Proceedings of the Second International Conference on Knowledge Discovery and Data Mining (KDD'96)*, pages 146 – 151, Portland, Oregon, Aug. 1996. AAAI Press.

36. H. Mannila and H. Toivonen. Multiple uses of frequent sets and condensed representations. In *Proceedings of the Second International Conference on Knowledge Discovery and Data Mining (KDD'96)*, pages 189 – 194, Portland, Oregon, Aug. 1996. AAAI Press.

37. H. Mannila and H. Toivonen. On an algorithm for finding all interesting sentences. In *Cybernetics and Systems, Volume II, The Thirteenth European Meeting on Cybernetics and Systems Research*, pages 973 – 978, Vienna, Austria, Apr. 1996.

38. H. Mannila, H. Toivonen, and A. I. Verkamo. Discovering frequent episodes in sequences. In *Proceedings of the First International Conference on Knowledge Discovery and Data Mining (KDD'95)*, pages 210 – 215, Montreal, Canada, Aug. 1995.

39. C. J. Matheus, G. Piatetsky-Shapiro, and D. McNeill. Selecting and reporting what is interesting. In U. M. Fayyad, G. Piatetsky-Shapiro, P. Smyth, and R. Uthurusamy, editors, *Advances in Knowledge Discovery and Data Mining*, pages 495 – 515. AAAI Press, Menlo Park, CA, 1996.

40. R. Meo, G. Psaila, and S. Ceri. A new SQL-like operator for mining association rules. In *Proceedings of the 22nd International Conference on Very Large Data Bases (VLDB'96)*, 1996. To appear.

41. K. Mulmuley. *Computational Geometry: An Introduction Through Randomized Algorithms*. Prentice Hall, New York, 1993.

42. B. Padmanabhan and A. Tuzhilin. Pattern discovery in temporal databases: A temporal logic approach. In *Proceedings of the Second International Conference on Knowledge Discovery and Data Mining (KDD'96)*, pages 351–354, 1996.

43. A. Savasere, E. Omiecinski, and S. Navathe. An efficient algorithm for mining association rules in large databases. In *Proceedings of the 21st International Conference on Very Large Data Bases (VLDB'95)*, pages 432 – 444, Zurich, Swizerland, 1995.

44. J. Schlimmer. Using learned dependencies to automatically construct sufficient and sensible editing views. In *Knowledge Discovery in Databases, Papers from the 1993 AAAI Workshop (KDD'93)*, pages 186 – 196, Washington, D.C., 1993.

45. W. Shen, K. Ong, B. Mitbander, and C. Zaniolo. Metaqueries for data mining. In U. M. Fayyad, G. Piatetsky-Shapiro, P. Smyth, and R. Uthurusamy, editors, *Advances in Knowledge Discovery and Data Mining*, pages 375–398. AAAI Press, Menlo Park, CA, 1996.

46. M. Siegel. Automatic rule derivation for semantic query optimization. Technical Report BUCS Tech Report # 86-013, Boston University, Computer Science Department, Dec. 1986.

47. R. Srikant and R. Agrawal. Mining quantitative association rules in large relational tables. In *Proceedings of ACM SIGMOD Conference on Management of Data (SIGMOD'96)*, pages 1–12, Montreal, Canada, 1996.

48. H. Toivonen. Sampling large databases for association rules. In *Proceedings of the 22nd International Conference on Very Large Data Bases (VLDB'96)*, pages 134 – 145, Mumbay, India, Sept. 1996. Morgan Kaufmann.

49. D. A. White and R. Jain. Algorithms and strategies for similarity retrieval. Technical Report VCL-96-101, Visual Computing Laboratory, University of California, San Diego, 9500 Gilman Drive, Mail Code 0407, La Jolla, CA 92093-0407, July 1996.

Conjunctive Query Containment Revisited

(Extended Abstract)

Chandra Chekuri*
Anand Rajaraman**

Department of Computer Science, Stanford University

Abstract. We consider the problems of conjunctive query containment and minimization, which are known to be NP-complete, and show that these problems can be solved in polynomial time for the class of *acyclic queries*. We then generalize the notion of acyclicity and define a parameter called *query width* that captures the "degree of cyclicity" of a query: in particular, a query is acyclic if and only if its query width is 1. We give algorithms for containment and minimization that run in time polynomial in n^k, where n is the input size and k is the query width. These algorithms naturally generalize those for acyclic queries, and are of practical significance because many queries have small query width compared to their sizes. We show that we can obtain good bounds on the query width of Q using the *treewidth* of the incidence graph of Q. Finally, we apply our containment algorithm to the practically important problem of finding equivalent rewritings of a query using a set of materialized views.

1 Introduction

Testing query containment and equivalence are fundamental problems of database theory, and are central to global query optimization in database systems. Conjunctive queries are an important class of database queries, equivalent in expressive power to SPJ queries in the relational algebra. We consider the classical problem of testing containment of conjunctive queries. The problem is well-known to be NP-complete [CM77]. In view of its practical significance, considerable attention has been devoted to finding classes of conjunctive queries that admit polynomial-time time algorithms for equivalence and minimization [ASU79a, ASU79b, JK83]. *Acyclic queries* have been extensively studied in the context of query optimization in distributed database systems, and are well-known to have desirable algorithmic properties [Yan81].

In this paper, we first present polynomial-time algorithms to test the containment of an arbitrary conjunctive query in an acyclic query and to minimize

---

* Email: chekuri@cs.stanford.edu. Supported by NSF Award CCR-9357849, with matching funds from IBM, Mitsubishi, Schlumberger Foundation, Shell Foundation, and Xerox Corporation.

** E-mail: anand@cs.stanford.edu. Supported by NSF grant IRI-92-23405, ARO grant DAAH04-95-1-0192, and USAF contract F33615-93-1-1339.

an acyclic query. We then introduce a new parameter of a query called the *query width*, and show that the acyclic queries are precisely the class of queries with query width 1. We generalize the query containment and minimization algorithms to arbitrary queries such that their running time is polynomial in n^k, where n is the input size and k is the query width. These results are significant not only because they naturally generalize the algorithms for acyclic queries, but also because most commonly encountered queries have small query width compared to their sizes. We relate query width to *treewidth*, an extensively studied graph-theoretic parameter, and show that we can obtain good bounds on the query width from the treewidth of the *incidence graph* of the query.

There are close connections between query containment and the problem of answering queries using materialized views [LMSS95]. This problem has recently received considerable attention because of its numerous applications, which include speeding up query evaluation, querying heterogeneous information sources, mobile computing, and maintaining physical data indepedendence ([LMSS95] provides references). For example, the Information Manifold project [LRO96] represents the contents of heterogeneous information sources as views on a common set of base relations. A query Q is "solved" by a program that uses the views to obtain information from the sources.

We consider in this paper the problem of finding an equivalent rewriting of a conjunctive query Q using a set of views $\mathcal{V}$ defined by conjunctive queries, when Q does not use repeated predicates, and show how our algorithms for query containment can be modified for this problem. A restricted variant of this problem, where neither Q nor the views in $\mathcal{V}$ use repeated predicates, is known to be NP-complete [LMSS95].

This paper is organized as follows. Section 2 presents the basic definitions and defines the problems we consider. Section 3 introduces acyclicity, query width, and treewidth, and describes how these concepts relate to one another. In Section 4 we present our algorithms for query containment, and in Section 5 we modify these algorithms to obtain algorithms for answering queries using views. Section 6 describes related work, and Section 7 concludes by describing some open problems.

2   Preliminaries

We assume a fixed set of predicates, called the *database predicates*, over which queries are posed and views are defined. All queries in this paper are *conjunctive queries*, defined in the conventional manner [Ull89]. We say query Q_1 is *contained* in query Q_2, denoted by $Q_1 \subseteq Q_2$, if for every state of the relations corresponding to the database predicates, the relation corresponding to the head of Q_1 is a subset of the relation corresponding to the head of Q_2. We say that Q_1 is *equivalent* to Q_2, denoted by $Q_1 \equiv Q_2$, if $Q_1 \subseteq Q_2$ and $Q_2 \subseteq Q_1$.

A *containment mapping* from Q_1 to Q_2 is a mapping from the variables of Q_1 to the variables and constants of Q_2 that maps each subgoal of Q_1 to a subgoal of Q_2 and also maps the head of Q_1 to the head of Q_2. For conjunctive queries, $Q_1 \subseteq Q_2$ if and only if there is a containment mapping from Q_2 to Q_1. The problems of testing whether $Q_1 \subseteq Q_2$ and $Q_1 \equiv Q_2$ are both NP-complete [CM77].

A *view* is a conjunctive query with a unique head predicate. Let Q be a query and $\mathcal{V}$ a set of views over the same set of database predicates. Let Q' be a query over the view predicates in $\mathcal{V}$. We extend the notions of containment and equivalence in the natural manner and make statements such as $Q \subseteq Q'$ and $Q \equiv Q'$. We call Q' an *equivalent rewriting* of Q using $\mathcal{V}$ if $Q' \equiv Q$.

Example 1. Suppose we have relations $part(Pname, Type)$, $supp(Sname, Saddr)$, $sales(Part, Supplier, Customer)$, and $cust(Cname, Caddr)$. Query Q asks for the types of parts bought by customers who have the same address as some supplier. Query Q' asks for types of parts sold by suppliers such that a customer at the same address buys parts of the same type.

$$Q: q(T) :- sales(P, S, C) \;\&\; part(P, T) \;\&\; cust(C, A) \;\&\; supp(S', A)$$
$$Q' : q(T) :- sales(P, S, C) \;\&\; part(P, T) \;\&\; part(P', T) \;\&\;$$
$$sales(P', S', C') \;\&\; cust(C, A) \;\&\; supp(S', A)$$

In Section 4, we present a polynomial-time algorithm to verify that $Q' \subseteq Q$.

Suppose we have the materialized views V_1, V_2, and V_3 shown below. View V_1 relates customers with the types of parts they buy, V_2 gives the address of each customer who buys some part, and view V_3 gives the address of each supplier.

$$V_1 : v_1(C_1, T_1) :- sales(P_1, S_1, C_1) \;\&\; cust(C_1, A_1) \;\&\; part(P_1, T_1)$$
$$V_2 : v_2(C_2, A_2) :- sales(P_2, S_2, C_2) \;\&\; cust(C_2, A_2)$$
$$V_3 : v_3(S_3, A_3) :- supp(S_3, A_3)$$

The query Q can be equivalently rewritten using the views as follows:

$$C : q(T) :- v_1(C, T) \;\&\; v_2(C, A) \;\&\; v_3(S', A)$$

We can save a join by using the materialized views to answer the query. □

To test whether C is an equivalent rewriting of Q, we construct the *expansion* E of C by replacing each view predicate in the body of C by its definition, using different local variables for the expansion of each view predicate. It is easily seen that $C' \equiv E$. Since Q and E are defined over the same sets of database relations, we can use containment mappings between them to test their equivalence and containment, and hence the equivalence and containment of Q and C. For example, the expansion of C in Example 1 is

$$E : q(T) :- sales(P_1, S_1, C) \;\&\; cust(C, A_1) \;\&\; part(P_1, T) \;\&\;$$
$$sales(P_2, S_2, C) \;\&\; cust(C, A) \;\&\; supp(S', A)$$

It can easily be verified that $E \equiv Q$, and so $C \equiv Q$.

The problem of finding an equivalent rewriting of a query Q using a set of views $\mathcal{V}$ was shown to be NP-complete by Levy et al. [LMSS95]. They show that the problem remains NP-complete even when the query and the views contain no repeated predicates. In this paper we present a polynomial-time algorithm for the equivalent rewriting problem, provided the query satisfies certain conditions to be defined in Section 3.

We now define some terminology. We use *argument* to mean either a variable or a constant that appears in a query, and *query term* to mean either an argument or a query subgoal. A *variable mapping* is a function that maps a set of variables to a set of arguments. A set of variable mappings $\phi_1, \ldots, \phi_n$, whose domains are different but perhaps overlapping, are said to be *consistent* if there do not exist variable A and integers i and j such that $\phi_i(A) \neq \phi_j(A)$. If $\phi_1, \ldots, \phi_n$ are consistent, we define their *union mapping*, ϕ, to be the variable mapping whose domain is the union of the domains of $\phi_1, \ldots, \phi_n$, and $\phi(A) = B$ if there exists some i, $1 \leq i \leq n$ such that $\phi_i(A) = B$. Variable mappings are defined to be the identity mapping on predicate symbols and constants, and so we can apply a variable mapping to any query term with the obvious meaning. If $\bar{A}$ is a tuple of arguments in the domain of a variable mapping ϕ, then $\phi(\bar{A})$ is a tuple over the set of attributes $\bar{A}$, where the value of each attribute is its image under ϕ.

A *partial mapping* ϕ from query Q to Q' is a variable mapping that maps some subset of the variables of Q to variables of Q', such that if X_i is the ith head argument of Q and $\phi(X_i) = Y_i$, then Y_i is the ith head argument of Q'. A *containment mapping* from Q to Q' is therefore a partial mapping whose domain is the set of all variables of Q.

3   Acyclicity, Query Width, and Treewidth

3.1   Acyclic Queries

It is often profitable to represent a conjunctive query as a hypergraph. The nodes of the hypergraph are the constants and variables in the query. There is one hyperedge corresponding to each query subgoal, that includes the variables and constants occuring as arguments in that subgoal. Figure 1 shows the hypergraphs corresponding to queries Q and Q' of Example 1.

In the rest of this paper, we restrict ourselves for simplicity of exposition to queries whose hypergraphs are connected. However, our results generalize in a straightforward manner to queries with disconnected hypergraphs.

Let E and F be hyperedges of hypergraph $\mathcal{G}$ such that the nodes in $E - F$ are *unique to* E; that is, they appear in no other hyperedge of $\mathcal{G}$. Then we call E an *ear*, the removal of E from $\mathcal{G}$ *ear removal*, and say that "E is removed in favor of F." The *GYO-reduction* of a hypergraph [Gra79, YO79] is obtained by removing ears until no further ear removals are possible. A hypergraph is *acyclic* if its GYO-reduction is the empty hypergraph; otherwise it is *cyclic*.

A query is cyclic (acyclic) if its hypergraph is cyclic (acyclic). If Q is an acyclic query, an *elimination tree* of Q is a rooted tree constructed as follows. Choose some sequence of ear removals for the hypergraph of Q. The tree has a node for each subgoal of Q, and E is a child of F in the tree whenever the hyperedge corresponding to E is eliminated in favor of the hyperedge corresponding to F in the chosen ear removal sequence.

Example 2. The hypergraph of query Q (Figure 1(a)) is acyclic. Figure 2 shows one possible elimination tree for this hypergraph. The hypergraph of Q' (Figure 1(b)) is cyclic, because it contains no ear and is its own GYO-reduction.

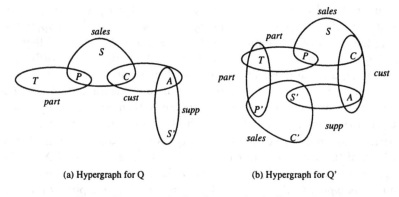

(a) Hypergraph for Q   (b) Hypergraph for Q'

Fig. 1. Hypergraphs for the queries in Example 1.

Suppose Q is an acyclic query, and T is an elimination tree for Q. An important observation that follows from the definition of the elimination tree is that for any argument X of Q, the subgoals that mention X form a connected subtree of T. It is this "connectedness property" of acyclic queries that enables a polynomial-time query containment algorithm for such queries (Section 4).

Our algorithms for acyclic queries assume the elimination tree as an input. Tarjan and Yannakakis [TY84] present a simple linear-time algorithm that tests whether Q is acyclic and if so, constructs an elimination tree for it.

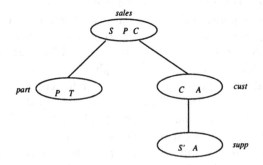

Fig. 2. Elimination tree for hypergraph in Figure 1(a).

3.2 The Width of a Query

It is natural to ask whether we can generalize the notion of query acyclicity in some way. Ideally, we would like to classify queries according to some parameter k that measures their "degree of cyclicity," such that we can design query containment algorithms whose complexity increases with k. In this section we present such a measure, which we call the *query width*.

A *query decomposition* of Q is a tree $T = (I, F)$, with a set $X(i)$ of subgoals and arguments associated with each vertex $i \in I$, such that the following conditions are satisfied:

- For each subgoal s of Q, there is an $i \in I$ such that $s \in X(i)$.
- For each subgoal s of Q, the set $\{i \in I \mid s \in X(i)\}$ induces a (connected) subtree of T.
- For each argument A of Q, the set

$$\{i \in I \mid A \in X(i)\} \cup \{i \in I \mid A \text{ appears in a subgoal } s \text{ such that } s \in X(i)\}$$

induces a (connected) subtree of T.

The *width* of the query decomposition is $\max_{i \in I} |X(i)|$. The *query width* of Q is the minimum width over all its query decompositions.

Example 3. Suppose *red* and *blue* are relations that represent the set of red and blue arcs in a directed graph G. Queries Q_2 and Q_3 below ask for blue arcs in subgraphs of G that satisfy certain properties.

$$Q_2 : q_2(A, B) : - \ blue(A, B) \ \& \ red(B, C) \ \& red(C, D) \ \& \ red(D, B)$$
$$Q_3 : q_3(X, Y) : - \ blue(X, Y) \ \& \ red(Y, Z) \ \& red(Z, Y) \ \& \ red(Z, Z)$$

It can be verified that Q_2 is cyclic. Figure 3(a) shows a query decomposition (of width 2) of Q_2; it can be shown that the query width of Q_2 is in fact 2. Section 4 presents an efficient algorithm to test whether $Q_3 \subseteq Q_2$. □

The elimination tree of an acyclic query (with one subgoal at each node) is a query decomposition of width 1, and acyclic queries have width 1. Moreover, the query decomposition with the smallest number of nodes for a query of width 1 is also an elimination tree. The following proposition summarizes these observations.

Proposition 1. *A query is acyclic if and only if its query width is 1.*

3.3 Treewidth

Computing the query width of a query Q is NP-complete. Our algorithms assume that given a query Q and some constant k, we can determine efficiently whether its query width is bounded by k and if so, construct a query decomposition of width no more than k. It is open whether there is a polynomial-time algorithm

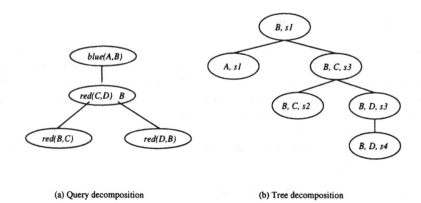

(a) Query decomposition   (b) Tree decomposition

Fig. 3. A query decomposition and a tree decomposition for query Q_2 in Example 3

for the above problem. However, we can obtain an upper bound on the query width by using the closely related notion of *treewidth*.

The *incidence graph* $G_Q = (V, E)$ of query Q has a vertex for each argument and for each subgoal of Q. There is an edge between an argument X and a subgoal s whenever X occurs in s. Figure 4 shows the incidence graph of query Q_2 from Example 1, where we use s_1, s_2, s_3, s_4 to denote the subgoals of Q_2 in order from left to right.

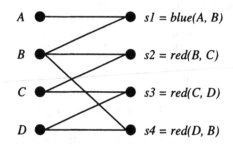

Fig. 4. The incidence graph for the query Q_2.

A *tree decomposition* of a graph $G = (V, E)$ is a tree $T = (I, F)$, with a set $X(i) \subseteq V$ associated with each vertex $i \in I$, such that the following conditions are satisfied:

- For each $v \in V$, there is an $i \in I$ with $v \in X(i)$.
- For all edges $(v, w) \in E$, there is an $i \in I$ with $v, w \in X(i)$.
- For each $v \in V$, the set $\{i \in I \mid v \in X(i)\}$ induces a (connected) subtree of T.

The *width* of the tree decomposition is $\max_{i \in I} |X(i)| - 1$. The *treewidth* of G is the minimum width over all its tree decompositions. [3] Figure 3(b) shows a tree decomposition (width 2) of the incidence of graph in Figure 4.

The *treewidth of a query* is the treewidth of its incidence graph. We can show easily that every tree decomposition of the incidence graph of Q is also a query decomposition of Q. (For example, Figure 3(b) is another query decomposition for query Q_2.) Therefore, the query width of a query Q is certainly not more than one greater than its treewidth (due to the -1 in the definition of treewidth). In fact, we can show the following result, where $tw(Q)$ is the treewidth of Q and $qw(Q)$ is the query width of Q.

Proposition 2. *For any query Q, $tw(Q)/a \leq qw(Q) \leq tw(Q)$, where a is the maximum predicate arity in Q.*

We assume that all predicate arities are bounded by some constant in this paper, and so Proposition 2 implies that the treewidth approximates the query width to within a constant factor. Proposition 2 is useful because treewidth is an extensively studied concept in graph theory. Bodlaender [Bod93] presents an efficient algorithm to determine, for a given k, whether the treewidth of a graph is bounded by k. The running time of the algorithm is exponential in k but linear in the size of the graph.

Theorem 3 [Bod93]. *For all $k \in N$, there exists a linear time algorithm that tests whether a given graph $G = (V, E)$ has treewidth at most k, and if so, outputs a tree decomposition of G with treewidth at most k which has at most $|V| - k$ nodes.*

4   Algorithms for Query Containment

Section 4.1 presents a polyomial-time algorithm to test whether $Q' \subseteq Q$, when Q is an acyclic query (there are no restrictions on Q'). Our approach is to construct partial mappings from Q to Q' and successively merge partial mappings until we either can no longer merge mappings or have found a containment mapping from Q to Q'. The connectedness property allows us to merge partial mappings in polynomial time. In Section 4.2 we extend the algorithm to work with query decompositions of arbitrary width for Q. Given a decomposition of width k, the algorithm runs in time polynomial in n^k where n is the sum of the sizes of Q and Q'.

4.1   Containment Algorithm for Acyclic Queries

Let $T = (I, F)$ be an elimination tree for Q, and let s_i be the subgoal of Q corresponding to node $i \in I$. The algorithm maintains a relation $Map_i(\bar{A}_i)$ at each node i. The attributes $\bar{A}_i$ of the relation are the arguments of s_i (repeated arguments appear only once in $\bar{A}_i$). We use S_i to denote the set of subgoals in

---

[3] The -1 in the definition of width ensures that trees have treewidth 1.

the subtree rooted at i. In the algorithm below, $\ltimes$ denotes the natural semijoin operator.

Algorithm AcyclicContainment

1. Initialize the relations as follows. For each partial mapping ϕ from Q to Q' that maps s_i to some subgoal of Q', the tuple $\phi(\bar{A}_i)$ is in $Map_i(\bar{A}_i)$.
2. Process tree nodes bottom-up as follows. Suppose i is a node of T all of whose children have been processed. For each child j of i:

$$Map_i(\bar{A}_i) := Map_i(\bar{A}_i) \ltimes Map_j(\bar{A}_j)$$

3. $Q' \subseteq Q$ if and only if the relation at the root of T is nonempty.

Example 4. Figure 5 shows the relations created by the algorithm when the elimination tree in Figure 2 is used to determine whether $Q' \subseteq Q$ in Example 1. The attribute names at each node give the relation schema for that node. Step 1 creates the relations in dashed boxes and Step 2 results in the relations in the solid boxes. The numbers at the nodes show the order in which they are processed in Step 2. We conclude that $Q' \subseteq Q$ since the relation at the root is nonempty after Step 2. □

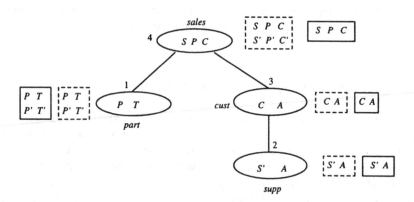

Fig. 5. Running Algorithm AcyclicContainment on Example 1 using the tree in Figure 2.

Lemma 4. *Algorithm AcyclicContainment correctly determines whether $Q' \subseteq Q$.*

Proof: We use induction on the number of nodes processed, with the following induction hypothesis: After node i is processed, tuple $t \in Map_i(\bar{A}_i)$ if and only if there is a partial mapping ϕ from Q to Q' whose domain is the set of subgoals S_i, such that $\phi(\bar{A}_i) = t$. Thus, when the root of T has been processed, the relation at the root is nonempty if and only if there is a containment mapping from Q to Q'.

The induction hypothesis holds for the leaves, because of the way the relations are initialized in Step 1. For the induction, assume that we have processed internal node i with children $j_1, \ldots, j_r$, and let $t \in Map_i$. Step 1 ensures that there is a partial mapping ψ from Q to Q' with domain s_i such that $\psi(\bar{A}_i) = t$. Step 2 assures us that for each j_k, there is a tuple $t_k \in Map_{j_k}$ that agrees with t on the attributes in $\bar{A}_i \cap \bar{A}_{j_k}$. By the induction hypothesis, there is a partial mapping ϕ_k from Q to Q' with domain S_{j_k} such that $\phi_k(\bar{A}_{j_k}) = t_k$.

The mappings ψ and ϕ_k are consistent. To see this, suppose X is a variable in the domains of both ϕ_k and ψ. By the connectedness property, $X \in \bar{A}_{j_k}$ and $X \in \bar{A}_i$. Since t and t_k agree on their common attributes, ψ and ϕ_k agree on X. Moreover, the mappings $\psi, \phi_1, \ldots, \phi_r$ are also consistent. To see this, suppose X is a variable in the domains of ϕ_k and ϕ_l. By the connectedness property, $X \in \bar{A}_{j_k}$, $X \in \bar{A}_{j_l}$, and $X \in \bar{A}_i$. Therefore, ψ, ϕ_k and ϕ_l agree on X. Let ϕ be the partial mapping from Q to Q' that is the union of $\psi, \phi_1, \ldots, \phi_r$. Then ϕ satisfies the conditions of the induction hypothesis.

Conversely, let ϕ be a partial mapping with domain S_i. Let $\phi_1, \ldots, \phi_r$ be the projection of ϕ on the sets of variables in $S_{j_1}, \ldots, S_{j_r}$, and let ψ be the projection of ϕ on the variables in s_i. By the induction hypothesis, there is a tuple $t_k \in Map_{j_k}$, $k = 1, \ldots, r$, such that $\phi_k(\bar{A}_{j_k}) = t_k$. After Step 1, there is a tuple $t \in Map_i$ such that $\psi(\bar{A}_i) = t$. Since t agrees with the tuples $t_1, \ldots, t_r$ on all common attributes, it will remain in Map_i after the sequence of joins in Step 2. □

Theorem 5. *Algorithm AcyclicContainment determines whether $Q' \subseteq Q$ in time $O(N_Q N_{Q'} \log N_{Q'})$ using space $O(N_Q N_{Q'})$, where N_Q and $N_{Q'}$ are the sizes of Q and Q', respectively.*

Proof (Sketch). Correctness follows from Lemma 4. The space and time complexities follow from the observation that the cardinality of each relation Map_i is bounded by the number of subgoals in Q', and the number of such relations is exactly the number of subgoals in Q. The semijoins in Step 2 have to implemented as sort-merge semijoins to achieve the time complexity in the theorem. □

Corollary 6. *Given an acyclic query Q, there is an algorithm to minimize Q in time $O(N_Q^3 \log N_Q)$ using space $O(N_Q^2)$, where N_Q is the size of Q.*

4.2 Generalizing the Algorithm

We now generalize Algorithm AcyclicContainment to test whether $Q' \subseteq Q$, where we are given a query decomposition $T = (I, F)$ of width k for Q. Let $X(i)$ be the set of terms associated with node i of T. As before, we associate a relation $Map_i(\bar{A}_i)$ with node i, where $\bar{A}_i$ is constructed as follows:

1. For each argument $A \in X(i)$, $A \in \bar{A}_i$.
2. For each subgoal $s \in X(i)$, $s \in \bar{A}_i$.
3. For each subgoal $s \in X(i)$, and each argument A that occurs in s, $A \in \bar{A}_i$.

We call attributes of type 1 and 2 *independent attributes* and attributes of type 3 *dependent attributes* (the reason for the nomenclature will become apparent later). Let $S(i)$ denote the set of terms associated with the nodes in the subtree of T rooted at i. The algorithm for query containment is now identical to Algorithm AcyclicContainment except for the initialization step.

Algorithm QueryContainment

1. (Initialize.) For each partial mapping ϕ from Q to Q' that maps all the terms in $X(i)$, include the tuple $\phi(\bar{A}_i)$ in Map_i.
2. (Propagate bottom-up.) Process tree nodes bottom-up as follows. Suppose i is a node of T all of whose children have been processed. For each child j of i:

$$Map_i(\bar{A}_i) := Map_i(\bar{A}_i) \bowtie Map_j(\bar{A}_j)$$

3. $Q' \subseteq Q$ if and only if the relation at the root of T is nonempty.

Example 5. Figure 6 shows the relations created by the algorithm when testing whether $Q_3 \subseteq Q_2$ in Example 3. We use the query decomposition in Figure 3(a) for Q_2. (We could have used the decomposition in Figure 3(b) as well.) In the figure $s_1, \ldots, s_4$ are the subgoals of Q_2 from left to right and $c_1, \ldots, c_4$ are the subgoals of Q_3 from left to right. The relation schema is show at each node, with independent attributes followed by dependent attributes. Step 1 creates the relations in the dashed boxes, and Step 2 results in the relations in the solid boxes. We conclude the $Q_3 \subseteq Q_2$ since the relation at the root is nonempty after Step 2. □

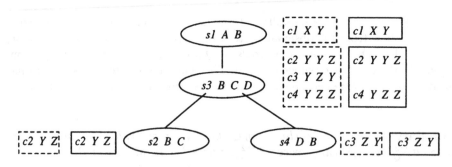

Fig. 6. Running Algorithm QueryContainment

Theorem 7. *Given a tree decomposition of width k for Q, algorithm QueryContainment determines whether $Q' \subseteq Q$ in time $O(k^2 N_Q N_{Q'}^k \log N_{Q'})$ using space $O(N_Q N_{Q'}^k)$, where N_Q and $N_{Q'}$ are the sizes of Q and Q', respectively.*

5 Algorithms for Answering Queries using Views

Let $p_1, \ldots, p_n$ be distinct predicates, and let Q be the query

$$Q : q(\bar{X}) \; :- \; p_1(\bar{X}_1) \; \& \; \ldots \; \& \; p_n(\bar{X}_n)$$

We wish to determine whether there is an equivalent rewriting of Q using an arbitrary set of views $\mathcal{V}$.

Call $V \in \mathcal{V}$ an *interesting view* if there is a variable mapping ϕ that maps the subgoals of V into subgoals of Q (ϕ need not map the head of V to the head of Q). The mapping ϕ is unique for a given interesting view V: since Q has no repeated predicates, there is a unique destination for each subgoal of V. Let $V_1, \ldots, V_m$ be the interesting views in $\mathcal{V}$ with associated mappings $\phi_1, \ldots, \phi_m$, and let $v_i(\bar{Y}_i)$ be the head of view V_i. Then the *canonical rewriting of Q using $\mathcal{V}$* is

$$C : q(\bar{X}) \; :- \; v_1(\phi_1(\bar{Y}_1)) \; \& \; \ldots \; \& \; v_m(\phi_m(\bar{Y}_m))$$

Example 6. In Example 1, all three views V_1, V_2, and V_3 are interesting for query Q. The rewriting C is the canonical rewriting in this case. □

Lemma 8. *There is an equivalent rewriting of Q using $\mathcal{V}$ if and only if $C' \subseteq Q$, where C' is the expansion of the canonical rewriting C.*

Proof. (If.) Suppose $C' \subseteq Q$. We will show that $Q \subseteq C'$; it follows that $Q \equiv C'$ and C is an equivalent rewriting of Q using $\mathcal{V}$. Let S_i denote the set of subgoals contributed to C' by the expansion of $v_i(\phi_i(\bar{Y}_i))$. There is a unique variable mapping ψ_i that maps the subgoals in S_i to subgoals of Q, corresponding to the unique mapping ϕ_i from V_i to Q. Moreover ψ_i is the identity on the variables in $\phi_i(\bar{Y}_i)$. For any i and j, the only variables common to the subgoals in S_i and S_j occur in $\phi_i(\bar{Y}_i)$ and $\phi_j(\bar{Y}_j)$. Since ψ_i and ψ_j are both the identity mapping on these variables, ψ_i and ψ_j are consistent. It follows that $\psi_1, \ldots, \psi_m$ is a consistent set of mappings. Let ψ be the union mapping of $\psi_1, \ldots, \psi_m$. Then ψ is a containment mapping from C' to Q, showing that $Q \subseteq C'$.

(Only if.) Conversely, suppose the following is an equivalent rewriting of Q using $\mathcal{V}$:

$$R : q(\bar{X}) \; :- \; u_1(\bar{Z}_1) \; \& \; \ldots \; \& \; u_l(\bar{Z}_l)$$

Let R' be the expansion of R. Since $Q \equiv R'$, there is a containment mapping τ from Q to R' and a containment mapping ρ from R' to Q. The projection of ρ on to the expansion of u_i maps the subgoals of the corresponding view to subgoals to Q, and so u_i is an interesting view for $i = 1, \ldots, l$. Let us assume without loss of generality that u_i is identical to v_i, $i = 1, \ldots, l$.

Consider the query T defined as follows:

$$T : q(\bar{X}) \; :- \; v_1(\rho(\bar{Z}_1)) \; \& \; \ldots \; \& \; v_l(\rho(\bar{Z}_l))$$

Let T' be the expansion of T. We have constructed T from R in a such a manner as to ensure that T is an equivalent rewriting of Q and $T' \equiv Q$. Since there is a unique mapping ϕ_i from each interesting view V_i to Q, it must be the case that $\phi_i(\bar{Y}_i) = \rho(\bar{Z}_i)$. Thus, each subgoal in T is also a subgoal of the canonical rewriting C, and therefore $C \subseteq T$ and $C' \subseteq T'$. Since $T' \equiv Q$, we have shown that $C' \subseteq Q$. □

Theorem 9. *Let Q be a query without repeated predicates and $\mathcal{V}$ a set of views. Given a query decomposition of width k for Q, there is an algorithm to test whether there is an equivalent rewriting of Q using $\mathcal{V}$ in time $O(k^2 N_Q |\mathcal{V}|^k \log |\mathcal{V}|)$ and space $O(N_Q |\mathcal{V}|^k)$, where N_Q is the size of Q and $|\mathcal{V}|$ is the size of $\mathcal{V}$.*

Proof. Follows from Lemma 8 and Theorem 7. □

The size of the canonical rewriting depends on the number of interesting views and is independent of the size of Q. We can modify the query containment algorithms of Section 4 slightly to obtain a rewriting that uses no more subgoals than the query. With each tuple t in a relation at a node of the query decomposition, we must store also the names of the views whose subgoals participate in the partial mapping corresponding to t. After Step 2 of the containment algorithm, we traverse the tree top-down and choose a set of consistent tuples, one from each node of the tree. We can then drop all but the views corresponding to the chosen tuples from the canonical rewriting C to obtain a shorter rewriting D such that $D \equiv Q$.

Theorem 10. *Let Q be a query without repeated predicates and $\mathcal{V}$ a set of views, such that Q has n subgoals. Given a query decomposition of width k for Q, there is an algorithm that tests whether there is an equivalent rewriting of Q using $\mathcal{V}$, and if so, produces a rewriting of Q using $\mathcal{V}$ that has no more than n subgoals. The algorithm runs in time $O(k^2 N_Q |\mathcal{V}|^k \log |\mathcal{V}|)$ and uses space $O(N_Q |\mathcal{V}|^k)$, where N_Q is the size of Q and $|\mathcal{V}|$ is the size of $\mathcal{V}$.*

6 Related Work

Aho et al. [ASU79a, ASU79b] gave polynomial-time minimization and equivalence algorithms for conjunctive queries corresponding to *simple tableaux*. Their results were extended by Johnson and Klug [JK83] to the class of *fanout-free queries*. The classes of fanout-free queries and queries with simple tableaux are incomparable to the classes of queries considered in this paper. The algorithms of Aho et al. and Johnson and Klug also differ from ours in that they cannot be generalized to test query containment instead of query equivalence. Recently, Qian [Qia96] showed independently that acyclic queries admit polynomial time algorithms for containment and minimization. Our work treats acyclic queries as a special case of queries with width 1, and so Qian's algorithm for query containment falls out as a special case of ours.

Yang and Larson [LY85, YL87] considered the problem of finding rewritings for SPJ queries using SPJ views. In their analysis, they considered what amounts to 1-1 mappings from the views to the query, and therefore their algorithm can miss some rewritings. The problem of finding equivalent rewritings was studied formally by Levy et al. [LMSS95], who showed the problem to be NP-complete.

Rajaraman et al. [RSU95] extended the results of Levy et al. to queries and views with *binding patterns*. Chaudhuri et al. [CKPS95] considered the problem of finding rewritings for SPJ queries and views, when the queries and views use bag semantics instead of the usual set semantics. They also suggest a way to extend a traditional relational query processor to choose between different rewritings based on their costs, a question we do not address in this paper. Qian [Qia96] presents a polynomial-time algorithm that, given an acyclic query Q and a set of views V, determines whether there is a rewriting using V that is contained in (but not necessarily equivalent to) Q. Levy et al. [LRU96] study the problem of finding an equivalent rewriting when the set of views is possibly infinite, albeit encoded in some finite fashion. The Information Manifold system [LRO96] implements heuristics that speed up the search for a rewriting of a query by eliminating irrelevant views.

Acyclic queries and acyclic database schemes have been studied extensively because their structural properties permit efficient algorithms. Several algorithms for acyclic database schemes were given by Yannakakis [Yan81]. Our query containment algorithm for acyclic queries is closely related to the one in [Yan81] for computing projections of acyclic joins. Treewidth is extensively studied in the graph-theoretic literature, and several intractable problems admit polynomial-time algorithms on graphs of constant treewidth [Bod93].

7 Open Problems

Our work raises some interesting open problems. While we obtained bounds on the query width of Q based on the treewidth of its incidence graph, it would be useful to have an efficient algorithm that produces query decompositions of small query width, analogous to the algorithm of Bodlaender [Bod93] for decompositions of small treewidth. The connectedness property of acyclic queries leads to several efficient algorithms [Yan81]; it may be possible to generalize many of these algorithms to queries of small query width. Finally, we would like to extend our results to queries with binding patterns [RSU95] and queries with built-in predicates.

Acknowledgements

The inspiration for considering the treewidth of the incidence graph came from the work of Khanna and Motwani [KM96]. We also thank Jeff Ullman for comments on earlier versions of this paper.

References

[ASU79a] A.V. Aho, Y. Sagiv, and J.D. Ullman. Efficient optimization of a class of relational expressions. *ACM Transactions on Database Systems*, 4(4):435–454, December 1979.

[ASU79b] A.V. Aho, Y. Sagiv, and J.D. Ullman. Equivalence of relational expressions. *SIAM Journal on Computing*, 8(2):218–246, May 1979.

[Bod93] H.L. Bodlaender. A linear time algorithm for finding tree-decompositions of small treewidth. In *Proceedings of the 25th ACM Symposium on the Theory of Computing*, pages 226–234, 1993.

[CKPS95] S. Chaudhuri, R. Krishnamurthy, S. Potamianos, and K. Shim. Optimizing queries with materialized views. In *Proceedings of the Eleventh International Conference on Data Engineering*, pages 190–200, 1995.

[CM77] A.K. Chandra and P.M. Merlin. Optimal implementation of conjunctive queries in relational databases. In *Proceedings of the Ninth ACM Symposium on Theory of Computing*, pages 77–90, 1977.

[Gra79] M.H. Graham. On the universal relation. Technical report, University of Toronto, Ontario, Canada, 1979.

[JK83] D.S. Johnson and A. Klug. Optimizing conjunctive queries that contain untyped variables. *SIAM Journal on Computing*, 12(4):616–640, November 1983.

[KM96] S. Khanna and R. Motwani. Towards a syntactic characterization of PTAS. In *Proceedings of the 28th ACM Symposium on the Theory of Computing*, 1996.

[LMSS95] A.Y. Levy, A.O. Mendelzon, Y. Sagiv, and D. Srivastava. Answering queries using views. In *Proceedings of the Fourteenth ACM Symposium on Principles of Database Systems*, pages 95–104, 1995.

[LRO96] A.Y. Levy, A. Rajaraman, and J.J. Ordille. Querying heterogeneous information sources using source descriptions. In *Proceedings of the 22nd International Conference on Very Large Data Bases*, 1996.

[LRU96] A.Y. Levy, A. Rajaraman, and J.D. Ullman. Answering queries using limited external query processors. In *Proceedings of the Fifteenth ACM Symposium on Principles of Database Systems*, pages 227–237, 1996.

[LY85] P.A. Larson and H.Z. Yang. Computing queries from derived relations. In *Proceedings of the Eleventh International Conference on Very Large Data Bases*, pages 259–269, 1985.

[Qia96] X. Qian. Query folding. In *Proceedings of the Twelfth International Conference on Data Engineering*, 1996.

[RSU95] A. Rajaraman, Y. Sagiv, and J.D. Ullman. Answering queries using templates with binding patterns. In *Proceedings of the Fourteenth ACM Symposium on Principles of Database Systems*, pages 105–112, 1995.

[TY84] R.E. Tarjan and M. Yannakakis. Simple linear-time algorithms to test chordality of graphs, test acyclicity of hypergraphs, and selectively reduce acyclic hypergraphs. *SIAM Journal on Computing*, 13(3):566–579, 1984.

[Ull89] J.D. Ullman. *Principles of Database and Knowledge-Base Systems, Volume II: The New Technologies*. Computer Science Press, Rockville, MD, 1989.

[Yan81] M. Yannakakis. Algorithms for acyclic database schemes. In *Proceedings of the Seventh International Conference on Very Large Data Bases*, pages 82–94, 1981.

[YL87] H.Z. Yang and P.A. Larson. Query transformation for PSJ-queries. In *Proceedings of the Thirteenth International Conference on Very Large Data Bases*, pages 245–254, 1987.

[YO79] C.T. Yu and M.Z. Ozsoyoglu. An algorithm for tree-query membership of a distributed query. In *Proceedings of IEEE COMPSAC*, pages 306–312, 1979.

Semantics and Containment of Queries with Internal and External Conjunctions

Gösta Grahne[1]*, Nicolas Spyratos[2] and Daniel Stamate[2]

[1] Department of Computer Science, P.O. Box 26 (Teollisuuskatu 23)
FIN-00014 University of Helsinki, Finland
email: grahne@cs.helsinki.fi
[2] Université de Paris-Sud, LRI, U.R.A. 410 du CNRS, Bât. 490,
F-91405 Orsay Cedex, France
email: {spyratos,daniel}@lri.lri.fr

Abstract. We study conjunctive queries that combine information from multiple sources. The need for combining information is manifest for instance in multimedia systems. It has recently been recognized that query semantics for these systems should be based on some quantitative model, such as fuzzy logic. Further complications arise, however, since the semantics used *internally* by subsystems, and the semantics used *externally* to combine information, are not necessarily the same.

In this paper we give a solution based on general multivalued logics with lattice-based semantics. The internal and external semantics are tied to each other through the concept of a *bilattice*. Queries using both internal level and external level conjunctions have a natural semantics in bilattices. We then show that homomorphism techniques from core database theory carry over to query containment for internal/external conjunctive queries in the bilattice-setting. We also show that the computational complexity of determining containment of internal/external conjunctive queries is in general Π_2^p-complete, and NP-complete in some restricted cases.

1 Introduction

In this paper we are interested in the evaluation of conjunctive queries that combine information provided by multiple sources. That is, the data used in the evaluation of queries can reside in different database systems as well as in a variety of non-database data servers.

A typical example is a multimedia information system, where a query can access data in a number of different subsystems (sound-, image-, text-subsystem etc.). Each subsystem provides the answer to a subquery and the system must then combine these answers in order to provide the answer to the overall query.

There are, however, several questions that arise in this context. We shall illustrate these questions using an example. Consider an application of a store

---

* Research conducted while the first author was visiting at Université de Paris-Sud, Laboratoire de Recherche en Informatique.

that sells compact disks and assume that we want to produce a list of albums by Oscar Peterson, sorted according to their jazziness. To do this we use two sources of information:

- A relation $A(AlbumNo, Artist)$ residing on a relational database, and
- The estimates of an expert as to the type (jazzy, funky, ... etc) of the music announced on the cover of the albums. Let us think of these estimates as of a relation $E(AlbumNo, Type)$ residing on a sound-subsystem. Each tuple in relation E is associated with a number, say a real between 0 and 1, indicating the experts' opinion as to whether the album is of the type (0 if the expert thinks that the music of the album is not at all of the type). The expert could for instance be an approximate pattern matching algorithm that looks if words from the language of jazz occur in samples from the CD's.

The multimedia query Q that we want to answer is then a conjunct of two atoms as follows:

$$Q(X) \leftarrow A(X, oscar Peterson) \,\&\, E(X, jazz)$$

In order to evaluate this query, we must evaluate the body for every given album a. Now, the atom $A(a, oscar Peterson)$ can be associated with *true* or *false* depending on whether $A(a, oscar Peterson)$ is in the relation or not. The atom $E(a, jazz)$, on the other hand, can be associated with any real value between 0 and 1. So the question is: with what value should $Q(a)$ be associated? In other words, what is the definition of the conjunction & in this case?

In a recent paper [Fag96], Fagin suggests a solution based on fuzzy logic and gives algorithms for efficient evaluation of conjunctive queries assuming the properties of "strictness" and "monotonicity." Following his approach, each atom can be associated with a real number between 0 and 1. Thus $A(a, oscar Peterson)$ can be associated with either 0, meaning *false*, or 1, meaning *true*, whereas $E(a, jazz)$ can be associated with any real number between 0 and 1, according to the experts' estimate. The conjunction & can be defined to be the *min*-function, and thus $Q(a)$ is associated with the smaller of the values for $A(a, oscar Peterson)$ and $E(a, jazz)$.

A further complication arises, however, from the fact that a multimedia information system is usually "on top of" various subsystems, and may have no control over the semantics of these subsystems. For example, suppose that the multimedia system actually is "underneath" a supersystem, and that this supersystem has access to a second multimedia system. In the second multimedia system, there is the traditional relation $A(AlbumNo, Artist)$, and in a sound-subsystem there are estimates $E'(AlbumNo, Type)$ of a second approximate pattern matcher, perhaps with a different scoring matrix, or different samples, or different definitions of jazziness etc. Then the supersystem should evaluate the following query

$$Q(X) \leftarrow$$
$$[A(X, oscar Peterson) \& E(X, jazz)] \text{ and}$$
$$[A(X, oscar Peterson) \& E'(X, jazz)]$$

where *and* is the conjunction used by the supersystem to combine the information from the subsystems. The conjunction *and* is not necessarily the same as the conjunction & used by the multimedia servers. As suggested by Fagin [Fag96], perhaps the most natural way to account for this is to define two conjunctions: the *internal conjunction*, to be used by the multimedia systems, and the *external conjunction*, to be used by the supersystem in combining the information from the various subsystems.

For instance, suppose each tuple in the relations is associated with *pairs* of real numbers between 0 and 1. A pair $\langle x, y \rangle$ for a tuple in the expert relations can be thought of as a weight of evidence *for* and *against*, respectively. The pattern matcher mentioned before contributes with x, and when the pattern is changed to, say, a language of "flatness," then y describes degree of match with this language. If we now have a tuple $E(a, jazz)$ with value $\langle x, y \rangle$, and a tuple $E'(a, jazz)$ with value $\langle z, w \rangle$, then how should these two values be combined? If one wants to extend Boolean logic, then one option is $\langle min(x, z), max(y, w) \rangle$, when *true* is $\langle 1, 0 \rangle$, and *false* is $\langle 0, 1 \rangle$. This type of conjunction is therefore suitable at the internal level (for &). However, another possibility for the external *and*, which Fitting [Fit91] calls "the consensus operator", is $\langle min(x, z), min(y, w) \rangle$. This gives rise to another logic with $\langle 1, 1 \rangle$ (inconsistent) as maximal truth-value, and $\langle 0, 0 \rangle$ (undefined) as minimal truth-value.

In this paper, we generalize the above example, and consider a set of autonomous systems connected in a network. Each system is capable of performing both internal conjunction and external conjunction. These conjunctions are the same for every system. We assume that a query, in a given system, is the external conjunction of subqueries. In turn, each subquery is the internal conjunction of atoms residing in one system. If we denote the external conjunction by $\otimes$, and the internal conjunction by $\wedge$, then the queries that we consider are of the form:

$$Q \leftarrow Q_1 \otimes Q_2 \otimes \cdots \otimes Q_n$$

where each subquery Q_i is of the form:

$$Q_i \leftarrow A_1^i \wedge A_2^i \wedge \cdots \wedge A_{m_i}^i,$$

where the A_j^i:s are atomic formulas.

The semantics of the queries are given by multivalued logics with two orderings, the *truth ordering* and the *knowledge ordering*, corresponding to internal and external conjunction, respectively. Our model is based on recent works by Fitting [Fit91, Fit93], using the concept of bilattice introduced by M. Ginsberg [Gin88]. In the framework of the model, we study the problem of containment between conjunctive queries, which is a central problem in query optimization. We show for instance, that in the bilattice framework the complexity of conjunctive query containment under both "internal" and "external" equivalence simultaneously is one level higher in the polynomial time hierarchy [Sto77] than in the classical case, i. e. the problem is Π_2^p-complete.

We emphasize that issues of efficient query evaluation in the framework considered here are very different from those in traditional database systems. Concrete evaluation methods are studied by Fagin [Fag96]. He assumes only internal

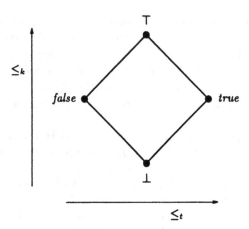

Fig. 1. The logic *FOUR*

conjunction, the semantics of which is based on fuzzy logic. Our framework generalizes the one of Fagin in the sense that we can have two different multivalued logics, one for internal conjunction, and one for external conjunction. The two logics have a combined semantics given by the bilattice. On the other hand, Fagin's approach is more general in the sense that the requirements for internal conjunction, called "strictness" and "monotonicity," follow from lattice axioms.

The rest of this paper is organized as follows: In section 2 we present the bilattice semantics and introduce our database model and queries with internal and external conjunctions. In section 3, we show that containment of internal/external conjunctive queries can be determined using homomorphism techniques. These results are related to (although incomparable with) theorems recently discovered by Ioannidis and Ramakrishnan [IR95]. In section 4 we analyze the computational complexity of determining containment of external/internal conjunctive queries. It turns out that the problem is in general Π_2^p-complete, and NP-complete when the queries use only one type of conjunction. These results are established using the homomorphism theorems and other characterizations from the previous section.

2   The Framework

In [Fit91] Fitting uses bilattices as truth-value spaces for information combined from several sources. The simplest bilattice is called *FOUR*, and it is basically Belnap's four-valued logic [Bel77]. The bilattice *FOUR* is depicted in Figure 1.

In the bilattice *FOUR* each subsystem can compute its internal conjunction (and disjunction) using classical two-valued logic (the horizontal axis). Information is combined using external conjunction (the vertical axis). Intuitively we combine conflicting truth-valued information into undefined (the bottom element in the vertical order). This can be generalized as follows.

Definition 1. A bilattice is a triple $\langle \mathcal{B}, \leq_t, \leq_k \rangle$, where $\mathcal{B}$ is a nonempty set, and $\leq_t$ and $\leq_k$ are partial orders each giving $\mathcal{B}$ the structure of a lattice with a top and bottom.

Meet and join under order $\leq_t$ are denoted $\vee$ and $\wedge$, and meet and join under $\leq_k$ are denoted $\oplus$ and $\otimes$. Top and bottom under $\leq_t$ are denoted *true* and *false*, and top and bottom under $\leq_k$ are denoted $\top$ and $\bot$. A bilattice is said to be *interlaced* if the meet and join for each partial order are monotone with respect to the other order. That is, if $a \leq_t b$ and $c \leq_t d$, then $a \otimes c \leq_t b \otimes d$, and similarly for other combinations of operations and orders.

By abuse of notation we will sometimes talk about the bilattice $\mathcal{B}$ when the orders are irrelevant or understood from the context.

A bilattice is said to be *nontrivial* if the bilattice *FOUR* can be isomorphically embedded in it. Fitting has shown the following:

Proposition 2. *[Fit91] In any nontrivial interlaced bilattice,*

$$true \oplus false = \top, \; true \otimes false = \bot$$
$$\top \vee \bot = true, \top \wedge \bot = false$$

The following lemma will be useful in the sequel.

Lemma 3. *In any nontrivial interlaced bilattice $\mathcal{B}$,*

$$\top \wedge a >_k \bot, \qquad true \otimes b >_t false$$

for any elements a and b of $\mathcal{B}$.

A bilattice is said to be *distributive* if the meet for each partial order distributes over the join of that partial order and over the meet and join of the other partial order, and similarly for the join of each partial order. In other words, $a \wedge (b \vee c) = (a \wedge b) \vee (a \vee c)$, $a \wedge (b \otimes c) = (a \wedge b) \otimes (a \wedge c)$, and ten other similar laws hold. An easy exercise yields the following

Proposition 4. *[Fit91] A distributive bilattice is interlaced.*

The bilattice *FOUR* is distributive. The bilattice mentioned in the introduction, with pairs of reals between 0 and 1 as truth-values is formally $\langle [0,1] \times [0,1], \leq_t, \leq_k \rangle$ where $\langle x, y \rangle \leq_t \langle z, w \rangle$ iff $x \leq z$ and $w \leq y$, and $\langle x, y \rangle \leq_k \langle z, w \rangle$ iff $x \leq z$ and $y \leq w$. In this bilattice $\langle x, y \rangle \wedge \langle z, w \rangle = \langle min(x,z), max(y,w) \rangle$, and $\langle x, y \rangle \otimes \langle z, w \rangle = \langle min(x,z), min(y,w) \rangle$. This bilattice is also distributive.

In distributive bilattices the following interesting property holds.

Lemma 5. *Let $\mathcal{B}$ be a distributive bilattice, and $\{a_1, \ldots, a_n, b_1, \ldots, b_m\}$ a subset of $\mathcal{B}$, where $n \geq m$. Then*

$$(a_1 \wedge b_1) \otimes \ldots \otimes (a_m \wedge b_m) \otimes a_{m+1} \otimes \ldots \otimes a_n \leq_t$$
$$(a_1 \wedge b_1) \otimes \ldots \otimes (a_m \wedge b_m) \otimes a_{m+1} \otimes \ldots \otimes a_n \otimes (a_1 \wedge \ldots \wedge a_m)$$

The dual property, obtained by interchanging $\otimes$ and $\wedge$ and replacing $\leq_t$ by $\leq_k$, also holds.

For a proof, let us denote $(a_1 \wedge b_1) \otimes \ldots \otimes (a_m \wedge b_m) \otimes a_{m+1} \otimes \ldots \otimes a_n$ with φ. Then we have to show that $\varphi \leq_t \varphi \otimes (a_1 \wedge \ldots \wedge a_m)$. From $(a_i \wedge b_i) \leq_t a_i$ and $\varphi \leq_t \varphi$, we get by interlacing laws $\varphi \otimes (a_i \wedge b_i) \leq_t \varphi \otimes a_i$, for every $i \in \{1, \ldots, m\}$. As $\varphi \otimes (a_i \wedge b_i) = \varphi$, we get $\varphi \leq_t \varphi \otimes a_i$ for every i as above. Using now lattice laws it follows that $\varphi \leq_t (\varphi \otimes a_1) \wedge \ldots \wedge (\varphi \otimes a_m)$. As the bilattice is distributive, we have $(\varphi \otimes a_1) \wedge \ldots \wedge (\varphi \otimes a_m) = \varphi \otimes (a_1 \wedge \ldots \wedge a_m)$, and therefore $\varphi \leq_t \varphi \otimes (a_1 \wedge \ldots \wedge a_m)$.

We assume from here on that the bilattices are distributive, unless explicitly stated otherwise.

Next we consider the natural generalizations of relations and database instances. An ordinary relation can be seen as a relation where each tuple is adorned with *true* or *false*. If $\mathcal{B}$ is a bilattice, then a $\mathcal{B}$-*adorned relation* corresponding to a predicate A is a relation called also A, where each tuple t is adorned with an element $a \in \mathcal{B}$; such a tuple is denoted by $A(t) : a$, unless the relation is understood from context, in which case we may write it $t : a$. A $\mathcal{B}$-*adorned instance* is a set of $\mathcal{B}$-adorned relations. We note that Ioannidis and Ramakrishnan [IR95], and Chaudhuri and Vardi [CV93] have recently studied adorned relations. Our framework is however more general, in the sense that the adornments (labels) come from a a "two dimensional" bilattice. Furthermore, a tuple can occur in the same relation with several labels. Since there are two partial orders, there will be two notions of equivalence. We shall shortly illustrate this by an example. When the bilattice $\mathcal{B}$ is irrelevant or understood from the context, we shall sometimes omit $\mathcal{B}$ and simply talk about adorned relations and instances.

Definition 6. Let R and S be adorned relations over the same schema. Then we say that R is truth-smaller (knowledge-smaller) than S, if for each tuple $t : a$ in R, there is a tuple $u : b$ in S, such that $t = u$ and $a \leq_t b$ (respectively $a \leq_k b$).

These are clearly partial pre-orders. If we have both $R \leq_t S$ and $S \leq_t R$, then we say that R and S are *truth equivalent*, and similarly for *knowledge equivalence*.

Example 1. Let R be the relation $\langle t : true, t : false, u : \top, u : \bot \rangle$. Then R is truth-equivalent to the relation $\langle t : true, u : \top, u : \bot \rangle$, and R is knowledge-equivalent to the relation $\langle t : true, t : false, u : \top \rangle$.

A *conjunctive query* Q is a formula of the form

$$head \leftarrow body,$$

where *head* is a function-free atomic formula of the form $R(x_1, \cdots, x_n)$. All the variables x_i in R have to appear in *body*. A body is defined inductively as follows:

1. An atomic formula $R(x_1, \cdots, x_m)$, where R is a relation name and the x_i's are variables or constants, is a body.
2. If A and B are bodies, then so are $A \wedge B$, and $A \otimes B$.
3. Nothing else is a body

Let I be an instance, and $Q = head \leftarrow body$ a conjunctive query. Furthermore, let θ be an assignment of Q into I, that is, a mapping from the variables in Q to constants in I. Then the *result due to θ of Q over I*, denoted $Q_\theta(I)$, is the set of all adorned tuples $head\theta : c$, such that for each atom $R(x_1, \cdots, x_m)$ in *body*, the tuple $R(\theta(x_1), \cdots, \theta(x_m))$ occurs with some label in I.[3] The value of the label c is defined recursively as follows.

1. If *body* is of the form $A \circ B$, where $\circ \in \{\wedge, \otimes\}$, and $head\theta : a$ is in $(head \leftarrow A)_\theta(I)$, and $head\theta : b$ is in $(head \leftarrow B)_\theta(I)$, then $c = a \circ b$.
2. If *body* is of the form $R(x_1, \cdots, x_m)$, and the tuple $R(\theta(x_1), \cdots, \theta(x_m))$ occurs with label a in I, then $c = a$.

The result of a query Q over an instance I, denoted $Q(I)$, is then defined to be $\cup_\theta Q_\theta(I)$, where θ is any assignment of Q into I.

3 Containment of conjunctive queries

We are now ready to define containment of queries over labelled instances.

Definition 7. Let P and Q be conjunctive queries. Then we say that P is *truth-contained* in Q (P is *knowledge-contained* in Q), denoted $P \leq_t Q$ (resp. $P \leq_k Q$), if for every instance I it is true that $P(I) \leq_t Q(I)$ (resp. $P(I) \leq_k Q(I)$). If we have both $P \leq_t Q$ ($P \leq_k Q$) and $Q \leq_t P$ (resp. $Q \leq_k P$), we say that P and Q are *truth-equivalent*, denoted $P \equiv_t Q$ (we say that P and Q are *knowledge equivalent*, denoted $P \equiv_k Q$). If we have both $P \equiv_t Q$ and $P \equiv_k Q$, we write $P \equiv Q$.

Containment is of course relative to a given bilattice $\mathcal{B}$, and should really be written $P \leq_t^\mathcal{B} Q$ and $P \leq_k^\mathcal{B} Q$. We shall however omit the superscript.

The notion of homomorphism is essential in containment of conjunctive queries [AHV95]. In the context of our work, the notion of homomorphism is defined as follows.

Definition 8. Let P and Q be two conjunctive queries whose heads are compatible (*i. e.* they represent relations of the same arity). A *homomorphism* $h : Q \rightarrow P$ is a total function from the variables and constants of Q to the variables and constants of P such that if x and y are variables appearing in the same argument position in the head of Q and P respectively, then $h(x) = y$, and if $R(x_1, \cdots, x_n)$ appears in Q, then $R(h(x_1), \cdots, h(x_n))$ appears in P. Furthermore, h has to be the identity on constants.

We will assume *w. l. o. g.* that all queries use a designated predicate symbol, say H, in their heads. (The predicate symbol H has no fixed arity.) The first result concerns containment of queries that only use either external or internal conjunctions.

---

[3] As usual, the mapping θ is extended to be the identity on constants. Furthermore, $E\theta$ where E is a formula, a query, or a vector is obtained from the expression E by replacing every variable x in E with $\theta(x)$.

Theorem 9. *Let P and Q be conjunctive queries that only use $\wedge$ (respectively only use $\otimes$) in their bodies. Then $P \leq_t Q$ (resp. $P \leq_k Q$) if and only if there exists a homomorphism $h : Q \to P$.*

Indeed, let Q be $H(\mathbf{x}) \leftarrow A_1(\mathbf{x}_1) \wedge \cdots \wedge A_n(\mathbf{x}_n)$, and let P be $H(\mathbf{y}) \leftarrow B_1(\mathbf{y}_1) \wedge \cdots \wedge B_m(\mathbf{y}_m)$, such that $H(\mathbf{x})$ and $H(\mathbf{y})$ are compatible (here $\mathbf{x}, \mathbf{x}_1, \ldots, \mathbf{y}, \mathbf{y}_1, \ldots$, are vectors of variables). Suppose we have a homomorphism h from Q to P. That is, $h(\mathbf{x}) = \mathbf{y}$, and for each $i \in \{1, \cdots, n\}$ there is a $j_i \in \{1, \ldots, m\}$, such that $A_i(h(\mathbf{x}_i)) = B_{j_i}(\mathbf{y}_{j_i})$. Let I be an instance, and $H(\mathbf{t}) : b$ an adorned tuple in $P(I)$. Obviously, there is an assignment θ such that $\mathbf{y}\theta = \mathbf{t}$ and $b = b_1 \wedge \cdots \wedge b_m$, where $\{B_1(\mathbf{y}_1)\theta : b_1, \cdots, B_m(\mathbf{y}_m)\theta : b_m\} \subseteq I$. Let σ be $\theta \circ h$. From the construction of σ, it follows that $\{A_1(\mathbf{x}_1)\sigma : b_{j_1}, \cdots, A_n(\mathbf{x}_n)\sigma : b_{j_n}\} \subseteq I$. Let $a = b_{j_1} \wedge \cdots \wedge b_{j_n}$. Now we can conclude that $H(\mathbf{x})\sigma : a$ belongs to $Q(I)$. It follows from the definition of the lattice join $\wedge$ that $b \leq_t a$. Since $H(\mathbf{y})\theta = H(\mathbf{x})\sigma$, we have that $P(I) \leq_t Q(I)$.

Conversely, suppose now that $P \leq_t Q$. Let the set of variables occurring in P be $\{y_1, \ldots, y_p\}$. Suppose w. l. o. g. that the constants in $\{1, \cdots, p\}$ do not occur in P or Q. Let θ be the map $y_i \mapsto i$. Then θ is a bijection from $\{y_1, \ldots, y_p\}$ to $\{1, \ldots, p\}$. Let I be the instance $\{B_1(\mathbf{y}_1)\theta : true, \cdots, B_m(\mathbf{y}_m)\theta : true\}$. Obviously, $H(\mathbf{y})\theta : true$ is in $P(I)$, and as $P(I) \leq_t Q(I)$, it follows that $H(\mathbf{y})\theta : true$ is in $Q(I)$. Thus there must be an assignment σ, such that $\mathbf{x}\sigma = \mathbf{y}\theta$, or equivalently $\theta(\mathbf{y}) = \sigma(\mathbf{x})$. That is, $\mathbf{y} = \theta^{-1}(\sigma(\mathbf{x}))$. Define h as $\theta^{-1} \circ \sigma$. As $H(\mathbf{x})\sigma : true$ is in $Q(I)$, it must be that $\{A_1(\mathbf{x}_1)\sigma : true, \cdots, A_n(\mathbf{x}_n)\sigma : true\} \subseteq I$. From the construction of I, it follows that for each $i \in \{1, \cdots, n\}$ there is a $j_i \in \{1, \ldots, m\}$, such that $A_i(\mathbf{x}_i)\sigma = B_{j_i}(\mathbf{y}_{j_i})\theta$, so $A_i = B_{j_i}$ and $\mathbf{x}_i\sigma = \mathbf{y}_{j_i}\theta$, or equivalently $\mathbf{y}_{j_i} = h(\mathbf{x}_i)$. That is, $A_i(h(\mathbf{x}_i)) = B_{j_i}(\mathbf{y}_{j_i})$, and as $h(\mathbf{x}) = \mathbf{y}$, the mapping h is a homomorphism from Q to P.

Ioannidis and Ramakrishnan [IR95] have recently proved a similar homomorphism characterization for annotated instances, where the annotations form a structure called a "label system of type A." We note that there are lattices that are not "label systems of type A," and that there are "label systems of type A" that are not lattices. Fuzzy logic, however, is both a lattice and a "label system of type A."

Next we characterize containment of queries whose bodies contain both $\wedge$ and $\otimes$. We will need two notions of normal form. A query Q is said to be in *truth-normal form* if it is of the form

$$head \leftarrow Q_1 \otimes Q_2 \otimes \cdots \otimes Q_n$$

where each Q_i is of the form:

$$A_1^i \wedge A_2^i \wedge \cdots \wedge A_{m_i}^i,$$

and the A_j^i's are atomic. Likewise, a query Q is in *knowledge-normal form* if it is of the form

$$head \leftarrow Q_1 \wedge Q_2 \wedge \cdots \wedge Q_n$$

where each Q_i is of the form:

$$A_1^i \otimes A_2^i \otimes \cdots \otimes A_{m_i}^i,$$

with atomic A_j^i's.

If Q is a query, then its normal forms will be denoted Q^t and Q^k, respectively. Every query can be transformed into truth-normal form or knowledge-normal form recursively as follows: Let E be the body of Q. We denote by E^t the truth-normal form of E. If E is an atom, then $E^t = E$. If $E = E_1 \otimes E_2$, then $E^t = E_1^t \otimes E_2^t$. If $E = E_1 \wedge E_2$, let E_1^t be $F_1 \otimes F_2 \otimes \cdots \otimes F_n$ and let E_2^t be $G_1 \otimes G_2 \otimes \cdots \otimes G_m$. Then E^t is built as $\bigotimes_{i,j}(F_i \wedge G_j)$. The knowledge-normal form is obtained similarly. Note that in the introduction we assumed that the queries were in truth-normal form. Notice also that, as the two conjunctions are associative and commutative, there are actually several truth-normal forms for a query. Then Q^t denotes some chosen element from the set of truth-normal forms of Q, and similarly for Q^t. The normal form transformation can be implemented for instance as an ordered rewriting system. Transforming into normal form does not necessarily preserve equivalence, unless the two conjunctions are distributive with respect to each other. In general, the following relationships hold between a query and its normal forms.

Lemma 10. $Q \leq_k Q^t$, and $Q \leq_t Q^k$ in any interlaced bilattice $\langle B, \leq_t, \leq_k \rangle$. If $\mathcal{B}$ is distributive, then in addition $Q \equiv Q^t$, and $Q \equiv Q^k$.

The proof of the lemma is an easy induction on the structure of the normal forms, using the interlacing or distribution laws.

Now Theorem 9 can be generalized to conjunctive queries using both external and internal conjunctions.

Theorem 11. Let $C \leftarrow \bigotimes_i P_i$ and $Q = D \leftarrow \bigotimes_i Q_i$ be queries in truth-normal form (let $P = C \leftarrow \bigwedge_i P_i$ and $Q = D \leftarrow \bigwedge_i Q_i$ be queries in knowledge-normal form). Then $P \leq_t Q$ (resp. $P \leq_k Q$) in a distributive bilattice if and only if both of the following hold

1. For each P_i in the body of P there is a Q_j in the body of Q, such that there is a homomorphism from the query $D' \leftarrow Q_j$ to the query $C' \leftarrow P_i$, where the head C' is obtained from C by projecting on the variables appearing in P_i, and similarly for D'.

2. For each Q_j in the body of Q there are atoms $C_1, \ldots, C_k$ in the body of P, such that there is a homomorphism from the query $D' \leftarrow Q_j$ to the query $C' \leftarrow C_1 \wedge \ldots \wedge C_k$ (resp. to the query $C' \leftarrow C_1 \otimes \ldots \otimes C_k$), where D' and C' are obtained as above.

The *if* part follows from applying Theorem 9 and Lemma 5.

For the *only if* part and point 1, suppose the set of variables occurring in P is $\{y_1, \cdots, y_p\}$, and let θ be the map $y_i \mapsto i$. Suppose then that $P_i = C_{i_1} \wedge \cdots \wedge C_{i_n}$. Let I be the instance containing the adorned tuples $C_{i_j}\theta$: *true*, for all $j \in$

$\{1,\ldots,n\}$, and the adorned tuples $A\theta$: *false*, for all atoms A that occur in the body of P, but not in P_i. It follows from Lemma 3 that there is an adorned tuple $C\theta$: c in $P(I)$, such that $c >_t$ *false*. Since $P(I) \leq_t Q(I)$, there must be an adorned tuple t : d in $Q(I)$, such that $c \leq_t d$, and consequently $d >_t$ *false*. That is, C and D are compatible and there is a conjunct $Q_j = D_{j_1} \wedge \cdots \wedge D_{j_m}$ in the body of Q, and an assignment σ, such that $(D' \leftarrow Q_j)_\sigma(I)$ contains an adorned tuple $D'\sigma$: d', where $d' >_t$ *false* since $d' = $ *false* would entail $d = $ *false*. This means that I has to contain all the adorned tuples of the form $D_{j_i}\sigma$: *true*, for all $i \in \{1,\ldots,m\}$. The desired homomorphism can now be defined as in the proof of Theorem 9.

For the *only if* part and point 2, suppose there is a Q_j in the body of Q, such that there is no set $\{C_1,\ldots,C_k\}$ of atoms from the body of P, for which we can find a homomorphism from the query $D' \leftarrow Q_j$ to the query $C' \leftarrow C_1 \wedge \cdots \wedge C_k$. Once again, let $\{y_1,\cdots,y_p\}$ be the variables occurring in P, and let θ be the map $y_i \mapsto i$. Consider the instance I, where I contains $A\theta$: *true*, for all atoms A in the body of P. Then the adorned tuple $C\theta$: *true* is in $P(I)$. Since we assumed that $P \leq_t Q$, there must be an assignment σ such that the following requirements are satisfied: $D\sigma$ and $C\theta$ contain the same tuple t, $D\sigma$: *true* belongs to $Q(I)$, and furthermore the result $(D' \leftarrow Q_j)_\sigma(I)$ contains the adorned tuple $D'\sigma$: *true*. Suppose $Q_j = D_{j_1} \wedge \cdots \wedge D_{j_m}$. Consider the mapping $h = \theta^{-1} \circ \sigma$. Then $h(D_{j_i})$ is in the body of P, for $i \in \{1,\ldots,m\}$; a contradiction to our counterassumption that no such homomorphism exists.

The Sagiv-Yannakakis theorem [SY80] for containment of unions of conjunctive queries comes as a special case, if we take union to be $\otimes$ in the trivial bilattice with $\mathcal{B} = \{$*true*, *false*$\}$, *false* $\leq_t$ *true* and *true* $\leq_k$ *false*. (Strictly speaking, in the trivial bilattice we only need condition 1 of Theorem 11.) Likewise, the generalization provided by Ioannidis and Ramakrishnan [IR95] is another special case of Theorem 11 in a similar trivial structure, where $\leq_k$ is the inverse of $\leq_t$.

If the bilattice is not distributive, we need to restrict our attention to the following case. Consider a partition of the set of predicates in our language. Call each block in this partition a server. Let $P = C \leftarrow \bigotimes_i P_i$ be a query in truth-normal form. Then we say that P is *well distributed* over the server-partition, if all predicates in each P_i in the body of P are from the same server, and if two predicates come from different P_i and P_j in the body of P, then they belong to different servers. Queries combining information from multiple sources are exactly of this kind.

Now we have the following.

Theorem 12. *Let $P = C \leftarrow \bigotimes_i P_i$ and $Q = D \leftarrow \bigotimes_i Q_i$ be queries well distributed over the same server-partition. Then $P \leq_t Q$ in a possibly non-distributive interlaced bilattice if and only if both of the following hold*

1. *As in Theorem 11.*
2. *For each Q_j in the body of Q there is a P_i in the body of P, such that there is a homomorphism from the query $D' \leftarrow Q_j$ to the query $C' \leftarrow P_i$.*

Here we apply Theorem 9 and the interlacing laws. The *only if* part for point 2 is similar to the proof Theorem 11. If the queries P and Q are in truth-normal form, but not well distributed, then the conditions in Theorem 12 are only sufficient.

4 The complexity of containment

Theorem 13. *Let P and Q be queries in truth or knowledge-normal form. Then the problem of testing whether $P \leq_t Q$ or $P \leq_k Q$, respectively, is NP-complete.*

The problem is NP-hard, since existence of homomorphism between classical conjunctive queries is NP-complete [CM77]. The problem is in NP, since as a consequence of Theorem 11, it is the intersection of polynomially many problems (existence of homomorphisms) in NP.

The complexity remains the same in non-distributive bilattices, if we restrict ourselves to well distributed queries. Formally we have:

Corollary 14. *Testing for truth-containment of well distributed queries in a possibly non-distributive, interlaced bilattice is NP-complete.*

For strong containment of queries both internal and external conjunctions we have the following result.

Theorem 15. *Let P and Q be queries in truth or knowledge-normal form. Then the problem of testing whether both $P \leq_t Q$ and $P \leq_k Q$, in a distributive bilattice, is Π_2^p-complete.*

Suppose that P and Q are in truth-normal form. From Theorem 12 we know that testing for $P \leq_t Q$ is in NP. We then need to test if $P \leq_k Q$. We can check if $P^k \not\leq_k Q^k$ as follows. Guess (in NP) a conjunct P_i of P^k and consult an oracle to see if there is a conjunct Q_j of Q^k, such that $P_i \leq_k Q_j$. From Theorem 13 we know that this can be done by an NP-oracle. If the oracle answers "no" output "yes." On the other hand, if indeed $P^k \leq_k Q^k$, then the oracle will never answer "no." Since $P^k \not\leq_k Q^k$ thus is seen to be in Σ_2^p, the problem $P^k \leq_k Q^k$ is in Π_2^p. The lower bound is established reducing a $\forall\exists$-quantified Boolean formula into two queries P and Q, if $P \leq_t Q$, then the formula is true iff $P \leq_k Q$.

The case where P and Q are in knowledge-normal form is symmetric to the one above.

It follows that testing for $P \leq_t Q$ or $P \leq_k Q$, when P and Q are not in any normal form, is Π_2^p-complete. Formally:

Corollary 16. *Let P and Q be queries not necessarily in any normal form. Then the problem of testing whether $P \leq_t Q$ or $P \leq_k Q$, respectively, in a distributive bilattice, is Π_2^p-complete.*

These complexity results generalize the Sagiv-Yannakakis Π_2^p-completeness result [SY80] from the trivial bilattices mentioned after Theorem 11 to general distributive bilattices.

5 Conclusion

Queries combining information from multiple sources have a natural semantics in bilattices. Determining containment of queries under bilattice semantics can be done through homomorphism techniques. Computationally, the problem is Π_2^p-complete. If the interlaced bilattice is not distributive, and the queries are not well distributed, then only a sufficient condition for queries in normal form can currently be given. It is not known if containment of non-well distributed queries is decidable when the semantics is given by a non-distributive interlaced bilattice, let alone if the queries in this case are not in any normal form.

References

[AHV95] Abiteboul S., Hull R., and Vianu V. *Foundations of Databases*. Addison-Wesley, Reading Ma. 1995.

[Bel77] Belnap N. D., Jr. A useful four-valued logic. In: J. Michael Dunn and G. Epstein (Eds.), *Modern Uses of Multiple-Valued Logic*, Reidel, 1977, pp. 89–148.

[CM77] Chandra A. K. and Merlin P. M. Optimal implementation of conjunctive queries in relational databases. *Proc. 9th Annual ACM Symp. on the Theory of Computing*, pp. 77–90.

[CV93] Chaudhuri S. and Vardi M. Optimization of real conjunctive queries. *Proc. 12th ACM Symp. on Principles of Database Systems*, pp. 59–70.

[Fag96] Fagin R. Combining fuzzy information from multiple systems. *Proc. 15th ACM Symp. on Principles of Database Systems*.

[Fit91] Fitting M. Bilattices and the semantics of logic programming. *J. Logic Programming* 11, 91–116.

[Fit93] Fitting M. The family of stable models. *J. Logic Programming* 17, 197–225.

[Gin88] Ginsberg M. L. Multivalued logics: a uniform approach to reasoning in artificial intelligence. *Computational Intelligence* 4, pp. 265–316.

[IR95] Ioannidis Y. E. and Ramakrishnan R. Containment of conjunctive queries: beyond relations as sets. *ACM Transactions on Database Systems* 20:3, pp. 288–324.

[SY80] Sagiv Y. and Yannakakis M. Equivalences among relational expressions with the union and difference operators. *J. ACM* 27:4, pp. 633–655.

[Sto77] Stockmeyer L. J. The polynomial-time hierarchy. *Theoret. Comput. Sci.* 3, pp. 1–22.

Efficient Complete Local Tests for Conjunctive Query Constraints with Negation

Nam Huyn [*]

Stanford University

Abstract. We consider the problem of incrementally checking global integrity constraints without using all the relations under constraint. In many application areas such as collaborative design, mobile computing and enterprise information systems, total data availability cannot be assumed. Even if all base data is available, some of it may incur such a high cost that its use should only be considered as a last resort. Without looking at all the base data, how can one meaningfully check a constraint for violation? When the constraint is known to be satisfied prior to the update, the state of the relations that are available (aka local) can in principle be used to infer something about the relations that are not available (aka remote). This observation is the basis for the existence of tests that guarantee that data integrity is preserved under a given update, without looking at all the base data.

In order to make integrity maintenance *practical*, the challenge is to find those tests that are *most general* (we call them *Complete Local Tests* or CLT's in short) and that are *efficient* to generate and execute. This paper addresses the problem of finding efficient CLT's for an important class of constraints that are very common in practice: constraints expressible as conjunctive queries with negated subgoals (abbreviated CQC¬.) We show that for single updates, all CQC¬ constraints admit a CLT that can be expressed in nonrecursive Datalog¬ when the predicates for the remote relations are not repeated in the constraint query. We then extend this result to a larger class of constraints and to certain sets of updates.

1 Introduction

The problem of incrementally checking global integrity constraints without using all the participating relations is important in many global information systems where base data is not totally available. In some cases, information access may be restricted for security reasons. In other cases, remote data sources may be disconnected temporarily due to mobility requirements. Cost may also be a factor in deciding not to use certain information sources if not absolutely needed. In some cases, we can optimize constraint maintenance in a distributed environment by first performing local checks for potential constraint violations before considering more expensive global checks. Consider a university information system as depicted in Fig. 1. While the databases are independently managed at their own site, they are subject to a global integrity constraint that students may

[*] This work was supported by ARO grant DAAH04-95-1-0192.

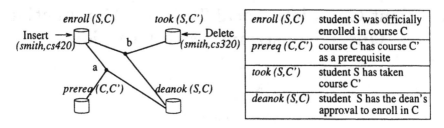

Fig. 1. University information system.

not enroll in a course unless they have either taken all the prerequisites for the course or obtained a special approval from the dean to enroll. This enrollment policy can be stated by the following integrity constraint:

$$(\forall\ S, C, C')\ enroll(S, C) \wedge prereq(C, C') \Rightarrow took(S, C') \vee deanok(S, C) \quad (1)$$

The databases may be disconnected due to network failure during which updates are allowed as long as the system remains globally consistent. Consider the insertion of a new tuple $enroll(smith, cs420)$. Let us see how we can guarantee that the insertion is safe in each of the following three scenarios.

1. Node a fails and relation $prereq$ becomes inaccessible. It is safe to enroll $smith$ in $cs420$ if he already has approval from the dean. Alternatively, consider the students who were enrolled in $cs420$ without using dean's approval (assuming there is one). Anyone of these students must have satisfied all the prerequisites for $cs420$. All these prerequisites must be among $\mathcal{P}$, the courses that all these students have taken. $\mathcal{P}$ is shown in Fig. 2 with hashed lines. If $smith$ has taken all courses in $\mathcal{P}$, he must have satisfied all the prerequisites for $cs420$.

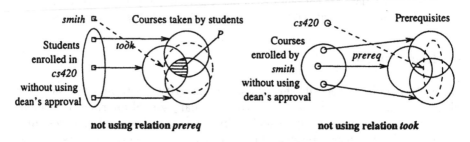

Fig. 2. Preserving data integrity under different scenarios.

2. Node b fails and relation $took$ becomes inaccessible. Again, approval from the dean is one way to safely enroll $smith$. Alternatively, we want to make sure $smith$ has taken all the prerequisite courses for $cs420$. Obviously, we cannot directly check this condition since relation $took$ is not available. Fortunately, there is an indirect method that considers the prerequisites for all courses

smith was enrolled in without using the dean's approval. If these prerequisites include all of *cs*420's prerequisites, we can conclude that *smith* has indeed taken all *cs*420's prerequisites. Fig. 2 illustrates this test.

3. Both nodes fail and none of the relations *prereq*, *took* and *deanok* is accessible. There is no way to ensure *smith*'s enrollment is legitimate.

While these tests obviously guarantee that data integrity is preserved under a given update, we also wish them to be as general as possible. Indeed, a degenerate test procedure that always results in predicting potential violation is certainly sound but too conservative to be of practical use. The challenge is to find the *most general* of these tests when they exist. Such most general tests are called *Complete Local Tests* (or just Complete Tests or CLT's in short) and can be formalized as follows:

- A CLT only looks at the instance of the local [2] base relations and the update instance.
- When the test is satisfied, global consistency is guaranteed to be preserved, regardless of the instance of remote relations. When it is not satisfied, there is some instance of the remote relations such that global consistency is not preserved.

Constraints of the form $(\forall \bar{U})(g_1 \wedge \ldots \wedge g_m \Rightarrow h_1 \vee \ldots \vee h_n)$, such as (1), are very common in practice. These constraints are used to specify that for a combination of data $(\bigwedge_i g_i)$ to be legitimate, it must have a "cover" among the h_j's (i.e., a tuple in the relation for some h_j that legitimizes the combination). These constraints have an equivalent query form in which the database is queried for violations, i.e., combinations of data that have no cover. The database is consistent if the constraint query returns no answers. In query form, the constraints of interest are represented as Datalog queries $panic :- g_1, \ldots, g_m, \neg h_1, \ldots, \neg h_n$. For this reason, we call them *Conjunctive-Query Constraints with Negation*, or $CQC^\neg$ in short. Besides the query form for $CQC^\neg$'s, the logic form will also be used to explain our reasoning.

This paper mainly considers the problem of finding not only most general tests for constraints whose query involves negation in general and for $CQC^\neg$'s in particular, but also tests that can be *efficiently* implemented such as first order queries. The $CQC^\neg$ class is shown in Fig. 3 as the shaded oval. Because of the presence of negation in the query, many questions that have practical significance are not immediately obvious. Do $CQC^\neg$'s admit test procedures that are complete and that can be efficiently generated? Do $CQC^\neg$'s admit CLT's that can be efficiently executed, i.e., in time polynomial in the size of the local relations? Can these CLT's be expressed as first order queries so they can be executed using conventional query-evaluation engines? In this paper, we establish the following results:

---

[2] For the rest of this paper, we choose to use the local/remote terminology purely to keep it consistent with [G94]. We say that a relation is "local" merely to indicate that it is available for use but not necessarily that is is physically local. Similar, "remote" is synonymous to "not available" for use.

- For single updates to local relations, all CQC¬'s admit complete local tests that can be expressed as nonrecursive Datalog queries with negation, provided each remote predicate has a single occurrence in the constraint query (shown as a dashed arc labeled "Our work" in Fig. 3). Using different techniques we recently developed but have not described in this paper, our results are extended to cover the entire conjunctive-query (CQ) class by lifting the restriction of no repeated predicates.
- These results are extended to a larger class of constraints and arbitrary sets of insertion updates and to certain sets of deletion updates to the local relations.
- All solution tests can be generated in time at most exponential in the size of the constraints. We give the solutions in a form that makes their expression in (safe) nonrecursive Datalog¬ (and other traditional query languages such as SQL) straightforward.

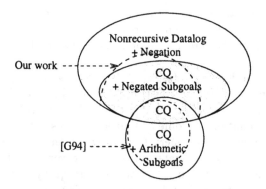

Fig. 3. Constraint classes for the CLT problem

Related Work. The notions of local tests and completeness were first introduced in [G94, GSUW94] and were embodied in an actual system supporting collaborative design in building construction [TH93]. The most powerful result for CLT's that can be found in [G94] applies to a subset of conjunctive-query constraints with arithmetic and handles only insertion updates and single local subgoals (shown as a dashed circle in Fig. 3). Negation was considered in [G94] but only for local tests that are not complete. The approach used in [G94] for finding complete tests is based on containment of conjunctive queries with arithmetic comparisons, and only in some restricted cases, a closed form solution for the CLT's (as queries) can be obtained by expanding and simplifying the containment tests.

In [LS93] a larger class of Datalog programs with negation was considered, but for a different though closely related problem: the problem of detecting queries independent of updates not looking at any relations. The problem of consistency maintenance considered in this paper is also closely related to the problem of view self-maintenance (see [TB88, GB95, H96b]) as follows: checking CQC¬ constraints reduces to checking if a given view instance is independent of a given update, but the latter problem is still open for CQ views with negation and with an arbitrary number of remote predicates. In fact, a subclass of this problem, namely that of checking if a given view instance gains new tuples under a given update to some local relation, reduces to our problem and can be solved using the results presented in this paper.

Alternative to containment-based approach. The problem of maintaining $CQC^\neg$'s can be reduced to that of testing containment of unions of conjunctive queries with negation and $\neq$ comparison. For instance, when l and g are available (with L and G as extensions) but h and r are not, maintaining the constraint $panic :- l(X), \neg g(X, Z), \neg h(X, Z), r(Z)$. under the insertion of $l(a)$ reduces to testing $Q_a \subseteq \bigcup_{t \in L} Q_t$, where Q_s denotes the boolean query $panic :- \neg g(s, Z), \neg h(s, Z), r(Z)$. To eliminate predicate g (whose extension is *given*) from Q_s, the trick is to rewrite Q_s as

$$panic :- \neg h(s, Z), r(Z), \bigwedge_{(x,z) \in G} (s \neq x \vee Z \neq z).$$

which in turn can be expanded into a union of conjunctive queries with negation and $\neq$. [LS93] gave an algorithm for testing such containments, which unfortunately has a complexity exponential in the size of the given relations in our problem (the queries have an exponential number of rules, and the rules have a number of subgoals the size of the given relations). Furthermore, it is not clear if one can always turn the algorithm for testing containment into a first order query independent of the extension of the given relations. While a containment-based approach cannot be easily applied to efficiently maintain $CQC^\neg$'s, the "university" example used earlier seems to suggest that an alternative but more direct approach can be used instead to find CLT's. The approach we offer in this paper essentially amounts to compile-time generation of runtime tests.

Paper Outline. The rest of this paper is organized as follows. In the next section, we provide some basic concepts on maintaining $CQC^\neg$ constraints, state assumptions and present our notation and terminology conventions. In Section 3, we illustrate our approach to the problem of finding complete tests by showing the concepts and the reasoning used in deriving complete local tests for our running example. We then present the main results of this paper in Sections 4 and 5. Finally in Section 6, we summarize our work and discuss possible extensions.

2 Preliminaries

Datalog$^\neg$. In this paper, integrity constraints (and their complete tests if any) are modeled as queries expressed by Datalog$^\neg$ programs. A Datalog$^\neg$ program is a collection of Horn rules that may have negated subgoals in their bodies. These rules are assumed to be *safe* (see [Ull88]), and when a program has both recursion and negation, stratified negation is assumed. Predicates used in a Datalog$^\neg$ program are partitioned into EDB predicates and IDB predicates. EDB predicates are those that only occur in rule bodies and represent base relations that are under constraint. Among the IDB predicates, there is a distinguished predicate called the *query predicate* that generates answers for the query. The following variable naming convention will be used in all Datalog$^\neg$ programs as well as in logic sentences: variable names always start in upper case, constant names in lower case.

Constraints. We mainly focus on constraints expressed by conjunctive queries with negation (CQC$^\neg$), that is, Datalog$^\neg$ programs consisting of a single rule of the form *panic* :- $g_1, \ldots, g_m, \neg h_1, \ldots, \neg h_n$., where the g_i's and h_i's denote positive literals with EDB predicates. In order to ensure safe use of negation, variables used in the h_i's must occur among the g_i's. The body in the rule above is called the *constraint query*. When the constraint query has an answer, the constraint is violated.

Since some of the EDB relations are local and others remote, we introduce a notation that makes the local vs remote distinction explicit. This notation also makes variable use in subgoals explicit. Thus, for the remainder of this paper, CQC$^\neg$'s are represented as

$$panic :- P(\bar{X}, \bar{Y}), \bigwedge_{i \in L} \neg Q_i(\bar{X}_i, \bar{Y}_i, \bar{Z}_i), \bigwedge_{j \in M} \neg \boldsymbol{Q_j}(\bar{X}_j, \bar{Y}_j, \bar{Z}_j), \boldsymbol{R}(\bar{Y}, \bar{Z}). \qquad (2)$$

- $P(\bar{X}, \bar{Y})$ denotes a conjunction of zero or more positive local subgoals (i.e. subgoals with local predicates), and $R(\bar{Y}, \bar{Z})$ a conjunction of zero or more positive remote subgoals. $\bar{X}$ denotes the set of variables that are used in positive local subgoals but not in positive remote subgoals, $\bar{Y}$ denotes the set of variables used in some positive local subgoal and some positive remote subgoal, and $\bar{Z}$ denotes the set of variables that are used in positive remote subgoals but not in positive local subgoals. Thus $\bar{X}, \bar{Y}, \bar{Z}$ are mutually disjoint. Note the use of boldface in the constraint query (2) to emphasize the fact that the subgoals in R are remote.
- The negated subgoals are partitioned into two subsets indexed by L and M: L indexes the negated local subgoals, that is, for $i \in L$, $Q_i(\bar{X}_i, \bar{Y}_i, \bar{Z}_i)$ denotes a subgoal with some local predicate; M indexes the negated remote subgoals, that is, for $j \in M$, $Q_j(\bar{X}_j, \bar{Y}_j, \bar{Z}_j)$ denotes a subgoal with some remote predicate. Also note the use of boldface in (2) for these remote Q_j's.
- $\bar{X}_i \subseteq \bar{X}$, $\bar{Y}_i \subseteq \bar{Y}$, $\bar{Z}_i \subseteq \bar{Z}$ are assumed for all $i \in L$ and $i \in M$ to ensure safe use of negation.

Unless explicitly stated otherwise, we use $\bar{a}$ (resp. $\bar{b}$, $\bar{c}$) to denote a vector of constants of the same arity as $\bar{X}$ (resp. $\bar{Y}, \bar{Z}$). When $\bar{X}_i \subseteq \bar{X}$, $\bar{a}_i$ denotes the projection of $\bar{a}$ onto the variables in $\bar{X}_i$. We will use $\bar{X} =_M \bar{X}'$ as a shorthand for $\bigwedge_{j \in M} \bar{X}_j = \bar{X}'_j$, representing the fact that the two vectors $\bar{X}$ and $\bar{X}'$ agree over the variables in all $\bar{X}_j$'s. Given some index $h \in L$, we will use L_h^+ to denote the set of indices $i \in L$ such that $\bar{Z}_i \subseteq \bar{Z}_h$. L_h^+ represents the negated local subgoals that do not use Z-variables other than those in $\bar{Z}_h$. $L_h^-(= L - L_h^+)$ denotes the indices for the remaining negated local subgoals.

Updates. Given a constraint and accessibility information about the EDB predicates as in (2), we only consider insertion and deletion updates to the local EDB relations. These updates are modeled as a set ΔP (resp. ΔQ_i) of tuples to be added to or deleted from the subquery $P(\bar{X}, \bar{Y})$ (resp. local subquery $Q_i(\bar{X}_i, \bar{Y}_i, \bar{Z}_i)$). For no loss of generality, we assume that when inserting a given ΔP into P, no tuples from ΔP is already in P. Similarly, when deleting a given ΔP from P, we assume all tuples from ΔP are already in P. The same assumption applies to the local ΔQ_i.

We will say that an update is *safe* (with respect to given local relations) if the update preserves global data consistency (with respect to a given constraint).

3 Extended example

In this section, we will go through the process of finding a complete local test for our running example. We will present the formal results for the general case in the next section. Recall from Section 1 the problem of finding complete tests for constraint (1) repeated here for convenience

$$(\forall \; S, C, C') \; enroll(S, C) \wedge prereq(C, C') \Rightarrow took(S, C') \vee deanok(S, C) \quad (3)$$

when relation *prereq* is remote. We first consider a simple insertion and later a simple deletion.

Characterizing when a simple insertion is safe. Suppose we want to insert *enroll*($smith, cs420$). To safely enroll *smith* in $cs420$, we must ensure that he has either obtained approval from the dean or taken all the prerequisites. In other words, a *cover* must be found for any tuple ($smith,cs420,C'$) where C' is a prerequisite for $cs420$. This condition is formalized as follows (by substituting S for *smith* and C for $cs420$ in (3)):

$$[(\forall C') \; prereq(cs420, C') \Rightarrow took(smith, C')] \vee deanok(smith, cs420) \quad (4)$$

The problem is that relation *prereq* is not available and we cannot directly look up the prerequisites for $cs420$. In order to eliminate the "unknown" $prereq(cs420, C')$ from (4), we must be able to "bound" $cs420$'s prerequisites or else, our "adversary" will be able to prevent *smith* from legally enrolling in $cs420$ by inventing prerequisites *smith* never took. We have just used a simple *adversary argument* to deal with the unknown, in which an imaginary adversary is trying to cause constraint violations by controlling the unknown. The adversary is able to do so if the following *boundability condition* is not satisfied (i.e., when every student uses dean's approval to enroll in $cs420$, the prerequisites no longer matter):

$$(\exists S) \; [enroll(S, cs420) \wedge \neg deanok(S, cs420)] \quad (5)$$

A key observation is that the adversary *is not totally free* to choose a state for *prereq* and must still respect the constraint that all past enrollments in $cs420$

were legal (by substituting C for $cs420$ in (3)):

$$(\forall S)\ enroll(S, cs420) \wedge \neg deanok(S, cs420)$$
$$\Rightarrow (\forall C')\ [prereq(cs420, C') \Rightarrow took(S, C')] \tag{6}$$

Boundability condition (5) amounts to requiring that constraint (6) is not vacuously satisfied. Constraint (6) also gives the bound we call $possible\text{-}cs420\text{-}prereq(C')$ representing all classes commonly taken by students without using dean's approval and formalized as:

$$possible\text{-}cs420\text{-}prereq(C') \stackrel{\text{def}}{\equiv}$$
$$(\forall S)\ enroll(S, cs420) \wedge \neg deanok(S, cs420) \Rightarrow took(S, C') \tag{7}$$

This bound is tight and the complete test for safe insertion is obtained by replacing unknown $prereq(cs420, C')$ in (4) with the bound $possible\text{-}cs420\text{-}prereq(C')$, and by attaching the boundability condition:

$$deanok(smith, cs420)\ \vee$$
$$(5) \wedge (\forall C')\ possible\text{-}cs420\text{-}prereq(C') \Rightarrow took(smith, C') \tag{8}$$

Ensuring test is finitely evaluable. Condition (8) would be easy to implement as a Datalog⌐ program (or in any traditional query language) if we know how to *finitely* evaluate $possible\text{-}cs420\text{-}prereq(C')$. The problem is that the current definition of $possible\text{-}cs420\text{-}prereq(C')$ in (7) is not safe. If every student uses dean's approval to enroll in $cs420$, then relation $possible\text{-}cs420\text{-}prereq$ would not be finite. Without changing its logical meaning, $possible\text{-}cs420\text{-}prereq(C')$ can simply be redefined to be safe by incorporating the boundability condition and by making it explicit that the values for C' actually come from relation $took$:

$$possible\text{-}cs420\text{-}prereq(C') \stackrel{\text{def}}{\equiv}$$
$$(\exists S)\ enroll(S, cs420) \wedge \neg deanok(S, cs420) \wedge took(S, C')\ \wedge$$
$$(\forall S)\ enroll(S, cs420) \wedge \neg deanok(S, cs420) \Rightarrow took(S, C')$$

The complete test (8) for safely inserting $enroll(smith, cs420)$ is expressed by the following nonrecursive Datalog⌐ program using `safeinsert` as the query predicate:

```
enroll-cs420-no-dean(S) :- enroll(S,cs420), ¬deanok(S,cs420).
            union(C') :- enroll-cs420-no-dean(S), took(S,C').
  not-a-cs420-prereq(C') :- union(C'), enroll-cs420-no-dean(S),
                            ¬took(S,C').
possible-cs420-prereq(C') :- union(C'), ¬not-a-cs420-prereq(C').
           notcovered :- possible-cs420-prereq(C'),
                            ¬took(smith,C').
           safeinsert :- deanok(smith,cs420).
           safeinsert :- enroll-cs420-no-dean(S),
                            ¬notcovered.
```

Deriving complete test for a simple deletion. Now suppose we want to delete $took(smith, cs320)$. For a deletion to be safe, we want to avoid situations where the tuple to be deleted is the sole way to legitimize the existence of certain tuples in other relations. If $smith$ was enrolled in a course that has $cs320$ as prerequisite, we must ensure that he was able to do so only with the dean's approval. In other words, any combination $(smith, C, cs320)$ that uses $took(smith, cs320)$ as a cover, must have an *alternative cover* to be found in $deanok$, the only choice of local relations left. This condition is formalized as

$$(\forall C)\ [enroll(smith, C) \wedge prereq(C, cs320)] \Rightarrow deanok(smith, C) \qquad (9)$$

Since $prereq(C, cs320)$ is unknown, the same idea of bounding courses having $cs320$ as prerequisite applies here as well, using the fact that prior to the deletion, there was no enrollment violations involving courses having $cs320$ as prerequisite:

$$(\forall C)\ prereq(C, cs320) \Rightarrow [(\forall S)\ enroll(S, C) \Rightarrow took(S, cs320) \vee deanok(S, C)]$$

The bound we call *possible-cs320-prereqfor*(C), is found on the right hand side of the implication above:

$$possible\text{-}cs320\text{-}prereqfor(C) \stackrel{\text{def}}{\equiv}$$
$$(\forall S)\ enroll(S, C) \Rightarrow took(S, cs320) \vee deanok(S, C) \qquad (10)$$

By eliminating unknown $prereq(C, cs320)$ from (9) using its bound (10), we obtain the following complete test for the safe deletion of $took(smith, cs320)$:

$$(\forall C)\ enroll(smith, C) \wedge possible\text{-}cs320\text{-}prereqfor(C) \Rightarrow deanok(smith, C)$$

This test can be directly implemented as the following nonrecursive Datalog⁻ program with **safedelete** as the query predicate:

```
enroll-no-dean(S,C) :- enroll(S,C), ¬deanok(S,C).
          forbid(C) :- enroll-no-dean(S,C),
                       ¬took(S,cs320).
possible-cs320-prereqfor(C) :- enroll-no-dean(S,C), ¬forbid(C).
             unsafe :- enroll-no-dean(smith,C),
                       possible-cs320-prereqfor(C).
         safedelete :- ¬unsafe.
```

4 General Case of Single Updates

We now present solutions for the problem of finding complete tests for general CQC⁻ constraints, that is, constraints of the form

$$panic :\!- P(\bar{X}, \bar{Y}), \bigwedge_{i \in L} \neg Q_i(\bar{X}_i, \bar{Y}_i, \bar{Z}_i), \bigwedge_{j \in M} \neg Q_j(\bar{X}_j, \bar{Y}_j, \bar{Z}_j), \boldsymbol{R}(\bar{Y}, \bar{Z}).$$

under the restriction that no remote predicate has multiple occurrences among the subqueries R and Q_j for $j \in M$, and under the restriction of single updates, i.e., when only one of the subqueries P or Q_i's for $i \in L$ changes, and only one tuple is either added to or removed from the subquery under change. We will successively consider the following three cases that have nontrivial solutions: (1) P vacuous (i.e. P has no conjuncts); (2) R vacuous; and (3) P and R nonvacuous (i.e. each has one or more conjuncts). The only remaining case that we are not considering here (for single updates) has a trivial solution which we can immediately state now: when there are no negated subgoals, inserting $P(\bar{a}, \bar{b})$ is safe if and only if $(\exists \bar{X}) P(\bar{X}, \bar{b})$ (see [H96atr]) and the net effect of removing anything from P is *always safe*. Due to space limitation, we omit all formal proofs and implementations in Datalog⁻, which can be found in [H96atr]. We prove sufficiency of all the test conditions in this section by case analysis, and their necessity by case analysis and counterexample construction.

4.1   No positive local subgoals

When there are no positive local subgoals, the constraint takes on a special form where there are neither X-variables nor Y-variables:

$$panic :- \bigwedge_{i \in L} \neg Q_i(\bar{Z}_i), \bigwedge_{j \in M} \neg \boldsymbol{Q}_j(\bar{Z}_j), \boldsymbol{R}(\bar{Z}).$$

Single insertions into the local Q_i's are always safe since the constraint query is antimonotonic in these Q_i's (i.e., the constraint query never gain tuples when tuples are added to the Q_i's). The following theorem gives a CLT solution for the general case of no positive local subgoals under single deletions.

Theorem 1. *(Deletion) Let $h \in L$ and let $\bar{c}$ be a vector of constants of the same arity as $\bar{Z}_h$. The following is a CLT for the safe deletion of $Q_h(\bar{c})$:*

$$\bigvee_{i \in L_h^+, i \neq h} Q_i(\bar{c}_i).$$

Intuitively, we want to make sure that any tuple $(\bar{Z})$ that uses $Q_h(\bar{c})$ as a cover, has an alternative cover to be found among the local Q_i's other than Q_h. We cannot count on the remote Q_j's to provide cover since they are controlled by the adversary. Also, since the variables outside of $\bar{Z}_h$ are totally controlled by the adversary, we are reduced to find cover among the local Q_i's that only use variables in $\bar{Z}_h$.

4.2   No positive remote subgoals

When there are no positive remote subgoals, the constraint takes on a special form where there are neither Y-variables nor Z-variables:

$$panic :- P(\bar{X}), \bigwedge_{i \in L} \neg Q_i(\bar{X}_i), \bigwedge_{j \in M} \neg \boldsymbol{Q}_j(\bar{X}_j).$$

The following theorems give solution CLT for the general case of no positive remote subgoals under a single insertion and a single deletion.

Theorem 2. *(Insertion) The following is a CLT for the safe insertion of $P(\bar{a})$:*

$$[\bigvee_{i \in L} Q_i(\bar{a}_i)] \vee (\exists \bar{X})[P(\bar{X}) \wedge (\bar{X} =_M \bar{a}) \wedge \bigwedge_{i \in L} \neg Q_i(\bar{X}_i)]$$

When a local cover cannot be found for the newly inserted $P(\bar{a})$, a remote cover must be found, albeit not directly. The trick here is to look for tuples in P that have no local cover (and thus must have used a remote cover), and that are "indistinguishable" from tuple $(\bar{a})$ from the remote point of view.

Theorem 3. *(Deletion) Let $h \in L$ and let $\bar{a}$ be a vector of constants of the same arity as $\bar{X}_h$. The following is a CLT for the safe deletion of $Q_h(\bar{a})$:*

$$(\forall \bar{X}) \quad P(\bar{X}) \wedge \bar{X}_h = \bar{a} \wedge \bigwedge_{i \in L, i \neq h} \neg Q_i(\bar{X}_i)$$
$$\Rightarrow (\exists \bar{X}')(P(\bar{X}') \wedge (\bar{X}' =_M \bar{X}) \wedge \bigwedge_{i \in L} \neg Q_i(\bar{X}'_i))$$

Any tuple $(\bar{X})$ in P that uses $Q_h(\bar{a})$ as a cover prior to its deletion and that has no other local covers, must have a remote cover which can be indirectly found if we can find some tuple $(\bar{X}')$ in P that has no local cover and that is indistinguishable from $(\bar{X})$ from the remote point of view.

4.3 Both positive local and remote subgoals present

Generalizing on the extended example in Section 3, the following theorems give the complete test solutions for the general case when both positive local and remote subgoals are present. The reader is warned that the test expressions are rather complex. This complexity is partly due to the generality of the results, which unify simpler results from more specialized subcases. Immediately following the theorems, we will briefly give an intuitive account of various subexpressions in the tests and point out opportunities when the test expressions can be drastically simplified.

In the following theorem for insertion, we use $\bar{Z}_I$ to denote the union of all variables from $\bar{Z}_i$ for all $i \in I$, for a given set I of indices.

Theorem 4. *(Insertion) The following is a CLT for the safe insertion of $P(\bar{a}, \bar{b})$:*

$$\underbrace{\bigvee_{i \in L, \bar{Z}_i = \emptyset} Q_i(\bar{a}_i, \bar{b}_i)}_{(i)} \vee [\underbrace{(\exists \bar{X}) \, (P(\bar{X}, \bar{b}) \wedge \bar{X} =_M \bar{a}) \wedge}_{(ii)}$$
$$\underbrace{\bigwedge_{I \subseteq L, I \neq \emptyset} (\forall \bar{Z}_I) \, [\phi_{\bar{a}\bar{b}}^I(\bar{Z}_I) \Rightarrow \bigvee_{i \in L, \bar{Z}_i \subseteq \bar{Z}_I} Q_i(\bar{a}_i, \bar{b}_i, \bar{Z}_i)]]}_{(iii)} \quad (11)$$

where $\phi_{\bar{a}\bar{b}}^{I}(\bar{Z}_I)$ is defined as:

$$\bigwedge_{i \in I} (\exists \bar{X})\,[P(\bar{X},\bar{b}) \wedge (\bar{X} =_M \bar{a}) \wedge Q_i(\bar{X}_i, \bar{b}_i, \bar{Z}_i)]$$

$$\wedge (\forall \bar{X})\,[P(\bar{X},\bar{b}) \wedge (\bar{X} =_M \bar{a}) \Rightarrow \bigvee_{i \in I} Q_i(\bar{X}_i, \bar{b}_i, \bar{Z}_i)]$$

Intuitively, we want to find a cover for any tuple $(\bar{a},\bar{b},\bar{Z})$ such that $R(\bar{b},\bar{Z})$. The local covers provided by subexpression *(i)* in (11) are the simplest since no Z-variables are involved. When these simple local covers fail, the situation becomes more complicated since we now have to not only find cover for these Z-values but also bound them. Roughly speaking, subexpression *(ii)* represents the boundability condition (analogous to (5) in the extended example), and the $\phi_{\bar{a}\bar{b}}^{I}(\bar{Z}_I)$'s are the bounds (analogous to (7) in the extended example). The implication *(iii)* essentially provides cover for the Z-values once bounded.

Note how all nonempty subsets $I \subseteq L$ are involved in testing for inclusion of the Z-values. This extra complexity is needed to make sure that the $\phi_{\bar{a}\bar{b}}^{I}(\bar{Z}_I)$ queries can be finitely evaluated, especially when the negated subgoals Q_i's are allowed to use arbitrarily different subsets of Z-variables. To appreciate this small but important point, consider the formula $(\forall\, Z_1, Z_2)[(\forall X)(p(X) \Rightarrow (q_1(X, Z_1) \vee q_2(X, Z_2)))] \Rightarrow [r_1(Z_1) \vee r_2(Z_2)]$. Even if relation p is nonempty, this formula is not safe since the number of pairs (Z_1, Z_2) that satisfy the left hand side of the top level implication may be unbounded. Since we only need to bound their projections onto Z_1 or Z_2, a solution is to generate the values *for each subset* of the Z-variables using the following safe queries

$$\varphi_1(Z_1) \overset{\text{def}}{\equiv} (\exists X)(p(X) \wedge q_1(X, Z_1)) \wedge (\forall X)(p(X) \Rightarrow q_1(X, Z_1))$$

$$\varphi_2(Z_2) \overset{\text{def}}{\equiv} (\exists X)(p(X) \wedge q_2(X, Z_2)) \wedge (\forall X)(p(X) \Rightarrow q_2(X, Z_2))$$

$$\varphi_{12}(Z_1, Z_2) \overset{\text{def}}{\equiv} (\exists X)(p(X) \wedge q_1(X, Z_1)) \wedge (\exists X)(p(X) \wedge q_2(X, Z_2)) \wedge$$
$$(\forall X)(p(X) \Rightarrow (q_1(X, Z_1) \vee q_2(X, Z_2)))$$

and test each of these subsets using the following equivalent but safe formula:

$$(\forall\, Z_1)\,[\varphi_1(Z_1) \Rightarrow r_1(Z_1)]\, \wedge$$
$$(\forall\, Z_2)\,[\varphi_2(Z_2) \Rightarrow r_2(Z_2)]\, \wedge$$
$$(\forall\, Z_1, Z_2)\,[\varphi_{12}(Z_1, Z_2) \Rightarrow (r_1(Z_1) \vee r_2(Z_2))]$$

The following theorem for deletion uses the notation $\bar{Z}_I =_{I,h} \bar{c}$ (for some $I \subseteq L_h^-$, some $h \in L$, and some vector $\bar{c}$ of constants of same arity as $\bar{Z}_h$) that needs to be clarified: the left hand side represents constant values for variables in $\bar{Z}_I$; the right hand side represents constant values for variables in $\bar{Z}_h$; when $\bar{Z}_I$ and $\bar{Z}_h$ have no variables in common, the comparison is vacuously satisfied; otherwise, there must be agreement over the common variables.

Theorem 5. *(Deletion) Let $h \in L$ and let $\bar{a}$ (resp. $\bar{b}$, $\bar{c}$) be a vector of constants of the same arity as $\bar{X}_h$ (resp. $\bar{Y}_h$, $\bar{Z}_h$). The following is a CLT for the safe deletion of $Q_h(\bar{a}, \bar{b}, \bar{c})$:*

$$(\forall \bar{X}, \bar{Y})[\ [P(\bar{X}, \bar{Y}) \wedge \eta_{\bar{a}\bar{b}\bar{c}}(\bar{X}, \bar{Y})]$$

$$\Rightarrow (\exists \bar{X}')(\psi_{\bar{b}\bar{c}}(\bar{X}', \bar{Y}) \wedge \bar{X}' =_M \bar{X})] \wedge$$

$$\bigwedge_{I \subseteq L_h^-, I \neq \emptyset} (\forall \bar{X}, \bar{Y}, \bar{Z}_I)[\ [P(\bar{X}, \bar{Y}) \wedge \eta_{\bar{a}\bar{b}\bar{c}}(\bar{X}, \bar{Y}) \wedge \xi_{\bar{b}\bar{c}}^I(\bar{X}, \bar{Y}, \bar{Z}_I)]$$

$$\Rightarrow \bigvee_{i \in L_h^-, \bar{Z}_i \subseteq \bar{Z}_I} Q_i(\bar{X}_i, \bar{Y}_i, \bar{Z}_i)] \tag{12}$$

where $\eta_{\bar{a}\bar{b}\bar{c}}$, $\psi_{\bar{b}\bar{c}}$ and $\xi_{\bar{b}\bar{c}}^I$ are defined by:

$$\eta_{\bar{a}\bar{b}\bar{c}}(\bar{X}, \bar{Y}) \stackrel{\text{def}}{\equiv} \bar{X}_h = \bar{a} \wedge \bar{Y}_h = \bar{b} \wedge \bigwedge_{i \in L_h^+, i \neq h} \neg Q_i(\bar{X}_i, \bar{Y}_i, \bar{c}_i)$$

$$\psi_{\bar{b}\bar{c}}(\bar{X}, \bar{Y}) \stackrel{\text{def}}{\equiv} P(\bar{X}, \bar{Y}) \wedge \neg Q_h(\bar{X}_h, \bar{b}, \bar{c}) \wedge \bigwedge_{i \in L_h^+, i \neq h} \neg Q_i(\bar{X}_i, \bar{Y}_i, \bar{c}_i)$$

$$\xi_{\bar{b}\bar{c}}^I(\bar{X}, \bar{Y}, \bar{Z}_I) \stackrel{\text{def}}{\equiv} (\forall \bar{X}')[(\psi_{\bar{b}\bar{c}}(\bar{X}', \bar{Y}) \wedge \bar{X}' =_M \bar{X}) \Rightarrow \bigvee_{i \in I} Q_i(\bar{X}'_i, \bar{Y}_i, \bar{Z}_i)]$$

$$\wedge [\bar{Z}_I =_{I,h} \bar{c}]$$

Intuitively, each tuple $(\bar{X}, \bar{Y}, \bar{Z})$ in $P(\bar{X}, \bar{Y}) \wedge R(\bar{Y}, \bar{Z})$ that uses $Q_h(\bar{a}, \bar{b}, \bar{c})$ as a cover, must have some alternative cover. The second line in (12) essentially provides cover for these tuples. However, the Z-values, especially for those variables not in $\bar{Z}_h$, must be bounded. Intuitively, the first line in (12) essentially provides the boundability conditions, and the $\xi_{\bar{b}\bar{c}}^I$'s define the bounds (analogous to (10) in the extended example). As with the test for insertion, all nonempty subsets $I \subseteq L_h^-$ need to be considered here to make sure that $\xi_{\bar{b}\bar{c}}^I$ can be finitely evaluated.

Simplifications. When the index set over which a conjunction or a disjunction ranges becomes empty, the conjunction (resp disjunction) can be treated as vacuous truth (resp falsity), enabling test expressions to simplify. For instance, when there are no negated local subgoals, the complete test for safe insertion simplifies to $(\exists \bar{X})[P(\bar{X}, \bar{b}) \wedge \bar{X} =_M \bar{a}]$. Another source of complexity in the test expressions was introduced in order to make their evaluation safe. However, by carefully factoring out the Q_i's that use no Z-variables, and by grouping together those that use the same subset of Z-variables, drastic simplifications can be achieved. For instance, when there are no negated remote subgoals and all the negated local subgoals use the same Z-variables (say $\bar{Z}$), the insertion test degenerates to $(\exists \bar{X})P(\bar{X}, \bar{b}) \wedge (\forall \bar{Z})(\phi_{\bar{b}}(\bar{Z}) \Rightarrow \bigvee_{i \in L} Q_i(\bar{a}_i, \bar{b}_i, \bar{Z}))$ where $\phi_{\bar{b}}(\bar{Z})$ is defined to be $(\exists \bar{X})[P(\bar{X}, \bar{b}) \wedge \bigvee_{i \in L} Q_i(\bar{X}_i, \bar{b}_i, \bar{Z})] \wedge (\forall \bar{X})[P(\bar{X}, \bar{b}) \Rightarrow \bigvee_{i \in L} Q_i(\bar{X}_i, \bar{b}_i, \bar{Z})]$. Thus, there are nontrivial classes of constraints whose CLT can be generated in time polynomial in the size of the constraints. More opportunities for simplification are explained in [H96atr].

4.4 Beyond CQC⌐ constraints

The results we just presented are not limited to CQC⌐ constraints as defined in (2). In fact, P and the local Q_i's may be *any query* not involving remote EDB's, as long as their updates can be computed from the EDB updates. This observation alone already allows us to extend the results to a considerably larger class of constraints. In addition, subqueries R and the remote Q_j's may be any query not involving local EDB's, as long as the Q_j's instances can be "arbitrarily realized" and R's instances can be "arbitrarily realized as singletons". We allow for instance $Q_j(\bar{X}_j, \bar{Y}_j, \bar{Z}_j)$ to actually represent $(\exists \bar{T}_j)\ q(\bar{X}_j, \bar{Y}_j, \bar{Z}_j, \bar{T}_j)$ for some remote predicate q, where the T-variables have been projected out. Thus, our complete test results can be used to enforce familiar data dependencies such as inclusion and tuple generating dependencies. We also allow for instance $R(\bar{Y}, \bar{Z})$ to represent the union of conjunctive queries $R_k(\bar{Y}, \bar{Z})$'s as long as no predicate occurs more than once in these queries. Thus, our results are also applicable to a limited form of union of CQC⌐'s.

5 Sets of Updates

Section 4 gave CLT solutions under single updates. These solutions are now extended to insertion sets and deletion sets. Due to space limitation, we will just briefly mention the results. The formal results and their proofs can be found in [H96atr]. In the following, we assume $L = \{1, \ldots, m\}$ and $h \in L$.

- Insertions to positive subgoals are *independently testable*: the complete test under the insertion of $(\Delta P, \Delta Q_1, \ldots, \Delta Q_m)$ is the conjunction, for t ranging over ΔP, of CLT under the insertion of $(t, \Delta Q_1, \ldots, \Delta Q_m)$. The CLT's for the latter type of insertion updates generalize the results from previous section by replacing some occurrences of Q_i in the test expression with $Q_i \cup \Delta Q_i$.

- Deletions from the same negated subgoal are independently testable: the complete test under the deletion of $(\Delta P, \Delta Q_h)$ is the conjunction, for t ranging over ΔQ_h, of CLT under the deletion of $(\Delta P, t)$. The CLT's for the latter type of deletion updates generalize the results from previous section by replacing some occurrences of P in the test expression with $P - \Delta P$.

- Deletions from multiple negated subgoals are *testable in chain*: testing safety of deletion update $(\Delta Q_1, \ldots, \Delta Q_m)$ can be done by testing safety of deletion update (ΔQ_i) in the instance of the local relations that results from deleting $(\Delta Q_1, \ldots, \Delta Q_{i-1})$ from the original instance.

6 Conclusion

In this paper, we considered CQC⌐'s for which, while an important class of constraints, the problem of finding efficient CLT's remained open. We solved the CLT problem for general CQC⌐ constraints for single updates when remote predicates have single occurrences in the constraint queries. We gave complete test solutions in a form that can easily be implemented in SQL. The time to generate these tests is at most exponential in the size of the given constraint. We also pointed out opportunities for substantially reducing the complexity of these tests. Since all the tests can be implemented in nonrecursive Datalog¬, executing them takes time at most polynomial in the size of the local relations.

Throughout this paper, we have assumed single occurrences of the remote predicates in the constraint query. This restriction was needed to ensure that it is always possible to choose an instance of the remote EDB relations such that arbitrary answers of the subqueries R and Q_j's can be realized. If the restriction is ignored, while all tests remain sound, their completeness can no longer be guaranteed. Indeed, if we allow multiple occurrences of the remote predicates, new dependencies are created within and among the instances of R and Q_j's. This observation suggests that for a test to be complete, the dependencies, induced by the particular structure of the remote queries on their results, must be embodied in the test's condition. When repeated remote predicates are allowed but only within R, we show in [H96atr] how our techniques can be extended to derive CLT's. Essentially, under the insertion of $P(\bar{a}, \bar{b})$, instead of looking for tuples $(\bar{X}, \bar{Y})$ in P that satisfy $\bar{Y} = \bar{b}$ (among other conditions), the search is extended to tuples whose $\bar{Y}$ may now take any value from some "closure" of $R(\bar{b}, \bar{Z})$. This closure degenerates to $\{\bar{b}\}$ when R has no repeated predicates.

Acknowledgments. We thank Jeff Ullman and Serge Abiteboul for their valuable comments regarding both technical contents and presentation of this material.

References

[G94]   Gupta A.: *Partial Information Based Integrity Constraint Checking.* PhD Thesis, Stanford University, November 1994.

[GB95]   Gupta A. and Blakeley J. A.: Using Partial Information to Update Materialized Views. In *Information Systems,* 20(8), pp. 641–662, 1995.

[GSUW94]   Gupta A., Sagiv Y., Ullman J. D. and Widom J.: Constraint Checking with Partial Information. *Proc. 13th ACM Symp. on PODS,* 1994, pp. 45–55.

[H96atr]   Huyn N.: Testing CQC¬ constraints under limited data access. *Unpublished Technical Report* available as URL http://www-db.stanford.edu/pub/papers/cqcnclt-tr.ps.

[H96b]   Huyn N.: Efficient View Self-Maintenance. *Proc. ACM Workshop on Materialized Views,* 1996, pp. 17–25.

[LS93]   Levy A. and Sagiv Y.: Queries Independent of Updates. *Proc. 19th International Conf. on Very Large Data Bases,* 1993, pp. 171–181.

[TH93]   Tiwari S. and Howard H. C.: Constraint Management on Distributed AEC Databases. *Fifth International Conf. on Computing in Civil and Building Engineering,* ASCE, 1993, pp. 1147–1154.

[TB88]   Tompa F. W. and Blakeley J. A.: Maintaining Materialized Views Without Accessing Base Data. In *Information Systems,* 13(4), pp. 393–406, 1988.

[Ull88]   Ullman J. D.: *Principles of Database and Knowledge-Base Systems,* Volumes 1 and 2. Computer Science Press, 1988.

Selection of Views to Materialize in a Data Warehouse

Himanshu Gupta

Department of Computer Science
Stanford University
hgupta@cs.stanford.edu

Abstract. A data warehouse stores materialized views of data from one or more sources, with the purpose of efficiently implementing decision-support or OLAP queries. One of the most important decisions in designing a data warehouse is the selection of materialized views to be maintained at the warehouse. The goal is to select an appropriate set of views that minimizes total query response time and the cost of maintaining the selected views, given a limited amount of resource, e.g., materialization time, storage space etc.

In this article, we develop a theoretical framework for the general problem of selection of views in a data warehouse. We present competitive polynomial-time heuristics for selection of views to optimize total query response time, for some important special cases of the general data warehouse scenario, viz.: (i) an AND view graph, where each query/view has a unique evaluation, and (ii) an OR view graph, in which any view can be computed from *any one* of its related views, e.g., data cubes. We extend the algorithms to the case when there is a set of indexes associated with each view. Finally, we extend our heuristic to the most general case of AND-OR view graphs.

1   Introduction

A *data warehouse* is a repository of integrated information available for querying and analysis [IK93, Wid95]. Figure 1 illustrates the architecture of a typical warehouse [WGL+96]. The information stored at the warehouse is in the form of views, referred to as *materialized views*, derived from the data in the sources. In order to keep a materialized view consistent with the data at sources, the view has to be *incrementally maintained* [ZGMHW95, GM95]. This maintenance of views incurs what is known as *view maintenance* or *update costs*.

In this paper, we concentrate on the problem of selecting an appropriate set of materialized views, one of the most important design decisions in designing a data warehouse. Given some storage space constraint, the problem is to select a set of derived views to minimize total query response time and the cost of maintaining the selected views. We refer to this problem as the *view-selection problem*.

Related work on this problem has been as follows. [HRU96] presents and analyzes algorithms for selection of views in the special case of "data cubes."

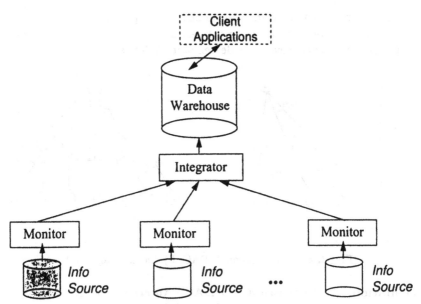

Fig. 1. A typical data warehouse architecture

Gupta et al. in [GHRU96] extend their result to selection of views and indexes in data cubes. Both these works ignore update costs. [RSS96] looks at the problem of augmenting a given set of materialized views with an *additional* set of views that may reduce the total maintenance cost.

The rest of the paper is organized as follows. In the next section, we develop a theoretical framework for the view-selection problem. In the following two sections, we present and analyze heuristics for some special cases. In Section 5, we present an algorithm for the general view-selection problem in a data warehouse. Finally, we conclude in Section 6.

2 View-Selection Problem Formulation

2.1 AND-OR View Graphs

In this subsection, we develop a notion of an AND-OR view graph, which is one of the inputs to the view-selection problem. We start by defining the notions of expression DAGs for queries or views.

Definition 2.1 (Expression A-DAG) An *expression A-DAG* (AND-DAG) for a query or a view V is a directed acyclic graph having the base relations as "sinks" (no outgoing edges) and the node V as a "source" (no incoming edges). If a node/view u has outgoing edges to nodes $v_1, v_2, \ldots, v_k$, then *all* of the views $v_1, v_2, \ldots, v_k$ are required to compute u and this dependence is indicated by drawing a semicircle, called an *AND arc*, through the edges $(u, v_1), (u, v_2), \ldots, (u, v_k)$. Such an AND arc has an operator[1] and a cost associated with it, which is the

---

[1] The operator associated with the AND arc is actually a k-ary function involving operations like join, union, aggregation etc.

cost incurred during the computation of u from $v_1, v_2, \ldots, v_k$.

The *evaluation cost* of a node u in an expression A-DAG is the sum of the costs associated with each of its descendant's AND arc. □

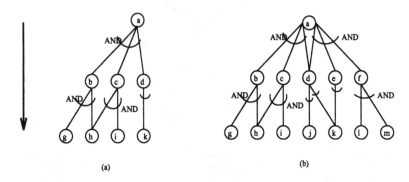

(a)   (b)

Fig. 2. a) An expression A-DAG, b) An expression AO-DAG

Definition 2.2 (Expression AO-DAG) An *expression AO-DAG* for a view or a query V is a directed acyclic graph with V as a source and the base relations as sinks. Each nonsink node has associated with it one or more AND arcs, each binding a *subset* of its outgoing edges. As in the previous definition, each AND arc has an operator and a cost associated with it. More than one AND arc at a node depicts multiple ways of computing that node. □

Definition 2.3 (AND-OR View Graph) A graph G is called an *AND-OR view graph* for the views (or queries) $V_1, V_2, \ldots, V_k$ if for each V_i, there is a subgraph G_i in G which is an expression AO-DAG for V_i. Each node u in an AND-OR view graph has the following parameters associated with it: f_u (frequency of the queries on u), S_u (space occupied by u), and g_u (frequency of updates on u). For example, the graph in Figure 2(b) is an AND-OR view graph for any subset of the views a through f. □

Note that in an AND-OR view graph, if a view u can be computed from the views $v, u_1, u_2, \ldots, u_k$ and the view v can be computed from $v_1, v_2, \ldots, v_l$, then u can also be computed from $u_1, u_2, \ldots, u_k, v_1, v_2, \ldots, v_l$.

2.2 Constructing an AND-OR View Graph

Given a set of queries $Q_1, Q_2, \ldots, Q_k$ to be supported at a warehouse, we construct an AND-OR view graph for the queries as follows. We first construct an expression-AO DAG D_i for each query Q_i in the set. An AND-OR view graph G for the set of queries can then be constructed by "merging" the expression AO-DAGs $D_1, D_2, \ldots, D_k$. Each node in the AND-OR view graph G will represent a view that could be selected for materialization, and these are the only views considered for materialization.

For a query Q_i we construct its expression AO-DAG D_i to consist of alternate "useful" ways of evaluating Q_i from the given base relations, in the presence of other queries/views. Roussopoulos in [Rou82] considers exactly this problem. The objective of his analysis is to identify all possible (useful) ways to produce the result of a view, given other view definitions and base relations.

2.3 The View-Selection Problem

Given an AND-OR view graph G and a quantity S (available space), the *view-selection problem* is to select a set of views M, a subset of the nodes in G, that minimizes the sum of total query response time and total maintenance cost, under the constraint that the total space occupied by M is less than S.

More formally, let $Q(u, M)$ denote the cost of answering a query u (also a node of G) using the set M of materialized views in the given view graph G. $Q(u, M)$ is the evaluation cost of the cheapest embedded expression A-DAG for u in G whose sinks belong to the set $M \cup L$, where L is the set of sinks in G. Here, without loss of generality, we have assumed that the sinks in G are always available for computation as they represent the base tables at the source(s). Thus, $Q(u, \phi)$ is the cost of answering the query on u directly from the source(s). Let $U(u, M)$ be the maintenance cost for the view u in the presence of the set of materialized views M and the set of sinks, L.

So, given an AND-OR view graph G and a quantity S, we wish to select a set of views/nodes $M = \{V_1, V_2, \ldots, V_m\}$, that minimizes $\tau(G, M)$, where

$$\tau(G, M) = \sum_{i=1}^{k} f_{Q_i} Q(Q_i, M) + \sum_{i=1}^{m} g_{V_i} U(V_i, M),$$

under the constraint that $\sum_{v \in M} S_v \leq S$.

The view-selection problem is NP-hard even for the special case of an AND-OR graph where each AND arc binds at most one edge, and when the update frequencies are zero. There is a straightforward reduction from **minimum set cover**.

2.4 Benefit of a Set of Selected Views

Let C be an arbitrary set of views in a view graph G. The *benefit* of C with respect to M, an already selected set of views, is denoted by $B(C, M)$ and is defined as $\tau(G, M) - \tau(G, M \cup C)$, where τ is the function defined above. The benefit of C per unit space with respect to M is $B(C, M)/S(C)$, where $S(C)$ is the space occupied by the views in C. Also, $B(C, \phi)$ is called the *absolute benefit* of the set C.

Monotonicity Property The benefit function B is said to satisfy the *monotonicity property* for M with respect to disjoint sets (of views) $O_1, O_2, \ldots, O_m$ if $B(O_1 \cup O_2 \ldots \cup O_m, M) \leq \sum_{i=1}^{i=m} B(O_i, M)$.

The monotonicity property of the benefit function is important for the greedy heuristics to deliver competitive (within a constant factor of optimal) solutions. For a given instance of AND-OR view graph, if the optimal solution O can be partitioned into disjoint subsets of views $O_1, O_2, \ldots, O_m$ such that the benefit function satisfies the monotonicity property w.r.t. $O_1, O_2, \ldots, O_m$, then we guide the greedy heuristic to select, at each stage, an optimal set (of views) of type that includes O_i for all $i \leq m$. Such a greedy heuristic is guaranteed to deliver a solution whose benefit is at least 63% of the optimal benefit, as we show later.

3 AND View Graph

In this section we consider a special case of the view-selection problem in AND-OR view graphs. Here, we assume that each AND arc binds all the outgoing edges from a node. This case depicts the simplied scenario where each view has a unique way of being computed. We call such a graph G an *AND view graph*, where a node can be computed from *all* of its children. As before, each AND arc has an operator and a cost associated with it. An AND view graph for a set of queries is just a "merging" of the expression A-DAGs of the queries.

3.1 Motivation

The general view-selection problem can be approximated by this simplified problem of selecting views in an AND view graph. Given a set of queries supported at the warehouse, instead of contructing an AND-OR view graph as in Section 2.2, we could run a multiple-query optimizer [Sel88, CM82] to generate a global plan, which is essentially an AND view graph for the queries. Such a global plan takes advantage of the common subexpressions among the queries.

3.2 Selection of Views in an AND View Graph

In this subsection, we present heuristics for solving the view-selection problem in AND view graphs without update costs. Later, we extend it to a special case of AND view graphs with update costs. We note here that the view-selection problem in AND view graphs is not known to be NP-complete.

Problem: Given an AND view graph G without updates and a quantity S, find a set of views M that minimizes the quantity $\tau(G, M)$, under the constraint that the total space occupied by the views in M is at most S.

Algorithm 3.1 <u>Greedy Algorithm</u>

Given: G, an AND-OR view graph, and S, the space constraint.
BEGIN
    $M = \phi$;   /* M = set of structures selected so far. */
    while $(S(M) < S)$
        Let C be the view which has the maximum benefit per unit space
            with respect to M.
        $M = M \cup C$;
    end while;
    return M;
END.

Greedy Algorithm We present a simple greedy heuristic for selecting views. At each stage, we select a view which has the maximum benefit per unit space at that stage. See Algorithm 3.1. The running time of the greedy algorithm is $O(kn^2)$, where n is the number of nodes in the graph and k is the number of stages used by the algorithm.

Observation 1 *In an AND view graph without updates, the benefit function B satisfies the monotonicity property for any M with respect to arbitrary set of views $O_1, O_2, \ldots, O_m$.*

Theorem 3.1 *For an AND view graph G without updates and a quantity S, the greedy algorithm produces a solution M that uses at most $S + r$ units of space, where r is the size of the largest view in G. Also, the absolute benefit of M is at least $(1 - 1/e)$ times the optimal benefit achievable using as much space as that used by M.*

Proof. It is easy to see that the space used by the greedy algorithm solution, $S(M)$, is at most $S + r$ units. Let $k = S(M)$. Let the optimal solution using k units of space be O and the absolute benefit of O be B.

Consider a stage at which the greedy algorithm has already chosen a set G_l occupying l units of space with "incremental" benefits $a_1, a_2, \ldots, a_l$. The absolute benefit of G_l is thus $\sum_{i=1}^{l} a_i$. Surely the absolute benefit of the set $O \cup G_l$ is at least B. Therefore, the benefit of the set O with respect to $G_l, B(O, G_l)$, is at least $B - \sum_{i=1}^{l} a_i$.

Using Observation 1, it is easy to show by contradiction that there exists a view O_i in O such that $B(O_i, G_l)/|O_i| \geq B(O, G_l)/k$. The benefit per unit space with respect to G_l of the set C selected by the algorithm is at least that of O_i, which is at least $(B - \sum_{i=1}^{l} a_i)/k$. Distributing the benefit of C over each of its unit spaces equally (for the purpose of analysis), we get $a_{l+j} \geq (B - \sum_{i=1}^{l} a_i)/k$, for $0 < j \leq S(C)$. As this is true for each set C selected at any stage, we have the set of equations viz. $B \leq ka_j + \sum_{i=1}^{j-1} a_i$, for $0 < j \leq k$.

Multiplying the jth equation by $(\frac{k-1}{k})^{k-j}$ and adding all the equations, we get $A/B \geq 1 - (\frac{k-1}{k})^k \geq 1 - 1/e$, where $A(= \sum_{i=1}^{k} a_i)$ is the absolute benefit of M. ∎

Greedy-Interchange Algorithm We present another heuristic called the "greedy-interchange" algorithm which starts with the solution produced by the greedy algorithm (Algorithm 3.1) and then improves the solution by interchanging a view already selected with some view not selected.[2] It iteratively performs such interchanging until the solution cannot be improved any further by an interchange. See Algorithm 3.2.

Unfortunately, not much can be proved about the competitiveness of the solution produced by the greedy interchange algorithm except that it is obviously at

---

[2] When views occupy different amounts of space, more than one view may have to be added/removed.

least as good as the greedy algorithm. Moreover, the running time of the greedy interchange algorithm is unbounded. We believe that the greedy interchange algorithm in practice would perform much better than the greedy algorithm.

Algorithm 3.2 Greedy-Interchange Algorithm

Given: G, an AND-OR view graph, and S, the space constraint.
           Assume that all views occupy the same amount of space.
BEGIN
    Run the greedy algorithm and let M be the solution returned.
    repeat
        Let (C_1, C_2) be a pair of views such that $C_1 \in M$ and the absolute
           benefit of $(M - C_1) \cup C_2$ is greater than that of M.
        $M = (M - C_1) \cup C_2$;
    until (no such pair (C_1, C_2) exists);
    return M;
END.

3.3 Incorporating Update Costs

Unfortunately, the benefit function may not satisfy the monotonicity property when there are update costs. To see this informally, consider a view C_1 which *helps* in maintaining another view C_2. Hence, the benefit of $C_1 \cup C_2$ might be more than the sum of their benefits individually. However, the benefit function does satisfy the monotonicity property for a special case as shown in the following lemma.

Lemma 1. *In an AND view graph, the benefit function B satisfies the monotonicity property for any M with respect to sets consisting of single views, if the update frequency g_v at any view v is less than its query frequency f_v.*

Proof. It suffices to prove that $B(v, \phi) \geq B(v, M)$ for any view v and a set of views M.

Let A be the set of (not necessarily proper) ancestors of v in the AND view graph G, and let $M_A = A \cap M$. Let D be the set of those ancestors of v which do not have any descendants in the set M.

We have $B(v, \phi) = \sum_{x \in A} f_x(Q(x, \phi) - Q(x, v)) - g_v U(v, \phi)$. Note that, $Q(x, \phi) - Q(x, v) = Q(v, \phi)$ in an AND view graph for any ancestor x of v. Therefore, we get $B(v, \phi) = \sum_{x \in A} f_x Q(v, \phi) - g_v U(v, \phi)$.

For $B(v, M)$, when M has already been selected, v reduces the query costs of only the nodes in D. Therefore, $B(v, M) = \sum_{x \in D} f_x(Q(x, M) - Q(x, M \cup \{v\})) - g_v U(v, M) + \sum_{x \in M_A} g_x(U(x, M) - U(x, M \cup \{v\}))$.

The last term on the right hand side is due to reduction in the update costs of nodes in M_A as a result of the inclusion of v.

As $U(x, M) - U(x, M \cup \{v\}) \leq Q(v, M), \leq Q(v, \phi)$ for any $x \in M_A$, and $(Q(x, M) - Q(x, M \cup \{v\})) = Q(v, M)$ for $x \in D$, we get $B(v, M) \leq \sum_{x \in D} Q(v, M) - g_v U(v, M) + \sum_{x \in M_A} Q(v, \phi)$.

Let M_D be the set of descendants of v in M and let $Q(M_D, \phi) = \sum_{x \in M_D} Q(x, \phi)$. Using $U(v, \phi) - U(v, M) \leq U(M_D, \phi) \leq Q(M_D, \phi)$, and $M_A \cup D \cup \{v\} \subseteq A$, we get $B(v, \phi) - B(v, M) \geq \sum_{x \in D} f_x(Q(v, \phi) - Q(v, M)) + f_v Q(v, \phi) - g_v(Q(M_D, \phi))$. Now as $Q(v, \phi) - Q(v, M) = Q(M_D, \phi)$, we get $B(v, \phi) - B(v, M) \geq 0$. ∎

Theorem 3.2 *Consider an AND view graph G, where for any view the update frequency is less than its query frequency. For such a graph G, the greedy algorithm produces a solution M whose absolute benefit is at least $(1 - 1/e)$ times the optimal benefit achievable using as much space as that used by M.* ∎

3.4 AND View Graph with Indexes

In this section, we generalize the view-selection problem in an AND view graph by introducing indexes for each node/view. In the presence of indexes the cost of computation depends upon the indexes being used to execute the operation. As indexes are built upon their corresponding views, an index can be materialized only if its corresponding view has already been materialized. Thus, selecting an index without its view does not have any benefit and hence, the benefit function may not satisfy the monotonicity property for arbitrary sets of structures.[3] We assume that if an index is not materialized, then it is never "computed" while answering user queries.

We need to introduce a slightly different cost model for the AND view graphs with indexes. In an AND view graph with indexes, there may be multiple edges from a node u to v, possibly one for each index of v. Instead of associating costs with the arcs, we associate a label (i, t_i) with each edge from u to v. The cost $t_i (i > 0)$[4] can be thought of as the cost incurred in accessing the relation (as many times as required to compute u) at v using its ith index. In addition, we have a k-ary monotonically increasing cost function associated with every arc that binds k edges.

Consider a node u which has k outgoing edges to nodes $v_1, v_2, \ldots, v_k$ and let the k-ary cost function associated with the arc binding all these outgoing edges be f. Then, the cost of computing u from all its children $v_1, v_2, \ldots, v_k$ using their $i_1, i_2, \ldots, i_k^{th}$ indexes respectively is $f(t_{i_1}, t_{i_2}, \ldots, t_{i_k})$, where there is an edge from u to v_j, for $0 < j \leq k$, with a label (i_j, t_{i_j}).

Problem: Given a quantity S and an AND view graph G with indexes. Associated with each edge is a label (i, t_i), $i \geq 0$, and there is a cost function associated with each arc, as described above. Assume that there are no updates.

Find a set of structures M that minimizes the quantity $\tau(G, M)$, under the constraint that the total space occupied by the structures in M is at most S.

Inner-Level Greedy Algorithm The inner-level greedy algorithm works in stages. At each stage, it selects a subset C, which consists either of a view and some of its indexes selected in a greedy manner, or a single index whose view has already been selected in one of the previous stages.

---

[3] A structure is a view or an index.

[4] When $i = 0$, t_0 is the cost in accessing v without any of its indexes.

Algorithm 3.3 Inner-Level Greedy Algorithm

Given: G, a view graph with indexes, and S, the space constraint.
BEGIN
   $M = \phi$;   /* M = Set of structures selected so far */
   while $(S(M) < S)$
      $C = \phi$; /* Best set containing a view and some of its indexes */
      for each view v_i **not** in M
        $IG = \{v_i\}$; /* IG = Set of v_i and some of its indexes selected */
                                    /* in a greedy manner */
        while $(S(IG) < S)$ /* Construct IG */
           Let I_{ic} be the index of v_i whose benefit per unit space w.r.t.
              $(M \cup IG)$ is maximum.
           $IG = IG \cup I_{ic}$;
        end while;
        if $(B(IG, M)/S(IG) > B(C, M)/|C|)$ **or** $C = \phi$
           $C = IG$;
      end for;
      for each index I_{ij} such that its view $v_i \in M$
        if $B(I_{ij}, M)/S(I_{ij}) > B(C, M)/S(C)$
           $C = \{I_{ij}\}$;
      end for;
      $M = M \cup C$;
   end while;
   return M;
END.

Each stage can be thought of as consisting of two phases. In the first phase, for each view v_i we construct a set IG_i which initially contains only the view. Then, one by one its indexes are added to IG_i in the order of their incremental benefits until the benefit per unit space of IG_i with respect to M, the set of structures selected till this stage, reaches its maximum. That IG_i having the maximum benefit per unit space with respect to M is chosen as C. In the second phase, an index whose benefit per unit space is the maximum with respect to M is selected. The benefit per unit space of the selected index is compared with that of C, and the better one is selected for addition to M. See Algorithm 3.3.

The running time of the inner-level greedy algorithm is $O(k^2 m^2)$, where m is the total number of structures in the given AND view graph and k is the maximum number of structures that can fit in S units of space, which in the worst case is S.

Observation 2 *In an AND view graph with indexes and without updates, the benefit function B satisfies the monotonicity property for any M with respect to arbitrary sets of structures $O_1, O_2, \ldots, O_m$, where each O_i consists of a view and some of its indexes.*

Theorem 3.3 *For an AND view graph with indexes and a given quantity S, the inner-level greedy algorithm (Algorithm 3.3) produces a solution M that uses at most $2S$ units of space. Also, the absolute benefit of M is at least $(1 - 1/e^{0.63}) = 0.467$ of the optimal benefit achievable using as much space as that used by M, assuming that no structure occupies more than S units of space.*

Proof. It is easy to see that $S(M) \leq 2S$. Let $k = |M|$. Let the optimal solution be O, such that $S(O) = k$ and the absolute benefit of O be B.

Consider a stage at which the Inner-level greedy algorithm has already chosen a set G_l occupying l units of space with "incremental" benefits $a_1, a_2, a_3 \ldots a_l$. The absolute benefit of the set $O \cup G_l$ is at least B. Therefore, the benefit of the set O with respect to G_l, $B(O, G_l)$, is at least $B - \sum_{i=1}^{l} a_i$.

If O contains m views, it can be split into m disjoint sets $O_1, O_2, \ldots, O_m$, such that each O_i consists of a view and its indexes in O. By the monotonicity property of B w.r.t. the sets $O_1, \ldots, O_m$, $B(O, G_l) \leq \sum_{i=1}^{m} B(O_i, G_l)$. Now, it is easy to show by contradiction that there exists at least one O_i such that $B(O_i, G_l)/S(O_i) \geq B(O, G_l)/k$. The benefit per unit space of the set C, selected by the Inner-level greedy algorithm at this stage, is at least 0.63 times $B(O_i, G_l)/S(O_i)$. This follows from the result of Theorem 4.1 on the performance guarantee of the simple greedy algorithm (skipping some tedious details here.) Let $k' = 0.63$. Distributing the benefit of C over each of its unit spaces equally (for the purposes of analysis), we get $a_{l+j} \geq k'(B - \sum_{i=1}^{l} a_i)/k$, for $0 \leq j < S(C)$. As this is true for each set C selected at any stage, we have the set of equations viz. $B \leq \frac{k}{k'} a_j + \sum_{i=1}^{j-1} a_i$, for $0 < j \leq k$.

Let $k'' = k/k'$. Multiplying the jth equation by $(\frac{k''-1}{k''})^{k-j}$ and adding all the equations, we get $A/B \geq 1 - (\frac{k''-1}{k''})^k \geq 1 - (\frac{k''-1}{k''})^{k''k'} \geq 1 - 1/e^{0.63}$, where $A(= \sum_{i=1}^{k} a_i)$ is the absolute benefit of M. ∎

4 OR View Graph

In this section we consider those AND-OR view graphs in which each AND arc binds exactly one edge. We call such a AND-OR view graph G an *OR view graph*, where a node can be computed from any one of its children.

4.1 Motivation

A specific model of a data warehouse is a data cube. *Data cubes* are databases where a critical value, e.g., **sales**, is organized by several dimensions, for example, sales of automobiles organized by model, color, etc. Queries in such a system are of the usually ask for a breakdown of **sales** by some of the dimensions. Therefore, we can associate an aggregate view, called a *cube*, V_α with each subset α of the dimensions. A view V_α is essentially a result of a "Select α, Sum(**sales**); group by α" SQL query over the base table. An aggregate view V_α can be computed from a view V_β iff $\alpha \subseteq \beta$.

In the data cube, the AND-OR view graph is an OR view graph, as for each view there are zero or more ways to construct it from other views, but each way involves only one other view. Hence, all the results developed in this section for OR view graphs apply to data cubes. As OLAP databases have very few or no updates, we assume that there are no update costs throughout this section.

4.2 View Selection in an OR View Graph

In this subsection, we present algorithms for solving the view-selection problem for OR view graphs without update costs. This generalizes the problem considered by Harinarayan et al. in [HRU96] for selection of cubes in a data cube. We prove that the greedy algorithm (Algorithm 3.1) proposed by them performs with the same performance guarantee even in this setting of an OR view graph. A variant of this problem known as the *K-median* has also been studied in a different context of facility location [CFN77].

Problem: Given an OR view graph G and a quantity S, find a set of views M that minimizes the quantity $\tau(G, M)$, under the constraint that the total space occupied by the views in M is at most S. Assume that there are no updates.

Observation 3 *In an OR view graph without updates, the benefit function B satisfies the monotonicity property for any M with respect to arbitrary sets of views $O_1, O_2, \ldots, O_m$.*

Theorem 4.1 *For an OR view graph G without updates and a given quantity S, the greedy algorithm produces a solution M that uses at most $S + r$ units of space, where r is the size of the largest view in G. Also, the absolute benefit of M is at least $(1 - 1/e)$ times the optimal benefit achievable using as much space as that used by M.* ∎

Recently, Feige in [Fei96] showed that the `minimum set-cover` problem cannot be approximated within a factor of $(1 - o(1)) \ln n$, where n is the number of elements, using a polynomial time algorithm unless $P = NP$. There is a very natural reduction of the `minimum set-cover` problem to our problem of view selection in OR view graphs. The reduction shows that no polynomial time algorithm for the view-selection problem in OR view graphs can guarantee a solution of better than 63% for all inputs unless $P = NP$ [Che96].

Greedy Interchange Algorithm Cornuejols et al. in [CFN77] show for their similar facility location problem through extensive experiments that in most cases the running time of greedy interchange is a little less than 1.5 times the running time of the greedy algorithm, and that it returns a much better solution than that returned by the greedy algorithm.

4.3 OR view graph with Indexes

As in the case of AND view graphs, we generalize the view-selection problem in OR view graphs by introducing indexes for each node/view. In an OR view graph G with indexes, each edge from a node u to v has a label (i, t_i) associated, where $t_i (i > 0)$ is the cost of computing u from v using its ith index and t_0 is the cost of computing u from just v.

Problem: Given a quantity S and an OR view graph G with indexes, find a set of structures M that minimizes the quantity $\tau(G, M)$, under the constraint that the total space occupied by the structures (views and indexes) in M is at most S. Assume that there are no updates.

Observation 4 *In an OR view graph with indexes and without updates, the benefit function B satisfies the monotonicity property for any M with respect to disjoint sets of structures $O_1, O_2, \ldots, O_m$, where each O_i consists of a view and some of its indexes.*

Theorem 4.2 *The Inner-level greedy algorithm produces a solution M that uses at most $2S$ units of space. Also, the absolute benefit of M is at least $(1-1/e^{0.63}) = 0.467$ of the optimal benefit achievable using as much space as that used by M, assuming that no structure occupies more than S units of space.* ∎

5 View Selection in AND-OR View Graphs

In this section, we try to generalize our results developed in the previous sections to the view-selection problem in general AND-OR view graphs. We present here an AO-greedy algorithm that could take exponential time in the worst case, but has a performance guarantee of 63%. We also present a multi-level greedy algorithm which is a generalization of the inner-level greedy algrorithm (Algorithm 3.3). We give a different formulation of the view-selection problem in AND-OR graphs, for the sake of simplifying the description of the algorithm.

Definition 5.1 (Query-View Graph) A query-view graph G is a bipartite graph $(Q \cup \zeta, E)$, where Q is the set of queries to be supported at the warehouse and ζ is a subset of the powerset of V, the set of views. An edge (q, σ) is in E iff the query q can be answered using the views in the set σ, and the cost associated with the edge is the cost incurred in answering q using σ. There is also a frequency f_q associated with each query $q \in Q$. We assume that there is a set $\rho \in \zeta$ (the set of base tables) such that $(q, \rho) \in E$ for all $q \in Q$.[5] Note that an arbitrary AND-OR view graph can be converted into an equivalent query-view graph. □

Problem (View Selection in Query-View Graphs): Given a quantity S and a query-view graph $G = (\zeta \cup Q, E)$, select a set of views $M \subseteq V$ that minimizes the total query response time,[6] under the constraint that the total space occupied by the views in M is at most S.

---

[5] A query-view graph can be looked upon as an OR graph, as a query $q \in Q$ can be computed by any of the *set* of views σ where $(q, \sigma) \in E$.

[6] Though we ignore update costs, it can be incorporated by adding possibly additional nodes in ζ and additional edges in F_ζ (defined later).

5.1 AO-Greedy Algorithm for Query-View Graphs

We define an *intersection graph* F_ζ of ζ as a graph having ζ and D as its set of vertices and edges respectively such that an edge $(\alpha, \beta) \in D$ if and only if the set of views α and β intersect.

The AO-greedy algorithm works in stages as follows. At each stage, the algorithm picks a connected subgraph H of F_ζ whose corresponding set of views V_H (union of the sets of views corresponding to the vertices of H) offers the maximum benefit per unit space at that stage. The set of views V_H is then added to the set of views already selected in previous stages. The algorithm halts when the space occupied by the selected views exceeds S.

We omit the proof of the following theorem due to space constraints.

Observation 5 *An optimal solution O of the view-selection problem in query-view graph G is of the form $O = \cup_{\sigma \in \Gamma} \sigma$, where $\Gamma \subseteq \zeta$.*

Theorem 5.1 *For a query-view graph without updates and a quantity S, the AO-greedy algorithm produces a solution M that uses at most $2S$ units of space. Also, the absolute benefit of M is at least $(1 - 1/e)$ times the optimal benefit achievable using as much space as that used by M.* ∎

For a query-view graph $G = (\zeta \cup Q, E)$ corresponding to an OR view graph, the AO-greedy algorithm behaves exactly as the greedy algorithm (Algorithm 3.1), taking polynomial time for OR view graphs.

5.2 Multi-level Greedy Algorithm

In this section, we generalize the inner-level greedy algorithm (Algorithm 3.3) to multiple inner-levels of greedy selection in query-view graphs. We try to modify the AO-greedy algorithm for query-view graphs in an attempt to improve its running time at the expense of its performance guarantee.

Consider a query-view graph $G = (Q \cup \zeta, E)$ and its intersection graph F_ζ such that there is a view v where $v \in \sigma$ for each node σ in F_ζ.[7] If no such v exists, then run AO-greedy algorithm on G. Let ζ' be the set obtained by removing v from each element of ζ and F_ζ' be its corresponding intersection graph. We select a set of views U whose benefit per unit space is close to that of the optimal.

Let $F_1, F_2, \ldots, F_k$ be the connected components of F_ζ'. We select the set of views U in a greedy manner. Initially the set U contains just v. Then, at each stage, we select a set of views J, corresponding to a subgraph in some component F_i, that has the maximum benefit per unit space. The set of views J is then added to the set U being maintained. We continue adding views to U till the total benefit per unit space of U cannot be further improved.

It is not difficult to show that the benefit per unit space of U at least 63% of the benefit per unit space of V_H, the set of views whose benefit per unit space is

---

[7] The technique developed here can be easily generalized to the case when F_ζ has $l > 1$ connected components $G_1, G_2, \ldots, G_l$, each satisfying the property that for some v_i, $v_i \in \sigma$ for each vertex σ in G_i.

the maximum among the connected subgraphs in F_ζ. The algorithm continues by interatively picking a new set U and adding it to the set of already selected views M, until the space occupied by M exceeds S.

This algorithm could still take exponential time because of the need to consider all possible subgraphs of F_i. We could apply the above technique recursively for the graphs F_i, selecting a set of views U_i whose benefit is within 63% of the benefit of an optimal set of views in F_i. Applying this technique recursively r times yields the *r-level greedy algorithm*. We omit the proof of the following theorem.

Theorem 5.2 *For a query-view graph G and a given quantity S, the r-level greedy algorithm delivers a solution M that uses at most $2S$ units of space. Also, the benefit of M is at least $1 - (1/e)^{0.63^r}$ of the optimal benefit achievable using as much space as that used by M, assuming that no view occupies more than S units of space. The r-level greedy algorithm takes $O((kn)^{2r})$ time, excluding the time taken at the final level. Here, k is the maximum number of views that can fit in S units of space.* ∎

For a given instance one could estimate the value of r such that at the rth level the graphs F_i are small constant-size graphs. The last level would then take only a constant amount of time.

For an OR view graph I with indexes, its equivalent query-view graph $G = (\zeta \cup Q, E)$ is such that each element $\sigma \in \zeta$ consists of a single view and one of its indexes.[8] Hence, at the first stage itself, the graphs obtained consist of nodes representing single indexes. For such a query-view graph, the 1-level inner greedy algorithm behaves exactly the same as the inner-level greedy algorithm (Algorithm 3.3) on OR view graphs with indexes.

6 Conclusions and Future Directions

In this paper, we have developed a theoretical framework for the general problem of selection of views in a data warehouse. We have presented competitive polynomial-time heuristics for some important special cases of the problem that occur in practice. We have presented proofs showing that the algorithms are guaranteed to provide a solution that is within a constant factor of the optimal.

There are still a lot of questions which remain unanswered and need considerable attention. Noteworthy among them are:

1. Are there competitive polynomial-time heuristics for other special cases like AND-OR *trees* or binary AND-OR view trees, even without updates or when optimizing just update costs? Are there heuristics which optimize total query benefit under the constraint of total maintenance time ?

2. Can we prove any negative results about the approximability of the view-selection problem?

---

[8] Under the assumption that an index is never computed to answer a query.

We believe that the techniques developed in this paper would offer significant insights into the greedy heuristic and the nature of the view-selection problem in a data warehouse. We hope that the view-selection problem would invoke substantial interest in the database theory community.

Acknowledgements

I would like to express my thanks to my advisor, Prof. Jeff Ullman, for his constant encouragement and insightful suggestions.

References

[CFN77]   G. Cornuejols, M. L. Fisher, and G. L. Nemhauser. Location of bank accounts to optimize float: An analytic study of exact and approximate algorithm. *Management Science*, 23(8):789–810, 1977.

[Che96]   Chandra Chekuri. Personal Communication, 1996.

[CM82]   U. S. Chakravarthy and J. Minker. Processing multiple queries in database systems. *Database Engineering*, 5(3):38–44, September 1982.

[Fei96]   U. Feige. A threshold of ln n for approximating set cover. In *Proc. of the 28th annual ACM Symp. on the Theory of Comp.*, pages 314–318, 1996.

[GHRU96]   H. Gupta, V. Harinarayan, A. Rajaraman, and J. Ullman. Index selection in OLAP. Unpublished manuscript. Stanford University, 1996.

[GM95]   A. Gupta and I.S. Mumick. Maintenance of materialized views: Problems, techniques, and applications. *IEEE Data Eng. Bulletin, Special Issue on Materialized Views and Data Warehousing*, 18(2):3–18, 1995.

[HRU96]   V. Harinarayan, A. Rajaraman, and J. Ullman. Implementing data cubes efficiently. In *ACM SIGMOD Intl. Conf. on Mngt. of Data*, 1996.

[IK93]   W.H. Inmon and C. Kelley. *Rdb/VMS: Developing the Data Warehouse.* QED Publishing Group, Boston, Massachussetts, 1993.

[Rou82]   N. Roussopoulos. The logical access path schema of a database. *IEEE Transaction in Software Engineering*, SE-8(6):563–573, November 1982.

[RSS96]   K. A. Ross, Divesh Srivastava, and S. Sudarshan. Materialized view maintenance and integrity constraint checking: Trading space for time. In *Proc. of the ACM SIGMOD Int. Conf. on Mngt. of Data*, 1996.

[Sel88]   Timos K. Sellis. Multiple query optimization. *ACM Transactions on Database Systems*, 13(1):23–52, March 1988.

[WGL+96]   J. Wiener, H. Gupta, W. Labio, Y. Zhuge, H. Garcia-Molina, and J. Widom. A system prototype for warehouse view maintenance. In *Workshop on Materialized Views: Tech. and App.*, 1996.

[Wid95]   J. Widom. Research problems in data warehousing. In *Proc. of the 4th Intl. Conf. on Info. and Knowledge Mngt.*, pages 25–30, 1995.

[ZGMHW95] Y. Zhuge, H. Garcia-Molina, J. Hammer, and J. Widom. View maintenance in a warehousing environment. In *Proceedings of the ACM SIGMOD Intl. Conf. on Mngt. of Data*, pages 316–327, 1995.

Total and Partial Well-Founded Datalog Coincide

Jörg Flum[I]   Max Kubierschky[I]   Bertram Ludäscher[II]

[I] Mathematische Fakultät, Universität Freiburg,
Eckerstr. 1, 79104 Freiburg, Germany
{flum,maku}@ruf.uni-freiburg.de

[II] Institut für Informatik, Universität Freiburg,
Am Flughafen 17, 79110 Freiburg, Germany
ludaesch@informatik.uni-freiburg.de

Abstract. We show that the expressive power of well-founded Datalog does not decrease when restricted to total programs (it is known to decrease from Π_1^1 to Δ_1^1 on infinite Herbrand structures) thereby affirmatively answering an open question posed by Abiteboul, Hull, and Vianu [AHV95]. In particular, we show that for every well-founded Datalog program there exists an equivalent *total* program whose only recursive rule is of the form

$$win(\bar{X}) \leftarrow move(\bar{X}, \bar{Y}), \neg\, win(\bar{Y})$$

where *move* is definable by a quantifier-free first-order formula. This yields a nice new normal form for well-founded Datalog and implies that it is sufficient to consider draw-free games in order to evaluate arbitrary Datalog programs under the well-founded semantics.

1 Introduction

The well-founded semantics (WFS) [VGRS88, VG93] has become popular as an intuitive and "well-behaved"[1] semantics for the language of logic programs containing negative cyclic dependencies, like the famous program P_{game}:

$$win(X) \leftarrow move(X, Y), \neg\, win(Y).$$

A position X in a game is won, if there is a move to some position Y which is not won (since then the opponent has to move). WFS assigns a partial (3-valued) model $WFS(P, D)$ to every logic program P and database D. The third truth-value *undefined* is assigned if the truth of an atom A depends negatively on itself and there is no other "well-founded" derivation for A leading to true. Consider for example a move graph for P_{game} consisting of the edges $move(a, b), move(b, a), move(b, c)$ and $move(c, d)$. Under the well-founded

---

[1] Dix [Dix95] formally defines this notion using certain weak principles, and shows that WFS is the weakest well-behaved extension of the generally accepted stratified semantics [ABW88].

semantics, $win(d)$ is false, since there are no moves from d. Consequently, $win(c)$ is true, since it is possible to move from c to d. On the other hand, $win(a)$ and $win(b)$ are undefined since a is won iff b is not won, and b is won iff a is not won. This corresponds nicely to the fact, that the positions a and b in the game are *drawn*: the player moving from b has no winning strategy (moving to c would leave the opponent in a won position), but she can enforce a game of infinite length by moving from b to a and thus avoid losing.

Another aspect of languages which has always played an important role in database theory is expressive power, i.e., the class of queries definable in a language. The query associated with a logic program P and database D is defined in terms of the *true* atoms of WFS(P, D) (hence *undefined* and *false* atoms belong to the complement of the query). Van Gelder showed that Datalog evaluated under WFS is equivalent to (least) fixpoint logic [VG89, VG93].

A natural question arising is: What is the expressive power of programs which never yield the truth value *undefined*, i.e. which are *total* for all databases D? For logic programs over infinite Herbrand structures, the restriction to total programs results in loss of expressive power from Π_1^1 to Δ_1^1 [Sch95]. For Datalog programs, the question has been posed by Abiteboul et. al. [AHV95] and remained open so far. We give the somewhat surprising[2] answer that on finite structures, i.e. for well-founded Datalog, there is no loss of expressive power.[3]

As it turns out, games play a crucial role in our solution: using a normal form for fixpoint logic, we first show that every Datalog program can be viewed as a game between two players. Thus, the ubiquitous *win-move* example is raised retroactively to an elegant normal form for well-founded Datalog. The drawn positions of the game are exactly the undefined atoms of the well-founded model. The second result is that for every game one can find an equivalent game which is *draw-free*, i.e. all positions in the game are either won or lost. This implies, that total well-founded Datalog and well-founded Datalog have the same expressive power.

The paper is structured as follows. In Section 2 the required concepts and terminology are briefly introduced. They are based on [AHV95], [VG93, AB94] (for WFS) and [EF95] (for fixpoint logic). In Section 3 we first introduce games and then show our main result, the reduction of games to draw-free games.

---

[2] Indeed, in [VG93] van Gelder writes: *"This suggests that the alternating fixpoint on normal programs captures the negation of positive existential closures (such as transitive closure), but not the negation of positive universal closures (such as well-foundedness)."* The generalization of WFS to *general logic programs*, i.e., with first-order rule bodies avoids – at least for some examples – undefined atoms in the well-founded model (cf. [Che95]).

[3] In [Kub95], the second author has obtained a normal form theorem for LFP. Rewriting programs as logic formulas, the first author realized that Kubierschky's result can be used to solve the problem by Abiteboul et. al. The present exposition is due to the third author.

2 Preliminaries

A *database schema* (or *relational schema*) σ is a finite set of relation symbols $r_1, \ldots, r_k$ with associated arities $\alpha(r_i) \geq 0$. Let *dom* be a fixed and countable underlying domain. A *database instance* (*database*) over σ is a finite structure $D = (U, r_1^D, \ldots, r_k^D)$ with finite universe $U \subseteq dom$ and relations $r_i^D \subseteq U^{\alpha(r_i)}$.

Let $inst(\sigma)$ denote the set of all database instances over σ. A *k-ary query* q over σ is a computable function on $inst(\sigma)$ such that (i) $q(D)$ is a k-ary relation on U, and (ii) q is preserved under isomorphisms, i.e. for every isomorphism π of D, $q(\pi(D)) = \pi(q(D))$. Thus, a query defines a k-ary *global relation* on $inst(\sigma)$.

A *query language* $\mathcal{L}$ is a set of expressions together with a semantics which maps every expression $\varphi \in \mathcal{L}$ to a query (over some σ). The *expressive power* of a query language $\mathcal{L}$ is the class of all queries definable in $\mathcal{L}$. $\varphi \in \mathcal{L}_1$ is *equivalent to* $\psi \in \mathcal{L}_2$ if they express the same query. We say that $\mathcal{L}_1$ is *at most as expressive as* $\mathcal{L}_2$, denoted by $\mathcal{L}_1 \leq \mathcal{L}_2$, if for every expression in $\mathcal{L}_1$ there is an equivalent expression in $\mathcal{L}_2$. Both languages have the *same expressive power*, written as $\mathcal{L}_1 \equiv \mathcal{L}_2$, if $\mathcal{L}_1 \leq \mathcal{L}_2$ and $\mathcal{L}_2 \leq \mathcal{L}_1$. $\mathcal{L}$ may denote both the language and the class of queries definable in it.

Notation. Following logic programming notation, we write domain variables in upper case like X, X', Y. Constants like x, y, a and relation symbols like $win, move$ are denoted in lower case.

$\bar{T}$ denotes a vector of n terms $T_1, \ldots, T_n$ (variables or constants).

$\tilde{T}$ denotes n-ary repetition of T, i.e. a vector $T, T, \ldots, T$.

We write $\varphi(\bar{X})$ to emphasize that all free variables of φ are among $\bar{X}$; if we write only φ, nothing is said about the free variables of φ.

Well-Founded Datalog. A *Datalog*$^\neg$ program P is a finite set of rules of the form

$$H \leftarrow B_1, \ldots, B_n, \neg C_1, \ldots, \neg C_m$$

where the head H is an atom, all B_i, C_j are atoms or equalities $T_1 = T_2$ where T_1, T_2 are terms. A rule where $n = m = 0$ is called a *fact*.

The signature σ_P of P is partitioned into a set $idb(P)$ of relation symbols of P occurring in some head of P and $edb(P)$ of relation symbols occurring only in the bodies of rules.

Fix a program P and a database D over $edb(P)$. A *ground instance* of a rule is obtained by substituting constants from D for all variables; $ground(P, D)$ denotes the set of all such ground instances of rules of P, and $\mathcal{B}_{P,D}$ denotes the set of all ground instances of atomic formulas of P.

Let $Y \subseteq \mathcal{B}_{P,D}$. For $X \subseteq \mathcal{B}_{P,D}$ let

$$T_P^Y(X) := \{ H \mid (H \leftarrow B_1, \ldots, B_n, \neg C_1, \ldots, \neg C_m) \in ground(P, D)$$
$$\text{with } (B_i \in D \text{ or } B_i \in X) \text{ for all } 1 \leq i \leq n$$
$$\text{and } C_j \notin Y \text{ for all } 1 \leq j \leq m \}$$

Then T_P^Y is a monotone operator. Let $\Gamma_P(Y) := \mathrm{lfp}(T_P^Y)$ be its least fixpoint. The operator Γ_P is antimonotone (observe how Y is used in T_P^Y), i.e., $Y_1 \subseteq Y_2$ implies $\Gamma_P(Y_2) \subseteq \Gamma_P(Y_1)$. It follows that Γ_P^2 ($:= \Gamma_P \circ \Gamma_P$) is a monotone operator; thus it has a least and a greatest fixpoint $\mathrm{lfp}(\Gamma_P^2)$ and $\mathrm{gfp}(\Gamma_P^2)$. These are used to define the truth value of a ground atom A under the *well-founded semantics* $\mathrm{WFS}(P,D)$ for a given program P and database D:

$$\mathrm{WFS}(P,D)(A) := \begin{cases} true & \text{if } A \in \mathrm{lfp}(\Gamma_P^2) \\ false & \text{if } A \notin \mathrm{gfp}(\Gamma_P^2) \\ undef & \text{if } A \in \mathrm{gfp}(\Gamma_P^2) \setminus \mathrm{lfp}(\Gamma_P^2) \end{cases} \qquad (\star)$$

Definition 2.1 (W-Datalog, W-Datalog$_2$)

A program P is called *total* (or *2-valued*) if *for all databases D* there is no ground atom A with $\mathrm{WFS}(P,D)(A) = undef$.

Let W-Datalog denote the set of Datalog$^-$ programs evaluated under the well-founded semantics, W-Datalog$_2$ is the set of *total* W-Datalog programs. □

Using the true atoms of the well-founded semantics, P defines for every relation $r \in idb(P)$ a query $q_{P,r}$ over $edb(P)$:

$$q_{P,r}: \; D \mapsto \{\bar{x} \mid \mathrm{WFS}(P,D)(r(\bar{x})) = true\} \qquad (\star\star)$$

We may assume w.l.o.g. that P contains one distinguished relation symbol $answer \in idb(P)$. This uniquely associates a query with every Datalog program P.

Least Fixpoint Logic. Let FO be the set of first-order formulas. By closing FO under least fixpoints of positive formulas we obtain *least fixpoint logic* LFP. The set of LFP-formulas is given by the following rules:[4]

$$\frac{}{\varphi} \text{ if } \varphi \text{ is an atom}; \quad \frac{\varphi}{\neg\varphi}; \quad \frac{\varphi,\psi}{\varphi \wedge \psi}; \quad \frac{\varphi}{\exists X\varphi}; \quad \frac{\varphi}{[\mathrm{LFP}_{R(\bar{X})}\, \varphi]\bar{V}} \text{ if } (+)$$

where $(+)$ is the proviso that the inductive relational variable R occurs only *positively* (i.e., under an even number of negations) in φ, and $\bar{X}, \bar{V}$ are $\alpha(R)$-ary tuples of variables.[5] The semantics of LFP-formulas is given by a relation $D \models \psi$ as usual. In particular, for $\psi(\bar{U}, \bar{V}) = [\mathrm{LFP}_{R(\bar{X})}\, \varphi(R, \bar{X}, \bar{U})]\bar{V}$ and $\bar{u}, \bar{v}$ in D:

$$D \models \psi(\bar{u}, \bar{v}) :\Leftrightarrow \bar{v} \in R_{\bar{u}}^\infty$$

where $R_{\bar{u}}^0 := \emptyset$, $R_{\bar{u}}^{i+1} := \{\bar{x} \mid D \models \varphi(R_{\bar{u}}^i, \bar{x}, \bar{u})\}$ and $R_{\bar{u}}^\infty := \bigcup_{i \in \mathbb{N}} R_{\bar{u}}^i$. Every LFP-formula $\psi(\bar{X})$ defines a query q_ψ as follows:

$$q_\psi: \; D \mapsto \{\bar{x} \mid D \models \psi(\bar{x})\}$$

Using $(\star)$ and $(\star\star)$ one can easily show W-Datalog $\leq$ LFP.

---

[4] In fixpoint formulas, relational variables are denoted in upper case.

[5] $\forall, \vee$ and $\to$ are viewed as abbreviations. For notational convenience, we only consider variables $\bar{V}$ instead of terms $\bar{T}$ in the last rule.

3 A Normal Form for Well-Founded Datalog

Abiteboul et. al. raised the question whether one can find for each W-Datalog program an equivalent *total program* [AHV95, pp. 397,401,403]. In other words, is W-Datalog $\leq$ W-Datalog$_2$? (W-Datalog$_2$ $\leq$ W-Datalog holds trivially.) When restricted to *ordered databases*, this is obviously the case, since S-Datalog (stratified Datalog) is equivalent to LFP (and thus captures PTIME) on ordered databases, and WFS is 2-valued for S-Datalog (see e.g. [AHV95]).

As we will show, the question can also be answered affirmatively in the absence of order. First, using results of van Gelder [VG89] and Grohe [Gro94], we show that every W-Datalog program can be transformed into a normal form which corresponds to a certain game. The main result is that one can reduce such games to draw-free games, which is equivalent to the fact that the corresponding W-Datalog program is total.

3.1 Games

A *game* is a finite structure $G = (V, move^G)$ with signature $\sigma = \{move\}$ and universe V. V are the *positions* (or *vertices*), $move^G \subseteq V \times V$ the set of possible *moves*.

The game is played with a pebble by two players I and II in *rounds*. Each round consists of two moves. Initially, I starts the game from some position x_0. A player can move from x to y iff $(x, y) \in move^G$. A player loses in x, if she cannot move; she wins in x, if she can move to a position in which the opponent loses. A position $x \in V$ is *won* (for I) if I can always win the game starting at x, no matter how II moves. Conversely, $x \in V$ is *lost* (for I) if II can always win the game, no matter how I moves. A position x is *drawn* if x is neither lost nor won. Observe that the presence of cycles in $move^G$ is necessary but not sufficient for the existence of drawn positions in G.

If x is won, the *length* of x, denoted $|x|$, is the number of rounds which are necessary for I to win, provided both players play optimal (i.e., each player tries to win as quickly or to lose as slowly as possible). If x is lost or drawn, let $|x| = \infty$. A game is called *draw-free* if no position in V is drawn.

Games have a very elegant and intuitive representation in W-Datalog in the form of the famous *win-move* example. Indeed this example has always been used to demonstrate that WFS handles negation in a nice and intuitive way.

Definition 3.1 (W-Datalog^G) Let W-Datalog^G be the class of W-Datalog programs P which have a single recursive rule of the form

$$win(\bar{X}) \leftarrow move(\bar{X}, \bar{X}'), \neg\, win(\bar{X}')$$

where $\bar{X}$ and $\bar{X}'$ have the same arity ≥ 1, and a rule of the form

$$answer(\bar{U}) \leftarrow win(\bar{T})$$

where $\bar{U}$ are variables occurring in $\bar{T}$. All other rules of P are nonrecursive, contain neither *win* nor *answer*, and are *semipositive*, i.e., negation is allowed only in front of *edb* relations.[6]

Let W-Datalog$_2^G$ be the set of *total* programs in W-Datalog^G. □

The simplest program in W-Datalog^G is P_G:

$$win(X) \leftarrow move(X, X'), \neg win(X').$$
$$answer \leftarrow win(x_0).$$

One easily verifies that P_G represents games, i.e., for every game $G = (V, move^G)$, x_0 is won/lost/drawn in G iff $\text{WFS}(P_G, G)(answer) = true/false/undef$.

We use the following theorems to show that an arbitrary W-Datalog program can be transformed into a W-Datalog^G program:

Theorem 3.2 (W-Datalog ≡ LFP, [VG89])
For every W-Datalog program there is an equivalent LFP-formula and vice versa.

Theorem 3.3 (Bounded Skolem Normal Form, [Gro94])
Every LFP-formula with free variables $\bar{U}$ is equivalent to a formula $\psi(\bar{U})$ of the form

$$\exists V[\text{LFP}_{W(\bar{X})} \ \varphi_0(\bar{X}, \bar{U}) \vee \exists \bar{Y} \forall \bar{Z}(\varphi(\bar{X}, \bar{Y}, \bar{Z}, \bar{U}) \rightarrow W(\bar{Z}))]\widetilde{V}$$

where φ_0, φ are quantifier-free first-order formulas not containing W.

Theorem 3.2 and Theorem 3.3 imply that for every W-Datalog program P, there is an equivalent LFP-formula ψ in bounded Skolem normal form. In the sequel, we show how to obtain an equivalent program $P_\psi \in$ W-Datalog^G by viewing ψ as a game.

Diagrams. As an auxiliary notation for games, we make use of *diagrams* as the one depicted in Fig. 1 (we do not need a formal definition). With every diagram d and structure D we associate a game $G_{d,D} = (V, move^{G_{d,D}})$ as follows:

Let $\bar{X} = X_1, \ldots, X_n$ be the unprimed variables of the diagram d, and let $Sq = \{s_1, \ldots, s_m\}$ be the (white and black) "squares" of d. Then the positions of $G_{d,D}$ are

$$V = \{(s, \bar{x}) \mid s \in Sq, \bar{x} \in D^n\} .$$

The possibles moves between positions are given by the edges in d:

$((s, \bar{x}), (s', \bar{x}')) \in move^{G_{d,D}}$ iff there is an edge $s \xrightarrow{\Theta} s'$ in d, and (i), (ii) hold:

(i) for all X_i such that X_i' is *not* $\exists$-quantified in Θ, we have $x_i' = x_i$.
(ii) if Θ contains a quantifier-free formula $\varphi(\bar{X}, \bar{X}')$, then $D \models \varphi(\bar{x}, \bar{x}')$.

---

[6] A rule r is *nonrecursive* if no literal in the body of r is depending – directly or indirectly via other rules – on the atom in the head of r, see e.g. [AHV95].

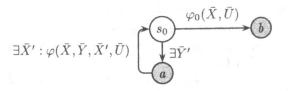

$$move(s_0, \bar{X}, \bar{Y}, \bar{U}, \ a, \bar{X}', \bar{Y}', \bar{U}') \leftarrow \bar{X}' = \bar{X}, \bar{U}' = \bar{U}.$$
$$move(s_0, \bar{X}, \bar{Y}, \bar{U}, \ b, \bar{X}', \bar{Y}', \bar{U}') \leftarrow R_{\varphi_0}(\bar{X}, \bar{U}), \bar{X}' = \bar{X}, \bar{Y}' = \bar{Y}, \bar{U}' = \bar{U}.$$
$$move(a, \bar{X}, \bar{Y}, \bar{U}, \ s_0, \bar{X}', \bar{Y}', \bar{U}') \leftarrow R_{\varphi}(\bar{X}, \bar{Y}, \bar{X}', \bar{U}), \bar{Y}' = \bar{Y}, \bar{U}' = \bar{U}.$$
$$R_{\varphi_0}(\bar{X}, \bar{U}) \leftarrow \dots$$
$$R_{\varphi}(\bar{X}, \bar{Y}, \bar{Z}, \bar{U}) \leftarrow \dots$$
$$win(S, \bar{X}, \bar{Y}, \bar{U}) \leftarrow move(S, \bar{X}, \bar{Y}, \bar{U}, \ S', \bar{X}', \bar{Y}', \bar{U}'), \neg\, win(S', \bar{X}', \bar{Y}', \bar{U}').$$
$$answer(\bar{U}) \leftarrow win(s_0, \widetilde{V}, \bar{Y}, \bar{U}).$$

Fig. 1. Reduction from Bounded Skolem Normal Form to a Game

$G_{d,D}$ can be viewed as a game played with a *sequence of pebbles* $(S, X_1, \dots, X_n)$ whose actual value $(s, x_1, \dots, x_n)$ is a position in $G_{d,D}$: the pebble S is on some square s in d, the pebbles X_i are on elements x_i of D. The players of $G_{d,D}$ move alternately between white and black squares (player I) or vice versa (player II). The pebbles can be moved from $(s, \bar{x})$ to $(s', \bar{x}')$ only if there is an edge $s \overset{\Theta}{\longrightarrow} s'$ in d, and if additionally the old positions $\bar{x}$ of the X-pebbles and their new positions $\bar{x}'$ satisfy the conditions (i) and (ii) above. In particular, all pebbles X_i have to remain on their positions during a move unless X_i' is $\exists$-quantified in Θ.

Every diagram d with unprimed variables $\bar{X}$ can be directly translated into the definition of the move relation $move(S, \bar{X}, \ S', \bar{X}')$ of the game $G_{d,D}$ such that for the resulting W-Datalog^G program P_d we have WFS$(P_d, D)(win(s, \bar{x})) = true/false/undef$ iff $(s, \bar{x})$ is won/lost/drawn in $G_{d,D}$. This translation is straightforward and should be clear from Fig. 1. Now we are in position to prove

Theorem 3.4 (W-Datalog $\leq$ W-Datalog^G)
For every W-Datalog program P there is an equivalent program $P_G \in$ W-Datalog^G.

Proof. Let P be a W-Datalog program. By Theorems 3.2 and 3.3 there is an equivalent LFP-formula $\psi(\bar{U})$ in bounded Skolem normal form. We view $\psi(\bar{U})$ as the game depicted by the diagram in Fig. 1. As explained before, the program P_ψ in Fig. 1 can be directly obtained from the diagram and represents this game.

Since φ_0 and φ in the diagram are quantifier-free FO-formulas, the rules defining the equivalent *idb* relations $R_{\varphi_0}(\bar{X}, \bar{U})$, $R_{\varphi}(\bar{X}, \bar{Y}, \bar{Z}, \bar{U})$ of P_ψ can be chosen semipositive and nonrecursive.

The idea behind the game is as follows: Player I wants to prove that some

$\bar{X}$ are in the least fixpoint $W_{\bar{u}}^{\infty}$ of Theorem 3.3. Player II wants to prove the contrary. $\bar{U}$ are fixed parameters and passed around unchanged.

If $\varphi_0(\bar{X},\bar{U})$ holds, I can move from s_0 to b and win, since there are no moves from b. The other possibility for I to win is the move to a. I can win by moving to a if she chooses some $\bar{Y}$ such that for all $\bar{Z}$ for which $\varphi(\bar{X},\bar{Y},\bar{Z},\bar{U})$ holds, $W(\bar{Z})$ also holds. In terms of the game, this means that $\bar{Z}$ has to be established as a won position for I *in the next round*. This is achieved by substituting $\bar{X}'$ for $\bar{Z}$ in $\varphi(\bar{X},\bar{Y},\bar{Z},\bar{U})$ as in Fig. 1, which "feeds back" the new $\bar{X}$ in place of $\bar{Z}$ in the fixpoint process. By induction one can verify that (for all $\bar{y}$):

$$win(s_0,\bar{x},\bar{y},\bar{u}) \in \Gamma_{P_{\psi}}^{2k} \Leftrightarrow \bar{x} \in W_{\bar{u}}^{k} \quad ,$$

which is the case iff I wins the game in s_0 in k rounds. Therefore,

$$win(s_0,\bar{x},\bar{y},\bar{u}) \in \mathrm{lfp}(\Gamma_{P_{\psi}}^{2}) \Leftrightarrow \bar{x} \in W_{\bar{u}}^{\infty} \quad ,$$

which implies

$$answer(\bar{u}) \in \mathrm{lfp}(\Gamma_{P_{\psi}}^{2}) \Leftrightarrow \text{ for some } v : \tilde{v} \in W_{\bar{u}}^{\infty}$$
$$\Leftrightarrow D \models \psi(\bar{u}) \quad ,$$

where D is the structure which is implicit in the definition of $W_{\bar{u}}^{k}$ and $\Gamma_{P_{\psi}}$. ∎

Remark. We have chosen as Theorem 3.3 the normal form of [Gro94] since it allows a particularly short translation into a game. Theorem 3.4 can also be proven from the following more familiar normal form theorem:

Theorem 3.5 ([Imm86])
Every LFP-formula is equivalent to a formula of the form $[\mathrm{LFP}_{R(\bar{x})}\varphi]\bar{T}$ *where* φ *is a FO-formula.*

Sketch of a proof of Theorem 3.4 using Theorem 3.5: By induction on FO-formulas define a diagram d_{φ} such that $G_{d_{\varphi},D}$ reflects the evaluation of φ in D. In order to convert d_{φ} to a diagram d_{ψ} for $\psi = [\mathrm{LFP}_{R(\bar{x})}\varphi]\bar{T}$, substitute all arrows with label containing R into appropriate loops back to the start of d_{φ} (use that φ is positive in R). Convert d_{ψ} into a W-Datalog^G program as described above.

3.2 Reduction from Games to Draw-Free Games

It remains to show that for each game, there is an equivalent draw-free game. We present an informal proof emphasizing the idea of the construction.[7]

Theorem 3.6 (W-Datalog^G ≤ W-Datalog$_2^G$)
For every W-Datalog^G program there is an equivalent program in W-Datalog$_2^G$.

---

[7] The presented reduction is due to [Kub95] which also contains the details of a proof of a normal form for LFP implying Theorem 3.6.

Proof. The main problem consists in avoiding drawn positions. In the absence of an order on the domain it seems particularly difficult to limit the length of the game in order to eliminate drawn positions, e.g. we cannot use a counter for that purpose.

The basic idea is to limit the length of a game by comparing it to a game of maximal length. Two games are compared by playing them independently but synchronously. Thus, we construct a new game $2G$ which simulates these two games on the original structure G. To do so, we need two pebbles – one for each game in G. Call these the *clock pebble* $\bar{Y}$ (on position $\bar{y}$ in G) and the *verify pebble* $\bar{X}$ (on position $\bar{x}$ in G).[8] The game played with the clock pebble is used to limit the length of the game played with the verify pebble. The latter plays the role of the pebble in the original game G.

Initially, player I claims that the verify pebble is on a won position, i.e. $|\bar{x}| < \infty$. II places the clock pebble on $\bar{y}$ and claims that $|\bar{y}|$ is the maximal length of a won position in the game. If this is true, I and II can compare $|\bar{x}|$ and $|\bar{y}|$ and thus verify the original claim of I. The difficulty remains that both players have to agree upon the choice of $\bar{y}$. To solve this, one has to design $2G$ in such a way, that II can be disproved if she "cheats" by choosing a $\bar{y}$ which is not maximal.

The new game $2G$ is constructed as follows (cf. Fig. 3): We use two macros $1\,\text{round}(\bar{X})$ and $1\,\text{round}(\bar{Y})$ to denote a round of moves of the pebbles on $\bar{x}$ and $\bar{y}$ in G, respectively (Fig. 2). Note that in the simulated game G, I moves first in $1\,\text{round}(\bar{X})$ while II moves first in $1\,\text{round}(\bar{Y})$.

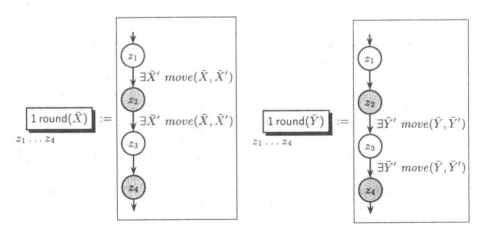

Fig. 2. Macro Definitions

Like above, the diagram in Fig. 3 defines a set of semipositive nonrecursive rules for the new relation $move(S, \bar{X}, \bar{Y},\ S', \bar{X}', \bar{Y}')$. Thus, if the move relation

---

[8] As noted before, $\bar{X} = X_1, \ldots, X_n$ is a sequence of pebbles on positions $\bar{x}$; analogously for $\bar{Y}$.

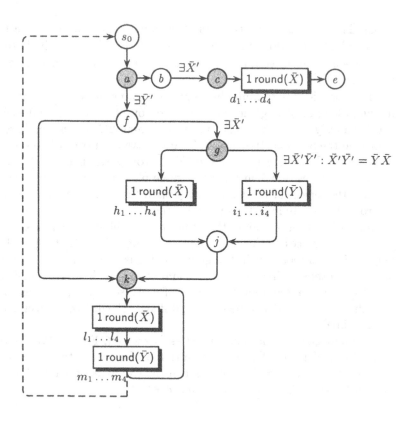

Player I	Player II
$s_0 \to a$ $\|\bar{x}\| < \infty$, "the length of $\bar{x}$ is finite, ie $\bar{x}$ is won"	$a \to b$ $\neg \exists \bar{x} : \|\bar{x}\| < \infty$, "there is no $\bar{x}$ in G which is won"
$b \to c$ $\exists \bar{x} : \|\bar{x}\| = 1$, "I show you a new $\bar{x}$ which is won in 1 round"	$a \to f$ $\exists \bar{y} : \|\bar{y}\| < \infty, \|\bar{y}\|$ maximal, $\|\bar{x}\| > \|\bar{y}\|$, "$\bar{y}$ is finite, of maximal length and shorter than $\bar{x}$"
$f \to k$ $\|\bar{x}\| \le \|\bar{y}\|$, "$\bar{y}$ is not shorter than $\bar{x}$"	$k \to l_1$ $\|\bar{x}\| > \|\bar{y}\|$, "you can't win on $\bar{x}$ in time"
$f \to g$ $\|\bar{y}\| < \infty, \exists \bar{x} : \|\bar{x}\| = \|\bar{y}\| + 1$, "$\bar{y}$ is finite, but not of maximal length: I show you a new $\bar{x}$ which is 1 round longer"	$g \to h_1$ $\|\bar{x}\| > \|\bar{y}\| + 1$, "$\bar{x}$ is more than 1 round longer than $\bar{y}$: I give you a lead of 1 round $\bar{x}$ and you lose"
$j \to k$ $\|\bar{x}\| \le \|\bar{y}\|$, "$\bar{y}$ is not shorter than $\bar{x}$"	$g \to i_1$ $\|\bar{x}\| \le \|\bar{y}\|$, "your chosen $\bar{x}$ is not longer than my $\bar{y}$: let us swap the pebbles on $\bar{x}$ and $\bar{y}$ and give me a lead of 1 round in $\bar{y}'$: then you lose on $\bar{x}$ against the clock"
$l_1 \to l_2$ $\|\bar{x}\| \le \|\bar{y}\|$, "I can win in time"	

Fig. 3. Draw-Free Game $2G$ and Implicit Claims of I and II.

of the original G (used in the macros of Fig. 2) is n-ary, the new move relation of $2G$ is $2(n+1)$-ary. For a given answer relation $answer(\bar{U}) \leftarrow win(\bar{X})$ in P_G, the new answer relation of P_{2G} is defined as

$$answer(\bar{U}) \leftarrow win(s_0, \bar{X}, \bar{Y}).$$

It is easy to see that I wins in $1\,round(\bar{X})$ if $|\bar{x}| = 1$, and II wins $1\,round(\bar{Y})$ if $|\bar{y}| = 1$.

Assume for the moment that the dashed edge $m_4 \to s_0$ in Fig. 3 is absent. The loop $l_1 \to m_4 \to l_1$ compares the lengths of $\bar{x}$ and $\bar{y}$: I wins this comparison if $|\bar{x}| < \infty$ and $|\bar{x}| \leq |\bar{y}|$, while II wins if $|\bar{y}| < \infty$ and $|\bar{y}| < |\bar{x}|$.

To get a better understanding of the construction of $2G$, we explain the diagram in Fig. 3 as a dialog between I and II, where each move corresponds to a claim of the moving player. Observe that each claim of a player contradicts the previous claim of the opponent, and that each false claim can indeed be disproved using the corresponding moves in the diagram.

Using the diagram and the implicit claims of the players, it should be clear that I wins $(s_0, \bar{x}, \bar{y})$ in $2G$ (for arbitrary $\bar{y}$) if I wins $\bar{x}$ in G, and II wins $(s_0, \bar{x}, \bar{y})$ in $2G$ if $\bar{x}$ is lost or drawn (for I) in G. Thus the new game $2G$ is *determinate* for positions $(s_0, \bar{x}, \bar{y})$.

However $2G$ may still contain positions which are drawn: Consider e.g. $(l_1, \bar{x}, \bar{y})$ where $\bar{x}$ and $\bar{y}$ are drawn in G. Then II gets no chance of refuting the claim that $\bar{x}$ is won in G, hence $(l_1, \bar{x}, \bar{y})$ is also drawn in $2G$. In order to allow II to defeat such false claims, the dashed edge is needed. By moving along $m_4 \to s_0$, II can win and refute I by choosing the maximal $\bar{y}$ in the move $a \to f$.

The final obstacle is that one has to verify that if $\bar{x}$ is won in G, then II cannot delay the game infinitely using the edge $m_4 \to s_0$. Indeed $|\bar{x}|$ decreases each time the game reaches m_4:

(a) if II chooses in a some $\bar{y}$ with $|\bar{y}| \geq |\bar{x}|$, then I has to move along $f \to k$ thereby enforcing that at least $1\,round(\bar{X})$ is played.

(b) if II chooses $|\bar{y}| < |\bar{x}|$, then I chooses a new $\bar{x}$ with $|\bar{x}| = |\bar{y}| + 1$. Independent of the choice of II ($g \to h_1$ or $g \to i_1$), the new $\bar{x}$ will be at least one smaller, when m_4 is reached.

Summarizing, this shows that (for arbitrary $\bar{y}$)

- I wins $(s_0, \bar{x}, \bar{y})$ in $2G$ iff $\bar{x}$ is won in G, and
- II wins $(a, \bar{x}, \bar{y})$ in $2G$ iff $\bar{x}$ is lost or drawn in G.
- No positions $(s, \bar{x}, \bar{y})$ in $2G$ are drawn.

∎

Putting everything together, we have

$$\text{W-Datalog} \overset{\text{Theorem 3.4}}{\leq} \text{W-Datalog}^G \overset{\text{Theorem 3.6}}{\leq} \text{W-Datalog}_2^G \leq \text{W-Datalog}$$

which proves

Corollary 3.7 (W-Datalog $\equiv$ W-Datalog$_2$)

For every well-founded Datalog program, there is an equivalent total program.

Acknowledgements. The third author would like to thank JÜRGEN DIX, WOLFGANG MAY and CHRISTIAN SCHLEPPHORST for many fruitful discussions, and his co-authors for illuminating insights into the realm of finite model theory and games.

References

[AB94]   K. R. Apt and R. N. Bol. Logic Programming and Negation: A Survey. *Journal of Logic Programming*, 19/20:9–71, 1994.

[ABW88] K. R. Apt, H. Blair, and A. Walker. Towards a Theory of Declarative Knowledge. In J. Minker, editor, *Foundations of Deductive Databases and Logic Programming*, pages 89 – 148. Morgan Kaufmann, 1988.

[AHV95] S. Abiteboul, R. Hull, and V. Vianu. *Foundations of Databases*. Addison Wesley, 1995.

[Che95] W. Chen. Query Evaluation in Deductive Databases with Alternating Fixpoint Semantics. *ACM Transactions on Database Systems*, 20(3):239–287, 1995.

[Dix95] J. Dix. Semantics of Logic Programs: Their Intuitions and Formal Properties. In A. Fuhrmann and H. Rott, editors, *Logic, Action and Information*. de Gruyter, 1995.

[EF95]   H.-D. Ebbinghaus and J. Flum. *Finite Model Theory*. Perspectives in Mathematical Logic. Springer, 1995.

[Gro94] M. Grohe. *The Structure of Fixed-Point Logics*. PhD thesis, Universität Freiburg, 1994. http://logimac.mathematik.uni-freiburg.de/preprints/groh12-94-{1,2,3}.ps.

[Imm86] N. Immerman. Relational Queries Computable in Polynomial Time. *Information and Control*, 68:86–104, 1986.

[Kub95] M. Kubierschky. Remisfreie Spiele, Fixpunktlogiken und Normalformen. Master's thesis, Universität Freiburg, 1995. http://logimac.mathematik.uni-freiburg.de/preprints/kub95.ps.

[Sch95] J. S. Schlipf. Complexity and Undecidability Results in Logic Programming. *Annals of Mathematics and Artificial Intelligence*, 15(III-IV), 1995.

[VG89]   A. Van Gelder. The Alternating Fixpoint of Logic Programs with Negation. In *Proc. ACM Symposium on Principles of Database Systems*, pages 1–10, 1989.

[VG93]   A. Van Gelder. The Alternating Fixpoint of Logic Programs with Negation. *Journal of Computer and System Sciences*, 47(1):185–221, 1993.

[VGRS88] A. Van Gelder, K. Ross, and J. Schlipf. Unfounded Sets and Well-Founded Sematics for General Logic Programs. In *Proc. ACM Symposium on Principles of Database Systems*, pages 221–230, 1988.

Fine Hierarchies of Generic Computation *

Jerzy Tyszkiewicz

Mathematische Grundlagen der Informatik,
RWTH Aachen, Ahornstraße 55,
D-52074 Aachen, Germany.
jurek@informatik.rwth-aachen.de

Abstract. Suppose that you are a user of a commercial relational database, accessible over the Internet, whose owner has decided to copy the price lists of the US telephone companies — first order queries are for free just like local calls, because they are local by the theorem of Gaifman [6]. All recursive queries, being potentially non-local, are charged, for simplicity let us assume $1.00 for a Boolean query. Non-Boolean queries are certainly not allowed, because the user would require all the data to be sent to him by issuing the first order identity query, and then manipulate with it himself, without any pay.

These are the rules. Well, what is your strategy, to compute all you want to know about the database, paying as little as possible? And how much will the total price be?

We answer this question, showing that the question whether you can get your answer without any costs at all, depends on whether or not the theories of databases in the provided query language are finitely axiomatizable.

Thus, assuming there is a limit on the number of variables allowed in queries, if the database query language is the fixpoint logic, you can get everything for free. When it is Datalog however, even with inequality and negation of the edb's, you have to pay. We present a method, which for graphs of n vertices costs about $ \log_2 \log_2 n$. Thus querying a graph with 1 Terabyte vertices costs $7.00. We demonstrate that this price cannot be substantially reduced without causing a large computational overhead.

1 Introduction

At the heart of the story in the abstract of this paper is the question:

Is it possible to evaluate recursive queries in nonrecursive query languages, perhaps by means of evaluating many nonrecursive ones and analyzing such obtained data? I.e., is it possible to compensate for the lack of recursion in the queries by computational power outside of the query language?

We attempt to characterize query languages in which it is possible, and determine how many recursive queries are really necessary, if it is impossible.

---

* This research has been supported by a Polish KBN grant 8 T11C 002 11 and by the German Science Foundation DFG.

1.1 A longer explanation of the problem

It seems that querying databases and analyzing such obtained data are becoming two completely separated tasks. Namely databases are more and more frequently offered through the Internet or other networks, and the remote user can query them with the provided queries, but any further manipulation with the retrieved data must be done on his local machine. The owner of the database simply is not interested in allowing remote users to perform time and memory consuming computations on his machine — he offers the data and takes care, that they are evaluated in the most effective way. And last but not least, the security factor is also important here.

Let us look at consequences which result from this separation.

First of all, the abilities of the end user are limited not directly by the expressive power of the query language, but by the expressive power of the *reflexive programming in the query language*, i.e., by abilities of application programs which may dynamically create and evaluate queries during computation. Therefore query languages whose expressive powers differ in the plain sense may appear to be equivalent in our scenario. If this happens to the recursive and nonrecursive queries in some language, we can legitimately say that the external computational power can compensate for the lack of recursion in the query language.

The answer to the above question can a priori depend on the complexity restrictions we impose on the programs. Further, the computational cost of the end user does not depend directly on the computational complexity of queries he issues any more. Perhaps the network transmission delay can be much more important factor for him, or waiting time to get his query evaluated because of many users querying the same data at the same time — in these cases the number of used queries becomes the main complexity measure. And certainly what remains important for him is the complexity of analyzing the data he gets.

1.2 Our results

First of all, we show that the question whether the lack of recursion in L can be compensated for by external computational power is generally equivalent to the old-fashioned logical question, whether complete L-theories are finitely axiomatizable or not and whether these axiomatizations can be effectively found.

We study in more detail two query languages, which have finite models with non-finitely-axiomatizable theories, namely Datalog with k variables, inequality and negation of edb's $\text{Datalog}^k(\neq, \neg)$ and its nonrecursive fragment $\text{FO}^k(\exists)$, which is (equivalent to) the existential fragment of first order logic with k variables. We show that one cannot emulate the recursion present in $\text{Datalog}^k(\neq, \neg)$ at all, even using unlimited computational power on the application level, but with only $\text{FO}^k(\exists)$ queries.

Then we attempt to measure, how much logics on two levels of this hierarchy differ, i.e., how many sentences of the stronger logic have to be evaluated, in addition to the sentences of the weaker one, to compute anything that can be computed with the unlimited access to queries of the stronger language. We prove that any function computable in polynomial time using Datalog^k($\neq$, $\neg$) queries can be still computed in polynomial time using only $\log_2 \log_2 n$ such recursive queries, the rest of them being replaced by nonrecursive ones, and that there are functions, which require that many recursive queries. We show also that this bound is optimal, up to a constant factor, whose decreasing however costs increasing the degree of the polynomial bounding computation time. Therefore for structures of 1 Terabyte ($= 10^{12}$) elements 7 recursive queries are necessary and already suffice.

2 Preliminaries

The space limitations do not allow us to define all the notions we are going to investigate or use in this paper. The general reference texts which cover everything what is necessary to read this paper are Abiteboul, Hull and Vianu [1] and Ebbinghaus and Flum [5]. In fact, each of these books alone already does it.

2.1 L-generic functions

Let L be a query language. We call two structures $\mathbb{A}$ and $\mathbb{B}$ L-equivalent, $\mathbb{A} \equiv_L \mathbb{B}$ in symbols, if for every sentence $\varphi \in L$ holds $\mathbb{A} \models \varphi \Leftrightarrow \mathbb{B} \models \varphi$.

A function from the set Fin of all finite structures into $\mathbb{N}$ is called L-generic iff for every two L-equivalent structures $\mathbb{A}$ and $\mathbb{B}$ holds $f(\mathbb{A}) = f(\mathbb{B})$. In other words, $\ker f \supseteq \equiv_L$, i.e., equivalence classes of $\ker f$ are unions of equivalence classes of $\equiv_L$.

L-generic functions provide a generalization of the notion L-generic definability of classes of finite structures, which can be seen as considering L-generic functions into $\{0, 1\}$.

An L-generic function $f : \text{Fin} \to \mathbb{N}$ is called an L-bijection iff f is surjective and $\ker f = \equiv_L$. f can be naturally considered as a bijective mapping of $\equiv_L$-equivalence classes into $\mathbb{N}$, from which the name comes.

2.2 L-generic computation model

We define now the *reflective relational machines* in the sense of Abiteboul, Papadimitriou and Vianu [2], which is in turn an extension of the model of *loosely coupled relational machines* of Abiteboul and Vianu [3].

Let L be a query language, closed under query composition. A *reflective relational L-machine* (RM(L) machine for short) is defined as follows.

It consists of a standard deterministic Turing machine component, including finite control and several work tapes. In addition it has a *relational store*, consisting of infinitely many relations R_i, $i = 1, 2, \ldots$ of fixed arities over some fixed finite set. These relations are provided as an input for the machine. One of the work tapes is distinguished to be the *L-query tape*, on which the machine can write arbitrary L-query of any finite subsignature of $\langle R_1, R_2, \ldots \rangle$, followed by # and a natural number. Upon entering a special state ex the query is evaluated in one step on the actual contents of the store, and the result is placed in the relation whose number is the second part of contents of the query tape. In case the second number is 0, the query on the tape should be a sentence. Then the output (*true* or *false*), which is obtained analogously in one step, is used to determine the next state of the machine, along with the symbols seen by heads on the standard tapes.

The initial configuration of the machine is as usually, where the relational store contains the input: it can be an arbitrary finite structure A of a fixed signature $\varrho = \langle R_1, \ldots, R_m \rangle$. The remaining relations $R_{m+1}, R_{m+2}, \ldots$ are set initially empty and will play the rôle of work registers.

We can now easily define, what it means, that a reflexive L-machine M computes a total function $f : \mathrm{Fin}(\varrho) \to \mathrm{N}$, or a total query $q : \mathrm{Fin}(\varrho) \to \mathrm{Fin}$.

It is possible to extend the above definition to query languages which are not closed under query composition. In this case we have to adopt additional restriction in the $\mathrm{RM}(L)$ model to make sure, that the machine cannot overcome limitations of the query language. One obvious and always applicable restriction is to forbid the use on non-Boolean queries. In some other context there are, however, other restrictions which assure us of this. In this paper we assume by the Boolean restriction only.

3   The Hierarchies in General

It is clear from the definition, that any function computable by a $\mathrm{RM}(L)$ machine is L-generic and that they are recursive in the standard sense. Our main goal in the paper is to investigate limitations concerning computability of L-generic functions by such machines. In a sense the maximal computational power is achieved when there is an $\mathrm{RM}(L)$-computable L-bijection f. Then the ability to compute any given L-generic function g by an $\mathrm{RM}(L)$-machine is just a recursion-theoretic question, namely whether there is a function $h : \mathrm{N} \to \mathrm{N}$ such that $g = h \circ f$.

It may happen, however, that for any an $\mathrm{RM}(L)$-computable function f holds $\ker f \supsetneq \equiv_L$. In this case some recursive and L-generic functions remain noncomputable for $\mathrm{RM}(L)$, even if at the same time $\equiv_L$ is decidable. (In the other case that $\equiv_L$ is undecidable it is trivial and thus uninteresting.) If it is so, then it is possible that some extension of $L' \supseteq L$ with the same indistinguishability relation is stronger in the sense, that $\mathrm{RM}(L')$ machines can compute more functions than $\mathrm{RM}(L)$ machines.

First of all, we isolate the main reason for it, being that L-theories of some finite structures are not finitely axiomatizable in L, or that these axiomatizations exist but are not effectively computable.

Further we consider naturally occurring recursion-theoretic and complexity-theoretic hierarchies within extensions of L sharing the same indistinguishability relation $\equiv_L$.

3.1 Fine hierarchies of generic computation

We define as follows:

Definition 1. If L, L' are two query languages, then we write $L \preccurlyeq L'$ if every RM(L)-computable function Fin $\to$ N is RM(L')-computable, as well. If the inverse relation holds too we write $L \approx L'$; if it does not we write $L \prec L'$.

This opens us the possibility to investigate hierarchies of query languages w.r.t. $\preccurlyeq$. We can distinguish two types of hierarchies: those where inequalities follow from strict inclusions between indistinguishability relations, and *fine hierarchies,* which stratify query languages sharing the same indistinguishability relation. The fine hierarchies are the topic of this paper.

First the question, if any fine hierarchies at all exist, and if so, when, should be answered.

Definition 2. We say that the L-theory of a structure A is *finitely axiomatizable in L* iff there is a finite $T \subseteq L$ such that for any finite structure B holds A $\equiv_L$ B whenever the equivalence A $\models \varphi \Leftrightarrow$ B $\models \varphi$ holds for every $\varphi \in T$.

If this is the case, we say that T *provides a finite axiomatization for* A. Note that we do not require A $\models T$, so T as such is not an axiomatization of the L-theory of A. Only T together with the pattern of truth values of the sentences from T in A is such an axiomatization. We choose this definition because not all of the logics we are going to deal with are closed under negation.

First we analyze the connections between the existence of fine hierarchies and the existence of finite axiomatizations of L-theories of finite structures.

Theorem 3. *Let L be a query language, such that the relation $\models$ between L-sentences and finite models is recursive and $\equiv_L$ is recursive.*

Then every recursive L-generic function is computable by some RM(L) *iff the following two conditions are satisfied:*

FA1 *L-theory of each finite model is finitely axiomatizable.*
FA2 *There exists a recursive function FA from* Fin *into finite subsets of L such that FA(A) provides a finite axiomatization for* A, *for each* A $\in$ Fin.

Proof. ($\Leftarrow$) We will show that there exists an L-bijection $f :$ Fin $\to$ N, computable by some RM(L) machine M.

Let $A_1, A_2, \ldots$ be any recursive enumeration of Fin.

The machine M we need proceeds as follows. Given A as input, M starts enumerating (encodings of) finite structures A_i for $i = 1, 2, \ldots$. For each enumerated structure it computes the set T_i of L-sentences providing a finite axiomatization for A_i, queries A and A_i with all queries in T_i (A is queried by queries written on the L-tape, while for A_i it is achieved by computing on encodings, done entirely on the work tapes) and compares the results, determining thereby whether A $\equiv_L A_i$. It stops this procedure when the first A_k is found for which this equivalence holds. Certainly such A_k will be eventually found, because A itself must appear somewhere in the enumeration of finite structures. Note that outputting k at this moment already yields a function with kernel equal to $\equiv_L$, which need not be surjective however. In order to remedy this, M determines which structures among $\mathbb{A}_1, \ldots, \mathbb{A}_{k-1}$ are $\equiv_L$-equivalent — it is possible either using sets T_i or the standard algorithm for $\equiv_L$. The output of M is then the number of distinct $\equiv_L$-equivalence classes represented among $\mathbb{A}_1, \ldots, \mathbb{A}_{k-1}$. As it is easy to verify, this is already an L-bijection.

($\Rightarrow$) The other direction we begin with a preliminary fact.

Lemma 4. *If the relation $\equiv_L$ is recursive, then there exists a recursive L-bijection.*

Proof. The proof is analogous to the just presented proof of ($\Leftarrow$) of the Theorem. The only difference is that the device computing the L-bijection is a standard Turing machine, and its input $\mathbb{A}$ is given as encoding. Therefore it does not need the sets T_i to determine $\equiv_L$-equivalence of the input with other structures, because the algorithm for $\equiv_L$ suffices. $\qquad\square$

Turning back to the proof of the Theorem, $\equiv_L$ is recursive, so by Lemma 4 there exists a recursive L-bijection f, which is in turn computable by some $\mathrm{RM}(L)$ machine M, by our assumption. Let $\mathbb{A}$ be a finite structure. Consider the computation of M on $\mathbb{A}$. The set of queries used by M in this computation provides a finite axiomatization for $\mathbb{A}$. Indeed, if there was another structure $\mathbb{B}$ with $\mathbb{A} \not\equiv_L \mathbb{B}$, but in which these queries gave the same results, then the computation of M in $\mathbb{B}$ would be identical as in $\mathbb{A}$ and would therefore result in the same output $f(\mathbb{A})$, thus contradicting L-bijectivity of f.

The above procedure can be used to determine recursively sets of sentences providing finite axiomatizations for finite structures, required in FA2. $\qquad\square$

It may seem strange, but FA1 does not imply FA2 in general. A suitable example will be presented in the full version of the paper.

3.2 Examples

A natural example of the finitely axiomatizable case, where the fine hierarchy collapses, is the well-known hierarchy of logics $\mathrm{FO}^k \subseteq \mathrm{LFP}^k \subseteq \mathrm{PFP}^k \subseteq \mathrm{L}^k_{\infty\omega}$, in which all members share the same indistinguishability relation. Since it is known, that FO^k-theories of finite models are finitely axiomatizable by so-called Scott sentences (see Dawar, Lindell and Weinstein [4]), and since they can be effectively determined, it follows that among all recursive extensions of FO^k within $\mathrm{L}^k_{\infty\omega}$ the fine generic computation hierarchy collapses, which has been indeed known since the work of Abiteboul and Vianu [3]. There are other proofs of this fact, which do not refer to finite axiomatizability directly, like e.g. in author's [9]. The conclusion is that the lack of recursion on the level of query language (FO^k) can be substituted by computing power on the level of the application program.

Another example is the existential first order logic $\mathrm{FO}(\exists)$. As noted in [9], the indistinguishability relation of this logic is the isomorphism relation, finite models have always finitely axiomatizable theories, and these axiomatizations are effectively computable in the sense of FA2 in Theorem 3. Indeed, the set providing a finite axiomatization for $\mathbb{A}$ can be chosen to consist of two sentences: one of them asserts that $\mathbb{A}$ is a substructure of the structure at hand (and should be true), and the second asserts that there are at least $|\mathbb{A}|+1$ elements in the structure at hand (and should be false). It follows that any recursive isomorphism-invariant function is $RM(FO(\exists))$-computable. In particular, the lack of recursion in this logic can be fully compensated for by the computational power outside of the query language. Another and interesting questions is whether it can be done efficiently. It can be shown that, e.g., any $RM(FO(\exists))$ machine computing the transitive closure query must use at least $\frac{1}{2}\log n$ variables in structures of cardinality n, while in Datalog just three variables suffice.

3.3 Complexity of L-generic functions

We introduce the notions of complexity of L-generic functions computed by $RM(L)$ machines as follows:

Definition 5. Let $K \subseteq L$ be two query languages with the same indistinguishability relation, and let $f : \text{Fin} \to \mathbb{N}$ be an L-generic function.

$f \in \text{TIME}_L(t(n))$ iff there is an $RM(L)$ machine computing f and using at most $t(n)$ time for input structures of cardinality n. Evaluation of a query costs a unit time.

$f \in L\text{-QUERY}_K(q(n))$ iff there is an $RM(L)$ machine computing f and querying its input at most $q(n)$ times with queries from $L\setminus K$, for input structures of cardinality n.

Complexity classes, in which functions obey simultaneously more resource bounds are defined as usual. E.g., $f \in [L\text{-QUERY}_K(q(n)), \text{TIME}(t(n))]$ iff there is an $RM(L)$ machine computing f and using at most $q(n)$ queries from $L \setminus K$ and time at most $t(n)$ for input structures of cardinality n.

Notions like e.g. PTIME_L are defined in the obvious way. $\text{TIME}_L(\infty)$ will be used to denote the set of all total functions computable by $RM(L)$ machines.

Now we can show that in reasonable cases fine hierarchies of generic computation have always a top element, which is moreover easily accessible from lower levels.

Proposition 6. *Let L be any query language such that $\equiv_L$ is decidable. Then there exists a query language $L^\top \supseteq L$ such that $\equiv_{L^\top} = \equiv_L$ and all recursive L-generic functions are computable by $RM(L^\top)$.*

Moreover, for any recursive, nondecreasing and unbounded function $f : \mathbb{N} \to \mathbb{N}$ holds

$$\text{TIME}_{L^\top}(\infty) = L^\top\text{-QUERY}_L(f(n)).$$

Proof. Fix any recursive L-bijection h, which exists by Lemma 4. Now let $h^\top : \text{Fin} \to \{0,1\}^\omega$ be defined by $h^\top(\mathbb{A}) = 1^{h(\mathbb{A})}0^\omega$.

Now let $L^\top = L \cup L'$, where L' consists entirely of Boolean queries φ_i, defined by

$$\varphi_i(\mathbb{A}) = \text{the } i\text{-th bit of } h^\top(\mathbb{A}).$$

It is immediate to verify that $\equiv_{L^\top} = \equiv_L$.

Let us now verify, that there is an $RM(L^\top)$-machine M, which can compute our L-bijection h using only few $L^\top \setminus L$ queries.

For this purpose let $F : \mathbb{N} \to \mathbb{N}$ be an arbitrarily fast growing recursive function. The machine M we need queries its input structure $\mathbb{A}$ with $\varphi_{F(i)}$ for $i = 1, 2, \ldots$ until it finds i such that the query is false. In virtue of the definition of $h^\top$ this implies that $h(\mathbb{A}) < F(i)$. Then the machine, working all the time on its work tapes, finds by brute force search representatives of all $\equiv_L$-classes, whose h-values are at most $F(i) - 1$. It is an effective procedure, because h is surjective and we compute as long as all of the values appear. Then, having already all the representatives, M starts evaluating all L-sentences in them, until it finds a finite subset $K \subseteq L$ such that all these representatives have different K-theories. Finally, it queries its input structure $\mathbb{A}$ with all sentences of K, determining thereby a representative $\mathbb{B}$ with $\mathbb{B} \equiv_L \mathbb{A}$, and then outputs $h(\mathbb{B})$, which is by the definition of an L-bijection equal to $h(\mathbb{A})$.

It is easy to see, that choosing F growing fast enough, we can assure that the number of queries from $L^\top \setminus L$ necessary in this computation is smaller than any given recursive, nondecreasing and unbounded function of the cardinality of the input. $\qquad\square$

Note that the proof suggests a kind of trade-off between $L^\top$-QUERY$_L$ complexity and the standard computational complexity. Namely, the faster F grows, the less queries from $L^\top \setminus L$ are needed, but more time and space is necessary in the remaining computation. E.g., when F is exponential and $h(\mathbb{A})$ happens to be only a little bit larger than $F(m) - 1$, then the number of structures considered in the computation will be exponentially larger than necessary. Moreover, the process of creating the set K is exponential in the number of structures to be considered itself.

Observe, however, that the simple algorithm, just querying the consecutive bits of $h^\top(\mathbb{A})$ works in time $O(h(\mathbb{A}) \cdot T_h(n))$, where $T_h(n)$ is the complexity of evaluating h. So in this case the overhead is not that bad.

We can show a lower bound, as well.

Proposition 7. *Suppose that every finite consistent set of L-sentences has infinitely many different extensions to a complete theory, i.e., to an L-theory of a finite structure. (Quite formally, for every $\mathbb{A}$ and every finite T there is a finite structure $\mathbb{B} \not\equiv_L \mathbb{A}$ such that $\mathbb{A} \models \varphi \Leftrightarrow \mathbb{B} \models \varphi$ for all $\varphi \in T$.)*

Let $L' \supsetneq L$ be such that L' and L have the same indistinguishability relation and any recursive L-generic function is $RM(L')$-computable. Then there exist recursive L-generic functions such that any $RM(L')$ machine computing them must use unbounded number of queries from $L' \setminus L$ during the computation.

Proof. Let f be any recursive L-bijection, which exists by Lemma 4. By our assumption, f is $\mathrm{RM}(L')$-computable. Suppose to the contrary, that the there is an $\mathrm{RM}(L')$ machine computing this function using at most m queries from $L' \setminus L$ for any input.

Then there are finitely many $\mathrm{RM}(L)$ machines $M_1, \ldots, M_w$ such that for every $\mathbb{A}$ holds $M_i(\mathbb{A}) = f(\mathbb{A})$ for at least one $i \leq w$. Indeed, we obtain M_i as follows: they simulate M, and, whenever M attempts to evaluate in the input a sentence not in L, M_i supplies it with the answer, which is encoded in its finite control. The answers are organized in a list, and are assigned to non-L queries in the order of appearance in the computation of M. So we need $w = 2^m$ such machines, one for each possible sequence of m results of evaluations of $L' \setminus L$ queries. Certainly most of the machines compute nonsense, but at least one provides the true answers, and therefore computes the correct output.

Let $\mathbb{A}_1$ be any finite model. At least one of the machines, w.l.o.g. M_1, when run on $\mathbb{A}_1$, stops and outputs $f(\mathbb{A}_1)$. But M_1 uses only a finitely many L-sentences in this computation, and there must be a structure $\mathbb{A}_2 \not\equiv_L \mathbb{A}_1$ such that all sentences evaluated by M_1 have the same truth values in $\mathbb{A}_2$ as in $\mathbb{A}_1$. So M_1 run on $\mathbb{A}_2$ computes precisely as in $\mathbb{A}_1$ and outputs $f(\mathbb{A}_1)$, thus making an error. So there must be another machine, w.l.o.g. M_2, which run on $\mathbb{A}_2$ halts and outputs $f(\mathbb{A}_2)$. But then similarly there must exist $\mathbb{A}_3$, $\equiv_L$-inequivalent to both $\mathbb{A}_1$ and $\mathbb{A}_2$, but such that $M_1(\mathbb{A}_3) = f(\mathbb{A}_1)$ and $M_2(\mathbb{A}_3) = f(\mathbb{A}_2)$. Therefore there must be a third machine M_3 with $M_3(\mathbb{A}_3) = f(\mathbb{A}_3)$, and so on. Continuing in this manner, we easily find that there exists an input structure on which all the machines $M_1, \ldots, M_w$ make an error, and thus arrive at a contradiction, finishing our proof. $\qquad\square$

4   Existential First Order Logic and Datalog

In this section we are going to investigate two natural and widely studied query languages, namely Datalog with negation of edb's and inequalities and its recursion-free fragment, i.e., existential first order logic. Due to reasons, which are explained in §3.2, we consider the k-variable fragments of these query languages, denoted respectively by $\mathrm{Datalog}^k(\neq, \neg)$ and by $\mathrm{FO}^k(\exists)$. Their indistinguishability relations are equal and decidable, even in PTIME, as it has been shown by Kolaitis and Vardi [7].

Since the names of the two above query languages will appear very frequently in this section, we introduce abbreviations: $\mathrm{Datalog}^k(\neq, \neg)$ will appear as D^k and $\mathrm{FO}^k(\exists)$ as F^k.

The query languages we consider in this section are not closed under query composition, which is a consequence of the fact they are not closed under negation. On the other hand, unrestricted $\mathrm{RM}(L)$ machines can compose queries. Therefore we impose the universal restriction, namely to Boolean queries, which works for any query language.

4.1 Emergence of the hierarchy

It is known from the work of Rosen and Weinstein [8], that the hierarchy must exist, because there are finite models, whose theories in neither F^k nor D^k are finitely axiomatizable in the respective logics. We improve them a little bit to the form of the following.

Theorem 8. *For every $k > 2$ and every constant c holds*

$$D^k\text{-QUERY}_{F^k}(c) \subsetneq \text{TIME}_{D^k}(\infty), \qquad (1)$$

$$(D^k)^\top\text{-QUERY}_{D^k}(c) \subsetneq \text{TIME}_{(D^k)^\top}(\infty). \qquad (2)$$

Proof. The strictness of the first inclusion will follow from the next theorem.

The strictness of the second is a simple improvement of the argument of Rosen and Weinstein, so we leave it out, because of space limitations. □

In particular, (1) and (2) imply the existence of the hierarchy

$$F^k \prec D^k \prec (F^k)^\top \approx (D^k)^\top. \qquad (3)$$

Now we establish precise distances between levels in this hierarchy, based on the number of queries, if no other complexity restrictions are imposed.

Theorem 9. *For any recursive, nondecreasing and unbounded function $f : \mathbb{N} \to \mathbb{N}$ holds:*

$$\text{TIME}_{D^k}(\infty) \subseteq D^k\text{-QUERY}_{F^k}(f(n)) \qquad (4)$$

$$\text{TIME}_{(F^k)^\top}(\infty) \subseteq (F^k)^\top\text{-QUERY}_{D^k}(f(n)) \qquad (5)$$

Proof. Inclusion (5) follows from the general fact. Inclusion (4) follows by an argument quite similar to that used in the proof of Theorem 10 below. It is therefore left out. □

4.2 Tradeoffs

As we have already noted after proof of Proposition 6, there seems to be a kind of tradeoff between complexity measured in terms of time and space and the complexity measured in terms of the number of queries. What we prove now, is that this tradeoff really exists, and the time price of decreasing the number of queries has to be paid. We do it analyzing the first strict inclusion in the hierarchy (3). The second strict inclusion there is much less interesting because $(F^k)^\top$ appearing in it is a kind of an artificial closure operator, which is not even uniquely determined, and the author is unaware of any natural query language $\approx$-equivalent to it.

Theorem 10. *For every k holds*

$$\text{PTIME}_{D^k} = [\text{PTIME}_{D_k}, D^k\text{-QUERY}_{F^k}(\log\log n)] \tag{6}$$

and for each $k > 2$ and each m there is a constant c such that

$$\text{TIME}_{D^k}(n^2) \nsubseteq [\text{TIME}_{D_k}(n^m), D^k\text{-QUERY}_{F^k}(c\log\log n)]. \tag{7}$$

In particular, if $\lim_{n\to\infty} q(n)/\log\log n = 0$, then

$$[\text{PTIME}_{D_k}, D^k\text{-QUERY}_{F^k}(q(n))] \subsetneqq \text{PTIME}_{D^k}. \tag{8}$$

Proof. We begin with (6). Suppose that M is a RM(D^k) and computes a function f, making at most n^m steps of computation in structures of cardinality n. W.l.o.g. we can assume $m > k > 2$.

We are going to construct an RM(D^k) machine N witnessing that $f \in [\text{PTIME}_{D_k}, D^k\text{-QUERY}_{F^k}(\log\log n)]$. Generally it simulates the behaviour of M. It is equipped with a counter, which counts steps of computation of M. (Recall that queries are evaluated in one step of M, so we count one step for them in the simulation, whatever N really does emulating this action of M.) N has a special query buffer for storing D^k queries to be evaluated later.

The following pseudo-Pascal program represents the algorithm realized by N. The integer valued variable *max* is initialized to 17 and *counter* to 0.

> **begin**
> > **do**
> > > emulate and count consecutive steps of the computation of M, replacing each evaluation of a query $\varphi \in D^k$ by evaluation of its *max*-step unwinding, which is in F^k; if this unwinding evaluates to *false*, then add the original query φ to the buffer
> >
> > **until** *counter* = *max* or M halts;
> > evaluate the disjunction of all queries in the buffer;
> > **if** the result is *false* and M halted
> > > **then**
> > > > output the output of M and halt
> > >
> > > **else**
> > > > empty the buffer;
> > > > *counter* := 0;
> > > > *max* := *max*^{m};
> >
> > **endif;**
> **goto** begin;

First let us see, that N is total and computes the same function as M. Indeed, suppose that $|\mathbb{A}| = n$. Then the computation of M in $\mathbb{A}$ takes at most n^m steps, and the deepest induction in a D^k query used in this computation requires at most $n^k \leq n^m$ steps. Since each execution of all statements in the outer **goto**-loop causes max to increase, eventually the value of max is at least n^m. Then in the next full emulation of M all approximations of D^k queries by F^k queries evaluate to correct answers, and M simulated with these results halts within max steps. Moreover, the disjunction of all queries stored in the buffer must evaluate to *false*, and consequently N halts and outputs what M does, which is the correct value. On the other hand, the only way N can halt is when M halts in the last simulation and all queries in this simulation evaluate to their true results, which in virtue of the above analysis leads to the correct output.

Now let us consider the complexity of N. Note that each cycle of emulation, including tests and resetting of buffer and integer variables, requires time polynomial (of some fixed degree) in the value of max and precisely one $D^k \setminus F^k$ query.

The value of max is never greater than n^{2m}. Indeed, any complete simulation performed with $max \geq n^m$ ends by outputting the value of $f(\mathbb{A})$ and halting. So in the worst case the last unsuccessful emulation is performed with $max = n^m - 1$, and then the next one, with $max = (n^m - 1)^m < n^{2m}$, already halts.

Finally, the outer **goto** loop is executed at most as many times as there are necessary to achieve n^{2m}, starting from 17 and rising the value each time to the m-th power. This number is easily seen to be at most $\log \log n$. This provides us the last two facts we need: the number of D^k queries is at most $\log \log n$, and the running time of N is bounded by $p(n) \cdot \log \log n$, for some fixed polynomial p. Therefore $f \in [\text{PTIME}_{D_k}, D^k\text{-QUERY}_{F^k}(\log \log n)]$.

The proof of (7) will be sketched only. We begin it with some preliminaries: The set of all satisfiable F^k sentences of any fixed vocabulary has a model, and even a finite model. Namely, every structure of this vocabulary, which has a substructure satisfying the *extension axiom* ϵ_k *with k variables* satisfies all satisfiable F^k sentences. Such structures exist in a great number, e.g., a randomly chosen directed graph of size 2^{k^2} already satisfies ϵ_k (for directed graphs) with probability very close to 1. See Rosen and Weinstein [8].

Let us fix a sequence $w = w_1 w_2 \ldots w_l \in (\mathbb{N} \cup \{\infty\})^*$. We construct a structure $\mathbb{A}(w)$ as follows: We begin with two disjoint directed chains (included in unary relations E_0, E_1, respectively) of length $|w|$. The beginning point of E_0 is marked by a constant b_0, and that of E_1 by b_1.

We fix a finite directed graph $G \models \epsilon_{k+1}$ and one of its vertices. The choice of both is unimportant. Let g denote the cardinality of the vertex set of G.

Now we add to the two-chain graph we have had $2|w|$ disjoint copies of G, identifying the distinguished vertices in the copies with elements in the chains.

Finally for each $i \leq |w|$, if $w_i \in \mathbb{N}$, we connect the i-th elements in E_0 and E_1 by a chain made of w_i new vertices; otherwise we do not add anything.

Let for $w \in (\mathbb{N} \cup \{\infty\})^*$ the string $\hat{w} \in \{0,1\}^*$ be defined as $\hat{w}_1 \hat{w}_2 \ldots \hat{w}_l$, where $\hat{w}_i = 1$ iff $w_1 \in \mathbb{N}$.

Paths of finite length joining vertices in $\mathbb{A}(w)$ mark bits of $\hat{w}$, like on Fig. 1 below.

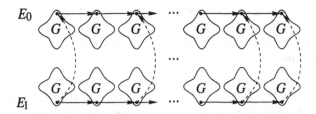

Fig. 1. An example of a structure $\mathbb{A}(w)$. In this case $\hat{w} = 101\ldots011$.

We assume the following lemma without proof.

Lemma 11. *Let $w \in (\mathbb{N} \cup \{\infty\})^*$ and let w' be obtained from w by replacing an occurrence of ∞ by $s \in \mathbb{N}$.*

Then $\mathbb{A}(w)$ and $\mathbb{A}(w')$ are indistinguishable by sentences $\varphi \in \mathrm{F}^k$ with less than s quantifiers, i.e., for all such sentences φ holds $\mathbb{A}(w) \models \varphi \Leftrightarrow \mathbb{A}(w') \models \varphi$.

$\square$

The function we are interested in is defined by $f : \mathbb{A}(w) \mapsto \hat{w}$. (It is not too difficult to extend it to a function defined for all finite structures and $\mathrm{RM}(\mathrm{D}^k)$-computable.)

Suppose M is an $\mathrm{RM}(\mathrm{D}^k)$ machine computing our function in polynomial time, say n^m. Let $q_M(n)$ denote the D^k-$\mathrm{QUERY}_{\mathrm{F}^k}$ complexity of M.

[1] We begin with $l = 10$, say, choose $w = \infty^{10}$, construct the structure $\mathbb{B}_0 = \mathbb{A}(\infty^{10})$ and run M on this structure. In this computation M must use at least one $\mathrm{D}^k \setminus \mathrm{F}^k$ query. Indeed, suppose to the contrary that M uses only F^k queries. Due to the time bound, their length, and therefore the number of quantifiers in each of them as well, is bounded by $s_0 = (20g)^m$. Then M run on $\mathbb{B}_1 = \mathbb{A}((s_0 + 1)\infty^9)$ has during the whole computation identical answers of queries as in the computation on $\mathbb{B}_0$ by Lemma 11, and therefore it halts and outputs 0^{10}, which is a contradiction with assumption that it computes f.

We get $q_M(20g)) \geq 1$.

[2] Let us now consider the computation of M on $\mathbb{B}_1$. We claim M must use at least two $\mathrm{D}^k \setminus \mathrm{F}^k$ queries.

Indeed, suppose to the contrary that M uses only one $\mathrm{D}^k \setminus \mathrm{F}^k$ query and finishes its computations with the right answer. Certainly the use of this query is forced by identity of computations of M on our input and on $\mathbb{B}_0$ up to the point of using the first $\mathrm{D}^k \setminus \mathrm{F}^k$-query.

This time the computation uses at most $s_1 = (20g + s_0 + 1)^m$ time, and so is the maximal possible number of quantifiers in the used F^k queries. Let us see what happens to the computation of M on $\mathbb{B}_2 = \mathbb{A}((s_0 + 1)(s_1 + 1)\infty^8)$. Again M uses in this computation its first $\mathrm{D}^k \setminus \mathrm{F}^k$ query exactly as in the computation on $\mathbb{B}_0$. The answer must be different as in $\mathbb{B}_0$, however, because otherwise M would have halted and answered 0^{10}. So the answer is identical as in $\mathbb{B}_1$, and, since all the remaining queries used by M in $\mathbb{B}_1$ are from $\mathbf{F}^k$, and moreover $\mathbb{B}_1$ and $\mathbb{B}_2$ do not differ w.r.t. $\mathbf{F}^k$ queries with less than $s_1 + 1$ quantifiers, which follows from Lemma 11, the machine halts and answers 10^9, which yields a contradiction.

So $q_M(20g + (20g)^m + 1) \geq 2$.

[3] We consider the computation of M on $\mathbb{B}_2$. We claim this computation must use at least three $\mathbf{D}^k \setminus \mathbf{F}^k$ queries. Indeed, suppose to the contrary it uses only two queries. The first of them is caused by the computation on $\mathbb{B}_0$ and the second by the computation on $\mathbb{B}_1$. Similarly as before, the first query must give the same result in $\mathbb{B}_1$ and in $\mathbb{B}_2$ (the opposite of the result in $\mathbb{B}_0$), so the results of the second one must be different, to prevent M from answering 10^9 in $\mathbb{B}_2$. Let $s_2 = (20g + s_0 + 1 + s_1 + 1)^m$. Now we consider $\mathbb{B}_3 = A((s_0 + 1)(s_1 + 1)(s_2 + 1)\infty^7)$ and the computation of M on this structure. And again, until a third $\mathbf{D}^k \setminus \mathbf{F}^k$ query is used, this computation must be identical as in $\mathbb{B}_2$, and since the remaining computation of M in $\mathbb{B}_2$ uses only $\mathbf{F}^k$ queries and they give in $\mathbb{B}_3$ the same results (by Lemma 11), actually the third $\mathbf{D}^k \setminus \mathbf{F}^k$ query is never used and M halts in $\mathbb{B}_3$ answering 110^8, which yields a contradiction.

So $q_M(20g + (20g)^m + 1 + (20g + (20g)^m + 1)^m + 1) \geq 3$.

[...] Continuing in the same manner we get finally $q_M(n_i) \geq i$ for each $i \leq 9$, where $n_1 = 20g$ and $n_{i+1} = n_i + n_i^m + 1 \leq (n_i + 1)^m$. It is elementary that $n_i \leq (40g)^{m^{i-1}}$.

Then we do not have any more place to play and we have to increase the length of the initial word, to, say, 100. Repeating the same construction we conclude $q_M(n_i) \geq i$ for each $i \leq 99$, where $n_1 = 100g$ and $n_{i+1} = n_i + n_i^m + 1 \leq (n_i + 1)^m$. It is again elementary that $n_i \leq (400g)^{m^{i-1}}$.

In total this makes $q_M(n_i) \geq i$ for some $n_i \leq (4(i + 1)g)^{m^{i-1}}$, for every i.

It follows by a simple computation that $q_M(n) \geq c \log \log n$ for infinitely many n and some constant c, which depends on m solely.

The construction of an $\text{RM}(\mathbf{D}^k)$ machine computing f in quadratic time is left for the reader as an exercise. $\square$

There is an interesting methodological consequence of the results we have proven. It is a kind of common opinion that pebble games and computational complexity are the main determinants of the expressiveness of query languages. And to some extent it is so indeed: in order to verify whether a given class of graphs is definable in, say, LFP, one has to check (1) whether it is compatible with $\equiv_{FO^k}$ for some k, and for this task suitable games are sound and complete; and (2) whether its time complexity w.r.t. $\text{RM}(FO^k)$ is within PTIME in appropriate sense. It has been shown by Abiteboul and Vianu [3] that these two conditions are necessary and already suffice.

In our case a pebble game appropriate for Datalog has been found by Kolaitis and Vardi [7]. But now there is a life beyond the games. We have just found functions which are in PTIME and are $\mathbf{F}^k$-generic, but which remain noncomputable by $\text{RM}(\mathbf{F}^k)$ machines, no matter how much time and space they are allowed to use. It seems therefore that the games for Datalog and existential first order logic are a little bit too strong when compared to the logics.

5 Conclusions

In this paper we have started investigating whether the lack of recursion in a query language can be compensated for by the computational power outside of the query language—namely by replacing a recursive query by a sequence of nonrecursive queries plus an analysis of such obtained data. We believe that this question can soon become of practical relevance, corresponding to the situation of a user querying a database over the net.

Using reflexive relational machines, computing functions from finite structures into natural numbers as a computation model, we have shown that the answer is positive iff complete theories in the query language are finitely axiomatizable and these finite axiomatizations are effectively computable.

Then we have investigated in more depth the non-finitely axiomatizable situation encountered in Datalog with bounded number of variables, enriched by inequality and negation of edb's. We have shown that in this case every function computable in PTIME with unlimited access to recursive queries can be computed using only $\log \log n$ recursive queries, the rest of them being replaced by nonrecursive ones. Moreover, this result is optimal, because there are functions which require this number of recursive queries.

Acknowledgments. The author would like to express his sincere thanks to Eric Rosen, who, among other valuable comments, has suggested the use of Lemma 11 in the proof of Theorem 10. The anonymous referees provided constructive criticism, which have helped me to improve the presentation of my results.

References

1. S. Abiteboul, J. Hull and V. Vianu, *Foundations of Databases*, Addison-Wesley, 1995.
2. S. Abiteboul, C. Papadimitriou and V. Vianu, The power of reflective relational machines, in: *Proc. 9th Symposium on Logic in Computer Science*, 1994, pp. 230–240.
3. S. Abiteboul and V. Vianu, Generic computation and its complexity, in: *Proc. ACM SIGACT Symp. on the Theory of Computing*, 1991, pp. 209–219.
4. A. Dawar, S. Lindell and S. Weinstein, Infinitary logic and inductive definability over finite structures, *Information and Computation*, **119**, 1995.
5. H.-D. Ebbinghaus and J. Flum, *Finite Model Theory*, Springer Verlag, 1995.
6. H. Gaifman, On local and nonlocal properties, in: J. Stern (ed.), *Logic Colloquium '81*, North Holland, 1982, pp. 105–135.
7. Ph. Kolaitis and M. Vardi, On the expressive power of Datalog: tools and a case study, in: *Proceedings of the 9th Symposium on Principles of Database Systems*, 1990, pp. 46–57.
8. E. Rosen and S. Weinstein, Preservation theorems in finite model theory, in: D. Leivant (ed.), *Logic and Complexity*, Springer Verlag, 1995.
9. J. Tyszkiewicz, On the Kolmogorov expressive power of Boolean query languages, to appear in *Theoretical Computer Science*.
   Preliminary version appeared in: G. Gottlob, M.Y. Vardi (eds.), *Proc. ICDT'95*, Lecture Notes in Computer Science 893, Springer Verlag, pp. 97–110

Local Properties of Query Languages

Guozhu Dong[1]   Leonid Libkin[2]   Limsoon Wong[3]

[1] Dept of Computer Science, University of Melbourne, Parkville, Vic. 3052,
Australia, Email: dong@cs.mu.oz.au
[2] Bell Laboratories/Lucent Technologies, 600 Mountain Avenue, Murray Hill, NJ
07974, USA, Email: libkin@research.bell-labs.com
[3] BioInformatics Center & Institute of Systems Science, Singapore 119597, Email:
limsoon@iss.nus.sg

Abstract. Expressiveness of database query languages remains the major motivation for research in finite model theory. However, most techniques in finite model theory are based on Ehrenfeucht-Fraisse games, whose application often involves a rather intricate argument. Furthermore, most tools apply to first-order logic and some of its extensions, but not to languages that resemble real query languages, like SQL.

In this paper we use *locality* to analyze expressiveness of query languages. A query is local if, to determine if a tuple belongs to the output, one only has to look at a certain predetermined portion of the input.

We study local properties of queries in a context that goes beyond the pure first-order case, and then apply the resulting tools to analyze expressive power of SQL-like languages. We first prove a general result describing outputs of local queries, that leads to many easy inexpressibility proofs. We then consider a closely related *bounded degree* property, which describes the outputs of queries on structures that locally look "simple," and makes inexpressibility proofs particularly easy. We prove that every local query has this property. Since every relational calculus (first-order) query is local, these results can be viewed as "off-the-shelf" strategies for inexpressibility proofs, which are often easier to apply than the games. We also show that some generalizations of the bounded degree property that were conjectured to hold, fail for relational calculus.

We then prove that the language obtained from relational calculus by adding grouping and aggregates (essentially plain SQL), has the bounded degree property, thus solving an open problem. Consequently, first-order queries with Härtig and Rescher quantifiers have the bounded degree property. Finally, we apply our results to show that SQL and relational calculus are incapable of maintaining the transitive closure view even in the presence of certain kinds of auxiliary data.

1   Introduction

One major issue in the study of database query languages is their expressive power. Given a query language, it is important to know if the language has enough power to express certain queries. Most database languages have limited power; for example, the relational calculus and algebra cannot express the transitive closure of a graph or the parity test. A large number of tools have been developed for first-order logic (or equivalently, the relational calculus); these include Ehrenfeucht-Fraisse games [1, 13], locality [13, 16], 0-1 laws [1, 13], Hanf's technique [15], the bounded degree property [23]. We are especially interested in local properties of queries, first introduced by Gaifman [16]. These state that the result of a query can be determined by looking at "small neighborhoods" of its arguments.

Expressiveness of database query languages remains the major motivation for research in finite model theory. However, most of those tools developed are modified Ehrenfeucht-Fraisse games, whose application often involves a rather intricate argument. Furthermore, most current tools are applicable only to first-order logic and some of its extensions (like fragments of second-order logic [15], infinitary logics [5], logics with counting [20], etc.); but they do not apply to languages that resemble real query languages, like SQL.

The goal of this paper is to give a thorough study of local properties of queries in a context that goes beyond the pure first-order case, and then apply the resulting tools to analyze expressive power of SQL-like languages.

Languages like SQL differ from the relational calculus in that they have grouping constructs (modeled by the SQL GROUPBY) and aggregate functions such as COUNT and AVG. After some initial investigation of extended relational languages was done in [21, 25], first results on expressive power appeared in [8]. However, the results of [8] were based on the assumption that the deterministic and nondeterministic logspace are different, and thus questions on expressive power of SQL-like languages remained open.

In the past few years, several researchers explored the connection between relational languages with aggregate functions and languages whose main data structures are bags rather than sets. Among the issues that were studied are interdefinability of their primitives [4, 22, 18], complexity [18], optimization [7], equational theories [17] and, finally and most recently, the limitations of their expressive power [23, 24]. In particular, it was shown in [23] that the transitive closure of a graph remains inexpressible even when grouping and aggregation are added to the relational calculus. For a survey of this area, see [19].

Since there was no tool available for studying languages with aggregate functions, in [23] we tried to find a property possessed by the queries in our language, which is not possessed by the transitive closure of a graph. Let a query q take a graph as an input and return a graph. Then we say that it has the *(graph) bounded degree property* if for any k, if all in- and out-degrees in an input graph G do not exceed k, then the number of distinct in- and out-degrees in the output graph $q(G)$ is bounded by some constant c, that depends only on k and q, and not on the graph G. It is clear that the transitive closure query violates this property: just look at the transitive closure of a chain graph.

We have been able to prove that the bounded degree property holds for every relational calculus graph query [23]. We have also demonstrated that it is a very convenient tool for establishing expressivity bounds, often much easier to apply than the games or other tools. However, we were not able to prove in [23] that it extends to languages with aggregation. Instead, we showed inexpressibility of the transitive closure in such a language by a direct brute-force argument, analyzing the properties of queries restricted to special classes of inputs (multicycles).

The question of whether relational calculus with grouping and aggregate functions has the bounded degree property was the main open problem left in [23]. We also mentioned a possible approach towards solving this problem. The proof of the bounded degree property for relational calculus was based on Gaifman's result that first-order formulae are *local*, in the sense as defined in [16]. The locality result in [16] has two parts, and only one was used in our proof in [23]. It says that in order to determine if a formula $\phi(\vec{x})$ is satisfied on a tuple $\vec{a}$, one only has to look at a small neighborhood of $\vec{a}$ of a predetermined size. (The second part deals with sentences, and is irrelevant for the discussion here.) Thus, we thought that it is of interest to give a general study of queries that satisfy this notion of locality.

The purpose of this paper is twofold. First, we give a general study of local queries, their expressive power, and more general notions of the bounded degree property. Second, we prove locality of certain queries in an SQL-like language and show that this is enough to confirm that it has the bounded degree property.

Organization In the next section, we introduce the notations in such a way that the presentation of the results about locality and bounded degree properties can be applied to a number of different languages, including first-order logic and some of its extensions. We give a formal definition of local queries, and note that every relational calculus query is local.

In Section 3, we prove the main result about expressiveness of local queries. We show that the number of different in- and out-degrees realized in the output of a graph query on an arbitrary structure is bounded above by the number of nonisomorphic neighborhoods realized in the input structure, such that the radius of these neighborhoods depends only on the query. We demonstrate some expressiveness bounds that immediately follow from this result.

The main result of Section 4 is that every local query has the bounded degree property. We also show how this result can be used to establish expressiveness bounds in the presence of some auxiliary data.

In Section 5 we look at some generalizations of the bounded degree property that one migh expect to be true, and show that they fail even for first-order graph queries.

In Section 6, we introduce a theoretical SQL-like language that extends relational calculus with grouping and aggregate functions, and prove that it is local when restricted to unordered flat relations whose degrees are bounded by a constant. Therefore, the language has the bounded degree property over flat relations without ordering on the domain elements. This implies that it cannot express the transitive closure. It also follows that first-order queries with Härtig and Rescher (equicardinality and majority) quantifiers have the bounded degree property. In Section 7 we apply our results to incremental maintenance of views, and show that SQL and relational calculus are incapable of maintaining the transitive closure view even in the presence of certain kinds of auxiliary data.

Complete proofs of all the results can be found in [10].

2 Notations

We study queries on finite relational structures. A relational signature τ is a set of relation symbols $\{R_1, ..., R_l\}$, with an associated arity function. In what follows, $p_i(> 0)$ denotes the arity of R_i. By τ_n we mean τ extended with n new constant symbols. We use graphs in many examples; we denote the signature of graphs by τ_{gr}, which consists of one binary predicate (for the edges).

A structure is written as $\mathcal{A} = \langle A, \overline{R}_1, \ldots, \overline{R}_l \rangle$, where A is a finite set called the carrier and $\overline{R}_i$ is the interpretation of R_i, which is a subset of A^{p_i}. The class of τ-structures is denoted by STRUCT$[\tau]$. When no confusion can arise, we write R_i in place of $\overline{R}_i$. We use the symbol $\cong$ to denote isomorphism of structures.

We would like to make our results general enough to apply to a variety of languages. To this end, we assume that a **query** is a formula $\psi(x_1, \ldots, x_m)$, where $x_1, ..., x_m$ are free variables. We also assume the notion of $\models$ between structures and formulas. (You may think of ψ as a first-order formula in the language of τ, and $\models$ as the usual satisfaction relation.) Associated with a query $\psi(x_1, \ldots, x_m)$ is a mapping Ψ of structures from STRUCT$[\tau]$ to STRUCT$[S_m]$, where S_m is a symbol of arity m, defined by $\Psi(\mathcal{A}) = \langle A, \{(a_1, \ldots, a_m) \in A^m \mid \mathcal{A} \models \psi(a_1, \ldots, a_m)\}\rangle$. If $m = 2$, the output of a query is a graph, and we speak about **graph queries**. For convenience, queries are denoted by lower case Greek letters; the associated mappings of structures are denoted by the corresponding upper case Greek letters.

The following definitions are quite standard; see [13, 16]. Given a structure $\mathcal{A}$, its **graph** $\mathcal{G}(\mathcal{A})$ is defined as $\langle A, E \rangle$ where (a, b) is in E iff there is a tuple $\vec{t} \in \overline{R}_i$ for some i such that both a and b are in $\vec{t}$. It is also called the **Gaifman graph** of a structure, cf. [15]. The distance $d(a, b)$ is defined as the length of the shortest path from a to b in $\mathcal{G}(\mathcal{A})$. Note that the triangle inequality holds: $d(a, c) \leq d(a, b) + d(b, c)$. Given $a \in A$, its r-**sphere** $S_r(a)$ is $\{b \in A \mid d(a, b) \leq r\}$. Note that $a \in S_r(a)$. For a tuple $\vec{t}$, $S_r(\vec{t}) = \bigcup_{a \in \vec{t}} S_r(a)$.

Given a tuple $\vec{t} = (t_1, \ldots, t_n)$, its r-**neighborhood** $N_r(\vec{t})$ is defined as a τ_n structure

$$\langle S_r(\vec{t}), \overline{R}_1 \cap S_r(\vec{t})^{p_1}, \ldots, \overline{R}_k \cap S_r(\vec{t})^{p_k}, t_1, \ldots, t_n \rangle$$

That is, the carrier of $N_r(\vec{t})$ is $S_r(\vec{t})$, the interpretation of the relations in τ is obtained by restricting them to the carrier, and the n extra constants are the elements of $\vec{t}$.

Given a structure $\mathcal{A}$, we define an equivalence relation $a \approx_d b$ iff $N_d(a) \cong N_d(b)$. We also define $\mathrm{ntp}(d, \mathcal{A})$ to be the number of $\approx_d$ equivalence classes in $\mathcal{A}$. That is, $\mathrm{ntp}(d, \mathcal{A})$ is the number of isomorphism types of d-neighborhoods in $\mathcal{A}$.

Now we can give our main definition.

Definition 1. Given a query $\psi(x_1, \ldots, x_m)$, its **locality index** is a number $r \in \mathbb{N}$ such that, for every $\mathcal{A} \in$ STRUCT$[\tau]$ and for every two m-ary vectors $\vec{a}, \vec{b}$ of elements of A, it is the case that $N_r(\vec{a}) \cong N_r(\vec{b})$ implies $\mathcal{A} \models \psi(\vec{a})$ iff $\mathcal{A} \models \psi(\vec{b})$. If no such r exists, the locality index is ∞. A query is **local** if it has a finite locality index. A language is **local** if every query in it is local. $\square$

Are there any interesting examples of local queries? An answer to this is provided by Gaifman's locality theorem [16] which implies, in our terminology, the following fact.

Fact 1 *Every first-order (relational calculus) query is local.* □

However, even the simplest fragment of second-order logic, monadic Σ_1^1, is not local. It is not hard to construct a nonlocal query using connectivity test for undirected graphs, which is definable in monadic Σ_1^1 [3].

We shall see later that there are other interesting examples of local queries, though restricted to some classes of structures. We define these restricted classes of structures below. They play a central role in the paper.

For a graph G, its **degree set** $deg\_set(G)$ is the set of all possible in- and out-degrees that are realized in G. By $deg(G)$ we denote the cardinality of $deg\_set(G)$; that is, the number of different in- and out-degrees realized in G. We also define similar notions for arbitrary structures. Given a relation $\overline{R}_i$ in a structure $\mathcal{A}$, $degree_j(R_i, a)$ is the number of tuples in $\overline{R}_i$ whose jth component is a. Then $deg\_set(\mathcal{A})$ is defined as the set of all $degree_j(R_i, a)$ for $\overline{R}_i \in \mathcal{A}$ and $a \in \mathcal{A}$. Finally, $deg(\mathcal{A})$ is the cardinality of $deg\_set(\mathcal{A})$.

The class of τ-structures $\mathcal{A}$ with $deg\_set(\mathcal{A}) \subseteq \{0, 1, \ldots, k\}$ is denoted by $\text{STRUCT}_k[\tau]$. We shall see that many queries in relational calculus augmented with grouping and arithmetic constructs (this is essentially plain SQL) are local when restricted to inputs from $\text{STRUCT}_k[\tau]$, for any fixed k. We also see from this that first-order queries with Härtig and Rescher quantifiers are local when restricted to the same structures.

As was mentioned before, a certain notion of uniform behavior of queries on $\text{STRUCT}_k[\tau_{\text{gr}}]$ was introduced earlier in [23]. We say that a graph query $\psi(x, y)$ has the **graph bounded degree property** if there exists a function $f : \mathbb{N} \to \mathbb{N}$ such that $deg(\Psi(G)) \leq f(k)$ for any $G \in \text{STRUCT}_k[\tau_{\text{gr}}]$. It was shown in [23] that every first-order graph query has the graph bounded degree property.

3 Expressiveness of Local Queries

The goal of this section is to prove a general theorem characterizing outputs of local graph queries. Informally, our main result says this. If ψ is a local query, then the Gaifman graph of $\Psi(\mathcal{A})$ cannot be much more complex than the structure $\mathcal{A}$ itself. We first prove a theorem that states this result for graph queries. From this and a lemma that determines the locality rank of a query defining the Gaifman graph, we obtain our main result.

Recall that for any structure $\mathcal{A}$, the parameter $deg(\mathcal{A})$ shows how complex the structure looks globally. That is, how many different degrees are realized in it. The parameter $ntp(d, \mathcal{A})$, for any fixed $d \geq 0$, shows how many distinct small neighborhoods are realized in $\mathcal{A}$. The first result of this section shows the connection between the parameter $ntp(d, \cdot)$ on an input to a local *graph* query and the parameter $deg(\cdot)$ on the output. It can be interpreted as saying that output of a local graph query cannot be much more complex than its input.

Theorem 2. *Let $\psi(x,y)$ be a graph query on τ-structures of finite locality index r. Then for any $\mathcal{A} \in \mathrm{STRUCT}[\tau]$,*

$$deg(\Psi(\mathcal{A})) \leq 2 \cdot \mathsf{ntp}(3r+1, \mathcal{A})$$

In fact, the number of distinct in-degrees in $\Psi(\mathcal{A})$ is at most $\mathsf{ntp}(3r+1, \mathcal{A})$, and the number of distinct out-degrees in $\Psi(\mathcal{A})$ is at most $\mathsf{ntp}(3r+1, \mathcal{A})$.

Proof sketch. The key to our theorem is the following observation.

Lemma 3. *Let $r > 0$, $d \geq 3r+1$, and let $a \approx_d b$. Then there is a permutation π on $S_{d-r}(a,b)$ such that for every $x \in S_{d-r}(a,b)$, it is the case that $N_r(a,x) \cong N_r(b, \pi(x))$.*

To show how lemma 3 implies the theorem, let $G' = \langle V, E' \rangle$ be $\Psi(\mathcal{A})$. Let $d = 3r+1$. Let $a \approx_d b$. For every $x \notin S_{2r+1}(a,b)$, $N_r(a,x) \cong N_r(b,x)$, since $N_r(a) \cong N_r(b)$ and $d(a,x), d(b,x) > 2r+1$. Thus, $(a,x) \in E'$ iff $(b,x) \in E'$ by locality. Furthermore, by Lemma 3, for every $x \in S_{2r+1}(a,b)$, $(a,x) \in E'$ iff $(b, \pi(x)) \in E'$ by locality and the property of π. Hence a and b have the same outdegrees. A similar argument shows that a and b have the same indegrees. Hence $degset(G')$ has at most $2 \cdot \mathsf{ntp}(d, G)$ elements. $\square$

Let us give two simple applications to demonstrate the usefulness of Theorem 2 in establishing expressiveness bounds. The second of these will be generalized in the next section into a powerful result that lets us eliminate Ehrenfeucht-Fraisse games from many inexpressibility proofs.

Corollary 4. *No local query can define the transitive closure of a graph.*

Proof. Suppose $\psi(x,y)$ of locality index r defines the transitive closure. Consider chains, *i.e.* graphs of the form $C_n = \{(a_0, a_1), \ldots, (a_{n-1}, a_n)\}$ with all a_is distinct. Then $deg(\Psi(C_n)) = n+1$. For every $d \geq 0$, there are at most $2d$ non-isomorphic d-neighborhoods in a chain. Thus, $deg(\Psi(G)) \leq 4(3r+1)$, by Theorem 2. Hence, ψ cannot define the transitive closure. $\square$

Corollary 5. *Every local graph query has the graph bounded degree property.*

Proof. If all in- and out-degrees in G are bounded by k, then the maximum number of non-isomorphic d-neighborhoods depends only on k and d. Combining this with Theorem 2, we see that there is a bound on $deg(\Psi(G))$ that depends only on k and the locality index of ψ. $\square$

The statement of Theorem 2 is not completely satisfactory, since it only deals with graph queries. To generalize it to arbitrary queries, we look at the Gaifman graphs of the outputs. Recall that $\mathcal{G}(\mathcal{A})$ denotes the Gaifman graph of $\mathcal{A}$.

Theorem 6. *Let $\psi(x_1, \ldots, x_n)$, $n \geq 2$, be a query on τ-structures of finite locality index $r > 0$. Then there is a number m that depends only on n and r such that, for any $\mathcal{A} \in \mathrm{STRUCT}[\tau]$, the number of distinct degrees in the Gaifman graph of $\Psi(\mathcal{A})$ does not exceed $\mathsf{ntp}(m, \mathcal{A})$. In fact,*

$$deg(\mathcal{G}(\Psi(\mathcal{A}))) \leq \mathsf{ntp}(3^{n-1}r + (3^{n-1} - 1)/2, \mathcal{A})$$

Proof sketch. We prove this theorem by reduction to graph queries. Given a query $\psi(x_1, \ldots, x_n)$, $n > 2$, define $\psi'(x_1, \ldots, x_{n-1})$ by letting $\mathcal{A} \models \psi'(a_1, \ldots, a_{n-1})$ iff for some $a \in A$, and for some index $0 \leq i \leq n-1$, it is the case that $\mathcal{A} \models \psi(a_1, \ldots, a_i, a, a_{i+1}, \ldots, a_{n-1})$.

Lemma 7. *Let $\psi(x_1, \ldots, x_n)$ be of locality rank $r > 0$. Then $\psi'(x_1, \ldots, x_{n-1})$ is of locality rank $3r + 1$.*

To prove the theorem, first note that if $\psi(x, y)$ is a graph query of locality rank r, and $\psi^*(x, y)$ is such that $\mathcal{A} \models \psi^*(a, b)$ iff $\mathcal{A} \models \psi(a, b)$ or $\mathcal{A} \models \psi(b, a)$, then ψ^* also has locality rank r.

For an arbitrary query $\psi(x_1, \ldots, x_n)$, $n > 2$, define $\psi_1(x_1, \ldots, x_{n-1}) = \psi'(x_1, \ldots, x_{n-1})$, $\psi_2(x_1, \ldots, x_{n-2}) = \psi_1'(x_1, \ldots, x_{n-2})$, etc., until we obtain $\phi(x, y) = \psi_{n-2}(x, y)$. It is easy to see that $\mathcal{A} \models \phi(a, b)$ iff (a, b) is in the Gaifman graph of $\Psi(\mathcal{A})$. From Lemma 7, we see that the locality rank of ϕ is $3^{n-2} r + (3^{n-2} - 1)/2$. Now the theorem follows from the observation made above, Theorem 2, and the fact that $\mathcal{G}(\Psi(\mathcal{A}))$ is undirected. □

4 Bounded Degree Property

A very convenient form of the locality property is called the *bounded degree property*. It says that for structures from $\mathrm{STRUCT}_k[\tau]$ (that is, τ-structures in which no degree exceeds k), there is an upper bound on $deg(\Psi(\mathcal{A}))$ that depends only on ψ and k. A special case of this property is the graph bounded degree property mentioned in Section 2. It was established for first-order graph queries in [23] (see also Corollary 5).

Definition 8. A query $\psi(x_1, \ldots, x_m)$ is said to have the **bounded degree property**, or **BDP**, if there is a function $f_\psi : \mathbb{N} \to \mathbb{N}$ such that $deg(\Psi(\mathcal{A})) \leq f_\psi(k)$ for every $\mathcal{A} \in \mathrm{STRUCT}_k[\tau]$. □

This property can be used as an easy-to-apply tool for establishing expressiveness bounds of query languages. Assume that it is known that every query in a language $\mathcal{L}$ has the BDP. To show that some query q is not definable in $\mathcal{L}$, one has to find a number k and a class $\mathcal{C}$ of input structures in $\mathrm{STRUCT}_k[\tau]$ such that $q(\mathcal{A})$ can realize arbitrarily large degrees on structures $\mathcal{A}$ from $\mathcal{C}$. This is exactly the idea of the proof of Corollary 4. The usefulness of BDP for proving expressiveness bounds on first-order graph queries was demonstrated in [23].

The main result of this section is the following.

Theorem 9. *Every local query has the bounded degree property.*

Proof sketch. Fix a query $\psi(x_1, \ldots, x_m)$ of locality rank r. Fix a structure $\mathcal{A}$ in $\mathrm{STRUCT}_k[\tau]$. Without loss of generality assume $m > 1$, $r > 0$ and $A \neq \emptyset$. Let $p = \sum_i p_i$. Let $s_\mathcal{A}(d)$ be the maximum size of $S_d(a)$ for $a \in A$. Under these assumptions, we claim

Lemma 10. *Let* $d = (2m - 2)(2r + 1)$. *Suppose* $a \approx_d b$ *and* $S_d(a) \cap S_d(b) = \emptyset$. *Then* $|degree_i(a) - degree_i(b)| \leq (2s_A(d))^{m-1}$ *for any* $i \leq m$. □

From this lemma we derive that $deg(\Psi(A)) \leq m \cdot s^m \cdot 2^{1+m+ls^p}$, where $s = s_A((4m - 4)(2r + 1))$. Finally, since $deg\_set(A) \subseteq \{0, \ldots, k\}$, there is an upper bound on $s_A(n)$ that depends on n, k, and p only, from which the bounded degree property follows. □

Let us discuss some implications of this result. As a start, we note that the graph bounded degree property result from [23] applies only to queries from graphs to graphs. One may ask what happens in the presence of auxiliary information, such as the successor relation. Since the successor relation only adds 0 and 1 to the degree set, we obtain immediately

Corollary 11. *The graph bounded degree property of first-order queries continues to hold in the presence of a successor relation.* □

But what happens if relations more complex than the successor are allowed? For instance, auxiliary relations whose degrees are not bounded by any constant, but are still not very large? We can answer this question by using the (slightly modified) notion of moderate degree from [15], and the estimate on the number of in- and out-degrees obtained in the proof of Theorem 9.

Consider a class of structures $C \subseteq \text{STRUCT}[\tau]$ for some relational vocabulary τ. Define a function $s_C : \mathbb{N} \to \mathbb{N}$ by letting $s_C(n)$ be the maximal possible in- or out-degree in some n-element structure $A \in C$. Given an increasing function $g(n)$ such that $g(n)$ is not bounded by any constant, we say that C is of $g(n)$-**moderate degree** if $s_C(n) \leq \log^{o(1)} g(n)$. That is, we have a function $\delta : \mathbb{N} \to \mathbb{N}$ such that $\lim_{n \to \infty} \delta(n) = 0$ and $s_C(n) \leq \log^{\delta(n)} g(n)$. When g is the identity, we have the definition of moderate degree of [15].

Proposition 12. *Let* ψ *be a local query. Let* C *be a class of structures of* $g(n)$-*moderate degree. Then there is* $N \in \mathbb{N}$ *such that for any* $A \in C$ *with* $card(A) = n > N$, *we have* $deg(\Psi(A)) < g(n)$. □

The transitive closure of a chain has as many distinct degrees as there are links in the chain. It is thus not definable by a local query even when auxiliary data of moderate degree are available. Now, using the fact that the transitive closure of a chain is FO-complete for DLOGSPACE [14], we obtain

Corollary 13. *Let* P *be a problem complete for DLOGSPACE under FO reductions. Then* P *is not definable by a local query even in the presence of relations of moderate degree.* □

The converse to Theorem 9 is not true. That is, there is a non-local query that has the bounded degree property. Indeed, let $\psi(x, y)$ be a graph query defined as follows. If G is the union of disjoint chains having a unique longest chain, then $G \models \psi(x, y)$ iff (x, y) is an edge in the unique longest chain in G; otherwise, $G \not\models \psi(x, y)$ for all x, y. It is clear that ψ has the bounded degree property but violates locality. Nevertheless, it should be pointed out that the relational algebra augmented with this query ψ does not have the bounded degree property.

5   Stronger Bounded Degree Properties

The reader may have noticed a certain asymmetry in the statement of the bounded degree property: We make an assumption about the degree *set* $deg\_set(\mathcal{A})$, and give a conclusion that there is an upper bound on the degree *count* $deg(\Psi(\mathcal{A}))$. So, the question arises: Can the bounded degree property be strengthened? In what follows, we present two most obvious attempts to strengthen it. It was conjectured that both of them hold for first-order logic, but we show that this is not the case. Consequently, not all local queries possess these stronger properties.

Definition 14. A query ψ has the **strong bounded degree property**, or SBDP, if there exists a function $f_\psi : \mathbb{N} \to \mathbb{N}$ such that $deg(\Psi(\mathcal{A})) \leq f_\psi(deg(\mathcal{A}))$ for any structure $\mathcal{A}$. $\square$

Definition 15. A query ψ has the **interval bounded degree property**, or IBDP, if there exists a function $f_\psi : \mathbb{N} \to \mathbb{N}$ such that $deg(\Psi(\mathcal{A})) \leq f_\psi(k)$ for any structure $\mathcal{A}$ with $\max deg\_set(\mathcal{A}) - \min deg\_set(\mathcal{A}) \leq k$. $\square$

It is easy to see that the SBDP implies the IBDP and the IBDP implies the BDP. It turns out, somewhat unexpectedly, that there are first-order graph queries that do not have them.

Theorem 16. *There are first-order graph queries that do not have the interval bounded degree property. Consequently, they do not have the strong bounded degree property either.*

Thus, in contrast to Theorem 9, we conclude that

Corollary 17. *There are local queries that do not possess the interval or the strong bounded degree properties.* $\square$

In the remainder we sketch the main construction of Theorem 16. We need to construct a first-order graph query that does not have the IBDP. First fix $n > 3$, four disjoint sets $X = \{x_1, \ldots, x_n\}$, $Y = \{y_1, \ldots, y_n\}$, $C = \{e_1, \ldots, e_n\}$, $D = \{d_1, \ldots, d_n\}$, and a permutation $\pi : \{1, \ldots, n\} \to \{1, \ldots, n\}$. Define the graph G_π as follows. Its set of nodes N is $X \cup Y \cup C \cup D \cup \{a, b, c\}$. Its edges are given as follows:

- There are loops (a, a), (b, b), (c, c) and also edges (b, c) and (c, b).
- For each $i < n$, there are edges (x_i, x_{i+1}) and (y_i, y_{i+1}).
- For each $i \leq n$, there is an edge $(x_i, y_{\pi(i)})$.
- For each $i \leq n$, there are edges (a, x_i), (x_i, a), (b, y_i), (y_i, b), (c, y_i), (y_i, c).
- For each $i \leq n$ and $j \leq n$, there are edges (x_i, e_j), (e_j, y_i), (y_i, d_j), (d_j, x_i).

Define the graph G_n as the disjoint union of G_π for all permutations π. That is, G_n has $n!$ connected components and $(4n + 3) \cdot n!$ nodes. It follows straightforwardly from the construction that $deg\_set(G_\pi) = \{n, n+1, n+2, n+3, n+4\}$.

Next, we define a query Ψ as follows: In some component G_π, in the output we get an edge from a to y_i iff we have $\pi(x_{l+1}) = y_{i+1}$ where $x_l = \pi^{-1}(y_i)$. One can now show that Ψ is first-order definable, but $deg(\Psi(G_n))$ depends on n. $\square$

6 Aggregation, SQL, and the Bounded Degree Property

In this section, we investigate locality and the bounded degree property in the context of SQL-like languages. We start by briefly describing the syntax and semantics of the theoretical SQL-like language to be analyzed. Two main features that distinguish (plain) SQL from the relational calculus are grouping (the SQL GROUPBY operator) and aggregate functions (such as COUNT and AVG). Our languages incorporate these features in a clean analyzable way. We then show how the notions of locality and bounded degree extend to queries in our language. The main result is that queries naturally representing those on $STRUCT_k[\tau]$ are local for every fixed k. Consequently, such queries have the BDP, and thus many inexpressibility proofs carry over from the first-order case to SQL.

Let us start with the syntax and semantics of our SQL-like language. The data types that can be manipulated in the language are given by the grammar:

$$s ::= b \mid \mathbb{B} \mid \mathbb{Q} \mid s_1 \times \cdots \times s_n \mid \{s\}$$

Elements of the base type b are drawn from an unspecified infinite domain. The type $\mathbb{B}$ contains the two Boolean objects *true* and *false*. The type $\mathbb{Q}$ contains the rational numbers. Elements of the product type $s_1 \times \cdots \times s_n$ are n-tuples whose ith component is of type s_i. Finally, elements of the set type $\{s\}$ are finite sets whose elements are of type s.

We present the language incrementally. We start from $\mathcal{NRC}(=)$, which is equivalent to the usual nested relational algebra [2, 6]. To obtain our SQL-like language we add arithmetic and a summation operation to model aggregation. The syntax of $\mathcal{NRC}(=)$ is given below.

$$\frac{}{true : \mathbb{B}} \quad \frac{}{false : \mathbb{B}} \quad \frac{x^s : s \quad c : \mathbb{Q}}{} \quad \frac{e_1 : \mathbb{B} \quad e_2 : s \quad e_3 : s}{if\ e_1\ then\ e_2\ else\ e_3 : s} \quad \frac{e_1 : s \quad e_2 : s}{e_1 = e_2 : \mathbb{B}}$$

$$\frac{e : s_1 \times \cdots \times s_n}{\pi_i\ e : s_i} \quad \frac{e_1 : s_1 \quad \cdots \quad e_n : s_n}{(e_1, \ldots, e_n) : s_1 \times \cdots \times s_n}$$

$$\frac{}{\{\}^s : \{s\}} \quad \frac{e : s}{\{e\} : \{s\}} \quad \frac{e_1 : \{s\} \quad e_2 : \{s\}}{e_1 \cup e_2 : \{s\}} \quad \frac{e_1 : \{t\} \quad e_2 : \{s\}}{\bigcup\{e_1 \mid x^s \in e_2\} : \{t\}}$$

We often omit the type superscripts as they can be inferred. Let us briefly recall the semantics, cf. [6]. Variables x^s are available for each type s. Every rational constant is available. The operations for Booleans, tupling and projections are standard. $\{\}$ forms the empty set. $\{e\}$ forms the singleton set containing e. $e_1 \cup e_2$ unions the two sets e_1 and e_2. Finally, $\bigcup\{e_1 \mid x \in e_2\}$ maps the function $f = \lambda x.e_1$ over all elements in e_2 and then returns their union; thus if e_2 is the set $\{o_1, \ldots, o_n\}$, the result of this operation would be $f(o_1) \cup \cdots \cup f(o_n)$. For example, $\bigcup\{\{(x, x)\} \mid x \in \{1, 2\}\}$ evaluates to $\{(1, 1), (2, 2)\}$.

Given a type s, the **height** of s is defined as the nesting depth of set brackets in s. For example, the usual flat relations (sets of tuples of base types) have height 1. Given an expression e, the **height** of e is defined as the maximal height of all types that appear in the typing derivation of e. For example, $\bigcup\{\bigcup\{\{(x,y)\} \mid x \in R\} \mid y \in S\}$ is an expression of height 1 if both R and S are flat relations. It is known [26, 28] that when restricted to expressions of height 1, $\mathcal{NRC}(=)$ is equivalent to the usual relational algebra. We also write $\mathcal{NRC}(=_b)$ when the equality test is restricted to base types b, $\mathbb{B}$, and $\mathbb{Q}$. We sometimes list the free variables in an expression in brackets like: $e(R, x)$.

As was mentioned, the practical database language SQL extends the relational calculus by having arithmetic operations, a group-by operation, and various aggregate functions such as AVG, COUNT, SUM, MIN, and MAX. It is known [6] that the group-by operator can already be simulated in $\mathcal{NRC}(=)$. The others need to be added. The arithmetic operators are the standard ones: $+$, $-$, $\cdot$, and $\div$ of type $\mathbb{Q} \times \mathbb{Q} \to \mathbb{Q}$. We also add the order on the rationals: $\leq_{\mathbb{Q}} \colon \mathbb{Q} \times \mathbb{Q} \to \mathbb{B}$. As to aggregate functions, we add just the following construct

$$\frac{e_1 : \mathbb{Q} \quad e_2 : \{s\}}{\sum\{\!| e_1 \mid x^s \in e_2 |\!\} : \mathbb{Q}}$$

The semantics is this: map the function $f = \lambda x. e_1$ over all elements of e_2 and then add up the results. Thus, if e_2 is the set $\{o_1, \ldots, o_n\}$, it returns $f(o_1) + \cdots + f(o_n)$. For example, $\sum\{\!| 1 \mid x \in X |\!\}$ returns the cardinality of X. Note that this is different from adding up the values in $\{f(o_1), \ldots, f(o_n)\}$; in the example above, doing so yields 1 as no duplicates are kept. To emphasize that duplicate values of f are being added up, we use bag (multiset) brackets $\{\!| \; |\!\}$ in this construct.

We denote this theoretical reconstruction of SQL by $\mathcal{NRC}^{\text{aggr}}$. That is, $\mathcal{NRC}^{\text{aggr}}$ has all the constructs of $\mathcal{NRC}(=)$, the arithmetic operations $+, -, \cdot$ and $\div$, the summation construct $\sum$ and the linear order on the rationals.

Let us provide two examples to demonstrate how typical SQL queries involving aggregate functions can be implemented in $\mathcal{NRC}^{\text{aggr}}$. For the first example, consider the query that computes the total expenditure on male employees in various departments in a company. Let $EMP : \{name \times salary \times sex \times dept\}$ be a relation that tabulates the name, salary, sex, and department of employees. The query in SQL is SELECT dept, SUM(salary) FROM EMP WHERE sex = 'male' GROUPBY dept. It can be expressed in $\mathcal{NRC}^{\text{aggr}}$ as $\bigcup\{\{(\pi_{dept}\, x, \sum\{\!| \text{if } \pi_{dept}\, x = \pi_{dept}\, y \text{ then if } \pi_{sex}\, y = \text{'male' then } \pi_{salary}\, y \text{ else } 0 \text{ else } 0 \mid y \in EMP |\!\})\} \mid x \in EMP\}$. For the second example, consider the query that computes the number of distinct salaries of male employees in various departments in the same company. The query in SQL is SELECT dept, COUNT(distinct salary) FROM EMP WHERE sex = 'male' GROUPBY dept. Note that in this query, duplicate salary figures in a department are eliminated before counting. It can be expressed in $\mathcal{NRC}^{\text{aggr}}$ as $\bigcup\{\{(\pi_{dept}\, x, \sum\{\!| 1 \mid y \in \bigcup\{\text{if } \pi_{dept}\, z = \pi_{dept}\, x \text{ then if } \pi_{sex}\, z = \text{'male' then } \{\pi_{salary}\, z\} \text{ else } \{\} \text{ else } \{\} \mid z \in EMP\}|\!\})\} \mid x \in EMP\}$.

In fact, it is known [23] that all possible nested applications of all SQL aggregate functions mentioned above can be implemented in $\mathcal{NRC}^{\text{aggr}}$. It is also known [23] that $\mathcal{NRC}^{\text{aggr}}$ has the conservative extension property and thus its expressive power depends only on the height of input and output and is independent of the height of intermediate data. So to conform to SQL, it suffices to restrict our input and output to height at most one.

Before, we assumed queries to be formulae $\psi(x_1, \ldots, x_m)$, mapping structures of some relational vocabulary τ into m-ary relations, defined by $\Psi(A) = \langle A, \{(a_1, \ldots, a_m) \mid a_1, \ldots, a_m \in A, A \models \psi(a_1, \ldots, a_m)\}\rangle$. Now we have to show how $\mathcal{NRC}^{\text{aggr}}$-expressions correspond to queries. After this, we shall be able to transfer the notions of locality and bounded degree to $\mathcal{NRC}^{\text{aggr}}$.

First, we model τ-structures as tuples of objects of types of the form $\{b \times \ldots \times b\}$, with the arities corresponding to those of the symbols in τ. We shall abbreviate $b \times \ldots \times b$, m times, as b^m. A **relational query** over STRUCT$[\tau]$ in $\mathcal{NRC}^{\text{aggr}}$ is an $\mathcal{NRC}^{\text{aggr}}$ expression e of type $\{b^m\}$, whose free variables have types $\{b^{p_1}\}, \ldots, \{b^{p_l}\}$, where p_i is the arity of the ith symbol in τ. Given such an expression, which we write as $e(R_1, \ldots, R_l)$ or $e(\vec{R})$, it can be considered as a query ψ_e as follows. We let, for a τ-structure A over the domain of type b,

$$A \models \psi_e(a_1, \ldots, a_m) \text{ iff } (a_1, \ldots, a_m) \in e(A)$$

In other words, the Ψ_e corresponding to the query ψ_e is precisely e. (This is true because $(a_1, \ldots, a_m) \in e(A)$ implies that all a_is are in the carrier of A.)

Now, for each relational query e, we say that it is local if ψ_e is, and e's locality rank is that of ψ_e. Similarly, we define the bounded degree property of relational queries in $\mathcal{NRC}^{\text{aggr}}$. Finally, we say that a query is local on a class of structures $\mathcal{C} \subset \text{STRUCT}[\tau]$ if the condition in the definition of locality is satisfied on every structure from $\mathcal{C}$ (but not necessarily on every structure in STRUCT$[\tau]$).

Our main result is:

Theorem 18. *For any fixed k, every relational query in $\mathcal{NRC}^{\text{aggr}}$ is local on* STRUCT$_k[\tau]$.

Proof sketch. The proof relies on the following key lemma which gives us a very convenient 'normal form' of $\mathcal{NRC}^{\text{aggr}}$ queries when restricted to structures of degrees at most k. The normal form is a chain of *if-then-else* statements where each branch is a relational calculus expression, and all uses of aggregate functions can only appear in the conditions of these *if-then-else* statements.

Lemma 19. *Let $\vec{R}$ denote a vector of relations of degree at most k, $e(\vec{R}) : s$ be an $\mathcal{NRC}^{\text{aggr}}$-expression, with s of height at most 1. Then $e(\vec{R})$ is equivalent to an expression of the form if $\mathcal{P}_1(\vec{R})$ then $e_1(\vec{R})$ ... else if $\mathcal{P}_d(\vec{R})$ then $e_d(\vec{R})$ else $e_{d+1}(\vec{R})$, where each $e_j(\vec{R})$ is in $\mathcal{NRC}(=_b)$ and d depends only on k and e.* $\square$

This normal form result gets complicated aggregate functions out of the way. We can now prove our theorem. Let $\vec{R}$ denote a structure in STRUCT$_k[\tau]$ whose elements are of base type b. Let $e(\vec{R})$ be a relational query in $\mathcal{NRC}^{\text{aggr}}$. By Lemma 19, we can assume that $e(\vec{R})$ has the form *if $\mathcal{P}_1(\vec{R})$ then $e_1(\vec{R})$ ... else if $\mathcal{P}_d(\vec{R})$ then $e_d(\vec{R})$ else $e_{d+1}(\vec{R})$*, where each $e_i(\vec{R})$ is in $\mathcal{NRC}(=_b)$. Since $\mathcal{NRC}(=)$ enjoys the conservative extension property [28], each e_i can be defined in relational calculus. By Fact 1, every ψ_{e_i} has some finite locality index r_i. From this we immediately conclude that ψ_e has locality index $\max_i r_i$. $\square$

From here, applying verbatim the proof of Theorem 9, we conclude

Corollary 20. *Relational queries in $\mathcal{NRC}^{\mathrm{aggr}}$ have the bounded degree property.*

We immediately conclude from Corollary 20 that

Corollary 21. *(cf. [23]) $\mathcal{NRC}^{\mathrm{aggr}}$ cannot express the following queries: (deterministic) transitive closure of a graph, connectivity test, testing for a (binary, ternary, etc.) tree. This continues to hold when a built-in successor relation or any other built-in relations whose degrees do not exceed a fixed number k are available on the nodes.* □

Recall that Härtig and Rescher quantifiers are two generalized quantifiers for equal cardinality and bigger cardinality respectively. Since these tests can be done in $\mathcal{NRC}^{\mathrm{aggr}}$, we obtain:

Corollary 22. *Every first-order query with Härtig and Rescher quantifiers has the bounded degree property.* □

7 Applications to Incremental Recomputation

Since relational calculus has a limited expressive power and cannot compute queries such as transitive closure, one often stores the results of these queries as materialized database views. Once the underlying database changes, the changes must be propagated to the views as well. In the case when a view is defined in relational calculus, or at least in the same language in which update propagations are specified, the problem of incremental maintenance has been studied thoroughly. However, few papers [11, 9, 12, 27] addressed the issue of maintaining queries such as the transitive closure in first-order or $\mathcal{NRC}^{\mathrm{aggr}}$.

It was shown [9] that, in the absence of auxiliary data, recursive queries such as transitive closure and same generation cannot be maintained in relational calculus or even in SQL. It was conjectured in [9, 12] that this continues to be true in the presence of auxiliary data. Using the results developed in previous sections, we can address this question partially. In particular, we now show that maintenance of some recursive queries remains impossible even if auxiliary data of moderate or low degree are available.

We also consider the same-generation query over a graph having two label symbols A and B. Such a graph can be conveniently represented by two relations, one for edges labeled A and the other for B, which need not be disjoint. We use A and B to name these two relations. Then x and y are in the same generation with respect to A and B iff there is a z such that there is a walk from x to z in A and a walk from z to y in B that are equal in length.

Theorem 23. *Neither transitive closure nor same-generation can be maintained in the relational calculus when auxiliary data of moderate degree are available.*

Proof sketch. The main idea of the proof of non-maintainability of both transitive closure and same-generation [9] is essentially this: Suppose there is an expression $g(I, I^+, t)$ that, given an input I, the result of a query I^+ on I, and a tuple t in I, produces the output of the query on $I - \{t\}$. Then both proofs in [9] show how to use this assumption to produce an expression in first-order logic plus g that computes the transitive closure of a chain. Since the construction of [9] does not assume any auxiliary data, we can apply it here to obtain that, if either query is maintainable in first-order in the presence of auxiliary data of moderate degree, then with such auxiliary data the transitive closure of a chain is computable, which contradicts Corollary 13. $\qquad\square$

Using essentially the same argument, but employing Corollary 21 in place of Corollary 13, we can also prove that

Corollary 24. *Neither transitive closure nor same-generation can be maintained in $\mathcal{NRC}^{\mathrm{aggr}}$ in the presence of auxiliary data whose degrees are bounded by a constant.* $\qquad\square$

8 Future Work

There are many open questions we would like to address in the future. We are interested in developing techniques for proving languages local. So far, there appears to be no commonality between Gaifman's proof of locality for first-order [16] and our proof of (restricted) locality of $\mathcal{NRC}^{\mathrm{aggr}}$. We also believe that this restriction can be eliminated, but we have not been able to prove it.

Conjecture 1 *Every relational query in $\mathcal{NRC}^{\mathrm{aggr}}$ is local.*

The previous results do not seem to apply to ordered structures: indeed, by taking any input and returning the graph of the underlying linear order, we violate the bounded degree property. Thus, it does not hold in $\mathcal{NRC}^{\mathrm{aggr}}(\leq_b)$, which is $\mathcal{NRC}^{\mathrm{aggr}}$ augmented with a linear order on type b. However, we still believe that the bounded degree property can be partially recovered:

Conjecture 2 *Every relational query in $\mathcal{NRC}^{\mathrm{aggr}}(\leq_b)$ that is order-independent has the bounded degree property.*

Acknowledgements. We thank Moshe Vardi for suggesting the extension from Theorem 2 to Theorem 6, and Tim Griffin for a careful reading of the manuscript. Part of this work was done while Wong was visiting the University of Melbourne and Bell Laboratories. Wong would like to thank these organizations and fellow coauthors for their hospitality during this work.

References

1. S. Abiteboul, R. Hull, V. Vianu, *Foundations of Databases*, Addison Wesley, 1995.
2. S. Abiteboul, P. Kanellakis. Query languages for complex object databases. *SIGACT News*, 21(3):9–18, 1990.
3. M. Ajtai and R. Fagin. Reachability is harder for directed than for undirected graphs. *Journal of Symbolic Logic*, 55(1):113–150, March 1990.

4. J. Albert. Algebraic properties of bag data types. In *VLDB'91*, pages 211–219.
5. J. Barwise et al eds., *Model-Theoretic Logics*. Springer-Verlag, 1985.
6. P. Buneman, S. Naqvi, V. Tannen, L. Wong. Principles of programming with complex objects and collection types. *Theoretical Computer Science*, 149 (1995), 3–48.
7. S. Chaudhuri, M. Y. Vardi, Optimization of *real* conjunctive queries, In *PODS'93*.
8. M.P. Consens, A.O. Mendelzon, Low complexity aggregation in GraphLog and Datalog, *Theoretical Computer Science* 116 (1993), 95–116.
9. G. Dong, L. Libkin, L. Wong. On impossibility of decremental recomputation of recursive queries in relational calculus and SQL. In *Database Progr. Lang.'95*, Springer Electronic Workshops in Computing, 1996.
10. G. Dong, L. Libkin, L. Wong. Local properties of query languages, Tech. Memo, Bell Labs, 1995.
11. G. Dong and J. Su. Incremental and Decremental Evaluation of Transitive Closure by First-Order Queries. *Information and Computation*, 120(1):101–106, 1995.
12. G. Dong and J. Su. Space-bounded FOIES. In *PODS'95*, pages 139–150.
13. H.-D. Ebbinghaus and J. Flum. *Finite Model Theory*. Springer Verlag, 1995.
14. K. Etessami, Counting quantifiers, successor relations, and logarithmic space, *in* Conf. on Structure in Complexity Theory, 1995.
15. R. Fagin, L. Stockmeyer, M. Vardi, On monadic NP vs monadic co-NP, *Information and Computation*, 120 (1994), 78–92.
16. H. Gaifman, On local and non-local properties, *in* Logic Colloquium '81, North Holland, 1982.
17. T. Griffin, L. Libkin, Incremental maintenance of views with duplicates, In *SIGMOD'95*, pages 319–330.
18. S. Grumbach, T. Milo, Towards tractable algebras for bags, *Journal of Computer and System Sciences*, 52 (1996), 570–588.
19. S. Grumbach, L. Libkin, T. Milo and L. Wong. Query languages for bags: expressive power and complexity. *SIGACT News*, 27 (1996), 30–37.
20. S. Grumbach and C. Tollu. On the expressive power of counting. *Theoretical Computer Science* 149(1): 67–99, 1995.
21. A. Klug, Equivalence of relational algebra and relational calculus query languages having aggregate functions, *Journal of the ACM* **29**, No. 3 (1982), 699–717.
22. L. Libkin, L. Wong, Some properties of query languages for bags, In *DBPL'93*, Springer, 1994.
23. L. Libkin, L. Wong, Query languages for bags and aggregate functions. *JCSS*, to appear. Extended abstract in *PODS'94*, pages 155–166.
24. L. Libkin, L. Wong, On representation and querying incomplete information in databases with bags, *Information Processing Letters* **56** (1995), 209–214.
25. G. Ozsoyoglu, Z. M. Ozsoyoglu, V. Matos, Extending relational algebra and relational calculus with set-valued attributes and aggregate functions, *ACM Transactions on Database Systems* 12, No. 4 (1987), 566–592.
26. J. Paredaens and D. Van Gucht. Converting nested relational algebra expressions into flat algebra expressions. *ACM TODS*, 17(1):65–93, March 1992.
27. S. Patnaik and N. Immerman. Dyn-FO: A parallel dynamic complexity class. In *PODS'94*, pages 210–221.
28. L. Wong, Normal forms and conservative properties for query languages over collection types, *JCSS* 52 (1996), 495–505.

Expressiveness and Complexity of Active Databases

Philippe Picouet[1] and Victor Vianu[2]*

[1] E.N.S.T., 46 rue Barrault, 75013 Paris, France, picouet@inf.enst.fr
[2] U.C. San Diego, CSE 0114, La Jolla, CA 92093-0114, vianu@cs.ucsd.edu

Abstract. The expressiveness and complexity of several active database prototypes are formally studied. First, a generic framework for the specification of active databases is developed. This factors out the common aspects of the prototypes considered, and allows studying various active database features independently of any specific prototype. Furthermore, each of the prototypes can be specified by specializing certain parameters of the framework. The prototypes considered are ARDL, HiPAC, Postgres, Starburst, and Sybase. Using their formal specifications, the prototypes are compared to each other with respect to expressive power. The results provide insight into the programming paradigm of active databases, the interplay of various features, and their impact on expressiveness and complexity.

1 Introduction

The ability of a database to react to specified events is an increasingly common requirement in advanced database systems. This has led to the emergence of active databases, which provide a qualitatively new paradigm of interaction between the database and the outside world. Numerous models for active databases have been proposed and several major prototypes produced [CCCR+90, MD89, SKdM92, Sto86, WF90] (see also [WC95]). However, many basic aspects of active databases remain little understood, and foundational work in the area is still scarce (e.g., see [AHW95, BM91, HJ91b, FT95, PV95]). Active databases are notoriously complex and hard to deal with. In evaluating existing prototypes and designing future ones, one would benefit from clear answers to questions such as: Which features of current execution models are cosmetic, and which are central to their functionality? Can execution models be simplified? When are two execution models equivalent? This paper addresses such basic questions. Its objective is to understand the computational paradigm introduced by several representative active database prototypes and systems, and particularly the impact of various active database features on their relative expressive power and complexity.

* Work performed in part while this author was visiting E.N.S.T.; supported in part by the National Science Foundation under grant IRI-9221268.

We consider the following prototypes and systems: ARDL [SKdM92], HiPAC [D+88, HLM88, CBB+89, MD89], Postgres [Sto86], Starburst [WF90, Wid91], and Sybase [Syb87]. These are quite diverse, and generally incomparable due to various idiosyncrasies. In order to meaningfully compare the computational paradigms they provide, we make certain simplifying assumptions, spelled out in the paper. For example, we assume the model is relational, events are semantic rather than syntactic, and the execution model is deterministic.

The basic scenario in all prototypes is the following. External programs issue updates to the database. The active database monitors these updates and periodically performs actions in response to specified update events. The actions result in further updates. The control is passed back and forth between the external program and the trigger system, typically at the boundaries of SQL statements. Active database semantics is usually specified in highly procedural terms by the "execution model" of the system. The final update of the database results from the combined effect of the external program and the trigger program. Consequently, we define the semantics of a trigger program as the mapping associating to each external program the final update performed on the database. The external programs we consider are essentially embedded SQL programs, in the style of C+SQL. Thus, equivalent trigger programs must generate the same final database update for each C+SQL external program.

In order to be able to make formal statements about the prototypes, we provide precise procedural semantics for each of them, subject to our unifying assumptions. To do this effectively, we first describe a generic active database framework which factors out the common aspects of all prototypes considered. Then each prototype description is obtained as a specialization of the generic framework by specifying certain parameters. The parameters include: the type of delta relations used, the coupling modes, the scheduling discipline, etc. We believe that the articulation of the generic framework is an important contribution of this paper. First, this provides a skeleton that allows precise, unambiguous specification of various active databases. Second, the generic framework provides a convenient abstraction that allows discussing and comparing various active database features independently of specific prototypes. Indeed, our first group of results does just that. We examine immediate and deferred triggering within the general framework, and the impact of various types of delta relations and scheduling disciplines within each coupling mode. For example, we show that immediate triggering generates computations of complexity limited to EXPTIME (and lower with some types of delta relations) whereas deferred triggering can generate arbitrary computations (but stays within PSPACE if no multiple rule occurrences are allowed in deferred queues). Such complexity results allow to understand the computational characteristics of various combinations of active database features.

The next group of results looks at the specific prototypes and compares them with respect to expressive power. We obtain a complete classification of the five prototypes, summarized in Figure 3. Results on the complexity of the prototypes are summarized in Figure 2.

Previous foundational work on active databases has mainly focused on proposing powerful models or programming constructs that generalize the main active database systems. Thus, [FT95] provides a model that subsumes most active database prototypes. [HJ91b] introduces a programming language for manipulating "deltas", that can be used to uniformly specify a variety of computations encountered in active databases. In [BM91], an object-oriented model for active databases is introduced. The model uses a very flexible trigger mechanism based on nested transactions. It is shown that the model can simulate the main features of active database systems in a uniform fashion. [AHW95] studies an important problem in practical active database systems: the termination and confluence of production rules.

The present paper builds upon our work in [PV95]. We introduced there a simple, abstract framework for active databases, capturing the interaction of external programs with trigger systems and based on *relational machines* (first introduced in [AV91a, AV95]). These are Turing machines augmented with a relational store, modeling computation in the style of C+SQL. Although very useful for formalizing the basic paradigm of active databases, the model based on relational machines does not make the fine distinctions needed to understand the relative expressiveness of the prototypes and the impact of various features. The general framework developed in the present paper lies much closer to the actual prototypes and fulfills this role.

The paper is organized as follows. The Preliminaries review informally some basic concepts of active databases. The generic framework for active databases is developed in Section 3. The impact of various active database features on expressiveness and complexity is investigated in Section 4 within the generic framework. Section 5 contains the results on the prototypes, and brief conclusions are provided in Section 6.

This paper is based on portions of the thesis [Pic95] and the related journal article [PV] (which subsumes the present paper as well as [PV95]). All proofs can be found there.

2 Preliminaries

Active databases support the automatic triggering of updates in response to "events". These responses are typically specified by so called "ECA" rules of the form:

$$\textbf{on } \langle \textit{ event } \rangle \textbf{ if } \langle \textit{ condition } \rangle \textbf{ then } \langle \textit{ action } \rangle$$

Although events may range over various external and internal phenomena, most prototypes restrict events to database updates. Conditions typically involve the current database and some information about the event. Some systems allow conditions to look at more than one version of the database state, e.g., corresponding to the state before the event and the state after the event. Accessing past states is usually done by keeping incremental information in so called *delta* relations. Deltas are relations private to the trigger system and persistent between calls to the trigger system within the same user transaction. In principle, the *action* may be a call to an arbitrary routine. In many cases in relational systems, the action will involve a sequence of insertions, deletions and modifications, and in object-oriented systems it will involve one or more method calls. Note that this may in turn trigger other rules.

A fundamental aspect of active databases concerns the choice of an execution model. We outline several possible ones. Suppose that a user transaction $t = c_1; \ldots; c_n$ is issued, where each of the c_i's is an atomic command. In the absence of active database rules, application of t will yield a sequence

$$\mathbf{I}_0, \mathbf{I}_1, \ldots, \mathbf{I}_n$$

of database states, starting with the original state $\mathbf{I}_0$, and where each state $\mathbf{I}_{i+1}$ is the result of applying c_{i+1} to state $\mathbf{I}_i$. If rules are present, then a different sequence of states might arise. Under *immediate* firing, a rule is essentially fired as soon as its event and condition becomes true; under *deferred* firing, rule application is delayed until after the state $\mathbf{I}_n$ is reached; and under *separate* firing, a process is spawned for the rule action, and executed concurrently with other processes. In the most general execution models, each rule is assigned its own "coupling-mode" (i.e., immediate, deferred, or separate), which may be further refined by associating a coupling-mode between event and condition testing, and between condition testing and action execution.

There is a wide variety of choices for execution models. The prototypes we examine illustrate some of the main ones. In order to meaningfully compare the prototypes, we make in this paper the following unifying assumptions:

- The database model is relational.
  For prototypes specified in other models (such as object-oriented) this requires recasting their models into a relational framework.
- Triggers have access to database relations, as well as to private relations used for bookkeeping. The private relations are persistent between invocations of the trigger system within the same user transaction.
- Events consist of insertions and deletions of tuples into relations (we do not consider modifications). We only consider here semantic events, although some active databases react to syntactic insertions and deletions (such systems are not covered by our framework). Actions are programs causing insertions and deletions of sets of tuples into relations; these use the database state(s) and private relations available to the trigger. Composite events are not considered but can be simulated (e.g., composite events specified by regular expressions can be detected by finite automata maintained in private relations).
- The semantics is deterministic.
  If several rules are triggered simultaneously, a preset priority among them is assumed to ensure determinism. For systems with nondeterministic tuple-at-a-time semantics (e.g., Postgres), we assume the data is ordered and events

consist of insertions and deletions of single tuples (thus we assume Postgres only operates on ordered databases and in conjunction with external programs operating one tuple at a time). If subtransactions are executed concurrently, we ignore the nondeterminism that might arise from the concurrency control, and assume instead a serial execution in order of priority.

The above-listed assumptions result in ignoring or slightly modifying certain features of the prototypes. We aimed at retaining the essential aspects of the data manipulation and execution models of each prototype.

What is the semantics of a trigger program? In the basic active database scenario, the input to a trigger program t is an external program e. The output is the database update resulting from the combined effect of the external program and the trigger program, denoted $t[e]$. Thus, (following the definition provided in [PV95]), we take the semantics of a trigger program t to be the mapping associating to each external program e the aforementioned database update, $t[e]$. This induces a notion of equivalence of trigger programs: two trigger programs t and t' are equivalent if for all external programs e, $t[e] = t'[e]$. Based on this definition, we can next compare trigger languages. We say that trigger language T is *subsumed* by trigger language T' if for each trigger program t in T there exists a trigger program t' in T' such that t and t' are equivalent. And two languages T and T' are *equivalent* if T subsumes T' and T' subsumes T. To make this formal, we need to precisely define (i) what an "external program" is, and (ii) the execution model of trigger programs in each language, in conjunction with the external programs.

Part (ii) is the subject of the next section. For (i), we use a very powerful language modeling SQL embedded in a complete programming language (e.g., C+SQL). We use as a convenient abstraction the language $while_N$ (first defined in [Cha81]). The language provides relation variables $P, Q, R, ...$ and integer variables $i, j, ...$ The basic instructions are $R := \varphi$ where R is a relational variable and φ is a first-order (FO) query (this assigns the answer of φ to R); *increment(i)*, *decrement(i)* where i is an integer variable. We also assume that each program begins with a special instruction *start* and ends with a special instruction *halt*. Additionally, there are two looping constructs: *while* φ *do* ... where φ is a FO condition on the database, and *while* $i > 0$ *do* ... where i is an integer variable. Note that this provides computation in the spirit of C+SQL, where a computationally complete language interacts with the database by FO queries/updates. In particular, $while_N$ expresses all queries and updates over ordered databases (i.e. databases providing a total order relation on domain elements) [Cha81].

Let **D** be a (public) database schema. External programs generally use private relations in addition to those in **D**. As we shall see, trigger programs are set off by updates to database relations. We will call an instruction $R := \varphi$ where $R \in \mathbf{D}$, a *database update instruction* of the external program.

Occasionally, we will need to consider restricted external languages. We mention two. The language *while* is $while_N$ without integer variables. The language FO* consists of line programs whose instructions are assignments $R := \varphi$, where R is a relation variable and φ is an FO query. Finally, the simplest language we consider is *setflag*, whose programs consist of a single instruction setting some boolean flag (propositional variable) to true.

If T is a trigger language and E an external language, $T[E]$ denotes the set of all updates resulting from the joint effect of external programs in E and trigger programs in T.

3   Generic Framework for Active Databases

The generic framework we present in this section extracts a common skeleton for the specific prototypes considered later. Once this is available, each prototype can be concisely specified by specializing the framework, in particular by providing certain parameters. We believe that such a framework is of interest in its own right, as a common vehicle for specifying in a precise manner the execution models of various trigger systems.

We begin by specifying the syntax of programs in the generic framework, then elaborate on delta relations and queues, and finally provide the semantics of trigger programs.

Syntax. A trigger program t is a 7-tuple $< \mathbf{D}, \mathbf{R}, rules, cpl, ev, pri, \Delta\text{-}type >$ where

- $\mathbf{D}$ is the (public) database schema.
- $\mathbf{R}$ is the schema of t, denoted $sch(t)$, and $\mathbf{D} \subseteq \mathbf{R}$. The relations in $\mathbf{R} - \mathbf{D}$ are the *private relations* of t.
- *rules* is a set of rules over $sch(t)$. A rule is an expression of the form

$$condition \rightarrow action$$

  where *condition* is an FO sentence and *action* is an external program. Recall that the most general external programs we consider are $while_N$ programs. Further information on the relations accessible by conditions and actions is given below.
- *cpl* is a mapping from *rules* to $\{imm, def\}$ providing the *coupling mode* of each rule (immediate or deferred).
- *ev* is a multi-valued mapping from *rules* to the set $\{R^+, R^- \mid R \in sch(t)\}$ called the *event* mapping of t (R^+ represents insertions into R and R^- deletions from R).
- *pri* is a mapping from *rules* into $\{1, \ldots, |rules|\}$, called the *priority* mapping of t.
- $\Delta\text{-}type$ is a mapping from *rules* to $\{global, local\text{-}fixed, local\text{-}fluid\}$.

The meaning of the mappings *cpl, ev* and *pri* is quite intuitive. We elaborate on the delta relations and the $\Delta\text{-}type$ mapping next.

Delta relations. Let t be a trigger program as above. For each $R \in \mathbf{R}$, t uses so called *delta relations* Δ_R^+ and Δ_R^- of the same arity as R. Let $sch(t) = \mathbf{R}$, and $sch_\Delta(t) = \{\Delta_R^+, \Delta_R^- \mid R \in \mathbf{R}\}$. The delta relations in $sch_\Delta(t)$ contain incremental information among two database instances. The particular instances involved are determined in different ways in various contexts and systems.

A given rule r accesses only the delta relations associated to its triggering event(s). More precisely, let $sch(ev(r)) = \{\Delta_R^x \mid R^x \in ev(r)\}$. Then the condition of the rule is an FO sentence over $sch(t) \cup sch(ev(r))$ and *action* is an external program over the same schema, which can access but not modify delta relations.

There are three main ways in which delta relations are used in trigger programs:

- Delta relations can record incremental information between the initial database instance and the current instance: Δ_R^+ keeps the tuples inserted into R and Δ_R^- keeps the tuples deleted from R since the beginning of the computation. These relations are updated *automatically* every time a database update instruction is executed (by the external program or some rule action). These delta relations can be accessed by rules as global variables, unless this is overridden by a local variable declaration as below. We refer to this type of delta relation as *global*.
- Delta relations may record incremental information between the database instance at the time of triggering of some rule, and the current instance. The delta relation in question is then treated by the triggered rule as a local variable. As before, its value evolves automatically. We refer to this mode of utilization of delta relations as *local-fluid*.
- Finally, delta relations may be accessed as local variables as above, except that they record incremental information between two *fixed* database instances; their values do not evolve. This mode is referred to as *local-fixed*.

When rules are triggered, they are placed in a queue of rule occurrences – immediate or deferred, according to the coupling mode specified by the *cpl* mapping. An occurrence of a rule may or may not be parameterized by a delta relation. More specifically, if Δ-$type(r) = global$ then there is no parameter. When the rule is executed, any reference to delta relations concerns the current values of the global delta relations. If Δ-$type(r) \in \{local\text{-}fixed, local\text{-}fluid\}$ the occurrence of the rule is parameterized by its delta relation(s) in $sch(ev(r))$. This is denoted by $r(\Delta_R^+)$, $r(\Delta_R^-)$, $r(\Delta_R^+, \Delta_R^-)$, etc. Here again there are two possibilities. If Δ-$type(r) = local\text{-}fixed$, the value of the delta relation(s) passed as parameter does not change since the time the rule is triggered. If Δ-$type(r) = local\text{-}fluid$, the value is local but evolves automatically by keeping track of the updates to the relevant relation. This is described in more detail below.

We will use the following convenient notation for the evolution of delta relations. A *transition* over $sch(t)$ is a pair of database instances $\tau = (\mathbf{I}, \mathbf{J})$ over $sch(t)$. For $R \in sch(t)$, the delta relations associated with τ, denoted $\Delta_R^x(\tau)$ for $x \in \{+, -\}$, are defined by $\Delta_R^+(\tau) = \mathbf{J}(R) - \mathbf{I}(R)$ and $\Delta_R^-(\tau) = \mathbf{I}(R) - \mathbf{J}(R)$.

Suppose we have current delta relations Δ_R^x, $x \in \{+, -\}$, and a new transition τ occurs. The delta relations are updated as follows. The new Δ_R^+ is denoted by $\tau^+(\Delta_R^+, \Delta_R^-)$ and is defined as $(\Delta_R^+ - \Delta_R^-(\tau)) \cup (\Delta_R^+(\tau) - \Delta_R^-)$. Similarly, the new Δ_R^- is denoted by $\tau^-(\Delta_R^+, \Delta_R^-)$ and is defined as $(\Delta_R^- - \Delta_R^+(\tau)) \cup (\Delta_R^-(\tau) - \Delta_R^+)$.

This in effect accumulates the delta relations Δ_R^x and $\Delta_R^x(\tau)$, in a manner similar to the *weak merge* operator of [HJ91a].

Let $\tau_1 = (\mathbf{I}, \mathbf{J})$, $\tau_2 = (\mathbf{J}, \mathbf{K})$ and $\tau_2 \circ \tau_1 = (\mathbf{I}, \mathbf{K})$ be transitions over $sch(t)$. It is easy to verify that for each $R \in sch(t)$ and $x \in \{+, -\}$, $\Delta_R^x(\tau_2 \circ \tau_1) = \tau_2^x(\Delta_R^+(\tau_1), \Delta_R^-(\tau_1))$.

Queue Manipulations. A rule queue is a sequence of rule occurrences, possibly parameterized (the empty queue is denoted by ϵ). The above notation is extended to queues as follows. Let q be a queue $r_1 \ldots r_n$ and τ be a transition. Then $\tau(q)$ denotes the queue $\tau(r_1) \ldots \tau(r_n)$, where $\tau(r_i) = r_i$ if $\Delta\text{-}type(r_i) \in \{global, local\text{-}fixed\}$, and $\tau(r_i) = r(\tau(sch(ev(r))))$ if $r_i = r(sch(ev(r)))$ and $\Delta\text{-}type(r) = local\text{-}fluid$.

There are two kinds of queues: q_{imm} holds rules whose coupling mode is immediate, while q_{def} holds rules whose coupling mode is deferred. At various points in the execution of the program, new rule occurrences are added to the queues. Also, two queues q and q' (which can be immediate or deferred) may be combined to yield new immediate and deferred queues. The way this is done is system dependent. We therefore do not specify in the generic framework a particular discipline for these operations. Instead, we parameterize the semantics by the following three functions:

- $add(r, q)$ returns the queue resulting from adding rule r to the queue q;
- $merge_{imm}(q, q')$ returns the immediate queue resulting from the merging of q and q'.
- $merge_{def}(q, q')$ returns the deferred queue resulting from the merging of q and q'.

Furthermore, we assume that the three functions perform queue manipulations of low complexity. More precisely, each mapping is computable in polynomial time (in the number of rules in the input), where comparison and insertion/deletion of rule occurrences are counted as single operations. This captures very general scheduling disciplines and covers all prototypes.

Semantics. We next describe the semantics of trigger programs. Recall that the semantics of a trigger program t is a mapping from external programs e in $while_N$ to updates $t[e]$ over $\mathbf{D}$. Given t and e, the update $t[e]$ is defined as follows. The definition comprises two main phases:

1. e and t take turns taking control of the computation; e starts out, then t takes control following each execution of an instruction $R := \varphi$ of e, where $R \in \mathbf{D}$ (recall that these are called *database update instructions* of e). When this happens, events are detected and new rules are triggered, both immediate and deferred. The immediate queue is executed until empty, generating a new database instance and deferred queue. Then control is passed back to e, and so on until e halts. At this point the first phase ends; its output is a new database instance and a queue of deferred rules.
2. The deferred rules are executed, producing a final database instance.

We next elaborate on (1) and (2) above. We use the following mutually recursive procedures:

- *exec-program* takes as input a 4-tuple $(f, s, \mathbf{I}, q)$ where f is an external program, s is the *start* instruction or a database update instruction of f, $\mathbf{I}$ a database instance, and q a queue of rules; its output is a pair $(\mathbf{I}', q')$ where $\mathbf{I}'$ is a new database instance, and q' a new queue of rules. The inputs of *exec-program* represent the current (start or database update) instruction in the execution of f, the current database instance, and the current q_{def}. The outputs represent the database instance and the queue of deferred rules after f has halted and all immediate queues have been executed.
- *exec-imm* takes as input a triple $(\mathbf{I}, q_{imm}, q_{def})$ where $\mathbf{I}$ is a database instance, q_{imm} is an immediate queue, and q_{def} a deferred queue. It outputs a pair $(\mathbf{I}', q'_{def})$, where $\mathbf{I}'$ is a new database instance and q'_{def} a new deferred queue, both resulting from the execution of the immediate queue of rules q_{imm}.

Once *exec-program* and *exec-imm* are defined, the update $t[e]$ is defined as follows. Suppose the input database instance is $\mathbf{I}$. The global values of the delta relations are initialized to empty.

1. run *exec-program*$(e, start, \mathbf{I}, \epsilon)$. This either does not end – in which case the result is undefined – or it ends with output $(\mathbf{J}, q_{def})$.
2. execute the following pseudo-code program, where $(\mathbf{J}, q_{def})$ is the output of the first phase:

$$q_{imm} := q_{def}; \ q_{def} := \epsilon; \mathbf{db} := \mathbf{J}$$
$$\textbf{while } q_{imm} \neq \epsilon \textbf{ do}$$
$$\textbf{begin}$$
$$(\mathbf{db}, q_{def}) := exec\text{-}imm(\mathbf{db}, q_{imm}, \epsilon);$$
$$q_{imm} := q_{def};$$
$$\textbf{end};$$
$$\textbf{return db}$$

It remains to describe the programs *exec-program* and *exec-imm*. We begin with *exec-program*. On input $(f, s, \mathbf{I}, q_{def})$, *exec-program* does the following. First, run f on $\mathbf{I}$ starting from instruction s, until a new database update instruction u of f is executed, or the *halt* instruction is reached. In the latter case, *exec-program* stops and outputs $(\mathbf{I}, q_{def})$. Otherwise, let the new database instance at that point be $\mathbf{I}'$ and τ denote the transition $(\mathbf{I}, \mathbf{I}')$. The transition τ affects the global delta relations: each global value of Δ_R^x is replaced by $\tau(\Delta_R^x)$, $x \in \{+, -\}$. The deferred queue q_{def} evolves as well: it is replaced by $\tau(q_{def})$. Next, immediate and deferred rules are triggered as follows. A rule r is triggered if for some $R^x \in ev(r)$, $\Delta_R^x(\tau) \neq \emptyset$ $(x \in \{+, -\})$.

When a rule r is triggered, r is placed in the immediate queue if $cpl(r) = imm$ or in the deferred queue if $cpl(r) = def$. If $\Delta\text{-}type(r) \in \{local\text{-}fixed, local\text{-}fluid\}$, the rule r is parameterized with values for the local delta relations $\Delta_R^x \in sch(ev(r))$. Specifically, in both cases $\Delta_R^x = \Delta_R^x(\tau)$, $x \in \{+, -\}$. The immediate queue q_{imm} consists of the triggered rules, possibly parameterized, for which $cpl(r) = imm$, in increasing order of their priorities as specified by the pri mapping. Next, the triggered rules r for which $cpl(r) = def$ are added to q_{def} by repeated application of the add function, in arbitrary order (it turns out that the order is irrelevant in the various definitions of add as they occur in systems).

We now have an immediate queue q_{imm} which needs to be executed. This is done using procedure $exec\text{-}imm(\mathbf{I}', q_{imm}, q_{def})$, which returns (if it terminates) a new database instance $\mathbf{J}$ and a new deferred queue q'_{def}. It is now time to resume the execution of f, starting from the database update instruction u last executed. Thus, $exec\text{-}program(f, u, \mathbf{J}, q'_{def})$ is executed. This concludes the recursive definition of $exec\text{-}program$.

We now proceed with the description of $exec\text{-}imm$. On input $(\mathbf{I}, q_{imm}, q_{def})$, $exec\text{-}imm$ does the following. If $q_{imm} = \epsilon$ then $exec\text{-}imm$ stops and outputs $(\mathbf{I}, q_{def})$. Otherwise, let r be the first rule occurrence in q_{imm}; r is of the form $condition \to action$, where $condition$ is an FO sentence over $sch(t) \cup sch(ev(r))$ and $action$ is an external program over the same schema, which does not modify delta relations. If $\Delta\text{-}type(r) = global$ then the global values of the delta relations are used, otherwise the local values (fixed or fluid) provided as parameters are used instead. If $condition$ is true, the procedure $exec\text{-}program(action, start, \mathbf{I}, \epsilon)$ is run. If it terminates, an output $(\mathbf{J}, q''_{def})$ is produced. Let τ denote the transition $(\mathbf{I}, \mathbf{J})$. Let q'_{imm} be q_{imm} from which the first rule in the queue is removed and to which τ is applied, and $q'_{def} = \tau(q_{def})$. New immediate and deferred queues are obtained according to the mappings $merge_{imm}$ and $merge_{def}$. Thus, $exec\text{-}imm$ is executed on new input $(\mathbf{J}, merge_{imm}(q'_{imm}, q''_{def}), merge_{def}(q'_{def}, q''_{def}))$.

This concludes the mutually recursive definition of $exec\text{-}imm$ and $exec\text{-}program$, and also the description of the semantics of t.

We shall refer to the generic framework described in this section as *Generic*.

Specializations

Descriptions of the prototypes considered in this paper can be obtained by specializing the generic framework presented above. These descriptions, omitted here due to space limitations, can be found in [PV]. They are based on "snapshots" of the prototypes, as presented in [WC95]. Additionally, recall that we are making certain unifying assumptions, outlined in Section 2.

4 Impact of active database features on expressive power

We next examine in more detail the impact on expressive power of various active database features, using *Generic* as a vehicle to unify the discussion. We organize the discussion around coupling modes: immediate triggering, deferred triggering, and their interaction.

We begin by developing some notation for several specializations of the generic framework. The prototypes correspond to some of these specializations.

Restrictions to the generic framework are denoted by specifying restrictions on *action* (rule actions), *cpl*, Δ-*type*, and the deferred or immediate queues. The restrictions on the queues involve specifying the $add, merge_{imm}$ and $merge_{def}$ mappings, or stipulating some properties that they must satisfy. For example, q_{def}: *bounded* might require that the mappings be defined so that the length of the deferred queues is statically bounded. Specializations of *Generic* are then denoted in the following style:

Generic(action: while, cpl: def, Δ-type: global, q_{def}: bounded)

This means that rule actions are restricted to *while* programs, all rules are deferred and use global delta relations, and $add, merge_{imm}$ and $merge_{def}$ are defined such that the deferred queues have statically bounded length. The notation will be self-explanatory, or spelled out when needed.

In the remainder of the paper, we will present two types of expressiveness results. The first type compares trigger languages with respect to subsumption and equivalence. Such are the results of Figure 3, providing the subsumption relationships for the prototypes. The second type of result looks at the power of a trigger language T to express updates in conjunction with some external language E, i.e. characterizes $T[E]$. In order for this to tell us something meaningful about T, the power of E should not overwhelm that of T. In fact, it is useful to minimize the power of E by restricting it to *setflag*, whose programs are limited to setting off the trigger program by turning on a boolean flag.

The second type of expressiveness result is related to the first. If $T[setflag]$ and $T'[setflag]$ are not equal then T and T' cannot be equivalent. This allows us to prove nonequivalence results about trigger languages.

4.1 Immediate triggering

We begin by examining the computational characteristics of immediate triggering. Recall that in the generic framework, immediate queues can generally be nested. Among the active database prototypes with immediate triggering, there are two main approaches to the nesting of immediate queues: (i) allow unbounded nesting (ii) ensure that the nesting is statically bounded. We examine both approaches here.

What is the computational power of immediate triggering with unbounded nesting? It turns out that this essentially provides EXPTIME computation. Intuitively, to perform the bookkeeping involved in immediate triggering with unbounded nesting, one needs a pushdown store. The remainder of the computation is in PSPACE. To arrive at the EXPTIME characterization, we use a result by Cook relating Turing machines with an auxiliary deterministic pushdown automaton (dpda) to time-bounded Turing machines. In particular, it is shown in [C71] that the PSPACE Turing machines with an auxiliary dpda express precisely EXPTIME. Thus, we are able to show the following:

Theorem 1. (i) *All updates expressed by* Generic(action: while, cpl: imm)[setflag] *are in* EXPTIME.

(ii) Generic(action: while, cpl: imm)[setflag] *expresses precisely the* EXPTIME *updates on ordered databases.*

Let us now consider bounded nesting. More precisely, let *Generic(action: while, cpl: imm, q_{imm}: bounded)* denote the common framework restricted so that rule actions are *while* programs, the coupling mode is immediate, and the depth of nesting of immediate queues is statically bounded. One would expect that the boundedness restriction on nesting of immediate queues would drastically reduce expressiveness. Although likely, this is far from obvious. Indeed, we can show that the complexity of updates expressed with bounded nesting (with *setflag* external programs) is PSPACE. However, it is open whether PSPACE $\neq$ EXPTIME. We are then able to show:

Theorem 2. *If* PSPACE $\neq$ EXPTIME *then* Generic(action: while, cpl: imm, q_{imm}: bounded) *is strictly subsumed by* Generic(action: while, cpl: imm).

Theorems 1 and 2 continue to hold if rule actions are restricted to FO* programs.

4.2 Deferred triggering

We next consider *Generic* restricted to deferred triggering. Recall that, when only deferred rules are present, there is just one deferred queue at any given time (as opposed to immediate triggering, where there may be nested immediate queues). However, unlike the immediate queues, the deferred queue is not generally statically bounded.

Also recall from the description of the generic framework that the deferred queue is treated as an immediate queue when executed.

The computational power of unrestricted deferred triggering is, in some sense, complete. More precisely, there is no complexity bound on the computations that may be generated, and all updates can be expressed if the database is ordered. In the following, the restriction "*queues*: HiPAC" means that the queue manipulation mappings are defined as in HiPAC.

Theorem 3. Generic(action: while, cpl: def, Δ-type: local-fluid, queues: HiPAC) [setflag] *expresses the same updates as* while$_N$, *and all updates on ordered databases.*

Some prototypes limit the power and complexity of deferred triggering by placing restrictions upon the deferred queue. We consider two kinds of restrictions. The first disallows multiple occurrences of rules in the deferred queue. The second allows multiple occurrences of a rule, but only if the occurrences are parameterized by distinct delta relations. For the first restriction, we denote the fact that the mapping *add* is defined so that there are no multiple occurrences of a rule in queues by *queues: no-multiple-rules*. We can show the following:

Theorem 4. (i) *All updates expressible in* Generic(action: while, cpl: def, queues: no-multiple-rules)[setflag] *are in* PSPACE.
(ii) Generic(action: while, cpl: def, queues: no-multiple-rules)[setflag] *expresses precisely the* PSPACE *updates on ordered databases.*

Consider now the second type of restriction: suppose that multiple occurrences of rules are allowed, but only with distinct delta relations (this allows unbounded queues). Denote this restriction by *queues: no-multiple-Δ*. We then obtain a trigger language lying strictly between deferred triggering with bounded queues and deferred triggering with unrestricted multiple occurrences of rules. Before showing this, we need the following complexity characterization:

Theorem 5. (i) *All updates expressible in* Generic(action: while, cpl: def, queues: no-multiple-Δ)[setflag] *are in* EXPSPACE.
(ii) Generic(action: while, cpl: def, queues: no-multiple-Δ)[setflag] *expresses precisely the* EXPSPACE *updates on ordered databases.*

We also note that Theorem 5 continues to hold if rule actions are limited to FO* programs instead of *while*. Indeed, *while* actions can be simulated using cascading rules with FO* actions.

We can now show:

Theorem 6. Generic(action: while, cpl: def, queues: no-multiple-rules) *is strictly subsumed by* Generic(action: while, cpl: def, queues: no-multiple-Δ) *which is strictly subsumed by* Generic(action: while, cpl: def, queues: HiPAC).

Immediate vs. deferred triggering A natural question comes up at this point: how does the power of immediate triggering compare to that of deferred triggering? In general, the two are incomparable. First, one cannot expect deferred triggering to simulate immediate triggering. Indeed, immediately triggered rules can change the public database and thus affect the execution of the external program. This cannot be done by deferred rules. On the other hand, immediate triggering cannot generally simulate deferred triggering because the former cannot detect when the execution of the external program has ended. Things are further complicated by the fact that deferred triggering is generally more powerful *computationally* than immediate triggering. Thus, it is generally not the case that immediate triggering subsumes deferred triggering even if immediate triggering can explicitly test for the end of the execution of the external program.

Suppose we wish to design an active database with immediate and deferred triggering, where the computational discrepancy between the two coupling modes is eliminated. It is clear that one has to use a triggering discipline where deferred rules recursively generated in the course of the execution of immediate rules can be reintegrated into the immediate queue, thus providing immediate triggering with the computational power of deferred rules. While this cannot be done in any of the prototypes, it can be achieved by a hybrid restriction which mixes elements of the queuing disciplines of Starburst and HiPAC. Such a hybrid system is described in [PV].

5 Expressiveness and complexity of the prototypes

We summarize in this section our results on the expressiveness and complexity of the five prototypes. For prototypes P allowing both immediate and deferred rules (i.e. ARDL and HiPAC), we denote by $P(imm)$ and $P(def)$ the restrictions of P allowing only immediate, respectively deferred rules. Many results follow from the study in the previous section of active database features within the general framework.

The first results on the prototypes establish the expressiveness of ARDL, ARDL(imm), ARDL(def), Starburst, and Sybase in conjunction with the external language *setflag*.

Theorem 7. *ARDL*[setflag], *ARDL*(imm)[setflag], *ARDL*(def)[setflag], *Starburst*[setflag], *and Sybase*[setflag] *express precisely the* PSPACE *updates on ordered databases.*

We next consider Postgres and HiPAC, which are no longer within PSPACE. Our formalization of Postgres is somewhat of a special case, since it works only on ordered databases and with tuple-at-a-time external programs in *while*, so all statements assume these restrictions.

Theorem 8. (i) *Postgres*[while] *expresses precisely the* EXPTIME *updates on ordered databases.*
(ii) *HiPAC*(imm)[setflag] *expresses precisely the* EXPTIME *updates on ordered databases, and HiPAC*(def)[setflag] *expresses all computable updates on ordered databases.*

We now establish one of the main results of the paper. This provides a complete classification of the prototypes considered, with respect to subsumption and equivalence.

Theorem 9. *The relationships in Figure 3 hold among the prototypes (and their immediate and deferred restrictions, where appropriate).*

Remark: Further equivalences among prototypes hold if we assume that immediate rules can test explicitly whether the execution of the external program has ended. Specifically:
(i) ARDL(imm), ARDL, and Sybase become equivalent, and
(ii) ARDL(def) and Starburst are both subsumed by the three prototypes above.

6 Conclusions

This paper makes two main contributions. First, it provides a generic framework for active databases that allows to concisely and unambiguously specify various execution models. We illustrated this for five representative prototypes: ARDL,

HiPAC, Postgres, Starburst, and Sybase, subject to certain unifying assumptions. Second, the paper uses the formal specifications of the generic framework and prototypes to investigate the computational paradigm of active databases with respect to expressiveness and complexity.

The generic framework was used to study various active database features independently of any specific prototype. We organized the investigation around coupling modes, immediate and deferred, and considered within each the impact of features such as the types of delta relations used, and queuing disciplines. We obtained results on the complexity and expressive power of various combinations of features. For example:

- The complexity of immediate triggering is essentially EXPTIME, even without delta relations. If the depth of nesting of immediate queues is bounded (as is the case in several prototypes), the complexity goes down to PSPACE.
- Deferred triggering is computationally more powerful than immediate triggering, since there is no complexity bound in this case. Complexity bounds are obtained under various restrictions on the queuing disciplines. If no multiple occurrences of rules are allowed in queues, then the complexity becomes PSPACE. If multiple occurrences of rules are allowed but only with distinct delta relations as parameters, then the complexity is EXPSPACE. The complexity results induce results on the relative expressive power of the various restrictions.

The complexity results are summarized in Figure 1.

Using some of the results obtained within the general framework, we studied the five prototypes and classified them completely with respect to subsumption and equivalence (Figure 3). We also characterized their complexity (Figure 2).

We believe that the results obtained in this paper provide insight into the programming paradigm of active databases, the interplay of various features, and their impact on expressiveness and complexity. In particular, they indicate which features are cosmetic, and which are central to expressiveness. They also provide useful information for the design of new trigger systems with desirable properties (as exemplified by the hybrid system mixing elements of Starburst and HiPAC).

One should keep in mind that the results described here are dependent upon the unifying assumptions made about the prototypes. Many aspects of active databases, such as syntax-based events, nondeterministic semantics, object-oriented features, real-time aspects, etc, were left out in the interest of simplicity. Such aspects are nonetheless important, and deserve separate investigation.

References

[AV91a]   S. Abiteboul and V. Vianu. Generic computation and its complexity. In *Proc. ACM SIGACT Symp. on the Theory of Computing*, pages 209–219, 1991.

[AV91b]   S. Abiteboul and V. Vianu. Datalog extensions for database queries and updates. *Journal of Computer and System Sciences*, 43(1), pages 62–124, 1991.

[AV95]   S. Abiteboul and V. Vianu. Computing with first-order logic. *Journal of Computer and System Sciences*, 50(2), pages 309–335, 1995.

[AHW95]   A. Aiken, J. Widom and J.M. Hellerstein. State analysis techniques for predicting the behavior of active database rules. *ACM Transactions on Database Systems* 20(1), pages 3–41, 1995.

[BM91]   C. Beeri and T. Milo. A model for active object oriented databases. In *Proc. of Intl. Conf. on Very Large Data Bases*, pages 337–349, 1991.

[CCCR+90] F. Cacace, S. Ceri, S. Crespi-Reghizzi, L. Tanca, and R. Zicari. Integrating object-oriented data modeling with a rule-based programming paradigm. In *Proc. ACM SIGMOD Int'l. Conf. on the Management of Data*, pages 225–236, 1990.

[Cha81]   A. K. Chandra. Programming primitives for database languages. In *Proc. ACM Symp. on Principles of Programming Languages*, pages 50–62, 1981.

[CBB+89]   S. Chakravarthy, et. al. Hipac: a research project in active time-constrained databases management. Technical report, Xerox Advanced Information Technology, July 1989.

[C71]   S.A. Cook. Characterizations of pushdown machines in terms of time-bounded computers. *J. of the ACM*, 18(1), pages 4–18, 1971.

[D+88]   U. Dayal et al. The HiPac project: Combining active databases and timing constraints. In *ACM SIGMOD Record*, 1988.

[FT95]   P. Fraternali and L. Tanca. A structured approach for the definition of the semantics of active databases. *ACM Transactions on Database Systems* 20(4), pages 414–471, 1995.

[HLM88]   M. Hsu, R. Ladin and D.R. McCarthy. An execution model for active data base management systems. In *Proc. Int'l. Conf. on Data and Knowledge Bases*, pages 171–179, Jerusalem, 1988.

[HJ91a]   R. Hull and D. Jacobs. Language constructs for programming active databases. In *Proc. of Intl. Conf. on Very Large Data Bases*, pages 455–468, 1991.

[HJ91b]   R. Hull and D. Jacobs. On the semantics of rules in database programming languages. In J. Schmidt and A. Stogny, editors, *Next Generation Information System Technology: Proc. of the First International East/West Database Workshop, Kiev, USSR, October 1990*, pages 59–85. Springer-Verlag LNCS, Volume 504, 1991.

[MD89]   D. McCarthy and U. Dayal. The architecture of an active database management system. In *Proc. ACM SIGMOD Int'l. Conf. on the Management of Data*, pages 215–224, 1989.

[Pic95]   P. Picouet. *Puissance d'expression et Consistance sémantique de bases de données actives* (Expressive Power and Semantic Consistency of Active Databases.) PhD thesis, Ecole Nationale Supérieure de Télécommunications, Paris, 1995.

[PV95]   P. Picouet and V. Vianu. Semantics and expressiveness issues in active databases. In *Proc. ACM Symp. on Principles of Database Systems*, 1995.

[PV]   P. Picouet and V. Vianu. Semantics and expressiveness issues in active databases. Invited to special issue of *JCSS*, to appear.

[SKdM92]   E. Simon, J. Kiernan, and C. de Maindreville. Implementing high level active rules on top of a relational dbms. In *Proc. of Intl. Conf. on Very Large Data Bases*, pages 315–326, 1992.

[Sto86]   M. Stonebraker et.al.   A rule manager for relational database systems. Technical Report, *The Postgres Papers*, Electronics Research Lab, UCB/ERL M86/85, U. of California, Berkeley, 1986.

[Syb87]   Sybase, Inc. Transact-sql user's guide. Technical report.

[WF90]   J. Widom and S. J. Finkelstein. Set-oriented production rules in relational database systems. In *Proc. ACM SIGMOD Int'l. Conf. on the Management of Data*, pages 259–264, 1990.

[Wid91]   J. Widom. Deduction in the Starburst production rule system. Technical report, IBM Almaden Research, 1991.

[WC95]   J. Widom and S. Ceri. *Active Database Systems: Triggers and Rules for Advanced Database Processing*. Morgan-Kaufmann, Inc., San Francisco, California, 1995.

Restrictions of *Generic*		T[*setflag*]
coupling mode	queue management	ordered DB
immediate	bounded	PSPACE
coupling	unbounded	EXPTIME
deferred	no-multiple-rules	PSPACE
coupling	no-multiple-Δ	EXPSPACE
	no restriction	all

Fig. 1. Expressive power and complexity of main restrictions of the Generic framework

Coupling mode	Prototypes	T[*setflag*] ordered DB
Immediate coupling	Sybase	PSPACE
	ARDL(*imm*)	PSPACE
	HiPAC(*imm*)	EXPTIME
	Postgres ordered DB tuple at a time semantics	EXPTIME
deferred coupling	ARDL (*def*)	PSPACE
	Starburst	PSPACE
	HiPAC(*def*)	all
mixed coupling	ARDL	PSPACE
	HiPAC	all

Fig. 2. Expressive power and complexity of prototypes

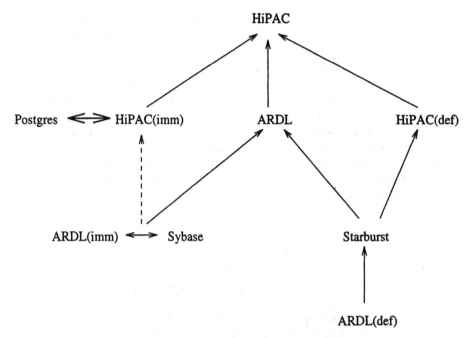

Fig. 3. Relative expressiveness of prototypes. Solid single arrows indicate strict subsumption. The broken single arrow indicates subsumption, and strict subsumption assuming that PSPACE ≠ EXPTIME. The double solid arrow indicates equivalence. The double boldfaced arrow indicates equivalence on ordered databases and tuple-at-a-time external programs.

A Model Theoretic Approach to Update Rule Programs

N. Bidoit and S. Maabout *

LIPN. CNRS URA1507
Université de Paris XIII. Institut Galilée.
Avenue J.B. Clément. 93430 Villetaneuse, France.
email : {nicole.bidoit, sofian.maabout}@ura1507.univ-paris13.fr

Abstract. Semantics of active rules is generally defined by execution models. The lack of a clean declarative semantics threats active system reliability. In this paper, a declarative semantics for update rules based on the well founded semantics of Datalog programs is investigated. The validation of our proposal proceeds by demonstrating it for static and transition integrity constraint enforcement.

Keywords: active databases, update, constraint, well-founded semantics.

1 Introduction

Active database is a new promising technology [AHV95]. Several active database languages and models have been proposed and several prototypes or commercial systems have been developed [WC96]. Foundational work is also emerging [Wid92, FT95, PV95]. The active database paradigm provides DBMS with a new component called "trigger system". The trigger system supports automatic triggering of actions, usually updates, in response to events which are in general updates too. Languages designed to express triggers are based on ECA (Event-Condition-Action) rule. Active databases have been widely investigated for implementing integrity constraint enforcement and seem to provide a well-suited framework for developing repair techniques.

The semantics of trigger systems is generally defined by means of execution models and the behavior of complex active rule sets is very difficult to predict. The main problems arising are: termination, confluence and also conflicting updates [S+95, AHW95]. One of the major argument in favor of active systems is that they subtract semantics from applications. However active databases cannot be trusted as long as the above problems are not answered: semantics represents a major problem for active databases.

This paper focuses on the semantics of rule-based update programming. An update rule is an ECA rule where event and action are restricted to updates. One feature of the update rules considered in this paper is that "negative events" are

---

* This work was partially supported by the GDR : 1140. CNRS

allowed in the body of rules and meant to capture the absence of these events. The well-founded semantics [VRS91] is investigated as a well-suited formalism for deriving updates given a set of input updates, a database instance and update rules. Although operational semantics of update rules is out of the scope of this paper, we are very much convinced that providing a procedural semantics that conforms to the declarative abstract one is mandatory. With regards to the well-founded semantics several proposals have been made and prototypes implementing top-down evaluation with memoing technic do exist [SSW94].

Our work is articulated with two kinds of properties: fundamental properties concerning update derivation and optional properties related to the updated database. We claim that updates derived from an update program should be conflict free, well-founded and well-supported. Roughly speaking, a set of updates is well-founded if for each update (e.g. insertion) the dual update (deletion) is proved "false". The notion of well supported update simply requires that update rules be managed as production rules rather than as logic formulas. Minimal change, maximal knowledge, priority to input updates and stability are properties linking the initial database and the updated database. We believe that fulfilling these properties may depend on the application. This last group of properties is indeed discussed for static integrity maintenance and transition constraint enforcement. The organization of the paper follows the introductory presentation.

2 Notation and Basic Definitions

We briefly review the logic programming terminology. We consider an alphabet consisting of a non empty finite set of constants $Cons$, a finite set of variables Var, and a set of base-predicate symbols $\Pi_b = \{P, Q, R \ldots\}$. To each base-predicate $P \in \Pi_b$ we associate two predicates $+P$ and $-P$ with the same arity as P called *update-predicates*. The predicate $+P$ (resp. $-P$) is called *insertion-predicate*, (resp. *deletion-predicate*). The notions of atom, literal and fact are defined as usual. Update-atoms, update-literals and update-facts are respectively atoms, literals and facts built up from update-predicates. If I is a set of literals, then $\neg I$ denotes the set $\{\neg \ell | \ell \in I\}$. An update rule ρ is an expression of the form:

$$\rho : E_1, \ldots, E_n, L_1, \ldots, L_m \longrightarrow A \tag{1}$$

where E_i is an update-literal, L_j a base literal and A an update-atom. We define: $Event(\rho) = \{E_1, \ldots, E_n\}$, $Cond(\rho) = \{L_1, \ldots, L_m\}$, $Body(\rho) = Event(\rho) \cup Cond(\rho)$ and $Head(\rho) = A$. An update program $\mathcal{P}$ is a finite set of rules. Intuitively, following the semantics of ECA rules, an update rule ρ intends to express that when the events in $Event(\rho)$ are detected, if the $Cond(\rho)$ is satisfied then the action $Head(\rho)$ is executed. Note here that, a negative event literal $\neg A$ is interpreted intuitively by: the event A does not occur.

A partial interpretation I is a set of ground literals such that, if $POS(I)$ and $NEG(I)$ denote respectively the positive and the negative literals of I, then $POS(I) \cap \neg NEG(I) = \emptyset$. An interpretation I satisfies a ground literal ℓ, denoted

$I \models \ell$, iff $\ell \in I$ and I satisfies a ground rule ρ iff whenever $Body(\rho) \subseteq I$ then $Head(\rho) \in I$. If $\mathcal{P}$ is an update program, then $Inst(\mathcal{P})$ denotes the set of all possible instantiations of the rules in $\mathcal{P}$ by using the constants in $\mathcal{P}$. I is a model of $\mathcal{P}$ iff I satisfies all ground rules of $Inst(\mathcal{P})$.

Well Founded Semantics: Now we briefly review the well founded semantics of Datalog⁻ programs. The reader is referred to [VRS91] for an extensive presentation on this topic. Note that update programs are Datalog⁻ programs. The well founded semantics of a Datalog⁻ program $\mathcal{P}$ is defined by means of a fixpoint operator WF composed by two operators: the immediate consequence operator $T^{\in}$ and the non founded operator NF. Let I be a partial interpretation. Then:

- $T_{\mathcal{P}}^{\in}(I) = \{Head(\rho) | \rho \in Inst(\mathcal{P}) \text{ and } \forall \ell \in Body(\rho) : \ell \in I\}$
- A set of facts U is unfounded w.r.t. I, iff:
  $\forall p \in U, \forall \rho \in Inst(\mathcal{P}) : [Head(\rho) = p] \Longrightarrow \exists \ell \in Body(\rho) : [\neg \ell \in I \text{ or } \ell \in U].$
  $NF_{\mathcal{P}}(I)$ is defined as the greatest unfounded set of facts w.r.t. I.

Now, consider the sequence $(I_i)_{(i \geq 0)}$ of partial interpretations defined by:
$$I_0 = \emptyset \qquad\qquad I_{i+1} = WF_{\mathcal{P}}(I_i) = T_{\mathcal{P}}^{\in}(I_i) \cup \neg NF_{\mathcal{P}}(I_i)$$
$I_{(i \geq 0)}$ is increasing (i.e. $POS(I_j) \subseteq POS(I_{j+1})$ and $NEG(I_j) \subseteq NEG(I_{j+1})$) and, because the domain is finite, there exists an integer k such that $I_k = I_i$ for all $i \geq k$. The well founded model of $\mathcal{P}$ is the fixpoint I_k.

Let $\mathcal{B}_P$ denote the Herbrand base of $\mathcal{P}$. The well founded model $\mathcal{M}$ of $\mathcal{P}$ is total if $POS(\mathcal{M}) \cup \neg NEG(\mathcal{M}) = \mathcal{B}_P$.

We consider (simple) incomplete databases defined by means of a three valued logic [Fit85]. A database instance is given by a set of true facts, and by a set of *unknown* facts. This representation of incomplete databases is the trivial alternative to the classical representation based on true and false facts.

Definition 1 - Database. A database schema $\mathcal{S}$ is simply given by a set Π_b of base-predicates. A database instance Δ is a pair $< POS(\Delta), UNK(\Delta) >$ where $POS(\Delta)$ and $UNK(\Delta)$ are disjoint sets of facts. The facts in $POS(\Delta)$ (resp. in $UNK(\Delta)$) are positive (resp. unknown) facts. If $UNK(\Delta) = \emptyset$, then Δ is total (or complete). If $\mathcal{B}$ is the set of all possible base facts built up from $Const$ and Π_b, then $NEG(\Delta) = \mathcal{B} \setminus [POS(\Delta) \cup UNK(\Delta)]$.

3 Update Semantics

This section introduces a semantics of update programs based on the well founded semantics. We start by exposing the general updating process and properties, independently of any semantics. First, input of updates (insertions and deletions) are requested either by the user or the system. Then given a database ruled by an update program, these input updates lead to derive new updates. **Up_Der** denotes an update derivation mapping which takes as input a database instance, a set of updates and an update program and returns a set of updates.

The effect of the input updates on a database instance is the application of the derived updates thus producing a new database instance. *Apply* denotes an update application mapping which takes as input a database instance and a set of updates and returns a new database. The mapping defining the semantics of update programs is denoted **Up_Sem**, it takes as input a database, a set of updates and an update program and returns a database instance. It is defined by composition of **Up_Der** and *Apply*.

$$
\begin{array}{c}
\\
\text{database instance } \Delta \\
\text{input update} \quad \delta \\
\text{update program} \quad \mathcal{P}
\end{array}
\left.\begin{array}{c}
\\
\\
\\
\end{array}\right\}
\quad
\begin{array}{c}
\text{derived updates} \\
\downarrow \\
\textbf{Up\_Der} \qquad \delta' \\
\longrightarrow
\end{array}
\quad
\begin{array}{c}
\text{database instance} \\
\downarrow \\
\textit{Apply} \qquad \Delta' \\
\longrightarrow
\end{array}
$$

$$\textbf{Up\_Sem}$$

3.1 Update derivation properties

The scope of the next properties is the mapping **Up_Der**. We claim that they are mandatory. The first definition intends to define update sets in general and introduces a basic property: derived updates should not contain conflicting or contradictory updates.

Definition 2 - Conflict Free Update. An update is a partial interpretation δ which contains only ground update-literals. δ^+ (resp. δ^-) denotes the set of insertion-literals (resp. deletion-literals) of δ. δ is called *conflict free* iff $POS(\delta^+) \cap POS(\delta^-) = \emptyset$.

In our framework, **input** updates will be restricted to conflict-free sets of ground update-atoms [2]. In the remaining of the paper, $\mathcal{P}$ is an update program, Δ is a database instance and δ is an input update.

Our claim is that derived updates should be well-founded. Informally, this property aims at enforcing that an insertion (resp. deletion) of a fact is feasible only if *it can be proved* that the corresponding deletion (resp. insertion) is not required.

Definition 3 - Well Founded Update. An update δ is well founded if for each ground update-atom $+p$ (resp. $-p$) in δ, $\neg{-p}$ (resp. $\neg{+p}$) belongs also to δ.

Durable change introduced in [Zan95] intends to enforce triggering of update rules only by updates which will belong to the final derived update set. This property was previously formalized in logic programming as *supported* [ABW87] and *justified* [BH89] interpretations. Below, we recall the definition of *well supported interpretations* of [Fag91].

---

[2] Input updates are either user's request or are gathered of the database application/transaction.

Definition 4 - Well-Supported. Let $\mathcal{P}$ be a program and I an interpretation[3]. I is *well supported* by $\mathcal{P}$ if there exists a well-founded ordering $<$ on the Herbrand base $B_{\mathcal{P}}$ of $\mathcal{P}$ such that for all ground atom p, $p \in I$ implies $\exists \rho \in Inst(\mathcal{P})$: $(Body(\rho) \subseteq I$ and $q < p$ for all $q \in POS(Body(\rho)))$.

Intuitively, if an update is well supported by a program $\mathcal{P}$, then it is not derived from itself using $\mathcal{P}$.

3.2 Database update properties

Let us now turn to properties of the mapping Up_Sem. Recall that Up_Sem is defined as the composition of the mappings Up_Der and *Apply*. These properties may or may not be desirable depending on the application environment.

Dealing with incomplete information leads naturally to compare the information contents of databases. In many situations given two databases satisfying the same properties, e.g. integrity constraints, one may prefer the more informative database, that is the database leaving as less as possible facts unknown.

Definition 5 - Knowledge Ordering. Let Δ_1 and Δ_2 be two instances. Δ_1 is *more informative than* Δ_2, denoted $\Delta_1 \succeq \Delta_2$, iff $UNK(\Delta_1) \subseteq UNK(\Delta_2)$.

The *minimal change* property is another classical property. It will be discussed in section 4 and requires introducing a distance between incomplete databases. This is done by extending in a straightforward way the notion of distance between two complete databases.

Let Δ, Δ_1 and Δ_2 be database instances over the same schema. $\div$ is the symmetric set difference operator. $|\Delta_1, \Delta_2| = [POS(\Delta_1) \div POS(\Delta_2)] \bigcup [UNK(\Delta_1) \div UNK(\Delta_2)]$. We say that Δ_1 is closer to Δ than Δ_2 is iff $|\Delta, \Delta_1| \subseteq |\Delta, \Delta_2|$.

Traditionally, the application of an update δ over an initial database Δ_{init} produces a database Δ_δ obtained by just adding each p into Δ_{init} if $+p \in \delta$ and removing each p from Δ_{init} if $-p \in \delta$. If we consider $\mathcal{F}$ as the family of instances satisfying some constraints, Δ_δ may not belong to $\mathcal{F}$. The minimal change property simply says that, in this case, instead of Δ_δ, the result of the update δ is the database belonging to $\mathcal{F}$ which is as close as possible to the database Δ_δ in terms of changes. Formally,

Definition 6 - Minimal Change. The instance Δ_{min} of $\mathcal{F}$ satisfies the minimal change w.r.t. the initial instance Δ_{init} and the input update δ iff:
$$\forall \Delta \in \mathcal{F} : |\Delta_\delta, \Delta| \subseteq |\Delta_\delta, \Delta_{min}| \Rightarrow |\Delta_\delta, \Delta| = |\Delta_\delta, \Delta_{min}|.$$

Input update priority expresses that the input update should have a visible final effect. The formal definition takes into account that, in our framework, databases may be incomplete and also that input updates may be in conflict with derived updates.

Definition 7 - Input Update Priority. The mapping Up_Sem gives priority to input update iff for each $+p \in \delta$ (resp. $-p \in \delta$) either $p \in POS(\Delta')$ (resp. $p \in NEG(\Delta')$) or $p \in UNK(\Delta')$ where $\Delta'=$Up_Sem$(\Delta, \delta, \mathcal{P})$.

---

[3] Think of I as a set of updates.

Although in a loose manner, this property entails that an elementary input update is never rejected: if p is subject of an insertion then the status of p in the new database is either true or unknown but p **cannot be false**.

Stability is a very simple property: an update semantics is stable if it reduces to the identity mapping for empty input update. More precisely:

Definition 8 - Stability. The update semantics mapping Up_Sem is stable for $\mathcal{P}$ iff: $\text{Up\_Sem}(\Delta, \delta, \mathcal{P}) = \Delta' \Rightarrow \text{Up\_Sem}(\Delta', \emptyset, \mathcal{P}) = \Delta'$.

Given some definition of Up_Sem, stability may hold for a given update program and not for another one. The motivation for such a property follows.

Let us consider a transition as a pair of database instances. A family $\mathcal{T}$ of transitions is called stable iff for each transition (Δ_1, Δ_2) in $\mathcal{T}$, the transitions (Δ_1, Δ_1) and (Δ_2, Δ_2) belong to $\mathcal{T}$. For instance if $\mathcal{C}$ is a set of **static** integrity constraints, the set of transitions (Δ_1, Δ_2) such that Δ_1 and Δ_2 satisfy $\mathcal{C}$ is stable. Clearly, if an update program $\mathcal{P}$ is meant to *generate* a stable family of transitions then stability is expected for $\mathcal{P}$. The contrary is expected when the transition family is not stable. Stability is further discussed in section 4.

Domain independence usually requires that the answers to a query specified for instance by a logic program be independent of the evaluation domain. In our framework, domain independence focuses on the update semantics mapping Up_Sem and can be rephrased by: the database resulting from an input update on an initial database given an update program should be independent of the evaluation domain.

Definition 9 - Domain Independence. Let $\mathcal{H}$ be the set of constants in $\mathcal{P} \cup \delta \cup \Delta$, $D_1 \supseteq \mathcal{H}$ and $D_2 \supseteq \mathcal{H}$, $\mathcal{P}_1$ and $\mathcal{P}_2$ the instantiations of $\mathcal{P}$ built up from D_1 and D_2 respectively. The update semantics Up_Sem is domain independent iff $\forall D_1, D_2 \supseteq \mathcal{H}$: $\text{Up\_Sem}(\Delta, \delta, \mathcal{P}_1) = \text{Up\_Sem}(\Delta, \delta, \mathcal{P}_2)$.

3.3 Well founded semantics

This section is devoted to show that the well founded (w.f.) semantics can be easily adapted and is well-suited in order to define update derivation (Up_Der). Of course, our proposal is investigated with regards to the properties introduced in the previous sub-sections.

First, a slight rewriting of update rules is done. Recall that we expect derived update to be well founded and thus an update rule ρ like $Body(\rho) \longrightarrow +p$ is naturally read like a default rule [Rei80]: if the *prerequisite* $Body(\rho)$ is "true", and if it is "consistent" to assume the *justification* $\neg\neg p$, then derive *the consequence* $+p$. It is well-known now that the w.f. semantics provides a well-suited formalism for approximating default reasoning [BF91].

Thus, in the remaining, we assume that for each update rule ρ with head $+P(\tilde{x})$ (resp. $-P(\tilde{x})$), [4] $Body(\rho) \ni \neg -P(\tilde{x})$ (resp. $\neg +P(\tilde{x})$).

---

[4] $\tilde{x}$ is a tuple of terms.

When specifying a query as a Datalog program $\mathcal{P}$, in order to define the answer of $\mathcal{P}$ on the input database Δ, Δ is embedded into $\mathcal{P}$. In our framework, updating is specified by a Datalog program $\mathcal{P}$ and in order to define the derived update, we need to embed into $\mathcal{P}$ the input database and the input update. This is done by adding the following rules to $\mathcal{P}$ producing a new update program denoted $\mathcal{P}_{\delta,\Delta}$:

1. $\longrightarrow p$ (resp. $\neg p \longrightarrow p$) for each fact p in $POS(\Delta)$ (resp. in $UNK(\Delta)$).
2. $\neg{-}p \longrightarrow {+}p$ (resp. $\neg{+}p \longrightarrow {-}p$) for each ${+}p \in \delta$ (resp. ${-}p \in \delta$).

In order to understand the embedding of an unknown fact p by the rule $\neg p \longrightarrow p$, it suffices to note that p will be unknown in the w.f. model of any update program containing this rule, since it is the only one which defines p.

The update derivation mapping defined below uses the w.f. semantics in a straightforward manner.

Definition 10 - Up_Der_WF. The mapping Up_Der_WF is defined by :
Up_Der_WF$(\Delta, \delta, \mathcal{P})$ is the greatest update included in the w.f. model[5] of $\mathcal{P}_{\delta,\Delta}$.

This first attempt to define update derivation fulfills all update derivation properties previously introduced.

Proposition 11. *Up_Der_WF(Δ, δ, $\mathcal{P}$) is conflict free, well founded, and well supported by $\mathcal{P}_{\delta,\Delta}$.*

In order to make the update process complete, we need to precise what is the effect of an (derived) update on a database i.e. to define the mapping *Apply*.

Definition 12. Let δ be a conflict free update and Δ a database instance. $Apply(\delta, \Delta) = \Delta'$ with:
- $POS(\Delta') = \{p | {+}p \in \delta\} \cup \{p | p \in POS(\Delta) \text{ and } \neg{-}p \in \delta\}$.
- $UNK(\Delta') = \{p | p \notin POS(\Delta') \cup NEG(\Delta')\}$ where
- $NEG(\Delta') = \{p | {-}p \in \delta\} \cup \{p | p \in NEG(\Delta) \text{ and } \neg{+}p \in \delta\}$.

Note that *Apply* makes persistent all positive facts of the initial database whose deletion is not required (see $POS(\Delta')$). The dual remark can be made concerning $NEG(\Delta')$.

Because Up_Der_WF is conflict free, its composition with *Apply*, denoted Up_Sem_WF, is well-defined. We are now ready to investigate the update semantics Up_Sem_WF with regards to database update properties. As the reader will see, this study leads to introduce variants of the initial proposal for update derivation.

The first modification of the update derivation mapping is based on a different embedding of unknown facts. Observe that, given an interpretation I and a rule ρ, ρ is satisfied by I as soon as one of its body literal is unknown.

---

[5] Note that due to the embedding of the database Δ in $\mathcal{P}$, the w.f. model of $\mathcal{P}_{\delta,\Delta}$ contains base-facts as well as event-facts.

Example 1. Let $\delta = \{+p\}$, $\Delta = <\emptyset, \{q\}>$ and $\mathcal{P} = \{+p, q, \neg\neg r \longrightarrow +r\}$.
$\mathcal{P}_{\delta,\Delta} = \{\rho_1 : \neg\neg p \longrightarrow +p; \rho_2 : \neg q \longrightarrow q; \rho_3 : +p, q, \neg\neg r \longrightarrow +r\}$. The body of ρ_3 contains the unknown fact q which leads to derive that $+r$ is unknown in the w.f. model $\mathcal{M}$ of $\mathcal{P}_{\delta,\Delta}$. Hence, Up_Sem_WF$(\Delta, \delta, \mathcal{P}) =< \{p\}; \{q, r\} >$. Notice that r becomes unknown because $+r$ is unknown. If we consider the interpretation I obtained from $\mathcal{M}$ by considering $+r$ as false, we still have a model of $\mathcal{P}_{\delta,\Delta}$.

Definition 13 - Up_Der_WFU. Let $\mathcal{P}_{\delta,\Delta}^{\mathcal{K}}$ be the update program obtained from $\mathcal{P}_{\delta,\Delta}$ by removing all rules ρ such that there exists ℓ in Body(ρ) with UNK$(\Delta) \cap \{\ell, \neg\ell\} \neq \emptyset$. The update derivation mapping Up_Der_WFU is defined by: Up_Der_WFU$(\Delta, \delta, \mathcal{P})$ is the greatest update included in the well founded model of $\mathcal{P}_{\delta,\Delta}^{\mathcal{K}}$. The update semantics mapping Up_Sem_WFU is defined as the composition of Up_Der_WFU and *Apply*.

The update derivation mapping Up_Der_WFU satisfies the conflict free (its composition with *Apply* is well-defined), the well-founded and well-supported properties. Moreover, the update derivation mapping Up_Der_WFU is better than Up_Der_WF from the point of view of knowledge maximization.

Proposition 14. The database instance *Up_Sem_WFU$(\Delta, \delta, \mathcal{P})$* is more informative than the database instance *Up_Sem_WF$(\Delta, \delta, \mathcal{P})$*.

Example 1. (**Continued**) The simplified program is $\mathcal{P}_{\delta,\Delta}^{\mathcal{K}} = \{\rho_1 : \neg\neg p \longrightarrow +p\}$. Thus, Up_Sem_WFU$(\Delta, \delta, \mathcal{P}) =< \{p\}; \{q\} >$ which is more informative than the database Up_Sem_WF$(\Delta, \delta, \mathcal{P})$.

Lemma 15. The update semantics *Up_Sem_WF* and *Up_Sem_WFU* both give priority to input updates.

If knowledge maximization is the major goal, it may seem appropriate to reject the input updates introducing incomplete information in the updated database. We propose below a new update derivation mapping leading to an update semantics that violates on purpose the input priority property.

Definition 16 - Up_Der++. Let Up_Der be either Up_Der_WF or Up_Der_WFU. Let $\beta=$Up_Der$(\Delta, \delta, \mathcal{P}) \cap \delta$. The mapping Up_Der++ is defined by:
$$\text{Up\_Der++}(\Delta, \delta, \mathcal{P}) = \text{Up\_Der}(\Delta, \beta, \mathcal{P}).$$

The update set β contains the subset of the initial input updates which are derivable. Thus the intuitive idea behind the definition of Up_Der++ is: first updates are derived from the input updates, then input updates which are not derivable are discarded and finally a new step of update derivation is performed.
The update derivation mapping Up_Der_WF++ and Up_Der_WFU++ are obviously conflict free, well founded and well supported. In the following, Up_Sem_WF++ (resp. Up_Sem_WFU++) denotes the update semantics based on Up_Der_WF++ (resp. Up_Der_WFU++). We use Up_Sem++ to state properties satisfied by both mappings.

Proposition 17. 1. Let β be defined as above. *Up_Der++$(\Delta, \delta, \mathcal{P}) \cap \beta=\beta$*.

2. *Up_Der++ does not give priority to input update.*
3. Let $\Delta' = Up\_Sem++(\Delta, \delta, \mathcal{P})$. Let $+p$ (resp. $-p$) be in δ such that $p \in UNK(\Delta')$. Let $\delta' = \delta - \{+p\}$ (resp. $\delta - \{-p\}$). Then $p \in UNK(\Delta'')$ where $\Delta'' = Up\_Der++(\Delta, \delta', \mathcal{P})$.
4. $Up\_Sem\_WFU++(\Delta, \delta, \mathcal{P}) \succeq Up\_Sem\_WFU(\Delta, \delta, \mathcal{P})$.

The third item tells us that if an input update, let say $+p$, finally introduces an unknown information about p in the new database, it is due to some conflicting update but the conflict is not due to the input update $+p$ itself.

The update semantics Up_Sem_WFU++ has a very interesting feature: it preserves completeness of database instances as soon as the update program is stratifiable [ABW87]. We should insist that stratification is only required on the update program, not the update program with embedded input database and update.

Proposition 18. *If $\mathcal{P}$ is stratifiable and if the instance Δ is complete then $Up\_Sem++(\Delta, \delta, \mathcal{P})$ is complete.*

Recall that stability is not a property which is desirable for all update programs. A sufficient condition on update programs ensuring that their associated update semantics mapping is stable, is given now.

Proposition 19. *Let ρ be an update rule. The expansion of ρ denoted $Exp(\rho)$ is the set of rules obtained by replacing each base-literal p (resp. $\neg p$) in $body(\rho)$ by $(p \wedge \neg -p) \vee +p$ (resp. by $(\neg p \wedge \neg +p) \vee -p$) and then by unfolding the rule to eliminate disjunctions. Up_Sem_WFU++ is stable for $\mathcal{P}$ if:*

1. $\nexists \rho \in \mathcal{P} : Cond(\rho) = \emptyset$ and $NEG(Event(\rho)) = Event(\rho)$, and
2. $\forall \rho \in \mathcal{P} : NEG(Event(\rho)) = Event(\rho)$ and $Cond(\rho) \neq \emptyset \Rightarrow Exp(\rho) \subseteq \mathcal{P}$.

Example 2. Let $\mathcal{P} = \{+p, \neg -r \longrightarrow +r; \neg +q, \neg +r \longrightarrow -r\}$. Consider $\Delta = \, < \emptyset, \emptyset >$ and $\delta = \{+p\}$. $\Delta' = Up\_Sem++(\Delta, \delta, \mathcal{P}) = \, < \{p\}; \{r\} >$, while $Up\_Sem++(\Delta', \emptyset, \mathcal{P}) = \, < \{p\}; \emptyset >$. The second rule of $\mathcal{P}$ does not satisfy the first condition.

To conclude this section, we examine domain independence for Up_Sem++. Classically, we propose a sufficient condition on update programs to guarantee domain independence.

Definition 20.   – A rule ρ is *semi_allowed* (resp. *allowed*) if each variable appearing in ρ appears in a positive literal in ρ (resp. in $Body(\rho)$). These properties are generalized to programs.
  – $\mathcal{P}^-$ denotes the rules of $\mathcal{P}$ having a delete-atom in the head.
  – $\mathcal{P}$ is *restricted* iff $\mathcal{P} \backslash \mathcal{P}^-$ is allowed and $\mathcal{P}^-$ is semi_allowed.

Proposition 21. *If the update program $\mathcal{P}$ is restricted then Up_Sem++ is domain independent for $\mathcal{P}$.*

Example 3. $\mathcal{P} = \{\neg P(x, y, z), R(z), \neg + Q(x, y, t) \longrightarrow -Q(x, y, t)\}$ is restricted. Note that viewed as a query, this program is not domain independent.

4 Integrity Constraints & Rule derivation

For static and transition constraints we show how to generate an update program in order to enforce consistency. Results on correctness, minimal change and stability are discussed at the end of the section.

4.1 Static Constraints

A lot of research have been done on rule derivation in order to maintain database integrity (see for example [Ger94, CFPT94]). We focus our attention on static constraints expressed by:

$$\forall \tilde{x} : [P_1(\tilde{x}_{P_1}) \wedge \ldots \wedge P_n(\tilde{x}_{P_n}) \Rightarrow \exists \tilde{y} : (Q_1(\tilde{x}_{Q_1}, \tilde{y}_{Q_1}) \vee \ldots \vee Q_m(\tilde{x}_{Q_m}, \tilde{y}_{Q_m}))]$$
$$\text{where } \tilde{x} = \bigcup_{i=1}^{n} \tilde{x}_{P_i}, \ \tilde{y} = \bigcup_{i=1}^{m} \tilde{y}_{Q_i}, \ \bigcup_{j=1}^{n} \tilde{x}_{Q_j} \subseteq \tilde{x}.$$

Let $\mathcal{C}$ be a set of constraints and Δ be a database instance. Δ violates $\mathcal{C}$ iff $\exists c \in \mathcal{C}, \exists$ substitution $\theta : \Delta \models \neg c\theta$.

Example 4. Let $\Delta =< \{P(a)\}, \{Q(a)\} >$ and $\mathcal{C} = \{c : \forall x(P(x) \Rightarrow Q(x))\}$. Δ does not violate c because the implication is not false; it is unknown.

The production of update rules from $\mathcal{C}$ is defined in four steps (see the appendix for an illustration).

First step: Each constraint is rewritten as a denial (like in [SK87]):
$\rho_c \equiv P_1(\tilde{x}_{P_1}), \ldots, P_n(\tilde{x}_{P_n}), \neg Q_1(\tilde{x}_{Q_1}, \tilde{y}_{Q_1}), \ldots, \neg Q_m(\tilde{x}_{Q_m}, \tilde{y}_{Q_m}) \longrightarrow$
Notice that this rule may not be allowed (variables in $\tilde{y}_{Q_j}$ do not appear in a positive literal). In order to remedy this, for each negative literal $\neg Q_j(\tilde{x}_{Q_j}, \tilde{y}_{Q_j})$, we introduce a deductive rule $Q_j(\tilde{x}_{Q_j}, \tilde{y}_{Q_j}) \longrightarrow Q'_j(\tilde{x}_{Q_j})$ and replace ρ_c by
$P_1(\tilde{x}_{P_1}), \ldots, P_n(\tilde{x}_{P_n}), \neg Q'_1(\tilde{x}_{Q_1}), \ldots, \neg Q'_m(\tilde{x}_{Q_m}) \longrightarrow$
Q'_j is an *auxiliary predicate*. Let us denote by $\mathcal{P}_1$ this set of rules.
Second step: For each denial $\rho_c = \ell_1, \ldots, \ell_n, \neg \ell_{n+1}, \ldots, \neg \ell_m \longrightarrow$ in $\mathcal{P}_1$ we derive an update rule ρ which is one of the following rules

$$\ell_1, \ldots, \ell_n, \neg \ell_{n+1}, \ldots, \neg \ell_{i-1}, \neg \ell_{i+1}, \ldots, \neg \ell_m, \neg - \ell_i \longrightarrow + \ell_i \text{ or}$$
$$\ell_1, \ldots, \ell_{i-1}, \ell_{i+1}, \ldots, \ell_n, \neg \ell_{n+1}, \ldots, \neg \ell_m, \neg + \ell_i \longrightarrow - \ell_i$$

The program $\mathcal{P}_2$ is the set of deductive rules of step 1 and the above update rules.
Third step: Notice that some rules in $\mathcal{P}_2$ may have in their head an insert atom built up from an *auxiliary predicate* (e.g. $+Q'(\tilde{x})$). Hence, these insertions need to be translated into insertions on base predicates. For this purpose, a special constant $\bot$ is introduced. For every $\rho \in \mathcal{P}_2$ such that $Head(\rho) = +Q'(\tilde{x})$ and Q' is an auxiliary predicate, replace $Head(\rho)$ by $+Q(\tilde{x}, \bot)$ and $\neg - Q'(\tilde{x})$ in $Body(\rho)$ by $\neg - Q(\tilde{x}, \bot)$. The new program is denoted $\mathcal{P}_3$.
Fourth step: Replace each $\rho \in \mathcal{P}_3$ by its expansion $Exp(\rho)$ (see Proposition 19 for the definition of $Exp(\rho)$). The obtained program is denoted by $\mathcal{P}_C$.

4.2 Transition Constraints

A transition constraint expresses a condition on two consecutive instances. A database transition is denoted by a pair (Δ_0, Δ_1) where Δ_0 is the initial instance and Δ_1 is the final/next instance. A transition constraint is expressed by:

$$\forall \tilde{x} : \bigwedge_{i=1}^{m_1} P_i(\tilde{x}_{P_i}) \bigwedge_{j=1}^{m_2} \vec{Q}_j(\tilde{x}_{Q_j}) \Rightarrow \exists \tilde{y} : \bigvee_{k=1}^{n_1} R_k(\tilde{x}_{R_k}, \tilde{y}_{R_k}) \bigvee_{l=1}^{n_2} \vec{S}_l(\tilde{x}_{S_l}, \tilde{y}_{S_l})$$

The arrow above a predicate intends to refer to the instance of this predicate in the final state of a transition. With this notation, satisfaction of transition constraints is straightforward. The production of update rules from a set C of transition constraints is defined in four steps (see the appendix for an illustration).

First step: (same as in 4.1)

Second step: For each denial $\vec{E}_1, \ldots, \vec{E}_m, \neg \vec{F}_1, \ldots, \neg \vec{F}_n, B_1, \ldots, B_n \longrightarrow$ in $\mathcal{P}_1$ where B_i are base literals and E_i, F_j are base atoms, we derive an update rule ρ which is one of the following rule

$$+E_1, \ldots, +E_{i-1}, +E_{i+1}, \ldots, +E_m, -F_1, \ldots, -F_k, B_1, \ldots, B_n, \neg + E_i \longrightarrow -E_i \text{ or}$$
$$+E_1, \ldots, +E_m, -F_1, \ldots, -F_{i-1}, -F_{i+1}, -F_k, B_1, \ldots, B_n, \neg - F_i \longrightarrow +F_i$$

It is obvious that "repairing" a transition constraint violation can only be done on arrowed predicates. The new program is $\mathcal{P}_2$.

Third Step: (same as in 4.1)

Fourth Step: For each $\rho \in \mathcal{P}_3$, replace $+E_i$ (resp. $-F_j$) by $+E_i \vee (E_i \wedge \neg - E_i)$ (resp. $-F_j \vee (\neg F_j \wedge \neg + F_j)$).

Notice that, unlike for static constraints, base literals are not transformed here. We denote the obtained program by $\mathcal{P}_C$.

4.3 Results:

In the remaining, C is a set of static/transition constraints and $\mathcal{P}_C$ is the associated update program. The first result states that our translation of constraints into update program is valid for static constraints and transition constraints.

Proposition 22. *Let* $\Delta' = Up\_Sem++(\Delta, \delta, \mathcal{P}_C)$.

- *$\mathcal{P}_C$ is a restricted program.*
- *If C is a set of static constraints, then Δ' satisfies C.*
- *If C is a set of transition constraints, then the transition (Δ, Δ') satisfies C.*

The previous result does not assume that the initial database satisfies the static constraints. This entails that update programs generated from static constraints can really be used to restore consistency, not only to maintain consistency.

Recall from section 3, that stability is expected for the update programs enforcing static constraints, but not for transitions constraints[6].

---

[6] It is immediate to see that transition families satisfying transitions constraints are not stable in general.

Proposition 23. *If C is a set of static constraints then the update semantics* Up_Sem++ *is stable for $\mathcal{P}_C$.*

Example 5. Let $c : \vec{p}, q \longrightarrow$ be a transition constraint from which we derive $\mathcal{P}_c = \{q, \neg+p \longrightarrow -p\}$. Consider the database $\Delta_0 =< \emptyset; \emptyset >$ and the input update $\delta = \{+p, +q\}$. Up_Sem_WFU++$(\Delta_0, \delta, \mathcal{P}_c) =< \{p, q\}; \emptyset >$.
Clearly, (Δ_0, Δ_1) satisfies c. However, the reader should notice that the transition (Δ_1, Δ_1) does not satisfy c and that Up_Sem_WFU++$(\Delta_1, \emptyset, \mathcal{P}_c) =< \{p\}; \emptyset >$.

The following proposition links minimal change and knowledge maximization. Intuitively, it states that in the context of complete databases, instances satisfying C and making less changes than the instance $\Delta_{\mathcal{P}}$ computed by the update program $\mathcal{P}_C$ (associated to C) are less informative.

Proposition 24. *Let Δ_{init} be a database and Δ_δ obtained by just inserting into Δ_{init} the fact p whenever $+p \in \delta$ and removing p if $-p \in \delta$.*

Let $\Delta_{\mathcal{P}} =$Up_Sem++$(\Delta_{init}, \delta, \mathcal{P}_c)$. If Δ_{init} and $\Delta_{\mathcal{P}}$ are both total, and if there is no occurrence of the special constant $\perp$, then for any Δ satisfying the static constraints of C and for any Δ such that the transition (Δ_{init}, Δ) satisfies C, we have: $\qquad |\Delta_\delta, \Delta| \subset |\Delta_\delta, \Delta_{\mathcal{P}}| \Rightarrow \Delta_{\mathcal{P}} \succ \Delta.$

Occurrences of $\perp$ can be avoided. This is technical and not developed here. The above proposition entails that:

Corollary 25. *If Δ_{init} and $\Delta_{\mathcal{P}}$ are total and if $\Delta_\delta \in C$ (resp. $(\Delta_{init}, \Delta_\delta) \in C$) then $\Delta_{\mathcal{P}} = \Delta_\delta$.*

5 Related Works

Due to space limitation, we focus on related works based on *fixpoint semantics* or *model theoretic semantics* of logic programs. [Ras94] considers a restricted class of update programs which satisfy a notion of stratification. Update rules are partitioned into deductive rules (having an insertion in their heads) and integrity rules (having a deletion in their heads). By transforming update programs UP into logic programs LP, [Ras94] show that the semantics of UP given by means of a non deterministic operator coincides with one of the stable models [GL88] of LP. Recall that in our approach, we do not make a distinction between both kinds of rules. The work of [Zan95] is directly founded on the semantics of $Datalog_{1S}$ [BCW93]. Conflict detection is handled by adding special rules to the update program. When a conflict is detected, all derived updates are canceled and the external program (transaction) which triggered the rules is aborted. Note that in our framework, conflicting updates do not stop the derivation of updates, neither do they stop the database updating process. The effect of conflicting updates in our approach is local. [GMS96] proposes an inflationary fixpoint semantics with parameterizable conflict resolution strategies. Parameterization is simply done by giving the choice between deletion and insertion.

No discussion is provided on integrity maintenance and this approach lacks of validating work. [MT95] investigates revision programs implementing integrity constraints. A declarative semantics of revision programs is provided based on stable model semantics (whose computation is exponential). In [BM96], we proceed to a more detailed comparison and we show that our approach provides a reasonable approximation of their proposal, in terms of semantics and moreover of tractability. [HLS95] studied the integration of update rules into Datalog¬ databases. Update rules serve to derive exceptions of the facts derived by the query rules. The problems arising with this approach are (i) only one literal may appear in the body of the update rules, (ii) the update rules are considered as constraints, but surprisingly, the update process does not entail that the database semantics always satisfies the constraints.

6 Conclusion

In this paper we have proposed and discussed a well-founded semantics of update programs. Our approach provides a treatment of conflicting updates, termination and non-determinism. We also have tried to evaluate the reliability of our approach with regards to a number of properties. Nevertheless, this work leaves open several topics. Our definition of update programs allows us mixing deductive rules with update rules. The appendix provides an example of the use of such feature which needs to be investigated in depth. We are currently examining how to generate update programs from constraints in order to guarantee completeness of database instances as well as characterizing constraints for which this is feasible. In this paper we have focused essentially on the semantics of update rules. Our proposal needs to be embedded in the general setting of active databases (for instance using the formalism of [PV95]) in order to have a better validation of our approach with respect to event detection and coupling strategies, semantic consistency, expressiveness etc. We have started a naive implementation of our semantics using the XSB system of [SSW94]. This implementation needs to be continued and improved.

Acknowledgments: We are grateful to the anonymous referees for their useful comments. Unfortunately, due to space limitation, we have not been able to answer all their suggestions.

References

[ABW87] K. Apt, H. Blair, A. Walker. Towards a Theory of Declarative Knowledge. In *Foundations of Deductive Databases and Logic Programming*. J. Minker Editor. Morgan Kauffman Publishers. 1987.

[AHV95] S. Abiteboul, R. Hull, V. Vianu. Foundations of Databases. Addison-Wesley. 1995

[AHW95] A. Aiken, J. Hellerstein, J. Widom. Static Analysis Techniques for Predicting the Behavior of Active Database Rules. In *ACM TODS 1995*, 20(1): 3-41, 1995.

[BCW93] M. Baudinet, J. Chomicki, P. Wolper. Temporal Deductive Databases. In *Temporal Databases: Theory, Design and Implementation*. Benjamin/Cummings 1993.

[BF91] N. Bidoit, C. Froidevaux. General Logic Databases and Programs: Default Logic Semantics and Stratification. In *Information and Computation*.91: 15-54, 1991.

[BH89] N. Bidoit, R. Hull. Minimalism, Justification and Non-Monotonicity in Deductive Databases. *JCSS* 38(2): 290.325. 1989.

[BM96] N. Bidoit, S. Maabout. Update Rule Programs Related to Revision Programs. *NMELP Workshop*, in conjunction with JICSLP'96, Bonn, Germany. 1996

[CFPT94] S. Ceri, P. Fraternali, S. Paraboshi, L. Tanca. Automatic Generation of Production Rules for Integrity Maintenance. In *ACM TODS*. 1994.

[Fag91] F. Fages. A New Fixpoint Semantics for General Logic Programs Compared with the Well-Founded and the Stable Model Semantics. *In New Generation Computing* 9(4), 1991.

[Fit85] M. Fitting. A Kripke-Kleene Semantics for Logic Programs. In *Journal of Logic Programming*. 2: 295-312. 1985.

[FT95] P. Fraternali, L. Tanca. A Structured Approach for the Definition of the Semantics of Active Databases. In *ACM TODS*.20(4):414-471. 1995.

[GL88] M. Gelfond and V. Lifschitz. The Stable Semantics for Logic Programs. In *5th International Symposium on Logic Programming*. MIT Press. 1988.

[GMS96] G. Gottlob, G. Moerkotte, V.S. Subrahmanian. The PARK Semantics for Active Databases. In *Proceedings of EDBT'96*. Avignon, France, 1996.

[Ger94] M. Gertz. On Specifying the Reactive Behavior on Constraint Violations. *Proceedings of RIDE 94*. Houston, USA. 1994.

[HLS95] M. Halfeld Ferrari Alves, D. Laurent, N. Spyratos. Update Rules in Datalog Programs. In *Proceedings of LPNMR'95*. LNAI 928. June 1995.

[MT95] V. Marek and M. Truszczynski. Revision Programming, Database Updates and Integrity Constraints. In *Proceedings of ICDT'95*. Prague, January, 1995.

[PV95] P. Picouet, V. Vianu. Semantics and Expressiveness Issues in Active Databases. In *Proceedings of PODS95*. pp: 126-138. San Jose. 1995.

[Ras94] L. Raschid. A Semantics for a Class of Stratified Production System Programs. In *Journal of Logic Programming*. Vol21, Numb 1, pp 31-57. August 1994.

[Rei80] R. Reiter. A Logic for Default Reasoning. In *Artificial Intelligence*. 1980.

[S+95] A.P.J.M. Siebes, J.F.P van den Akker, M.H. van der Voort. (Un)decidability Results for Trigger Design Theories. *Report CS-R9556* CWI. Amsterdam. 1995.

[SK87] F. Sadri, R. Kowalski. A Theorem-Proving Approach to Database Integrity. In *Foundations of Deductive Databases and Logic Programming*. J. Minker Editor. Morgan Kauffman Publishers. 1987.

[SSW94] K. Sagonas, T. Swift, D. S. Warren. *XSB* as an Efficient Deductive Database Engine. In *Proccedings of ACM Sigmod Conference*. 1994.

[VRS91] A. van Gelder, K. A. Ross, J. S. Schlipf. The Well-founded Semantics for General Logic Programs. In *Journal of the ACM*. vol:38. 1991.

[WC96] J. Widom, S. Ceri (eds). Active Databases: Triggers and Rules for Advanced Database Processing. Morgan-Kaufman, Inc. San Francisco, 1996.

[Wid92] J. Widom. A Denotational Semantics for the Starburst Production Rule Language. *SIGMOD Record, 21(3)*, September 1992.

[Zan95] C. Zaniolo. Active Database Rules with Transaction-Conscious Stable-Model Semantics. In *Proceedings of DOOD'95*, LNCS: 1013. Singapore, December 1995.

Appendix A : Static Constraints

Consider the predicates $Emp(N, S, D)$, $Dept(D, C)$ where N, S, D, C are short-hands for Name, Salary, Department and City, and the constraint

$$\forall x, y, z : [Emp(x, y, z) \Rightarrow \exists t : Dept(z, t)]$$

The program associated to this constraint is one of the following:

$$\mathcal{P}_C = \left\{ \begin{array}{c} Dept(z, t), \neg - Dept(z, t) \longrightarrow Dept'(z) \\ +Dept(z, t) \longrightarrow Dept'(z) \\ \neg Dept'(z), \neg + Emp(x, y, z) \longrightarrow -Emp(x, y, z) \end{array} \right\}$$

or

$$\mathcal{P}_{C'} = \left\{ \begin{array}{c} Dept(z, t), \neg - Dept(z, t) \longrightarrow Dept'(z) \\ +Dept(z, t) \longrightarrow Dept'(z) \\ Emp(x, y, z), \neg - Emp(x, y, z), \neg - Dept(z, \bot) \longrightarrow +Dept(z, \bot) \\ +Emp(x, y, z), \neg - Dept(z, \bot) \longrightarrow +Dept(z, \bot) \end{array} \right\}$$

Appendix B : Transition Constraints

Consider the constraint: *A person can be enrolled as the manager of Department d if she/he was already an employee in the Department d.* It is expressed by:

$$\forall x : [\overrightarrow{Manager}(x, d) \Rightarrow \exists y : Emp(x, y, d)]$$

This constraint is expressed by

$$Emp(x, y, d) \longrightarrow Emp'(x, d)$$
$$\neg Emp'(x, d), \overrightarrow{Manager}(x, d) \longrightarrow$$

From the constraint above, the only update program we can derive is

$$Employee(x, d, y) \longrightarrow Employee(x, d)$$
$$\neg Employee'(x, d), \neg + Manager(x, d) \longrightarrow -Manager(x, d)$$

Appendix C : Constraints with Recursive Predicates

Consider the classical bill of material example. Consider the predicate P where $P(x, y)$ means that y is part of x. The predicate SP (SubPart) is defined by the rules $P(x, y) \longrightarrow SP(x, y)$ and $P(x, y), SP(y, z) \longrightarrow SP(x, z)$.

Now, consider the constraint which says that an item cannot be a subpart of itself. This can be stated by the denial: $\{P(x, y), SP(y, x) \longrightarrow\}$, [7] from which, we can derive the rules:

$$SP(y, x), \neg + P(x, y) \longrightarrow -P(x, y) \quad \bigg| \quad P(x, y), \neg - P(x, y), SP(y, z) \longrightarrow SP(x, z)$$
$$P(x, y), \neg - P(x, y) \longrightarrow SP(x, y) \quad \bigg| \quad +P(x, y), SP(y, z) \longrightarrow SP(x, z)$$
$$+P(x, y) \longrightarrow SP(x, y) \quad \bigg|$$

---

[7] Notice that the same constraint can also be expressed by $SP(x, x) \longrightarrow$.

Abstract Interpretation of Active Rules and Its Use in Termination Analysis

James Bailey, Lobel Crnogorac, Kotagiri Ramamohanarao
and Harald Søndergaard

Dept. of Computer Science, University of Melbourne, Parkville Vic. 3052, Australia
E-mail: {jbailey,lobel,rao,harald}@cs.mu.oz.au

Abstract. The behaviour of rules in an active database system can be difficult to predict, and much work has been devoted to the development of automatic support for reasoning about properties such as confluence and termination. We show how abstract interpretation can provide a generic framework for analysis of active rules. Abstract interpretation is a well-understood, semantics-based method for static analysis. Its advantage, apart from generality, lies in the separation of concerns: Once the underlying semantics has been captured formally, a variety of analyses can be derived, almost for free, as *approximations* to the semantics. Powerful general theorems enable simple proofs of global correctness and uniform termination of specific analyses. We outline these ideas and show, as an example application, a new method for termination analysis. In terms of precision, the method compares favourably with previous solutions to the problem. This is because the method investigates the flow of data rather than just the syntax of conditions and actions.

1 Introduction

An active database is a system which provides the functionality of a traditional database and additionally is capable of automatically reacting to state changes, both internal and external, without user intervention. This functionality is achieved by means of active rules or triggers. Active rules are useful in diverse applications such as workflow systems, audit trails, and maintenance of statistics. When multiple triggers are defined in a system, however, their interactions can be difficult to analyse, and interaction analysis is currently an important area of research. A key property which needs to be examined in this context is that of termination [2, 5, 11, 3, 4, 9, 8]. In this paper, we present an approach to rule analysis, based on abstract interpretation, which goes beyond the checking of syntax. The analysis propagates sophisticated dataflow information about calling patterns and how different rules interact. An important advantage of the technique is that it can be used for examining a wide variety of rule properties. We apply our method to the particular problem of rule termination and are able to obtain more precise answers for many types of rule sets.

The remainder of this paper is structured as follows. We provide a brief survey of termination analysis and an introduction to the principles of abstract interpretation. We then present the semantics of our active database language in a denotational form and also define an extension of it called the collecting semantics. We show how to approximate the collecting semantics using a simple rule language as an example. Next, we put this approximate collecting semantics to use in termination analysis. A discussion of how this could be extended to a more realistic rule language is also given. Finally, we discuss the results obtained and outline some directions for future research.

1.1 Termination

A rule set is said to terminate if, for any initial database state and any initial triggering event, rules cannot activate each other indefinitely. Obviously, this is a desirable property, since infinite triggering behaviour could make a system unusable. Yet it is undecidable in the general case whether an arbitrary rule set terminates. Previous work has suggested the use of either syntactic analysis, local semantic analysis, or a combination of both for detecting termination.

One of the first studies of active rule termination analysis was due to Aiken, Widom and Hellerstein [2] who introduced an abstraction called the *triggering graph*. In a triggering graph, the rules are represented by vertices and the possibility that execution of one rule can cause the execution of another rule is captured by a directed arc between two vertices. An acyclic triggering graph implies definite termination of a set of rules. This idea was refined by Karadimce and Urban [9]. Baralis and Widom [5] suggested another type of graph, the *activation graph*. Again rules are represented by vertices, but this time an arc indicates that the action of one rule may satisfy the condition of another rule. Here too, acyclicity means definite termination, but generating the graph is non-effective. Baralis *et al.* [3] presented the *rule reduction method*, combining the use of triggering and activation graphs. Any vertex which does not have both an incoming triggering and activation arc, can be removed from the graph (along with its outgoing arcs). If this procedure results in all vertices being removed, then the rule set must terminate.

Van der Voort and Siebes [11] consider the termination problem in an object-oriented rule system. The focus is on deciding termination in a fixed number of steps. The proofs make use of typical database states and the reasoning has some resemblance to a dataflow style of analysis. The general termination problem is not discussed, however, and details of the algorithms are unclear.

In an alternative approach by Baralis *et al.* [4], termination analysis happens at run time. The method presented in this paper, although static, does have features in common with this dynamic method, since we are effectively "running" the rule set, albeit in an approximate manner. The dynamic method is fundamentally limited, however, in that it can't analyse rules which can create new constants.

1.2 Abstract Interpretation

Abstract interpretation has proven a useful tool for analysis of imperative, functional and logic programs [1, 7, 10]. It has numerous applications in compiler

*	none	odd	even	any
none	none	none	none	none
odd	none	odd	even	any
even	none	even	even	even
any	none	any	even	any

Input	No branch	Yes branch
none	none	none
odd	odd	none
even	none	even
any	odd	even

Table 1. Approximating multiplication (left) and the *even* test (right)

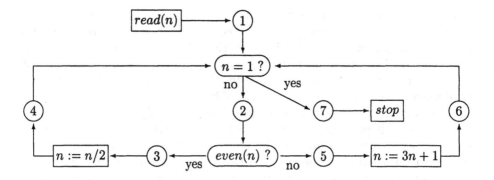

Fig. 1. A flow diagram for the $3n + 1$ example

optimisation and program transformation. The idea is to infer and collect information about a program's run time properties and its operational aspects. This information is known as the collecting semantics of a program.

The semantic domain of a program is approximated by an "abstract" domain, essentially a coarse grained version of the semantic domain. The operations of a program are approximated by abstract operations. Consider a program to be analysed whose semantic domain is $\mathcal{Z}$, the set of integers, and whose operations are the arithmetic operations $\{+, -, *, /\}$, the comparison functions, $\{<, >, =\}$, as well as tests $\{odd(\cdot), even(\cdot)\}$. The semantic domain could be approximated by descriptions $\{none, even, odd, any\}$ and the arithmetic operations simply according to the well-known "rules of parities". For example, Table 1 shows how multiplication is approximated (left table), as well as the approximation of the test *even* (right table).

Now consider the approximate computation of the flow diagram in Figure 1. Each arc of the diagram corresponds to a program point, and is labelled with a number. The computation involves iterating towards a fixpoint. The iteration proceeds by following arcs from the goal and updating program points until the values at each point have stabilised. Table 2 shows how the states iterate towards a fixpoint assuming n is *any* at point 1. The last step yields a fixpoint. The result of the analysis justifies transformation of the program so as to avoid a number of tests; for example, the statement $n := 3n+1$ can be replaced by $n := (3n+1)/2$.

Step	(1,	2,	3,	4,	5,	6,	7)
0	(any,	none,	none,	none,	none,	none,	none)
1	(any,	any,	none,	none,	none,	none,	odd)
2	(any,	any,	even,	none,	odd,	none,	odd)
3	(any,	any,	even,	any,	odd,	even,	odd)
4	(any,	any,	even,	any,	odd,	even,	odd)

Table 2. Approximate computation to a fixpoint from an initial state

Even though the actual computation may never terminate, the approximate computation always terminates. This is because the analysis is monotone with respect to the natural ordering of the descriptions, namely $d \leq d'$ iff $(d = none) \vee (d = d') \vee (d' = any)$. Annotations are only allowed to "grow" with respect to that ordering. In particular, where two or more arcs run together, the result is taken to be their least upper bound. We return to this point in Section 3.

2   A Collecting Semantics for Active Rules

We use denotational semantics to formally specify the execution of our active database model as a fixpoint computation. Analysis then consists of finding an approximation to the least fixpoint. Our basic execution model is similar to that assumed by Baralis *et al.* [3]:

1. If there is no triggered rule then exit.
2. Select the highest priority triggered rule.
3. Evaluate the condition of the selected rule.
4. If the condition is true then execute the action of the selected rule.

The action that executes in step 4 can trigger further rules by causing events and thus 1-2-3-4 can repeat forever. We assume that an initial triggering event occurs within a transaction and this immediately initiates rule processing which will either continue indefinitely or terminate and allow the next statement in the transaction to execute (essentially immediate coupling mode). In the denotational definition, we have made the following important choices.

- Whenever there are several triggered rules to choose from, we deterministically select one according to a priority scheme. This is quite a sensible choice, since it automatically imposes confluence on the rule set.
- Pending rules are represented as a set. This means that a rule cannot have multiple instances triggered simultaneously.

We now give a denotational definition of the execution model. The definition captures the essence of our model and is similar in spirit to those of Widom [12] and Coupaye and Collet [6].

A database is modelled by a collection of variables. *Dbs* is the domain of database states. A database state associates each variable with its value. *Rule* is the domain of rules. Assume that a fixed set R_0 of rules is given. In the following we define the meaning $\mathcal{M}$ of R_0. To keep the definition readable, we do this without direct reference to R_0. We assume that a function, *triggered*, when given a rule r, will yield the set $R \subseteq R_0$ of rules that could be triggered by the execution of r.

The meaning $\mathcal{M}$ of R_0 is a function which, given a set R of initially triggered rules and an initial database state d, yields a new database state. Since non-termination is a possibility, $\mathcal{M}$ is in fact partial. We model this by allowing for a result, $\bot$, signifying undefinedness. That is,

$$\mathcal{M} : \mathcal{P}(Rule) \rightarrow Dbs \rightarrow Dbs_\bot$$

where $Dbs_\bot = Dbs \cup \{\bot\}$ with ordering $d \leq d'$ iff $d \in \{\bot, d'\}$

Since rules can activate each other recursively, the meaning $\mathcal{M}$ is naturally given as a fixpoint characterisation. $\mathcal{M}$ is defined to be the least $P : \mathcal{P}(Rule) \rightarrow Dbs \rightarrow Dbs_\bot$ (wrt the pointwise ordering) satisfying:

$$
\begin{aligned}
P(R)(d) = \ &\text{if } R = \emptyset \text{ then } d \\
&\text{else let } r = select(R) \\
&\qquad R' = triggered(r, d) \cup (R \setminus \{r\}) \\
&\qquad d' = \mathcal{R}(r)(d) \\
&\text{in } P(R')(d')
\end{aligned}
$$

It is straightforward to show that $\mathcal{M}$ is well-defined. The right-hand side reads as follows: If no rules are pending then the current database state is the final result. Otherwise the rule r with highest priority is selected, and the set of pending rules is updated by removing r and adding whichever rules r triggers. The effect of r on the database state is given by a function $\mathcal{R}$ which gives the meaning of r as a state transformer $Dbs \rightarrow Dbs$. A rule consists of an event, condition and a set of actions. It produces a new state and a set of events. The function $\mathcal{R}$ gives the meaning of a rule as the result of applying its actions to the current state. If the condition of the rule evaluates to *false* in the current database state then the resulting state is just the current state. The exact definition of $\mathcal{R}$ depends on the rule language and its definition is of no interest here, but the details would be straightforward. In the next section we consider a specific language.

For analysis purposes we are interested not only in the result of the computation, but also in all the database states that are obtained at intermediate points in the execution. For this reason the denotational definition is changed into a so-called *collecting semantics* [7, 10]. The idea is to use a history to record all the possible combinations (set of pending rules, database state) that occur. The domain $Hist = \mathcal{P}(Rule) \rightarrow \mathcal{P}(Dbs)$ is used for this. For example, if at some stage we encounter a set R of pending rules in a current database state d, then the entry for R will be updated to include d. Notice that the rule r which would have been activated next is the rule in R which has the highest priority. This leads to the following definition of a collecting semantics: $\mathcal{C} : \mathcal{P}(Rule) \rightarrow Dbs \rightarrow Hist$ is defined by

$$C(R)(d) = C'(R)(d)(\lambda R . \emptyset)$$

where C' is the least $P : \mathcal{P}(Rule) \rightarrow Dbs \rightarrow Hist \rightarrow Hist$ satisfying

$$P(R)(d)(h) = \text{let } h' = update(R)(d)(h) \text{ in}$$
$$\text{if } R = \emptyset \text{ then } h'$$
$$\text{else let } r = select(R)$$
$$R' = triggered(r, d) \cup (R \setminus \{r\})$$
$$d' = \mathcal{R}(r)(d)$$
$$\text{in } P(R')(d')(h')$$

Again, it is possible to show that $\mathcal{C}$ is well-defined. The function $update$: $\mathcal{P}(Rule) \rightarrow Dbs \rightarrow Hist \rightarrow Hist$ handles the updating of history entries. Namely,

$$update(R)(d)(h)(R') = \begin{cases} h(R) \cup \{d\}, \text{ if } R = R' \\ h(R), \qquad \text{otherwise} \end{cases}$$

In other words, $update(R)(d)(h)$ is a new history which is identical to h, except its value for R has had $\{d\}$ added.

The collecting semantics is not finitely computable in general, as infinite sets of database states may be generated. It represents the *ideal* information needed for many analysis tasks. In the next section we consider how to finitely approximate the collecting semantics, so as to obtain correct, albeit less precise, dataflow information in finite time.

3 Approximating the Collecting Semantics

Recall the following basic fixpoint-theoretical notions. A *preordering* on a set D is a binary relation that is reflexive and transitive. A *partial ordering* is a preordering that is antisymmetric. Given a partially ordered set (*poset*) D, for any subset S of D, $a \in D$ is an *upper bound* for S if for all $x \in S$, $x \leq a$. Moreover, a' is the *least upper bound* (lub) of S, if a' is an upper bound for S, and for each upper bound a, $a' \leq a$. When it exists, we denote the (unique) least upper bound of S by $\sqcup S$. Dually, the *greatest lower bound* $\sqcap S$ can be defined. A partially ordered set for which every subset S possesses both a least upper bound and a greatest lower bound is a *complete lattice*. A (possibly empty) subset Y of X is a *chain* if for all $y, y' \in Y, y \leq y' \vee y' \leq y$.

Our interest in complete lattices should be clear. Although we have not made it explicit in our semantic definitions, the definitions are fixpoint characterisations. Complete lattices thus help ensure well-definedness. The idea in the following is to replace the large lattice of database states by a more crude (smaller) lattice of approximate database states. Once we have made the notion of "approximates" precise, we only need to devise ways of manipulating approximations in a manner faithful to the way the basic operations of the given database language manipulate proper database states.

In the $3n + 1$ example in Section 1 we dealt informally with the notion of approximation. More formally we can specify the meaning of *none*, *even*, *odd*, and *any* by mapping each to the set of integers it stands for:

$$\gamma(none) = \emptyset$$
$$\gamma(even) = \{z \in \mathcal{Z} \mid z \text{ is even}\}$$
$$\gamma(odd) = \{z \in \mathcal{Z} \mid z \text{ is odd}\}$$
$$\gamma(any) = \mathcal{Z}$$

We can also give, for each set of integers, the best approximation available:

$$\alpha(S) = \begin{cases} none, & \text{if } S = \emptyset \\ even, & \text{if } S \neq \emptyset \text{ contains only even numbers} \\ odd, & \text{if } S \neq \emptyset \text{ contains only odd numbers} \\ any, & \text{if } S \neq \emptyset \text{ contains both even and odd numbers} \end{cases}$$

These two functions form a *Galois connection* which is the basic tool for formalising "correct approximation" in abstract interpretation. We refer to them as the *concretization function* and *abstraction function*, respectively. Similarly the domain and codomain for α are called the concrete and abstract domains, respectively. In the example, α and γ are monotonic and

$$S \subseteq \gamma(\alpha(S)), \text{ for all } S \in \mathcal{P}(\mathcal{Z})$$
$$d = \alpha(\gamma(d)), \text{ for all } d \in \{none, even, odd, any\}$$

More generally, a Galois connection is a quadruple (γ, α, U, V) where U and V are posets and $\alpha(v) \leq u \iff v \leq \gamma(u)$, for all $u \in U, v \in V$. Approximation is defined as follows:

$$u \text{ appr } v \iff v \leq \gamma(u).$$

There are standard ways of extending this notion to composite domains, such as Cartesian products and function spaces [10].

The powerful correctness theorem that we have alluded to can now be explained. Assume we have two chains, $\{u_i\}_{i \in I}$ and $\{v_i\}_{i \in I}$, such that u_i *appr* v_i for each $i \in I$. Then $\bigsqcup_{i \in I} u_i$ *appr* $\bigsqcup_{i \in I} v_i$. In this sense, local correctness automatically implies global correctness. If we guarantee correct manipulation of approximations by all basic operations, then we automatically approximate least fixpoints correctly. Moreover, the design of approximate operations does not need to be *ad hoc*. For each operation $f : V \to V$ on the concrete domain, the Galois connection determines a unique best approximation $f' : U \to U$, namely $f' = \alpha \circ f \circ \gamma$.

We now make these points more specific, by considering example concrete and abstract domains. The rule language we consider is of the usual Event-Condition-Action form. Variables range over $\mathcal{Z}$.

- An event is of the form $U(X)$ which means "update variable X." It is triggered by any assignment to X.

- A condition is a conjunction of simple conditions. A simple condition is a test of the form $X = n$ or $X = Y$, where X and Y are variables and n is an integer.
- An action is a sequence of simple actions. A simple action is an assignment of the form $X{:=}Y$ or $X{:=}n$.

As an example abstract domain let us use the set

$$Adom = \mathcal{Z} \cup \{\bot, neg, pos, nonpos, nonzero, nonneg, \top\}.$$

The function $\gamma : Adom \to \mathcal{P}(\mathcal{Z})$, defined by

$$\gamma(d) = \begin{cases} \emptyset, & \text{if } d = \bot \\ \{d\}, & \text{if } d \in \mathcal{Z} \\ \{n \in \mathcal{Z} \mid n < 0\}, & \text{if } d = neg \\ \{n \in \mathcal{Z} \mid n > 0\}, & \text{if } d = pos \\ \{n \in \mathcal{Z} \mid n \leq 0\}, & \text{if } d = nonpos \\ \{n \in \mathcal{Z} \mid n \neq 0\}, & \text{if } d = nonzero \\ \{n \in \mathcal{Z} \mid n \geq 0\}, & \text{if } d = nonneg \\ \mathcal{Z}, & \text{if } d = \top \end{cases}$$

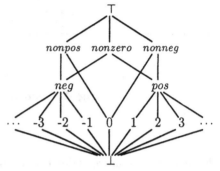

Fig. 2. The abstract domain *Adom*

gives the meaning of elements of *Adom*. The domain's Hasse diagram is shown in Figure 2. The ordering is induced by the subset ordering on $\mathcal{P}(\mathcal{Z})$.

The collecting semantics is approximated in two steps, as indicated in Figure 3. Assuming a finite set *Var* of database variables, a database state is a finitely based function in $Dbs = Var \to \mathcal{Z}$. First the domain $\mathcal{P}(Dbs)$ is replaced by $Var \to \mathcal{P}(\mathcal{Z})$. This involves an approximation by which the set of functions F is approximated by the single function f' defined by

$$f'(V) = \{n \mid f(V) = n \text{ for some } f \in F\}.$$

(It is straightforward to show that this determines a Galois connection between the two domains.) Next the domain $Var \to \mathcal{P}(\mathcal{Z})$ is replaced by $Var \to Adom$. Here the approximation is induced by the *appr* relation: the function $f' : Var \to Adom$ approximates $f : Var \to \mathcal{P}(\mathcal{Z})$ if $f'(V)$ *appr* $f(V)$ for all variables V.

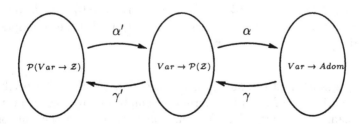

Fig. 3. The two steps needed to approximate sets of database states

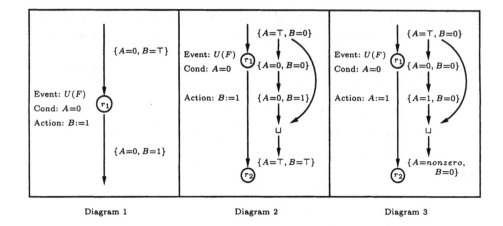

Diagram 1   Diagram 2   Diagram 3

Fig. 4. Approximate execution of rules

Example 1. Let us consider the approximate execution of rules. Recall that a rule is seen as a database state transformer. The meaning of a rule here has type $(Var \to Adom) \to (Var \to Adom)$ and a denotational definition is straightforward. We omit the details, giving instead, in Figure 4, a few examples of "approximate" rule behaviour.

Diagram 1 shows the result of executing a rule. In the initial database state, A is 0, while nothing is known about B. This is sufficient to guarantee that the action $B:=1$ is executed, so the resulting database state has $A = 0$ and $B = 1$.

Diagram 2 considers the case where a rule's condition involves an indefinite variable A. We proceed by case analysis. In case $A = 0$, action $B:=1$ results in a database state which has $A = 0$ and $B = 1$. Alternatively, no action is taken, so $A = nonzero$ and $B = 0$. The least upper bound of these two (the junction labelled '⊔' represents this operation) is the state $A = \top$ and $B = \top$.

Diagram 3 shows an example of a *self-disactivating* rule. The rule r_1 makes its own condition *false*. The resulting approximate database state is sufficiently precise that we can detect self-disactivation in this case. It is obtained as the least upper bound of $\{A = 1, B = 0\}$ and $\{A = nonzero, B = 0\}$. The latter state is a *sharpening* of the original $\{A = \top, B = 0\}$, incorporating the assumption that the condition $A = 0$ was false. ∎

The example illustrated the approximate execution of rules. The result of executing an entire set of rules is determined simply by approximating the collecting semantics. In particular, the function that updates the "history" remains the same except that its type is $\mathcal{P}(Rule) \to Dbs' \to Hist' \to Hist'$, where $Dbs' = Var \to Adom$ and $Hist' = \mathcal{P}(Rule) \to \mathcal{P}(Var \to Adom)$.

4 Termination Analysis

A rule set is said to terminate if, for any initial database state and any initial triggering event, rules cannot activate each other indefinitely. A termination detection algorithm will typically return either an answer that the rule set *definitely* terminates or an answer that it *may* terminate. The approximate semantics developed so far can be used for this type of analysis. Essentially, if, during approximate execution, we never encounter the same (pending rule set, approximate database state) combination twice, then the rules must terminate. Only finitely many such combinations are possible, in spite of *Adom* being infinite, this is because rules are unable to create new constants. Ways to relax this restriction are examined in section 5.

We now look at two examples of termination analysis. After that we give an algorithm based on what we have developed so far. We stress that, although the first example is taken from a paper which only deals with a 0–1 language, we read the rules as elements of a more expressive language, in which variables can take any integer value. Still we obtain comparable or better precision. That is, we improve expressiveness and precision simultaneously.

Example 2. This example of non-terminating behaviour is due to Baralis *et al.* Figure 5 shows the rule system.

A solid arc from one rule to another indicates that the first rule's action can trigger the event of the second rule (the *triggering graph* [2]). For example, there is a solid arc from r_3 to r_1 because r_3 contains the action $F:=1$ which causes the event of r_1 to trigger. The dashed arcs represent the *activation graph* [5]. Thus, there is a dashed arc from rule r_2 to rule r_1 because r_2 contains the action $A:=0$ which can make the condition of r_1 true. The triggering and activation graphs are used in the

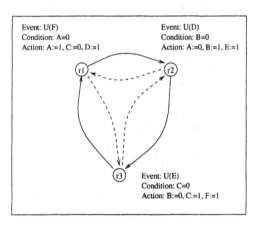

Fig. 5. Triggering/activation graph

rule reduction algorithm [3]. In this example the rule reduction algorithm cannot eliminate any rules and so the rule set is deemed possibly non-terminating. This is a precise statement since this rule set is non-terminating in general (for example, if A and B are both 0 initially and r1 is triggered).

In Table 3, trace 1 gives the trace of execution for a method based on abstract interpretation. After six steps our algorithm detects a repeating state (3 and 6) and possible non-termination is signalled. ∎

trace 1

Step	A	B	C	D	E	F	set
0	T	T	T	T	T	T	$\{r_1\}$
1	1	T	0	1	T	T	$\{r_2\}$
2	0	1	0	1	1	T	$\{r_3\}$
3	0	0	1	1	1	1	$\{r_1\}$
4	1	0	0	1	1	1	$\{r_2\}$
5	0	1	0	1	1	1	$\{r_3\}$
6	0	0	1	1	1	1	$\{r_1\}$

trace 2

Step	A	B	C	D	E	F	set
0	T	T	T	T	T	T	$\{r_1\}$
1	1	T	0	1	T	T	$\{r_2\}$
2	0	1	1	1	1	T	$\{r_3\}$

Table 3. Traces of execution

Example 3. Now change r_2 slightly, adding $C:=1$ to its actions. Trace 2 shows the trace of the resulting computation. Our algorithm signals termination after two steps, outperforming the rule reduction algorithm, as the triggering/activation graph remains the same as in Figure 5. Our algorithm yields a better result because it is able to mimic the dataflow of the real execution. Note that we only show traces assuming that r_1 was the first rule activated. In practice it would be necessary to give additional traces for when r_2 or r_3 is initially activated. ∎

The algorithm follows the outline provided by the collecting semantics, but additional features have been added to obtain a precise termination analysis.

```
For each rule r_0 do
    For each set R do h[R] := ∅
    For each variable V do d[V] := T
    R = {r_0}
    While R ≠ ∅
        if d ∈ h[R] then (* we have met this state before *)
            report "rules may not terminate"; exit
        else h[R] := h[R] ∪ {d}
        r := select(R)
        R' := triggered(r) ∪ (R \ {r})
        if must_satisfy(d, cond(r)) then d := eval(action(r), d)
        else if may_satisfy(d, cond(r)) then
            if R = {r} then d := eval(action(r), d) (*assume cond(r) true *)
            else d := sharpen(d, cond(r)) ⊔ eval(action(r), d);
                R' := mark(triggered(r)) ∪ (R \ {r})
        else R' := R \ {r} (* must not satisfy *)
        R := R'
    end While
    report "rules must terminate"
```

Since database states are approximate, the evaluation of a rule condition can have three outcomes:

1. The function *must_satisfy* takes an approximate database state d and a condition c and returns true iff c holds for *every* database state approximated by d and the selected rule is not marked. If it returns true then the function *eval* is called to yield the state that results after the rule's action has been executed.

2. The function *may_satisfy* takes the same arguments and returns true iff c holds for *some* database state approximated by d. In general we should then take the least upper bound of two possible results: d itself (if r is not activated) and $eval(action(r), d)$ (in case r is activated). However, we can improve on this: If r was the only rule pending then we can disregard the result of not activating r, since it will not be used. Furthermore, knowing that d does not satisfy the condition of r can sometimes allow a *sharpening* of d before taking its least upper bound with $eval(action(r), d)$. The function *sharpen* is for this purpose. For example, with $d(A) = \top$ and the condition $A = 0$, we know that $d(A) = nonzero$ is correct when the test fails. For safety reasons, sharpening is constrained to only have an effect when there are no more than two rules in the pending set and a rule is marked if triggered as the result of a *may_satisfy* rule.

3. In the remaining case, the rule will definitely not be activated, so it is simply removed from the set of pending rules. No new rules can be triggered.

Notice that the algorithm assumes that exactly one rule is initially triggered. However, it is a simple modification to allow arbitrary initial configurations, by making R and d parameters.

Theorem 1. *If our algorithm signals that the rule set is terminating, then the rule set terminates for any initial database state and triggering event.* ∎

Theorem 2. *The abstract interpretation algorithm always terminates.* ∎

Let us compare our algorithm with the rule reduction method for a language where variables can only take the values 0 or 1. For the rule reduction method to remove a rule, either it has no incoming triggering arc or no incoming activation arc. In case of no incoming triggering arc, no other rule can trigger it and thus our algorithm will never be able to consider it for execution. In case of no incoming activation arc, the rule must be self-disactivating and no other rule's action can make it true. Hence, our algorithm executes it a finite number of times and without state repetition. Let us state this result as a lemma:

Lemma 3. *Every rule that is eliminated by the rule reduction algorithm is executed a finite number of times and without state repetition by the abstract interpretation algorithm.* ∎

We now claim that the abstract-interpretation-based algorithm is at least as precise as the rule reduction method for simple conditions in the 0-1 rule language. To prove this, we only need to show that it signals termination whenever the rule reduction algorithm reports termination. Suppose the rule reduction algorithm reports termination. This implies it is able to reduce the input set of rules to the empty set. This means that every rule in the rule set is eventually eliminated. By Lemma 3, the abstract interpretation algorithm will eventually be unable to execute any rule and thus it signals termination. Thus we have:

Proposition 4. *The abstract interpretation algorithm, applied to the 0-1 rule language is uniformly at least as precise as the rule reduction method provided the rule set only contains simple conditions.* ∎

Note that for simple triggering graphs (that is, where each rule can trigger at most one other rule), Proposition 4 also holds for compound conditions. In the case of non-simple graphs, we can modify our algorithm such that we keep a disjunction of variable dependencies and thus still achieve greater precision.

5 Extending the Rule Language

The previous section defined an algorithm to handle a language which was unable to construct new constant values. It is straightforward to extend this to a language which uses arithmetic and inequalities, however, provided we are willing to sacrifice some precision. The extension necessitates we alter the way we update our history of database states. Instead of adding a new state to the set of previous states, we only record one entry for each pending set and incrementally refine its value by taking the least upper bound with new states as they arise. This implies some loss of precision in our analysis, but guarantees termination. The advantage is that termination and correctness of this new algorithm come almost for free, owing to the framework's flexibility. Also, by more complex choices of abstract domain, we can regain precision at the expense of efficiency.

We now consider how we would approximate the collecting semantics of a more complex rule language. We wish to examine rules which can perform relational algebra operations on a relational database. For this, it is necessary that we be able to represent the state of the database as we conduct our analysis. The following theorem states that we could do this using just variables which have the value 0 or 1, subject to certain restrictions.

Theorem 5. *Suppose we have a relational database with a schema such that every attribute of a relation has a finite, ordered domain. It is possible to represent the contents of any possible database state by a finite number of 0-1 variables.* ∎

This is true because it is possible to finitely enumerate the tuples that could occur. The presence of a tuple can be signified by '1' and its absence by '0'. The order on attributes allows us to construct an index to access any combination of attribute values. The truth value of a relational algebra condition can be determined by testing the values of the appropriate 0-1 variables, and the effect of a relational algebra action can be captured by appropriate assignments.

Therefore, in principle, if we have finite, ordered domains, we can use the method previously described to analyse for properties in a rule system which uses relational algebra. Obviously, the complexity of this procedure would be prohibitive for large domains, so we now sketch ways in which it could be reduced. The first thing to note is that we only need to simulate relations which are used by rules, the rest can be ignored. Second, if we are analysing for termination, then as a first pass one of the graph based methods such as the rule reduction method can be used to highlight which rules *may* be part of cycles, all other rules can be disregarded. The abstract interpretation method can then be used to conduct a more refined termination analysis of the relevant rules. Third, we need not store every previous database state in a history, but can in fact store delta relations as in [4] which describe the differences between successive states. Fourth, if we have information on some semantic properties of the data, such as functional dependencies and constraints, this can be used to eliminate further potential database states. Fifth, if the complexity is still too high, we can sacrifice some precision by abstracting the attribute domains (e.g by range compression).

6 Conclusion

We have suggested abstract interpretation as a tool to help solve static analysis problems for active rules. The approach has a number of advantages:

- The approach is generic, so that the same formal machinery can help solve a variety of problems.
- It is well-understood and based on a solid mathematical foundation.
- Termination (of the analysis) does not require complicated *ad hoc* proofs. Simple properties of the abstract domain (finiteness, ascending chain property, and others) suffice to guarantee termination.
- Correctness proofs are simplified, since global correctness follows automatically whenever basic operations are approximated correctly.
- The technique allows/forces one to think in semantic terms and conveniently separate two concerns: approximation and implementation [10].
- The technique can be used for analysis of other properties in a rule system such as the detection of redundant rules or determination of the reachability of particular database states as a result of trigger activation (which has applications in the static analysis of transactions).

This paper contains an example of an abstract domain and its use for termination analysis for active rules. The intention has been to demonstrate applicability and show how, by simple means, we can improve on previous "syntactic" methods. However, the termination analysis is far from definitive. Much more work is needed to design abstract domains that are useful for practical active databases. Here 'useful' means both 'sufficiently expressive' and 'efficiently realisable'. One possibility that should not be overlooked is the mixing of technologies to form hybrid methods, so that for example relatively expensive abstract interpretation is replaced by cheaper methods once analysis time exceeds a given limit.

Although we sketched in Section 5 how our method can be extended for more complex cases, it is not clear how feasible this will be when extensions for relational algebra are incorporated. There are several other avenues for future work:

- Exploring other abstract domains, in particular for interval analysis.
- Experimentally comparing the precision of termination analysis using abstract interpretation with that of current syntactic methods.
- Exploring the effect of non-determinism.
- Applying abstract interpretation to other problems in active databases, such as confluence and optimisation of conditions.

References

1. S. Abramsky and C. Hankin, editors. *Abstract Interpretation of Declarative Languages.* Ellis Horwood, 1987.
2. A. Aiken, J. Widom, and J. M. Hellerstein. Behavior of database production rules: Termination, confluence and observable determinism. In *Proceedings of the ACM SIGMOD International Conference on Management of Data*, pages 59–68. ACM Press, 1992.
3. E. Baralis, S. Ceri, and S. Paraboschi. Improved rule analysis by means of triggering and activation graphs. In T. Sellis, editor, *Rules in Database Systems*, Lecture Notes in Computer Science 985, pages 165–181. Springer-Verlag, 1995.
4. E. Baralis, S. Ceri, and S. Paraboschi. Run-time detection of non terminating active rule systems. In *Proceedings of the Fourth International Conference on Deductive and Object Oriented Databases*, pages 38–54, Singapore, 1995.
5. E. Baralis and J. Widom. An algebraic approach to rule analysis in expert database systems. In *Proceedings of the 20th International Conference on Very Large Databases*, pages 475–486, Santiago, Chile, 1994.
6. T. Coupaye and C. Collet. Denotational semantics for an active rule execution model. In *Proceedings of the Second International Workshop on Rules in Database Systems*, pages 36–50, Athens, Greece, 1995.
7. P. Cousot and R. Cousot. Abstract interpretation and application to logic programs. *Journal of Logic Programming*, 13(2&3):103–179, 1992.
8. A. Karadimce and S. Urban. Conditional term rewriting as a formal basis for analysis of active database rules. In *Proceedings of the Fourth International Workshop on Research Issues in Data Engineering*, pages 156–162, Houston, Texas, 1994.
9. A. Karadimce and S. Urban. Refined triggering graphs: A logic based approach to termination analysis in an active object-oriented database. In *Proceedings of the 12th International Conference on Data Engineering*, New Orleans, Louisiana, 1996.
10. K. Marriott, H. Søndergaard, and N. D. Jones. Denotational abstract interpretation of logic programs. *ACM Transactions on Programming Languages and Systems*, 16(3):607–648, 1994.
11. L. Van der Voort and A. Siebes. Termination and confluence of rule execution. In *Proceedings of the Second International Conference on Information and Knowledge Management*, Washington DC, 1993.
12. J. Widom. A denotational semantics for Starburst production rule language. *ACM SIGMOD Record*, 21:4–9, 1992.

Structural Issues in Active Rule Systems

James Bailey, Guozhu Dong and Kotagiri Ramamohanarao

Dept. of Computer Science, University of Melbourne, Parkville Vic. 3052, Australia
E-mail: {jbailey,dong,rao}@cs.mu.oz.au

Abstract. Active database systems enhance the functionality of traditional databases through the use of active rules or 'triggers'. There is little consensus, though, on what components should be included in a rule system. In this paper, the expressive power of some simple active database rule systems is examined and the effect of choosing different features studied. Four important parameters of variation are presented, namely the rule language, the external query language, the meta rule language and the pending rule structure. We show that each of these is highly influential in determining the expressiveness of the rule system as a whole, and that an appreciation of them can serve as a basis for understanding the broader picture of system behaviour.

1 Introduction

Traditional database systems provide a mechanism for storing large amounts of data and an interface for manipulating and querying this data. They are, however, passive in the sense that their state can only change as a result of outside influences. In contrast, an active database is a system providing the functionality of a traditional database and additionally is capable of reacting automatically to state changes, both internal and external, without user intervention. This functionality is achieved by active rules or triggers. Applications have been found in areas such as workflow management, view management and constraint maintenance [7, 4, 3]. Additionally, many different prototype systems have been built. Despite this, less progress has been made with regard to the theory of active database rules. An understanding of how various features of rule syntax and semantics can affect the properties of active database rules is still in its infancy. Our aim in this paper is to illustrate the expressiveness of simple active rule systems and note the effect of making certain changes in their functionality. We study four dimensions of variation, namely

- The mechanism used to record pending rules for execution
- The rule language
- The external query/update language
- The meta rule language

We measure the power of a rule system by the set of external event histories that it can recognise. This metric helps us focus upon the potency of active rules as a programming language mechanism. It differs from most work on active databases, since the attention is less on using rules to react to changes in the database, but rather on using them as a tool to carry out computation. Through the use of this model, we are able to demonstrate two key results. The first is that even a very basic rule language can have power comparable to a Turing machine. The second is that the expressiveness of the rule system as a whole is acutely sensitive to a small change in any of the above dimensions. Each of these has important implications for language designers.

The remainder of this paper is structured as follows. The next subsection presents some related work and Section 2 presents the definitions to be used in the paper. Section 3 looks at the implications of varying the rule execution structure. In Section 4, meta rules are introduced and analysed. Section 5 looks at changing the rule and query language and it brings a database perspective to the results we have obtained. Lastly, we provide some conclusions and look at future directions.

1.1 Related Work

In [11], the concept of the relational machine is presented as useful for simulating an active database. It is essentially a Turing machine which has restricted access to a relational store via first order queries and is designed to capture the spirit of a database query language embedded in a host programming language such as C. An active database system is modelled by two relational machines, one replicating the external query system and the other duplicating the set of active rules. Using this model, statements can be made about the power of various simplified prototype systems. Our work in this paper is essentially complementary to this approach. Our aim is not so much to construct an all embracing formalism for active databases, but rather to focus on some of the elements that affect the power of the rule system. Also, we treat certain aspects not covered in [11] such as syntactic events. Our work is also complementary to [9], where a programming language which employs the delayed update or *delta* is defined. This can be used to express the semantics of some active database systems.

In [10], methods for specifying meta rules to manage execution of the rule set as a whole are presented. Although we also consider meta rules, our interest is primarily in the additional computational power they can add to a rule system and not on how to use them for static reasoning about rule behaviour.

2 Preliminaries

We begin by presenting the core active rule language used in this paper. It follows the so-called ECA format

$$on \text{ event } if \text{ condition } then \text{ action}$$

The following 0-1 language was used as a simple example language in [2].

Definition 1. 0-1 Language

- Events are of the form U(X) which we understand to mean 'update the variable X'. They are thus triggered by an assignment statement on this variable[1].
- A condition is a conjunction of simple conditions. A simple condition is a test of the form *Var=0* or *Var=1*
- An action is a sequence of simple actions. A simple action is an assignment of the form *Var=0* or *Var=1*. □

Thus a typical 0-1 rule might be

$$\text{On } U(A)$$
$$\text{If } C = 0 \land D = 1 \land T = 1$$
$$\text{Then } T = 0 \, ; \, B = 1$$

The basic execution model used is:

0. A sequence of external events occurs, each of which may trigger some rules. Control is then passed to the rule system.
1. If there are no triggered rules then exit
2. Select a rule to execute from the pending rule structure
3. Evaluate the condition of the selected rule
4. If the condition is true then execute the action of the selected rule

The action executed in step 4 can cause further (internal) events which trigger other rules and these will be added in turn to the pending rule structure. Thus the steps 1-2-3-4 can potentially loop forever.

We now define what we mean by the power of a set of active database rules. The definition focuses on the power of rules as a programming language construct. The rule system is seen as a recogniser for external event sequences. Using this definition we can describe rule expressiveness in terms of formal language theory. As a result, it becomes easy to compare the expressiveness of different constructs and various corollaries on decidability can be obtained for free.

Definition 2. Rule Power

Suppose we have an alphabet E of external events and a set of rules R. Then L(R) denotes the set of external event sequences accepted by R. A sequence $w \in E^*$, known as an *external event history*, is said to be accepted by R if the computation of R, after input of the external event history w, halts in an accepting state.[2] □

---

[1] We don't require that the new value has to be different from the old one for an update to be registered.

[2] A state of the rule system is described by the values of its 0-1 variables. We designate a number of these states as *accepting states*.

Definition 3. Let H_p represent a set of external event histories. A rule set R is said to characterise H_p if L(R) = H_p. □

We are interested in situations such as H_p = the set of regular histories or H_p = the set of recursively enumerable histories.

3 Pending Rules

The first feature we investigate is the nature of the pending rule structure. The most straightforward choice is to make it a set and whenever a rule needs to be selected from it, the one with highest priority is chosen. We assume rules are totally ordered by priority. The implications of a set are that it can contain only one instance of any particular rule and thus there is a bound on the size of the set. More complex choices are to use a queue (like HiPAC [8]) or a stack (like NAOS [6]) to record the pending rules. These may contain multiple instances of a rule and thus are unbounded in size. Rule selection is done by taking the rule on top of the stack or queue. When a rule is triggered it is placed on top of the stack or on the bottom of the queue and if more than one rule is activated at once then they are placed on in order of highest priority.

We now state an interesting and perhaps surprising result about rules in a 0-1 language.

Theorem 4. *A 0-1 trigger system with a queue characterises the set of recursively enumerable external event histories.*

Proof(sketch): We will show that we can build a set of 0-1 triggers with queue to recognise any external event history that a Turing machine can. We show equivalence to Post machines [12] instead of Turing machines however. A Post machine has exactly the same power as a Turing machine and is like a pushdown automaton which uses a queue instead of a stack. It consists of an alphabet of input symbols and a number of states including a START state. In each state one can move to another state after reading and removing a symbol from the front of the queue and/or possibly adding an element(s) to the end of the queue. The machine doesn't have a separate input tape unit, but rather the input string is initially loaded into the queue before execution. Acceptance of a string is defined by whether the machine halts in an accepting state.

A Post machine's transition is of the form *(state, symbol, state', symbol')*

- *state* is the machine's current state
- *symbol* is the symbol on top of the queue
- *state'* is the new state the machine will go to
- *symbol'* is the symbol to place on the bottom of the queue

To translate this machine into 0-1 rules, we define the following variables.

- A special variable V_{accept} to indicate an accepting state

- A special variable V_ϵ, this will allow us to deal with the situation when the empty word is put on to the queue
- A special variable V_{flag} to help with mutual exclusion
- For each machine symbol a, the variable V_a
- For each machine state p, the variable V_p

We group transitions together according to symbol. Suppose the group for symbol a is the following:

$$(p,\, a,\, p_1,\, w_p)$$
$$(q,\, a,\, q_1,\, w_q)$$

These can be translated into the following rules.

R_a	R_{a_p}	R_{a_q}
On $U(V_a)$	On $U(V_a)$	On $U(V_a)$
If true	If $V_p=1$ and $V_{flag}=1$	If $V_q=1$ and $V_{flag}=1$
$V_{flag}=1$	Then $V_p=0$; $V_{p_1}=1$;	Then $V_q=0$; $V_{q_1}=1$;
	$V_{w_p}=1$; $V_{flag}=0$	$V_{w_q}=1$; $V_{flag}=0$

The variable V_{flag} ensures that only one of R_{a_p} and R_{a_q} is executed. Rule R_a resets V_{flag} so that other rules may use it. These rules are ordered from left to right so that R_a has the highest priority. If p is an accepting state, then we also include the action $V_{accept}=1$ in rule R_{a_p}, similarly for state q and rule R_{a_q}.

We also need a rule in order to empty the queue when an accepting state is entered. Its priority is less than R_a and larger than R_{a_p} and R_{a_q}.

$R_{a_{empty}}$
On $U(V_a)$
If $V_{accept}=1$
Then $V_{flag}=0$

We have thus shown how the state transitions of the Post machine can be replicated by 0-1 rules. To complete the picture, we assume the rules are initially placed in the queue by a sequence of external events firing (this corresponds to the Post machine's input string) as described in section 2 and the variables V_s (corresponding to the START state s) and V_{accept} are initialised to 1. We also designate the START state as an accepting state since this allows us to accept ϵ (the empty event history). A 0-1 rule computation halts once the queue is empty. □

Since we can simulate a Turing machine, it then immediately follows that

Corollary 5. *Termination is undecidable for a 0-1 trigger system with a queue.* □

The next two theorems consider what happens when we replace the queue by a stack or a set. We observe that there is a dramatic loss of power for these structures. One reason for this is to do with the way rules are placed on the pending structure. Execution of rules can only begin once the entire external event history (in the form of rules) has been put in the pending rule structure. Hence the stack/set is being used as both a source of the history and also as an aid to computation. Contrast this situation with the operation of a machine such as a pushdown automaton, where a separate read only input is available. Here, the input string does not 'interfere' with intermediate computations on the stack. We could eliminate this interference by changing our semantics so that control is passed to the trigger system after each external event, but we would then want the ability to be able to terminate with a non-empty stack/set so it could then process the next external event and this would violate the spirit of active rule execution.

Theorem 6. *A 0-1 trigger system with a stack characterises the set of regular external event histories.* $\square$

Theorem 7. *A 0-1 trigger system with a set can accept any external event history which can be described by a formula using the connectives $\wedge$, $\neg$ and $\vee$ to combine statements of the form $\diamondsuit\ e_k$. $\diamondsuit\ e_k$ holds at position j in a history iff the event e_k has occurred at position j or some preceding position.* $\square$

Once again, using results from formal language theory we can state

Corollary 8. *Termination is decidable for a 0-1 trigger system with a set or a stack*

4 Meta Rules

Meta rules are used for managing the behaviour of the set of active rules. We have already seen an example of a meta rule in the form of the priority mechanism used to order the set of rules. We now consider complex events which can be thought of as a type of meta level construct for combining events.

Many active rule languages have a facility for specifying complex events. These are combinations of various primitive events. One needs to be careful, however, about specifying their semantics, since even seemingly simple operators may have a variety of interpretations [5].

The operator we will consider is the sequence operator. An event E=e1;e2 occurs if the event e1 followed by the event e2 occurs. The event consumption semantics we choose is a cumulative one and is intuitively 'match an e2 with each unconsumed e1 before it' (in real life this could correspond to tracking all deposits preceding a big withdrawal). Figure 1 illustrates this with six different occurrences of the event E. The numeric labels on the arcs indicate the complex event ordering i.e 1 occurs before 2, 2 occurs before 3 etc. When multiple rules

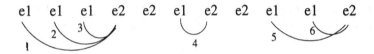

Fig. 1. Cumulative Consumption Semantics

are activated at once (e.g 1,2 and 3), they are pushed onto the stack in reverse order of firing (i.e 3 then 2 then 1).

Suppose we assume that our rule system has the power to recognise a complex event of the type just discussed. The following theorem tells us that it makes the system as powerful as when we had a queue earlier.

Theorem 9. *A 0-1 trigger system with a stack and the cumulative event sequence operator characterises the set of recursively enumerable external event histories.*

Proof(sketch): The proof is similar to that of Theorem 4. We will only need to show that it is possible to place a rule at the bottom of the stack to show that the stack can behave like a queue. For each rule in the rule set, we associate with it an identifier event. So for Rule $R1$ we have E_{R1}, Rule $R2$ we have E_{R2} etc. We also have a special event called E_{bottom}. Using these events we create another set of rules that are activated on complex events.
For rule $R1$ we would create another rule $R1'$ of the form

$$R1'$$
$$\text{On } E_{R1}; E_{bottom}$$
$$\text{if C1'}$$
$$\text{then A1'}$$

where C1' and A1' are the same as $R1$'s condition and action respectively.

Now suppose we wish to place rule $R5$ on the bottom of the stack and the stack already has a number of rules on it. We first set a variable called the consumption flag. This will make sure the condition of each rule in the stack is false and will also cause an event to be fired when that rule is considered. e.g If $R1$ is on top of the stack in consumption mode, then it will be removed and the event E_{R1} will be fired. Similar events will be fired for every other rule on the stack. Once the bottom of the stack is reached (detectable by an appropriate marker rule[3]), we do two things. Firstly we fire the event E_{R5} (since we want to put rule $R5$ on the bottom of the stack), then we fire the event for the marker rule followed by event E_{bottom} and lastly we turn consumption mode off. The firing of E_{bottom} causes all the rules with complex events defined above to be placed

---

[3] For this, it is necessary to assume the external event history is always begun by a distinguished event e_{marker} which places the marker rule in the stack.

back on the stack in reverse order of the firing of their E_{R_k} event. Thus the stack is the same as it was originally, but with rule $R5$ on the bottom. □

There are clearly many other types of meta rules which can be defined. A couple of examples are meta rules which prohibit two rules occupying the pending set simultaneously and meta rules which require a particular rule to be in the pending set for another rule to be added to it. The extra power meta rules provide to the rule system lies in their ability to control the flow of the system in non standard ways.

Remark: Suppose we have a meta rule which deterministically removes one instance of a certain rule from the pending set whenever a particular rule is added. Then it is straightforward to recognise the external event history $\{e_1^n e_2^n \mid n \geq 1\}$ using a 0-1 rule system with stack.

5 Language Variation

5.1 Trigger Language

We now turn our attention to the timing of activation of the components in an E-C-A rule. Current active database systems address this by incorporating the notion of coupling modes [8]. Each rule can be triggered in either of two modes.

- Immediate: The rule is placed into the pending rule structure immediately after the event occurs and control is then transferred to the rule set by the external query system (or if the event was generated internally by the rule system, then it will retain control).
- Deferred: If a rule is triggered, then it is placed into the pending rule structure only after the structure has become empty (until which time the rule can be thought of as occupying a separate 'deferred' pending structure). If a rule is triggered by an external event, then control is not passed to the rule system unless the event is the last operation in the history. Deferred mode corresponds to postponing rule execution until the end of a transaction, just before the commit phase.

In our semantics described in Section 2, we effectively assumed deferred coupling mode for rules activated triggered by external events and immediate coupling mode for rules triggered by internal events. If we relax this restriction, then we can get increased rule power.

Theorem 10. *A 0-1 trigger system with a stack and the option of immediate and deferred coupling modes for all rules, characterises the set of recursively enumerable external event histories.*

Proof(sketch): As in Theorem 9, we will just show that it is possible to place a rule at the bottom of the stack. First, suppose that for every rule we define two variants, one in immediate mode and one in deferred mode. Assume also, that we have a flag indicating whether we currently want to activate rules in deferred mode or in immediate mode. Suppose we want to place Rule $R5$ at the bottom of the stack, we set the flag to deferred and this will ensure that every rule on the stack is reactivated in deferred mode and then removed. Thus the stack will be emptied and conceptually we'll have a new stack containing all the rules activated in deferred mode, but with their original order reversed. We now activate rule $R5$ in deferred mode (we can set a flag to remember to do this as soon as we reach a marker rule indicating the bottom of the stack) and then carry out the deferred activation process once again, for each element on the stack. We then reset the flag to indicate immediate mode. We now have a new stack with the order as it was initially and rule $R5$ on the bottom. $\square$

5.2 External Query Language

Query Augmentation We now address the question of whether the type of rule languages presented are useful in a database context. On the surface it would seem not, since neither the condition or action involves any reference to or manipulation of database relations. We show, however, that such languages can be useful provided events can be triggered in a certain way.

We look at whether the rule system can allow a given external query language to obtain answers to queries that it couldn't normally. Assume we are using a relational database and let us consider the query *even* on a unary relation T

$$even(T)= \text{true if } |T| \text{ is even and false otherwise}$$

This query cannot be expressed by query languages such as *fixpoint, while or* $while_N$ on unordered databases [1]. It is possible to express this query using 0-1 active rules with stack and immediate coupling mode, however, if events can be generated in a tuple oriented fashion (i.e an event is triggered for each instance in the binding set).

Suppose a user asks the query *even*(T). Then this is translated into the statements

```
parity=1
add(tmp(X)) :- T(X)
if parity=1 then return true
else return false
```

The active database rules shown in figure 2 are instrumental in constructing the answer to the query. Assume R3 has higher priority than rule R2

As many instances of R1 will be placed on the stack as there are tuples in the relation T. As rules are removed from the stack for execution, they toggle the parity variable. We can thus determine the answer to the *even* query and this idea can be extended to performing tests such as $|T1| = |T2|$ etc.

R1	R2	R3
On add to relation tmp	On E2	On E3
If true	If parity=0	If parity=1 and flag=true
Then fire E2 ; fire E3;	Then parity=1;	Then parity=0
flag=true	flag=false	

Fig. 2. Rules for the parity query

Note that although this tuple oriented activation of events is deterministic, it would not be so if the rules were able to retain parameters containing information on how they were activated (e.g if the first instance of a rule was triggered by the tuple 'Fred'). We would then have to assume tuples to be accessed in some predefined order if we wished to retain determinism.

By the assumptions made in [11], it is not possible to express a query such as *even* using several major active database prototypes, yet we have shown how it can be done using tuple oriented triggering. In [13], it is shown how to express the query using the production rule language RDL1, which uses condition-action rules, but this language is not deterministic however.

Role of Events The preceding discussion raises the question of just what the role of events is in the 0-1 language. In section 3 they were primarily used as a convenient mechanism for controlling the activation of other rules. It is possible, however, to achieve the same functionality just with Condition-Action rules, provided we carefully choose our semantics. We will consider a C-A rule to be activated if its condition makes a transition from false to true. Suppose we want to simulate the E-C-A rule $R1$ by a C-A rule $R1'$.

$R1$	$R1'$
On E	
If C	If C and flag=true
Then A	Then A

For rule $R1'$ to be triggered, we perform the action 'flag=false;flag=true'. It is a moot point whether we've gained anything by doing this, since this method of activation is an event in everything except name. Indeed we may even have lost power, since it is unclear whether C-A rules with this semantics may compute the *even* query.

First Order Extensions We now briefly consider the implications of adding the ability to execute relational operations to our 0-1 rule language. Suppose that our 0-1 rules with queue can issue a first order query to a relational store and can assign the result of a first order query to the store (call this rule language $0\text{-}1_{FO}$). We can then claim that this system is equivalent computationally to the relational machine used by [11]. This provides an interesting perspective, since the results in [11] show that the active database system HiPAC [8] can be modelled by a relational machine. Therefore our $0\text{-}1_{FO}$ active rule language would have the ability to 'simulate' this complex prototype system, subject to [11]'s simplifying assumptions.

6 Conclusions and Future Work

We have examined some of the key features in an active database system and have seen that they can have a considerable impact on expressiveness. This is summarised in Figure 3 (the question marks in the set row indicate the problem is open at this time). We have also seen that even simple rule languages can

	Standard Configuration	Unrestricted Coupling	Cumulative Event
Set	Past Temporal Formula	?	?
Stack	Regular	Rec. Enum.	Rec. Enum.
Queue	Rec. Enum	Rec. Enum.	Rec. Enum.

Fig. 3. Rule Power Summary

be very powerful computationally in the presence of features such as a queue or complex events. This potential power can be used effectively for database queries, provided events can be generated in a sophisticated manner. More importantly, this power implies that many questions in regard to active behaviour will be undecidable.

In our future work, we plan to investigate the following directions:

- The effect of allowing conditions to look at more than one version of the database
- The effect of further types of meta rules
- The features needed in order to increase the power of a 0-1 rule system with a set
- The computational complexity of certain configurations of rule sets
- Investigating the relationship between the systems presented and various 'exotic' grammar types such as ordered grammars, timed grammars and grammars with control rules

References

1. S. Abiteboul, R. Hull, and V. Vianu. *Foundations of Databases.* Addison-Wesley, 1995.
2. E. Baralis, S. Ceri, and S. Paraboschi. Improved rule analysis by means of triggering and activation graphs. In T. Sellis, editor, *Rules in Database Systems*, Lecture Notes in Computer Science 985, pages 165–181. Springer-Verlag, 1995.

3. S. Ceri and J. Widom. Deriving production rules for constraint maintenance. In *Proceedings of the 16th International Conference on Very Large Databases*, pages 566–577, Brisbane, Australia, 1990.

4. S. Ceri and J. Widom. Deriving production rules for incremental view maintenance. In *Proceedings of the 17th International Conference on Very Large Databases*, pages 577–589, Barcelona, Spain, 1991.

5. S. Chakravarthy and D. Mishra. Snoop: An expressive event specification language for active databases. *Data and Knowledge Engineering*, 14(1):1–26, 1994.

6. C. Collet, T. Coupaye, and T. Svensen. Naos: Efficient and modular reactive capabilities in an object oriented database system. In *Proceedings of the 20th International Conference on Very Large Data bases*, pages 132–143, Santiago, Chile, 1994.

7. U. Dayal, M. Hsu, and R. Ladin. Organizing long running activities with triggers and transactions. In *Proceedings of the ACM-SIGMOD International Conference on the Management of Data*, pages 204–214, Atlantic City, 1990.

8. U. Dayal et al. The HiPAC project: Combining active databases and timing constraints. *ACM SIGMOD Record*, 17(1):51–70, 1988.

9. R. Hull and D. Jacobs. Language constructs for programming active databases. In *Proceedings of the 17th International Conference on Very Large Databases*, pages 455–468, 1991.

10. H. V. Jagadish, A. O. Mendelzon, and I. S. Mumick. Managing rule conflicts in an active database. In *Proceedings of the 14th ACM SIGMOD-SIGACT-SIGART Symposium on Principles of Database Systems*, Montreal, Canada, 1996.

11. P. Picouet and V. Vianu. Semantics and expressiveness issues in active databases. In *Proceedings of the 14th ACM SIGMOD-SIGACT-SIGART Symposium on Principles of Database Systems*, pages 126–138, San Jose, California, 1995.

12. E. Post. Finite combinatory processes-formulation I. *Journal of Symbolic Logic*, 1:103–105, 1936.

13. E. Simon and C. de Maindreville. Deciding whether a production rule is relational computable. In *Proceedings of The International Conference on Database Theory*, pages 205–222, 1988.

Discovering All Most Specific Sentences by Randomized Algorithms
Extended Abstract

Dimitrios Gunopulos[1] and Heikki Mannila[2] and Sanjeev Saluja[3]

[1] Max-Planck-Insitut Informatik, Im Stadtwald, 66123 Saarbrücken, Germany.
gunopulo@mpi-sb.mpg.de
[2] University of Helsinki, Dept. of Computer Science, FIN-00014 Helsinki, Finland.
Heikki.Mannila@cs.helsinki.fi.
Work supported by Alexander von Humbold-Stiftung and the Academy of Finland.
[3] Max-Planck-Institut Informatik, Im Stadtwald, 66123 Saarbrücken, Germany.
saluja@mpi-sb.mpg.de

Abstract. Data mining can in many instances be viewed as the task of computing a representation of a theory of a model or a database. In this paper we present a randomized algorithm that can be used to compute the representation of a theory in terms of the most specific sentences of that theory. In addition to randomization, the algorithm uses a generalization of the concept of hypergraph transversal. We apply the general algorithm, for discovering maximal frequent sets in 0/1 data, and for computing minimal keys in relations. We present some empirical results on the performance of these methods on real data. We also show some complexity theoretic evidence of the hardness of these problems.

1 Introduction

Data mining has recently emerged as an important application area [11]. The goal of data mining can briefly be stated as "finding useful high-level knowledge from large masses of data". The area combines methods and tools from databases, machine learning, and statistics.

A large part of current research in the area can be viewed as addressing instances of the following problem: given a language, a frequency criterion, and a database, find all sentences from the language that are true in the database and satisfy the frequency criterion. Typically, the frequency criterion states that there are sufficiently many instances in the database satisfying the sentence. Examples where this formulation works include the discovery of association rules, strong rules, episodes, and keys. Using this *theory extraction formulation* [19, 20, 23] one can formulate general results about the complexity of algorithms for various data mining tasks.

The algorithms for the above mentioned data mining tasks typically operate in a bottom-up fashion: first the truth and frequency of the simplest, most general, sentences from the language are evaluated against the database, and then the process continues for more specific sentences. While this approach works reasonably well in several cases, problems can arise when the theory to be extracted is large: there are lots of sentences to be output. An alternative method is to try to search for the most specific sentences from the language that satisfy the requirements: theses sentences determine the theory uniquely.

In this paper we present a randomized algorithm for locating the most specific true sentences satisfying the frequency criterion. Although our algorithm is randomized, it is complete, in the sense that it returns all most specific sentences. Briefly the method works as follows. We apply a randomized greedy search to locate some maximal elements from the language. We then use the simple fact that if some sets from an anti-chain are known, then every unknown set in the anti-chain must contain a *minimal transversal* of the *complements* of the known sets. The algorithm alternates between finding new random most specific true sentences and finding minimal transversals of the complements of the already discovered most specific true sentences, until no new most specific true sentence can be found.

We demonstrate this method by applying it to the problem of computing all maximal frequent sets of a 0/1 matrix for a given threshold, and to the problem of computing of all minimal keys, or functional dependences, in a relational database. The computation of maximal frequent sets is a fundamental data mining problem which is required in discovering association rules [1, 2]. Minimal keys can be used for semantic query optimization, which leads to fast query processing in database systems [22, 18, 5, 26]. Here we refer to possible keys that exist in a specific instance of a relational database and are not designed as such.

The computation of sentences of a theory is an enumeration problem. The computation involves listing combinatorial substructures related with the input. For enumeration problems one of the definitions of efficiency is that the running time of algorithm be bounded by a polynomial function of input and output sizes. Such an algorithm is called as an output-polynomial time algorithm. For the problems that we discuss in this paper, output-polynomial algorithms are not known. In the absence of such provably efficient algorithms, we view our algorithm as an efficient alternative which can perform well in practice.

The rest of this paper is organized as follows. In Section 2 we present a model of data mining which formally defines the theory extraction problem. In Section 3 we formulate our general algorithm in this setting. Section 4 adapts our algorithm to the well-studied problem of finding maximal frequent sets, and also gives some complexity-theoretic evidence of hardness of this problem. Empirical results on the behavior of the algorithm are also given. In Section 5 we adapt the general algorithm of Section 3 to the problem of finding keys of relations, and present some empirical results. Finally, in Section 6 we give a short conclusion.

2   Data mining as theory extraction

The model of knowledge discovery that we consider is the following [19, 23, 20]. Given a database $\mathbf{r}$, a language $\mathcal{L}$ for expressing properties or defining subgroups of the data, and a frequency criterion q for evaluating whether a sentence $\varphi \in \mathcal{L}$ defines a sufficiently large subclass of $\mathbf{r}$. The computational task is to find the theory of $\mathbf{r}$ with respect to $\mathcal{L}$ and q, i.e., the set $Th(\mathcal{L}, \mathbf{r}, q) = \{\varphi \in \mathcal{L} \mid q(\mathbf{r}, \varphi)$ is true$\}$.

We are not specifying any satisfaction relation for the sentences of $\mathcal{L}$ in $\mathbf{r}$: this task is taken care of by the frequency criterion q. For some applications, $q(\mathbf{r}, \varphi)$ could mean that φ is true or almost true in $\mathbf{r}$, or that φ defines (in some way) a sufficiently large or otherwise interesting subgroup of $\mathbf{r}$. The roots of this approach are in the use of *diagrams* of models in model theory (see, e.g., [7]). The approach has been used in various forms for example in [2, 8, 9, 16, 17, 21]. One should note that in contrast with, e.g., [8], our emphasis is on very simple representation languages.

Obviously, if $\mathcal{L}$ is infinite and $q(\mathbf{r}, \varphi)$ is satisfied for infinitely many sentences, (an explicit representation of) $Th(\mathcal{L}, \mathbf{r}, q)$ cannot be computed feasibly. Therefore for the above formulation to make sense, the language $\mathcal{L}$ has to be defined carefully. In case $\mathcal{L}$ is infinite, there are alternative ways of meaningfully defining feasible computations in terms of dynamic output size, but we do not concern ourselves with these scenarios. In this paper we assume that $\mathcal{L}$ is finite.

3 A randomized algorithm for computing $Th(\mathcal{L}, \mathbf{r}, q)$

We make the following assumption about language $\mathcal{L}$. There is a partial order $\preceq$ on the set of sentences of $\mathcal{L}$ such that q is monotone with respect to $\preceq$, that is, for all $\psi, \theta \in \mathcal{L}$ with $\theta \preceq \psi$ we have: if $q(\mathbf{r}, \psi)$, then $q(\mathbf{r}, \theta)$. [4] Denote by $rank(\psi)$ the *rank* of a sentence $\psi \in \mathcal{L}$, defined as follows. If for no $\theta \in \mathcal{L}$ we have $\theta \prec \psi$, then $rank(\psi) = 0$, otherwise $rank(\psi) = 1 + \max\{rank(\theta) \mid \theta \prec \psi\}$. For a sentence ψ, $rank(\psi)$ can be arbitrary large but finite. For $T \subset \mathcal{L}$, let T_i denote the set of the sentences of $\mathcal{L}$ with rank i.

The level-wise algorithm [23] for computing $Th = Th(\mathcal{L}, \mathbf{r}, q)$ proceeds by first computing the set Th_0 consisting of the sentences of rank 0 that are in Th. Then, assuming Th_i is known, it computes a set of *candidates*: sentences ψ with rank $i + 1$ such that all θ with $\theta \prec \psi$ are in Th. For each one of these candidates ψ, the algorithm calls the function q to check whether ψ really belongs to Th. This iterative procedure is performed until no more sentences in Th are found. This level-wise algorithm has been used in various forms in finding association rules, episodes, sequential rules, etc. [2, 3, 24, 23, 1, 13, 14, 25]. The drawback with this algorithm is that it always computes the whole set $Th(\mathcal{L}, \mathbf{r}, q)$, even in the cases where a condensed representation of Th using *most specific sentences* would be useful.

Given Th, a sentence $\psi \in Th$ is a *most specific* sentence of Th, if for no $\theta \in Th$ we have $\psi \prec \theta$. Denote by $MTh = MTh(\mathcal{L}, \mathbf{r}, q, \preceq)$ the set of most specific sentences of $Th(\mathcal{L}, \mathbf{r}, q)$ with respect to $\preceq$.

Our general algorithm for computing MTh is based on repeatedly computing new most specific sentences in Th. To compute one most specific sequence, we use the following randomized algorithm:

---

[4] Note that this description is a fairly severe one. For example, a q defined in terms of statistical significance does not satisfy this condition.

Algorithm A_Random_MSS Find a random most specific sentence from Th.

1. $i := 0$.
2. $\psi :=$ **true**.
3. While (there is an immediate specialization θ of ψ
   such that $q(\mathbf{r}, \theta)$ holds) do: select such a θ randomly and let $\psi := \theta$.
4. Output ψ.

The algorithm assumes that **true** $\in \mathcal{L}$, and proceeds to specialize it successively until a most specific sentence is found. In Step 2, if ψ is initialized with an arbitrary sentence $s \in Th$ instead of "true", then the algorithm will find a random most specific sentence s' such that $s \preceq s'$.

After the computation of one or more new most specific sentences in MTh, we compute the *minimal-orthogonal-elements* (abbr. *min-ortho-element*) with respect to the collection of most specific sentences found so far. Let S be the set of most specific sentences computed. A *minimal orthogonal element* with respect to S is a sentence ψ in $\mathcal{L}$, such that ψ is unrelated to all the sentences in S under $\preceq$ and for no sentence $\phi \prec \psi$, this property holds. The definition of minimal orthogonal elements is a natural extension of the minimal hypergraph transversal [6, 10]. Then we can show the following lemma:

Lemma 1 *Let S be a set of most specific sentences in MTh, and let T be the set of all minimal orthogonal elements with respect to S. Then, if there is a sentence γ in MTh which is not in S, then there is a sentence β in T such that $\beta \preceq \gamma$.*

Proof: Any new most specific sentence γ cannot be either above or below (with respect to $\preceq$) another most specific sentence. γ must therefore be unrelated to all the sentences in S. This means that either $\gamma \in T$ or there is a sentence $\gamma' \preceq \gamma$ that is also unrelated to all sentences in S. Since the rank of γ is finite the lemma follows. □

This property allows us to limit the search to these sentences which are above the min-ortho-elements with respect to $\preceq$. Denote by Algorithm *A_Random_MSS(ψ_{init})* the parameterized version of the Algorithm *A_Random_MSS*, which starts by initializing ψ with the sentence ψ_{init}. We can now give the general algorithm for finding all most specific sentences.

Algorithm All_MSS Finding all most specific sentences in Th.
   k_1 and k_2 are input parameters.

1. Run Algorithm *A_Random_MSS("true")* k_1 times and let S be the set of most specific sentences found.
2. While new most specific sentences are found:
   (a) Compute the set X of all *min-ortho-elements* with respect to S.
   (b) For each sentence $x \in X$:
       Run Algorithm *A_Random_MSS(x)*, k_2 times and add any new most specific sentence found to S.
3. Output S.

Theorem 2 *Given a database* **r**, *a language* $\mathcal{L}$, *a partial order* $\preceq$, *and a frequency criterion* q, *algorithm AlLMSS computes* $MTh(\mathcal{L}, \mathbf{r}, q, \preceq)$.

Proof: If there exist one most specific sentence, Step 1 results in a nonempty collection of most specific sentences. Let S be the collection of sentences, which are output in Step 3 at the end of the algorithm. Since the algorithm exited the while loop, it must be that in the last iteration of the while loop, S remained unchanged. By Lemma 1, if there is a most specific sentence γ not in S, there exist $x \in X$ such that $x \preceq \gamma$. So the algorithm *A_Random_MFS(x)* must have found at least one new maximal frequent set in the last iteration, a contradiction.

$\square$

Since the running time of the algorithm depends on k_1 and k_2, these values must be chosen suitably depending on the application of the algorithm.

Computing the min-ortho-elements is in general computationally non-trivial. In the problems we consider the problem reduces to the problem of computing the minimal traversals of a hypergraph, a problem for which no output polynomial algorithm is known [15]. We use a simple enumeration heuristic that attempts to cut down the number of sets that cannot be transversals. This algorithm is exponential in the worst case. In our experiments the randomized algorithm usually produces a good approximation to the collection MTh, so only a few iterations of the expensive transversal computation are needed. Also, note that the transversal computation does not involve the input data, but only elements of $\mathcal{L}$ instead; if the size of the input data is large, a complicated computation on $\mathcal{L}$ can still be cheaper than just reading the data once.

4 Finding frequent sets using the randomized algorithm

In this section, we discuss how to adapt the algorithms of the previous section to find maximal frequent sets of a $\{0,1\}$ matrix and threshold value σ. We first discuss association rules and how frequent sets arise in computation of association rules.

Given a 0/1 relation **r** with a set of attributes R (that is, a $\{0,1\}$ matrix with $|R|$ columns), an association rule is an expression $X \Rightarrow B$, where $X \subseteq R$ and $B \in R$. The intuitive meaning of such a rule is that if a row has an 1 in all attributes of X, then it tends also to have a 1 in column B.

An association rule has two values *support* and *confidence* associated with it, which are defined as follows. Given a set X of attributes of a relation **r**, *frequency* f(X,r) of X in **r** is the number of rows in **r** for which all attributes in X have a 1. The *support* of X in **r** is the fraction of these rows among all the rows of **r**. Given a rule $X \Rightarrow B$, the support of the rule is defined to be the support of $X \cup \{B\}$. The confidence of the rule is the fraction $f(X \cup \{B\}, \mathbf{r})/f(X, \mathbf{r})$.

The problem of mining association rules is to compute all association rules in a 0/1 relation such that the support of a rule is at least σ and the confidence at least γ. The first step in computing such association rules is to find all subsets of attributes (columns), whose support is at least σ. Such subsets are called the *frequent sets* of the relation **r** with threshold σ (or σ-frequent sets). A *maximal σ-frequent set* X of relation **r** is an σ-frequent set of **r** such that no proper superset of X is an σ-frequent set of **r**. The collection of all σ-frequent sets (resp. maximal σ-frequent sets) of relation **r** is denoted by $Fr(\mathbf{r}, \sigma)$ (resp. $MFr(\mathbf{r}, \sigma)$). Note that to identify all σ-frequent sets, it is enough to compute $MFr(\mathbf{r}, \sigma)$ because every frequent set is a subset of some maximal frequent set and conversely every subset of a maximal frequent set is a frequent set.

The computational problem that we study in this section is the following.

Problem 3 *Given a 0/1 relation **r** over attributes R, and a support value $\sigma \in [0, 1]$, find all maximal σ-frequent sets of **r**.*

We start by presenting two results which show the computational hardness of the above problem.

Theorem 4 *The problem of finding the number of σ-frequent sets of a given 0-1 relation **r** and a threshold $\sigma \in [0, 1]$ is #P-hard. In addition, the problem of deciding if there is a maximal σ-frequent set with at least t attributes for a given 0/1 relation **r**, and a threshold $\sigma \in [0, 1]$, is NP-complete.*

Proof: Finding the number of σ-frequent sets is shown to be #P-hard by reducing the problem of computing the number of satisfying assignments of a monotone-2CNF (shown to be #P-hard by [28]) to it.

Deciding if there is a maximal σ-frequent set with at least t attributes can be shown to be NP-complete by reducing the Balanced Bipartite Clique problem (known to be NP-complete, [12]), to it. □

This theorem rules out the possibility of an efficient algorithm which outputs the maximal frequent sets in the decreasing order of their size.

We now discuss a refinement of the algorithm of Section 3 for computing all maximal frequent sets. To use the framework of Section 3, we define $\mathcal{L} = \{X \mid X \subseteq R\}$, and let $q(\mathbf{r}, X)$ be true iff $s(X, \mathbf{r}) \geq \sigma$. Next, the relation $\preceq$ is defined by $X \preceq Y$ iff $X \subseteq Y$; it is easy to see that the monotonicity condition holds. We also have $X \preceq_1 Y$ iff $Y = X \cup \{A\}$ for some $A \in R$. A most specific sentence corresponds to a maximal frequent set.

A useful way to think about the maximal σ-frequent sets problem is the lattice that is formed by the subsets of R. The level i of the lattice includes all subsets of size i, and two subsets are connected if they are on consecutive levels and one is the subset of the other (see Figure 1.) Note that the collection of all maximal σ-frequent sets of a matrix and threshold σ, is an ideal of the boolean lattice over the set of columns (attributes) of the matrix. The lattice view makes also the drawbacks of the level-wise algorithm evident: it can be that Fr is large, but MFr is quite small.

To apply the general algorithm *A_Random_MSS*, we can use the lattice structure efficiently: the process can be seen as a random walk in the lattice. Given X, in order to select a random sentence/set Y such that $X \preceq_1 Y$ the only thing we have to do is to get a random element $A \in R \setminus X$ and let $Y = X \cup \{A\}$.

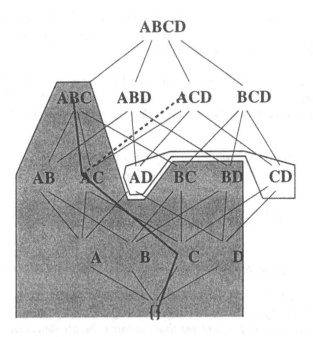

Fig. 1. A relation with four attributes. The shaded area represents the maximal σ-frequent sets found so far ($\{A, B, C\}, \{B, D\}$) and their subsets. The solid line represents a run of the algorithm for the permutation C, A, D, B. Any new maximal σ-frequent set must be a superset of $\{A, D\}$ or $\{C, D\}$.

Once a collection of maximal σ-frequent sets is found, any new maximal σ-frequent set cannot be subset or superset of a known maximal σ-frequent set. It follows that any new maximal σ-frequent set must include a set of attributes that is not a subset of any of the maximal σ-frequent sets found so far. Similarly for any new maximal σ-frequent set, there must be set of attributes such that it intersects every known maximal σ-frequent set and does not intersect the the new maximal σ-frequent set. We can express these conditions more succinctly using the concept of the *minimal transversal* of a hypergraph. A *minimal* transversal of a hypergraph is a transversal of the hypergraph with the property that no proper subset of it is also a transversal. Therefore, if we view a given collection C of maximal σ-frequent sets as a hypergraph, then any new maximal σ-frequent set F is a transversal of the hypergraph whose edges are the complements of the σ-frequent sets in C. In fact the following lemma is the equivalent of Lemma 1.

Lemma 5 *Let C be a collection of maximal σ-frequent sets of a relation, and F be a maximal σ-frequent set not in C. Then there exists a minimal transversal T of the hypergraph defined by the complements of the sets in C such that $T \subseteq F$.*

Therefore to discover a new maximal σ-frequent set, we have to start with a minimal transversal of the above type and extend it to a maximal σ-frequent set. We can now present the algorithm in detail. First we give the algorithm

A_Random_MFS, which finds a single random maximal σ-frequent set containing a given set S of attributes. This algorithm corresponds to the parameterized version of the algorithm *A_Random_MSS*.

Algorithm A_Random_MFS(S) Given a $\{0,1\}$ matrix M with attributes $R = \{A_1, \ldots, A_{|R|}\}$ and n tuples (rows), a threshold σ and the set S of attributes $\{A_{S_1}, \ldots, A_{S_l}\}$; find a maximal σ-frequent set F containing all the attributes in S.

1. Find a permutation p of $(1, \ldots, |R|)$ such that for $i \leq |S|$, $p(i) = S_i$, and for $i > |S|$, p is a random permutation of the attributes in the set $R \setminus S$.
2. Set $X = \emptyset$.
3. For $i = 1$ to $|R|$:
   (a) If $X \cup \{A_{p(i)}\}$ is a σ-frequent set, add $A_{p(i)}$ to X.
4. Return X

The following theorem shows the basic properties of the algorithm.

Theorem 6 *Let S be a σ-frequent set of relation $\mathbf{r}$. Then the algorithm A_Random_MFS(S) finds the lexicographically first (according to the ordering given by p) maximal σ-frequent set that contains the attributes in S. Its running time complexity is $O(|\mathbf{r}|)$.*

Proof: The basic operation of the algorithm is to add a new attribute in the σ-frequent set X. We keep the set of rows $\alpha(X, \mathbf{r})$ that support X as a vector $s = (s_1, \ldots, s_m)$. When attribute R_i is considered, we take the intersection of s and the i-th column of $\mathbf{r}$. This is the support of the set $X \cup R_i$. This process takes $O(m)$ time, so the total running time of the algorithm is $O(m|R|) = O(|\mathbf{r}|)$, linear to the size of the relation $\mathbf{r}$.

Note that with respect to a given permutation, a maximal frequent set F_1 is lexicographically smaller than another maximal frequent set F_2, if the smallest attribute (w.r.t. the order of attributes defined using permutation) in the symmetric difference of F_1 and F_2 is in F_1.

It is clear that the output set X is a maximal σ-frequent set. Assume that it is not the lexicographically first maximal σ-frequent set with respect to the ordering p that contains S. S has to be a frequent set itself and all the attributes of S are in the beginning of p. So all will be included in X in Step 3. Thereafter, the algorithm will add greedily into X attributes in the order given by p. Let $LF = \{R_{LF_1}, \ldots, R_{LF_k}\}$ be the lexicographically first maximal σ-frequent set with the attributes sorted according to p, and let P_i be the first attribute that is included to LF but not X. But the set $\{R_{LF_1}, \ldots, R_i\}$ is a frequent set, and therefore the algorithm would add P_i to X when it was considered. It follows that at the end of the algorithm F will represent the lexicographically smallest maximal σ-frequent set containing S. $\square$

The complete algorithm uses algorithm *A_Random_MFS*, and finds all maximal frequent sets. After finding some of the maximal frequent sets, it computes all the minimal transversals of the hypergraph as defined in the lemma, to focus the search on undiscovered maximal frequent sets. In the algorithm below, we omit the details of how transversals are computed.

Algorithm All_MFS Given a {0,1} relation **r** in the form of an $n \times m$ matrix M and a threshold σ, find all maximal σ-frequent sets. Parameters k_1, k_2 are positive integers.

1. Preprocess the matrix to remove all the columns (i.e. attributes) in which the number of 1's is less than σn.
2. Run algorithm *A_Random_MFS(ϕ)* k_1 times and let C be the set of maximal σ-frequent sets discovered in these runs.
3. While new maximal frequent sets are found:
   (a) Compute the set X of all minimal transversals of the hypergraph defined by complements of sets in C.
   (b) For each $x \in X$:
      Run algorithm *A_Random_MFS(x)* k_2 times and add any new maximal frequent set found to C.
4. Output S.

The following theorem is a corollary of Algorithm *All_MFS* and Theorem 2.

Theorem 7 *Given a 0/1 matrix M, and a threshold value σ, algorithm All_MFS finds all maximal σ-frequent sets of the input matrix M.*

We have implemented the algorithm *A_Random_MFS*, and we used the implementation to find maximal frequent sets in real data sets taken from the University of Helsinki. In these data sets each column represents a course offered, and the rows represent students. A given column has a 1 for each student that took this course and 0 for the rest. We have used two different threshold values, and we try to determine the rate at which the probabilistic algorithm finds new maximal frequent sets. We compare our results with the output of the level-wise algorithm ([1, 2]). These data sets are quite small for any serious data mining application. Our aim is not so much to claim that the randomized method would be a good way of computing maximal σ-frequent sets; rather we want to check the feasibility of the approach.

The preliminary results of our experiments are summarized in the following tables. In the first table we present the runs of the randomized algorithm. The two datasets have sizes of 2670×20 and 2836×129 respectively, and the threshold value σ was set to 100 and 400 rows. We run the algorithm for 500 to 4000 times before collecting the different maximal σ-frequent sets that had been found so far. The number of different maximal σ-frequent sets found is shown in the column *MFSs* found. The next column shows the total number of maximal σ-frequent sets, as reported by the level-wise algorithm. In the second table we tabulate the results of the level-wise algorithm runs on the same datasets.

Matrix Size	σ	Runs	MFSs found	MFSs present	Time (sec)
2670 × 20	100	500	78	93	15
2670 × 20	100	1000	86	93	26
2670 × 20	100	2000	88	93	50
2670 × 20	100	4000	89	93	99
2670 × 20	400	100	23	23	5
2670 × 20	400	500	23	23	14
2836 × 129	100	500	178	315	56
2836 × 129	100	1000	244	315	108
2836 × 129	100	2000	283	315	208
2836 × 129	100	4000	303	315	409
2836 × 129	400	100	27	27	18
2836 × 129	400	500	27	27	64

Matrix Size	σ	MFSs found	Time (sec)
2670 × 20	100	93	355
2670 × 20	400	23	6
2836 × 129	100	315	1512
2836 × 129	400	27	10

The implementation of our algorithm is in C++, and the running times for both algorithms were measured on a SPARCstation 5.

The experiments show that the randomized algorithm finds a big fraction of all the maximal frequent sets while the number of iterations is only about 5 times the total number of maximal frequent sets. In addition the randomized algorithm clearly outperforms the level-wise algorithm as long as the size of the maximal σ-frequent sets is relatively large. In our datasets this happens for a threshold value of 100.

However, as the number of iterations increase the number of discovered maximal frequent sets does not increase in proportion, but "levels off". By observing the datasets, we also noticed that the level-wise algorithm performs equivalently or slightly better when the size of maximal frequent sets are small.

Our observations suggest that by increasing the number of runs to a very large number, the advantage of finding more MFS is lost in the increase of the running time. So a better alternative can be to run the randomized algorithm a fixed number of times and then use the transversal computation to focus the search. We have implemented the algorithm for transversal computation and included it in an implementation of the algorithm *All_MFS*. We are currently testing it with more examples to see how much the computation of transversals help in speeding up the computation of all maximal frequent sets.

5 Finding Minimal Keys in Databases

In this section we discuss the computational problem of finding all minimal keys of a relational database and propose an algorithm for the problem based on the general algorithm of Section 3. We begin by defining what we mean by keys and describe an application in which it is useful to find all minimal keys. Let R be a relation schema, and $\mathbf{r}$ a relation over R. Then a set $X \subseteq R$ is a *key* of $\mathbf{r}$, if no two rows of $\mathbf{r}$ agree on every attribute in X. A *minimal key* is a key such that no proper subset of it is a key. Note that every key must contain some minimal key and conversely every superset of a minimal key is a key. Therefore the collection of all minimal keys of a relational database is a succinct representation of the set of all keys of the database. The computational problem that we consider here is the following:

Problem 8 *Given a relational database, compute all minimal keys that exist currently.*

The knowledge of all minimal keys in the relation instance can help in semantic query optimization. In this process, a database manager substitutes a computationally expensive query by a semantically equivalent query which can be processed much faster ([4]).

However, the problem of finding the minimal keys turns out to be a difficult one.

Theorem 9 *The problem of finding the number of minimal keys of a relation* r *is #P-hard.*

Proof: We present two polynomial time reductions. The first reduction is from the problem of computing the number of minimal vertex covers of a graph to the problem of computing the number of minimal set covers of a family of sets. The second reduction is from the problem of computing the number of minimal set covers of a family of sets to the problem of computing the number of minimal keys if the database. Since the problem of computing the number of minimal vertex covers of a graph is known to be #P hard [28], the theorem follows.

Recall that a vertex cover of a graph G is a set of vertices of G such that every edge of G is incident on at least one vertex in the set. Given a graph G with n vertices and m edges, define a family of sets $S_1, ..., S_n$ each of which is a subset of the set $\{1, 2, ..., m\}$, as follows. The set S_i has element j iff the jth edge of the graph is incident on the ith vertex. Note that a collection of sets $S_{i_1}, ..., S_{i_c}$ (for some c) from the family is a minimal set cover iff the set of vertices $\{i_1, ..., i_c\}$ is a minimal vertex cover of G. Therefore the number of minimal vertex covers of G is same as the number of minimal set covers of the family. This completes the first reduction.

We now discuss the second reduction. Given a family of sets $S_1, ..., S_n$ each of which is a subset of the universe set $\{1, 2, ..., m\}$, construct a relational database as follows. The database has m fields $f_1, ..., f_m$ and $n + 1$ records $R_0, ..., R_n$. The record R_0 will have value 0 in every field. For $1 \leq i \leq n$ and $1 \leq j \leq m$, the field f_j of record R_i will have value i if element i is present in the set S_j otherwise it will have value 0. A collection $S_{i_1}, ..., S_{i_c}$ is a *minimal* set cover of the family iff the set of fields $\{f_{i_1}, ..., f_{i_c}\}$ is a *minimal* key of the database. Therefore the number of minimal set covers of the family is same as the number of minimal keys of the database. □

We now discuss our algorithm for discovering all minimal keys of a relation. To keep an analogy with the problem of discovering maximal frequent sets, we will use the notion of an *anti-key*. An *anti-key* in a relation is a set of fields which is complement of some key of the relational database. A maximal anti-key is an anti-key such that no proper superset of it is an anti-key. Note that a set of fields is a maximal anti-key iff its complement is a minimal key. Therefore the problem of finding all minimal keys of a relation is equivalent to the problem of finding all maximal anti-keys of the relation. Note that the collection of all maximal anti-keys of a relation forms an ideal of the boolean lattice over the fields of the relation.

We first present an algorithm for finding a random maximal anti-key containing a given set of fields.

Algorithm A_Random_MAS(S) Given a relation r in the form of an $n \times m$ matrix M and a set $S = \{f_{i_1}, ..., f_{i_s}\}$ of s fields of the relation, find a random maximal anti-key which contains all the fields in the set, provided there exists one.

1. Find a permutation p of $(1, \ldots, m)$ such that for $i \le s$, $p(i) = i_s$, and for $i > s$, p is a random permutation of the numbers $\{1, \ldots, m\} \setminus \{i_1, \ldots, i_s\}$.
2. Set $A = \emptyset$.
3. For $i = 1$ to m:
   (a) If $A \cup \{f_{p(i)}\}$ is an anti-key, add $f_{p(i)}$ to A.
4. Return A

Theorem 10 *Given a relation r and a set S of fields, suppose there exist an anti-key which contains all the fields in S. Then the algorithm A_Random_MAK outputs the lex-smallest maximal anti-key with respect to the random permutation and which contains all the fields in S. The running time of the algorithm is $O(nm)$, assuming that the time to access any field of any record is constant.*

We now give the complete algorithm for finding all maximal anti-keys, which is analogous to the algorithm for finding all maximal frequent sets. Again we omit the details of how to find all minimal transversals of a hypergraph. First we point out that an analogue of the Lemma 5 holds also for the case of maximal anti-keys.

Lemma 11 *Given a collection C of maximal anti-keys of a relation, let K be a maximal anti-key not in C. Then there exists a minimal transversal T of the hypergraph defined by the complements of the sets in C such that $T \subseteq K$.*

Algorithm All_MAK Given a relational database in the form of $n \times m$ matrix M and find all maximal anti-keys. Parameters k_1, k_2, which are positive integers.

1. Run algorithm *A_Random_MAK(ϕ)* k_1 times and let C be the set of maximal anti-keys discovered in these runs.
2. While new anti-keys are being found:
   (a) Compute the set X of all minimal transversals of the hypergraph defined by complements of subsets in C.
   (b) For each $x \in X$: Run algorithm *A_Random_MAK(X)* k_2 times and add any new maximal anti-key found to C.
3. Output C.

We can now claim the following theorem.

Theorem 12 *Given a relational database* **r**, *algorithm All_MAK finds all current maximal anti-keys (and hence minimal keys) of* **r**.

In this section we present some experimental results obtained from an earlier implementation of a somewhat different algorithm to compute all keys. This algorithm uses the same general scheme, but attempts to compute minimal keys directly, instead of computing maximal anti-keys first. We implemented this algorithm, *All_K* in C++. To test the algorithm, we used two different relations with extremely complicated real data, which happen have a lot of keys, and four artificial relations, three of which have few keys and 1 has many keys. The size of the keys ranges from one to ten attributes. Parameters k_1, k_2 where set to 100.

Relation size	Number of keys present	Time (sec)
58×12	58	30
128×22	1258	6375
100×10	1	1
100×11	2	2
10000×11	2	388
11×20	1024	604

We remark that the second test case is an exceptionally complex one in terms of the size and structure of minimal keys of the input relation. We are planning more experiments to see the performance for large inputs and with respect to the level-wise algorithm.

6 Discussion

We have given a randomized algorithm for computing the representation of a theory in terms of its most specific sentences. We have also proposed an approach based on transversal computation to focus the search of the randomized algorithm on undiscovered sentences. This can be combined with the randomized algorithm to give an algorithm which can (provably) find all the most specific sentences. We have illustrated the application of the algorithm in two important data mining scenarios: computing all maximal σ-frequent sets of a 0/1 relation with threshold σ and computing all minimal keys of a relation.

We have conducted some experiments with our algorithms which indicate the benefits of using randomization over the earlier known level-wise approach. Though the preliminary results of the experiments show our algorithms to be promising, a lot more remains to be done to substantiate these promises. These include the scalability analysis and the tradeoff of transversal computation for focusing search against the level wise approach.

An issue we have not explored yet is to find a more efficient way to use transversals to guide the search. Currently we compute all the minimal transversals from scratch every time some new sentences is discovered. Some alternative strategies may result in faster algorithms. One possibility is to compute only one transversal at a time instead of all of them. Another possibility is to avoid computing the minimal transversals from scratch every time. Since the hypergraph (whose minimal transversals are computed) in a given iteration contains the hypergraphs for all previous iterations, it may be possible to compute the new set of minimal transversals by scanning the old set and dropping those which are no longer transversals and then computing only the newly formed transversals.

Another interesting possibility we plan to explore is to use the randomized algorithm in combination with the level-wise algorithm. The randomized algorithm for maximal σ-frequent sets can be used to select the right range for σ, as a preprocessing step to the level-wise algorithm of Agrawal et. al. [2].

References

1. R. Agrawal, T. Imielinski, and A. Swami. Mining association rules between sets of items in large databases. In *Proceedings of ACM SIGMOD Conference on Management of Data (SIGMOD'93)*, pages 207 – 216, May 1993.

2. R. Agrawal, H. Mannila, R. Srikant, H. Toivonen, and A. I. Verkamo. Fast discovery of association rules. In U. M. Fayyad, G. Piatetsky-Shapiro, P. Smyth, and R. Uthurusamy, editors, *Advances in Knowledge Discovery and Data Mining*, pages 307 – 328. AAAI Press, Menlo Park, CA, 1996.

3. R. Agrawal and R. Srikant. Mining sequential patterns. In *International Conference on Data Engineering*, Mar. 1995.

4. S. Bell. Deciding distinctness of query results by discovered constraints. *Manuscript*.

5. S. Bell and P. Brockhausen. Discovery of data dependencies in relational databases. Technical Report LS-8 14, Universität Dortmund, Fachbereich Informatik, Lehrstuhl VIII, Künstliche Intelligenz, 1995.

6. C. Berge. *Hypergraphs. Combinatorics of Finite Sets*. North-Holland Publishing Company, Amsterdam, 1989.

7. C. C. Chang and H. J. Keisler. *Model Theory*. North-Holland, Amsterdam, 1973. 3rd ed., 1990.

8. L. De Raedt and M. Bruynooghe. A theory of clausal discovery. In *Proceedings of the Thirteenth International Joint Conference on Artificial Intelligence (IJCAI-93)*, pages 1058 – 1053, Chambéry, France, 1993. Morgan Kaufmann.

9. L. De Raedt and S. Džeroski. First-order jk-clausal theories are PAC-learnable. *Artificial Intelligence*, 70:375 – 392, 1994.

10. T. Eiter and G. Gottlob. Identifying the minimal transversals of a hypergraph and related problems. *SIAM Journal on Computing*, 24(6):1278 – 1304, Dec. 1995.

11. U. M. Fayyad, G. Piatetsky-Shapiro, P. Smyth, and R. Uthurusamy, editors. *Advances in Knowledge Discovery and Data Mining*. AAAI Press, Menlo Park, CA, 1996.

12. M. Garey and D. Johnson. *Computers and Intractability - A Guide to the Theory of NP-Completeness*. W.H. Freeman, New York, 1979.

13. J. Han and Y. Fu. Discovery of multiple-level association rules from large databases. In *Proceedings of the 21st International Conference on Very Large Data Bases (VLDB'95)*, pages 420 – 431, Zurich, Swizerland, 1995.

14. M. Houtsma and A. Swami. Set-oriented mining of association rules. Research Report RJ 9567, IBM Almaden Research Center, San Jose, California, October 1993.

15. D. S. Johnson, M. Yannakakis, and C. H. Papadimitriou. On generating all maximal independent sets. *Information Processing Letters*, 27:119–123, 1988.

16. J.-U. Kietz and S. Wrobel. Controlling the complexity of learning in logic through syntactic and task-oriented models. In S. Muggleton, editor, *Inductive Logic Programming*, pages 335 – 359. Academic Press, London, 1992.

17. W. Kloesgen. Efficient discovery of interesting statements in databases. *Journal of Intelligent Information Systems*, 4(1):53 – 69, 1995.

18. A. J. Knobbe and P. W. Adriaans. Discovering foreign key relations in relational databases. In *Workshop Notes of the ECML-95 Workshop on Statistics, Machine Learning, and Knowledge Discovery in Databases*, pages 94 – 99, Heraklion, Crete, Greece, Apr. 1995.

19. H. Mannila. Aspects of data mining. In *Workshop Notes of the ECML-95 Workshop on Statistics, Machine Learning, and Knowledge Discovery in Databases*, pages 1–6, Heraklion, Crete, Greece, Apr. 1995.

20. H. Mannila. Data mining: machine learning, statistics, and databases. In *Proceedings of the 8th International Conference on Scientific and Statistical Database Management, Stockholm*, 1996. To appear.

21. H. Mannila and K.-J. Räihä. Design by example: An application of Armstrong relations. *Journal of Computer and System Sciences*, 33(2):126 – 141, 1986.

22. H. Mannila and K.-J. Räihä. Algorithms for inferring functional dependencies. *Data & Knowledge Engineering*, 12(1):83 – 99, Feb. 1994.

23. H. Mannila and H. Toivonen. On an algorithm for finding all interesting sentences. In *Cybernetics and Systems Research '96*, Vienna, Austria, Apr. 1996. To appear.

24. H. Mannila, H. Toivonen, and A. I. Verkamo. Discovering frequent episodes in sequences. In *Proceedings of the First International Conference on Knowledge Discovery and Data Mining (KDD'95)*, pages 210 – 215, Montreal, Canada, Aug. 1995.

25. A. Savasere, E. Omiecinski, and S. Navathe. An efficient algorithm for mining association rules in large databases. In *Proceedings of the 21st International Conference on Very Large Data Bases (VLDB'95)*, pages 432 – 444, Zurich, Swizerland, 1995.

26. J. Schlimmer. Using learned dependencies to automatically construct sufficient and sensible editing views. In *Knowledge Discovery in Databases, Papers from the 1993 AAAI Workshop (KDD'93)*, pages 186 – 196, Washington, D.C., 1993.

27. J. D. Ullman. *Principles of Database and Knowledge-Base Systems*, volume I. Computer Science Press, Rockville, MD, 1988.

28. L. G. Valiant. The complexity of enumeration and reliability problems. *SIAM Journal on Computing*, 8(3):410–421, 1979.

A Formal Foundation for Distributed Workflow Execution Based on State Charts

Dirk Wodtke and Gerhard Weikum

Department of Computer Science, University of the Saarland
P.O. Box 151150, D–66041 Saarbruecken, Germany
E–mail: {wodtke,weikum}@cs.uni–sb.de, WWW: http://www–dbs.cs.uni–sb.de/

Abstract. This paper provides a formal foundation for distributed workflow executions. The state chart formalism is adapted to the needs of a workflow model in order to establish a basis for both correctness reasoning and run–time support for complex and large–scale workflow applications. To allow for the distributed execution of a workflow across different workflow servers, which is required for scalability and organizational decentralization, a method for the partitioning of workflow specifications is developed. It is proven that the partitioning preserves the original state chart's behavior.

1 Introduction

Workflow management is a rapidly growing research and development area of very high practical relevance [GHS95, Mo96, VB96, WfMC95, Sh96]. Typical examples of (semi–automated) workflows are the processing of a credit request in a bank, the editorial handling and refereeing process for papers in an electronic journal, or the medical treatment of patients in a hospital. Informally, a workflow consists of a set of activities with explicitly specified control and data flow between the activities. An activity may invoke a transaction or some specific application (e.g., a portfolio assessment program), or it may simply prompt a human user for intellectual work. The results of an activity are propagated back to the workflow and may drive the further control flow. Activities are assigned to execution roles, which are dynamically filled by automated or human actors depending on the required skills and competence. Presently, virtually all commercial systems and most of the research prototypes lack a mathematically rigorous foundation, so that formal reasoning about the correctness of workflow executions is infeasible.

1.1 Problem Statement

The specification of a workflow is usually done via high–level graphical interfaces, e.g., by drawing nodes and arcs. This specification must be mapped into an internal representation that serves as the basis for execution. In many workflow management systems, the underlying internal representation uses an ad hoc model and thus lacks capabilities for formal correctness reasoning. In contrast, general–purpose specification formalisms for dynamic systems such as Petri nets, state charts, temporal logic, or process algebras, which are pursued in various research projects and a few products, come with a rich theory and thus provide an excellent basis for formal proofs. For the work in this paper we have adopted the method of state and activity charts by Harel et al. [Ha87a, Ha87b, Ha88, Ha90, i–Log91, HN95], which is perceived by practitioners as more intuitive and easier to learn than Petri nets yet has an equally rigorous semantics. In particular, state chart specifications are amenable to model checking [McM93, HK94], so that critical workflow properties that are expressible in temporal logic can be formally verified; an example would be that a credit request must be rejected if it turns out that the customer has insufficient collaterals.

Formal reasoning about specifications implicitly assumes a centralized execution model; there is no notion of distribution, interoperating workflow engines, and so on. So tools for formal reasoning must have access to the complete workflow specification in a uniform representation, regardless of whether the workflow may in reality span different autonomous business units of an enterprise or even different enterprises. In fact, however, distributed, decentralized execution of workflows is a mandatory requirement for complex, large–scale applications for two reasons. First, such applications may involve a very large number of concurrent workflow instances which impose a high load on the workflow engine. Consequently, scalability and availability considerations dictate that the overall workflow processing be distributed across multiple workflow engines that run on different servers, and this workload partitioning may itself require the partitioning of individual workflows. Secondly, whenever a workflow spans multiple business units that operate in a largely autonomous manner, it may be required that those parts of a workflow that are under the responsibility of a certain unit are managed on a server of that unit. Thus, the partitioning and distribution of a workflow may fall out naturally from the organizational decentralization.

1.2 Contribution of the Paper

So there seems to be an inherent incompatibility between the centralized view of tools for formal reasoning and the need for decentralized, distributed execution in a real–life setting, and the question arises as to how significant or insignificant formal proofs are when their underlying model deviates substantially from the actual execution. This paper aims to reconcile the centralized specification and distributed execution views by providing theoretical underpinnings for transforming a specification into a distributed execution scheme within the formal framework of state charts. To this end, we proceed in three major steps and make the following contributions:

1. We first develop a simplified operational semantics of state and activity charts that is tailored to the use for workflow specification. We assume that a workflow can be specified completely in this "canonical" form; specifications that are given in another language (e.g., in a scripting language such as FlowMark's FDL) can be converted into our state and activity chart dialect.

2. We assume that activities are intellectually assigned to business units according to their roles and responsibilities. Then a state and activity chart is partitioned such that all activities and corresponding states of one business unit constitute one partition. In this transformation process, we make use of the notion of orthogonal components of a state chart, which is the standard form to express parallel execution: the resulting partitions form orthogonal components. This representation is directly amenable to distributed execution.

3. The transformation process is formally defined as a mapping between state charts, which we refer to as "orthogonalization". The paper's major theoretical result is a theorem that this mapping is a homomorphism between state charts, which means that the transformation preserves the behavior of the specification. Thus, all formally derived properties of the centralized specification do provably carry over to the distributed execution scheme as well.

The work reported here is embedded in the MENTOR project [WWWK96a, WWWK96b] on "middleware for enterprise–wide workflow management" with emphasis on banking applications. This project uses the commercial state chart tool STATEMATE [Ha90, i–Log91] along with our own "glueing" software as a local workflow engine, and combines multiple instances of this engine for distributed execution using the TP monitor Tuxedo. The idea of transforming a centralized state chart specification into an equivalent collection of orthogonal components that is amenable to distributed execution has been introduced informally in [WWWK96a]; in the current paper we develop the formal underpinnings for this approach, thus justifying that centralized correctness reasoning and decentralized execution can indeed be reconciled. A formal approach with similar goals, albeit in a Petri net setting and unrelated to workflow, is presented in [Ho91]. However, this approach is extremely complex and restricted to simple place/transition nets (as opposed to richer Petri net variants such as predicate/transition nets).

The outline of the paper is as follows. Section 2 is an informal overview of state and activity charts. Section 3 gives the syntax and operational semantics of our simplified, workflow–specific state chart version. Section 4 presents the orthogonalization and partitioning of state charts, and develops the proof that this mapping is a homomorphism. Section 5 discusses further practical aspects of this approach. Due to length restrictions, some of the simpler definitions are given in an informal style in the paper. Full details can be found in [WW96].

2 Overview of the State Chart Specification Method

State and activity charts were originally developed for reactive systems (e.g., embedded control systems in automobiles) and have been quite successful in this area. They comprise two dual views of a specification.

Activities reflect the functional decomposition of a system and denote the "active" components of a specification; they correspond directly to the activities of a workflow. An *activity chart* specifies the data flow between activities, in the form of a directed graph with data items as arc annotations.

State charts reflect the behavior of a system in that they specify the control flow between activities. A state chart is essentially a finite state machine with a distinguished initial state and transitions driven by Event–Condition–Action rules (ECA rules). Each transition arc between states is annotated with an ECA triple. A transition from state X to state Y fires if the specified event E occurs and the specified condition C holds. The effect is that state X is left, state Y is entered, and the specified action A is executed. Conditions and actions are expressed in terms of data item variables, for example, those that are specified for the data flow in the corresponding activity chart; conditions and events may also refer to states and the modification of variables by means of special predicates like "in(s)" and "ch(v)" where s is a state and v is a variable. In addition, an action A can explicitly start or stop an activity and can generate an event E or set a condition C. ECA rules of this kind are notated in the form E[C]/A. Each of the three components may be empty. If all components are empty, then a transition can fire immediately; that is, a state change is possible without any precondition. Every state change in a state chart execution is viewed as one timestep; thus, state changes induce a discrete time dimension.

Two important additional features of state charts are *nested states* and *orthogonal components*. Nesting of states means that a state can itself contain an entire state chart. The semantics is that upon entering the higher–level state, the initial state of the embedded

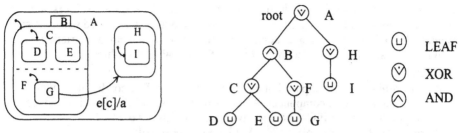

Fig. 1: Example of a state chart and its corresponding state tree

lower–level state chart is automatically entered, and upon leaving the higher–level state all embedded lower–level states are left. The possibility of nesting states is especially useful for the refinement of specifications during the design process, but this is not further considered in this paper. Orthogonal components denote the parallel execution of two state charts that are embedded in the same higher–level state (where the entire state chart can be viewed as a single top–level state). Both components enter their initial state simultaneously, and the transitions in the two components proceed in parallel, subject to the preconditions for a transition to fire.

The left portion of Fig. 1 shows an example chart with states A through I. Initial states are marked by an arc without source, and orthogonal components are separated by a dashed line within their corresponding higher–level state. For example, C and F are orthogonal components inside B, with D and G as their initial states. Only one of the transitions, namely, from G to H, has an explicit transition condition "e[c]/a".

3 Syntax and Operational Semantics of State Charts

In this section, we define the syntax and the operational semantics of a simplified version of state charts that is "tailored" to our application area of workflow management. Operational semantics of the full–fledged state chart formalism have been developed, for example, in [Ha87a, HN95, Hu88] (see [vB94] for a survey). However, these are unnecessarily complex for our purpose, mutually incompatible, and fall short of intuitive comprehensibility. For example, to cover a broad spectrum of application areas, an intricate timing model has been incorporated into these operational semantics that allows executing multiple "micro–step" actions within one time step. However, according to our experience with workflow applications, workflow specifications do not need the semantics of "micro steps" or related concepts (such as "chain reactions" within a step), but are served best by a "synchronous time model" in the sense of [HN95]. Thus, the following considerations, rather than inventing yet another state chart interpretation, aim to adapt the state chart formalism to the needs of a workflow model.

3.1 Syntax of State Charts

Definition 1: A state tree S_tree is a triple (S, types, acts), where
– S is a set of states,
– types is a function which defines for each state its type:
  $types_S$: S → {AND, XOR, LEAF},
– act_S is a function which maps each state onto its corresponding activity:
  act_S: S → Act.

The function act_S, which is not shown in Fig. 1 , defines an assignment of states to activities. In the workflow setting considered here, states capture the processing states of a workflow (e.g., waiting for the third review in an electronic submission workflow). A state is assigned to the activity that is in progress or about to be activated when the state is entered; note that assigning a state to exactly one activity is not a restriction, since activities can also be nested according to their functional relationships.

Definition 2:
- A *transition label*, is composed of an event component, E, a condition component, C, and an action component, A, and is written as: E[C]/A. E and A may be empty; in this case or if C=true, the trivial components are omitted.
- A *transition* $t = (s_1, s_2, lbl) \in (2^S \times S \times L)$ is composed of:
  - a set of source states, s_1, which is either a singleton or empty (i.e., $|s_1| \leq 1$),
  - a target state, s_2,
  - a transition label, lbl.

- A transition is called a *default transition* if source(t)=$\emptyset$.

The formal definition of the syntax of events, conditions, actions, and expressions is given in [WW96]. For example, there are events en(s) and conditions in(s) indicating that state s has been entered or is currently entered, respectively, and an event ch(el) indicating that element el has changed its value, and so on. These elements can be composed by using the operators of the propositional calculus to form expressions in a straightforward manner.

Definition 3: A *state chart* is a pair (S_tree, T), where
- S_tree is a tree of states,
- T is a set of transitions such that for each non–leaf state s the following holds:
  - if s is of type XOR, there exists exactly one default transition which has one of its children as its target,
  - if s is of type AND, its children must not be targets of default transitions.

The children of AND type states are referred to as orthogonal components (e.g., C and F in Fig. 1).

Note that the definition of activity charts is straightforward and will not be needed explicitly in the following. Informally, activity charts differ from state charts in that they have data flow connectors between activities instead of transitions between states, and activities are assigned to "modules", which in turn correspond to the servers of the various business units in an enterprise–wide workflow.

3.2 Operational Semantics of State Charts

We define the operational semantics of state charts in terms of "executing" a finite state machine, i.e., by identifying: (a) a set of states, (b) a state transition relation, (c) a set of initial states, and (d) a set of final states. With regard to state charts, parameter (a) is the set of *system configurations* which will be defined in Definition 10; parameter (b) is the *step function* which will be given by Definition 11; parameter (c) is the *initial system configuration* which will be defined in Definition 10; parameter (d) is not explicitly defined for state charts since the state chart execution does not necessarily need to terminate. Informally, we consider a state configuration as final when no transitions can fire anymore (regardless of further "external stimuli", i.e, user input).

Definition 4: Let S be a state chart. A *state configuration* cf of S is a set of states of S such that the following constraints hold:
- the root of the state tree of S is in cf,
- for each state which is in cf and of type AND, all its children are in cf,
- for each state which is in cf and of type XOR, exactly one of its children is in cf.

At each discrete point of time during the state chart execution, the state configuration denotes the set of currently entered states. The *initial state configuation*, cf_0, contains the root state, all children of type AND states which are in the initial state configuration, and one child of each type XOR state which is in the initial state configuration and which has children. In Fig. 1 the initial state configuration, cf_0, is {A, B, C, D, F, G}.

Definition 5: Let S be a state chart. Given the sets of primitive (i.e., explicitly named) conditions, C_p, primitive events, E_p, and variables, V_p, a *context* ct of S is a mapping of these conditions, events, and variables onto values:

$ct : C_p \cup E_p \cup V_p \rightarrow$ {true, false, generated} $\cup$ INT $\cup$ { $\perp$ }

where $\perp$ denotes the value "undefined".

The *initial context*, ct_0, is defined as false for primitive conditions and undefined (i.e., not generated) for primitive events and variables unless their initial values have not been set explicitly. For a given context, the values of expressions over variables and event as well as condition names can be computed inductively in a straightforward manner. This evaluation of expressions is done by the function *eval*.

A state configuration changes whenever at least one transition fires. In order to find out whether a transition fires at a given state configuration, two aspects need to be considered. First, one has to check whether the transition's source state is in the current state configuration. Second, it has to be determined whether the current values of the event and condition components of its transition label permit its firing, i.e., the event component has to evaluate to "generated" and the condition component has to evaluate to "true" under the eval function for the current context.

Definition 6: Given a state configuration cf_i, and a context ct_i, $i \geq 0$, a transition t=(src, trgt, E[C]/A), $t \in T$, *fires at timestep i* if and only if one of the following conditions holds:

- if src $\in cf_i \wedge$ eval(E, cf_i, ct_i) = generated $\wedge$ eval(C, cf_i, ct_i) = true (6.1)

- if src = $\emptyset$ and there exists a transition firing at the same step
  which has the type XOR parent of trgt as its target, (6.2)

- if src = $\emptyset$ and there exists a transition firing at the same step
  which has the type AND grandparent of trgt as its target. (6.3)

Informally, a transition fires in three cases: its source state is element of the current state configuration and its transition label evaluates to "generated" and to "true", respectively (6.1) (e.g., in Figure 1 the transition from G to H fires if G is in the current state configuration and the event and condition component of the transition label evaluate to "generated" and to "true", respectively); it is a default transition, and its target has a type XOR parent which is entered at the same timestep by the firing of another transition (6.2) (e.g., in Figure 1, the default transition which has I as its target fires when the transition from G to H fires); it is a default transition and its target has a type AND grandparent state which is entered at the same timestep by the firing of another transition (6.3). In the following, the set of transitions that fire at a given timestep i is denoted by τ_i.

Resulting from the firing of transitions, a new state configuration is computed:

Definition 7: Given a state configuration cf_{i-1}, a context ct_{i-1}, and the corresponding set of firing transitions τ_{i-1}, $i > 0$, the *state configuration at timestep i*, cf_i, is inductively defined as follows:

- if s $\in cf_{i-1} \wedge \neg \exists_{t \in \tau_{i-1}}$ s $\in$ source*(t) then s is in cf_i, (7.1)

- if $\exists_{t \in \tau_{i-1}}$ s $\in$ target*(t) then s $\in cf_i$ (7.2) where source*(t) and target*(t) are the sets of left and entered states, respectively, of the firing transitions. These two sets are formally defined in [WW96]. Informally, a state is an element of the new state configuration if it is already in the preceding state configuration and has not been left in timestep i–1 (7.1) or it is entered by the firing of a transition in timestep i–1 (7.2).

When a transition fires, the action component of its transition label is executed which may incur changes of the context by assigning new values to events, conditions, and variables. In addition to these assignments, users may generate external stimuli, i.e., generate events, set conditions, or write variables.

Definition 8: Given a context ct_{i-1} and a set of firing transitions τ_{i-1}, i>0.

- The *external stimuli of timestep i* are defined as follows:

  $es_i : C_p \cup E_p \cup V_p \rightarrow \{true, false, generated\} \cup INT \cup \{\perp\}$

$$es_i(x) = \begin{cases} generated, & \text{if } x \in E_p \land gen(x) \text{ has been entered at timestep } i \\ true & \text{, if } x \in C_p \land tr!(x) \text{ has been entered at timestep } i \\ false & \text{, if } x \in C_p \land fs!(x) \text{ has been entered at timestep } i \\ n & \text{, if } x \in V_p \land x:=n \text{ has been entered at timestep } i \\ \perp & \text{, otherwise} \end{cases}$$

- Let A(t) be the action component of transition t. The *assignments of timestep i* are defined as follows:

  $assign_i : C_p \cup E_p \cup V_p \rightarrow \{true, false, generated\} \cup INT \cup \{\perp\}$

$$assign_i(x) = \begin{cases} generated, & \text{if } x \in E_p \land \exists_{t\in\tau_{i-1}} gen(x) \in A(t) \land es_i(x) = \perp \\ true & \text{, if } x \in E_p \land \exists_{t\in\tau_{i-1}} tr!(x) \in A(t) \land es_i(x) = \perp \\ false & \text{, if } x \in E_p \land \exists_{t\in\tau_{i-1}} fs!(x) \in A(t) \land es_i(x) = \perp \\ n & \text{, if } x \in V_p \land \exists_{t\in\tau_{i-1}} (x := n) \in A(t) \land es_i(x) = \perp \\ es_i(x) & \text{, if } es_i(x) \neq \perp \\ \perp & \text{, otherwise} \end{cases}$$

In summary, assignments can be initiated by user interactions, in the case that es(x) is defined, or by the execution of actions that are part of transition labels of firing transitions. Note that the es(x) assignment has higher priority than the assignment initiated by the firing of a transition. Resulting from these assignments a new context of a state chart has to be computed.

Definition 9: Given the sets of conditions, C_p, events, E_p, and variables, V_p, the *context at timestep i* is defined as follows:

$ct_i : C_p \cup E_p \cup V_p \rightarrow \{true, false, generated\} \cup INT \cup \{\perp\}$

$$ct_i(x) = \begin{cases} assign_i(x), & \text{if } assign_i(x) \neq \perp & (9.1) \\ \perp & \text{, if } assign_i(x) = \perp \land x \in E_p & (9.2) \\ ct_{i-1}(x) & \text{, otherwise} & (9.3) \end{cases}$$

The context changes if there are explicit assignments due to user interaction or actions in transition labels (9.1). In addition, all events that have not been generated are set to undefined (i.e., "not generated") (9.2). This means that the generation of events is only

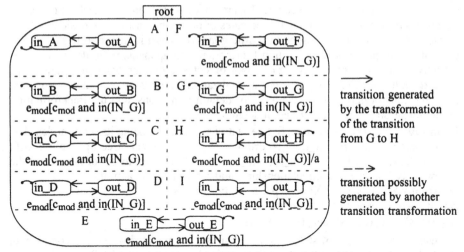

Fig. 2: Transformation of the state chart of Fig. 1

valid for one step. In contrast to events, the context of conditions and variables that are not subject to assignments is the same as in the previous step (9.3).

Now we are ready to define concisely the stepwise execution of a state chart.

Definition 10: Given a state configuration cf_i and a context ct_i, $i \geq 0$. The *system configuration* is defined as $sc_i := (cf_i, ct_i)$. The set of system configurations is denoted by $SC := \{sc_i \mid i \geq 0\} \subseteq CF \times CT$ where CF is the set of all possible state configurations and CT is the set of all possible contexts. The *initial system configuration* is denoted as sc_0.

Definition 11: Let SC be a set of system configurations. The *step* function is defined as follows:

$step : SC \rightarrow SC$

$step : sc_i \mapsto sc_{i+1}$, $i \geq 0$

Definition 12: A *state chart execution* is a sequence of system configurations: $sc_0, sc_1, sc_2, \ldots sc_n$, with $step(sc_i) = sc_{i+1}$, $i \geq 0$.

4 Orthogonalization and Partitioning of State Charts

In this section we present our method for the partitioning of workflow specifications. The partitioning transforms a state chart into a behaviorally equivalent state chart that is directly amenable to distributed execution in that each distributable portion of the state chart forms an orthogonal component. The first step towards a partitioned specification is thus called "orthogonalization". The outcome of this step is another state chart that can easily be partitioned. The proof that this transformation is indeed feasible in that it preserves the original state chart's behavior is cast into showing that the resulting "orthogonalized" state chart is a homomorphic image of the original specification. Note that we do not address the issue of "streamlining" or optimizing business processes by altering the invocation order of activities. We are solely concerned with preparing workflow specifications for distributed execution.

4.1 Orthogonalization of State Charts

The basic idea of the orthogonalization is that each state s of the original chart is simulated by an orthogonal component with two states in_s and out_s, thus keeping track of entering and leaving s. While this is straightforward, the technical difficulty is to adapt the transitions in the correct way. This involves augmenting the labels of the original chart's transitions by additional predicates of the form "in(in_s)". Consider the example of Figure 1. The corresponding orthogonalized chart is shown in Figure 2. For each of the original states, A through I, orthogonal components with identical names are generated, each one consisting of a pair of states, two interconnecting transitions, and a default transition. Next, the orthogonalization which is done in three steps, i.e., the state transformation, the generation of default transitions, and the transformation of the transitions, will be described in detail.

Definition 13: Given a state tree, S_tree, with S={s_1, ..., s_n} being its set of nodes. The *orthogonalized state tree* S_tree' := ortho$_{state}$(S_tree) is a state tree of height 3 with S':={root, s_1, ..., s_n, in_s_1, ..., in_s_n, out_s_1, ..., out_s_n} being its set of nodes and the following types, parent/child relationships, and assignments to activities:

type(root)=AND, type(s)=XOR, type(in_s)=type(out_s)=LEAF,

parent(s)=root, parent(in_s)=parent(out_s)=s,

act$_{S'}$(in_s)=act$_{S'}$(out_s)=act$_{S'}$(s) := act$_S$(s).

For each state s a triple of states, {s, in_s, out_s}, is generated where s becomes both child of the AND–type root of the orthogonalized state chart and XOR–type parent of in_s and out_s. The three generated nodes keep the assignment, act$_S$, of the original node.

Definition 14: Given the orthogonalized state tree with states S':={root, s_1, ..., s_n, in_s_1, ..., in_s_n, out_s_1, ..., out_s_n} and the initial state configuration, cf$_0$, of a state chart, the set of *generated default transitions*, T$_{default}$' is the following set of transitions on S': T$_{default}$' = { t' | source(t') = ∅ ∧ target(t') = in_s ∧ s ∈ cf$_0$} U

{ t' | source(t') = ∅ ∧ target(t') = out_s ∧ s ∉ cf$_0$}

Informally, an "in"–state becomes the target of a default transition if its corresponding state of the original state chart is element of the initial state configuration. Otherwise the corresponding "out"–state becomes the target of a default transition. Since in the example of Figure 1 cf$_0$ is {A, B, C, D, F, G}, in Figure 2 the target states of default transitions are in_A, in_B, in_C, in_D, in_F, in_G, and out_E, out_H, out_I.

Definition 15: Given a state chart with transition set T. Let S' be the state set of the corresponding orthogonalized state tree and let for each transition t=(s_j, s_k, E[C]/A)∈T source*(t) and target*(t) be the sets of left and entered states when t fires. The *orthogonalized transition set* is ortho$_{transition}$(T) with: ortho$_{transition}$(T):=

$$
U_{t∈T}
\begin{cases}
\{(in\_s, out\_s, E_{mod}[C_{mod}']) \mid s ∈ source^*(t)\} \, U & (15.1) \\
\{(out\_s_k, in\_s_k, E_{mod}[C_{mod}'] \, / \, A)\} \, U & (15.2) \\
\{(out\_s, in\_s, E_{mod}[C_{mod}']) \mid s ∈ target^*(t), \, s ≠ s_k\} & (15.3)
\end{cases}
$$

with: C$_{mod}$':= C$_{mod}$ and in(in_s_j)   (15.4)

C$_{mod}$:= C where all terms of the form "in(s)" are replaced by "in(in_s)" (15.5)

E$_{mod}$:= E where all terms of the form "en(s)" or "ex(s)" are replaced (15.6)

by "en(in_s)" or "ex(in_s)", respectively

Informally, each transition t is mapped onto at least two transitions. For each state which is left when t fires a transition which has the corresponding "out"–state as its target is generated (15.1) (e.g., in Figure 2 these are the transitions which interconnect the pairs of states (in_B, out_B), (in_C, out_C), (in_D, out_D), (in_E, out_E), (in_F, out_F), (in_G, out_G)). In addition, one transition is generated which has the corresponding "in"–state of target(t) as its target (e.g., in Figure 2 this is the transition interconnecting out_H and in_H). Note that this is the only transition which inherits the action component, a, from t (15.2). In addition, for each other state which is entered when t fires a transition which has the corresponding "in"-state as its target is generated (15.3) (e.g., in Figure 2 this is the transition interconnecting out_I and in_I).

Concerning the transition labels, the transition transformation extends the condition component of each transition label by the conjunctive term "in(s_j)" with s_j denoting the source state of t (15.4). Terms in event and condition components which are related to states are replaced by terms with adjusted state names (15.5), (15.6) (e.g., "en(state)" is changed to "en(in_state)"). In the example of Figure 2, the event and condition components of the transition label "e[c]/a" are extended to "$e_{mod}[c_{mod}$ and in(IN_G)]".

The above considerations are summarized in the following definition of an orthogonalized state chart.

Definition 16: Let s_chart = (S_tree, T) be a state chart, and let $ortho_{state}$(S_tree), $T_{default}$', $ortho_{transition}$(T) be the orthogonalized state tree, the generated set of default transitions, and the orthogonalized transition set of s_chart as defined above.

The *orthogonalized state chart* s_chart':=ortho(s_chart) is defined as (S_tree',T') with S_tree' := $ortho_{state}$(S_tree) and T' := $ortho_{transition}$(T) $\cup$ $T_{default}$'.

4.2 The Homomorphism Property

Now we are about to state the main result of the paper, namely, that the orthogonalized state chart of a given state chart preserves the original chart's behavior. There are several notions of "behavioral equivalence" discussed in the literature on reactive and concurrent systems (see, e.g., [MP92, Mil89]). However, we can exploit the specific nature of our simplified state chart version to introduce a simpler and, in our opinion, more elegant notion of behavioral equivalence. Intuitively, behavioral equivalence of two state charts means that both produce the same externally observable actions under the same external stimuli, where the observable actions in a workflow setting would be the invocation of workflow activities along with their actual parameters. This is certainly ensured if the two state charts exhibit equivalent transition sequences under the same external stimuli. The transition sequences in turn are uniquely determined by the step function of Definition 11, i.e., the operational semantics that we have defined and which holds uniformly for all state charts including those that result from the orthogonalization transformation. Now, by viewing a state chart as an algebraic structure with its system configurations as its carrier set and the step function as a unary operator, we can ensure equivalent transition sequences of two state charts by defining a homomorphism between the two algebras. Thus, we have to define a mapping between the system configurations of two state charts such that this mapping and the step operator commute.

Definition 17: Consider a state chart with state set, S={s_1, ... , s_n}, the set of state configurations, CF, the set of transitions, T, and the set of contexts, CT. Let S', CF', T', CT' be the corresponding sets of the orthogonalized state chart. The mappings h_{CF}, h_{CT}, and h_{SC} are defined as follows:

- *mapping of state configurations:* h_{CF}: CF$\rightarrow$CF'   (17.1)
  h_{CF}(cf)=cf'   with cf':={root, s_1, ... , s_n}$\cup${in_s|s$\in$cf}$\cup${out_s|s$\notin$cf},
- *mapping of contexts:* h_{CT}: CT$\rightarrow$CT'   (17.2)
  h_{CT}(ct)=ct i.e., the identity mapping,
- *mapping of system configurations:* h_{SC}: SC$\rightarrow$SC'   (17.3)
  h_{SC}(sc)=sc'   with: sc = (cf, ct), sc' := (h_{CF}(cf), h_{CT}(ct)).

For example, the initial state configuration of the state chart in Figure 1, {A, B, C, D, F, G}, is mapped onto the state configuration of the state chart of Figure 2, {root, A, B, C, D, E, F, G, H, I, in_A, in_B, in_C, in_D, in_F, in_G, out_E, out_H, out_I}.

The result that we are heading for is that the mapping h_{SC} is a homomorphism. We therefore introduce a step operator of the orthogonalized chart which we denote by step'. However, note that both the step operator of the original state chart and step' are defined by the generic function of Definition 11. It has to be proved that the following holds: $h_{SC}(step(sc)) = step'(h_{SC}(sc))$.

In the following, we proceed through a series of lemmas towards our main theorem. The proofs of the lemmas 1 and 2 and the full proof of Lemma 3 are contained in [WW96].

Lemma 1: Given a state chart, s_chart. Let s_chart' be a a state chart which differs from s_chart only in that the condition component of each transition label is further constrained in the following way: Each transition t=(source, target, E[C]/A) is changed into t'=(source, target, E[C and in(source)]/A). Let $t \in \tau_i$, $t' \in \tau_i'$ be firing transitions in timestep i of s_chart and s_chart', respectively. The following holds for the sets of firing transitions, τ and τ', of s_chart and s_chart', respectively: $t \in \tau_i \Leftrightarrow t' \in \tau_i'$ for all $i \geq 0$.

The lemma guarantees that by constraining the condition components of the transitions in the described manner, the transitions fire exactly at the same timestep as the corresponding original transitions. However, the question that needs to be answered is: Do the constrained transitions have the same effects on the state chart execution as the corresponding original transitions?

Lemma 2: Consider a state chart, s_chart. Let s_chart' be a state chart which differs from s_chart only in that the condition component of each transition label is further constrained as described in Lemma 1. Let $t \in \tau_i$, $t' \in \tau_i'$ be firing transitions in timestep i of s_chart and s_chart', respectively. Let EG(t), CST(t), CSF(t), AE(t) be the sets of generated events, the sets of conditions set to true and set to false, and the set of actions executed as a result of the firing of t, respectively. Let EG(t'), CST(t'), CSF(t'), and AE(t') be the according sets for transition t'. The following holds: EG(t) = EG(t'), CST(t) = CST(t'), CSF(t) = CSF(t'), AE(t)=AE(t') for all $t \in \tau_i$, $t' \in \tau_i'$ for all $i \geq 0$.

According to the lemma, the firing of transitions with constrained transition labels actually has the same effects as the corresponding original transitions; in particular, the same actions are executed (e.g., the same activities are started at the same timestep). From these lemmas we obtain:

Corollary 1: Let SC be the set of system configurations of a state chart s_chart. Let SC' be the set of system configurations of s_chart' which differs from s_chart only in that the condition component of each transition label is further constrained by adding the conjunctive term "in(source)" where source is the source state of the transition. The following property holds: For all timesteps $i \geq 0$, under the condition that $es_i(x)=es_i'(x)$ it holds: $sc_i=sc_i'$.

Informally, the meaning of the corollary is that by constraining the condition components of the transition labels the behavior of a state chart does not change. Next, we will concentrate on the relationship between the operational semantics (i.e., the step function) of a state chart and its orthogonalized representation.

Lemma 3: Let cf_i be the state configuration of a state chart s_chart at timestep $i \geq 0$. The state configuration of the orthogonalized state chart s_chart' at the same timestep is $h_{CF}(cf_i)$.

Proof Sketch (Lemma 3) We use induction to prove the lemma.

- Basis of the induction: The initial state configuration of s_chart', cf_0', is $h_{CF}(cf_0)$ where cf_0 is the initial state configuration of s_chart.
  Proof: Let the set of states of the original state chart be $S=\{s_1, \dots, s_n\}$. Because of Definitions 13 and 14, the initial state configuration of the orthogonalized state chart, cf_0', is: $\{root, s_1, \dots, s_n\} \cup \bigcup_{s \in cf_0}\{in\_s\} \cup \bigcup_{s \notin cf_0}\{out\_s\}$.
  This is exactly the set of states according to Definition 17.1, namely $h_{CF}(cf_0)$.
- Induction hypothesis: For each timestep $i>0$ the state configuration of s_chart', cf_i', is $h_{CF}(cf_i)$ with cf_i being the state configuration of s_chart at timestep i.
- The induction step is as follows: $cf_{i+1}' = h_{CF}(cf_{i+1})$
  Generally, cf_{i+1} is the state configuration that is reached from cf_i when the transitions in τ_i fire. Therefore,

$$h_{CF}(cf_{i+1}) = h_{CF}\left(cf_i \cup \bigcup_{t \in \tau_i}\{target^\bullet(t)\} - \bigcup_{t \in \tau_i}\{source^\bullet(t)\}\right)$$

For the computation of the right side of the above equation, we will use the following evidently correct computation rule for h_{CF}:
Let $S=\{s_1, \dots, s_n\}$ be a set of states, and let $S_1:=\{s_1, \dots, s_k\}$, $S_2 := S_1 \cup \{s_{k+1}\}$, and $S_3 := S_1 - \{s_k\}$ be subsets of S. The following computation rules hold for h_{CF}:

- $h_{CF}(S_2) = h_{CF}(S_1 \cup \{s_{k+1}\}) = h_{CF}(S_1) - \{out\_s_{k+1}\} \cup \{in\_s_{k+1}\}$
- $h_{CF}(S_3) = h_{CF}(S_1 - \{s_k\}) = h_{CF}(S_1) - \{in\_s_k\} \cup \{out\_s_k\}$

Applied to the above equation we obatin the following equation:

$$h_{CF}(cf_{i+1})=h_{CF}(cf_i) - \bigcup_{t \in \tau_i}\{out\_s | s \in target^\bullet(t)\} \cup \bigcup_{t \in \tau_i}\{in\_s | s \in target^\bullet(t)\}$$
$$- \bigcup_{t \in \tau_i}\{in\_s | s \in source^\bullet(t)\} \cup \bigcup_{t \in \tau_i}\{out\_s | s \in source^\bullet(t)\}$$

Because of the induction hypothesis, this is equivalent to:

$$h_{CF}(cf_{i+1})=cf_i' - \bigcup_{t \in \tau_i}\{out\_s | s \in target^\bullet(t)\} \cup \bigcup_{t \in \tau_i}\{in\_s | s \in target^\bullet(t)\}$$
$$- \bigcup_{t \in \tau_i}\{in\_s | s \in source^\bullet(t)\} \cup \bigcup_{t \in \tau_i}\{out\_s | s \in source^\bullet(t)\}$$

According to Definition 15, we substitute the above four unions. The outcome is as follows shown below:

$$h_{CF}(cf_{i+1})=cf'_i - \bigcup_{t' \in ortho_{transition}(t), t \in \tau_i}\{out\_s | target(t') = out\_s\}$$
$$- \bigcup_{t' \in ortho_{transition}(t), t \in \tau_i}\{in\_s | source(t') = in\_s\}$$
$$\cup \bigcup_{t' \in ortho_{transition}(t), t \in \tau_i}\{in\_s | target(t') = in\_s\}$$
$$\cup \bigcup_{t' \in ortho_{transition}(t), t \in \tau_i}\{out\_s | source(t') = out\_s\} \qquad (*)$$

According to Definition 7, cf_{i+1}' can be computed as follows:
$$cf_{i+1}'=cf_i' - \bigcup_{t' \in \tau_i}\{source^\bullet(t')\} \cup \bigcup_{t' \in \tau_i}\{target^\bullet(t')\}$$
Since, generally, $source^\bullet(t) = source(t) \wedge target^\bullet(t) = target(t)$ holds for all orthogonalized state charts and for all transitions t, this is equivalent to:
$$cf_{i+1}'=cf_i' - \bigcup_{t' \in \tau_i}\{source(t')\} \cup \bigcup_{t' \in \tau_i}\{target(t')\}$$
Both "out"–states and "in"–states can be elements of source(t') and target(t').
Therefore, we can write:
$$cf_{i+1}'=cf_i' - \bigcup_{t' \in \tau_i}\{out\_s | source(t') = out\_s \in cf_i'\}$$
$$- \bigcup_{t' \in \tau_i}\{in\_s | source(t') = in\_s \in cf_i'\}$$
$$\cup \bigcup_{t' \in \tau_i}\{in\_s | target(t') = in\_s \notin cf_i'\}$$

$$\cup \bigcup_{t' \in \tau_i'} \{out\_s | target(t') = out\_s \notin cf_i'\} \tag{**}$$

Two cases have to be considered:

<u>case 1</u>: $\tau_i' = ortho_{transition}(\tau_i)$

Obviously, in this case (*) and (**) are identical, i.e., $h_{CF}(cf_{i+1}) = cf_{i+1}'$ holds.

<u>case 2</u>: $\tau_i' \neq ortho_{transition}(\tau_i)$

Two cases have to be considered: First, there exists a transition in the orthogonalized state chart which fires at timestep i, however the corresponding transition in the original state chart does not fire. Secondly, there exists a transition which fires in the original state chart at timestep i whereas the corresponding transitions in the orthogonalized state chart, or at least one of them, does not fire.

<u>case 2.1</u>: Because of Definition 15, for each transition of the original state chart at least two transitions have been generated by the orthogonalization. Without loss of generality, we assume that by applying $ortho_{transition}$ to a transition $t=(s, r, E[C]/A)$ four transitions, $t'=\{t_1', t_2', t_3', t_4'\}$, have been generated. All transitions in t' have the same event and condition components, E_{mod} and C_{mod}', in their transition labels. In addition, all condition components contain the conjunctive term "in(in_s)". Suppose that for one transition, e.g., t_1', the following holds: $t_1' \in \tau_i'$, $t_1' \notin ortho_{transition}(\tau_i)$. From $t_1' \in \tau_i'$ it follows: $in\_s \in cf_i'$, $eval(E_{mod}, cf_i', ct_i')$=generated and $eval(C_{mod}', cf_i', ct_i')$=true $\Rightarrow eval(in(in\_s), cf_i', ct_i')$=true . Because of the assumption of case 2.1, $t \notin \tau_i$ must hold; however, from $ct_i'=ct_i$ and from the induction hypothesis it follows $eval(E, h_{CF}(cf_i), ct_i')$=generated, $eval(C, h_{CF}(cf_i), ct_i')$=true. $\Rightarrow$ To prevent t from firing $s \notin cf_i$ must hold. Because of the induction hypothesis, $cf_i'=h_{CF}(cf_i)$, it follows: $in\_s \in cf_i'$. This is a contradiction.

<u>case 2.2</u>: Without loss of generality, we suppose that by applying $ortho_{transition}$ to a transition $t=(s, r, E[C]/A)$ four transitions, $t'=\{t_1', t_2', t_3', t_4'\}$, have been generated. We assume that the following holds: $t'=\{t_1', t_2', t_3', t_4'\} \not\subset \tau_i'$, $t' \subseteq \{ortho_{transition}(\tau_i)\}$, with $t_1'=(in\_s, out\_s, E_{mod}[C_{mod}'])$, $t_2'=(out\_r, in\_r, E_{mod}[C_{mod}']/A)$, $t_3'=(in\_q, out\_q, E_{mod}[C_{mod}'])$, $t_4'=(out\_p, in\_p, E_{mod}[C_{mod}'])$. We assume that q is an element of $s\_r(t)$ and p is an element of $t\_r(t)$. In order to meet the assumption, it has to be proved that at least one of the transitions in t' cannot fire.

From $t \in \tau_i$ it follows: $s \in cf_i$, $eval(E, cf_i, ct)$=generated, $eval(C, cf_i, ct_i)$=true. From the induction hypothesis we know that $in\_s \in cf_i'$ holds. Furthermore, if there are any expressions in event or condition components of the transition labels of transitions in t' which refer to states, like en(s), in(s), etc., these expressions are translated into according "in"–expressions, e.g., en(in_s), in(in_s), etc. By this argument and knowing that $in\_s \in cf_i'$, and $ct_i=ct_i'$, it follows: $eval(E_{mod}, cf_i', ct_i')$=generated and $eval(C_{mod}', cf_i', ct_i')$=true

Considering Corollary 1, this means that the only thing that can prevent one of the transitions in t' from firing is that its source state is not in cf_i'. Since in T' are only transitions which interconnect "in"–states and "out"–states, this would imply that at least one of the following states must be in cf_i': out_s or in_r or out_q or in_p. However, (1) with regard to t_1', because of the induction hypothesis in_s is in cf_i', (2) with regard to t_2', if in_r would be in cf_i' then r would be in cf_i because of the induction hypothesis; but if s and r would be both elements of cf_i their least common ancestor would have to be a state of type AND; this would disallow that there existed a transition interconnecting s and r $\Rightarrow$ out_r $\in cf_i'$, (3) with regard to t_3', if out_q would be in cf_i' then q could not be an element of s_r(t) $\Rightarrow$ in_q$\in cf_i$', (4) with regard to t_4', if in_p would be in cf_i' then p could not be an element of t_r(t) $\Rightarrow$ out_p$\in cf_i$'. $\Rightarrow t' \subseteq \tau_i$ '. This is a contradiction.

Since both case 2.1 and case 2.2 lead to contradictions, the proof is completed.

Next, we will state a relevant property of h_{SC} that will be exploited in the proof of the main theorem.

Lemma 4: h_{SC} is injective.

Proof (Lemma 4)

We will first prove that h_{CF} is injective.

(Proof by contradiction) Assumption: $h_{CF}(cf_1)=h_{CF}(cf_2)$ and $cf_1 \neq cf_2$. Assuming that S is the set of states of the original state chart, it follows from the assumption: $\exists_{s \in S} s \notin cf_1 \wedge s \in cf_2$.

From $s \notin cf_1$ it follows: out_s$\in h_{CF}(cf_1) \wedge$ in_s$\notin h_{CF}(cf_1)$; from $s \in cf_2$ it follows: out_s$\notin h_{CF}(cf_2) \wedge$ in_s$\in h_{CF}(cf_1)$. This is in contradiction to the first assumption, $h_{CF}(cf_1)=h_{CF}(cf_2) \Rightarrow h_{CF}$ is injective.

Assuming that sc is (cf, ct), we know from Definition 17 that $h_{SC}(sc)$ is defined as the tuple $(h_{CF}(cf), h_{CT}(ct))$. Since h_{CF} is injective and h_{CT} is the identity mapping, it follows that h_{SC} is injective.

We are now prepared for a corollary describing the relationship between the sets of firing transitions of the original and the orthogonalized state chart. This result follows directly from Lemma 3.

Corollary 2: Let τ_i be the set of firing transitions of a state chart s_chart at timestep $i \geq 0$. The set of firing transitions of the orthogonalized state chart s_chart' at the same timestep is τ_i':=ortho$_{transition}(\tau_i)$.

Corollary 1, Lemma 3, Lemma 4, and Corollary 2 lead us to the following main theorem.

Theorem 1: The mapping h_{SC} which maps the system configurations of a state chart onto the system configuration of the corresponding orthogonalized state chart is a homomorphism; that is, for all timesteps $i \geq 0$ and for all system configurations sc_i of the original state chart the equation h_{SC} (step (sc_i)) = step' $(h_{SC}(sc_i))$ must hold, where step is the step function of the original state chart and step' that of the orthogonalized state chart (both defined by the operational semantics developed in Section 3).

Proof (Theorem 1): Since the step operator is actually a composite function, the formal derivation of the homomorphism needs to refer to the state configuration, cf, and the context, ct. It has to be shown that, for all state configurations, cf_i, and for all contexts, ct_i, step(cf_i, ct_i) results in the same system configuration as h_{SC}^{-1}(step'($h_{SC}(cf_i, ct_i)$).

Consider a state chart, s_chart=(S_tree, T), its state set, S = $\{s_1, ... , s_n\}$, and its set of transitions, T = $\{t_1, ... , t_m\}$. Let $cf_i = \{s_1, ... , s_p\}$ be the current state configuration, and let ct_i be the current context. First, we will orthogonalize the state chart: s_chart':=ortho(s_chart)=(S_tree', T') with S_tree':=ortho$_{state}$ (S_tree), T':=ortho$_{transition}$ (T)$\cup T_{default}$', and the transformed set of states, S':= $\{$root, $s_1, ... , s_p$, in_$s_1, ... ,$ in_s_n, out_$s_1, ... ,$ out_$s_n\}$. The proof is organized in four working steps:

working step (1): First, we will apply the step function to cf_i and ct_i, i.e., compute step(cf_i, ct_i):

Based on cf_i and ct_i, the set of firing transitions, τ_i, can be computed. Suppose that τ_i is $\{t_k, ..., t_l\}$. The firing of these transitions effects some states to be left: $\bigcup_{t \in \tau_i}\{$source$^{\bullet}(t)\}$ and some states to be entered: $\bigcup_{t \in \tau_i}\{$target$^{\bullet}(t)\}$. Without loss of generality, we assume that the set of left states is $\{s_1, ..., s_{j-1}\}$, and the set of entered states is $\{s_{p+1}, \ldots, s_q\}$. Therefore, cf_{i+1} is $\{s_j, \ldots, s_p, s_{p+1}, \ldots, s_q\}$. For the computation of the context ct_{i+1}, we assume that $CST(\tau_i)$, $CSF(\tau_i)$, $EG(\tau_i)$, and $EA(\tau_i)$, i.e, the sets of conditions set true, set false, the set of generated events, and the set of executed actions which result from the execution of the action components of the firing transitions, and the set of external stimuli $\{es_{i+1}(x)\}$ are known. Because of Definition 9, the new context, ct_{i+1}, is well–defined. Therefore, $step(cf_i, ct_i) = (cf_{i+1}, ct_{i+1})$.

<u>working step (2)</u>: Now, we will apply h_{CF} to cf_i and h_{CT} to ct_i:

$cf_i' := h_{CF}(cf_i) = \{s_1, \ldots, s_n, root, in\_s_1, \ldots, in\_s_p, out\_s_{p+1}, \ldots out\_s_n\}$, $ct_i' := h_{CT}(ct_i) = ct_i$.

<u>working step (3)</u>: Now, we will apply the step function to cf_i' and ct_i':

First, we will compute the set of firing transitions of the orthogonalized state chart, τ_i'. Because of Corollary 2, this set is $\tau_i'=ortho_{transition}(\tau_i)$.

With regard to the state configuration, we know from Definition 15 that each transition which is element of any $ortho_{transition}(t)$, $t \in \{t_k, \ldots, t_l\}$, has either a source state which is element of $\{in\_s \mid s \in source^*(t) \cap cf_i\}$ or a target state which is element of $\{in\_s \mid s \in target^*(t)\}$. Since all transitions in T' and thus all transitions in τ_i' interconnect pairs of "in"–states and "out"–states, the transitions in τ_i' interconnect the following pairs of states: $(in\_s_1, out\_s_1,), \ldots, (in\_s_{j-1}, out\_s_{j-1})$ and $(out\_s_{p+1}, in\_s_{p+1}), \ldots, (out\_s_q, in\_s_q)$. Since exactly all transitions in τ_i' fire, the states $in\_s_1, \ldots, in\_s_{j-1}, out\_s_{p+1}, \ldots, out\_s_q$ have to be deducted from the state configuration and the states $out\_s_1, \ldots, out\_s_{j-1}, in\_s_{p+1}, \ldots, in\_s_q$ have to be added to the state configuration. Therefore, the resulting state configuration is:

$cf_{i+1}'=\{s_1, \ldots, s_n, root, out\_s_1, \ldots, out\_s_{j-1}, in\_s_j, \ldots, in\_s_p, in\_s_{p+1}, \ldots, in\_s_q, out\_s_{q+1}, \ldots, out\_s_n\}$.

With regard to the context, the following holds: Updates of the context can only have their origin in the execution of action components of firing transitions or in external stimuli. The latter are the same as for the original state chart. Therefore, it remains to be proved that the same actions are executed: Since $ortho_{transition}(\tau_i)$ maps each firing transition of s_chart onto at least a pair of firing transitions in τ_i' and generates no additional action components of transition labels, and since for each action component of s_chart exactly one (identical) action component is generated by $ortho_{transition}$, the actions that are executed at timestep i in s_chart' are the same as in s_chart. Therefore, for the sets of conditions set true and false and for the set of generated events the following holds: $CST(\tau_i')=CST(\tau_i)$, $CSF(\tau_i')=CSF(\tau_i)$, $EG(\tau_i')=EG(\tau_i)$ and $EA(\tau_i')=EA(\tau_i)$.

<u>working step (4)</u>: Now, we will exploit the injectivity of h_{CF} (Lemma 4) in order to map sc_{i+1}' onto sc_{i+1}: $cf_{i+1} = h_{CF}^{-1}(cf_{i+1}') = h_{CF}^{-1}(\{s_1, \ldots, s_n, root, out\_s_1, \ldots, out\_s_{j-1}, in\_s_j, \ldots, in\_s_p, in\_s_{p+1}, \ldots, in\_s_q, out\_s_{q+1}, \ldots, out\_s_n\}) = \{s_j, \ldots, s_p, s_{p+1}, \ldots, s_q,\}$

$ct_{i+1} = h_{CT}^{-1}(ct_{i+1}') = ct_{i+1}$

Since the outcome of working step (4) and working step (1) are identical, h_{SC} is a homomorphism for all timesteps $i \geq 0$.

4.3 Partitioning of State and Activity Charts

The outcome of the orthogonalization is a state chart which consists of a set of orthogonal components. The final partitioning which transforms an orthogonalized state chart into a form that is amenable to distributed execution then falls out in a natural and straightforward manner. The orthogonalized state chart is decomposed along the boundaries of its orthogonal components, and all the resulting components with the same assignment to activities, act$_S$, are grouped together to form a new state chart.

In many cases, it is natural to further combine multiple activities into a coarser unit that corresponds to one business unit (e.g., a department). Assuming that each activity has been assigned to such a business unit all activities that belong to a business unit together with the corresponding state chart form a partition of the workflow.

Such partitions are the unit of distribution; that is, each partition may reside on a different server. Obviously, servers may have to communicate local state and context information to each other in order to ensure a synchronized evaluation of their local transition labels. A foolproof, still unoptimized solution would be that all servers mutually exchange all modified conditions, events, and variables after every time step. Using standard compiler techniques for data flow analysis, these communication steps can be restricted to the cases where the progress at one server may in fact potentially influence other servers. More details on this synchronization are discussed in [WWWK96a]. Note that in contrast to the orthogonalization, the correctness proof for the final partitioning is straightforward and thus omitted.

5 Practical Perspectives

Now that we have developed the formal underpinnings of our transformation approach, we will briefly discuss their applicability to a concrete workflow scenario. According to our experience in a collaboration with the Union Bank of Switzerland, state charts are still too formal in flavor and, therefore, not appropriate for wide use in a business environment. Rather high–level design tools for business process engineering or re–engineering (BPR) are preferred; these tools are geared for ease of use in the design process itself but cannot produce executable workflows. With this in mind, we suggest the following workflow design procedure: Workflow or business process specifications can be initially developed with BPR tools or the specification tools of the user's favorite commercial workflow system. Such a specification can be automatically converted into a state and activity chart specification (which is also shown in the figure). Next, the orthogonalization is carried out. Finally, the partitions that result from the orthogonalization are assigned to workflow servers, taking into account both the performance and availability requirements and the organizational responsibilities of the enterprise (e.g., one server for each involved department). Thus, the role of state and activity charts in a practical business environment, as we view it, is that of a canonical representation for the underlying execution engine (with rigorously defined semantics), into which other specifications can be converted and which may even serve as an exchange format across different workflow engines.

With regard to the correctness of state chart based workflow specifications, we have collected first practical experience with verification techniques. In particular, we have studied the validation of state chart properties by means of reachability tests (as supported by STATEMATE [Ha90]) and symbolic model checking (using the tool described in [HK94]). For example, a property that every credit request will eventually be granted or rejected, and that these two results exclude each other, can be easily expressed in the temporal logic CTL [Em90] and efficiently verified by means of model checking. On the other hand, given the inherent limitations of such verification techniques, we believe that a combination of verification and simulation is a viable approach towards higher confidence in the correctness of workflow specifications. The transformation approach developed in this paper contributes to this goal in that it justifies that verification and simulation can be applied to the centralized specification, and their results carry over to the actually distributed execution.

References

[Em90] E.A. Emerson, Temporal and Modal Logic, in: J. van Leeuwen (ed.), Handbook of Theoretical Computer Science, Elsevier, 1990

[GHS95] D. Georgakopoulos, M. Hornick, A. Sheth, An Overview of Workflow Management: From Process Modeling to Workflow Automation Infrastructure, Distributed and Parallel Databases, 3(2), 1995

[Ha87a] D. Harel, On the Formal Semantics of Statecharts, Proc. Symposium on Logics in Computer Science, Ithaca, New York, 1987

[Ha87b] D. Harel, Statecharts: A Visual Formalism for Complex Systems, Science of Computer Programming Vol.8, 1987

[Ha88] D. Harel, On Visual Formalisms, Communications of the ACM, 31(5), 1988

[Ha90] D. Harel et al., STATEMATE: A Working Environment for the Development of Complex Reactive Systems, IEEE Transactions on Software Engineering, 16(4), 1990

[HN95] D. Harel, A. Naamad, The STATEMATE Semantics of Statecharts, Technical Report, i–Logix Inc., October 1995

[HK94] J. Helbig, P. Kelb, An OBDD–Representation of Statecharts, Proc. European Design and Test Conference, 1994

[Ho91] R.P. Hopkins, Distributable nets, in: Rozenberg (ed.), Advances in Petrinets, LNCS 524, Springer, 1991

[Hu88] C. Huizing, Modelling Statecharts in a fully abstract way, in: Proc. CAAP, LNCS 299, Springer, 1988

[i–Log91] i–Logix Inc., Documentation for the Statemate System, 1991

[MP92] Z. Manna, A. Pnueli, The Temporal Logic of Reactive and Concurrent Systems, Springer, 1992

[McM93] K.L. McMillan, Symbolic Model Checking, Kluwer, 1993

[Mil89] R. Milner, Communication and Concurrency, Prentice Hall, 1989

[Mo96] C. Mohan, Workflow Management Systems: State of the Art on Research and Products, Tutorial Notes, Int. Conf. on Extending Database Technology, Avignon, 1996

[Sh96] A. Sheth (ed.), Proc. NSF Workshop on Workflow and Process Automation in Information Systems, Athens, 1996, http://lsdis.cs.uga.edu/activities/NSF–workflow/

[vB94] M. von der Beeck, A Comparison of Statechart Variants, in: Formal Techniques in Real–Time and Fault–Tolerant Systems, LNCS 863, Springer, 1994

[VB96] G. Vossen, J. Becker (eds.), Business Process Modelling and Workflow Management – Models, Methods, Tools (in German), International Thomson, 1996

[WW96] D. Wodtke, G. Weikum, A Formal Foundation for Distributed Workflow Execution Based on State Charts, Technical Report, University of Saarbruecken, 1996

[WWWK96a] D. Wodtke, J. Weissenfels, G. Weikum, A. Kotz Dittrich, The Mentor Project: Steps Towards Enterprise–wide Workflow Management, Proc. 11th International Conference on Data Engineering, New Orleans, 1996

[WWWK96b] J. Weissenfels, D. Wodtke, G. Weikum, A. Kotz Dittrich, The Mentor Architecture for Enterprise–wide Workflow Management, in: [Sh96]

[WfMC95] Workflow Management Coalition, 1995, http://www.aiai.ed.ac.uk/WfMC/

Incorporating User Preferences in Multimedia Queries

(Extended Abstract)

Ronald Fagin and Edward L. Wimmers

IBM Almaden Research Center
650 Harry Road
San Jose, California 95120-6099
email: fagin@almaden.ibm.com, wimmers@almaden.ibm.com

Abstract. In a multimedia database system, queries may be fuzzy: thus, the answer to a query such as *(Color='red')* may not be 0 (false) or 1 (true), but instead a number between 0 and 1. A conjunction, such as *(Color='red')* ∧ *(Sound='loud')*, is evaluated by first evaluating the individual conjuncts and then combining the answers by some scoring function. Typical scoring functions include the min (the standard scoring function for the conjunction in fuzzy logic) and the average. We address the question of how to permit the user to weight the importance of atomic subformulas. In particular, we give a semantics for permitting non-uniform weights, by giving an explicit formula (that is based on the underlying scoring function). This semantics permits an efficient implementation with a low database access cost in a multimedia database system in important cases of interest.

1 Introduction

A database system faces the task of responding to queries. In a traditional database system, all queries deal with Boolean values, since a property is either true or false. As queries over multimedia data become more prevalent, it is important to permit various shades of gray. For example, in searching for a red picture, the user is unlikely to want a Boolean value that says whether the picture is red or not. More likely, the user would prefer a "score" giving the redness of a particular picture.

In general, a user might want to query not only over a single multimedia property, but might wish to take into account several properties. For example, the user might be interested in a movie clip that has a predominantly red scene with a loud noise in the sound track. In this case, there is likely to be a score giving the redness of the scene and a different score giving the loudness of the sound. These two scores must be combined into a single score. One way to do this is to use fuzzy logic. Such an approach is taken by the Garlic system, which is being developed at the IBM Almaden Research Center, and which provides access to a variety of data sources, including multimedia. See [CHS+95, CHN+95] for a discussion of the Garlic system, and [Fa96] and [CG96] (along with Section 8 of this paper) for a discussion of algorithms with a low database access cost for computing distributed scores (where different "black boxes" produce the various scores that must be combined).

However, there is an additional problem that must be addressed. It is unlikely that the user equally values the attributes being queried. For example, the user might like to inform the multimedia system to give extra weight to the picture and less weight to the sound. In the user interface, *sliders* are often used to convey this information to the system. Sliders are bars on the screen that indicate the importance of each attribute. The user moves his mouse to slide an indicator along the bar in order to increase or decrease the weighting of a given attribute.

The contribution of this paper is to give an explicit formula for incorporating weights that can be applied no matter what the underlying method is for combining scores (the average, the min, etc.). The formula we give is surprisingly simple, in that it involves far fewer terms than we might have guessed. In addition, its database access cost is low. It has two further desirable properties. The first desirable property is that when all of the weights are equal, then the result obtained is simply the underlying method for combining scores. Intuitively, this says that when all of the weights are equal, then this is the same as considering the unweighted case. Another way to say this is that if the user does not see any sliders, then this is the same as if the sliders exist and are all set to a default value where the weights are equal. The second desirable property is that if a particular argument has zero weight, then that argument can be dropped without affecting the value of the result. It turns out that if these two desirable properties hold, then under one additional assumption (a type of local linearity), our formula gives the unique possible answer.

2 Examples

Assume that there are two scores, namely x_1 and x_2. These scores are numbers (typically between 0 and 1, where 1 represents a perfect match) that represent how well an object rates on a particular attribute. For example, x_1 might be a score indicating how red a picture is, and x_2 might be a score indicating how loud a sound is. How should these scores be combined to reflect an "overall score" that reflects both the redness and the loudness? Should we take the average of the scores? Or what should we do? Not surprisingly, there are many possible answers, depending on the issues at hand.

One context where this issue of combining scores arises is fuzzy logic. In particular, a score must be assigned to a conjunction $A_1 \wedge A_2$ that is a function of the scores of A_1 and A_2. In his original paper [Za65], Zadeh defined the score of $A_1 \wedge A_2$ to be the min of the scores of A_1 and A_2. Similarly, he defined the score of the disjunction $A_1 \vee A_2$ to be the max of the scores of A_1 and A_2. Zadeh's choices were later justified by a famous result of Bellman and Giertz [BG73], which was extended and simplified by Yager [Ya82], Voxman and Goetschel [VG83], Dubois and Prade [DP84], and Wimmers [Wi96]. They showed that min and max are the unique choices that should be assigned to the conjunction and disjunction, respectively, that fulfill certain natural conditions. There is a large literature on other possible choices for scoring functions in fuzzy logic: see, for example, the discussion in Zimmermann's textbook [Zi91].

The question of interest in our paper is as follows. Assume that some method, such as the average or the min, is given for combining scores. How do we modify this method if we decide now that we do not want to assign equal weight to the scores? In the example we gave earlier, assume that the user cares twice as much about the color of the picture as he does about the loudness of the sound. How should he combine the color score and the volume score to obtain an overall score? In the case of average, the answer is fairly clear. We would assign a weight $\theta_1 = 2/3$ to the color, and a weight $\theta_2 = 1/3$ to the volume. (The weights must sum to one, and the weight for color, namely θ_1, should be twice the weight θ_2 for volume.) We then take the weighted sum $\theta_1 x_1 + \theta_2 x_2$. But what if we are using a different underlying method than the average for combining scores?

For the rest of this section, we assume that as in standard fuzzy logic, the underlying method is to take the min. Assume again that we wish to weight the scores, where θ_1 is the weight for color, and θ_2 is the weight for volume. Then we cannot simply take the result to be $\theta_1 x_1 + \theta_2 x_2$. For example, if we are indifferent to color versus volume, so that we weight them equally with $\theta_1 = \theta_2 = 1/2$, then we would get the wrong answer by using $\theta_1 x_1 + \theta_2 x_2$, since this does not give us the min of x_1 and x_2. (We are assuming here that we use the underlying, or "unweighted", method for combining scores when the θ_i's are equal. Later, we shall make such assumptions explicit.) What should the answer be, as a function of x_1, x_2, and θ_1? (Here we do not need to include θ_2 as a parameter, since $\theta_2 = 1 - \theta_1$.)

Assume without loss of generality that $x_1 \leq x_2$. If $\theta_1 = 1/2$, then the answer should be x_1, since as we noted, when the weights are equal, we should use the unweighted method for combining, which in this case is the min. If $\theta_1 = 0$, then the answer should be x_2. This is under the assumption that when an argument has 0 weight, then it can be "dropped"; this is another assumption that will be made explicit later. Similarly, if $\theta_1 = 1$, so that $\theta_2 = 0$, then the answer should be x_1.

What about values of θ_1 other than 0, 1, or 1/2? Since the value is x_1 when $\theta_1 = 1/2$, it is reasonable to argue that the value should be x_1 whenever $\theta_1 \geq 1/2$; after all, if the value of x_2 becomes irrelevant (as long as it is bigger than x_1) for $\theta_1 = 1/2$, then surely it should be irrelevant for any larger value of θ_1, where we are weighting the first value (the x_1 value) even more highly. Another argument that the value should be x_1 whenever $\theta_1 \geq 1/2$ is that the value is x_1 for both $\theta_1 = 1/2$ and $\theta_1 = 1$, and so it should be the same for intermediate values. Later, we shall give a local linearity argument that says that the value should be x_1 whenever $\theta_1 \geq 1/2$. Furthermore, this local linearity argument says that the value when $\theta_1 < 1/2$ should be the appropriate linearly interpolated value between the value x_2 when $\theta_1 = 0$, and the value x_1 when $\theta_1 = 1/2$: this value is $2(x_1 - x_2)\theta_1 + x_2$.

What would we do when there are three arguments x_1, x_2, and x_3, and three weights θ_1, θ_2, and θ_3? Here the answer is not at all clear *a priori*. Our results enable us to answer this question, under reasonable assumptions. Our methods in this paper work for arbitrary scoring functions, not just average and min.

3 Definitions

We assume that we are given a finite index set $\mathcal{I}$, that intuitively represents the set of attributes. In the example we considered earlier, these attributes would include color and volume. We typically use I to denote some non-empty subset of $\mathcal{I}$. Let D be a set that represents the arguments of the scoring functions. In the case of fuzzy logic, we take D to be the closed interval $[0, 1]$. We shall take a *tuple X (over I)* to be a function with domain I and range D. We shall usually write x_i for $X(i)$. Let S be the set of possible scores; we shall take S to be an interval of real numbers.[1] In the case of fuzzy logic, S (like D) is the closed interval $[0, 1]$. A *scoring function b_I (over I)* is a function with domain D^I (the set of tuples over I) and range S, the set of scores. When $D = S$, as in fuzzy logic, the scoring function combines a collection of scores to obtain an overall score. In this case, it would certainly be natural to assume that $b_{\{i\}}(X) = x_i$; this says intuitively that the score when we restrict our attention to i is simply the value at i. For the sake of generality we do not assume that $b_{\{i\}}(X) = x_i$, even when $D = S$, since we never need this assumption.

Let $\mathcal{B}$ be a set of scoring functions that contains one scoring function b_I for each nonempty $I \subseteq \mathcal{I}$. This scoring function b_I is over I, that is, has domain D^I. We refer to $\mathcal{B}$ as an *unweighted collection of scoring functions*, to distinguish it from a weighted collection, which we shall define shortly.

A *weighting (over I)* is a function Θ with domain a nonempty index set $I \subseteq \mathcal{I}$ and range the closed interval $[0, 1]$, whose values $\Theta(i)$ sum to 1. Addition and scalar multiplication are defined in the usual way: $(\alpha \cdot \Theta)(i) = \alpha \cdot \Theta(i)$ for real numbers α, and $(\Theta + \Theta')(i) = \Theta(i) + \Theta'(i)$. We shall write θ_i for $\Theta(i)$.

Let $\mathcal{F}$ be a set of scoring functions that contains one scoring function f_Θ for each nonempty index set $I \subseteq \mathcal{I}$ and each weighting Θ over I. If Θ is over I, that is, has domain I, then the scoring function f_Θ is also over I, that is, has domain D^I. We refer to $\mathcal{F}$ as a *weighted collection of scoring functions*. This paper is concerned with the problem of obtaining a weighted collection of scoring functions from an unweighted collection of scoring functions in a way that is always applicable.

It is sometimes notationally convenient to define $b_I(X)$ even when the tuple X is not over I, but when X is over a superset of I. In this case, intuitively, the arguments outside of I are simply ignored. Formally, we let X' be the restriction of X to I, and define $b_I(X)$ to be $b_I(X')$. Similarly, when Θ is over I, and when X, X' are as above, we define $f_\Theta(X)$ to be $f_\Theta(X')$.

---

[1] We would like S to be an interval so that it is convex. We do not actually need S to be an interval of real numbers—it could just as well be an interval in an arbitrary ordered field. In particular, all of our results hold if S is taken to be an interval of rational numbers and each of the weights θ_i is a rational number.

If Θ is over I, we define the *support* of Θ to be the subset of I consisting of all $i \in I$ such that $\theta_i > 0$.

4 Desiderata

Assume that we are given an unweighted collection $\mathcal{B}$ of scoring functions. That is, intuitively, we are given a method of combining scores, such as the average or the min. We wish to define from the unweighted collection $\mathcal{B}$ a weighted collection $\mathcal{F}$ of scoring functions. That is, intuitively, we wish to decide how to combine scores when we weight the importance of the arguments. In this section, we consider two desirable properties for the relationship between $\mathcal{F}$ and $\mathcal{B}$. Later (Theorem 1), we shall show that under the additional natural assumption of a type of local linearity (that we also define in this section), there is a unique choice of $\mathcal{F}$ that satisfies these properties.

Our first desirable property relates $\mathcal{F}$ to $\mathcal{B}$: it says intuitively that each member of $\mathcal{F}$ with all of its weights equal should equal the corresponding member of $\mathcal{B}$. This corresponds to the intuition that $\mathcal{B}$ gives methods for obtaining an overall score in the case where no argument has higher weight than any other argument. Formally, denote the evenly-balanced weighting over I by E_I; thus, $(E_I)_i = 1/card(I)$ for each $i \in I$, where $card(I)$ denotes the cardinality of I. We say that the weighted collection $\mathcal{F}$ of scoring functions is *based on* the unweighted collection $\mathcal{B}$ of scoring functions if $f_{E_I} = b_I$ for every nonempty $I \subseteq \mathcal{I}$.

Our second desirable property says intuitively that if a particular argument has zero weight, then that argument can be dropped without affecting the value of the result. Formally, a weighted collection $\mathcal{F}$ of scoring functions is *compatible* if whenever Θ and X are over the same index set, and Θ' is the restriction of Θ to the support of Θ, then $f_\Theta(X) = f_{\Theta'}(X)$.

These two desirable properties are really essential—any method of going from an unweighted collection of scoring functions to a weighted collection that does not satisfy these two properties is seriously flawed. The weighted case must bear some relation to the unweighted case, and our notion of "based on" is the only natural choice. The notion of "compatibility" is also the only natural choice for handling zero weights.

These two properties are not sufficient to determine a unique weighted collection from an unweighted collection of scoring functions. We now give another property ("local linearity") that is quite reasonable, and that, together with the other two properties, does uniquely determine a weighted collection. Furthermore, this new property leads to a simple formula for scoring functions in the weighted case. We first need some more definitions.

Two weightings are called *order-equivalent* if they never "clash" by disagreeing on the order of importance of two components. More formally, assume that Θ, Θ' are weightings over I. Then Θ, Θ' are *order-equivalent* if there do *not* exist $i, j \in I$ with $\theta_i < \theta_j$ and $\theta'_j < \theta'_i$ both holding. For example, $(.2, .7, .1)$ and $(.3, .5, .2)$ are order-equivalent because in both cases, the second entry is biggest, the first entry is next-biggest, and the third entry is smallest. It is clear that order-equivalence is reflexive and symmetric. Order-equivalence is *not* transitive, since for example $(0,1)$ and $(1,0)$ are not order-equivalent, while $(0.5, 0.5)$ is order-equivalent to both $(0,1)$ and $(1,0)$.

We now define local linearity, and argue that it is fairly natural. Intuitively, local linearity says that the scoring functions act like a balance. If two weightings are order-equivalent, then local linearity demands that the weighting that is the midpoint of two order-equivalent weightings should produce a score that is the midpoint of the two scores produced by the given weightings. In fact, local linearity extends beyond the midpoint to any weighting that is a convex combination of two order-equivalent weightings: if a weighting is a convex combination of two weightings that are order-equivalent, then local linearity demands that the associated score should be the same convex combination of the scores associated with the given weightings. Formally, we say that a weighted collection $\mathcal{F}$ of scoring functions is *locally linear* if whenever Θ and Θ' are order-equivalent and $\alpha \in [0,1]$, then

$$f_{\alpha \cdot \Theta + (1-\alpha) \cdot \Theta'}(X) = \alpha \cdot f_{\Theta}(X) + (1-\alpha) \cdot f_{\Theta'}(X). \tag{1}$$

Our main theorem (Theorem 1) gives an explicit, simple formula for obtaining a weighted collection $\mathcal{F}$ of scoring functions from an unweighted collection $\mathcal{B}$ of scoring functions. The weighted collection $\mathcal{F}$ is based on $\mathcal{B}$, compatible, and locally linear. Furthermore, the theorem says that $\mathcal{F}$ is the unique such weighted collection of scoring functions.

A weighted collection $\mathcal{F}$ of scoring functions is *totally linear* if equation (1) always holds, even when Θ and Θ' are not necessarily order-equivalent. Although we argued above that local linearity is a reasonable assumption, we do not believe that total linearity is sensible to demand. When the order of importance of two components changes, a dramatic shift might occur, and there is no reason to assume that the score associated with the midpoint has any relation to the score associated with the endpoint weightings. It might even occur that the midpoint of two weightings is not order-equivalent to either weighting. For example, $(0.3, 0.4, 0.3)$ is the midpoint of $(0.1, 0.4, 0.5)$ and $(0.5, 0.4, 0.1)$ but is not order-equivalent to either one.

Indeed, as we shall see from Theorem 3, extending linearity to hold for all weightings and not merely the order-equivalent ones severely restricts the possible choices for the unweighted case. That is, total linearity of $\mathcal{F}$ can be obtained only for certain very restricted classes $\mathcal{B}$.

It is helpful to have a notation for selecting the most important (i.e., the largest) component of a weighting, down to the least important (i.e., the smallest) component of a weighting. A bijection σ that provides such a service is said to "order" the weighting. If σ orders a given weighting, then $\sigma(1)$ represents the most important component and $\sigma(m)$ represents the least important component (where m is the number of components). This is formalized in the next definition.

Assume that $m = card(I)$. A bijection σ from $\{1, \ldots, m\}$ onto I is said to *order* a weighting Θ over I if $\theta_{\sigma(1)} \geq \theta_{\sigma(2)} \geq \ldots \geq \theta_{\sigma(m)}$. It is easy to see that every weighting is ordered by some bijection σ. We define $\sigma[i]$ to be

$\{\sigma(1),\ldots,\sigma(i)\}$, for $1 \leq i \leq m$. Intuitively, if Θ is ordered by σ, then $\sigma[i]$ is the set of indices of the i largest θ_j's.

5 Main Theorem

We now give the main theorem of the paper. Let $\mathcal{B}$ be an unweighted collection of scoring functions. The theorem gives an explicit formula for a corresponding weighted collection $\mathcal{F}$ of scoring functions. As we shall explain, this formula is surprisingly simple, in that it involves far fewer terms than we might have guessed. Furthermore, the theorem says that this weighted collection is the unique one with the desirable properties we have discussed.

Theorem 1. *For every unweighted collection $\mathcal{B}$ of scoring functions, there exists a unique weighted collection $\mathcal{F}$ of scoring functions that is based on $\mathcal{B}$, compatible, and locally linear. Furthermore, if Θ and X are over I, if Θ is ordered by σ, and if $m = card(I)$, then*

$$f_\Theta(X) = m \cdot \theta_{\sigma(m)} \cdot b_{\sigma[m]}(X) + \sum_{i=1}^{m-1} i \cdot (\theta_{\sigma(i)} - \theta_{\sigma(i+1)}) \cdot b_{\sigma[i]}(X). \quad (2)$$

This formula (2) is both simple and simple to evaluate, given Θ and the b_I's. As an example of the formula, assume that $m = 3$, and $\theta_1 \geq \theta_2 \geq \theta_3$. Then formula (2) says that $f_{(\theta_1,\theta_2,\theta_3)}(x_1,x_2,x_3)$ equals

$$(\theta_1 - \theta_2) \cdot b_{\{1\}}(x_1) + 2 \cdot (\theta_2 - \theta_3) \cdot b_{\{1,2\}}(x_1,x_2) + 3 \cdot \theta_3 \cdot b_{\{1,2,3\}}(x_1,x_2,x_3).$$

We denote the family $\mathcal{F}$ of Theorem 1 by $\mathcal{F}(\mathcal{B})$. Note that if $b_I(X)$ is rational for each I, and if each θ_i is rational, then $f_\Theta(X)$ is also rational (cf. footnote 1 of Section 3). Note also that each of the m summands in (2) is nonnegative; this turns out to be useful for proving a later theorem (Theorem 4).

Clearly, we can rewrite (2) as a linear combination of the θ_i's: the result is

$$f_\Theta(X) = \theta_{\sigma(1)} \cdot b_{\sigma[1]}(X) + \sum_{i=2}^{m} \theta_{\sigma(i)} \cdot (i \cdot b_{\sigma[i]}(X) - (i-1) \cdot b_{\sigma[i-1]}(X)). \quad (3)$$

Unlike the situation with (2), some of the summands of (3) may be negative. Sometimes (such as in the derivation of Theorem 3) it is more useful to use (3) than (2).

The next result follows easily from Theorem 1.

Corollary 2. *Assume that Θ and X are over I, that Θ is ordered by σ, that $m = card(I)$, and that $f_\Theta(X) \in \mathcal{F}(\mathcal{B})$. Then there are $\alpha_1,\ldots,\alpha_m$ (with $\alpha_m = m \cdot \theta_{\sigma(m)}$) such that (1) $\alpha_i \geq 0$ for each i, (2) $\sum_{i=1}^{m} \alpha_i = 1$, and (3) $f_\Theta(X) = \sum_{i=1}^{m} \alpha_i \cdot b_{\sigma[i]}(X)$.*

Corollary 2 is rather surprising, since it is not clear *a priori* that f_Θ should depend only on $b_{\sigma[1]}, \ldots, b_{\sigma[m]}$, and not also on other b_I's. For example, when $m = 3$, each b_I is min, and $\theta_1 \geq \theta_2 \geq \theta_3$, then the formula for f_Θ is a convex combination of the three terms x_1, $\min(x_1, x_2)$, and $\min(x_1, x_2, x_3)$ only, and not of any of the terms x_2, x_3, $\min(x_1, x_3)$, or $\min(x_2, x_3)$. In general, f_Θ depends on only m of the $2^m - 1$ functions b_I. Thus, the formula is not only simple, but it is surprisingly simple.

At this point, it is perhaps worth commenting about the equality $\alpha_m = m \cdot \theta_{\sigma(m)}$ in Corollary 2. Now $0 \leq \theta_{\sigma(m)} \leq 1/m$ (the upper bound of $1/m$ follows from the fact that $m \cdot \theta_{\sigma(m)} = \alpha_m \leq 1$). Note that when $\theta_{\sigma(m)} = 1/m$ (so that $\Theta = E_I$), then $\alpha_m = 1$; then from Corollary 2 we see that $f_\Theta(X) = b_{\sigma[i]}(X)$. This reflects the fact that $\mathcal{F}$ is based on $\mathcal{B}$. Note that $b_{\sigma[m]}$ is the only member of $\mathcal{B}$ in $\sum_{i=1}^{m} \alpha_i \cdot b_{\sigma[i]}(X)$ of Corollary 2 whose index set is all of I. In particular, when $\theta_{\sigma(m)} = 0$, then the index set of every member of $\mathcal{B}$ in $\sum_{i=1}^{m} \alpha_i \cdot b_{\sigma[i]}(X)$ is contained in the proper subset $\{\sigma(1), \ldots, \sigma(i-1)\}$ of I. This corresponds to the fact that $\mathcal{F}(\mathcal{B})$ is compatible, that is, scores with zero weight do not affect the result. We note that the fact that $\alpha_m = m \cdot \theta_{\sigma(m)}$ turns out to be useful in the proof of Theorem 4.

We close this section with some intuitive remarks about the geometry behind obtaining the weighted collection of scoring functions from the unweighted collection. In fact, historically, this geometric intuition is what led us first to discover Theorem 1. We shall show how to determine a formula for f_Θ by induction on the number of nonzero entries of Θ. To start off the induction, note that if Θ has only one nonzero entry, so that $\theta_i = 1$ for some i, then then f_Θ is uniquely determined, since then $f_\Theta(X) = f_{E_{\{i\}}}(X) = b_{\{i\}}(X)$ from the fact that $\mathcal{F}$ is based on $\mathcal{B}$. Assume now that Θ has m nonzero entries. By compatibility, we can assume that Θ is over an index set I of size m. Let S be the $(m-1)$-dimensional hyperplane in m-dimensional Euclidean space (indexed by I), where S is defined by $\sum_{i \in I} \theta_i' = 1$. Let R be the (bounded) subregion of S where $\theta_i' \geq 0$ for each $i \in I$. For each $i \in I$, let B_i be the $(m-2)$-dimensional hyperplane that is the intersection of S with the $(m-1)$-dimensional hyperplane defined by $\theta_i' = 0$. Then the boundary B of R is the union of the B_i's. Each Θ' in B has at least one 0 entry. Therefore, by induction hypothesis (and by compatibility), we can assume that we already have determined a formula for $f_{\Theta'}$ for each Θ' in B. Now Θ is a linear combination of E_I and of some Θ' in B; say $\Theta = \alpha \cdot E_I + (1 - \alpha) \cdot \Theta'$, where $\alpha \in [0, 1]$. (In fact, we see from the uniqueness part of the proof of Theorem 1 that $\alpha = m \cdot \theta_{\sigma(m)}$ when Θ is ordered by σ.) We know that $f_{E_I} = b_I$, since $\mathcal{F}$ is based on $\mathcal{B}$, and by induction hypothesis we know a formula for $f_{\Theta'}$. By local linearity, we know that we can then take f_Θ to be $\alpha \cdot b_I + (1 - \alpha) \cdot f_{\Theta'}$. This turns out to give us the formula in the statement of Theorem 1.

6 Totally Linear Collections

When is the class $\mathcal{F}(\mathcal{B})$ not only locally linear, but even totally linear? Theorem 3 below tells us that this happens only in very limited circumstances, where the values of b_I with $card(I) > 1$ are completely determined by the values of b_I with $card(I) = 1$. In fact, under the assumption of total linearity, it follows from Theorem 3 below (in the fact that part 1 implies part 2) that $b_I(X)$ must be the average of $b_{\{i_1\}}(X), \ldots, b_{\{i_m\}}(X)$ if $I = \{i_1, \ldots, i_m\}$.

It is not surprising that if $f_\Theta(X)$ is the weighted average of $b_{\{i_1\}}(X), \ldots, b_{\{i_m\}}(X)$, weighted according to Θ, then $\mathcal{F}(\mathcal{B})$ is totally linear. The fact that part 1 implies part 3 in Theorem 3 below shows that this is the only possible way for $\mathcal{F}(\mathcal{B})$ to be totally linear.

Theorem 3. *The following are equivalent:*

1. *$\mathcal{F}(\mathcal{B})$ is totally linear.*
2. *$b_I(X) = (1/card(I)) \cdot \sum_{i \in I} b_{\{i\}}(X)$ holds whenever X is over I.*
3. *$f_\Theta(X) = \sum_{i \in I} \theta_i \cdot b_{\{i\}}(X)$ holds whenever Θ and X are over I.*

Under the natural assumption (discussed near the beginning of Section 3) that $b_{\{i\}}(X) = x_i$, part 3 says that $f_\Theta(X) = \sum_{i \in I} \theta_i \cdot x_i$, a simple linear combination.

7 Inherited Properties

So far the scoring functions have been completely arbitrary. In practice, these functions usually enjoy many properties such as continuity, monotonicity, etc. As we discuss in this section, these properties are inherited by scoring functions in the corresponding weighted family.

If X and X' are each tuples over the same index set I, let us write $X \geq X'$ if $x_i \geq x_i'$ for each $i \in I$, and $X > X'$ if $x_i > x_i'$ for each $i \in I$. Let f be a scoring function over I. We say that f is *monotonic* if $f(X) \geq f(X')$ whenever $X \geq X'$, and *strictly monotonic* if $f(X) > f(X')$ whenever $X > X'$. We certainly expect a scoring function to be monotonic: intuitively, if the individual scores according to X are each at least as big as the corresponding scores according to X', then the overall score of X should be at least as big as the overall score of X'. Similarly, we expect a scoring function to be strictly monotonic; if it is monotonic but not strictly monotonic, then there is a portion of the domain where the scoring function is insensitive. In fact, in Section 9 we shall mention an example of a scoring function that is monotonic but not strictly monotonic, that arises under a certain rule for obtaining weighted families of scoring functions; we feel that such a scoring function is undesirable. We also expect a scoring function to be continuous: slight changes in individual scores should lead to only slight changes in the overall score.

We now define a notion of a scoring function being *strict*. This notion will be important in Section 8. For this notion, we assume that, as in fuzzy logic, the domain D and the range S are both the closed interval $[0, 1]$. Intuitively, a scoring function is strict if it takes on the value 1 precisely when all of its arguments are 1. In making this definition precise, there is a slight subtlety, brought on by the fact that, for example, we have defined $b_I(X)$ whenever X is over a superset of I. Formally, we say that b_I is strict if whenever X is over I, then $b_I(X) = 1$ iff $x_i = 1$ for every $i \in I$. Strictness is certainly a property we would expect of any scoring function that is used to evaluate the conjunction. We now define strictness in the weighted case. Assume that Θ is over I. We say that f_Θ is strict if whenever X is over I, then $f_\Theta(X) = 1$ iff $x_i = 1$ for every $i \in I$. Furthermore, we say that f_Θ has full support if the support of Θ is I. We would not expect f_Θ to be strict unless f_Θ has full support.

A scoring function f is called *translation-preserving* if $f(X') = f(X) + a$ provided $x_i' = x_i + a$ for every i in the domain of X. The idea behind a translation-preserving scoring function is that if all the input scores are increased by the same amount, then the output score is increased by that same amount. Unlike the situation with continuity and monotonicity, we do not necessarily expect a scoring function to be translation-preserving. Of course, the min function is translation-preserving. In fact, as we shall discuss later (Proposition 7), min is the unique monotonic, translation-preserving scoring function (up to boundary conditions).

A scoring function f *satisfies betweenness* if $\min X \leq f(X) \leq \max X$ for every X. This says that the resulting score lies between the smallest and largest of its arguments. This is certainly a natural property that we would expect scoring functions to enjoy. A scoring function f *satisfies identity* if $f(x, ..., x) = x$ for every x in the domain D. This says that if all of the "input scores" are equal, then the resulting output score has this same value. It is clear that if a scoring function satisfies betweenness, then it also satisfies identity.

The next theorem says that the properties we have discussed in this section are inherited by the weighted family of scoring functions.

Theorem 4. 1. *If every scoring function in $\mathcal{B}$ is continuous (resp. is monotonic, is strictly monotonic, is translation-preserving, satisfies betweenness, satisfies identity), then every scoring function in $\mathcal{F}(\mathcal{B})$ is continuous (resp. is monotonic, is strictly monotonic, is translation-preserving, satisfies betweenness, satisfies identity) as well.*

2. *If every scoring function in $\mathcal{B}$ is strict, then every scoring function in $\mathcal{F}(\mathcal{B})$ that has full support is strict as well.*

We next consider a property that is a property not of an individual scoring function, but of a class of scoring functions. We would like to show that some sort of symmetry is inherited by weighted collections from unweighted ones. Normally, a function is called symmetric if it is unchanged by any permutation of its arguments. In our setting, this translates to saying that we can take any permutation of the indices without changing the result. We now formally define the notion of symmetry. In this definition, $\circ$ represents functional composition, and $\delta(I)$ represents the image of the set I under the function δ when I is a subset of the domain of δ.

An unweighted collection $\mathcal{B}$ of scoring functions is called *symmetric* if $b_{\delta(I)}(X) = b_I(X \circ \delta)$ for each permutation δ of $\mathcal{I}$, each nonempty $I \subseteq \mathcal{I}$, and each $X \in D^{\delta(I)}$. A weighted collection $\mathcal{F}$ of scoring functions is called *symmetric* if $f_\Theta(X) = f_{\Theta \circ \delta}(X \circ \delta)$ for each permutation δ of $\mathcal{I}$, each Θ over $\delta(I)$, and each $X \in D^{\delta(I)}$. (Note that f_Θ and X are over $\delta(I)$, and that $f_{\Theta \circ \delta}$ and $X \circ \delta$ are over I.) Being symmetric means intuitively that we do not distinguish among the arguments.

Theorem 5. *If $\mathcal{B}$ is symmetric, then $\mathcal{F}(\mathcal{B})$ is symmetric.*

Note that the average and the min are symmetric scoring functions. In fact, we believe that most naturally-occurring scoring functions are symmetric. In some circumstances, there might be a reason to treat the arguments differently and thereby take a nonsymmetric scoring function. One such scenario could arise if, say, all of the scores about one particular attribute are guaranteed to be at most 1/2, but this is not true about the other attributes. Assume that in this case we are "designing" a scoring function with two arguments x_1 and x_2, where x_1 is guaranteed to be at most 1/2. Instead of, say, taking the scoring function to be the average $(x_1 + x_2)/2$, it would probably be more reasonable to "normalize" and take $(2x_1 + x_2)/2$ as a scoring function. This leads to a family that is not symmetric.

8 Low Database Access Cost

Garlic [CHS+95, CHN+95] is a multimedia information system being developed at the IBM Almaden Research Center. It is designed to be capable of integrating data that resides in different database systems as well as a variety of non-database data servers. A single Garlic query can access data in a number of different subsystems. An example of a nontraditional subsystem that Garlic accesses is QBIC [NBE+93] ("Query By Image Content"). QBIC can search for images by various visual characteristics such as color, shape, and texture. In [Fa96], the first author developed an efficient algorithm for evaluating conjunctions in such a system, when the conjuncts are independent. In this section, we show that this algorithm can be carried over to the weighted case.

Let us begin with an example, where we deal first with the unweighted case. Consider again the fuzzy conjunction *(Color='red')* $\land$ *(Sound='loud')*. We denote this query by Q. Assume that two different subsystems deal with color and sound (for example, QBIC might deal with color). Garlic has to piece together information from both subsystems in order to answer the query Q. Let I be the index set {Color, Sound}, and let o be an object. Assume that the redness score of object o, as determined by the subsystem dealing with color, is x_1, and the loudness score of object o, as determined by the subsystem dealing with sound, is x_2. Then, in the setup of this paper, we would take the overall score of object o under query Q to be $b_I(x_1, x_2)$. Thus, the overall score is determined by applying the relevant scoring function (namely, b_I) to the redness score and the loudness score.

Let us say that we are interested in finding the top 10 answers to query Q (that is, the 10 objects with the highest overall scores, along with their scores). One way to do this would be to evaluate the query on every single object in the database, and take the 10 objects with the highest overall scores (ties would be broken arbitrarily). The problem with this naive algorithm is that there is a very high database access cost[2]: every single object in the database must be accessed. The first author [Fa96] gives an algorithm that is much more efficient, provided that the conjuncts are independent. He shows that if the scoring function (in this case, b_I) is monotonic, then the database access cost is of the order of the square root of the number of objects in the database. (More precisely, it is shown that if there are m conjuncts, and N objects in the database, then the database access cost for finding the top k objects in the database is $O(N^{(m-1)/m}k^{1/m})$, with arbitrarily high probability. For details about the probabilistic assumptions, see [Fa96].) Furthermore, it is shown that if the scoring function is strict, then this is optimal.

What about the weighted case, where, say, we care twice as much about the color as about the sound? It follows from Theorem 4 that if every scoring function in $\mathcal{B}$ is monotonic and strict, then every scoring function in $\mathcal{F}(\mathcal{B})$ that has full support is monotonic and strict as well. Now the upper bound in [Fa96] depends only on the scoring functions being monotonic, and the matching lower bound depends only on the scoring functions being strict. Therefore, we have the following theorem.

Theorem 6. *Assume that every scoring function in $\mathcal{B}$ is monotonic and strict. There is an algorithm $\mathcal{A}$ for finding the top k answers to the query determined by $f_\Theta \in \mathcal{F}(\mathcal{B})$. If the support of Θ consists of m independent attributes, then the database access cost for algorithm $\mathcal{A}$ is $O(N^{(m-1)/m}k^{1/m})$ with arbitrarily high probability, and this is optimal.*

9 Related Work

There is much work in the economics literature about indifference curves. This includes work on computing optimal indifference curves (which depend on user-supplied weightings). Since the focus there is on computing optimality and the focus in this paper is on combining scores in a way that preserves desirable properties, the other work is only tangentially related. See [KR76] for a more complete discussion.

We now discuss two methods from the literature for obtaining a weighted family of scoring functions from an unweighted family, and compare them with our approach. Each of these methods deals only with certain unweighted families, rather than, as in our approach, with arbitrary unweighted families.

---

[2] The cost model, including the definition of "database access cost", is defined formally in [Fa96]. Intuitively, the database access cost corresponds to the number of elements accessed in the database.

Method 1: The first method is inspired by a paper by Dubois and Prade [DP86]. It deals with the case where the min function is used in the unweighted case (in fact, the title of Dubois and Prade's paper is "Weighted Minimum and Maximum Operations in Fuzzy Set Theory"). Their underlying scenario and goals are actually quite different from ours (for example, instead of dealing with probabilities θ_i, they deal with possibility distributions [Za78]). Nonetheless, it is instructive to compare the explicit formula that they obtain for the "weighted min", and see how it fares under our criteria.

Assume again that the range of scores is $[0, 1]$. Let X be a vector over I, let $b_I(X) = min_{i \in I}\{x_i\}$ and let

$$f_\Theta(X) = \min_{i \in I}\left\{\max\left\{1 - (\theta_i/M), x_i\right\}\right\}, \tag{4}$$

where $M = \max_{i \in I}\{\theta_i\}$. It is easy to check that $\mathcal{F}$ is a compatible collection of scoring functions that is based on $\mathcal{B}$. Note that $\mathcal{F}$ is not locally linear.

An attractive feature of this formula for f_Θ is that it is simple, it is continuous, monotonic, and strict, it satisfies betweenness and identity, and the corresponding family is symmetric. Since it is monotonic and strict, it follows that for this choice of f_Θ, there is an algorithm $\mathcal{A}$ as in Theorem 6 such that the last sentence of that theorem holds. However, the formula in (4) is not strictly monotonic. For example, let $\theta_1 = 2/3$ and $\theta_2 = 1/3$. The reader can easily verify that $f_\Theta(.7, .3)$ and $f_\Theta(.8, .4)$ are each equal to .5. In fact, it is easy to verify that if $x_2 \leq .5 \leq x_1$, then $f_\Theta(X) = .5$. This is undesirable, since it says intuitively that f_Θ is insensitive to its arguments in this region.

Also, f_Θ is not translation-preserving, since $f_\Theta(.8, .4) \neq f_\Theta(.7, .3) + .1$. We consider this undesirable because, as the following proposition shows, the essence of min (the underlying scoring function) is that it is monotonic and translation-preserving. That is, up to boundary conditions, it is uniquely determined by being monotonic and translation-preserving.

Proposition 7. min *is the unique monotonic, translation-preserving function f on $[0, 1]$ for which $f(0, 1) = 0 = f(1, 0)$.*

The formula (4) is computationally a little simpler than (2). Therefore, there might be situations, where, say, computational simplicity is more important than strict monotonicity and translation invariance, when (4) would be preferable to use rather than (2).

Method 2: The second method is from a paper by Salton, Fox and Wu on information retrieval [SFW83], and deals with the case where a version of the Euclidean distance is used in the unweighted case.

Assume again that the range of scores is $[0, 1]$. Let X be a vector over I, let

$$b_I(X) = \sqrt{\frac{\sum_{i \in I} x_i^2}{card(I)}}, \tag{5}$$

and let

$$f_\Theta(X) = \sqrt{\frac{\sum_{i \in I} \theta_i^2 x_i^2}{\sum_{i \in I} \theta_i^2}}. \tag{6}$$

It is easy to check that $\mathcal{F}$ is a compatible collection of scoring functions that is based on $\mathcal{B}$. Note that $\mathcal{F}$ is not locally linear. Unlike other scoring functions we have discussed, these take us out of the rationals.

The formula (6) is quite reasonable: it gives a natural generalization of the unweighted formula (5); it is continuous, strictly monotonic, and strict, it satisfies betweenness and identity, and the corresponding family is symmetric. It is not translation-preserving, but we would not expect it to be, since the formula in the unweighted case is not translation-preserving.

As was the case with Method 1 in this section, the formula for f_Θ, namely (6), is computationally easier than our formula (2) in this case, since only one square root is involved in (6), whereas m square roots are involved in (2). Also, as with Method 1 in this section, because of monotonicity and strictness, it follows that for this choice (6) of f_Θ, there is an algorithm $\mathcal{A}$ as in Theorem 6 such that the last sentence of that theorem holds.

One possible objection to (6) is that it is not clear why θ_i^2, rather than θ_i, is being used in the formula; either seems like a reasonable alternative. In fact, QBIC [NBE+93] also uses a variation of Euclidean distance, and in the weighted case uses θ_i rather than θ_i^2. Because of the specific form of the formula (5) for b_I (the unweighted case), there is a natural extension to f_Θ (the weighted case), which is (6). This is often not the situation; min is a good example.

The point of this example is that for certain special unweighted collections $\mathcal{B}$, there may be a natural way to obtain a weighted collection that is not the weighted collection $\mathcal{F}(\mathcal{B})$ that our methodology gives us. In fact, the extension (6) is more in the spirit of the unweighted case (5) than our extension (2). But our methodology has the advantage that it *always* gives us a (simple) way to obtain a weighted collection of scoring functions from an unweighted collection, no matter what the unweighted collection is.

10 Summary

The typical user query in a multimedia system asks for "good" matches (as indicated by a score) rather than "perfect" matches (as indicated by a Boolean value of 0 or 1). There are many possible methods for combining subscores into a single score. These methods include combining functions such as average, min, etc. Of course, it is rare that users wish to give equal weight to all components. This paper presents, by means of a surprisingly simple formula, a general method that extends any unweighted collection $\mathcal{B}$ of scoring functions to a weighted collection $\mathcal{F}(\mathcal{B})$ of scoring functions. This general method preserves a number of desirable properties, such as continuity and monotonicity. Furthermore, $\mathcal{F}(\mathcal{B})$ is the only weighted collection that is based on $\mathcal{B}$, compatible, and locally linear.

11 Acknowledgements

We thank Joe Halpern for many useful discussions and for the suggestion that we extend our results to include the non-symmetric case. We also thank Laura Haas and Joe Halpern for comments on the paper.

References

[BG73] R. Bellman and M. Giertz, On the Analytic Formalism of the Theory of Fuzzy Sets, *Information Sciences* **5** (1973), pp. 149–156.

[CG96] S. Chaudhuri and L. Gravano, Optimizing Queries over Multimedia Repositories, *Proc. ACM SIGMOD Conference*, 1996, pp. 91–102.

[CHS+95] M. J. Carey, L. M. Haas, P. M. Schwarz, M. Arya, W. F. Cody, R. Fagin, M. Flickner, A. W. Luniewski, W. Niblack, D. Petkovic, J. Thomas, J. H. Williams, and E. L. Wimmers, Towards Heterogeneous Multimedia Information Systems: the Garlic Approach, RIDE-DOM '95 (5th Int'l Workshop on Research Issues in Data Engineering: Distributed Object Management), 1995, pp. 124–131.

[CHN+95] W. F. Cody, L. M. Haas, W. Niblack, M. Arya, M. J. Carey, R. Fagin, M. Flickner, D. S. Lee, D. Petkovic, P. M. Schwarz, J. Thomas, M. T. Roth, J. H. Williams, and E. L. Wimmers, Querying Multimedia Data from Multiple Repositories by Content: the Garlic Project, *IFIP 2.6 3rd Working Conference on Visual Database Systems (VDB-3)*, 1995.

[DP84] D. Dubois and H. Prade, Criteria Aggregation and Ranking of Alternatives in the Framework of Fuzzy Set Theory, in *Fuzzy Sets and Decision Analysis* (H. J. Zimmermann, L. A. Zadeh, and B. Gaines, Eds.), TIMS Studies in Management Sciences **20** (1984), pp. 209–240.

[DP86] D. Dubois and H. Prade, Weighted Minimum and Maximum Operations in Fuzzy Set Theory, *Information Sciences* **39** (1986), pp. 205–210.

[Fa96] R. Fagin, Combining Fuzzy Information from Multiple Systems, *Fifteenth ACM Symp. on Principles of Database Systems*, 1996, pp. 216–226. Full version appears in http://www.almaden.ibm.com/cs/people/fagin/pods96rj.ps

[KR76] R. L. Keeney and H. Raiffa, *Decisions with Multiple Objectives: Preferences and Value Tradeoffs*, John Wiley & Sons, New York (1976).

[NBE+93] W. Niblack, R. Barber, W. Equitz, M. Flickner, E. Glasman, D. Petkovic, and P. Yanker, The QBIC Project: Querying Images by Content Using Color, Texture and Shape, *SPIE Conference on Storage and Retrieval for Image and Video Databases* (1993), volume 1908, pp. 173–187. QBIC Web server is http://wwwqbic.almaden.ibm.com/

[SFW83] G. Salton, E. A. Fox, and H. Wu, Extended Information Retrieval, *Comm. ACM* **26**,12 (1983), pp. 1022–1036.

[VG83] W. Voxman and R. Goetschel, A Note on the Characterization of the Max and Min Operators, *Information Sciences* **30** (1983), pp. 5–10.

[Wi96] E. L. Wimmers, Minimal Bellman-Giertz Theorems, to appear.

[Ya82] R. R. Yager, Some Procedures for Selecting Fuzzy Set-Theoretic Operations, *International Journal General Systems* **8** (1982), pp. 115–124.

[Za65] L. A. Zadeh, Fuzzy Sets, *Information and Control* **8** (1965), pp. 338–353.

[Za78] L. A. Zadeh, Fuzzy Sets as a Basis for a Theory of Possibility, *Fuzzy Sets and Systems* **1** (1978), pp. 3–28.

[Zi91] H. Zimmermann, *Fuzzy Set Theory*, Kluwer Academic Publishers, Boston (1991).

Queries and Computation on the Web*

Serge Abiteboul[1] ** and Victor Vianu[2]

[1] Computer Science Department, Stanford University, Stanford, CA 94305-9045
[2] Univ. of California at San Diego, CSE 0114, La Jolla, CA 92093-0114

Abstract. The paper introduces a model of the Web as an infinite, semi-structured set of objects. We reconsider the classical notions of genericity and computability of queries in this new context and relate them to styles of computation prevalent on the Web, based on browsing and searching. We revisit several well-known declarative query languages (first-order logic, Datalog, and Datalog with negation) and consider their computational characteristics in terms the notions introduced in this paper. In particular, we are interested in languages or fragments thereof which can be implemented by browsing, or by browsing and searching combined. Surprisingly, stratified and well-founded semantics for negation turn out to have basic shortcomings in this context, while inflationary semantics emerges as an appealing alternative.

1 Introduction

The World Wide Web [BLCL+94] is a tremendous source of information which can be viewed, in some sense, as a large database. However, the nature of the Web is fundamentally different from traditional databases and raises qualitatively new issues. Its main characteristics are its global nature and the loosely structured information it holds. In this paper, we consider some fundamental aspects of querying the Web.

We use as a model of the Web an abstraction that captures its global nature, and the semi-structured information it holds. Perhaps the most fundamental aspect of our model is that we view the Web as infinite. We believe this captures the intuition that exhaustive exploration of the Web is –or will soon become– prohibitively expensive. The infiniteness assumption can be viewed as a convenient metaphor, much like Turing machines with infinite tapes are useful abstractions of computers with finite (but potentially very large) memory. Note that our approach is fundamentally different from previous attempts to model infinite data (e.g. [HH93, KKR90]) which focus on finitely representable databases. In contrast, we do not assume the Web is finitely represented. Instead, we view it as

---

* Work supported in part by the National Science Foundation under grant number IRI-9221268.

** This author's permanent position is INRIA-Rocquencourt, France. His work was supported in part by the Air Force Wright Laboratory Aeronautical Systems Center under ARPA Contract F33615-93-1-1339, and by the Air Force Rome Laboratories under ARPA Contract F30602-95-C-0119

a possibly nonrecursive infinite structure which can never be entirely explored. Our model leads to a focus on querying and computation where exploration of the Web is controlled. This raises issues akin to safety in classical databases.

The data model we use is similar to several models for unstructured data recently introduced, e.g., [Q⁺95, CACS94, BDS95]. The Web consists of an infinite set of objects. Objects have a value and/or may reference other objects via labeled links. The set of labels for each object is not fixed, unlike the attributes of a relation. Intuitively, an object can be viewed as a Web page; the value is the content of a page; labels provide links that allow navigating through the Web, in hypertext style.

We begin by exploring the notion of computable query in the context of the Web. Our model is along the lines of the computable queries of Chandra and Harel [CH80]. We introduce a machine model of computation on the Web that we call a Web machine. This works much like a Turing machine, but takes as input an infinite string and may produce an infinite answer. We also introduce two particular machine models that capture directly the main styles of computing used on the Web: browsing and searching. The *browser* machine model allows for navigational exploration of the Web. The *browse/search* machine additionally allows searching in the style of search engines.

Based on the Web machine, we define the notions of computability and eventual computability of queries. The latter notion arises from the fact that infinite answers to queries are allowed. A query is *computable* if its answer is always finite and computable by a halting Web machine. A query is *eventually computable* if there is a Web machine, possibly nonterminating, which eventually outputs each object in the answer to the query. Interesting connections hold with the browser machine and with the browse/search machine. We show that every generic and computable query is in fact computable by a browser machine. This confirms the intuition that browsing is in some sense the only way to control computation on the Web. We also show that the set of generic queries which are eventually computable by a Web machine is precisely the same as the set of generic queries which are eventually computable by a browse/search machine. Thus, everything can be done by a combination of browsing and searching.

To express queries, one needs query languages. We are interested in the ability of *declarative* database query languages to express queries on the Web. To this end, we revisit the classical languages FO (first-order logic), Datalog, and Datalog¬. The questions of interest for each language are the following: (i) Are the queries in the language computable or eventually computable? (ii) Which fragments of each language can be implemented by browsers and which by a combination of browsing and searching? We provide syntactic restrictions that guarantee computability by browsers or by browse/search machines in FO and Datalog⁽¬⁾.

One of the interesting results of the paper is with respect to negation. The "positive" fragment of FO is eventually computable. The addition of recursion yields no problem. However, negation brings trouble, and some simple FO queries are not eventually computable. The Datalog¬ languages yield some surprises:

the standard semantics, stratified and well-founded [GRS88], are ill-suited for expressing eventually computable queries, whereas the more procedural inflationary semantics [AV88, KP88] turns out to be naturally suited to express such queries, and thus has a fundamental advantage over the first two semantics.

Computation on the Web is still in its infancy, and it is premature to propose a definitive model. It is not yet clear what the right abstractions are. We believe that our model of the Web captures some essential aspects; future developments may confirm or invalidate this. Clearly, we have ignored in our investigation many important aspects, such as the communication costs associated with browsing and searching; the notion of locality; the essentially distributed nature of the Web and the fact that concurrent processes may participate in evaluating a query; updates; the fact that users are often satisfied with incomplete, imprecise or partially incorrect answers.

Query languages for the Web have attracted a lot of attention recently, e.g., W3QL [KS95] that focuses on extensibility, WebSQL [MMM96] that provides a formal semantics and introduce a notion of locality, or WebLog [LSS96] that is based on a Datalog-like syntax. Since HTML (the core structure of the Web) can be viewed as an instance of SGML, the work on querying structured document, e.g., [CACS94, GZC89] is also pertinent, along with work on querying semi-structured data (see [A97]). The work on query languages for hypertext structures, e.g., [MW95, CM89, MW93] is also relevant.

In the next section, we introduce Web machines, browser machines, and browse/search machines. We then formalize the notion of (eventually) computable query on the Web. The following section considers FO, Datalog and Datalog$^\neg$, and establishes connections to (eventual) computability, browsing, and searching. Finally, we provide some conclusions.

2   Computation on the Web

We model the Web as a set of semi-structured objects in the style of [Q$^+$95, BDS95]. More precisely, we view the Web as an infinite database over the fixed relational schema $\{Obj(oid), Ref(source,label,destination), Val(oid,value)\}$. The meaning of the above relations is as follows:

1. *Obj* provides an infinite set of objects.
2. Relation *Ref* specifies, for some of the objects, a *finite* set of links to other objects, each of which has a label. More precisely, $Ref(o_1,l,o_2)$ indicates that there is an edge labeled l between o_1 and o_2.
3. Relation *Val* specifies a value for some of the objects. Thus, $Val(o,v)$ specifies that object o has value v.

Intuitively, an object corresponds to a Web page. The value is the content of the page, and references model labeled links to other pages.

A *Web instance* is an *infinite* structure[3] over the above schema, satisfying the following constraints:

$Obj = \pi_{source}(Ref) \cup \pi_{oid}(Val)$; $\qquad$ *Val* satisfies the fd *source* $\rightarrow$ *value*;

$\pi_{destination}(Ref) \subseteq Obj$; $\qquad\qquad$ $\forall o \in Obj,\ \sigma_{source=o}(Ref)$ is finite.

Thus, each object must have a value or some references to other objects. An object can have at most one value and only finitely many references to other objects. Every referenced object must belong to the specified set of objects of the instance. The set of all Web instances is denoted **inst**(Web).

Let I be a Web instance. For each object o in $I(Obj)$, the *description* of o in I consists of the finite set of tuples in I whose first coordinate is o. Thus, the description of an object provides its outgoing links and/or its value. It does *not* provide the set of in-going links (which can be infinite). We may regard *Ref* as a labeled graph whose vertices are objects. We say that object o' is reachable from object o if this holds in the labeled graph given by *Ref*. The distance between two objects is also defined with respect to the *Ref* graph.

A first attempt

We wish to formalize the notion of a query on the Web. We first explore a straightforward extension of the classical notion of query, which we will soon refine. Let a query be a mapping on **inst**(Web) which associates to each Web instance I a subset of $I(Obj)$.

We wish to have a notion of *generic* and *computable* query that is appropriate for the Web. As in the classical definition proposed by Chandra and Harel [CH80], a query is *generic* if it commutes with isomorphisms over **inst**(Web). More precisely, a query q is *generic* if for each I and each one-to-one mapping ρ on the domain (extended to I in the obvious way), $q(\rho(I)) = \rho(q(I))$. Intuitively, this means that the result only depends on the information in I and is independent of any particular encoding chosen for I.

The definition of computability requires a departure from the classical definition, because inputs and outputs are possibly infinite. Let a *Web machine* be a Turing machine with three tapes: (1) a right-infinite input tape, (2) a two-way-infinite work tape, and (3) a right-infinite output tape. Initially, the input tape contains an infinite word (an encoding of the Web instance), and the work and output tapes are empty. The input tape head is positioned at the first cell. The moves are standard, except that the output tape head can only move to the right (so nothing can be erased once it is written on the output tape).

Web instances can be encoded on the input tape in a straightforward manner. Let α be a successor relation on all elements occurring in I (including oid's, labels, and values). For each element e occurring in I, let $enc_\alpha(e)$ be the binary representation of the rank of e in the ordering α. An instance I is encoded as

$$enc_\alpha(\widehat{o_1})\#\#enc_\alpha(\widehat{o_2})\#\#...enc_\alpha(\widehat{o_m})\#\#...$$

---

[3] All infinite structures mentioned in the paper are countable, unless otherwise specified.

where $o_1, o_2, ..., o_m, ...$ is the list of oid's in $I(Obj)$ in the order specified by α and for each i, $enc_\alpha(\widehat{o_i})$ is a standard encoding with respect to α of the description of o_i. (Recall that the description of o_i is the finite structure.)

Note that in the above encoding, the finite information about each object is clustered together. This has nontrivial consequences. Some of the results below do not hold otherwise. Our encoding presents the advantage that it models accurately the real situation on the Web (information is clustered around pages).

The output $q(I)$ of a query q on input I is a set of objects, that is encoded as $enc_\alpha(o_{i_1}) \# ... \# enc_\alpha(o_{i_k}) ...$, where $o_{i_1}, ... o_{i_k} ...$ are the objects in $q(I)$, in *some* order. No particular order is imposed on the presentation of objects in the answer, so many possible answers are possible. Allowing this flexibility is important for technical reasons, since some of the results below would not hold if we required that objects be output in lexicographical order. (Intuitively, one could not output an object o before being certain that no "smaller" object is in the answer). By slight abuse of notation, we denote any such presentation of the answer by $enc_\alpha(q(I))$.

Let us now make a first attempt at defining the notion of a computable query. A query q is *0-computable* (we will abandon soon this definition) if there exists a Web machine which on input $enc_\alpha(I)$ halts and produces $enc_\alpha(q(I))$ on the output tape, for each I in inst(Web) and each α. Note that every 0-computable query produces a finite answer for each input. A query q is *0-eventually computable* if there exists a Web machine whose computation on input $enc_\alpha(I)$ has the following properties:

- the content of the output tape at each point in the computation is a prefix of $enc_\alpha(q(I))$, and
- for each $o \in q(I)$, its encoding $enc_\alpha(o)$ occurs on the output tape at some point in the computation.

Note that if q is 0-eventually computable the Web machine is not required to terminate, even if $q(I)$ happens to be finite.

It turns out that the above definitions need some further refining. Indeed, as things stand, the only queries that are 0-computable are in some sense trivial. More precisely, we call a query q *trivial* if $q(I) = \emptyset$ for every Web instance I. We claim that every 0-computable query is trivial. (Note that there are nontrivial 0-*eventually* computable queries on infinite databases, e.g., the query that outputs the set of oid's.) The argument for 0-computable queries goes as follows. Suppose q is a 0-computable query and $q(I) \neq \emptyset$ for some input I. Let W be a Web machine that computes q. Observe that W only reads a finite prefix ω of $enc_\alpha(I)$. Now consider an instance $\bar{I}$ consisting of infinitely many isomorphic copies of I over disjoint sets of oid's and an ordering β on the elements of $\bar{I}$ such that ω is also a prefix of $enc_\beta(\bar{I})$. Clearly, $\bar{I}$ and β exist and by genericity $q(\bar{I})$ is infinite. This is a contradiction, since q is computable and therefore produces only finite answers. Similarly, there is no nontrivial 0-eventually computable query that always produces finite answers.

Observe that 0-computability makes sense on finite databases (and indeed corresponds to the standard notion of computability). However, we are concerned here with Web instances, which are infinite. Since terminating computation remains important in this context, we modify our notion of computability to allow for meaningful finite computations.

A second attempt

The source of the problem with our definitions so far is that any finite computation on $enc_\alpha(I)$ sees an arbitrary finite sample of I, determined by the encoding. This is unsatisfactory, because we clearly want to allow the possibility of meaningful finite computations. This leads naturally to the solution adopted all along in practice, which is to carry out the computation starting from a designated Web object. This particular object is then part of the input to the query.

This can be formalized as follows. A Web query is a mapping q associating to each Web instance I and object $o \in I(Obj)$, a subset $q(o, I)$ of $I(Obj)$. The object o is called the *source (of the query)*. The definitions of computable and eventually computable query are the same, except that the encoding of the input on the Web machine input tape is now $enc_\alpha(o)\#\#\#enc_\alpha(I)$. *We henceforth adopt the above definitions of Web query, computable query, and eventually computable query.*

Observe that the presence of a source object indirectly allows to refer to more that one "constant" vertex in a query. This can be done by linking the source object to other objects we wish to name, by edges with new labels.

Example 1. The notions of computable and eventually computable queries are illustrated by the following queries on input (o, I):

1. computable:
   - Find the objects reachable from o by a path labeled $a.b.c$ (an a-labeled edge, followed by a b-labeled edge, followed by a c-labeled edge).
   - Find the objects o' such that there is a path of length at most k from o to o'.
   - Find all objects lying on a cycle of length at most 3 which contains o.
2. eventually computable with possibly infinite answers (so not computable):
   - Find the objects reachable from o.
   - Find the objects referencing o.
   - Find the objects belonging to a cycle.
3. eventually computable with finite answers, but not computable:
   - Find the objects on the shortest cycle containing o.
   - Find the object(s) at the shortest distance from o that reference o.
4. not eventually computable:
   - Find all objects that do not belong to a cycle.
   - Find all objects which are not referenced by any other object.
   - Output o iff all objects reachable from o have non-nil references[4].

In particular, it is clear from the above examples that computable and eventually computable properties are not closed under complement.

---

[4] Nil references can be modeled by references to a special object named *nil*.

Browse and Search

The Web machine captures a very general form of computation on the Web. However, two particular modes of computation on the Web are prevalent in practice: *browsing* and *searching*. We next define two machine models that capture more directly such computation. The first, called a *browser machine*, models browsing. The second, called a *browse/search machine* models browsing and searching combined.

The idea underlying the browser machine is to access the Web navigationally, by following object references starting from the input object o. A browser machine has an infinite browsing tape, an infinite work tape, and a right-infinite output tape. It is equipped with a finite state control which includes a special state called *expand*. The computation of the machine on input (o, I) is as follows. Let α be a fixed successor relation on the elements of I. Initially, the browsing tape contains the encoding $enc_\alpha(o)$ of the source object o. If the *expand* state is reached at any point in the computation and the browsing tape contains the encoding $enc_\alpha(o')$ of some object o' in $I(Obj)$, this is replaced on the browsing tape by $enc_\alpha(\widehat{o'})$ (i.e., the encoding of the finite description of o', see earlier notation for encodings).

A query q is computable by a browser machine if there exists a browser machine which on input (o, I) halts and produces on the output tape the encoding of $q(o, I)$. The definition of query eventually computable by a browser machine is analogous.

Obviously, browser machines have limited computing ability, since they can only access the portion of the Web reachable from the input object. However, this is an intuitively appealing approach for controlling the computation. We next prove a result which confirms the central role of this style of computation in the context of the Web.

Theorem 1. *Every generic and computable Web query is browser computable.*

Proof. (Sketch): Since our formalism is a departure from familiar terrain, we provide some detail in this first proof. Let q be a generic and computable Web query and W a Web machine computing q. Let (o, I) be an input for q. Let I_o denote the subinstance of I consisting of descriptions of all objects reachable from o. If we show that $q(o, I) = q(o, I_o)$ we are done, since $q(o, I_o)$ is clearly computable by a browser machine. There is however one difficulty: I_o may be finite, in which case it is not a Web instance.

To fix this problem, let $\bar{I}_o$ be I_o augmented with an infinite set *New* of new objects with the same new value, say 0, and without references. Now $\bar{I}_o$ is surely a Web instance. For technical reasons, we also need to similarly augment I. Let $\bar{I}$ be I augmented with the objects in *New*. We will show that:

1. $q(o, I) = q(o, \bar{I})$, and
2. $q(o, \bar{I}) = q(o, \bar{I}_o)$.

For suppose that (1) and (2) hold. Then, $q(o, I) = q(o, \bar{I}_o)$. Now a browser machine W' can compute $q(o, I)$ by simulating the computation of $q(o, \bar{I}_o)$. The browser generates on a portion of its work tape an encoding of a prefix of (o, I_o), and starts simulating W on this input tape. Whenever W attempts to move past the right end of the input tape, W' extends the tape by either browsing I_o or (if I_o is finite and has already been exhausted), by generating the encoding of an object in New. Since objects in New are standard, their encodings can simply be made up by the browser.

To prove (1), let α be a successor relation on all elements of I. The computation of W on $enc_\alpha(o, I)$ halts after W has inspected a finite prefix ω of $enc_\alpha(o, I)$. Clearly, there exists a successor relation β on the elements of $\bar{I}$ such that ω is also a prefix of $enc_\beta(o, \bar{I})$. Thus, $q(o, I) = q(o, \bar{I})$.

The proof of (2) is similar, starting from the computation of W on input $(o, \bar{I}_o)$.

Remark. (i) Observe that the previous result does not hold without the assumption that Web instances are infinite. Consider the following query: on input (o, I), output o_1, o_2 if I consists precisely of o and two other objects o_1, o_2 pointing to o. This would be computable by a Web machine but not by a browser machine. (ii) In addition to computable queries, browser machines can also compute queries that are eventually computable but not computable (e.g., "Find all objects reachable from o"). However, there exist eventually computable queries which are not eventually computable by a browser machine, such as "Find all objects in I".

We next augment browser machines with a search mechanism. The search is essentially a selection operation on a relation in the schema, whose condition specifies a conjunction of a finite set of (in)equalities involving an attribute and a constant. Examples of selections are: (i) $\sigma_{value=SGML}(Val)$ that returns all tuples $Val(o, SGML)$ where o is an object whose value is "SGML"; (ii) $\sigma_{label=Department}(Ref)$ that selects all edges with label "Department"; (iii) $\sigma_{label=A \wedge destination=556}(Ref)$ that returns all edges with label A and oid 556 as destination; and (iv) $\sigma_{source=source}(Ref)$ that returns all edges. In general, a search triggers an eventually computable subquery, whose result may be infinite. This leads to the problem of integrating nonterminating subcomputations into the computation of a query. We adopt the following model.

A *browse/search machine* is a browser machine augmented with a right-infinite search-answer tape and a separate search-condition tape. There is a distinguished *search* state. The computation of the machine is nondeterministic. A search is triggered by writing a selection operation on the search-condition tape, then entering the search state. The search-answer tape functions similarly to the answer tape of an eventually computable query. Answers to previously triggered searches arrive on the search-answer tape at arbitrary times and in arbitrary order. More precisely, suppose the set of selections triggered up to some given point in the computation is $\{\sigma_1, \ldots, \sigma_n\}$. In any subsequent move of the machine, a (possibly empty) finite subset of the answers to some of the σ_i's is appended to the search-answer tape. This is non-deterministic. The order in which answers are produced is arbitrary. Each tuple in the answer to σ_i is prefixed by σ_i (everything is encoded in the obvious way). It is guaranteed that all answers to a triggered search will be eventually produced, if the computation does not terminate. However, note that there is generally no way to know at a given time if all answers to a particular search have been obtained.

The rest of the computation occurs as in the browser machine. A Web query q is computable by a browse/search machine if there exists a browse/search machine W such that *each* computation of W on input (o, I) halts and produces an encoding of $q(o, I)$ on the answer tape[5]. The definition of query eventually computable by a browse/search machine is analogous.

What is the power of browse/search machines? This is elucidated by the following result.

Theorem 2. *(i) A generic Web query is eventually computable iff it is eventually computable by a browse/search machine.*

(ii) A generic Web query is computable iff it is computable by a browse/search machine.

Proof. (Sketch): For (i), consider first a query that is eventually computable by a browse/search machine M. The *expand* operations of M are easy to simulate in finite time by a Web machine (but note that this uses the fact that the encodings of tuples describing a given object are clustered together). Searches are simulated as follows. For each selection, the Web machine scans the input tape from left to right in search of answers to the selection. When a tuple in the answer is found, its encoding is placed on a portion of the worktape that simulates the search-answer tape of M. The searches (which never terminate) are interleaved with the rest of the simulation in some standard way.

Conversely, suppose q is eventually computed by a Web machine W. A browse/search machine can simulate W as follows. First, it triggers a search on a selection condition true of all objects. As objects arrive on the search-answer tape, they are expanded and encoded on the work tape using *expand*. This is interleaved with a simulation of W on the portion of the input tape constructed so far.

Part (ii) follows immediately from Theorem 1.

3 Query Languages

It is tempting to use classical declarative query languages in the context of the Web. However, it is not clear to what extent such languages are appropriate in this framework. We examine this issue in light of the notions of (eventual) computability discussed so far. Specifically, we consider the languages FO (first-order logic), Datalog, and Datalog⌐. Due to space limitations, we assume familiarity with the above languages (e.g., see definitions in [AHV94]). All programs we

---

[5] However, it should be clear that a browse/search machine that uses the search feature in a nontrivial way cannot terminate.

consider here use as input the Web relations *Obj, Ref* and *Val*, as well as one constant *source* that is interpreted as the object o in an input instance (o, I).

For each language, we are interested in the following questions:

(i) are the queries in the language (eventually) computable?
(ii) which fragment of each language can be implemented by browsers?

As it turns out, conventional wisdom cannot be counted upon in this context. To begin with, FO is no longer a nice, tractable language: it expresses queries that are not eventually computable. We will see that negation is the main source of problems in the languages we consider. This is not surprising, given that neither the (eventually) computable queries nor the queries computable by browser machines are closed under complement. We therefore begin our discussion with languages without negation: positive FO (FO without negation or universal quantification, denoted FO^+) and Datalog. The following is easily shown.

Theorem 3. *All FO^+ and Datalog queries are eventually computable.*

In particular, every FO^+ and Datalog query can be implemented by a browse/search machine. Clearly, the fragments implementable by a browser machine are of special interest. Note that navigational languages proposed for the Web are implementable by browsers. In particular, the languages based on specification of paths from the source object using regular expressions (e.g., see [MMM96]), are fragments of Datalog implementable by browsers. We isolate fragments of Datalog and FO^+ (eventually) computable by browsers by a syntactic restriction on variables which limits their range to values reachable from the source. We provide the definition for Datalog (this induces an analogous restriction on FO^+, since this can be viewed as nonrecursive Datalog).

Definition 4. The set of *source-range-restricted* variables in a Datalog rule r is the minimum set of variables in r satisfying:

- if $R(\mathbf{u})$ occurs in the body of the rule, R is some idb predicate and x is one of the variables of $\mathbf{u}$, then x is source-range-restricted;
- if x is the source constant or x is source-range-restricted and $Ref(x, y, z)$ occurs in the body of the rule, then y, z are source-range-restricted; and
- if x is the source constant or x is source-range-restricted and $Val(x, y)$ occurs in the body of the rule, then y is source-range-restricted.

A rule is *source-safe* (ss) if all its variables are source-range-restricted. A program is *source-safe* if all its rules are source-safe.

For example, the first Datalog program below is source-safe, and it is eventually computable by a browser machine. The second program is not source-safe. It is eventually computable, but not by a browser machine alone.

$$
\begin{array}{ll}
\text{reachable nodes} & answer(source) \leftarrow \\
& answer(t') \qquad \leftarrow answer(t), Ref(t, x, t')
\end{array}
$$

$$
\begin{array}{ll}
\text{nodes leading} & answer(source) \leftarrow \\
\text{to the source} & answer(t) \qquad \leftarrow answer(t'), Ref(t, x, t')
\end{array}
$$

We can now show the following.

Theorem i *All ss-FO$^+$ queries are computable by a browser machine.*
(ii) All ss-Datalog queries are eventually computable by a browser machine.

We next consider languages with negation. As expected, things become more complicated. Even without recursion, one can easily express queries which are not eventually computable. Consider the FO query

$$\{x \mid Ref(source, A, x) \wedge \neg \exists y(y \neq source \wedge Ref(y, A, x))\}.$$

This asks for the (finite set of) objects x which are referenced with an edge labeled A by *source* and by no other object. It is easy to see that this query is not eventually computable.

Besides FO, we will consider Datalog$^\neg$ with stratified, well-founded, and inflationary semantics. To obtain fragments eventually computable by browser machines, it is natural to extend the source-safe restriction to these languages. The definition of ss-Datalog$^\neg$ is precisely the same as for Datalog, with the proviso that all occurrences of predicates required by the definition to ensure source-range-restriction must be *positive* occurrences. (More precisely, the definition is obtained by replacing "occurs" by "occurs positively" in the definition of source-safe for datalog.) A definition of source-safe FO program in the same spirit can be given (we omit the details). It is straightforward to show:

Theorem 5. *All queries in ss-FO are computable by a browser machine.*

Consider now ss-Datalog$^\neg$. This language provides some interesting surprises. The classical stratified and well-founded semantics do not appear to be well-suited to express eventually computable queries, whereas inflationary semantics is quite well-behaved. First, recall that in the finite case (i) FO is subsumed by stratified-Datalog$^\neg$ which is subsumed by Datalog$^\neg$ with well-founded semantics [GRS88], and (ii) Datalog$^\neg$ with well-founded semantics (with answers reduced to their positive portion[6]) is equivalent to Datalog$^\neg$ with inflationary semantics [Gel89]. In the infinite case, things are different: (i) continues to hold but (ii) does not.

It is quite easy to see that ss-Datalog$^\neg$ with stratified semantics expresses queries that are not eventually computable. For example, consider the stratified ss-Datalog$^\neg$ program:

$$
\begin{aligned}
R(source) &\leftarrow & R(t') &\leftarrow R(t), Ref(t, x, t') \\
R_1(t') &\leftarrow R(t), R(t'), Ref(t, A, t') & answer(t) &\leftarrow R(t), \neg R_1(t)
\end{aligned}
$$

The query asks for all vertices reachable from the source, without in-going edges labeled "A" from any other vertex reachable from the source. One can show that the stratified semantics (so also the well-founded semantics) of this query is not eventually computable.

For inflationary semantics, we are able to show:

---

[6] Recall that well-founded semantics uses a 3-valued model.

Theorem 6. *Every query in ss-Datalog¬ with inflationary semantics is eventually computable by a browser machine.*

Generally, there are queries which are eventually computable (and even computable) by a browser machine, which are not expressible in ss-Datalog¬ with inflationary semantics. An example of such a computable query is "Output o iff there is an even number of objects x such that $Ref(o, A, x)$." This is a familiar difficulty in the theory of query languages, and is due to the lack of an order on the domain. Let us consider Web instances augmented with a total order relation on all oid's in *Obj*. Call such a Web instance *ordered*. Also, a Web instance (o, I) is *source-infinite* if there are infinitely many objects reachable from o. Otherwise, the instance is called *source-finite*. We can show the following:

Theorem 7. *(i) The language ss-Datalog¬ with inflationary semantics expresses exactly the queries eventually computable by a browser machine on ordered, source-infinite Web instances.*
(ii) The language ss-Datalog¬ with inflationary semantics expresses exactly the queries computable by a browser machine in polynomial time (with respect to the number of objects reachable from source) on ordered, source-finite Web instances.

The proof involves a simulation of browser machines. The tape cells of the machine are encoded using indexes consisting of objects reachable from the source. Recall that browser machines may not terminate, so infinitely many cells may have to be encoded. This only works for source-infinite instances (even in the case when the browser machine itself only inspects finitely many objects reachable from the source). On source-finite instances ss-Datalog¬ with inflationary semantics can only construct polynomially many indexes for tape cells.

Theorem 7 allows to show an interesting connection between the ss-Datalog¬ languages with various semantics for negation.

Proposition 8. *On ordered Web instances, every query eventually computable by a browser machine that is expressible in ss-Datalog¬ with well-founded semantics is also expressible in ss-Datalog¬ with inflationary semantics.*

The proof uses the fact that on source-finite Web instances every ss-Datalog¬ program with well-founded semantics can be evaluated in time polynomial in the number of objects reachable from the source. Thus, Proposition 8 follows from a complexity/completeness argument rather than from an explicit simulation. It remains open to find a uniform simulation of ss-Datalog¬ with well-founded semantics which are eventually computable by browsers, by ss-Datalog¬ with inflationary semantics. It also remains open whether Proposition 8 holds for unordered Web instances.

In view of these results, ss-Datalog¬ with inflationary semantics emerges as a particularly appealing language in the context of the Web.

Remark. The notion of source-safety was developed to ensure that programs can be implemented by a browser. One could develop a less restrictive notion of safety geared towards eventual computability, which would guarantee that the program can be implemented by browsing and searching combined. Consider for instance Datalog$^{(\neg)}$. Recall that Datalog queries (without negation) are eventually computable with browse and search, while ss-Datalog$^{\neg}$ programs with inflationary semantics are eventually computable with browsers alone. One could relax the source-safety restriction of ss-Datalog$^{\neg}$ by allowing a mix of idb's defined by positive rules and idb's defined by source-safe rules. Hybrid rules that are neither positive nor source-safe are allowed if idb's occurring negatively are defined only by source-safe rules and variable occurring under negation are also bound to positive occurrences of some predicate. Such programs express (with inflationary semantics) queries eventually computable by browse and search. We omit the details here.

4 Conclusions

We explored some basic aspects of querying and computing on the Web. In doing so, we revisited and adapted fundamental concepts from the theory of database query languages, such as genericity and computability. There are substantial differences, arising from the fact that we model the Web as a semi-structured, infinite object. Some of our results can be viewed as *a posteriori* formal justification for much of the computation style adopted in practice in the context of the Web, based on browsing from a given source object.

We considered FO, Datalog and Datalog$^{\neg}$ in the context of the Web, and characterized them with respect to (eventual) computability. We also identified fragments in each language implementable by browsing alone. There were some surprises: FO is no longer the nicely behaved language we are used to from the finite case. And among semantics for negation in Datalog$^{\neg}$, stratified and well-founded semantics have fundamental shortcomings, whereas inflationary semantics emerges as particularly appealing in this context. Although it is unlikely that FO, Datalog, or Datalog$^{\neg}$ will be used as such to query the Web, the results can guide the design of more practical languages. In particular, we believe that the nice properties of source-safe Datalog$^{\neg}$ with inflationary semantics suggest useful ways to extend previously proposed languages based on browsing.

As emphasized in the introduction, our abstraction of the Web left out important aspects which we plan to include in future investigations. Perhaps the most important are the communication costs associated with browsing and searching, and the notion of locality. Locality could be introduced in our model by having two-sorted edges in the reference graph *Ref*: local and remote, with the added condition that each connected component of the subgraph of *Ref* consisting of local edges is finite. The fact that local browsing/searching is guaranteed to terminate can in turn be exploited at the language level by allowing explicit reference to local links in the language. Locality is indeed an explicit notion in some languages proposed for the Web [MMM96]. It is natural then to provide extended notions of safety based on locality of browsing and searching.

References

[A97]   S. Abiteboul. Querying semi-structured data. This proceedings.

[AHV94]   S. Abiteboul, R. Hull, and V. Vianu. *Foundations of Databases*. Addison-Wesley, Reading-Massachusetts, 1994.

[AV88]   S. Abiteboul and V. Vianu. Procedural and declarative database update languages. In *Proc. ACM PODS*, pages 240–250, 1988.

[BDS95]   P. Buneman, S. Davidson, and D. Suciu. Programming constructs for unstructured data. In *Proc. DBPL*, 1995.

[BLCL⁺94]   T. Berners-Lee, R. Cailliau, A. Luotonen, H. Nielsen, and A. Secret. The World-Wide Web. *Comm. of the ACM*, 37(8):76–82, 1994.

[CACS94]   V. Christophides, S. Abiteboul, S. Cluet, and M. Scholl. From structured documents to novel query facilities. In *Proc. ACM SIGMOD*, pages 313–324, 1994.

[CH80]   A.K. Chandra and D. Harel. Computable queries for relational data bases. *Journal of Computer and System Sciences*, 21(2):156–178, 1980.

[CM89]   M. P. Consens and A. O. Mendelzon. Expressing structural hypertext queries in graphlog. In *Proc. 2nd. ACM Conference on Hypertext*, pages 269–292, 1989.

[Gel89]   A. Van Gelder. The alternating fixpoint of logic programs with negation. In *Proc. ACM PODS*, pages 1–11, 1989.

[GRS88]   A. Van Gelder, K.A. Ross, and J.S. Schlipf. The well-founded semantics for general logic programs. In *Proc. ACM PODS*, pages 221–230, 1988.

[GZC89]   R. Güting, R. Zicari, and D. M. Choy. An algebra for structured office documents. *ACM TOIS*, 7(2):123–157, 1989.

[HH93]   D. Harel and T. Hirst. Completeness Results for Recursive Data Bases. In *Proc. ACM PODS*, pages 244–252, 1993.

[KKR90]   P. Kanellakis, G. Kuper, and P. Revesz. Constraint query languages. In *Proc. ACM PODS*, pages 299–313, 1990.

[KP88]   P. G. Kolaitis and C.H. Papadimitriou. Why not negation by fixpoint? In *Proc. ACM PODS*, pages 231–239, 1988.

[KS95]   D. Konopnicki and O. Shmueli. W3QS: A query system for the World Wide Web. In *Proc. of VLDB'95*, pages 54–65, 1995.

[LSS96]   V. S. Lakshmanan, F. Sadri, and I. N. Subramanian. A declarative language for querying and restructuring the Web. In *Proc. of 6th. International Workshop on Research Issues in Data Engineering, RIDE '96*, New Orleans, February 1996.

[MMM96]   G. Mihaila, A. Mendelzon, and T. Milo. Querying the World Wide Web. In *Proc. PDIS*, 1996. Also available in ftp://db.toronto.edu/pdis96.ps.Z.

[MW93]   T. Minohara and R. Watanabe. Queries on structure in hypertext. In *Proc. Foundations of Data Organization and Algorithms*, pages 394–411, Springer-Verlag, 1993.

[MW95]   A. O. Mendelzon and P. T. Wood. Finding regular simple paths in graph databases. *SIAM J. Comp.*, 24(6), pages 1235-1258, 1995.

[Q⁺95]   D. Quass et al. Querying semistructured heterogeneous information. In *Proc. DOOD*, pages 319–344, Springer-Verlag, 1995.

The Complexity of Iterated Belief Revision

Paolo Liberatore

Università di Roma "La Sapienza",
Dipartimento di Informatica e Sistemistica
Via Salaria 113, 00198 Rome, Italy
email: liberato@dis.uniroma1.it
http://www.dis.uniroma1.it/~liberato

Abstract. In this paper we analyze the complexity of revising a knowledge base when an iteration of this process is necessary. The analysis concerns both the classical problems of belief revision (inference, model checking, computation of the new base) and new issues, related to the problem of "committing" the changes.

1 Introduction

Belief revision is an active area in Databases, AI and philosophy. It has to do with the problem of accommodating new information into an older theory, and is therefore a central topic in the study of knowledge representation.

Suppose to have a knowledge base, represented with a propositional base K. When new information a arrives, the old base must be modified. If the new information is in contradiction with the old one, we must resolve the conflict somehow. The principle of minimal change is often assumed: the new knowledge base, that we denote with $K * a$, must be as similar as possible to the old one K. In other terms, the k.b. must be modified as little as possible. Many researchers give both general properties [AGM85, KM91] and specific methods (for example, [Dal88]) to resolve this conflict.

More recently, the studies have been focused on the iteration of this process. When, after a first revision, another piece of information arrives, the system of revision should take into account the first change. Roughly speaking, the program that makes this change on the knowledge base should not consider only facts which are currently true (the objective database), but also the revisions which have been done up to now.

In this paper we analyze the complexity of these frameworks. An analysis of the complexity of single-step (non-iterated) revision can be found in [EG92, LS96, Neb91, Neb94]. The key problem is of course to extract information from the revised k.b., or

> given a knowledge base K, a revision a, and a formula q, decide whether q is derivable from $K * a$, the revised knowledge base.

that is, given an old base and a revision, decide how much does it cost to extract information from the base obtained by revising the old one.

Iterating the process of revision, new problems arise. As will be clear in section 2, the operators defined in the literature need some extra information that depend on the history of the previous revisions. The size of this information becomes quickly exponential, thus we need a criterion to decide when the history becomes irrelevant, that is, when the changes can be "committed". At least, we need to know how many previous revisions the process must take into account.

2 Definitions

In this section we present the background and the terminology needed to understand the results of the rest of the paper. Throughout this paper, we restrict our analysis to a finite propositional language.

The *alphabet* of a propositional formula is the set of all propositional atoms occurring in it. Formulae are built over a finite alphabet of propositional letters using the usual connectives $\neg$ (not), $\vee$ (or) and $\wedge$ (and). Additional connectives are used as shorthands, $a \rightarrow b$ denotes $\neg a \vee b$, $a \equiv b$ is a shorthand for $(a \wedge b) \vee (\neg a \wedge \neg b)$ and $a \neq b$ denotes $\neg(a \equiv b)$.

An *interpretation* of a formula is a truth assignment to the atoms of its alphabet. A *model* M of a formula f is an interpretation that satisfies f (written $M \models f$). Interpretations and models of propositional formulae will be denoted as sets of atoms (those which are mapped into true). For example, the interpretation that maps the atoms a and c into true, and all the others into false is denoted $\{a, c\}$. We use W to denote the set of all the interpretations of the considered alphabet. A *theory* K is a set of formulae. An interpretation is a model of a theory if it is a model of every formula of the theory. Given a theory K and a formula f we say that K *entails* f, written $K \models f$, if f is true in every model of K. The set of the *logical consequence* of a theory $Cn(K)$ is the set of all the formulas implied by it. Given a propositional formula or a theory K, we denote with $Mod(K)$ the set of its models. We say that a knowledge base K *supports* a model M if $M \in Mod(K)$, or equivalently $M \models K$. A formula f is satisfiable if $Mod(f)$ is non-empty. Let $Form$ be the operator inverse to Mod, that is, given a set of models A, $Form(A)$ denotes one of the equivalent formulas that have A as set of its models.

2.1 General Properties of Revision

Revision attempts to describe how a rational agent incorporates new information. This process should obey the principle of minimal change: the agent should make as little changes as possible on the old knowledge base.

As a result, when a new piece of information is consistent with the old one, the revision process should simply add it to the agent's beliefs. The most interesting situation is when they are inconsistent. The postulates stated by Alchourron, Gärdenfors and Makinson (AGM postulates for now on) provide base principles for this process.

Given a knowledge base K (represented with a deductively closed set of formulas) and a formula a representing a new information to be incorporated in it, they denote with $K * a$ the result of this process. The AGM postulates attempt to formalize the principle of minimal change.

Katsuno and Mendelzon in [KM91] give a reformulation of AGM's postulates in terms of formulas, instead of complete theories. For our purposes, this representation is more suitable. They proved that the AGM postulates are equivalent to the following ones (notice that now $*$ is an operator that takes two propositional formulas k and a, and the result $k * a$ is a propositional formula).

KM1 $k * a$ implies a
KM2 If $k \wedge a$ is satisfiable, then $k * a = k \wedge a$
KM3 If a is satisfiable, then $k * a$ is also satisfiable
KM4 If $k_1 \equiv k_2$ and $a_1 \equiv a_2$ then $k_1 * a_1 \equiv k_2 * a_2$
KM5 $(k * p_1) \wedge p_2$ implies $k * (p_1 \wedge p_2)$
KM6 If $(k * p_1) \wedge p_2$ is satisfiable, then $k * (p_1 \wedge p_2)$ implies $(k * p_1) \wedge p_2$

In the same paper they give an elegant representation theorem of the AGM revisions. Let $\mathcal{W}$ be the set of all the interpretations. A linear preorder over $\mathcal{W}$ is a reflexive, transitive relation $\leq$ over $\mathcal{W}$, with the additional property that for all $I, I' \in \mathcal{W}$ either $I \leq I'$ or $I' \leq I$.

In the KM formalization, each revision operator $*$ is associated to a family of linear preorders $O = \{\leq_f \mid f \text{ is a formula}\}$ that have the so called property of faithfulness.

Definition 1. A family $O = \{\leq_f \mid f \text{ is a formula}\}$ of linear preorders is said to be faithful if and only if for each formula f the following conditions hold (we use $I <_f J$ to denote that $I \leq_f J$ holds but $J \leq_f I$ does not).

1. If $I, J \in Mod(f)$ then $I <_f J$ does not hold.
2. If $I \in Mod(f)$ and $J \notin Mod(f)$ then $I <_f J$ holds.
3. If $f_1 \equiv f_2$ then $\leq_{f_1} = \leq_{f_2}$

Note that the above definition does not impose constraints over a relation $\leq_f$ when $I, J \notin Mod(f)$. The following theorem shows how an AGM revision can be represented with a faithful family of preorderings.

Theorem 2 [KM91]. *A revision operator $*$ satisfies postulates KM1-KM6 if and only if there exists a faithful family $O = \{\leq_f \mid f \text{ is a formula}\}$ such that for all pairs of propositional formulas k and a, it holds*

$$Mod(k * a) = \min(Mod(a), \leq_k)$$

We can view $\leq_k$ as the order of plausibility induced by k, where $I <_k J$ means that I is considered more plausible than J to an agent believing k. The above formula means that the process of revision "chooses" the models of a that are considered more plausible.

2.2 Full Meet Revision

In this section we present a specific revision operator that has been proposed. The AGM's and KM's postulates imposes that when k and a are consistent then $k * a = k \wedge a$. Following Lehmann [Leh95], we call *mild* a revision that is consistent with the old information, *severe* otherwise.

The full meet revision [AGM85] is a "drastic" form of revision, that is, it preserves no information of the old k.b. if the revision is severe.

Definition 3. The full meet revision is defined as:

$$k *_{FM} a = \begin{cases} k \wedge a & \text{if consistent} \\ a & \text{otherwise} \end{cases}$$

As noticed by Alchourron, Gärdenfors and Makinson, this revision satisfies all the eight AGM's postulates and thus all the six KM's postulates. As a result, it can be expressed with a faithful family of linear preorderings. This family is:

$$FM = \{ \leq_k^{FM} \mid k \text{ is a formula, and } \leq_k^{FM} \text{ is defined as} \\ I \leq_k^{FM} J \text{ iff } I \in Mod(k) \text{ or } J \notin Mod(k) \}$$

Example 1. Let us consider the sequence $[p_1, p_2, p_3]$, where $p_1 = Form(\{I, L\})$, $p_2 = Form(\{L, M\})$ and $p_3 = Form(\{I, J, M\})$, and

$$I = \{a\} \quad J = \{b\} \\ L = \{a, b\} \quad M = \{a, b, c, d\}$$

After revising p_1 with p_2 the current knowledge is $p_1 * p_2 = p_1 \wedge p_2$, since p_1 and p_2 are consistent. If a new information p_3 arrives, the result of the second revision is $(p_1 \wedge p_2) * p_3 = p_3$, since $p_1 \wedge p_2$ and p_3 are inconsistent. Note that all the information given by p_1 and p_2 has been lost.

2.3 Iterated Revision Operators

In this section we summarize some iterated revisions proposed. A sequence of formulas is denoted with $[p_1, \ldots, p_m]$. The null sequence (the sequence with no elements) is denoted with $[\,]$. If P and Q are two sequences, $P \cdot Q$ denotes their concatenation. In the previous section we have introduced the notion of single-step revision, denoted with $k * a$. In a similar manner, if we have a sequence of revisions w.r.t. the formulas $p_1, \ldots, p_m$, this will be denoted as $k * [p_1, \ldots, p_m]$. We assume, without loss of generality, that the initial formula k contains no information, and denote $() * [p_1, \ldots, p_m]$ simply with $*[p_1, \ldots, p_m]$.

Natural Revision. Boutilier [Bou93] defines a revision model as a triple $\mathcal{M} = \langle W, R, \phi \rangle$, where W is a set of worlds with a valuation function ϕ, and R is a linear preorder relation over W. The relation R represents the plausibility of worlds, that is, if wRw' then the world w is considered more plausible than the world w'. For our purposes, W can be viewed as the set of all the models, and $\phi(M)$ as the function of evaluation of the atoms associated with the model M. The natural revision is defined as follows.

Let $\mathcal{M}_{[p_1,\ldots,p_{m-1}]} = \langle W, R, \phi \rangle$ be the revision model associated to a sequence $[p_1, \ldots, p_{m-1}]$. The natural revision maps this model into a new model $\mathcal{M}_{[p_1,\ldots,p_m]} = \langle W, R', \phi \rangle$ such that

1. If $I \in \min(Mod(p_m), R)$ then $\langle I, J \rangle \in R'$ for each J, and $\langle J, I \rangle \in R'$ only if $J \in \min(Mod(p_m), R)$.
2. If $I, J \notin \min(Mod(p_m), R)$, then $\langle I, J \rangle \in R'$ if and only if $\langle I, J \rangle \in R$.

We assume that the null sequence $[\,]$ is associated to the model $\mathcal{M}_{[\,]} = \langle W, R_0, \phi \rangle$, where $R_0 = W \times W$. Once determined $\mathcal{M}_{[p_1,\ldots,p_m]} = \langle W, R, \phi \rangle$, the natural revision is defined as

$$*_{NR}[p_1, \ldots, p_m] = Form(\min(W, R))$$

Example 2. Consider the sequence $[p_1, p_2, p_3]$, where p_1, p_2 and p_3 are as in the previous example. We have $W_{[\,]} = \langle W, R_0, \phi \rangle$ where $R_0 = W \times W$ by definition. For the sequence with only the first element the above rules gives $W_{[p_1]} = \langle W, R_1, \phi \rangle$ where R_1 is $\{\langle I, L \rangle, \langle L, I \rangle, \langle I, J \rangle, \langle I, M \rangle, \langle L, J \rangle, \langle L, M \rangle\}$ (for the sake of simplicity we write only the pairs that contain two elements in $\{I, J, L, M\}$)

The sequence with two formulas has model $W_{[p_1,p_2]} = \langle W, R_2, \phi \rangle$ where R_2 contains $\{\langle L, I \rangle, \langle I, M \rangle, \langle I, J \rangle\}$ and the other pairs implied by transitivity.

The complete sequence has model $W_{[p_1,p_2,p_3]} = \langle W, R_3, \phi \rangle$, where R_3 contains $\{\langle I, L \rangle, \langle L, J \rangle, \langle L, M \rangle\}$. Thus, the result of the revision is $Form(\min(W, R_3)) = Form(\{I\}) = p_1 \wedge p_3$. Note that p_2, although is consistent with p_3 and is considered more plausible than p_1, is not in the result.

Prioritized Iteration of Revision. Suppose to have a faithful family of orderings O, for example the family associated to the full meet revision. Consider a formula p_1 and its associated ordering $\leq_{p_1}^{FM}$. It holds $I \leq_{p_1}^{FM} J$ if, when we believe p_1, we consider the interpretation I more plausible than J.

Now, another formula p_2 arrives. What should be the plausibility ordering after revising p_1 with p_2? In other terms, what should be $\leq_{[p_1,p_2]}^{FM}$? Consider that p_2 is associated to the ordering $\leq_{p_2}^{FM}$. When both $I \leq_{p_1}^{FM} J$ and $I \leq_{p_2}^{FM} J$ hold (when these orderings agree), it is reasonable to assume $I \leq_{[p_1,p_2]}^{FM} J$.

Suppose instead that $I \not\leq_{p_1}^{FM} J$ but $I \leq_{p_2}^{FM} J$. Our guiding principle is that the new information is more reliable than the older one. As a result, $\leq_{p_2}^{FM}$ should be considered more reliable, and thus $I \leq_{[p_1,p_2]}^{FM} J$.

In general, we can state the following definition. Let $P = [p_1, \ldots, p_m]$ be a sequence. Its full meet prioritized associated ordering is defined inductively as follows ($I \cong J$ means that both $I \leq J$ and $J \leq I$ hold).

$$I \leq_{[p_1,\ldots,p_m]}^{FM} J \text{ if and only if } \begin{cases} I <_{p_m}^{FM} J \text{ or} \\ I \cong_{p_m}^{FM} J \text{ and } I \leq_{[p_1,\ldots,p_{m-1}]}^{FM} J \end{cases}$$

The prioritized iteration of full meet revision is defined as

$$*_{PR(FM)}[p_1, \ldots, p_m] = Form(\min(W, \leq^{FM}_{[p_1,\ldots,p_m]}))$$

Example 3. Consider again the sequence $[p_1, p_2, p_3]$ defined in the example 1. By definition $\leq^{FM}_{[p_1]}$ gives

$$I \cong^{FM}_{[p_1]} L <^{FM}_{[p_1]} J \cong^{FM}_{[p_1]} M$$

Applying the definition, $\leq^{FM}_{[p_1,p_2]}$ is

$$L <^{FM}_{[p_1,p_2]} M <^{FM}_{[p_1,p_2]} I <^{FM}_{[p_1,p_2]} J$$

and finally for $\leq^{FM}_{[p_1,p_2,p_3]}$ we obtain

$$M <^{FM}_{[p_1,p_2,p_3]} I <^{FM}_{[p_1,p_2,p_3]} J <^{FM}_{[p_1,p_2,p_3]} L$$

The result of the revision is $Form(\min(W, <^{FM}_{[p_1,p_2,p_3]})) = Form(\{M\}) = p_2 \wedge p_3$.

Ranked Revisions. Lehmann in [Leh95] defines a (widening) ranking model as a function $\mathcal{R} : \mathcal{N} \to 2^W - \emptyset$ (where $\mathcal{N}$ is the set of the non-negative integers), such that, for any $i, j \in \mathcal{N}$, if $i < j$ then $\mathcal{R}(i) \subseteq \mathcal{R}(j)$, and for any $I \in W$ there exists a number n such that $I \in \mathcal{R}(n)$. The meaning of $\mathcal{R}$ is the following: if $I \in \mathcal{R}(i)/\mathcal{R}(j)$ and $J \in R(j)$ with $i > j$ then J is considered more plausible than I.

Each ranking model induces an iterated revision operator. Let $\mathcal{M}$ be a ranking model. Any sequence of revisions $P = [p_1, \ldots, p_m]$ defines a rank $r(P)$ that is a number, and a set of models $p(P)$.

The definition of revision is by induction on the length of the sequence. If $P = [\,]$ then $p(P) = \mathcal{R}(0)$ and $r(P) = 0$, and $*_{RR(\mathcal{R})}P = Form(p(P))$. If $P = [p_1, \ldots, p_m]$ then, if there is in $p([p_1, \ldots, p_{m-1}])$ a model that satisfies p_m then $r(P) = r([p_1, \ldots, p_{m-1}])$ and $p(P) = p([p_1, \ldots, p_{m-1}]) \cap Mod(p_m)$. Furthermore, $*_{RR(\mathcal{R})}[p_1, \ldots, p_m] = Form(p(P))$.

If no interpretation in $p([p_1, \ldots, p_{m-1}])$ satisfies p_m, then $r(P)$ is the smallest number greater than $r([p_1, \ldots, p_{m-1}])$ such that there is a model in $\mathcal{R}(r(P))$ that satisfies p_m. Furthermore, $p(P) = \mathcal{R}(r(P)) \cap Mod(p_m)$ and $*_{RR(\mathcal{R})}[p_1, \ldots, p_m] = Form(p(P))$.

Notice that $\mathcal{R}$ is not changed by the introduction of new formulas in the sequence. The only effect of adding a formula in a sequence is to modify the set of current models $p(P)$, and the rank of the sequence $r(P)$. In all the other revision operators, instead, the plausibility ordering (however it is represented) is changed each time a formula is introduced in a sequence.

Example 4. In order to evaluate the revision of a sequence, we must specify the ranked model considered. Let $\mathcal{R}(M)$ be the number of the atoms in the interpretation M (or, the number of the atom that are mapped to true in the interpretation M). For the models I, J, L, and M defined in the example 1, we have $\mathcal{R}(I) = \mathcal{R}(J) = 1$, $\mathcal{R}(L) = 2$ and $\mathcal{R}(M) = 4$.

The sequence $[\ ]$ has by definition $r([\ ]) = 0$ and $p([\ ]) = \mathcal{R}(0)$. For $[p_1]$, consider that $p([\ ])$ and $Mod(p_1)$ share no model, thus the definition gives $r([p_1]) = 1$ and thus $p([p_1]) = \mathcal{R}(1) \cap Mod(p_1) = \{I\}$.

The formula p_2 does not support the model I, thus we have to increase the rank, that becomes $r([p_1, p_2]) = 2$, and hence $p([p_1, p_2]) = \{L\}$.

As a result, the final revision with p_3 is severe, thus the rank is increased once again: $r([p_1, p_2, p_3]) = 3$. The result is thus

$$Form(p([p_1, p_2, p_3])) = Form(\mathcal{R}(3) \cap Mod(p_3)) = Form(\{I, J\}) = \neg p_2 \wedge p_1$$

Transmutations. Williams in [Wil94] defines a class of iterated revision that operates on a generic logic with some constraints. We are interested only in the propositional version of her work.

An ordinal conditional function (OCF for now on), is a function C from the set of models to non-negative integers, such that there are some models assigned to the number 0. Extend C to sets of models: $C(A) = \min(\{C(I) | I \in A\}, \leq)$ where $\leq$ is the classical ordering between numbers. Transmutations work on sequences of pairs $(formula, number)$. The number associated to a formula is the degree of acceptance of the formula. Thus, $(a, 1)$ means that we have a low degree of confidence on the fact that a is true, while $(b, 100)$ means that we are almost sure that b is valid.

Two specific transmutations have been defined.

Conditionalization. Given the OCF C assigned to a sequence of pairs $P = [(p_1, i_1), \ldots, (p_{m-1}, i_{m-1})]$, the new OCF C' that corresponds to the sequence $P' = [(p_1, i_1), \ldots, (p_m, i_m)]$ is defined as the function C' such that $C'(I) = C(I) - C(Mod(p_m))$ if $I \models p_m$, and $C'(I) = C(I) - C(Mod(\neg p_m)) + i_m$ otherwise. Furthermore, the OCF assigned to the null sequence $[\ ]$ is the function that associates 0 to each model. The conditionalization of a sequence $[(p_1, i_1), \ldots, (p_m, i_m)]$ is defined as

$$*_{CT}[(p_1, i_1), \ldots, (p_m, i_m)] = Form(\{I \in \mathcal{W} | C(I) = 0\})$$

where C is the OCF assigned to P.

Adjustment. Given the OCF C assigned to $P = [(p_1, i_1), \ldots, (p_{m-1}, i_{m-1})]$, the new OCF C' assigned to $P' = [(p_1, i_1), \ldots, (p_m, i_m)]$ is defined as

1. If $i_m = 0$ then if $C(I) = C(Mod(\neg p_m))$ and $I \models \neg p_m$ then $C'(I) = 0$, otherwise $C'(I) = C(I)$.
2. If $i_m \geq C(Mod(\neg p_m))$ then a) if $I \in Mod(p_m)$ and $C(I) = C(Mod(p_m))$ then $C'(I) = 0$; b) if $I \in Mod(\neg p_m))$ and $C(I) < i_m$ then $C'(I) = i_m$; c) otherwise $C'(I) = C(I)$.
3. If $0 < i_m < C(Mod(\neg p_m))$ then a) if $I \in mod(p_m)$ and $C(I) = C(Mod(p_m))$ then $C'(I) = 0$; b) if $I \in mod(\neg p_m)$ and $C(I) = C(Mod(\neg p_m))$ then $C'(I) = i_m$; c) otherwise $C'(I) = C(I)$.

The adjustment of a sequence $[(p_1, i_1), \ldots, (p_m, i_m)]$ is defined as:

$$*_{AT}[(p_1, i_1), \ldots, (p_m, i_m)] = Form(\{I \in \mathcal{W} | C(I) = 0\})$$

Note that if $i_m = 0$ then the revision with (p_m, i_m) is actually a contraction, that is, the formula p_m is not true in the revised knowledge base.

Example 5. Consider the sequence $[(p_1, 1), (p_2, 1), (p_3, 1)]$. The conditionalization associates to the sequence $[(p_1, 1)]$ the OCF C_1 such that $C_1(I) = C_1(L) = 0$ and $C_1(J) = C_1(M) = 1$.

Introducing $(p_2, 1)$ in the sequence, the OCF C_1 is transformed into a new OCF C_2 defined as $C_2(L) = 0$, $C_2(M) = C_2(I) = 1$ and $C_2(J) = 2$.

The OCF C_3 associated to the whole sequence is defined as $C_3(I) = C_3(M) = 0$, $C_3(L) = C_3(J) = 1$. As a result,

$$*_{CT}[(p_1, 1), (p_2, 1), (p_3, 1)] = Form(\{M|C_3(M) = 0\}) = Form(\{I, M\})$$

It is also easy to see that $*_{AT}[(p_1, 1), (p_2, 1), (p_3, 1)] = p_3$.

2.4   Computational Complexity

We assume that the reader is familiar with the basic concepts of computational complexity. We use the standard notation of complexity classes that can be found in [Joh90]. Namely, the class P denotes the set of problems whose solution can be found in polynomial time by a *deterministic* Turing machine, while NP denotes the class of problems that can be resolved in polynomial time by a *non-deterministic* Turing machine. The class coNP denotes the set of decision problems whose complement is in NP. We call NP-hard a problem G if any instance of a generic problem NP can can reduced to an instance of G by means of a polynomial-time (many-one) transformation (the same for coNP hard). The class LOGSPACE is defined as the class of problems that can be resolved by a deterministic Turing machine using only a logarithmic amount of space.

Clearly, P $\subseteq$ NP and P $\subseteq$ coNP. We assume, in line with the prevailing assumptions of computational complexity, that these containments are strict, that is P $\neq$ NP and P $\neq$ coNP. Therefore, we call a problem that is in P *tractable*, and a problem that is NP-hard or coNP-hard *intractable* (in the sense that any algorithm resolving it would require a super polynomial amount of time in the worst case).

We also use higher complexity classes defined using oracles. In particular P^A (NP^A) corresponds to the class of decision problems that are solved in polynomial time by deterministic (nondeterministic) Turing machines using an oracle for A in polynomial time (for a much more detailed presentation we refer the reader to [Joh90]). All the problems we analyze reside in the *polynomial hierarchy*, that is the analog of the Kleene arithmetic hierarchy. The classes Σ_k^p, Π_k^p and Δ_k^p of the polynomial hierarchy are defined by

$$\Sigma_0^p = \Pi_0^p = \Delta_0^p = P$$

and for $k \geq 0$,

$$\Sigma_{k+1}^p = NP^{\Sigma_k^p}, \quad \Pi_{k+1}^p = co\Sigma_{k+1}^p, \quad \Delta_{k+1}^p = P^{\Sigma_k^p}.$$

Notice that $\Delta_1^p = \mathrm{P}$, $\Sigma_1^p = \mathrm{NP}$ and $\Pi_1^p = \mathrm{coNP}$. The class $\Delta_2^p[\log n]$, often mentioned in the paper, is the class of problems solvable in polynomial time using a logarithmic number of calls to an NP oracle. The definitions of hardness and completeness for all these classes are similar to those of NP-hardness and completeness. The prototypical Δ_2^p-complete problem is the following [Kre88]:

Definition 4 MAXLEXMOD. Given a propositional formula f using the letters of the alphabet $\mathcal{L} = \{x_1, \ldots, x_n\}$, decide if the maximal lexicographic model of f contains x_n.

Given a propositional formula t, its cardinality-based circumscription NCIRC(t) is the formula whose models are the minimal (w.r.t. number of atoms) models of t. The following problem [LS95] is complete for the class $\Delta_2^p[\log n]$.

Definition 5 INFNCIRC. Given two propositional formulas t and q, decide if NCIRC(t) $\models q$.

We use also the class D^p, that is defined as the set of problems that can be expressed as deciding if a string x belongs to a language L_1/L_2, where deciding whether $x \in L_1$ is an NP problem and $x \in L_2$ is a coNP one (for more details see [Joh90]). A D^p complete problem is the following.

Definition 6 CRITSAT. Given a set of clauses Π decide if it is unsatisfiable but any of its proper subsets is satisfiable.

The complexity of deciding $k * a \models q$ was studied by Eiter and Gottlob in [EG92]. Very briefly, for many revision operators it is Π_2^p-complete. The complexity of deciding whether $M \models k * a$ has been studied in [LS96].

3 Overview and Discussion of the Results

We have performed a thorough analysis of several computational aspects of iterated belief revision. In this section we explain which problems have been considered, and give an insight of the results. The results are presented in Table 1 and Table 2. Next section contains some proof sketches.

In the first table we report the complexity of the classical problems of belief revision, that is, deciding whether a formula is implied or not by a sequence of revisions (inference), whether a model is supported by the result of a revision (model checking), and the complexity of actually computing the result of revision, that is, to find the formula $*[p_1, \ldots, p_m]$.

More formally, the problem of inference is: given a sequence of formulas $p_1, \ldots, p_m$ and a formula q, decide if $*[p_1, \ldots, p_m] \models q$. The problem of model checking is to decide, given a sequence and a model M, if $M \models *[p_1, \ldots, p_m]$. The other problem, the computation, is to find a formula that is equivalent to $*[p_1, \ldots, p_m]$.

The first thing to notice is that for most operators the complexity of inference and model checking is Δ_2^p complete (and for all of them is *in* Δ_2^p). We remind

	inference	model checking	computation
Full Meet Iterated	$\Delta_2^p[\log n]$-hard in LOGSPACE^{NP}	D^p-hard in LOGSPACE^{NP}	NP equivalent
Natural Revision	Δ_2^p complete	Δ_2^p complete	NP equivalent
Adjustment	Δ_2^p complete	Δ_2^p complete	NP equivalent
Condizionalization	Δ_2^p complete	Δ_2^p complete	NP equivalent
Prioritized Full Meet Revision	Δ_2^p complete	coNP complete	NP equivalent
Ranked (general)	$\Delta_2^p[\log n]$-hard in Δ_2^p	D^p-hard in Δ_2^p	NP equivalent
Ranked (upper bound)	Δ_2^p complete	Δ_2^p complete	NP equivalent

Table 1. Complexity of inference, model checking and computation.

that the class Δ_2^p is the class of the problems that can be computed with a polynomial number of calls to a procedure that solves an NP problem.

This happens because the revisions can be computed using plausibility orderings (represented by OCF, or revision models, or ranks), and the plausibility ordering induced by a sequence $[p_1, \ldots, p_i]$ can always be determined from the ordering associated to $[p_1, \ldots, p_{i-1}]$ by solving a polynomial number of resolution of NP problems.

Some interesting observations can be made on the third column of Table 1. The first is that the revision of a sequence has always size polynomial in the total size of the sequence. This is in contrast with the results about many forms of one-step revision [CDLS95], for which it is not always possible to find a polynomial size formula that represents the result of the revision. The second observation is that all the operators have the same complexity (namely, NP-equivalent). The reason is that the class of the NP-equivalent problems contains all the problems that are at least NP-hard, and for which a polynomial number of calls to an NP oracle suffices to determine the result. Both these facts hold for the iterated revisions introduced.

Note also that there are two rows for the ranked revision. This happens because the ranked revisions are actually a class of revisions or, using the terminology of Nebel [Neb94], a scheme of revision. Let $\mathcal{R}$ be a ranking model. We

	equivalence with one formula	equivalence between sequences	minimality	minimal length
Full Meet Iterated	always	equal to inference	$O(1)$	1
Natural Revision	coNP complete	Δ_2^p complete	Δ_2^p complete	2^n
Adjustment	Δ_2^p complete	Δ_2^p complete	Δ_2^p complete	2^n
Condizionalization	D^p-hard in Δ_2^p	Δ_2^p complete	Π_2^p-hard in PSPACE	n
Prioritized Full Meet Revision	coNP complete	coNP complete	Π_2^p-hard in PSPACE	n
Ranked (general)	Δ_2^p	$\Delta_2^p[\log n]$-hard in Δ_2^p	Δ_2^p	4 if $el_\mathcal{R} = 0$
Ranked (upper bound)	Δ_2^p complete	Δ_2^p complete	Δ_2^p complete	4

Table 2. Complexity of equivalence and minimality.

denote $*_{RR(\mathcal{R})}$ the corresponding revision. In order to compute the complexity of this operator, some hypothesis are required.

1. The rank r such that $\mathcal{R}(r) = W$ can always be represented with $O(n)$ bits, where n is the number of atoms in the considered alphabet.
2. Deciding whether $I \in \mathcal{R}(r)$ is polynomial for any r.

These hypothesis restrict to a specific class of revisions. However, in this class there are different revision, that have different computational properties.

There are new aspects that must be considered in the iterated process of revision. Consider a sequence of revisions $[p_1, \ldots, p_m]$. The resulting k.b. $*[p_1, \ldots, p_m]$ in general does not suffice alone to evaluate a further revision if another formula p_{m+1} arrives. That is, if we store a $f \equiv *[p_1, \ldots, p_m]$ and forget the formulas $p_1, \ldots, p_m$, then we have not enough information to evaluate $*[p_1, \ldots, p_m, p_{m+1}]$. At any time, the revision process must take into account the history of the past revisions, or a suitable data structure representing it.

An important problem is decide when the "commitment" of the changes is possible, that is, when it is possible to replace a sequence $[p_1, \ldots, p_m]$ with a formula representing its revision $f \equiv *[p_1, \ldots, p_m]$.

More formally, we state the following definition.

Definition 7. Let $P = [p_1, \ldots, p_m]$ be a sequence and f be a formula. We say that P is equivalent to f w.r.t. a revision $*$ (written $P \equiv_* f$) if and only if for any sequence Q it holds $*P \cdot Q \equiv *[f] \cdot Q$.

More generally, it is useful to decide if a sequence is equivalent to another (hopefully shorter) one.

Definition 8. Let P, S be two sequences. We say that P is equivalent to S, w.r.t. a specific revision $*$, written $P \equiv_* S$, if and only if for any sequence Q it holds $*P \cdot Q \equiv *S \cdot Q$

The key problem is clearly to decide if a sequence is minimal, or is equivalent to a shorter one. Actually, for all the revisions it is possible to show that any sequence is equivalent to a sequence of a certain length independent to the length of the original sequence. For example, for the prioritized iteration of the full meet revision, any sequence is equivalent to a sequence of length n (the number of atoms in the formulas of the sequence). The complexity of resolving these problems is reported in Table 2.

The result of the last column for the ranked revision holds only if $el_{\mathcal{R}} = 0$, where $el_{\mathcal{R}}$ is the maximum number of consecutive empty levels of $\mathcal{R}$ (that is, it holds only if $\mathcal{R}$ has no empty level).

As one would expect, deciding the equivalence between sequences is more difficult than the problem of equivalence with one formula. Note however that this is not directly implied by the definitions: the first problem is to decide, given *two* sequences, if they are equivalent, while the second one is to decide, given *one* sequence if there exists a formula f equivalent to it. It could be possible, (for revisions not yet introduced) that this task of finding f makes the one formula equivalence problem more hard.

Deciding if a sequence is minimal turns out to be the most difficult problem, for each revision defined (exception made for the full meet revision, for which it is trivial). As a result, finding a minimal sequence equivalent to a given one is also an hard problem. However, a sequence does not need in general to be represented by the minimal one equivalent to it: a sub-optimal representation may meet the memory requirements.

The last column shows an interesting property of all the operators introduced: any sequence of length m is equivalent to a sequence whose length is independent to m. Namely, the length of these minimal sequences depends only on the number n of atoms in the considered alphabet. For long sequences ($m \gg n$) this can be useful.

4 Proof Sketches

In this section, we give proof sketches for some of the results of Table 1 and Table 2.

Theorem 9. *Inference for the natural revision is Δ_2^p complete.*

Proof (sketch). The membership in Δ_2^p follows from definition: the revision of a sequence is defined in terms of revision models, and the revision model of a sequence $[p_1, \ldots, p_m]$ can always be determined with a polynomial number of calls to a procedure that resolve an NP problem, if the revision model associated with $[p_1, \ldots, p_{m-1}]$ is known. However, representing a revision model in polynomial space is not a so trivial issue.

In order to prove hardness, we give a polynomial reduction from the problem MAXLEXMOD (see Section 2) to the problem of inference for the natural revision. Given a formula t on the alphabet $\{x_1, \ldots, x_n\}$, the natural revision applied to the sequence

$$P = [t, y_1, x_1 \equiv y_1, \ldots, y_n, x_n \equiv y_n]$$

has only one model I, and $I \cap \{x_1, \ldots, x_n\}$ is the maximal lexicographic model of t.

In order to prove it, consider that the maximal lexicographic model of t can be found with the following procedure:

```
s := t
for i := 1 to n do
    if s ∧ xᵢ is consistent
        then s := s ∧ xᵢ
        else s := s ∧ ¬xᵢ
    return Mod(s)
```

We can prove that the revision of the sequence P above "simulates" this algorithm.

Essentially, what happens is that the class of the minimal models w.r.t. the relation R (of the current revision model $\langle \mathcal{W}, R, \phi \rangle$) is exactly the set of models of the formula s of the procedure. For the first formula of the sequence this is true since the minimal models of the revision model associated to $[t]$ are exactly the models of t.

The introduction of y_i in the sequence "splits" the current class of minimal models in two: the minimal models that contain y_i form the new class of minimal models, while the other models (those without y_i) form a new class just above.

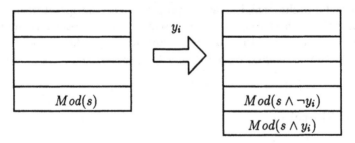

The introduction of $x_i \equiv y_i$ modifies this relation. If s is consistent with x_i, then in the minimal class there are already models that satisfies $x_i \equiv y_i$. Thus those models become the new minimal models of the relation. On the other case (if $s \wedge x_i$ is inconsistent) the minimal models of $x_i \equiv y_i$ are in the class $Mod(s \wedge \neg y_i)$, thus the new minimal class is $Mod(s \wedge \neg y_i \wedge \neg x_i)$.

Now, since the only model of $*_{NR}P$ is the maximal lexicographical model of t, we have that MAXLEXMOD is equivalent to $*_{NR}P \models x_n$. □

Theorem 10. *Any sequence is equivalent (w.r.t. the natural revision) to a sequence of length 2^n, where n is the number of atoms in the considered alphabet. Moreover, there are sequences of length 2^n that are minimal.*

Proof (sketch). A given sequence P is equivalent to a sequence S if the revision models induced by them are identical. Now, consider the revision model $\langle \mathcal{W}, R, \phi \rangle$ associated with P, and define

$$\mathcal{W}_0 = min(\mathcal{W}, R)$$

$$\vdots$$

$$\mathcal{W}_i = min(\mathcal{W}/\mathcal{W}_{i-1}, R)$$

Since $\mathcal{W}$ contains 2^n interpretation (for an alphabet of size n), there are at most 2^n non-empty classes $\{\mathcal{W}_0, \ldots, \mathcal{W}_k\}$. Now, consider the sequence

$$S = [Form(\mathcal{W}_k), \ldots, Form(\mathcal{W}_0)]$$

One can prove that S and P induce the same revision model. □

5 Conclusions and Related Work

In this paper we have studied a fundamental issue of knowledge bases, that is, the complexity of a process of iterated revisions. Apart from the classical problems of belief revision (inference, model checking) we have introduced and studied new problems related to the iteration (commitment, equivalence, minimality).

Some questions are still open. For example, it is not clear if the problem of minimality for $*_{CT}$ and $*_{PR(FM)}$ is Π_2^p complete, PSPACE complete or lies in some point of the polynomial hierarchy. However, as we will show in the full version of this paper, this problem is related to the problem of counting the classes of equivalence induced by a certain relation, and thus it is probably better characterized with one of the "counting classes", such as #P.

Note also that in this paper we have considered only the problem of revision, and not the related problem of update [GM95, FH94].

Finally, we relate our work with [EG93]. In that paper, the authors analyze the complexity of inference in the (simple) iteration of the revision introduced by Fagin, Ullman and Vardi (also known as Ginsberg's revision). Other issues, related to the conditional logics are studied there. In our work, instead, we want to characterize the new semantics introduced for iterated revision. We also introduced the problems of equivalence as a measure of the possibility of committing the changes on a knowledge base.

Acknowledgments

We thank to Marco Cadoli and Marco Schaerf for their comments on earlier versions of this paper. We also thank to the anonymous referees for their valuable suggestions.

References

[AGM85] C. E. Alchourrón, P. Gärdenfors, and D. Makinson. On the logic of theory change: Partial meet contraction and revision functions. *J. of Symbolic Logic*, 50:510–530, 1985.

[Bou93] Boutilier. Revision sequences and nested conditionals. In *Proc. of IJCAI-93*, pages 519–525, 1993.

[CDLS95] M. Cadoli, F. M. Donini, P. Liberatore, and M. Schaerf. The size of a revised knowledge base. In *Proc. of PODS-95*, pages 151–162, 1995.

[Dal88] M. Dalal. Investigations into a theory of knowledge base revision: Preliminary report. In *Proc. of AAAI-88*, pages 475–479, 1988.

[EG92] T. Eiter and G. Gottlob. On the complexity of propositional knowledge base revision, updates and counterfactuals. *AIJ*, 57:227–270, 1992.

[EG93] T. Eiter and G. Gottlob. The complexity of nested counterfactuals and iterated knowledge base revisions. In *Proc. of IJCAI-93*, pages 526–531, 1993.

[FH94] N. Friedman and J. Y. Halpern. A knowledge-based framework for belief change: Part II: Revision and update. In *Proc. of KR-94*, pages 190–200, 1994.

[GM95] G. Grahne and A. O. Mendelzon. Updates and subjunctive queries. *Information and Computation*, 2(116):241–252, 1995.

[Joh90] D. S. Johnson. A catalog of complexity classes. In J. van Leeuwen, editor, *Handbook of Theoretical Computer Science*, volume A, chapter 2. Elsevier, 1990.

[KM91] H. Katsuno and A. O. Mendelzon. Propositional knowledge base revision and minimal change. *AIJ*, 52:263–294, 1991.

[Kre88] M. V. Krentel. The complexity of optimization problems. *J. of Computer and System Sciences*, 36:490–509, 1988.

[Leh95] D. Lehmann. Belief revision, revised. In *Proc. of IJCAI-95*, pages 1534–1540, 1995.

[LS95] P. Liberatore and M. Schaerf. Relating belief revision and circumscription. In *Proc. of IJCAI-95*, pages 1557–1563, 1995.

[LS96] P. Liberatore and M. Schaerf. The complexity of model checking for belief revision and update. In *Proc. of AAAI-96*, pages 556–561, 1996.

[Neb91] B. Nebel. Belief revision and default reasoning: Syntax-based approaches. In *Proc. of KR-91*, pages 417–428, 1991.

[Neb94] B. Nebel. Base revision operations and schemes: Semantics, representation and complexity. In *Proc. of ECAI-94*, pages 341–345, 1994.

[Wil94] M. Williams. Transmutations of knowledge systems. In *Proc. of KR-94*, pages 619–629, 1994.

Expressive Power of Unary Counters

Michael Benedikt[1]   H. Jerome Keisler[2]

[1] Bell Laboratories, 1000 East Warrenville Rd., Naperville, IL 60566, USA, Email: benedikt@bell-labs.com
[2] University of Wisconsin, Madison Wisconsin 53706, Email: keisler@math.wisc.edu

Abstract. We compare the expressive power on finite models of two extensions of first order logic L with equality. $L(Ct)$ is formed by adding an operator $count\{x : \varphi\}$, which builds a term of sort $\mathbf{N}$ that counts the number of elements of the finite model satisfying a formula φ. Our main result shows that the stronger operator $count\{t(x) : \varphi\}$, where $t(x)$ is a term of sort $\mathbf{N}$, cannot be expressed in $L(Ct)$. That is, being able to count elements does not allow one to count terms.

This paper also continues our interest in new proof techniques in database theory. The proof of the unary counter combines a number of model-theoretic techniques that give powerful tools for expressivity bounds: in particular, we discuss here the use of indiscernibles, the Paris-Harrington form of Ramsey's theorem, and nonstandard models of arithmetic.

1   Introduction

Most database query languages are based on some version of first-order logic. However, practical query languages such as SQL generally supplement their pure first-order component with certain primitives, among them the ability to count over the database. An active line of research in database theory has been to model the impact of counting on a database language by studying extensions of first-order logic by *counting quantifiers* [16] [10]. The goal is to characterize the expressive power of various counting languages, and to identify those with and without good analytical and computational properties.

In [16] logics with n-ary counters $FO + C^n$ are introduced. A method of proving upper bounds on the complexity of these languages is introduced, relying on an Ehrenfeucht-Fraisse game construction for counting (see also [17]). This technique is used to prove a hierarchy theorem for this sequence of logics, in the case of unnested counters. The games are also exploited in [9] and [10] to get complexity bounds for languages allowing counting quantifiers of the form $\exists i$.

As opposed to the works cited above, we will consider languages with counting constructs that can interact with arbitrary expressions over the integers. We shall consider three extensions of first order logic formed by adding term-building operators which count the number of elements satisfying a formula. The smallest of these is a first-order logic with unary counters, like the language $FO + C^1$ considered in [16], but with arbitrary integer predicates applicable to the counters. This language is more similar in spirit to the rich two-sorted languages considered in [13] than to the more restricted ones of [10] and [9]. Although this language is extremely large, we will show some interesting limits on its expressive power by displaying two counting languages with more expressive power. In particular, we will show that it is impossible to count the number of equivalence classes of a binary relation in the language of unary counters, and it is impossible to count the number of connected components of a graph. Our results also serve to show that the ability to count the number of elements satisfying a property does not suffice to count the number of terms.

In the process, we will introduce modifications to the Ehrenfeucht-Fraisse argument that we think are interesting in its own right. We will make use of two model-theoretic techniques: nonstandard universes and indiscernibles. Indiscernibles and nonstandard models have shown up either implicitly or explicitly in several recent works in database theory [26] [4]. These techniques were recently used to settle a number of other problems concerning the expressive power of query languages [3], and they can be used to simplify the bookkeeping involved in many Ehrenfeucht-Fraisse arguments. We believe these techniques can be particularly helpful for proving expressivity bounds for languages involving aggregates.

As mentioned before, one of the principal reasons for studying the expressive power of query languages is to give insight into the design of languages with desirable properties. At the end of this paper we will apply our main theorem to show that a particular desirable property—the weakest precondition property—fails for a natural database language with unary counters.

Organization: Section 2 gives the definition of the languages we will deal with in this paper. Section 3 describes the nonstandard framework we use to analyze expressivity of queries, and gives some introductory examples of its usefulness. Section 4 outlines the proof of the main result. Section 5 gives a version of this result for a language similar to the tuple relational calculus with range-restriction, and gives an application of these results to the weakest precondition problem for this language.

2 Preliminaries

We give the notation for first-order logic and several counting languages.

Let L be a first-order language with equality and finitely many relation, function and constant symbols. Let U be an infinite set. When we talk about *finite L-structures*, we will mean structures whose domain is a finite subset of U. Let Λ be a countable set of relations and functions on the set N of natural numbers which contains at least equality and a constant for each $n \in N$, and remains fixed throughout our discussion.

Our first extension of L, denoted by $L(Ct)$, adds to L the term building operator

$$count\{x : \varphi(x, \ldots)\}$$

which bounds the variable x, and has a symbol for every element of Λ. The models for $L(Ct)$ are finite structures $\mathcal{A} = \langle A, \ldots \rangle$ with vocabulary L, and the count operator is interpreted in $\mathcal{A}$ as the cardinality of the set of all elements $x \in A$

which satisfy the formula φ in $\mathcal{A}$. Similarly, the term $\tau(\vec{y}) = count\{x : \varphi(x, \vec{y})\}$ defines a function that for each $\vec{y}$ returns the cardinality of elements in $\mathcal{A}$ satisfying $\varphi(x, \vec{y})$.

More precisely, the language $L(Ct)$ has terms of the two sorts U and $\mathbf{N}$. The terms of sort U are the same as for first order logic; in particular, the variables are of sort U. $L(Ct)$ has the usual first order rules for building formulas, plus

- For each formula φ and variable x, $count\{x : \varphi\}$ is a term of sort $\mathbf{N}$.
- If $t_1, \ldots, t_n$ are terms of sort $\mathbf{N}$, then $f(t_1, \ldots, t_n)$ is a term of sort $\mathbf{N}$, and $r(t_1, \ldots, t_n)$ is a formula for each n-ary function $f \in \Lambda$ (relation $r \in \Lambda$).

Our second extension of L, denoted by $L(Tm)$, adds to $L(Ct)$ the more general term-building operator

$$count\{t(x, \ldots) : \varphi(x, \ldots)\}$$

where φ is a formula and $t(x, \ldots)$ is a term of sort $\mathbf{N}$. In a model $\mathcal{A}$, it counts the number of distinct values of $t(x, \ldots)$ such that x satisfies φ in $\mathcal{A}$. Thus, we always have $count\{t(x, \ldots) : \varphi(x, \ldots)\} \leq count\{x : \varphi(x, \ldots)\}$.

Our third extension, $L(Ct, \mathbf{N})$, adds to $L(Ct)$ variables of sort $\mathbf{N}$ and quantifiers over variables of sort $\mathbf{N}$. The language $L(Ct, \mathbf{N})$ was considered in [16]. The main object of study in that paper was a language like $L(Ct, \mathbf{N})$ which had counts over n-tuples of variables of sort U, but did not allow nesting of counts.

In this paper we shall show that $L(Tm)$ and $L(Ct, \mathbf{N})$ are proper extensions of $L(Ct)$.

We remark that quantifiers of sort U can be eliminated from each of the languages $L(Ct)$, $L(Tm)$, and $L(Ct, \mathbf{N})$. An existential quantifier can be eliminated by replacing a formula $\exists x \varphi(x, \ldots)$ by $\neg count\{x : \varphi(x, \ldots)\} = 0$.

In a vocabulary L with function symbols, one might also consider the term builder $count\{s(x, \ldots) : \varphi(x, \ldots)\}$, where the term s is of sort U. This term builder is already definable in $L(Ct)$, because the equation

$$count\{s(x, \ldots) : \varphi(x, \ldots)\} = count\{z : \exists x(z = s(x, \ldots) \wedge \varphi(x, \ldots))\}$$

holds in all finite models.

3 Model-theoretic techniques and expressive bounds

We discuss here some model-theoretic techniques that are helpful for giving expressive bounds, and which will be used in the main result of Section 4.

3.1 Nonstandard Models

The work in [3] made use of nonstandard models and indiscernibles as techniques for analyzing expressivity bounds. Here we discuss them in more detail.

The naive approach to showing that a property Q is not expressible in some language $\mathcal{L}$ is to get two models that agree on all sentences of $\mathcal{L}$, but disagree on

Q. The problem immediately encountered in applying this technique in finite-model theory is the following: Any two finite models which satisfy the same sentences of a first order language L are isomorphic, and thus satisfy the same sentences of any reasonable logic, including $L(Ct)$, $L(Tm)$, and $L(Ct, \mathbf{N})$. The standard technique for circumventing this problem is via Ehrenfeucht-Fraisse games ([8], [7]). One decomposes the sentences of the logic into countably many fragments $\mathcal{L}_n$, and then constructs for each n two finite models M_n and N_n agreeing on fragment $\mathcal{L}_n$ but disagreeing on Q.

Here, we give an alternative to this construction. Inexpressibility bounds are obtained by finding two hyperfinite (meaning, informally for now, "infinitely large finite") models M and N agreeing on all queries in $\mathcal{L}$, but disagreeing on Q. The first virtue of this technique is as a way of abstracting away from the bookkeeping involved in Ehrenfeucht-Fraisse constructions. For example, if one is interested in showing the inexpressibility of connectivity within pure first-order logic, one need only look at the two hyperfinite graphs G_1 and G_2, where G_1 is a single hyperfinite cycle, while G_2 is the union of two hyperfinite cycles. A single game argument shows these two to be elementarily equivalent in first-order logic, but only one is connected, hence connectivity is not first-order definable.

The above example may appear to make the technique of nonstandard models useful more as a convenience than as an essential tool. However, the technique becomes particularly useful when dealing with expressivity results for higher-order logics. We will defer a more detailed discussion of the use of nonstandard models in higher-order languages to the full paper. The use of nonstandard universes (as opposed to elementary extensions) allows one to work with hyperfinite extensions of traditional aggregates constructs such as Counts, Sums, and set formers. For example, consider the query Q over complex objects (see [5],[25],) asking whether a given set of sets A contains two sets of differing parity. One can show this query to be inexpressible in the nested relational algebra [5], a higher-order analog of the relational algebra, by considering a natural counterexample: two hyperfinite structures S_1 and S_2, the first consisting of two hyperfinite sets of differing parity, the second consisting of two hyperfinite sets of the same parity. This argument can be formalized in a straightforward way using the definitions below, and can be easily generalized to higher-order queries. Arguments such as this are difficult to prove using other techniques (see the discussion in [20]) and can't be formalized using the 'flat' ultraproduct or elementary extension constructions. On the other hand, direct constructions using ultraproducts, when available, are often more concrete and more accessible in terms of exposition than the use of a nonstandard universe(compare, for example [3] and [24]).

In the previous paragraph, we spoke informally of hyperfinite structures. We now give some formal definitions, following the exposition in [3]:

For any set S, the **superstructure** $V(S)$ over S is defined as $V(S) = \bigcup_{n<\omega} V_n(S)$ where $V_1(S) = S$, and $V_{n+1}(S) = V_n(S) \cup \{X \mid X \subset V_n(S)\}$.

We will work with the structure $\langle V(S), \in \rangle$ considered as a structure for the first-order language for the epsilon relation. A **bounded-quantifier formula** in this language is a formula built up from atomic formulas by the logical connectives and the quantification: $\forall X \in Y$, $\exists X \in Y$, where X and Y are variables.

A **nonstandard universe** consists of a pair of superstructures $V(S)$ and $V(Y)$ and a mapping $*: V(S) \to V(Y)$ which is the identity when restricted to S (i.e. $*x = x$ for each x in S) and which satisfies

1. $Y = {}^*S$.
2. *(Transfer Principle)* For any bounded quantifier formula $\phi(v_1, \ldots, v_n)$ and any list $a_1, \ldots, a_n$ of elements from $V(S)$, $\phi(a_1, \ldots, a_n)$ is true in $V(S)$ if and only if $\phi({}^*a_1, \ldots, {}^*a_n)$ is true in $V(Y)$.

An element of $V(Y)$ is **standard** if it is in the image of the $*$-map. An element of $V(Y)$ is **internal** if it is in the downward transitive closure of the standard sets under $\in$. Elements of $V(Y)$ that are not internal are called **external**. An internal map is a map whose graph is an internal set.

We will assume that our universe also satisfies the following

3. *(Countable Saturation Principle)* For every standard A, and every countable collection $\Sigma(x, \vec{v})$ of bounded-quantifier formulas, and for every vector $\vec{c}$ of internal sets, if every finite subset of $\Sigma(x, \vec{c}/\vec{v})$ is satisfied in $V(Y)$ by some element of A, then $\Sigma(x, \vec{c}/\vec{v})$ is satisfied by an element of A.

We often omit the $*$ when convenient: for example, if $<$ is an ordering on a set A, and $x_1, x_2 \in {}^*A$, then we will write $x_1 < x_2$ rather than $x_1 {}^*{<} x_2$. If Q is a query on schema SC, and M is a $*$-database (an element of the set ${}^*DB$, where DB is the set of all SC-databases), then we will refer to $Q(M)$ rather than ${}^*Q(M)$.

For our proofs we take the base set S of $V(S)$ to be the disjoint union of the domain $\mathbb{U}$ from which our finite structures are taken and $\mathbb{N}$.

By a **$*$-finite set** we mean any set in the $*$-image of the collection of finite subsets of some standard set. Equivalently, an internal set B is $*$-finite if there is an internal bijection of B onto an initial segment of ${}^*\mathbb{N}$. In particular, we can talk about $*$-finite structures, which will have their underlying domains being contained in the $*$-image of the finite powerset of $\mathbb{U}$. By the transfer principle, such sets B have a well-defined cardinality, which is a (possibly nonstandard) positive integer, as well as a well-defined parity, sum, etc. By a **hyperfinite set**, we mean a $*$-finite set whose cardinality is not a standard integer. We similarly talk about hyperfinite structures, orderings etc. to mean those whose cardinality is a nonstandard integer.

We can now talk formally about hyperfinite structures. However, we cannot assume in general that the semantic function for a given logic will agree with the semantics obtained by considering the structure "externally". However, for first-order logic, we have the following result:

Proposition 1. *[3] Let L be a language for which each symbol is internal, and let M be an L-structure such that the domain of M is internal and the interpretation of each symbol in L is internal. Let $\phi(\vec{x})$ be a formula of L that has standard finite cardinality (i.e. number of symbols). Then the internal satisfaction predicate ${}^*\models$ agrees with the external satisfaction predicate $\models$ on ϕ. That is, if $\vec{c}$ is a finite sequence of parameters from M, then $M {}^*\models \phi(\vec{c})$ iff $M \models \phi(\vec{c})$.*

Given the above proposition we will not distinguish the two kinds of satisfaction predicates when we are dealing with finitary first-order ϕ's.

The nonstandard technique is now based on the following simple proposition:

Proposition 2. *[3] The following are equivalent for any boolean query Q on finite structures:*

- *There are two hyperfinite* * *− structures that agree on every query in the first-order language L but disagree on *Q.*
- *Q is not expressible in L.*

It is now easy to formalize the inexpressibility arguments mentioned in the beginning of the section. We can form, for example, a graph consisting of two hyperfinite chains (such a graph exists by transfer plus saturation), and show, by a single Ehrenfeucht game, that this graph , considered as an infinite structure, is elementarily equivalent to any graph consisting of a single hyperfinite cycle. The inexpressibility result now follows from Proposition 2.

3.2 Indiscernibles

Although the use of nonstandard models eliminates the need to construct countably many counterexample models, and relieves some of the combinatorial burden in a game argument, it may still be difficult to reason about elementary equivalence in an arbitrary hyperfinite structure.

To relieve the amount of analysis necessary in analyzing elementary equivalence, we will often want to restrict our attention to models whose algebraic structure is "as simple as possible". Indiscernibility is a method for capturing the intuition that the domain of our structures should have no unnecessary algebraic dependencies among its elements. This idea is implicit in many of the Ramsey-theoretic constructions used in Ehrenfeucht-Fraisse constructions [21],[26].

We now define indiscernibles formally. Let I be any ordered set. A sequence $B = \langle B_i \rangle_{i \in I}$, whose elements come from an infinite L-structure M is **indiscernible** if for every formula $\phi(\vec{x})$, ϕ is satisfied in M by either every increasing (in the order on I) subsequence of B or by no increasing subsequence of B. Indiscernibles are discussed at length in [6].

Within an indiscernible set, the logical structure of the model reduces to a simple ordering. Indiscernibles were used in algorithms for eliminating constraints from constraint queries in [3] [26] and [21].

An infinite set of indiscernibles need not exist in an arbitrary infinite structure. For example, considering the structure $M = \langle N, +, < \rangle$, we easily see that there can be no indiscernible set of size bigger than 1! However, it is easy to show, using saturation, that for any infinite structure, there is an infinite set of indiscernibles in the nonstandard extension $*M$: this makes the use of indiscernibles particularly powerful in conjunction with nonstandard methods.

In this work, we will consider the use of indiscernibles in collapsing logics with counting quantifiers to first-order logics. The construction in the next section will give an example of the use of indiscernibles to reduce every formula in the language $L(Ct)$ to a first-order formula. Since several previous expressibility bounds on aggregates make use of some sort of "Count Elimination" [19], we hope to investigate this phenomenon in more generality in forthcoming work.

4 Nonstandard Models and Unary Counters

Consider the logics $L(Ct)$, $L(Tm)$, and $L(Ct, \mathbf{N})$ defined in Section 2. We are interested in investigating the relative expressive powers of these languages, using the techniques mentioned above. In particular, we wish to show that $L(Ct)$ cannot express important properties expressible in $L(Tm)$, and $L(Ct, \mathbf{N})$. Our plan, of course, will be to find two nonstandard models which satisfy the same sentences of $L(Ct)$ but do not satisfy the same sentences of $L(Tm)$ or of $L(Ct, \mathbf{N})$.

Our first result will show that the language of unary counters $L(Ct)$ cannot count the number of equivalence classes in an equivalence relation, while $L(Ct, \mathbf{N})$ can express this. We now fix a particular first-order language L^0.

Definition 3. Let the language L^0 have one unary predicate symbol S and one binary predicate symbol E. Let θ be the following sentence of $L^0(Tm)$:

$$count\{count\{y : E(x, y)\} : x = x\} = count\{z : S(z)\}$$

If E is an equivalence relation, θ says that the number of distinct sizes of equivalence classes of E is equal to the number of elements of S.

Definition 4. Let θ^+ be the following sentence of $L^0(Ct, \mathbf{N})$:

$$\forall i[\forall j(Bit(j, i) \Leftrightarrow \exists x\ count\{y : E(x, y)\} = j) \Rightarrow Setcard(i) = count\{z : S(z)\}],$$

where i, j are variables of sort $\mathbf{N}$, $Bit(j, i)$ is true exactly when the jth bit of the binary representation of i is set, and $Setcard(i)$ is the cardinality of the set coded by the binary representation of i.

Since our arithmetic permits arbitrary functions on the integers, the predicates Bit and $Setcard$ are certainly expressible. Note that θ^+ expresses the same property as θ, that is, for every finite model C for L^0, C satisfies θ if and only if it satisfies θ^+. The sentence θ^+ does not have nested counts.

We shall prove the following theorem, which shows that neither θ nor θ^+ is expressible in $L^0(Ct)$, so that both $L(Tm)$ and $L(Ct, \mathbf{N})$ are proper extensions of $L(Ct)$.

Theorem 5. *For every sentence φ of $L^0(Ct)$ there is a finite model C in which θ is not equivalent to φ: i.e., the unary counter language cannot express θ.*

As mentioned above, our plan will be to find two nonstandard models which satisfy the same sentences of $L^0(Ct)$ but do not satisfy the same sentences of $L^0(Tm)$ or of $L^0(Ct, \mathbf{N})$.

We let $\mathcal{N}$ be the structure with universe set $\mathbf{N}$ and a symbol for $+$, $\times$, and every relation and function in the set Λ. For each *finite model $\mathcal{A}$ for L, each term t and formula φ of $L(Tm)$ is interpreted in the natural way, using the functions and relations on the extension $^*\mathcal{N}$. Terms of sort $\mathbf{N}$ are interpreted as functions with values in $^*\mathbf{N}$.

Our goal is to prove the following.

Theorem 6. *There exist *finite models $\mathcal{A}$ and $\mathcal{B}$ which satisfy the same sentences of $L^0(Ct)$ such that θ is false in $\mathcal{A}$ but true in $\mathcal{B}$.*

Given this theorem, the inexpressibility of θ in $L^0(Ct)$ now follows from the general results of the previous section.

The proof of this theorem will give a canonical example of the use of indiscernibles and nonstandard universes together. We will first show that a special set of indiscernibles exists, and then make use of them to prove Theorem 6.

We use the usual notation for intervals in $^*\mathbf{N}$; for example, $(J, K] = \{x \in {}^*\mathbf{N} : J < x$ and $x \le K\}$. By a *finite sequence in $^*\mathbf{N}$ we mean an an element of the star-image of the finite sequences in $\mathbf{N}$. By the transfer principle, each *finite sequence in $^*\mathbf{N}$ is a function $\vec{d} = \langle d_1, \ldots, d_H \rangle$ from the interval $(0, H]$ into $^*\mathbf{N}$ for some hyperinteger $H \in {}^*\mathbf{N}$.

Lemma 7. *There is a strictly increasing *finite sequence $\vec{d} = \langle d_1, \ldots, d_H \rangle$ in $^*\mathbf{N}$ such that $0 < d_1 < H$ and $\vec{d}$ is indiscernible in $^*\mathcal{N}$; that is, any two finite increasing subsequences of $\vec{d}$ satisfy the same first order formulas in $^*\mathcal{N}$.*

Proof. By the Paris-Harrington form of Ramsey's theorem, for every $e, r \in \mathbf{N}$ there exists $m \in \mathbf{N}$ such that for every partition $P : [m]^e \to r$ there is a subset $Q \subseteq m$ which is homogeneous for P and has size $|Q| \ge \min(Q)$. Then for each finite set φ of formulas in the language of $\mathcal{N}$ there is a strictly increasing finite sequence $\langle d_1, \ldots, d_h \rangle$ in $\mathbf{N}$ such that $0 < d_1 < h$ and $\vec{d}$ is indiscernible for φ. Using saturation once again on $^*\mathcal{N}$, it follows that there is a strictly increasing *finite sequence $\vec{d} = \langle d_1, \ldots, d_H \rangle$ in $^*\mathbf{N}$ such that $0 < d_1 < H$ and $\vec{d}$ is indiscernible in $^*\mathcal{N}$. $\square$

Hereafter we let $\vec{d} = \langle d_1, \ldots, d_H \rangle$ be as in Lemma 7, and put $d_0 = 0$.

Corollary 8. *H and d_1 are infinite, and $\frac{d_J}{d_{J-1}}$ is infinite for each $J \in (1, H]$ (i.e. for each standard integer n, $d_J > n \cdot d_{J-1}$) for each $J \in (1, H]$).*
The proofs are in the appendix.

We now define the *finite structures $\mathcal{A}$ and $\mathcal{B}$ for L^0.

Definition 9. Let $\mathcal{A} = \langle A, E, S \rangle$ where $A = (0, d_H]$, E is the equivalence relation on A with equivalence classes $(d_{J-1}, d_J], J \in (0, H]$, and $S = (0, d_1]$. Let $K = d_1$ and $\mathcal{B} = \langle B, F, S \rangle$ where $B = (0, d_K]$, $F = E \cap B \times B$, and $S = (0, d_1]$.

Lemma 10. *The sentence θ is false in $\mathcal{A}$ and true in $\mathcal{B}$.*

Lemma 11. *$\mathcal{A}$ and $\mathcal{B}$ satisfy the same sentences of $L^0(Ct)$.*
Lemma 10 is proved straightforwardly by insepection; the proof of Lemma 11 is quite involved, and can be found in the appendix.

5   Applications to weakest preconditions

We now outline a version of the previous results for a language L' whose concrete syntax is closer to existing database languages. The description we give below is based on the tuple relational calculus with range restriction [1], and on our analysis of the PRL constraint language [14] [15].

We have a signature $\{R_1, \ldots, R_n\}$, and for each $i \leq n$ a finite set of **attribute symbols** A_i. The **arity** of R_i is the cardinality of A_i. For each R_i we also fix a countably infinite set U_i. We now define our language L'.

We have variables of sort i for each $i \leq n$, and an integer sort. A formula will be built out of atomic formulas of the form:

- $x.a = y.b$ where x and y are variables of the same sort i, and a and b are symbols in A_i, or of the form
- $P(\tau_1, \ldots, \tau_n)$, where P is an integer predicate and the τ_j are terms of type integer.

Formulae are built up by the logical connectives and quantifications $\forall x \in R_i\ \phi(x)$, and $\exists x \in R_i\ \phi(x)$, where x has sort i.

Terms are built up via composition from atomic terms, which are of one of the forms:

1. $f(\vec{x})$, where f is a symbol for some function from tuples of integers to integers, and $\vec{x}$ is a tuple of variables of integer sort. The corresponding language $L'(Ct)$ adds the ability to form terms from formulas via the rule:
2. $Count\{x \in R_i : \phi(x)\}$, where x has sort i and ϕ is a formula.

The language $L'(Tm)$ further supplements this by permitting

3. $Count\{\tau(x) : x \in R_i \wedge \phi(x)\}$, where τ is a term.

A structure for L' consists of an assignment to each relational variable R_i of a finite collection of elements of the set of functions $U_i^{A_i}$ (i.e. tuples). Satisfaction relative to an assignment of variables is defined exactly as in the language $L(Ct)$.

Let our signature have two relations R and S, and let R have attributes a and b, while S has attributes c and d .

Theorem 12. *The $L'(Tm)$ sentence θ' below is not expressible in $L'(Ct)$:*

$$\theta' \equiv count\{x.a : x \in R \wedge x = x\} = count\{z \in S : z = z\}.$$

The proof is found in the appendix.

5.1   Preconditions and Definable transactions

Let $\mathcal{L}$ be any of the standard logical languages (first-order logic, infinitary logic, etc.). We let $s(\mathcal{L})$ denote the sentences of $\mathcal{L}$. We will talk about a database (that is, a finite structure as in the previous section) satisfying a sentence or open formula of $\mathcal{L}$: we mean this in the usual sense. By a **transaction** on databases, we mean simply any function mapping databases to databases. In the following discussion, we will let D range over databases for a particular signature, and T denote the set of database transactions for this signature. $TERM(\mathcal{L})$ denotes the set of terms of $\mathcal{L}$ and for Γ a collection of terms and D a database, we let $\Gamma(D)$ denote all elements obtained from applying a vector of terms in Γ to elements in the underlying set of D. That is:

$$\Gamma(D) = \{\vec{\tau}(\vec{y}) : \vec{y} \subset D \text{ and } \vec{\tau} \subset \Gamma\}$$

We now discuss two classes of transactions on finite models associated with $\mathcal{L}$. The definitions are taken from [2]. The class $\mathcal{WPC}(\mathcal{L})$ (transactions with *weakest preconditions* with respect to $\mathcal{L}$) is defined as

$$\{T \in T \mid \exists \text{ recursive } f : s(\mathcal{L}) \to s(\mathcal{L}) : \forall D \, \forall \alpha \in s(\mathcal{L}) : T(D) \models \alpha \Leftrightarrow D \models f(\alpha)\}$$

A transaction T has weakest preconditions for $\mathcal{L}$ if we can statically determine whether the database resulting from T will satisfy a constraint in $\mathcal{L}$.

The set of *L-definable* transactions is the collection

$$\mathcal{DEF}(\mathcal{L}) = \{T \mid \forall R \, \exists \, \mathcal{L} \text{ formula } \beta_R(\vec{x}) \, \exists \, \Gamma \subset TERM(\mathcal{L}) \text{ such that}$$
$$\forall D \, \forall \vec{t} : T(D) \models R(\vec{t}) \Leftrightarrow \vec{t} \subset \Gamma(D) \wedge D \models \beta_R(\vec{t})\}$$

The class of definable transactions are those that can be expressed using a finite set of $\mathcal{L}$ terms and $\mathcal{L}$ formulae.

In [2] it is observed that for first-order languages, we have containment, $\mathcal{DEF}(\mathcal{L}) \subset \mathcal{WPC}(\mathcal{L})$. That is, definable transactions all admit weakest preconditions. This is a desirable closure property for a query language to possess. [2] investigates weakest preconditions over a number of logics, and over a number of transaction languages. In [15],[2], and [14] applications of weakest precondition closure to database integrity maintenance are discussed.

Given the importance of weakest precondition closure for database query languages, it is important to see if natural extensions of the relational calculus, such as $L'(Ct)$, posess this closure property. It follows from the main result of this paper that containment does *not* hold for the language $L'(Ct)$.

Corollary 13. *There are $L'(Ct)$-definable transactions that do not posess weakest preconditions over $L'(Ct)$.*

6 Conclusions and future work

Languages with aggregate constructs are not nearly so well understood as the relational calculus. In particular, issues of optimization, complexity, safety, and expressiveness remain open for many models of aggregation. We are interested in developing a usable set of rewrite-rules for simplifying languages such as $L(Ct)$ and $L(Tm)$, and getting semantic characterizations of the definable transactions that are available (along the lines of Gaifman's locality theorem [11] or the bounded degree property of [19]).

We are interested in studying the relationship of the language $L(Tm)$ to various other counting languages (those discussed, for example, in [16]). In particular, it would be helpful to know whether languages with binary counters can express all sentences of $L(Tm)$, and similarly for n-ary counters.

Techniques for proving expressiveness bounds on query languages are hard to come by. We've presented here one technique for analyzing expressivity of query languages, based on the use of indiscernibles and nonstandard models, that we believe can be useful outside of the context of aggregates. In particular, we hope to investigate the interaction of these techniques with the use of Ehrenfeucht games for logics with counting [16] [12].

Questions in this work were motivated by considering the closure under weakest preconditions of various extensions of first-order logic. The closure of a specification language under weakest-preconditions of definable transactions is helpful for integrity constraint maintenance [2],[22],[23]. It is therefore important to find logics that include aggregate operators that have this closure property, are of manageable complexity, and allow for optimization and analysis. The results of this paper show that $L(Ct)$ is not closed under weakest-preconditions, and we suspect that the same is true for $L(Tm)$. We would like to discover natural weakest-precondition closed logics containing these languages.

Acknowledgements: The authors wish to thank the referees for several helpful comments, and Leonid Libkin for numerous improvements to the text.

References

1. S. Abiteboul, R. Hull, V. Vianu. *Foundations of Databases.* Addison-Wesley, 1995.
2. M. Benedikt, T. Griffin, and L. Libkin Verifiable properties of database transactions. In *Proceedings of 15th ACM Symposium on Principles of Database Systems*, pages 117–128, Montreal Canada, June 1996.
3. M. Benedikt, G. Dong, L. Libkin, L. Wong. Relational expressive power of constraint query languages. In *Proceedings of 15th ACM Symposium on Principles of Database Systems*, pages 5–17, Montreal Canada, June 1996.
4. M. Benedikt and L. Libkin. On the structure of queries in constraint query languages. In *Proceedings of 11th IEEE Symposium on Logic in Computer Science, New Brunswick, New Jersey* 1996.
5. P. Buneman, S. Naqvi, V. Tannen, L. Wong. Principles of programming with complex objects and collection types. *Theoretical Computer Science*, 149(1):3–48, 1995.
6. C. C. Chang and H. Jerome Keisler. *Model Theory.* North-Holland Elsevier 1990.
7. H.-D. Ebbinghaus and J. Flum. *Finite Model Theory.* Springer Verlag, 1995.
8. A. Ehrenfeucht. An application of games to the completeness problem for formalized theories. *Fundamentae Mathematicae*, 49:129–141, 1961.
9. K. Etessami. Counting quantifiers, successor relations, and logarithmic space. In *Proceedings of 10th IEEE Conference on Structure in Complexity Theory*, May 1995, pages 2–11.
10. K. Etessami and N. Immerman. Tree canonization and transitive closure. Tenth Annual IEEE Symposium on Logic in Computer Science. 1995.
11. H. Gaifman. On local and nonlocal properties. In J. Stern, editor, *Logic Colloquium '81*, pages 105–135. North -Holland, 1982.

12. Gradel, E. and Otto, M. Inductive definability with counting on finite structures. In E. Borger (ed.), *Computer Science Logic*, LNCS 702 Springer (1993), 231-247.

13. Erich Gradel and Yuri Gurevich. Metafinite model theory. In *Logic and Computational Complexity, International Workshop LCC'94* Indianapolis, IN,313-366.

14. T. Griffin and H. Trickey. Integrity Maintenance in a Telecommunications Switch. In IEEE Data Engineering Bulletin V. 17, No. 2., June 1994.

15. T. Griffin, H. Trickey, and C. Tuckey. Update constraints for relational databases. Technical Memorandum AT&T Bell Laboratories, 1992

16. S. Grumbach and C. Tollu. On the expressive power of counting. Fourth International Conference on Database Theory. 1992.

17. N. Immerman, E.S. Lander. Describing graphs: a first-order approach to graph canonization. In *Complexity Theory Retrospective*, pp. 59-81. Springer, 1990.

18. C. Karp. Finite quantifier equivalence. In *The Theory of Models*, edited by J. Addison, L. Henkin, and A. Tarski, North-Holland 1965, 407-412.

19. L. Libkin and L. Wong. New techniques for studying set languages, bag languages and aggregate functions. In *Proceedings of the 13th Conference on Principles of Database Systems*, Minneapolis MN, May 1994, pages 155–166.

20. L. Libkin and L. Wong. On representation and querying incomplete information in databases with bags. Information Processing Letters 56 (1995), 209-214

21. J. Paredaens, J. Van den Bussche, and D. Van Gucht. First-order queries on finite structures over the reals. In *Proceedings of 10th IEEE Symposium on Logic in Computer Science, San Diego, California*, pages 79–87, 1995.

22. X. Qian. An effective method for integrity constraint simplification. In *Fourth International Conference on Data Engineering*, 1988.

23. X. Qian. *The Deductive Synthesis of Database Transactions*. PhD thesis, Stanford University, 1989.

24. O.Belagradek, A. Stolboushkin, M. Tsaitlin. On order-generic queries. Manuscript. To appear.

25. V. Tannen, Tutorial: Languages for collection types, *in* "Proceedings of 13th Symposium on Principles of Database Systems," Minneapolis, May 1994.

26. J. Van Den Bussche and M. Otto. First-order queries on databases embedded in an infinite. structure. Information Processing Letters, to appear.

A Proofs

We will prove the remaining lemmas used to prove Theorem 6. Hereafter we let $\vec{d} = \langle d_1, \ldots, d_H \rangle$ be as in Lemma 7, and put $d_0 = 0$.

Proof of corollary 8. By indiscernibility, d_1 is infinite, and thus H is infinite. Since $\vec{d}$ is strictly increasing and $d_1 < H$, we have $2d_1 \leq d_H$. By indiscernibility, $2d_{J-1} \leq d_J$ for each $J \in (1, H]$, and by indiscernibility again, $2^n d_{J-1} \leq d_J$ for each J and each finite n. $\square$

Proof of lemma 11. We have $count\{x : S(x)\} = d_1$ in both $\mathcal{A}$ and $\mathcal{B}$. In $\mathcal{A}$, $count\{count\{y : E(x,y)\} : x = x\} = H > d_1$, so θ fails in $\mathcal{A}$. In $\mathcal{B}$, $count\{count\{y : E(x,y)\} : x = x\} = d_1$, so θ holds in $\mathcal{B}$. $\square$

It remains to show that $\mathcal{A}$ and $\mathcal{B}$ satisfy the same sentences of $L^0(Ct)$. In order to do this we introduce an auxiliary first order vocabulary L^1 and corresponding models $\mathcal{A}^1$ and $\mathcal{B}^1$.

Definition 14. Let $f : A \to (0, H]$ be the function such that $f(x) = J$ whenever $J \in (0, H]$ and $x \in (d_{J-1}, d_J]$. Let L^1 be a first order vocabulary with countably many unary relations $\min_n(x), \max_n(x)$ and countably many binary relations $x \preceq_n y$ for $n \in \mathbf{N}$. Let $\mathcal{A}^1$ be the model for L^1 with universe A such that

- $\mathcal{A}^1 \models \min_n(x)$ iff $f(x) \le n$,
- $\mathcal{A}^1 \models \max_n(x)$ iff $H - n \le f(x)$,
- $\mathcal{A}^1 \models x \preceq_n y$ iff $f(x) + n \le f(y)$.

Let $\mathcal{B}^1$ be the model for L^1 with universe B such that

- $\mathcal{B}^1 \models \min_n(x)$ iff $f(x) \le n$,
- $\mathcal{B}^1 \models \max_n(x)$ iff $K - n \le f(x)$,
- $\mathcal{B}^1 \models x \preceq_n y$ iff $f(x) + n \le f(y)$.

Lemma 15. *For every formula $\varphi(\vec{x})$ of $L^0(Ct)$ there is a formula $\varphi^1(\vec{x})$ of $L^1(Ct)$ such that for all $\vec{a}$ in A, $\mathcal{A} \models \varphi[\vec{a}]$ if and only if $\mathcal{A}^1 \models \varphi^1[\vec{a}]$, and for all $\vec{b}$ in B, $\mathcal{B} \models \varphi[\vec{b}]$ if and only if $\mathcal{B}^1 \models \varphi^1[\vec{b}]$.*
Proof: Put $(x = y)^1 = (x = y)$, $E(x, y)^1 = (x \preceq_0 y \wedge y \preceq_0 x)$, and $S(x)^1 = \min_1(x)$. Then use the formation rules in the obvious way to define φ^1 for arbitrary φ. $\square$

Definition 16. Let $\vec{a} \equiv_0 \vec{b}$ mean that $|\vec{a}| = |\vec{b}|$ and $(\mathcal{A}^1, \vec{a})$ and $(\mathcal{B}^1, \vec{b})$ satisfy the same atomic formulas of L^1. We use a similar notation for pairs of tuples which are both in A or in B.

Lemma 17. *$\mathcal{A}^1$ and $\mathcal{B}^1$ satisfy the same sentences of L^1. In fact, $\vec{a} \equiv_0 \vec{b}$ if and only if $(\mathcal{A}^1, \vec{a})$ and $(\mathcal{B}^1, \vec{b})$ satisfy the same formulas of L^1.*
Proof: Using the fact that we have $\preceq_n$ as an atomic relation in the language for each n, and the fact that $\mathcal{A}^1$ and $\mathcal{B}^1$ are countably saturated, we derive that the relation $\vec{a} \equiv_0 \vec{b}$ has the back and forth property. It follows that whenever $\vec{a} \equiv_0 \vec{b}$, player $\exists$ has a winning strategy in the Ehrenfeucht-Fraisse game with ω moves between $(\mathcal{A}^1, \vec{a})$ and $(\mathcal{B}^1, \vec{b})$. In addition, we have that the empty sequences from each model are $\equiv_0$-equivalent, since there are no atomic sentences in L^1. Thus $(\mathcal{A}^1, \vec{a})$ and $(\mathcal{B}^1, \vec{b})$ are elementarily equivalent by Karp's theorem in [18]. $\square$

Lemma 18. *Let $\Gamma(\vec{x})$ be a set of quantifier-free formulas of L^1 maximal consistent with the theory of $\mathcal{A}^1$ and let $\psi(\vec{x}, y)$ be a quantifier-free formula in L^1. Let $s = \mathrm{domain}(\vec{x}) \cup \{\min, \max\}$. There exist $\alpha_1, \ldots, \alpha_m \in s, \beta_1, \ldots, \beta_m \in \{-1, 1\}, \gamma_1, \ldots, \gamma_m \in \mathbf{Z}, \delta \in \mathbf{Z}$ such that whenever $(\mathcal{A}^1, \vec{a})$ satisfies $\Gamma(\vec{x})$,*

$$\mathrm{count}\{y : \psi(\vec{a}, y)\} = \delta + \sum_{j=1}^{m} \beta_j d_{f(a_{\alpha_j}) + \gamma_j},$$

and whenever $(\mathcal{B}^1, \vec{b})$ satisfies $\Gamma(\vec{x})$,

$$\mathrm{count}\{y : \psi(\vec{b}, y)\} = \delta + \sum_{j=1}^{m} \beta_j d_{f(b_{\alpha_j}) + \gamma_j},$$

with the convention that $f(a_{\min}) = f(b_{\min}) = 0$, $f(a_{\max}) = H$, *and* $f(b_{\max}) = K$.
Proof: Given $\Gamma(\vec{x})$, any quantifier-free formula $\psi(\vec{x}, y)$ of L^1 says that either y belongs to a subset of $\{x_i : i < |\vec{x}|\}$, or $y \notin \{x_i : i < |\vec{x}|\}$ and $f(y)$ belongs to a finite union of disjoint "intervals" with endpoints at a finite distance from elements of

$$\{f(x_i) : i \in s\}.$$

In the model $(\mathcal{A}, \vec{a})$, such an interval will have the form $(u + \gamma, u' + \gamma']$ where $\gamma, \gamma' \in \mathbf{Z}$ and u, u' belong to $\{f(x_i) : i \in s\}$. The number of elements y of A such that $f(y)$ belongs to such an interval is equal to the difference $d_{u'+\gamma'} - d_{u+\gamma}$. A similar computation holds for $(\mathcal{B}, \vec{b})$. $\square$

We now prove our main lemma, which shows that in the models $\mathcal{A}^1$ and $\mathcal{B}^1$ both quantifiers and counts can be eliminated.

Lemma 19. *For each formula φ of $L^1(Ct)$ there is a quantifier-free formula φ^1 of L^1 such that $\mathcal{A}^1 \models \varphi \Leftrightarrow \varphi^1$ and $\mathcal{B}^1 \models \varphi \Leftrightarrow \varphi^1$.*
Proof: We argue by induction on the complexity of φ. As remarked earlier, we may assume without loss of generality that φ has no quantifiers, because the existential quantifier $\exists x \psi(x, \ldots)$ may be replaced by $\neg count\{x : \psi(x, \ldots)\} = 0$. The hard case of the induction is the case where φ has the form

$$r(count\{y : \psi_i(\vec{x}, y)\} : i \leq j)$$

for some j-ary relation r on $\mathbf{N}$. For simplicity we let $j = 1$, so that

$$\varphi = r(count\{y : \psi(\vec{x}, y)\}).$$

By inductive hypothesis we have a quantifier-free formula $\psi^1(\vec{x}, y)$ of L^1 which is equivalent to ψ in both models.
Claim 1. Suppose $\vec{a} \equiv_0 \vec{b}$. Then $(\mathcal{A}^1, \vec{a}) \models \varphi$ if and only if $(\mathcal{B}^1, \vec{b}) \models \varphi$.
Proof of Claim 1: By the preceding lemma, $(\mathcal{A}^1, \vec{a})$ satisfies equation (18) and $(\mathcal{B}^1, \vec{b})$ satisfies the corresponding equation (18). The claim now follows by the indiscernibility of the sequence $\vec{d}$ in $^*\mathcal{N}$.
Claim 2. There is a quantifier-free formula $\varphi^1(\vec{x})$ of L^1 such that $\mathcal{A}^1 \models \varphi \Leftrightarrow \varphi^1$.
Proof of Claim 2: Let $\Sigma(\vec{x})$ be the set of all quantifier-free formulas $\sigma(\vec{x})$ of L^1 such that $\mathcal{A}^1 \models \varphi \Rightarrow \sigma$. Suppose $\mathcal{A}^1 \models \Sigma[\vec{a}]$. Then the set of formulas

$$\{\varphi(\vec{x})\} \cup \{\eta(\vec{x}) : \eta \text{ is quantifier-free in } L^1 \text{ and } \mathcal{A}^1 \models \eta[\vec{a}]\}$$

is finitely satisfiable in $\mathcal{A}^1$. Since $^*\mathcal{N}$ is saturated, this set of formulas is satisfiable in $\mathcal{A}^1$ by some tuple $\vec{c}$. Then $\mathcal{A}^1 \models \varphi[\vec{c}]$ and $\vec{a} \equiv_0 \vec{c}$. By Lemma 17 and the saturation of $^*\mathcal{N}$, there exists $\vec{b}$ in B such that $\vec{a} \equiv_0 \vec{b} \equiv_0 \vec{c}$. By Claim 1, $(\mathcal{B}^1, \vec{b}) \models \varphi$ and $(\mathcal{A}^1, \vec{a}) \models \varphi$. Thus every tuple which satisfies Σ in $\mathcal{A}^1$ satisfies φ. Since $^*\mathcal{N}$ is saturated, there is a finite conjunction $\varphi^1(\vec{x})$ of formulas in $\Sigma(\vec{x})$ such that $\mathcal{A}^1 \models \varphi \Leftrightarrow \varphi^1$, and the claim is proved.

Now let $\vec{b}$ be a tuple in B. By Lemma 17 and the saturation of $^*\mathcal{N}$, there exists $\vec{a}$ in A such that $\vec{a} \equiv_0 \vec{b}$. By Claim 2, $\mathcal{A}^1 \models (\varphi \Leftrightarrow \varphi^1)[\vec{a}]$. By Claim 1, $\mathcal{B}^1 \models (\varphi \Leftrightarrow \varphi^1)[\vec{b}]$. $\square$

Corollary 20. $\mathcal{A}^1$ and $\mathcal{B}^1$ *satisfy the same sentences of* $L^1(Ct)$. *Moreover,* $\mathcal{A}$ *and* $\mathcal{B}$ *satisfy the same sentences of* $L^0(Ct)$.

This completes the proof of Lemma 11, and hence Theorem 6.

Proof of Theorem 12. Fix some bijection K from the universe for tuples of S to the universe for tuples of R. Let $\mathcal{M}$ be the class of L' models of the form $M' = \langle R, S \rangle$ which satisfy

- the sets $\{x.a : x \in R\}$, $\{x.b : x \in R\}$, $\{x.c : x \in S\}$, are pairwise disjoint.
- $x.c = x.d$ for each $x \in S$, $- x.c \neq y.c$ for distinct x, y in S.
- For each x in S, $K(x.c)$ is in R.

We define a mapping F that maps $\mathcal{M}$ to models for the language L^0 defined previously. $F(M')$ is defined to have domain equal to R, the predicate S is interpreted by the K-image of the attributes of the relation S in M', and the interpretation of the binary predicate E is defined by $xEy \leftrightarrow x.a = y.a$.

We also define a mapping G from formulae and terms of $L(Ct)$ to formulae and terms (respectively) of $L'(Ct)$ as follows:

$G(x.a = y.a) = xEy$, where x and y are any two variables of sort R, (not necessarily distinct).

$G(x.c = y.c) = G(x.d = y.d) = G(x.c = y.d) = G(x.d = y.c) = x = y$, where x, y have sort S.

$G(x.att1 = y.att2) = false$, for all attribute/sort combinations not listed above.

$G(P(\tau_1, \ldots, \tau_n)) = P(G(\tau_1), \ldots, G(\tau_n))$, $G(\forall x \in R \; \phi(x)) = \forall x \; G(\phi(x))$

$G(\exists x \in R \; \phi(x)) = \exists x \; G(\phi(x))$, $G(\forall x \in S \; \phi(x)) = \forall x \; S(x) \wedge G(\phi(x))$

$G(\exists x \in S \; \phi(x)) = \exists x \; S(x) \wedge G(\phi(x))$, $G(f(\vec{x})) = f(\vec{x})$,

$G(Count\{x \in R : \phi(x)\}) = Count\{x : G(\phi(x))\}$.

Proposition 21. *1) The maps* F *and* G *are surjections. 2)* $M' \models \phi(\vec{x}) \leftrightarrow F(M') \models G(\phi(\vec{x}))$.

1) is proved by inspection and 2) by straightforward induction on complexity.

Theorem 12 now follows, since if there were a formula of $L'(Ct)$ expressing exactly those models that satisfy θ', then by applying the inverse of G to this formula we would get a sentence of $L(Ct)$ expressing exactly those models satisfying θ, contradicting the main theorem of the previous section.

Proof of Corollary 13. Consider the transaction T on structures for the signature SC defined above as follows: $R \Leftarrow \Pi_a(R)$, $S \Leftarrow S$, where $\Pi_a(R)$ is defined via $x \in \Pi_a(R) \leftrightarrow (\exists y \in R \; x.a = y.a \wedge x.b = y.a)$. Then T is clearly $L(Ct)$-definable. The precondition of the $L'(Ct)$-sentence $count\{y \in R : y = y\} = count\{z \in S : z = z\}$ is exactly the sentence θ' of Theorem 12 cited above, which is not expressible in $L'(Ct)$.

Concurrency Control Theory for Deferred Materialized Views

Akira Kawaguchi[1]   **Daniel Lieuwen**[2]   **Inderpal Singh Mumick**[3]
Dallan Quass[4]   **Kenneth A. Ross**[1]

[1] Columbia University, akira@cs.columbia.edu, kar@cs.columbia.edu.[‡]
[2] Bell Laboratories, lieuwen@research.bell-labs.com.
[3] AT&T Laboratories, mumick@research.att.com.
[4] Stanford University, quass@cs.stanford.edu.

Abstract. We consider concurrency control problems that arise in the presence of materialized views. Consider a database system supporting materialized views to speed up queries. For a range of important applications (*e.g.* banking, billing, network management), transactions that access materialized views would like to get some consistency guarantees—if a transaction reads a base relation after an update, and then reads a materialized view derived from the base relation, it expects to see the effect of the base update on the materialized view. If a transaction reads two views, it expects that the two views reflect a single consistent database state.

Such guarantees are not easy to obtain, as materialized views become inconsistent upon updates to base relations. *Immediate* maintenance re-establishes consistency within the transaction that updates the base relation, but this consistency comes at the cost of delaying update transactions. *Deferred* maintenance has been proposed to avoid penalizing update transactions by shifting maintenance into a different transaction (for example, into the transaction that reads the view). However, doing so causes a materialized view to become temporarily inconsistent with its definition. Consequently, transactions that read multiple materialized views, or that read a materialized view and also read and/or write base relations may execute in a non-serializable manner even when they are running under a strict two phase locking (2PL) protocol.

We formalize the concurrency control problem in systems supporting materialized views. We develop a serializability theory based upon conflicts and serialization graphs in the presence of materialized views. Concurrency control algorithms based on this theory are being developed in the SWORD/Ode database system.

[‡] The work of Akira Kawaguchi and Kenneth A. Ross was performed while visiting AT&T Bell Laboratories, and was also partially supported by a grant from the AT&T Foundation, by a David and Lucile Packard Foundation Fellowship in Science and Engineering, by a Sloan Foundation Fellowship, and by an NSF Young Investigator Award.

1   Introduction

A *view* is a derived relation defined in terms of base (stored) relations. A view thus defines a function from a set of base tables to a derived table; this function is typically recomputed every time the view is referenced. A view can be materialized by storing the tuples of the view in the database. Index structures can be built on the materialized view. Consequently, database accesses to the materialized view can be much faster than recomputing the view.

Importance of Materialized Views: Materialized views can be used to speed up the processing of complex queries. It is quicker to access a materialized view than to recompute the corresponding query from scratch. In this sense a materialized view is like a cache—a commonly used version of the data that can be accessed quickly. Materialized views are finding applications in domains such as data warehousing, mobile systems, data visualization, banking, billing, and network management [9, 15] where quick response to complex queries is critical.

Importance of Deferred View Maintenance: Like a cache, a materialized view gets out-of-date whenever the underlying base relations are modified. The process of making a materialized view consistent with the base relations from which it is derived is called *view maintenance*. A view can be maintained in an *immediate* or a *deferred* manner. Immediate view maintenance algorithms maintain the view inside the transaction that modifies the base relations, before the transaction commits. Immediate maintenance can significantly slow down update transactions, especially if the number of views is large. Deferred maintenance algorithms maintain the view *outside* the transaction that modifies the base relations. Deferred maintenance thus has minimal impact on update transactions. There exist workloads (such as when there are frequent updates to large tables and relatively infrequent reads, or alternating bursts of updates and reads) under which deferred maintenance performs better than immediate maintenance [6].

Importance of Serializability: Some application domains (*e.g.*, decision support) use materialized views, but do not require serializability guarantees. Often, the materialized views are stored in a separate database from the base data, and the only desirable property may be that the views be mutually consistent.

However, other applications (*e.g.*, banking, billing, and network management) can use materialized views, but require serializability guarantees. Queries in these environments usually run on the same database that supports on-line transaction processing because they need answers that reflect the *current* state of the database. Furthermore, queries that access complex derived data and could benefit from reading materialized views may appear in the same transaction with queries that access base data, with both sets of queries being expected to see a consistent database state. For example, in a telephone billing application, the summary of charges reported to a user or to a switch must match the detailed call data. A credit limit application in cellular or long distance telephone service would require that charges due to all telephone calls be included in the summary being read to determine whether the credit limit has been reached or not. Similarly, routing information stored as a view in a network switch must match base data in the switch.

Problem Addressed: The goal of our work is to provide serializability guarantees to transactions that access both base relations and materialized views when the views are maintained in a deferred manner. The problem is that by allowing transactions that update base relations to commit without updating the materialized views that are derived from those base relations, we allow the database to enter an inconsistent state temporarily. We need to ensure that no transaction is allowed to read any inconsistencies. This means that if a transaction reads both a base relation and a materialized view, it must see the effects of the same set of transactions in both. It is not permissible to allow a transaction to see the effects of a transaction in a base relation, and miss them when reading a materialized view. Similarly, if a transaction reads two materialized views, we must ensure that it sees the effects of the same set of transactions in both the views.

Summary of Contributions and Paper Outline: We show through motivating examples that naive application of (deferred) view maintenance and strict two-phase locking protocols is insufficient to guarantee serializability in a system supporting materialized views (Section 1.1). Section 2 describes the notation and background. We define what is meant for a schedule to be serializable in the presence of materialized views and extend serializability theory to cover materialized views in Section 3. Related work is discussed in Section 4, and we conclude in Section 5.

1.1 Motivating Examples

We present two examples that show that naive application of deferred view maintenance and strict 2PL is insufficient to guarantee serializability when transactions read materialized views. Inconsistencies arise even when the transaction reading the view does not modify base relations. Even more opportunities for inconsistency arise when the transaction reading the view also modifies base relations. We formalize our notion of serializability in the presence of materialized views in Section 3. For now, it is sufficient to think of serializability in the presence of materialized views as the following restriction: A transaction T_1 either always or never sees the effects of changes made by a transaction T_2, regardless of whether T_1 reads a base relation updated by T_2, or it reads a materialized view derived from a base relation updated by T_2.

Example 1. **Maintain at transaction start, or before the first view read:** In this example we show that two-phase locking, in conjunction with a policy of maintaining a view at the start of a transaction that reads the view or just before reading the view for the first time, is insufficient to guarantee serializability. Consider a materialized view V derived from the one-to-one join of two base relations R and S. (We shall use this view V throughout the rest of this paper.) Let V_X denote a tuple in view V derived from the tuple R_X in R and the tuple S_X in S. (Similarly V_Y is derived from R_Y and S_Y.) Transactions T_1 and T_2 are running concurrently. Figure 1a shows their execution history.

Time	T_1	T_2
1	$rl[V_X]$	
(Assume V is up to date;		
hence no maintenance is needed)		
2	$r[V_X]$	
3		$wl[R_Y]$
4		$w[R_Y]$
5		$u[R_Y]$
6		commit
7	$rl[R_Y]$	
8	$r[R_Y]$	
9	$rl[V_Y]$	
10	$r[V_Y]$	
(R_Y is inconsistent with V_Y!)		
11	$u[V_X], u[R_Y], u[V_Y]$	
12	commit	

(a) Maintain at transaction start

Time	T_1	T_2
1	$rl[V_X]$	
(Assume V is up to date;		
hence no maintenance is needed)		
2	$r[V_X]$	
3		$wl[R_X]$
4		$w[R_X]$
5		$u[R_X]$
6		commit
(Detect that V_X is out of date)		
7	$rl[R_X]$	
8	$wl[V_X]$	
(Upgrade lock on V_X to write-lock)		
9	$m[V_X]$	
(Maintain V_X from R_X ($m[V_X]$ is		
a macro for $r[R_X]$, $r[S_X]$, $w[V_X]$))		
10	$r[V_X]$	
(V_X has a different value than before!)		
11	$u[V_X], u[R_X]$	
12	commit	

(b) Maintain before each read

Fig. 1. Concurrency control anomalies for deferred materialized views

In the figure,

- $rl[R_X]$ means "Get a read-lock on tuple X in relation R,"
- $r[R_X]$ means "Read tuple X in relation R,"
- $wl[R_X]$ means "Get a write-lock on tuple X in relation R,"
- $w[R_X]$ means "Write tuple X in relation R,"
- $u[R_X]$ means "Unlock X in relation R."

When T_1 starts it detects that V is already completely up to date, so maintenance is not needed. T_1 reads V_X. It then tries to get a read-lock on R_Y, but in the meantime T_2 has obtained a write-lock on R_Y, so T_1 waits for T_2 to release that lock. After T_2 commits T_1 reads R_Y and V_Y. T_1 sees T_2's changes to R_Y, but it doesn't see T_2's changes to the corresponding tuple V_Y. Therefore, transaction T_1 sees an inconsistent database state, violating serializability.

Note that the schedule violates serializability even if the operations $rl[V_X]$ and $r[V_X]$ at time 1 and 2 are removed. However, by including these two operations we show that a policy to maintain a view just before the first time the view is read does not ensure serializability.

The previous example shows that simply maintaining the view once at the beginning of a transaction or just before first reading the view is insufficient to guarantee serializability, even when the schedule satisfies a strict two-phase locking protocol. The following example shows that maintaining the view before each read operation is also insufficient to guarantee serializability.

Example 2. **Maintain just before each read of the view:**
Figure 1b shows an execution history where the view is maintained before each read. When T_1 starts it detects that V is already completely up to date, so maintenance is not needed. T_1 reads V_X as before. Meanwhile, T_2 updates R_X and commits. When T_1 tries to re-read V_X, it notices that the view is now out of date, so it maintains V_X. It does this by obtaining a read lock on R_X, a write lock on V_X, and applying a *maintain* operation, denoted m. The maintain operation is a macro for reading all base relation tuples that contribute to the view tuple, then writing the view tuple. Tuple V_X now has a different value than the first time it was read, violating serializability. (Another alternative might be to not maintain a tuple that is out of date if it had been read previously in the transaction, but then the read of V_X would be inconsistent with a read of R_X.)

As illustrated by the previous examples, naive application of deferred view maintenance and strict 2PL is insufficient to guarantee serializability when transactions read materialized views. This paper extends serializability theory to handle transactions that read materialized views, especially when the views are maintained in a deferred manner. A view can be maintained within the reader's transaction or as a separate transaction. Maintaining the view in a separate transaction has performance advantages, but can lead to additional consistency problems.

2 Notation and Background

A database consists of a set of base relations and views. A read-write locking model is used for both base and view data. A view is defined by an SQL CREATE VIEW statement. All base relations and view names that appear in the FROM clause of the SQL statement (including subqueries) defining a view V are said to *derive* view V.

Definition 1. (Dependency Graph) The dependency graph $G(V)$ of a view is a directed graph, with a node for every base relation and view used in defining view V, either directly or through other views. There is an edge from a node N_1 to a node N_2 if N_1 derives view N_2.

Algorithms that compute changes to a view in response to changes to the base relations are called *incremental view maintenance* algorithms. A classification and survey of several view maintenance algorithms appears in [9]. View maintenance algorithms assume that the changes to the base relations are stored in one or more *delta* relations. In this paper, we will make the assumption that for every base relation R used in a view V, we have available a delta relation $\Delta R(V)$, containing all modifications (insertions, deletions, and updates) made to relation R since the last time view V was maintained. The particular algorithms used to obtain $\Delta R(V)$ and perform incremental maintenance are orthogonal to our discussion of concurrency control. We will abstract the maintenance algorithm for view V as the following maintain function:

1. Check if view V needs to be refreshed.
2. If yes, then:
   (a) Read all delta relations for view V.
   (b) Read all or part of the base relations in the dependency graph of V.
   (c) Write the changed tuples to the materialization of view V.

The second step of maintain updates the materialized view to bring it up-to-date, and will be called the *refresh*. Depending upon the SQL statement defining view V, it is possible that Step 2b is not required (as for single-relation selection and other self-maintainable views [8]). However, in general, Step 2b is needed.

A system has a choice about when to apply the incremental view maintenance algorithm—*immediate maintenance* within the transaction that modifies a base relation, or *deferred maintenance* outside the modifying transaction.

For immediate view maintenance, serializability between transactions that modify base relations and read materialized views can be guaranteed by using two-phase locking, with the following minor extension. If a transaction updates a base relation and then reads a materialized view derived from the base relation, the changes made by the transaction must be propagated into the view before the view is read so that the transaction sees the effects of its own writes. If a transaction that reads a view V does not modify base relations that derive V, then propagating changes to views at transaction commit is sufficient to obtain serializability.

Deferred maintenance may be done just before reading the view (lazy deferred), at regular intervals by a daemon process (periodic deferred), on demand by a user (also called periodic deferred), or it may be triggered by some other condition. An example of such a triggering condition is when the materialized view exceeds a tolerance range for inconsistency [18]. Deferred view maintenance breaks the serializability guarantee of two phase locking. Additional steps must be taken to guarantee serializability in the presence of deferred view maintenance.

There has been substantial work on concurrency control for databases with multiple versions of data or multiple copies (replicas) of data. This is relevant for materialized views because one can think of a materialized view as another "version" of the underlying data. The relationship between the present work and the theories of multi-version concurrency control and replica concurrency control are discussed in Section 4.

3   Serializability Theory for Materialized Views

Traditionally, views in databases have been *virtual*. Queries over virtual views are answered by accessing base data. We would like view maintenance to be *transparent* to the user of a database system. In other words, view maintenance may improve the *performance* of queries, but it may not change the *semantics* of queries over views. We require that a materialized view appear to the user as if it were a virtual view. Our extended notion of serializability, called *Mat-serializability*, incorporates this notion of transparency.

Definition 2. (Serializability for Materialized Views) A transaction history is *Mat-Serializable* iff it is equivalent to some serial execution of the same transactions with all materialized-view reads treated as virtual-view reads.

The serializability theory of materialized views can be seen as an extension of multi-version serializability theory to account for the following:

- Views are not copies of base tuples, but are derived using query functions.
- User histories contain operations over both views and base relations, as well as a maintain operation.

The reason that traditional concurrency control algorithms don't work in the presence of materialized views is that there is an implied relationship between tuples in a materialized view and tuples in the base relations on which the view is defined. This relationship is unknown to, and therefore not enforced by, traditional concurrency control algorithms, which treat base relations and views as independent lockable entities. The reason two-version concurrency control does not work is that the relationship between versions is complex, the user has access to both versions, and certification is not feasible before commit time.

In this section, we extend traditional serializability theory to include materialized views. We extend the traditional read-write conflict matrix to include new operations that apply to materialized views, and show that an execution history is Mat-Serializable iff a serialization graph with edges due to the new conflicts is acyclic.

3.1 Derivation Sets

We formally define the set of tuples in base relations that contribute to the derivation of a tuple in a view. For simplicity of presentation, we define this concept here for a single-block SQL query defining a view. Note that a predicate is said to be *local* if all the attributes referenced in the predicate are from the same relation.

Definition 3. (Localized query) Consider an arbitrary view V defined by a single-block SQL query. We construct the localized query V' from V by performing the following steps to V. First, we omit the GROUPBY and HAVING clauses, and omit any aggregated attributes from the SELECT clause. We then replace the WHERE clause by the strongest condition C that can be derived from the original WHERE clause, such that C consists only of local predicates and predicates relating attributes in the SELECT clause.

A localized query allows us to isolate those tuples in the underlying relations that, for some database extension, would affect the result of the query. This concept is formalized in the next definition.

Definition 4. (Derivation set) Let V be a view, let V' be its localized query, let t be a tuple with the arity of V, and let every attribute value of t be from the appropriate domain for V. (t may or may not actually be in the extension of the view.) Let t' be the restriction of t to the schema of V'. Instantiate the conditions of V' with the corresponding values from t', so that every remaining condition is a local selection condition on an input relation R in the FROM clause of V'. The *derivation set* of t in V, written as $ds(t)$ when V is understood from context, is defined as the set of all tuples in the schema of the FROM clause relations R that satisfy the conditions in the WHERE clause of V', and that have attribute values equal to those attributes of t specified in the SELECT clause (for those relations with selected attributes).

The derivation set represents the set of all tuples whose insertion, deletion or modification could potentially, for some database extension, affect the tuple t in the view. (For an update to a tuple, we need to check both the old and new value for membership in the derivation set.) It is important that we define the derivation set in a *database independent* way. We do not want to have to consult the database (which may be in the process of being updated) in order to determine the presence or absence of a conflict.

Example 3. The view V on the left has a localized query given on the right.

```
SELECT  Emp.EmpId, min(Deadline)
FROM    Emp, Works, Proj              SELECT Emp.EmpId
WHERE   Emp.EmpId = Works.EmpId       FROM   Emp, Works, Proj
        and Proj.ProjId = Works.ProjId  WHERE  Emp.EmpId = Works.EmpId
        and Proj.manager = 'Fred'            and Proj.manager = 'Fred'
GROUPBY Emp.EmpId
HAVING  min(Deadline) > 10/23/95
```

For the tuple $t = (123, 10/30/95)$, $ds(t)$ consists of (a) All Emp tuples with EmpId 123, (b) all Works tuples with EmpId 123, and (c) all Proj tuples with manager "Fred". We expect that any change to tuples in $ds(t)$ could affect t's presence in the view; a change of a tuple outside $ds(t)$ to a value in $ds(t)$ would also affect t.

3.2 Materialized View Histories and Virtual View Histories

Traditional serializability theory defines two basic operations on a data item: read and write. We need to distinguish the read of a view tuple from the read of a base relation tuple; hence we will denote a read operation on a view tuple as r^V, and a read operation on a base relation tuple as r. Since we assume view tuples are only maintained, not modified directly by transactions, the write operation in a user transaction, denoted w, applies only to tuples in base relations.

We also add a new maintenance operation, denoted m, that maintains a given view tuple t, similar to the macro $m[V_X]$ introduced in Figure 1b. The maintain operation $m[t]$ performs the following sequence of operations:

Check if tuple t in view V needs to be refreshed; *i.e.*, there has been a write to a tuple in $ds(t)$ since t was last maintained. If yes, then:

1. Read the tuples of the delta relations for V that are in $ds(t)$.
2. Read the tuples of the base relations in the dependency graph of V that are in $ds(t)$.
3. Write t.

Note that the check for a write is built in as a part of the m operation. *Actual* refresh is performed only when necessary; *i.e.*, when a modification to some tuple in the view tuple's derivation set has occurred since the last maintenance operation on the view tuple. We assume that, from the point of view of concurrency control, maintenance operations are done atomically. We assume that a view tuple is always maintained by reading the delta relations and base relation tuples in its derivation set. Even when a view is defined in terms of other views, we treat those views as virtual and only read base relation tuples to maintain the view.

Recall that an execution history is Mat-Serializable if it is equivalent to a serial ordering of the transactions with all materialized-view reads treated as virtual-view reads. The definition does not require that we treat a materialized-view read as a virtual-view read that occurs at the same point in time as the materialized-view read. Because views are materialized, they may correspond to database states that are slightly out of date. In fact, a materialized-view read is equivalent to a virtual-view read performed at the point in time when the view tuple was last maintained. So, it is possible to translate a materialized-view read to an earlier virtual-view read, so long as the validity condition specified in the following Definition 5 is satisfied.

Transactions in a *materialized view history* have operations r, w, m, and r^V, where r^V is interpreted as reading from the stored version of the view. Transactions in a *virtual view history* have operations r, w and r^V, where r^V is interpreted as reading from the virtual view, *i.e.*, from the corresponding base relations. (Note that we do not translate the r^V operation into a sequence of base relation read operations in the history.)

Definition 5. (Valid History) Let t be a tuple in a view. A materialized view history is *valid* if for every transaction T in the history that writes a tuple in $ds(t)$ and later reads t, there is a maintain operation on t (either in T or elsewhere) occurring between the write to $ds(t)$ and the read of t.

In order for a history to be valid, transactions must see the effects of their own writes on the view tuples they read. A valid history guarantees that when translating a materialized-view read to a virtual-view read, the virtual-view read does not occur before a previous write by the same transaction to a tuple in the derivation set of the view tuple.

Lemma 6. *A valid materialized-view history can be translated to an equivalent virtual-view history by translating all materialized-view tuple reads to virtual-view tuple reads performed at the point in time when the view tuple was last maintained, and omitting the maintain operations.*

	$r[u]$	$r^V[t]$	$w[u]$
$r[u]$	–	–	×
$r^V[t]$	–	–	×
$w[u]$	×	×	×

Table 1. Conflict Matrix

Lemma 6 guarantees that any valid history involving materialized views can be translated to an equivalent history involving virtual views. Let $virtual(H)$ be the virtual-view history that is equivalent to the valid materialized-view history H according to Lemma 6. By our definition of Mat-serializability, in order for a valid materialized-view history H to be Mat-Serializable, $virtual(H)$ must be serializable. An invalid materialized-view history cannot be translated to an equivalent virtual-view history, and hence cannot be Mat-Serializable, since transactions would not see the effects of their own earlier writes.

Table 1 extends the read-write conflict matrix to virtual-view histories, including reads of virtual views. In the table, t denotes a view tuple and u denotes a base relation tuple. In the conflict between $r^V[t]$ and $w[u]$, we assume u is a tuple in $ds(t)$. Note that there is no maintain operation in the conflict matrix, since maintenance operations do not appear in virtual view histories. Conflicts between r and w operations derive from the traditional read-write conflicts: If a read or write operation precedes and conflicts with another read or write operation in the history, it must precede the other in the equivalent serial history. Conflicts between r^V and w operations are similar. Consider any pair of $r^V[t]/w[u]$ operations in a virtual-view history. If the write precedes the view read, then the write must precede the view read in the equivalent serial history since the effect of the write is visible to the view reader. Conversely, suppose that the view read precedes the write. Then the view read must precede the write in the equivalent serial history because the view reader does not see the effect of the write.

3.3 Mat-Serialization Graphs

In this section, we show how to construct a serialization graph for histories that include maintaining and reading materialized views. We call the extended graph a *Mat-Serialization graph*. We show that a valid history is Mat-Serializable iff the Mat-Serialization graph is acyclic. We then describe two types of anomalies that can occur if cycles are allowed in the Mat-Serialization graph.

Recall that a traditional serialization graph is a directed graph whose nodes are transactions, and where there is an edge from transaction T_i to T_j if an operation by T_i precedes and conflicts with an operation by T_j. We define a Mat-Serialization graph for a materialized-view history H similarly, to include edges between transactions in $virtual(H)$ due to the conflicts presented in Table 1. The direction of an edge due to conflicts between (base relation) reads and writes is from the transaction containing the preceding operation to the transaction containing the succeeding operation as usual. The Mat-Serialization graph represents all of the dependencies on the equivalent virtual-view history $virtual(H)$ for a materialized-view history H.

Definition 7. (Mat-Serialization Graph) Let H be a valid materialized-view history. A Mat-Serialization graph of H is a directed graph with a node for each transaction in H, and an edge from transaction T_i to T_j if an operation of T_i precedes an operation of T_j in $virtual(H)$ where the two operations conflict according to Table 1.

Theorem 8. *A valid execution history is* Mat-Serializable *iff the Mat-Serialization graph for the history is acyclic.*

Theorem 8 states that a materialized-view history H is Mat-Serializable iff the serialization graph corresponding to its equivalent virtual-view schedule $virtual(H)$ is acyclic, and each transaction sees the effects of its own writes on the view tuples it reads. A proof of the theorem appears in [13]. It is interesting to examine why we do not need to consider conflicts involving maintenance operations. Intuitively, the reason is that the value written by a maintenance operation $m[t]$ is based solely upon previous writes to tuples in $ds(t)$, and not upon operations in the transaction doing the maintenance (unless the transaction doing the maintenance previously wrote tuples in $ds(t)$). It is acceptable to relax isolation and allow transactions to read the effects of maintenance operations in transactions that may be serialized later. This relaxation is possible so long as all writes to tuples in the derivation set of the maintained tuple that occur before the maintenance operation take place in transactions that are serialized before the view reader. The resulting histories are Mat-Serializable, even though if we thought of the views as regular base relations, with a conflict between a maintain operation and a subsequent view-read operation, they would not be serializable.

Anomalies: Let us now consider the effects of cycles in the Mat-Serialization graph. We demonstrate two anomalies caused by different types of cycles in the Mat-Serialization graph.

Missing Update Transaction T_1 reads a tuple t in a view. Transaction T_2 inserts, deletes, or modifies a tuple in the derivation set of t and commits. If transaction T_1 also reads the tuple written by T_2 (or attempts to read it in case of a delete), T_2's update will appear to be missing from the view.

Example 1 is a case of the missing update anomaly. The Mat-Serialization graph for Example 1 contains a cycle between transactions T_1 and T_2. There is an edge from T_2 to T_1 because R_Y is written at time 4 by transaction T_2 and later read at time 8 by transaction T_1. In addition, there is an edge from T_1 to T_2 because V_Y, which was assumed to be maintained before time 1, is read at time 10 by transaction T_1, and R_Y, which is in the derivation set of V_Y, is written at time

4 by transaction T_2. Even though V_Y is read by T_1 after the write of R_Y by T_2, the edge is from T_1 to T_2 because V_Y was last maintained before time 1, which precedes the write of R_Y by T_2.

Unrepeatable View Read Transaction T_1 reads a tuple t in a view. Transaction T_2 inserts, deletes, or modifies a tuple in the derivation set of t and commits. If t is maintained and T_1 later re-reads t, it will read a modified value or find that t has been deleted.

Example 2 is a case of the unrepeatable view read anomaly. Like Example 1, Example 2's Mat-Serialization graph contains a cycle between transactions T_1 and T_2. There is an edge from T_1 to T_2 because V_X, which was assumed to be maintained before time 1, is read at time 2 by transaction T_1, and R_X, which is in the derivation set of V_X, is written at time 4 by transaction T_2. There is an edge from T_2 to T_1 because R_X is written at time 4 by T_2, and V_X, which has R_X in its derivation set and is maintained at time 9, is read at time 10 by T_1.

3.4 Conflicts at View-Level Granularity

Using derivation sets to determine serializability is of interest if we have an efficient means to lock the derivation sets. When the derivation set consists of a single tuple and can easily be determined from the view tuple (as when the view is a replica of a base relation), it will be possible to lock the derivation set. In general, locking a derivation set requires predicate locks, and requires view maintenance algorithms that work at the tuple level rather than table level. In some cases, (e.g. when the view is defined by a join over a key) predicate locks can be realized using indices. However, general predicate locks are not available in most systems. Furthermore, current view maintenance algorithms maintain the entire view, rather than one tuple in the view. Therefore, it is important to consider concurrency control when maintenance is done at the *view-level granularity*. In the following we show that it is possible for algorithms based on view-level granularity to guarantee Mat-serializability.

At view-level granularity, the maintenance operation maintains an entire view, not just an individual view tuple, and obtains table-level locks on all base relations in the view's dependency graph. We continue to assume that operations reading view tuples, and reading and writing base relation tuples obtain tuple-level locks. Conflicts at view-level granularity are easily derived from the tuple-level conflicts of Table 1. We extend the conflict between a read of a view tuple and a write to a tuple in the view tuple's derivation set to include writes to any base relation in the dependency graph of the view. Conflicts between operations on base relation tuples continue to be at the tuple level.

When constructing the Mat-Serialization graph for a materialized-view history H, we construct edges between a view-read operation and a base relation write as before using $virtual(H)$. A history is valid if a write to a view in each transaction T is followed by a maintain operation on the view (either in T or elsewhere) before the view is next read by T.

Corollary 9. *An execution history is Mat-Serializable if the Mat-Serialization graph with conflicts at view-level granularity is acyclic, and the history is valid.*

Corollary 9 states that an execution history is Mat-Serializable if its Mat-Serialization graph for view-level conflicts is acyclic and if each transaction sees the effects of its own writes.

4 Related Work

View Maintenance: Most work on view maintenance [2, 4, 7, 10, 11, 12, 16] has dealt with automatic derivation of the maintain function from the view definition. [9] is a survey and classification of several view maintenance algorithms. [5] deals with deriving the maintain functions specifically for deferred maintenance. Our current work is different from all of the above in that we do not derive (or advocate) any particular maintenance algorithm.

Deferred view maintenance has been implemented in ADMS [17], and has also been proposed by [18, 19, 20]. [18, 19] consider only select-project views. They do not discuss concurrency, and avoid the problems presented here since (1) they do not store the base relations and views at the same node, (2) they assume that a transaction reads only one view, and (3) select-project views can be maintained without accessing base relations. [20] considers a data warehouse where a view is materialized over relations stored in remote autonomous databases. They consider a concurrency problem that arises in computing the maintain function itself, and propose a view maintenance algorithm that can work in *absence* of concurrency control between the warehouse and remote databases. [17] is most closely related to our work, and proposes a concurrency control algorithm to permit concurrent maintenance of several related views. However, they do not allow view reader transactions to modify base relations, and it is not clear whether they allow such transactions to even read base relations directly. Only select-join views are considered; it is not clear how the technique will generalize to other views. There is no discussion of serialization theory.

Multi-Version Concurrency Control: We can draw the following analogy between multi-version serializability theory [1] and the serializability theory of materialized views described in Section 3. The process of translating materialized-view histories into virtual-view histories captures the conflicts represented by version order edges in the multi-version serializability graph, and the validity condition is analogous to the requirement that a transaction read the same version that it writes. The main differences between multi-version concurrency control and concurrency control for materialized views are: (1) a materialized view is just a single extra version of (some of) the data, (2) both base data and materialized views are visible to the user, while versions are invisible to the user, and (3) multiple versions are simply copies of single data items while views are query functions of multiple data items.

Replicas: A materialized view can be seen as a complex form of replicated data. However, replica concurrency control [1] differs from our problem and solution in that: (1) Replicas are assumed to be interchangeable for readers, while view and base relations are not interchangeable, and (2) Replica management either causes updates to be propagated within the updating transaction (similar to immediate maintenance), or causes the reader to read a majority of copies. Our goal in using materialized views is to improve performance by reading derived data and (where possible) to avoid reading the base data; reading multiple copies of the data is not well-suited to enhancing performance.

5 Conclusion

In this paper we have identified an important new problem – concurrency control in database systems that support materialized views. We motivated the problem through examples and developed a serialization theory in the presence of materialized views.

Applications like billing, banking, retailing, and data warehousing all have needs for materialized views. Often performance and scalability make it desirable and/or necessary to maintain views in a deferred manner. Currently these applications materialize the views into base relations and write application code to maintain the views. However, if subsequent queries and transactions access both materialized views and base relations, or if they access multiple materialized views, inconsistent results can be obtained. There is currently no system support to ensure the consistency of materialized views in these applications.

This paper identifies the concurrency control problems that must be solved to support materialized views. This is the first paper on the topic of concurrency control for materialized views, and surely leaves several open questions. Are there notions of non-serializability that will be of interest in a system with materialized views? While there are workload scenarios (frequent updates to large tables and relatively infrequent reads, or alternating bursts of updates and reads) where doing deferred maintenance with table level read locks is helpful, there are also workload scenarios where using predicate locks will be of great value. What is the class of views for which predicate locks can be implemented efficiently?

Mat-Serializability doesn't give us any guarantees that the views read by transactions will be up to date. For example, a transaction that reads a single view might be serialized in the "distant past". In [13] we define an additional property, *currency*, that requires that a transaction T see at least the effects of all transactions that committed up to a certain time.

We have developed concurrency control algorithms based on the theory developed in this paper; these algorithms are currently being implemented in the SWORD/Ode database system [14].

References

1. P. A. Bernstein, V. Hadzilacos, and N. Goodman. *Concurrency Control and Recovery in Database Systems*. Addison-Wesley, 1987.
2. J. A. Blakeley, P. Larson, and F. W. Tompa. Efficiently Updating Materialized Views. In C. Zaniolo, editor, *Proceedings of ACM SIGMOD 1986 International Conference*, pages 61–71, Washington, D.C., May 1986.

3. M. Carey and D. Schneider, editors. *Proceedings of ACM SIGMOD 1995 International Conference*, San Jose, CA, May 1995.

4. S. Ceri and J. Widom. Deriving production rules for incremental view maintenance. In G. M. Lohman, A. Sernadas, and R. Camps, editors, *Proceedings of the Seventeenth VLDB Conference*, pages 108–119, Barcelona, Spain, September 1991.

5. L. Colby, T. Griffin, L. Libkin, I. S. Mumick, and H. Trickey. Algorithms for deferred view maintenance. In H. V. Jagadish and I. S. Mumick, editors, *Proceedings of ACM SIGMOD 1996 International Conference*, Montreal, Canada, June 1996.

6. L. Colby, A. Kawaguchi, D. Lieuwen, I. S. Mumick, and K. A. Ross. Implementing materialized views. Unpublished Manuscript, 1996.

7. T. Griffin and L. Libkin. Incremental maintenance of views with duplicates. In Carey and Schneider [3], pages 328–339.

8. A. Gupta, H. V. Jagadish, and I. S. Mumick. Data integration using self-maintainable views. In *Proceedings of the Fifth EDBT Conference*, Avignon, France, March 1996.

9. A. Gupta and I. S. Mumick. Maintenance of Materialized Views: Problems, Techniques, and Applications. *IEEE Data Engineering Bulletin, Special Issue on Materialized Views and Data Warehousing*, 18(2):3–19, June 1995.

10. A. Gupta, I. S. Mumick, and V. S. Subrahmanian. Maintaining views incrementally. In *Proceedings of ACM SIGMOD 1993 International Conference*, Washington, DC, May 1993.

11. E. N. Hanson. A performance analysis of view materialization strategies. In U. Dayal and I. Traiger, editors, *Proceedings of ACM SIGMOD 1987 International Conference*, pages 440–453, San Francisco, CA, May 1987.

12. H. V. Jagadish, I. S. Mumick, and A. Silberschatz. View maintenance issues in the chronicle data model. In *Proceedings of the Fourteenth PODS Symposium*, pages 113–124, San Jose, CA, May 1995.

13. A. Kawaguchi, D. Lieuwen, I. S. Mumick, D. Quass, and K. A. Ross. Concurrency control theory for deferred materialized views. Technical Memorandum, AT&T and Bell Laboratories, 1996.

14. A. Kawaguchi, D. Lieuwen, I. S. Mumick, D. Quass, and K. A. Ross. Implementing concurrency control for deferred view maintenance. Unpublished manuscript, 1996.

15. I. S. Mumick. The Rejuvenation of Materialized Views. In *Proceedings of the Sixth International Conference on Information Systems and Management of Data (CISMOD)*, Bombay, India, November 1995.

16. X. Qian and G. Wiederhold. Incremental recomputation of active relational expressions. *IEEE Transactions on Knowledge and Data Engineering*, 3(3):337–341, 1991.

17. N. Roussopoulos and H. Kang. Principles and techniques in the design of ADMS+. *IEEE Computer*, pages 19–25, December 1986.

18. A. Segev and W. Fang. Currency-based updates to distributed materialized views. In *Proceedings of the Sixth IEEE International Conference on Data Engineering*, pages 512–520, Los Angeles, CA, February 1990.

19. A. Segev and J. Park. Updating distributed materialized views. *IEEE Transactions on Knowledge and Data Engineering*, 1(2):173–184, June 1989.

20. Y. Zhuge, H. Garcia-Molina, J. Hammer, and J. Widom. View maintenance in a warehousing environment. In Carey and Schneider [3], pages 316–327.

Serializability of Nested Transactions in Multidatabases *

Ugur Halici[1], Budak Arpinar[2] and Asuman Dogac[2]

Software Research and Development Center
[1]Dept. of Electrical Engineering, [2]Dept. of Computer Engineering
Middle East Technical University (METU), 06531 Ankara Turkiye
halici@rorqual.cc.metu.edu.tr, {asuman, budak}@srdc.metu.edu.tr

Abstract. *The correctness of nested transactions for multidatabases differs from that of flat transactions in that, for nested transactions the execution order of siblings at each related site should also be consistent. In this paper we first propose a simple but powerful theory for the serializability of nested transactions in multidatabases and then a technique called Nested Tickets Method for Nested Transactions (NTNT). The NTNT technique provides correctness of nested transactions in multidatabases without violating the local autonomy of the participating DBMSs. The algorithm is fully distributed, in other words there is no central scheduler. The correctness of the NTNT technique is proved by using the developed theory.*

1 Introduction and Related Work

A multidatabase system (MDBS) is a software that allows global applications accessing data located in multiple heterogeneous, autonomous DBMSs by providing a single database illusion. A multidatabase environment supports two types of transactions: local transactions submitted directly to a single Local DBMS (LDBMS), and executed outside the control of MDBS and global transactions that are channeled through the MDBS interface and executed under the MDBS control. The objectives of a multidatabase transaction management are to avoid inconsistent retrievals and to preserve the global consistency in the presence of updates.

Transaction management has always been one of the most important parts of a DBMS [GR 93]. The research on transaction management for centralized DBMSs is first extended to distributed DBMSs [BHG 87, HD 89, HD 91] and then to multidatabases. The transaction management for flat transactions in multidatabases have received considerable attention in recent years and correctness criteria have been defined [ZE 93] and several concurrency control techniques have been suggested [BGS 92, ZE 93, GRS 94]. In [GRS 94]

---

* This work is partially being supported by the Turkish State Planning Organization, Project Number: AFP-03-12DPT.95K120500, by the Scientific and Technical Research Council of Turkey, Project Number: EEEAG-Yazilim5, by Motorola (USA) and by Sevgi Holding (Turkey)

a ticket method is suggested to enforce serializability of global transactions in a MDBS environment. However it has been observed that nested transactions are more suitable to distributed environments since they provide more general control structures and support reliable and distributed computing more effectively. Nested transactions [M 85] facilitate the control of complex persistent applications by enabling both fine-tuning of the scope of rollback and safe intra-transaction parallelism. As a result nested transactions have become integral parts of some important standards, e.g. OMG's Common Object Services Specification (COSS). OMG's transaction service specification supports nested transactions along with flat transactions in a distributed heterogeneous environment based on the CORBA architecture [OMG 94]. Yet, to the best of our knowledge there is no technique suggested for the correctness of nested transactions in multidatabases, although some multidatabase projects have decided to use nested transaction model in their implementations [HFBK 94, DDK 96].

Principles and realization strategies of multilevel transaction management is described in [W 91]. A multi-level transaction approach to federated DBMS transaction management is discussed in [SWS 91].

DOM Transaction Model [BOH 92] for multidatabases allows closed nested and open nested transactions. InterBase Transaction Model [ELLR 90] is based on nested transaction model and allows a combination of both compensatable and non-compensatable subtransactions. However the correctness theory has not yet been developed for the models mentioned above.

In this paper we have developed a simple, neat and powerful theory for the serializability of nested transactions in multidatabases. Note that the theory provided in [BBG 89] for nested transactions could have been generalized to multidatabases. However the theory developed in [BBG 89] is very general in the sense that it takes semantics of transactions into account by allowing compatible transactions. Thus to prove the correctness of a concurrency control technique, commutativity and pruning concepts are used. We are able to develop a simpler theory, provided in Section 3, by not taking the semantics of transactions into account.

We then present a technique called Nested Tickets Method for Nested Transactions (NTNT) that provides for the correct execution of nested transactions in multidatabases. It should be noted that the concurrency control techniques developed for flat multidatabase transactions do not provide for the correctness of nested transactions in multidatabases because for nested transactions a consistent order of global transactions is not enough; the execution order of siblings at all levels must also be consistent at all sites.

The main idea of NTNT technique is to give tickets to global transactions at all levels, that is, both the parent and the child transactions obtain tickets. Then each global (sub)transaction is forced into conflict with its siblings through its parent's ticket at all related sites. The recursive nature of the algorithm makes it possible to handle the correctness of different transaction levels smoothly. NTNT technique also produces correct executions for flat transactions, flat transactions being a special case of nested transactions.

NTNT technique is fully distributed and does not violate the autonomy of participating LDBMSs. A transaction manager using the NTNT technique is implemented within the scope of the METU Interoperable DBMS (MIND) project [DDK 96, DEO 96]. MIND is based on OMG's object management architecture and is developed on top of a CORBA [OMG 91] compliant ORB, namely, DEC's Object Broker. A generic database object is defined through CORBA IDL and an implementation is provided for each of the participating DBMSs (namely, Oracle7[2], Sybase[3], Adabas D[4] and MOOD (METU Object-Oriented DBMS) [DAO 95]). Among these DBMSs Sybase and Adabas D support nested transactions. Therefore the restrictions of a global transaction to Sybase and Adabas D servers can be nested transactions, the others are flat transactions.

The paper is organized as follows: In Section 2 nested transaction models for centralized and multidatabase systems are given. Section 3 introduces a serializability theory for nested transactions in multidatabases. In Section 4, NTNT technique and its correctness proof are presented. We conclude with Section 5.

2 Nested Transactions

A nested transaction is a tree of transactions, the subtrees of which are either nested or flat transactions. The transaction at the root of the tree is called the top-level transaction. The others are called subtransactions. A transaction's predecessor in the tree is called a parent and subtransaction at the next lower level is called a child. The ancestors of a transaction are the parent of the subtransaction and recursively the parents of its ancestors. The descendants of a transaction are the children of the transaction and recursively the children of its descendants. The children of one parent are called siblings. We use the term (sub)transaction to refer to both top-level transaction and subtransactions.

2.1 A Nested Transaction Model

In the following we summarize a nested transaction model [CR 91] that we use in our work. Let t_0 be the top-level transaction, t_p be a root or a subtransaction, t_c be a subtransaction of t_p, and t_a be the ancestors of t_c.

i. Abort Rule: All the children t_c must be aborted if the parent transaction t_p aborts. A child transaction can abort independently without causing the abortion of its ancestors.

ii. Commit Rule: The parent transaction t_p cannot *commit* until all its children t_c commit or abort. The child transaction will *finally commit* only if it has *committed* and all its ancestors have *finally committed*.

iii. Visibility Rule: The child transactions t_c can view the partial results of their ancestors t_a, plus any results from committed detached transactions. Also they can view the partial results of their committed siblings due to following delegation rule.

---

[2] Oracle7 is a trademark of Oracle Corp.

[3] Sybase is a trademark of Sybase Corp.

[4] Adabas D is a trademark of Software AG Corp.

iv. Delegation Rule: At commit, child transaction t_c delegates its objects to parent transaction t_p. So all changes done by a child transaction become visible to the parent transaction upon the child transaction's commit. The effects of delegation can be found in [CR 91].

v. Conflict Rule Between A Child Transaction and Its Ancestors: Consider a child transaction t_c and its ancestors t_a and conflicting operations p and q: t_a can not invoke q after t_c invokes p. □

It should be noted that rule v. prevents parent/child parallelism.

2.2 A Nested Transaction Model for Multidatabases

In distributed systems such as multidatabases, nested transaction model provides more general control structures to support reliable and distributed computing more effectively [HR 93].

A nested transaction submitted to a multidatabase may have to be executed in several LDBMSs if the related data is scattered across a number of sites. Operations submitted by (sub)transactions are executed by LDBMSs' Data Managers (DM) and they are called as DM operations. If a (sub)transaction in the hierarchy has a DM operation in a LDBMS, the operation is dispatched to the related site. If a LDBMS does not support nested transactions, their effect with respect to hierarchical domains of recovery can be simulated by using savepoints [GR 93].

Since each (sub)transaction of a nested transaction is failure-atomic, restrictions of a (sub)transaction to sites must be executed as an atomic unit. So, atomicity rule is defined for nested multidatabase transactions as follows:

Let t be a (sub)transaction and t^k be the restriction of t at sites $k = 1, 2, ..., n$.

i. Atomicity Rule: All the restrictions of a (sub)transaction t at sites $k = 1, 2, ..., n$ should be aborted if t aborts.

3 A Serializability Theory for Nested Transactions in Multidatabases

Before presenting the serializability theory of nested transactions in multidatabases, we provide an intuitive explanation.

It is possible to view a nested transaction as a tree, where the leaf nodes contain the DM operations and intermediate nodes represent the subtransactions. Note that this tree is not necessarily balanced. When a nested transaction is executed, the (sub)transactions that conflict on the same data item must be ordered in such a way that the order of their conflicting DM operations are preserved. Another important point is that when two subtransactions are ordered, this imposes an order between their parents. To be able to express these concepts formally we define an *ordered hierarchy* where the ordering imposed by the leaf nodes are delegated to the upper nodes in the hierarchy. With this ordered hierarchy definition it is possible to formally model an ordering within a

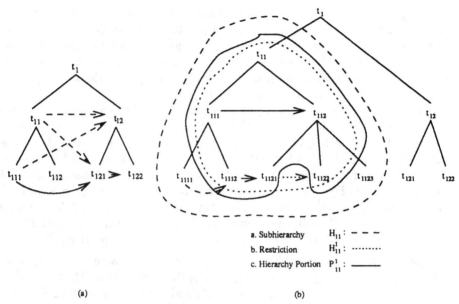

a. Subhierarchy H_{11} : – – –
b. Restriction H_{11}^1 : ·········
c. Hierarchy Portion P_{11}^1 : ———

(a)   (b)

Fig. 1. (a) Illustration of delegation axiom, (b) Subhierarchy, restriction, and hierarchy portion

tree. Furthermore by assuming an imaginary root transaction for all submitted transactions it is possible to model an execution history of nested transactions through the ordered hierarchy definition.

In order to extend the theory to distributed DBMSs, we define *restriction* of a hierarchy to represent the executions at different sites. And to extend the theory further to multidatabases, where there is no global control on local transactions, we define *global portion* and *local portions* of an execution.

Definition 1. An **ordered hierarchy** (or shortly a **hierarchy**) is a tuple $H = (\rightarrow, O, T)$ where O is a set of nodes, T is a tree on O, and $\rightarrow$ is a nonreflexive and antisymmetric relation on O satisfying the following axioms for any $a, b \in O$

   a. parent-child order[5] : $parent(a) \rightarrow a$
   b. transitivity: if $a \rightarrow b$ and $b \rightarrow c$ then $a \rightarrow c$
   c. delegation: if $a \rightarrow b$ and
      i. if $parent(b) \notin ancestors(a)$ then $a \rightarrow parent(b)$
      ii. if $parent(a) \notin ancestors(b)$ then $parent(a) \rightarrow b$.□

In fact the relation defined is an ordering relation with further restrictions imposed by Definition 1.a and 1.c. The closure obtained by by applying the axioms of the hierarchy definition repeatedly is denoted by *.

Figure 1.(a) presents an example to clarify the delegation axiom. Given an

---

[5] Note that ordered hierarchy definition takes only sibling parallelism into consideration assuming the conflict rule given in Section 2.1.v. Therefore we have chosen parent's preorder priority in Definition 1.a.

ordering $t_{111} \to t_{121}$, t_{111} and t_{12} (which is $parent(t_{121})$) are ordered as $t_{111} \to t_{12}$ (from Definition 1.c.i). Also t_{121} and t_{11} (which is $parent(t_{111})$) are ordered as $t_{11} \to t_{121}$ (from Definition 1.c.ii). Yet although t_{121} and t_{122} are ordered as $t_{121} \to t_{122}$, since t_{12} (which is $parent(t_{122})$) is also one of the $ancestors(t_{121})$, the order is not delegated upwards. Finally, t_{11} and t_{12} are ordered as $t_{11} \to t_{12}$ (from Definition 1.c.i and ordering $t_{11} \to t_{121}$).

Definition 2. Let $H = (\to, O, T)$ be a hierarchy, and T_i be a complete subtree of T rooted at the node $t_i \in O$, and let T_i^k be a part of T_i such that T_i^k is also a tree rooted at the node t_i but $leaves(T_i^k) \subseteq leaves(T_i)$. A **restriction** $\mathbf{H}_i^k$ is the tuple $H_i^k = (\to_i^k, O_i^k, T_i^k)$ where O_i^k is the set of nodes related to T_i^k and $\to_i^k$ is the restriction of the order $\to$ to O_i^k. If $T_i^k = T_i$ then the restriction is denoted as $H_i = (\to_i, O_i, T_i)$ and called as **subhierarchy**. A **hierarchy portion** $\mathbf{P}_i^k$ of H on restriction H_i^k is the hierarchy tuple $P_i^k = (\to_i^{Pk}, O_i^k, T_i^k)$ satisfying $\to_i^{Pk} \subseteq \to_i^k$. If T_i is T itself, then restriction and portion related to part T^k are denoted as $H^k = (\to^k, O^k, T^k)$ and $P^k = (\to^{Pk}, O^k, T^k)$ respectively.□

Figure 1.(b) shows: a subhierarchy H_{11} rooted at t_{11} with $\to_{11} = \{t_{1111} \to t_{1112}, t_{1112} \to t_{1121}, t_{1121} \to t_{1122}, t_{111} \to t_{112}\}^*$, a restriction H_{11}^1 with $\to_{11}^1 = \{t_{1112} \to t_{1121}, t_{1121} \to t_{1122}, t_{111} \to t_{112}\}^*$, and a hierarchy portion P_{11}^1 with $\to_{11}^{P1} = \{t_{1112} \to t_{1121}, t_{111} \to t_{112}\}^*$. Note that $\to_{11}^{P1} \subseteq \to_{11}^1 \subseteq \to_{11}$ and $leaves(T_{11}^1) \subseteq leaves(T_{11})$. In Figure 1.(b) transitive edges and edges from parent to child are not shown for the sake of simplicity.

Proposition 1. Given hierarchy $H = (\to, O, T)$ then a restriction $H_i^k = (\to_i^k, O_i^k, T_i^k)$ is also a hierarchy since it satisfies Definition 1.□

In the following definition, a partial order represents an irreflexive, antisymmetric, and transitive relation.

Definition 3. A hierarchy $H = (\to, O, T)$ is said to be **partially (totally) ordered** iff $\to$ is a partial (total) order on O.□

Definition 4. A subhierarchy $H_i = (\to_i, O_i, T_i)$ of a hierarchy $H = (\to, O, T)$ is said to be **isolated** in H iff for any $t_{im}, t_{in} \in O_i$, $t_l \in O - O_i - ancestors(t_i)$, the following holds: $not(t_{im} \to t_l \to t_{in})$ and either $t_l \to t_{im}$ or $t_{im} \to t_l$.□

Definition 5. A subhierarchy $H_i = (\to_i, O_i, T_i)$ of a hierarchy $H = (\to, O, T)$ is said to be **hierarchically isolated** in H iff every subhierarchy H_{ij} (including H_i itself) of H_i is isolated in H.□

Definition 6. A hierarchy $H = (\to, O, T)$ said to be **serial** if H itself is hierarchically isolated and $\to$ is a total order.□

Definition 7. A hierarchy $H = (\to, O, T)$ is said to be **serializable** if there exists a serial hierarchy $H^+ = (\to^+, O, T)$, such that $\to \subseteq \to^+$.□

Theorem 1. A hierarchy $H = (\to, O, T)$ is serializable iff $\to$ is a partial order.

Proof: (if) Consider the preorder traversal of T where the siblings are traversed in consistency with the order $\to$. If the siblings are not ordered by $\to$ then their traversal order is immaterial. Since $\to$ is a partial order and since $\to$ is closed under delegation axiom, such a traversal exists. Let $\to^+$ be the total order determined by such a preorder traversal. Obviously $\to \subseteq \to^+$ and $H^+ = (\to^+, O, T)$ is serial. Therefore $H = (\to, O, T)$ is serializable by definition.

(only if) Assume $H = (\to, O, T)$ is serializable and $\to$ is not a partial order

(Note that our partial order relation is irreflexive, antisymmetric and transitive). Since $\rightarrow$ is transitive by definition of a hierarchy, there should be $a \rightarrow a$ for some $a \in O$. However, this in turn implies that there is no total order satisfying $\rightarrow \subseteq \rightarrow^+$, which means H is not serializable.$\square$

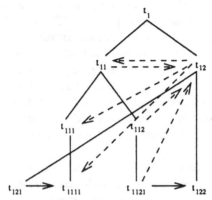

Fig. 2. An unserializable hierarchy

As an example to an unserializable hierarchy consider Figure 2. An initial order is given as $\{t_{121} \rightarrow t_{1111}, t_{1121} \rightarrow t_{122}\} \subseteq \rightarrow$. From the definition of ordered hierarchy, $\rightarrow$ also contains the following set obtained by applying the delegation axiom of Definition 1.c repeatedly: $\{t_{1121} \rightarrow t_{12}, t_{112} \rightarrow t_{12}, t_{11} \rightarrow t_{12}, t_{12} \rightarrow t_{1111}, t_{12} \rightarrow t_{111}, t_{12} \rightarrow t_{11}\}$. $\rightarrow$ is not a partial order because of $t_{12} \rightarrow t_{11}$ and $t_{11} \rightarrow t_{12}$ and hence the hierarchy in Figure 2 is not serializable.

Definition 8. A nested transaction T is a tree on $O = O_{dm} \cup O_{tr}$ where O_{dm} are the nodes representing the DM operations and O_{tr} are the nodes corresponding the abstract operations representing (sub)transactions, such that $\{leaves(T)\} = O_{dm}$ and $t = root(T)$ is the node representing the abstract operation corresponding to T and any subtree T_i rooted at $t_i \in \{child(t) - leaves(T)\}$ is a subtransaction defined recursively.$\square$

We assume an imaginary top-level transaction such that any transaction submitted by the users is a subtransaction of it. Thus it is possible to model the execution history of nested transactions as an ordered hierarchy.

Definition 9. An execution history is an ordered hierarchy $H = (\rightarrow, O, T)$ where T is a transaction on O and $\rightarrow = (\rightarrow_{dm} \cup \rightarrow_{ep})^*$ where $\rightarrow_{dm}$ is the ordering requirements on the leaf nodes due to execution order of conflicting DM operations, $\rightarrow_{ep}$ is the ordering requirement due to execution policy[6]. A

---

[6] If there are additional ordering requirements due to transactions $\rightarrow$ can be written as $\rightarrow = (\rightarrow_{dm} \cup \rightarrow_{ep} \cup \rightarrow_{ts})^*$ where $\rightarrow_{ts}$ is the transaction specific ordering requirements. However it is easier here to assume any execution policy to cover such requirements, that is $\rightarrow_{ts} \subseteq \rightarrow_{ep}$.

subhierarchy of an execution is called a subexecution and a hierarchy portion of it is called an execution portion.□

Two DM operations are in **conflict** if one of them is a write operation, they operate on the same data item and they belong to different parents in the transaction tree. Note that in the transaction tree, the parent of a DM operation is the (sub)transaction itself that issued the DM operation.

We take the serializability of an ordered hierarchy as the correctness criterion of executions. Therefore as a consequence of Theorem 1 an execution history $H = (\rightarrow, O, T)$ is correct iff $\rightarrow$ is a partial order. At this point it should be noted that to provide the correctness of executions it is sufficient to find a total order consistent with the order of conflicting DM operations. In other words $\rightarrow_{dm}$ is the order to be preserved. Yet, a concurrency control technique while trying to guarantee the consistent order of DM operations may introduce a more restrictive ordering. We denote the ordering that stems from the execution policy as $\rightarrow_{ep}$. As an example, in a technique that allows only serial executions, $\rightarrow_{ep}$ itself is a total order.

In centralized databases only a single site contributes to the execution and the serializability of the execution can be checked easily. In distributed databases there are several sites contributing to the execution.

Definition 10. A distributed execution $H = (\rightarrow, O, T)$ is an execution history such that $O_{dm} = \cup_k(O_{dm}^k)$ where O_{dm}^k is the set of DM operations on data items stored at site k, for $k = 1, .., n$. The execution of H at site k is the restriction $H^k = (\rightarrow^k, O^k, T^k)$ such that $leaves(T^k) = O_{dm}^k$.□

Notice that $O_{dm}^k \cap O_{dm}^l = \phi$ when $k \neq l$, however this is not true in general for O_{tr}^k and O_{tr}^l, since $O_{tr}^k \cap O_{tr}^l$ gives root nodes corresponding to subtransaction trees having DM operations at both sites.

$H = (\rightarrow, O, T)$ with restrictions $H^k = (\rightarrow^k, O^k, T^k)$ at site k, for $k = 1, .., n$, satisfies $O = \cup_k(O^k)$, $T = \cup_k(T^k)$, and $\rightarrow = (\cup_k \rightarrow^k)^*$. $\rightarrow$ contains the order enforced by the distributed execution policy, $\rightarrow_{dep}$ in addition to $\cup_k \rightarrow_{dm}^k$; on the other hand $\rightarrow^k$ contains also $\rightarrow_{dep}^k$.

In distributed DBMSs, the concurrency control information related to hierarchy restrictions are completely available and can be used to decide on the serializability of the execution. In distributed DBMSs the restriction $H^k = (\rightarrow^k, O^k, T^k)$ of H at site k is known.

However, in multidatabases, the complete information about H is not available. A local scheduler at site k knows only the local execution portion $L^k = (\rightarrow^{Lk}, O^k, T^k)$ where $\rightarrow^{Lk} \subseteq \rightarrow^k$ and does not have the complete information on the restriction $H^k = (\rightarrow^k, O^k, T^k)$.

Furthermore a global scheduler in multidatabases have knowledge only about global execution portion, $G = (\rightarrow^G, O^G, T^G)$ while a distributed DBMS scheduler has the complete information about $H = (\rightarrow, O, T)$.

Definition 11. On a multidatabase having sites $k = 1, .., n$, a **multisite execution** $H = (\rightarrow, O, T)$ is an execution history such that

- $O = O^G \cup (\cup_k O^{Lk})$, $O^G = \cup_k O^{Gk}$, and $T = T^G \cup (\cup_k T^{Lk})$, $T^G = \cup_k T^{Gk}$ and $\rightarrow = ((\cup_k \rightarrow^{Lk}) \cup \rightarrow^G)^*$,

- H has restrictions $H^k = (\rightarrow^k, O^k, T^k)$ at site k, for $k = 1, .., n$ where $O^k = O^{Gk} \cup O^{Lk}$ and $T^k = T^{Gk} \cup T^{Lk}$ with a local execution portion $L^k = (\rightarrow^{Lk}, O^k, T^k)$, $\rightarrow^{Lk} \subseteq \rightarrow^k$, $\rightarrow^{Lk} = (\rightarrow^{Lk}_{dm} \cup \rightarrow^{Lk}_{lep})^*$ where $\rightarrow^{Lk}_{lep}$ is the ordering enforced by local execution policy,
- H has restriction $H^g = (\rightarrow^g, O^G, T^G)$ to T^G with a global execution portion $G = (\rightarrow^G, O^G, T^G)$, $\rightarrow^G = ((\cup_k \rightarrow^{Gk}_{dm}) \cup \rightarrow_{gep})^*$ where $\rightarrow_{gep}$ is the ordering due to global execution policy, $\rightarrow^G \subseteq \rightarrow^g$,
- G has restriction $G^k = (\rightarrow^{Gk}, O^{Gk}, T^{Gk})$ at sites $k = 1, .., n$, $\rightarrow^{Gk} \subseteq \rightarrow^k$, $\rightarrow^{Gk} \subseteq \rightarrow^G$ and $\rightarrow^{Gk}_{dm} \subseteq \rightarrow^{Lk}_{dm}$ (but not necessarily $\rightarrow^{Gk} \subseteq \rightarrow^{Lk}$ or $\rightarrow^{Lk} \subseteq \rightarrow^{Gk}$).$\square$

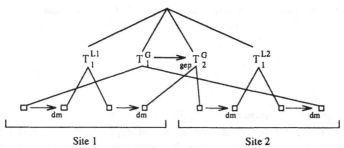

Fig. 3. A Multisite execution H

Figure 3 depicts a multisite execution H where the edges due to axioms of Definition 1 are not demonstrated for the sake of simplicity. Figure 4.(a) shows local execution portions L^1 and L^2 of H at site 1 and site 2 respectively. Note that local scheduler at site 1 does not have the complete knowledge of $\rightarrow^1$ which contains orderings that come from local scheduler at site 2 such as $T_2^G \rightarrow T_1^G$. This is symmetrically true for the local scheduler at site 2. Also ordering due to global execution policy is hidden from the local schedulers. In Figure 4.(a), these orderings which are not included in $\rightarrow^{L1}$ and $\rightarrow^{L2}$ are depicted as dotted lines and the delegated orderings are displayed as dashed lines. In Figure 4.(b), the global execution portion G of H is given. $\rightarrow^G$ does not contain orderings coming from local schedulers due to conflicting DM operations with local transactions at those sites and these orderings are also depicted as dotted lines.

One of the necessary condition for serializability of H is that $(\cup_k \rightarrow^k)^*$ should not introduce any cycles, which is not satisfied in the example shown in Figure 3 and Figure 4.

Definition 12. A multisite execution is said to be **EGOL (enforcing global order locally on siblings)** iff $a \rightarrow^{Gk} b$ implies $a \rightarrow^{Lk} b$ whenever $parent(a) = parent(b)$, and $a, b \in O^G$, and $a, b \in O^k$ for any $a, b \in O$.$\square$

Definition 13. A multisite execution is said to be **ELOT (enforcing local ordering transparency for siblings)** iff $a \rightarrow^{Lk} b$ implies $a \rightarrow^{Gk} b$ whenever $parent(a) = parent(b)$, and $a, b \in O^G$, and $a, b \in O^k$ for any $a, b \in O$.$\square$

If an execution is EGOL and ELOT, then the order of the siblings are con-

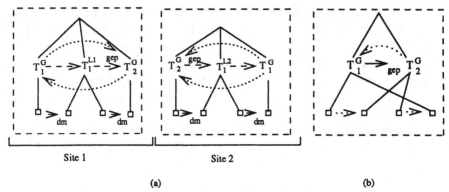

Fig. 4. (a) Local execution portions L^1 and L^2 of H at site 1 and site 2, (b) Global execution portion G of H

sistent at each site as shown in the following Lemma.

Lemma 1. If a multisite execution $H = (\rightarrow, O, T)$ is EGOL and ELOT then $a \rightarrow^{Lk} b$ implies $a \rightarrow^{Ll} b$ for any site k, l whenever $parent(a) = parent(b)$, and $a, b \in O^l$ and $a, b \in O^k$ for any $a, b \in O$.

Proof: $a \rightarrow^{Lk} b$ implies $a \rightarrow^{Gk} b$ by ELOT property which inturn implies $a \rightarrow^G b$ since $G^k = (\rightarrow^{Gk}, O^{Gk}, T^{Gk})$ is the restriction of G at sites k. $a \rightarrow^{Gl} b$ since $a, b \in O^l$ and since $G^l = (\rightarrow^{Gl}, O^{Gl}, T^{Gl})$ is the restriction of G at sites l. Furthermore, since the restriction is EGOL, $a \rightarrow^{Gl} b$ implies $a \rightarrow^{Ll} b$.□

Theorem 2. Let $H = (\rightarrow, O, T)$ be a multisite EGOL and ELOT execution having serializable local execution portions $L^k = (\rightarrow^{Lk}, O^k, T^k)$ at site k for $k = 1, .., n$. Then H is serializable iff the global portion $G = (\rightarrow^G, O^G, T^G)$ is serializable.

Proof: (if) Due to EGOL and ELOT properties of H and Lemma 1, and due to serializability of L^k for $k = 1, .., n$ and serializability of G; all the orderings in $\rightarrow^G$ and $\rightarrow^{Lk}$, $k = 1, .., n$ are consistent for any siblings a, b. Therefore a preorder traversal $\rightarrow^+$ (total order) of T exists for any siblings a and b such that $\rightarrow^+$ is consistent with the following:

1. If $a, b \in O^G$ and $a \rightarrow^G b$ then a is traversed before b,
2. If $a, b \in O^k$ and $a \rightarrow^{Lk} b$ for any k then a is traversed before b,
3. Otherwise the ordering of a and b is immaterial

and this preorder traversal satisfies $\rightarrow \subseteq \rightarrow^+$. Since $\rightarrow^+$ is a total order consistent with $\rightarrow$, H is serializable.

(only if) If H is serializable then $\rightarrow$ is a partial order by Theorem 1. Since $\rightarrow^G \subseteq \rightarrow$ by definition this in turn implies $\rightarrow^G$ is a partial order. Therefore H^G is serializable by Theorem 1.□

4   Nested Tickets Method for Nested Transactions

In this section, a technique for global concurrency control of nested transactions in multidatabases, called Nested Tickets Method for Nested Transactions (NTNT) is presented.

NTNT ensures global serializability of nested multidatabase transactions without violating autonomy of LDBMSs. It is assumed that LDBMSs' schedulers guarantee local serializability of nested transactions.

We present the NTNT technique by referring to the pseudocode of the algorithm. To be able to provide a neat recursive algorithm, we imagine all the global transactions to be children of a virtual transaction called OMNI. When OMNI transaction starts executing, it creates a siteTicket(OMNI) at each site whose default value is 0. Then we imagine that OMNI transaction executes forever. Since it is an imaginary transaction, it does not need to commit finally to make the updates of its children persistent.

$GlobalBegin(T_i^G)$ assigns a globally unique and monotonically increasing ticket number denoted as $TN(T_i^G)$ to all transactions denoted by T_i^G when they are initiated, that is, both the parent and the child transactions at all levels obtain a ticket. A Ticket Server object in MIND provides tickets and guarantees that any new subtransaction obtains a ticket whose value is greater than any of the previously assigned ticket numbers. Since any child is submitted after its parent, this automatically provides that any child has a ticket number greater than its parent's ticket. When the first DM read or DM write operation of a subtransaction T_i^G is to be executed at a local site, $LocalBegin(T_i^G, k)$ is executed which starts all ancestors of the subtransaction if they are not initiated at this site yet. Next, each child transaction reads the local ticket created by its parent at this site (this ticket is created for the children of $parent(T_i^G)$, i.e. $siblings(T_i^G)$), and checks if its own ticket value is greater than the stored ticket value in the ticket for $siblings(T_i^G)$ at this site. If it is not, the transaction T_i^G is aborted at all related sites and resubmitted to MIND using the algorithms given in $GlobalAbort(T_i^G)$ and $GlobalRestart(T_i^G)$. Otherwise, T_i^G sets the local ticket created by its parent to its own ticket value $(TN(T_i^G))$ and creates a site ticket, $siteTicket(T_i^G)$ with default value 0 for its possible future children. As a result, all siblings of a subtransaction accessing to some site k are forced into conflict through a ticket item created by the parent of these siblings at site k. The pseudocode of the algorithm to check ticket values is presented in $LocalCheckTicket(T_i^G, k)$. This mechanism makes the execution order of all siblings of a subtransaction to be consistent at all related sites since the execution is EGOL and ELOT by the use of tickets. In other words, the consistency of serialization order of the siblings are provided by guaranteeing them to be serialized in the order of their ticket numbers. If a transaction is validated using the $LocalCheckTicket(T_i^G, k)$ algorithm then its read and write operations on any item x are submitted to related LDBMS by $LocalWrite(x)$, $LocalRead(x)$ algorithms and committed by $GlobalCommit(T_i^G)$. $GlobalCommit(T_i^G)$ is executed after all children of T_i^G commit or abort due to Commit Rule in Section 2.1.ii. $GlobalCommit(T_i^G)$ coordinates the 2PC protocol and if all LDBMSs replied Ready then commits this subtransaction.

The NTNT Algorithm:

$GlobalBegin(T_i^G)$:

    Get global ticket for T_i^G so that

        $TN(T_i^G):=lastTicketNo+1$;

        $lastTicketNo:=TN(T_i^G)$; □

$LocalBegin(T_i^G, k)$:

    If parent(T_i^G, k) has not started at site k yet then

        $LocalBegin(parent(T_i^G), k)$;

        Forward begin operation for T_i^G as child of parent(T_i^G) to Local Transaction Manager

        (LTM) at site k;

    else

        Forward begin operation for T_i^G as child of parent(T_i^G) to LTM at site k;

    $LocalCheckTicket(T_i^G, k)$;

    If check FAILs then $GlobalRestart(T_i^G)$; □

$LocalCheckTicket(T_i^G, k)$:

    If T_i^G is not OMNI then

        If $siteTicket(parent(T_i^G)) > TN(T_i^G)$ then FAIL;

        else

            $siteTicket(parent(T_i^G)):=TN(T_i^G)$;

            create($siteTicket(T_i^G)$) at site k with default value 0; □

$LocalWrite(x)$, $LocalRead(x)$:

    If the site(x) is being visited for the first time by T_i^G then $LocalBegin(T_i^G, k)$;

    Forward the read/write operation to Local Data Manager on behalf of T_i^G; □

$GlobalAbort(T_i^G)$:

    for each related site send $LocalAbort(T_i^G)$ message to LTM at site k; □

$GlobalRestart(T_i^G)$:

    $GlobalAbort(T_i^G)$;

    $GlobalBegin(T_i^G)$; □

$GlobalCommit(T_i^G)$:

    wait until all children(T_i^G) commit or abort;

    for each related site k send $PrepareToCommit(T_i^G)$ message to LTM at site k;

    If all LTMs have replied Ready

        for each related site k send $Commit(T_i^G)$ message to LTM at site k;

    If any site fails to PrepareToCommit then $GlobalAbort(T_i^G)$; □

An Example: In the following, an example is provided to clarify the NTNT technique. Assume a multidatabase system with two LDBMSs at sites 1 and 2. User transactions can be arbitrarily nested and each (sub)transaction can issue read and write operations denoted as $r(a)$ and $w(a)$ respectively.

Figure 5 depicts the execution of two nested multidatabase transactions T_1^G and T_2^G, and a local transaction T_1^{L2}. Global transaction T_1^G has two subtransactions T_{11}^G and T_{12}^G, and T_2^G has one subtransaction T_{21}^G. At site 1, first T_1^G writes a, then T_{11}^G writes a, and then T_{21}^G reads a. Therefore, T_1^G and T_{21}^G directly conflict at site 1 and the serialization order of the transactions is $\{T_1^G \to T_{21}^G\} \subseteq \to^1$.

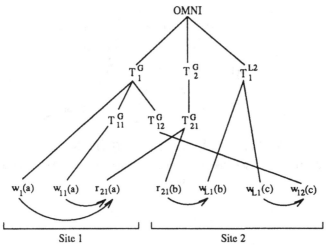

Fig. 5. A Schedule of Nested Multidatabase Transactions

Using the delegation axiom in Definition 1.c the serialization order of T_1^G and T_2^G at site 1 is $\{T_1^G \rightarrow T_2^G\} \subseteq \rightarrow^1$. At site 2, T_{21}^G reads b and later T_{12}^G writes c. Therefore, there is no direct conflict between T_{21}^G and T_{12}^G at site 2. However, a local transaction T_1^{L2} writes b and c, and thus T_{21}^G and T_{12}^G conflict indirectly at site 2. Therefore the serialization order is $\{T_{21}^G \rightarrow T_1^{L2} \rightarrow T_{12}^G\} \subseteq \rightarrow^2$ at site 2. Using the delegation axiom the serialization order of T_1^G and T_2^G at site 2 is $\{T_2^G \rightarrow T_1^G\} \subseteq \rightarrow^2$. Because of the local autonomy, the indirect conflict between siblings T_{12}^G and T_{21}^G at site 2 cannot be detected at the global level without a technique like NTNT. Although local schedules for nested transactions are serializable, the complete schedule is not serializable because the local schedules at sites 1 and 2 are not consistent with a total order $\{\rightarrow^1 \cup \rightarrow^2\} \subseteq \rightarrow$ defined on transactions T_1^G and T_2^G.

NTNT technique works for this example as follows: Assume the tickets obtained from the ticket server to be as follow: $TN(OMNI) = 0$, $TN(T_1^G) = 1$, $TN(T_2^G) = 2$, $TN(T_{11}^G) = 3$, $TN(T_{21}^G) = 4$, $TN(T_{12}^G) = 5$ and let $siteTicket$ $(OMNI) = 0$ at each site.

<u>Execution at site 1:</u>
T_1^G is accepted since $siteTicket(parent(T_1^G)) = siteTicket(OMNI) = 0 < TN(T_1^G) = 1$ and $siteTicket(OMNI)$ is set to 1 and $siteTicket(T_1^G)$ is created with default value 0. Thus $w_1(a)$ is executed. Since $siteTicket(parent(T_{11}^G)) = 0 < TN(T_{11}^G) = 3$, $siteTicket(parent(T_{11}^G))$ is set to 3 and $siteTicket(T_{11}^G) = 0$ is created and $w_{11}(a)$ is executed. Similarly $siteTicket(parent(T_2^G)) = siteTicket$ $(OMNI) = 1 < TN(T_2^G) = 2$, T_2^G is accepted and $siteTicket(OMNI)$ becomes 2 and $siteTicket(T_2^G)$ is created with default value 0. $r_{21}(a)$ is executed because $siteTicket(parent(T_{21}^G)) = 0 < TN(T_{21}^G) = 4$ and $siteTicket(parent(T_{21}^G))$ is set to 4 and $siteTicket(T_{21}^G)$ is created with default value 0.

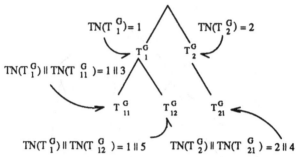

Fig. 6. Illustration of serialization order assignment through ‖ (concatenation) operation

Execution at site 2:

T_2^G is accepted since $siteTicket(parent(T_2^G)) = TN(OMNI) = 0 < TN(T_2^G) = 2$ and $siteTicket(OMNI)$ is set to 2. $siteTicket(T_2^G)$ is created with default value 0. T_{21}^G is accepted and $r_{21}(b)$ is executed since $siteTicket(parent(T_{21}^G)) = 0 < TN(T_{21}^G) = 4$. Yet T_1^G at site 2 is rejected and aborted at all sites since $siteTicket(parent(T_1^G)) = siteTicket(OMNI) = 2$ which is not less than $TN(T_1^G) = 1$.

Correctness Proof of the Method:

Theorem 3. NTNT method produces serializable multisite executions.

Proof: To prove the serializability of any $H = (\to, O, T)$ produced by NTNT method we apply Theorem 2 through the following steps: **1)** We have only sibling parallelism and all the siblings are enforced into conflict with each other through their parent's ticket at all related sites. When the local serialization orders of transactions are not consistent with their ticket numbers, they are aborted. In the global execution portion $G = (\to^G, O^G, T^G)$, $\to^G$ is a total order consistent with the alphabetical ordering of $TNO(a) = TNO(parent(a)) \| TN(a)$ for any subtransaction $a \in O^G$ where $TNO(parent(a)) \| TN(a)$ denotes the concatenation of the $TNO(parent(a))$ and the ticket of a as illustrated in Figure 6. Note that the alphabetical order for OMNI is $TNO(OMNI) = 0$. **2)** Since L^k is serializable, $\to^{Lk}$ is a partial order for $k = 1, .., n$ from Theorem 1. For any $a, b \in O^G$ if $parent(a) = parent(b)$ and $a, b \in O^k$, then a and b conflict on a common ticket item at site k and these siblings are enforced to be ordered in $\to^{Lk}$ in the order of their ticket numbers otherwise they are aborted. Therefore H is EGOL. **3)** Furthermore for every sibling $a, b \in O^G$, if $a, b \in O^k$ then they are enforced to be ordered in $\to^{Lk}$. Since $a \to^{Gk} b$ implies $a \to^{Lk} b$, and since $\to^{Lk}$ is a partial order, it is not possible to have $b \to^{Lk} a$. Hence H is ELOT.

Therefore due to Theorem 2 we have $H = ((\cup_k \to^{Lk}) \cup \to^G)^*, O, T)$ serializable.□

5 Conclusions

In this paper we have presented a theory for the serializability of nested transactions in multidatabases and then developed a technique called NTNT that provides for the correctness of nested transactions in multidatabases. To the best of our knowledge NTNT is the first technique to provide serializability of nested transactions in multidatabases. The correctness of the NTNT technique is proved by using the developed theory. Note that the theory developed is general enough to be applicable to correctness of future techniques.

References

[BBG 89]   C. Beeri, P. A. Bernstein, and N. Goodman. A Model for Concurrency in Nested Transaction Systems. Journal of the ACM, 36(2), 1989.

[BGS 92]   Y. Breitbart, H. Garcia-Molina, and A. Silberschatz. Overview of Multidatabase Transaction Management. VLDB Journal, 1(2), 1992.

[BHG 87]   P. A. Bernstein, V. Hadzilacos, and N. Goodman. Concurrency Control and Recovery in Database Systems. Addison Wesley, Reading, MA, 1987.

[BOH 92]   A. Buchman, M. T. Ozsu, M. Hornick, D. Georgakopulos, and F. A. Manola. A Transaction Model for Active Distributed Object Systems. In A. K. Elmagarmid (Ed.), Database Transaction Models for Advanced Applications, Morgan Kaufmann, San Mateo, CA., 1992.

[CR 91]   P. K. Chrysanthis, and K. Ramamritham. A Formalism for Extended Transaction Models. In Proc. of the 17th Int. Conf. on VLDB, Barcelona, 1991.

[DAO 95]   A. Dogac, M. Altinel, C. Ozkan, B. Arpinar, I. Durusoy, and I. Altintas. METU Object-Oriented DBMS Kernel. In Proc. of Intl. Conf. on Database and Expert Systems Applications, London, Sept. 1995, Lecture Notes in Computer Science, Springer-Verlag.

[DDK 96]   A. Dogac, C. Dengi, E. Kilic, G. Ozhan, F. Ozcan, S. Nural, C. Evrendilek, U. Halici, B. Arpinar, P. Koksal, and S. Mancuhan. METU Interoperable Database System. Demo Description, In Proc. of ACM Sigmod Intl. Conf. on Man. of Data, Montreal, June 1996.

[DEO 96]   A. Dogac, C. Dengi, and T. Ozsu. Building Interoperable Databases on Distributed Object Management Platforms. Communications of the ACM (to appear).

[ELLR 90]   A.K. Elmagarmid, Y. Leu, W. Litwin, and M. Rusinkiewicz. A Multidatabase Transaction Model for Interbase. In Proc. of the 16th VLDB Conf., Brisbane, Australia, 1990.

[GR 93]   J. Gray, and A. Reuter. Transaction Processing: Concepts and Techniques. Morgan Kaufmann, 1993.

[GRS 94]   D. Georgakopoulos, M. Rusinkiewicz, and A. P. Sheth. Using Tickets to Enforce the Serializability of Multidatabase Transactions. IEEE Transactions on Knowledge and Data Engineering, 6(1), 1994.

[HD 89]   U. Halici, and A. Dogac. Concurrency Control in Distributed Databases Through Time Intervals and Short Term Locks. IEEE Transactions on Software Engineering, 15(8), August 1989.

[HD 91]   U. Halici, and A. Dogac. An Optimistic Locking Technique for Concurrency Control in Distributed Databases. IEEE Transactions on Software Engineering, 17(7), July 1991.

[HR 93]   T. Harder, and K. Rothermel. Concurrency Control Issues in Nested Transactions. VLDB Journal, 2(1), 1993.

[HFBK 94]   G. Huck, P. Fankhauser, R. Busse, and W. Klas. IRO-DB: An Object-Oriented Approach towards Federated and Interoperable DBMS. In Proc. of ADBIS'94, Moscow, May 1994.

[M 85]   J. E. B. Moss. An Approach to Reliable Distributed Computing. MIT Press, 1985.

[OMG 91]   Object Management Group. The Common Object Request Broker: Architecture and Specification. OMG Document, December 1991.

[OMG 94]   Object Transaction Service. OMG Document, 1994.

[SWS 91]   H.-J. Schek, G. Weikum, and W. Schaad, A Multi-Level Transaction Approach to Federated DBS Transaction Management. In Proc. of Int. Workshop on Interoperability in Multidatabase Systems, Kyoto, 1991.

[W 91]   G. Weikum. Principles and Realization Strategies of Multilevel Transaction Management. ACM TODS, 16(1), 1991.

[ZE 93]   A. Zhang, and A. K. Elmagarmid. Theory of Global Concurrency Control in Multidatabase Systems. VLDB Journal 2(3), 1993.

Adding Structure to Unstructured Data

Peter Buneman[1] and Susan Davidson[1] and Mary Fernandez[2] and Dan Suciu[2]

[1] University of Pennsylvania, USA {peter,susan}@cis.upenn.edu
[2] AT&T Labs — Research, USA {mff,suciu}@research.att.com

Abstract. We develop a new schema for unstructured data. Traditional schemas resemble the type systems of programming languages. For unstructured data, however, the underlying type may be much less constrained and hence an alternative way of expressing constraints on the data is needed. Here, we propose that both data and schema be represented as edge-labeled graphs. We develop notions of conformance between a graph database and a graph schema and show that there is a natural and efficiently computable ordering on graph schemas. We then examine certain subclasses of schemas and show that schemas are closed under query applications. Finally, we discuss how they may be used in query decomposition and optimization.

1 Introduction

The ability to represent and query data with little or no apparent structure arises in several areas: biological databases, database integration, and query systems for the World-Wide Web[PGMW95, TMD92, BDHS96a, MMM96, QRS+95, KS95, CM90]. The general approach is to represent data as a labeled graph. Data values and schema information, such as field and relation names, are kept in one data structure, blurring the distinction between schema and instance.

Although these models merge schema and data, distinguishing between them is important, because schemas are useful for query decomposition and optimization and for describing a database's structure to its users. The biological database system ACeDB [TMD92] allows flexible representation of data, but also has a schema-definition language that limits the type and number of edges stored in a database. The OEM [PGMW95] model supports database integration by providing a structure in which most traditional forms of data (relational, object-oriented, etc.) can be modeled. Even the World-Wide Web, which appears to be completely unstructured, contains structured subgraphs. Fig. 1 depicts a fragment of the web site http://www.ucsd.edu, in which pages connecting schools, departments, and people are structured. Queries applied to this graph's link structure can benefit from structural information, for example, by knowing there exists at most one department on any path from the root to a leaf and that every paper is reachable from a department.

We describe a new notion of schema appropriate for an edge-labeled graph model of data. We use this model to formulate, optimize, and decompose queries for unstructured data [BDS95, BDHS96a, Suc96]. Informally, a database is an edge-labeled graph, and a schema is a graph whose edges are labeled with formulas. A database DB conforms to a schema S if there is a correspondence between the edges in DB and S, such that whenever there is an edge labeled a in DB, there is a corresponding edge labeled with predicate p in S such that

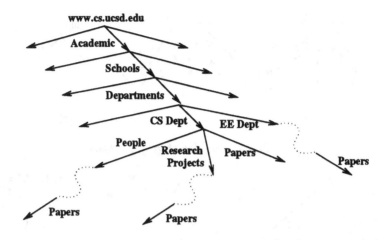

Fig. 1. A fragment of http://www.ucsd.edu.

$p(a)$ holds. This notion of conformance is a generalization of *similarity* [HHK95]. We investigate the properties of such schemas, and show that there is a natural subsumption ordering on schemas – a generalization of similarity. We then investigate a "deterministic" subclass of schemas and argue that it is appropriate to have deterministic schemas although data may be "nondeterministic". Finally, we examine queries on a database with a known schema and consider when we can compute a schema for the result of the query. We also discuss how schemas can improve the optimization and decomposition of queries in UnQL [BDHS96a].

2 Basic Definitions

Let $\mathcal{U}$ be the universe of all constants ($\mathcal{U} = Int \cup String \cup Bool \cup \ldots$). We adopt the data model of [BDHS96a], where a *graph database* is a rooted graph with edge labels in $\mathcal{U}$. Formally, $DB = (V, E, v_0)$, where V is a set of nodes, $E \subset V \times \mathcal{U} \times V$, and $v_0 \in V$ is a distinguished *root*. Fig. 1 is an example of a graph database. This model is powerful enough to encode relational databases, as illustrated in Fig. 2(a), which encodes a relation $R(A : Int, B : Int, C : String)$, but flexible enough to represent unstructured data, like Fig. 2(b) and (c). Sets, records, and variant nodes are equivalent in this model. Graphs may have arbitrary cycles and sharing. Two graphs are considered equal if they are *bisimilar* [BDHS96b]. Briefly, DB and DB' are bisimilar if there exists a binary relation $\approx$ from the nodes of DB to those of DB' such that (1) $v_0 \approx v_0'$ where v_0, v_0' are the two roots, and (2) whenever $u \approx u'$, then for every $u \xrightarrow{a} v$ in DB, there exists $u' \xrightarrow{a} v'$ in DB' such that $v \approx v'$, and for every $u' \xrightarrow{a} v'$ in DB', there exists $u \xrightarrow{a} v$ in DB such that $v \approx v'$.

In earlier work [BDHS96a], we introduced a notation for specifying graphs, e.g., the tree database in Fig. 2(c) is written as $\{tup \Rightarrow \{A, \{D \Rightarrow \{3\}\}\}\}$. Also, we defined a union operation on two graph databases in which their two roots are collapsed (Fig. 3(a)). For example, in Fig. 3(b) $DB_1 = \{a \Rightarrow \{b\}, c\}$, $DB_2 = \{a \Rightarrow \{d\}\}$, and $DB_1 \cup DB_2 = \{a \Rightarrow \{b\}, c, a \Rightarrow \{d\}\}$.

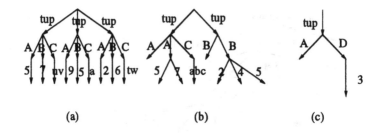

(a)   (b)   (c)

Fig. 2. Three examples of graph databases.

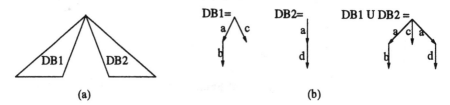

(a)   (b)

Fig. 3. Union of graph databases.

To define graph schema, consider a set of base predicates over $\mathcal{U}, P_1, P_2, \ldots$, such that the first order theory T generated by $\mathcal{U}$ (i.e. the first order sentences true in $\mathcal{U}$) is decidable. A *unary formula* is a formula with at most one free variable.

Definition 1. A graph schema is a rooted, labeled graph, in which the edges are labeled with unary formulas.

Although our results apply to every decidable theory, we use theories generated by unary predicates, with equality and with names for all constants in our universe. Typical predicates include $Int(x), String(x), Nat(x)$, and $Bool(x)$, which denote $x \in Int, x \in String, x \in Nat$, and $x \in Bool$, and user-defined unary predicates, $P(x)$. The theory has an equality operator, so we have predicates such as $x = 5$ and $x = $ "abc". Such a theory is decidable, because it admits quantifier elimination: e.g. $\exists y.(Int(x) \wedge Int(y) \wedge x \neq y)$ is equivalent to $Int(x)$.

Fig. 4 (a) depicts a graph schema S. By convention, we drop the free variable from unary formulas which are boolean combinations of unary predicates, thus writing A and $Int \vee String$ instead of $x = A$ and $Int(x) \vee String(x)$. Intuitively, a graph schema captures some knowledge about the structure of a graph database. In particular, the graph schema S says that a graph database that conforms to S has only *tup*-edges emerging from the root, possibly followed by A, B, or C edges, and these possibly followed by integers or strings respectively. The graph database encoding a relational database in Fig. 2(a) conforms to this graph schema, but the graph in Fig. 2(c) does not. The database in Fig. 2(b) also conforms to this schema, although it does not encode any relational database.

In schemas (c), (d), (e), (f) in Fig. 4, $isDept(x)$ and $isPaper(x)$ are user-defined predicates testing whether x is a string denoting a department (e.g., "Computer Science Department" or "Electrical Engineering Department") or a paper. Schema (d) says that there is at most one department on every path

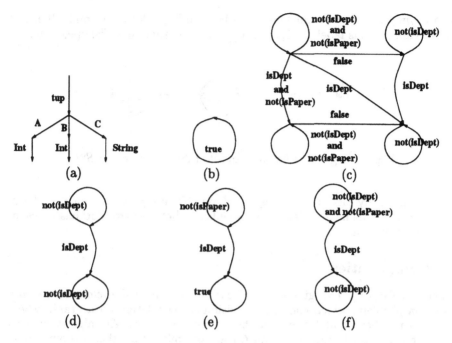

Fig. 4. Six examples of graph schema.

starting at the root, while that in (e) says that no paper edge may occur before a department edge. The database in Fig. 1 conforms to both these schemas.

Definition 2. A database DB *conforms* to a graph schema S, $DB \preceq S$, if there exists a *simulation* from DB to S, i.e. a binary relation $\preceq$ from the nodes of DB to those of S satisfying: (1) the root nodes of DB and S are in the relation $\preceq$, (2) whenever $u \preceq u'$ and $u \xrightarrow{a} v$ is an edge labeled a in DB, then there exists some edge $u' \xrightarrow{p} v'$ in S such that $p(a)$ is true and $v \preceq v'$.

A graph schema cannot enforce the presence of some label. This is consistent with the notion of schema in ACeDB [TMD92]. In particular, the empty database (one node, no edges) conforms to any graph schema S, i.e., $\emptyset \preceq S$. A graph schema cannot model variants, nor can it prevent a node from having several outgoing edges with the same label, as occurs in Fig. 2(b). Finally, any database DB can be viewed as a schema, by replacing every label a with the unary formula $x = a$, which gives us a notion of simulation between databases, $DB \preceq DB'$.

In keeping with our view that two graphs are considered equal if they are bisimilar, we can show that if $DB \preceq S$ and DB and DB' are bisimilar, then $DB' \preceq S$. However, note that $DB \preceq DB'$ and $DB' \preceq DB$ does not necessarily imply that DB, DB' are bisimilar.

Graph schemas can be viewed as infinite databases. For example, we view an edge $u \xrightarrow{Nat} v$ in S, as representing infinitely many edges, $u \xrightarrow{0} v, u \xrightarrow{1} v, u \xrightarrow{2} v, \ldots$. We call the *expansion* of S, denoted S^∞, the (possibly infinite) database obtained from replicating each edge in S once for every constant in the universe

$\mathcal{U}$ satisfying the unary formula on that edge. See Fig. 5 for an example. If any of the schema edges is labeled with the formula *false*, that edge disappears in S^∞.

Fig. 5. A graph schema S and its infinite expansion S^∞.

One can easily check that for any database DB and graph schema S, $DB \preceq S$ iff $DB \preceq S^\infty$. The latter relation is a simulation between two databases, one of which may be infinite.

3   Complexities

Paige and Tarjan [PT87] give an $O(m \log n)$ algorithm for the *relational coarsest partition* problem, which computes a bisimulation relation on a graph, where n is the number of nodes and m the number of edges. The algorithm tests whether two rooted graphs G_1 and G_2 are bisimilar: take their disjoint union G, compute a bisimulation $\approx$ on G, then test whether the two roots of G_1 and G_2 are in $\approx$. Although bisimulation and simulation are related, they require different algorithms. Henzinger, Henzinger, and Kopke [HHK95] have recently found an $O(mn)$ time algorithm to compute the simulation between two graphs with labeled nodes.

Neither algorithm applies directly to our framework, because they associate labels with nodes, not edges. We can reduce the problem of finding a (bi)simulation of two edge-labeled graphs with a total of n nodes and m edges to that of finding a (bi)simulation between two node-labeled graphs with a total of $m + n$ nodes and $2m$ edges. We split each labeled edge $x \xrightarrow{a} y$ into two unlabeled edges $x \to z \to y$, in which z is a new node labeled a, and we label all other nodes with a new, unique label. Finally, we compute a (bi)simulation for the new graphs, in time $O(2m \log(m + n)) = O(m \log m)$ for bisimulation, or $O((m + n)2m) = O(m^2)$ for simulation. We may assume $m \geq n$, because the graphs G_1, G_2 are connected, but unlike in [HHK95], we no longer necessarily have $m \leq n^2$. This still does not allow us to test $DB \preceq S$, because when we expand S into a database we get an infinite graph. We can, however, adapt the algorithm in [HHK95] to get:

Proposition 3. *Suppose one can test validity of sentences of the theory T in time t. Then there exists an algorithm for checking whether $DB \preceq S$ that runs in time $O(m^2 t)$. Here m is the total number of edges in DB and S, which are each assumed to be connected.*

4   Expressiveness of graph schemas

Graph schemas differ from relational or object-oriented schemas. A relational database has only one schema. A graph database, however, may conform to several graph schemas such as those in Fig. 4 (d) and (e). Moreover, there exists a schema S_T (Fig. 4 (b)) to which all graph databases conform. Since graph schemas are meant to capture partial information about the structure of data with the purpose of optimizing queries, we could store multiple graph schemas for the same data and offer multiple "hints" to a query optimizer.

The relationship between graph database and graph schemas raises several questions. First, given two graph schemas S and S', how do we know if S says more about some database than S'? How do we know that graph schemas S and S' are "equivalent", i.e. $DB \preceq S$ iff $DB \preceq S'$, for any DB? For example, the graph schema in Fig. 4(f) captures more information about a database than either schema in (d) or (e). Formally, if $[S] \stackrel{\text{def}}{=} \{DB \mid DB \preceq S\}$, then we want to check whether $[S] \subseteq [S']$ and $[S] = [S']$. We show that both $[S] \subseteq [S']$ and $[S] = [S']$ can be checked in polynomial time.

Second, given two graph schemas S and S', which express different constraints on a database, can we describe with a single graph schema S'' their combined constraints? We want some graph schema S'' such that $DB \preceq S \wedge DB \preceq S'$ iff $DB \preceq S''$. We show that S'' always exists. For example, when S, S' are those in Fig. 4 (d), (e), then S'' is the schema in (f).

Last, when $DB \npreceq S$, what "fragment" DB_0 of DB does conform to S? This question is important if we wish to use graph schema as *data guides* [Abi97]. Assume we optimize queries based on the assumption that the Web site in Fig. 1 follows schema S in Fig. 4 (d) as a guide. Since the schema does not enforce conformance it is unclear what the optimized query means. We show here that for any database DB and schema S there exists a canonical "fragment" DB_0 of DB that conforms to S. Moreover, whenever $DB \preceq S$, then DB_0 is DB. We can now state what we expect from an optimizer. Given a query Q and schema S, we expect a correct optimizer to produce an optimized query Q_{opt} such that for any database DB, $Q_{\text{opt}}(DB) = Q(DB_0)$. This implies that $Q_{\text{opt}}(DB) = Q(DB)$ whenever $DB \preceq S$.

4.1 Subsumption of graph schemas

We define schema subsumption and equivalence as follows.

Definition 4. Given two graph schemas S, S' we say that S *subsumes* S', in notation $S \preceq S'$, if there exists a binary relation $\preceq$ between the nodes of S and S' such that: (1) $v_0 \preceq v_0'$, where v_0, v_0' are the roots of S, S', (2) whenever $u \preceq u'$, for every labeled edge $u \stackrel{p}{\to} v$ in S and every $a \in \mathcal{U}$ s.t. $\mathcal{U} \models p(a)$, there exists an edge $u' \stackrel{p'}{\to} v'$ in S' s.t. $\mathcal{U} \models p'(a)$ and $v \preceq v'$. S and S' are *equivalent* if $S \preceq S'$ and $S' \preceq S$.

The subsumption relation, $S \preceq S'$, naturally extends the simulation relation between databases. Recall that a graph schema S represents its possibly infinite expansion, S^∞, i.e., an edge $x \stackrel{p}{\to} y$ represents infinitely many edges, one for each a for which $\mathcal{U} \models p(a)$. Each such edge may be simulated in S' by some unary formula. First, we choose $a \in \mathcal{U}$, then decide which edge $x' \stackrel{p'}{\to} y'$ in S' will "mimic" the edge $x \stackrel{p}{\to} y$ in S. For example, let $S = \{Int \vee String \Rightarrow \{5\}\}, S' = \{Int \Rightarrow \{Int\}, String \Rightarrow \{Int\}\}$, then $S \preceq S'$, because $\forall a \in \mathcal{U}$ for which $Int(a) \vee String(a)$ there is a corresponding edge in S'.

Proposition 5. $S \preceq S'$ *iff* $S^\infty \preceq S'^\infty$. *The latter is the simulation relation between (possibly infinite) databases.*

In particular, a database DB conforms to a graph schema S, $DB \preceq S$, iff DB when viewed as a graph schema subsumes S, for which we use the same notation $DB \preceq S$.

We now determine whether $S \preceq S'$. From [HHK95], this problem is decidable. Moreover, our algorithm in Fig. 6 checks whether $S \preceq S'$ in polynomial time.

Let $R \longleftarrow \{(u, u') \mid u \in nodes(S), u' \in nodes(S')\}$
while any change **do**
    find $(u, u') \in R$ and edge $u \xrightarrow{p} v$ in S
        such that $\mathcal{U} \models \exists a.p(a) \wedge (\bigwedge_{i=1,k} \neg p'_i(a))$

            where $u' \xrightarrow{p'_i} v'_i$, $i = 1, k$ are all edges from u' in S'
    $R \longleftarrow R - \{(u, u')\}$
return $((v_0, v'_0) \in R)$

Fig. 6. An algorithm checking whether $S \preceq S'$.

Proposition 6. *The algorithm in Fig. 6 checks in time $m^{O(1)}t$ whether $S \preceq S'$, where t is the time needed to check validity of a sentence in the theory T.*

We want to use this algorithm to check whether $[S] \subseteq [S']$. Corollary 8, which says that $[S] \subseteq [S']$ is equivalent to $S \preceq S'$, allows us to do that. To prove it, we observe that the subsumption relation $\preceq$ on graph schemas is preorder (from Proposition 5), and this allows us to define the least upper bound of a set of graph schemas, as in any preordered set. We review here the definition for completeness. Let $\mathcal{D}$ be a set of graph schemas. S is a *least upper bound* for $\mathcal{D}$ if (1) $\forall S_0 \in \mathcal{D}$, $S_0 \preceq S$, and (2) when another graph schema S' has this property, it follows that $S \preceq S'$. We use $\bigsqcup \mathcal{D}$ for the set of least upper bounds of $\mathcal{D}$. Since $\preceq$ is a preorder rather than an order relation, $\bigsqcup \mathcal{D}$ may have more than one element, but all are equivalent, i.e. $S, S' \in \bigsqcup \mathcal{D} \implies S \preceq S'$ and $S' \preceq S$. This justifies abbreviations like $\bigsqcup \mathcal{D} \preceq S'$ for $\exists S \in \bigsqcup \mathcal{D}, S \preceq S'$. The following theorem relates the order relation $\preceq$ to the meaning of a graph schema, $[S]$:

Theorem 7. *If $\mathcal{D} = [S]$ then $S \in \bigsqcup \mathcal{D}$.*

Before proving this result, we prove a corollary:

Corollary 8. $S \preceq S'$ *iff* $[S] \subseteq [S']$. *Hence S, S' are equivalent iff $[S] = [S']$.*

Proof. Obviously, $S \preceq S' \implies [S] \subseteq [S']$. The converse follows from Theorem 7, because $[S] \subseteq [S']$ implies $\bigsqcup[S] \preceq \bigsqcup[S']$, hence $S \preceq S'$.

Together, Corollary 8 and Proposition 6 imply that $[S] \subseteq [S']$ and $[S] = [S']$ are decidable in polynomial time. The rest of this subsection contains the proof of

Theorem 7, in which we approximate graph databases with trees. A *tree database* is a database whose graph is a finite tree. For a database DB, the *approximations* of DB is the set appr $(DB) = \{TDB \mid TDB$ a TDB $\preceq DB\}$. When DB is cycle-free, then appr (DB) is a finite set; when DB is a tree database itself, then $DB \in$ appr (DB). When DB has cycles, appr (DB) is infinite, and can be thought of as the set of all finite unfoldings of DB. Approximations allow us to infer simulations:

Proposition 9. appr $(DB) \subseteq$ appr (DB') *iff* $DB \preceq DB'$.

Proof. $DB \preceq DB'$ implies appr $(DB) \subseteq$ appr (DB'). For the converse, let u be some node in DB, and DB_u be the same graph database DB, but whose root is u. More precisely, when $DB = (V, E, v_0)$ then $DB_u = (V, E, u)$. We define the relation $\preceq$ from the nodes of DB to those of DB' to be $u \preceq u'$ iff appr $(DB_u) \subseteq$ appr $(DB'_{u'})$. Obviously, $v_0 \preceq v'_0$, where v_0, v'_0 are the roots of DB, DB' respectively. Now we have to prove that $\preceq$ is a simulation. Assume $u \preceq u'$ and let $u \overset{a}{\to} v$ be an edge in DB. The tree $(\{u, v\}, \{(u, a, v)\}, u)$ (consisting of a single edge $u \overset{a}{\to} v$ with root u) is in appr (DB_u), hence it is in appr $(DB'_{u'})$, so there exists at least one a-labeled edge leaving u'. Let $u' \overset{a}{\to} v'_1, \ldots, u' \overset{a}{\to} v'_k$ be the set of all such edges, $k \geq 1$. We use the fact that this set is finite and show that there exists some i s.t. appr $(DB_v) \subseteq$ appr $(DB'_{v'_i})$, implying $v \preceq v'_i$. Suppose by contradiction that this is not true: then for each $i = 1, k$ there exists some tree database $TDB_i \in$ appr (DB_v) s.t. $TDB_i \notin$ appr $(DB'_{v'_i})$. Consider the tree $TDB = \{a \Rightarrow (TDB_1 \cup \ldots \cup TDB_k)\}$. We have $TDB \in$ appr (DB_u), but $TDB \notin$ appr $(DB'_{u'})$ – a contradiction.

This proposition also holds for some infinite databases. Let us call some infinite database, DB, *label finite* if for any node u and label a, the set of outgoing edges $u \overset{a}{\to}$ is finite. From the proof of Proposition 9, we derive:

Corollary 10. *Let* appr $(DB) \subseteq$ appr (DB'), *with DB, DB' possibly infinite databases, but with DB' label-finite. Then $DB \preceq DB'$.*

Example 1. Let $DB = \{a \Rightarrow \{0, 1, 2, \ldots\}\}$ and $DB' = \{a \Rightarrow t_0, a \Rightarrow t_1, a \Rightarrow t_2, \ldots\}$, where $t_k = \{0, 1, \ldots, k-1, k+1, k+2, \ldots\}$. Then appr $(DB) =$ appr (DB') but $DB \not\preceq DB'$, proving that Corollary 10 fails when DB' is not label finite.

We now prove Theorem 7 using Proposition 9. We extend the notation appr to graph schemas, i.e. appr $(S) = \{TDB \mid TDB \preceq S, TDB$ is a tree d.b.$\} =$ appr (S^∞). Suppose S' satisfies $\forall DB \in \mathcal{D}, DB \preceq S'$: we have to prove $S \preceq S'$. First we show appr $(S) \subseteq$ appr (S'): $TDB \preceq S \Longrightarrow TDB \in \mathcal{D} \Longrightarrow TDB \preceq S' \Longrightarrow TDB \in$ appr (S'). Now we observe that S'^∞ is label-finite, hence Corollary 10 implies $S^\infty \preceq S'^\infty$. Finally Proposition 5 implies $S \preceq S'$.

4.2 GLB's and LUB's of graph schemas

Next, we show how to construct a schema S that expresses the combined constraints of two graph schemas S_1 and S_2. Given two schemas S_1 and S_2, we show that there exists a schema S s.t. $[S] = [S_1] \cap [S_2]$. Take the nodes of S to be pairs (u_1, u_2), with u_i a node in S_i, $i = 1, 2$, and take edges to be $(u_1, u_2) \overset{p_1 \wedge p_2}{\longrightarrow} (u_1, v_2)$, for any two edges $u_i \xrightarrow{p_i} v_i$ in S_i, $i = 1, 2$. One can show $[S] = [S_1] \cap [S_2]$. It follows that S is the greatest lower bound of S_1 and S_2, in notation $S_1 \sqcap S_2$. For example, when S_1, S_2 are given by Fig. 4(d) and (e), then $S_1 \sqcap S_2$ is given by the schema in (c) which is equivalent to that of (f), assuming the predicates *isDept* and *isPaper* are disjoint.

A similar fact does not hold for union or complement. Let us say that a set $\mathcal{D}$ of databases is *representable* if it is of the form $\mathcal{D} = [S]$ for some graph schema S. Then it is easy to show that any representable set $\mathcal{D}$ is an *ideal* [Gun92], i.e.: (1) $\mathcal{D}$ is nonempty, (2) $\mathcal{D}$ is downwards closed, i.e. $DB \preceq DB'$ and $DB' \in \mathcal{D}$ implies $DB \in \mathcal{D}$, and (3) $\mathcal{D}$ is directed, i.e. $DB_1, DB_2 \in \mathcal{D}$ implies $\exists DB \in \mathcal{D}$ s.t. $DB_1 \preceq DB$ and $DB_2 \preceq DB$. It follows immediately that, if $\mathcal{D}_1$ and $\mathcal{D}_2$ are representable, then the complement of $\mathcal{D}_1$ and $\mathcal{D}_1 \cup \mathcal{D}_2$ are, in general, not representable. Let $idl(\mathcal{D})$ denote the ideal generated by the set $\mathcal{D}$, i.e. $idl(\mathcal{D}) = \{DB_1 \cup \ldots \cup DB_k \mid \exists DB'_1, \ldots, DB'_k \in \mathcal{D}, \text{ s.t. } DB_i \preceq DB'_i, i = 1, k\}$. Then we can prove that when $\mathcal{D}_1, \mathcal{D}_2$ are representable, so is $idl(\mathcal{D}_1 \cup \mathcal{D}_2)$. For S_1, S_2 graph schemas representing $\mathcal{D}_1$ and $\mathcal{D}_2$ respectively, we define S to be their union(Section 2). It follows that $[S] = idl([S_1] \cup [S_2])$ and that S is the least upper bound of S_1, S_2, in notation $S_1 \sqcup S_2$.

4.3 Fragments of databases

Finally, we address the problem of finding for some database DB and graph schema S, a canonical "fragment" DB_0 of DB such that $DB_0 \preceq S$. This is important if we wish to use graph schemas as data guides [Abi97]. Instead of insisting that a database DB strictly conforms to some schema S, we require that there be a "large fragment" of DB which conforms to S. By "fragment" we mean a database DB_0 s.t. $DB_0 \preceq DB$. The name "fragment" is justified, because whenever $DB_0 \preceq DB$, there exists some graph DB' which is bisimilar to DB (hence, DB and DB' denote the same data) of which DB_0 is a subgraph. E.g. consider the graph schema S in Fig. 4 (a), and let $DB = \{tup \Rightarrow \{A, D \Rightarrow \{3\}\}\}$ be the database in Fig. 2(c). Then $DB_0 = \{tup \Rightarrow \{A\}\}$.

We observe that for any DB, S, the empty database $\emptyset$ (one node, no edges) is a fragment satisfying the requirement above, i.e. $\emptyset \preceq DB$ and $\emptyset \preceq S$. This is not the "canonical" fragment we want, because it is not the largest fragment under the simulation relation $\preceq$. By taking $DB_0 \overset{\text{def}}{=} DB \sqcap S$ we can prove:

Proposition 11. *For any graph database DB and graph schema S, there exists some database DB_0 s.t. (1) $DB_0 \preceq DB$ and $DB_0 \preceq S$, and (2) for any other database DB'_0 satisfying this property, $DB'_0 \preceq DB_0$. Moreover DB_0 can be computed in PTIME, and if $DB \preceq S$ then DB_0 is bisimilar to DB. We call DB_0 the* canonical fragment *of DB satisfying S.*

5 Determinism

Nodes in a schema have the potential to classify nodes in a database. This could be useful, for example, in a distributed environment, where we could use a schema to describe how such a database is distributed. For example, suppose that the database DB in Fig. 1 is distributed on two sites, such that all nodes before a department edge are located on site 1, while those after a department edge are on site 2. We could describe this formally using the schema in Fig. 4(d), which has two nodes u', v': database nodes conforming to u' will be on site 1, while those conforming to v' on site 2. However, the schema in Fig. 1(e) does not classify the nodes uniquely, because whenever we encounter an edge $u \xrightarrow{a} v$ in DB such that $isDept(a)$, we may either follow the edge $u' \xrightarrow{isDept} v'$ or the edge $u' \xrightarrow{not(isPaper)} u'$ in the schema. We say that the first schema is *deterministic*, while the second one is not.

In object-based graph database models, determinism is natural. For example, the semantics of ACeDB trees imposes that instance databases be deterministic, and in the Tsimmis data model, each node has a unique object identifier making the instance database deterministic. In our graph model, however, a deterministic representation of relational databases requires adding unnecessary object identifiers to sets. For example, in order to make the tree representation of a relational database in Fig. 2(a) deterministic we would use a different object identifier for every tup edge, say $tup1, tup2, tup3$. Determinism for graph schemas in any model, however, is natural. Note that the tree representation of the relational graph schema in Fig. 4 (a) for the database of Fig. 2(a) *is* deterministic.

We show that certain nondeterministic schemas are not equivalent to any deterministic ones. A natural question arises then: given a nondeterministic schema S, how can we best approximate it with a deterministic schema S_d ? We show here that a canonical S_d always exists.

We call an edge-labeled graph G *deterministic* if for every node x and label a, there exists at most one edge labeled a going out of x. This definition is not invariant under bisimulation[3]. A database DB is deterministic if there exists some deterministic graph bisimilar to it. Similarly, we call a graph schema S *deterministic* iff S^∞ is deterministic. The following is a sufficient condition for checking if a graph schema S is deterministic:

Proposition 12. *Let S be a graph schema. S is deterministic if for any node u and any two distinct edges $u \xrightarrow{p} v, u \xrightarrow{p'} v'$, we have $\mathcal{U} \models \neg(\exists x. p(x) \wedge p'(x))$.*

Deterministic graph schemas are important because of the following:

Proposition 13. *Let S be deterministic and TDB a tree database s.t. $TDB \preceq S$. Then TDB conforms to S "in a unique way". More precisely there exists a function φ from the nodes of TDB to those of S s.t. for any simulation $\preceq$ from TDB to S, and for every node u of TDB, $u \preceq \varphi(u)$.*

This follows from the observation that nodes in a tree database are in 1-1 correspondence with sequences of labels, $a_1 \ldots a_n$. Such a sequence is mapped uniquely into some node in S, because S is deterministic, and this defines the function φ. $\varphi(u)$ classifies nodes: u and v are in the same class iff $\varphi(u) = \varphi(v)$.

Deterministic schemas are less "expressive" than nondeterministic ones. For example, the nondeterministic graph schema $S = \{a \Rightarrow \{b\}, a \Rightarrow \{c\}\}$ is not equivalent to any deterministic graph schema, i.e. $[S] \neq [S_d]$ for any deterministic graph schema S_d. The "closest" we can get is the deterministic graph schema

---

[3] The tree $\{a\}$ is deterministic and bisimilar to the tree $\{a, a\}$; but the latter is not deterministic.

$S_d = \{a \Rightarrow \{b, c\}\}$. In general, for any nondeterministic graph schema S, there exists a "closest" deterministic graph schema S_d. The latter is constructed in a way reminiscent of the DFA equivalent to an NDFA:

Proposition 14. *For any graph schema S, there exists some deterministic graph schema S_d with the following properties: (1) $S \preceq S_d$, (2) whenever $S \preceq S'$ and S' is deterministic then $S_d \preceq S'$.*

The proof is based on a standard powerset construction and is given in [BDFS96].

An interesting case is when S is a database (i.e. all unary formulas on its edges are equalities with constants); then S_d is precisely the deterministic automata obtained from S. For the example in which $S = \{a \Rightarrow \{b\}, a \Rightarrow \{c\}\}$, we get $S_d = \{a \Rightarrow \{b, c\}\}$.

In general, the number of nodes in S_d is exponential in that of S. But when S is a tree database, then the number of nodes in S_d is less than or equal to that of S [Per90, pp.7]. When we generalize to unary formulas, then the number of nodes in S_d may be exponential, even when S is a tree. For example, let $S = \{p_1, p_2, \ldots, p_n\}$, then $S_d = \{r_0, r_1, \ldots, r_{2^n-1}\}$, where each $r_i = \bigvee_{j=0,n-1} q_j$, with $q_j = p_j$ or $q_j = \neg p_j$, depending on whether the j's bit in the binary representation of i is 1 or 0. Such arbitrary sets of unary formulas $p_1, p_2, \ldots, p_n$ rarely occur in practice, because the base predicates are either constants, or taken from a list of disjoint predicates, like $Int, String, Bool, Nat, isDept$. The graph schemas in Figure 4 have this property. Then we can prove:

Proposition 15. *Let S be a tree schema in which for every two distinct unary formulas $p(x), p'(x)$, either is a constant (i.e. of the form $x = a$), or they are disjoint (i.e. $\mathcal{U} \models \neg \exists x.(p(x) \wedge p'(x))$). Then S_d has at most as many nodes as S, and can be computed in polynomial time.*

6 Graph Schemas and Queries

In [BDHS96a], we propose UnQL, a language for querying and restructuring graph databases. UnQL is compositional, has a simple select ... where ... construct, supports flexible path expressions, and can express complex restructuring of the graph database. Consider the simple UnQL query Q:

$$\text{select } \{x \Rightarrow \{x\}\} \text{ where } \backslash x \leftarrow DB$$

Q takes a graph database of the form $\{a_1 \Rightarrow t_1, \ldots, a_n \Rightarrow t_n\}$ and returns the graph database $\{a_1 \Rightarrow \{a_1\}, \ldots, a_n \Rightarrow \{a_n\}\}$, i.e., Q doubles each edge in the first level of edges in DB.

Recall from Section 2 that graph schemas can be thought of as finite descriptions of infinite sets of databases, i.e. S defines the set $[S] = \{DB \mid DB \preceq S\}$. We consider whether, given a schema S and an UnQL query Q, we can describe the set $\{Q(DB) \mid DB \preceq S\}$ by a schema S'. This question is important for two reasons. First, we use graph schemas in query optimization of UnQL. Since UnQL is compositional, when we optimize a composed query $Q(DB) \overset{\text{def}}{=} Q_2(Q_1(DB))$ whose input conforms to some graph schema, $DB \preceq S$, we first optimize Q_1 according to graph schema S, then optimize Q_2 according to the graph schema of the set $\{Q_1(DB) \mid DB \preceq S\}$, hence the need to compute the latter. Second, UnQL queries can be used to define views, like $V \stackrel{\text{def}}{=} Q(DB)$. Given that $DB \preceq S$, we want to optimize queries against the view. This requires a graph schema for the set $\{Q(DB) \mid DB \preceq S\}$.

Given a graph schema S and a query Q, there is a natural way to compute a graph schema $Q(S)$, with the property: (∗) $\forall DB \preceq S$, $Q(DB) \preceq Q(S)$. Since UnQL queries are just graph transformations, we can compute $Q(S)$ much in the same way in which we compute $Q(DB)$. Where the construct is less obvious, we take a conservative action. For example, for a subquery $Q(DB) = \{x \Rightarrow DB\}$, having a free variable x bound in a surrounding context, we define $Q(S)$ to be $\{true \Rightarrow S\}$, or if any predicate $P(x)$ is known about the variable x (e.g. Q occurs in the then branch of an if $P(x)$ then ... else ... construct), then we take $Q(S) = \{P \Rightarrow S\}$. This ensures that (∗) holds, but $Q(S)$ may not necessarily get the tightest description of the set $\{Q(DB) \mid DB \preceq S\}$.

We omit the full description of $Q(S)$ from this abstract, but mention that $Q(S)$ can be computed in PTIME, and that it satisfies (∗). But (∗) can be trivially satisfied by taking $Q(S) = S_\top$ (Fig. 4 (b)), which is a maximal element in the partial order $\preceq$. We would like to make the claim $Q(S) = \bigsqcup\{Q(DB) \mid DB \preceq S\}$, thus showing that $Q(S)$ describes precisely the set $\mathcal{D} \stackrel{\text{def}}{=} \{Q(DB) \mid DB \preceq S\}$. Unfortunately, this does not hold. Worse, there are examples of simple queries Q and graph schema S for which $\bigsqcup \mathcal{D}$ does not exist. Consider the graph schema $S = \{Nat\}$ and the UnQL query Q from above. This query doubles every label in the database, e.g. on the database $DB = \{2, 4, 5\}$ Q returns $\{2 \Rightarrow \{2\}, 4 \Rightarrow \{4\}, 5 \Rightarrow \{5\}\}$. Our method computes the graph schema $S' = Q(S)$ to be $\{Nat \Rightarrow \{Nat\}\}$, but this is not $\bigsqcup \mathcal{D}$. The sequence of graph schemas $S_1, S_2, \ldots$ where $S_n = \{0 \Rightarrow \{0\}, 1 \Rightarrow \{1\}, \ldots, n \Rightarrow \{n\}, p_n \Rightarrow \{Nat\}\}$, with $p_n(x) = (x \neq 0 \wedge \ldots \wedge x \neq n \wedge Nat(x))$, forms an infinite, strictly descending chain of graph schemas, each offering a better approximation of $\mathcal{D}$. In fact, we can prove directly that $\mathcal{D}$ has no least upper bound.

Graph schemas cannot describe all sets of the form $\{Q(DB) \mid DB \preceq S\}$, because they cannot impose equality constraints on edges in the database. We can partially fix this by extending the notion of graph schema to allow equality constraints between certain values on edges. Formally, we define an *extended graph schema* with variables $z_1, \ldots, z_n$ to be a rooted graph (V, E, v_0), in which the edges are labeled with formulas as explained below, and with $n \geq 0$ distinguished subgraphs, denoted $G_{z_1}, \ldots, G_{z_n}$. Each subgraph G_z is called the *scope* of the variable z, and is given by (1) a set of nodes $V_z \subseteq V$, (2) a set of edges $E_z \subseteq E$, s.t. for every edge $u \rightarrow v$ in E_z, both u and v are in V_z, (3) a set of input nodes $I_z \subseteq V_z$, and (4) a set of output nodes $O_z \subseteq V_z$. We impose several conditions on extended graph schemas: (1) For every edge $u \rightarrow v$ entering some graph G_z (i.e. $u \notin V_z$ and $v \in V_z$), v is one of the inputs of G_z. (2) Similarly, every edge $u \rightarrow v$ leaving some graph G_z exits from an output node, $u \in O_z$. (3) Each formula labeling some edge in the scope of k variables $z_1, \ldots, z_k$ may have $k + 1$ free variables: $z_1, \ldots, z_k$ and a distinguished variable x as before. (4) The scopes of variables follow traditional rules in programming languages: for $z \neq z'$, either $G_z \subseteq G_{z'}$, or $G_{z'} \subseteq G_z$, or G_z and $G_{z'}$ are disjoint.

Graph schemas are particular cases of extended graph schemas with no variables ($n = 0$). As with graph schemas, an extended graph schema S can be modeled by its infinite expansion S^∞. Each graph G_z is replicated once for each value $z \in \mathcal{U}$, and their input and output nodes are collapsed. Fig. 7 contains two examples of extended graph schemas with one variable z. I_z has a single node in both (a) and (b); O_z is empty in (a) and has one node in (b). The expansion in (b) is incomplete: $not(0)$ should be further expanded with all atoms $a \in \mathcal{U}$, $a \neq 0$, etc. Unlike graph schemas, S^∞ may have infinitely many nodes. Some care is needed when collapsing the input and output nodes. In a formal definition presented elsewhere, we use ε edges to define S^∞ (see [BDHS96a] for a definition of ε edges).

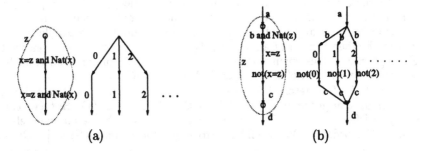

Fig. 7. Two examples of extended graph schemas and their expansions.

Since extended graph schemas are a more sophisticated way of specifying an infinite graph, we can extend previous results for graph schemas. We can define what it means for a database DB to conform to an extended graph schema S, $DB \preceq S$, and for an extended graph schema S to subsume some other extended graph schema S', $S \preceq S'$, etc. From [HHK95], both $DB \preceq S$ and $S \preceq S'$ are decidable. Unfortunately, S^∞ is not generally label-finite, and Theorem 7 fails in general for extended graph schemas. For example, take $S = \{a \Rightarrow \{Nat\}\}$. Then $S^\infty = DB$ with DB from Example 1, and $[S] = \text{appr}(DB)$. Take S' to be the graph $G = G_z = \{u \xrightarrow{x=a \wedge Nat(z)} v \xrightarrow{Nat(x) \wedge x \neq z} w\}$ with $I_z = \{u\}$ and $O_z = \emptyset$, then $S'^\infty = DB'$ of Example 1, and S' is an upperbound of $[S]$ but $S \npreceq S'$. Intuitively, S' is better than $S = \{a \Rightarrow \{Nat\}\}$ because it says that after each a-edge, at least one natural number is missing. Using two variables z_1, z_2 we can say that at least two natural numbers are missing, etc. In fact the set $[S]$ does not have a least upper bound in the preordered set of extended schemas. Fortunately, we can address this problem if we are restricted to deterministic extended graph schemas. More precisely, we can prove the following theorem, which is the most complex result of this paper. Here a *positive* UnQL query is a query whose translation into UnCAL does not use the only non-monotone operator in UnCAL, *isempty* (see [Suc96] for a more detailed discussion).

Theorem 16. *Let Q be a positive UnQL query. Then for every (extended) graph schema S there exists an extended graph schema $Q(S)$, computable in $PTIME$ such that: for every deterministic, extended graph schema S', if $\forall DB \preceq S \Rightarrow Q(DB) \preceq S'$, then $Q(S) \preceq S'$.*

The proof appears in [BDFS96]. For the UnQL query Q at the beginning of this section and schema $S = \{Nat\}$, $Q(S)$ is the schema in Fig. 7 (a).

7 Conclusions and Future Work

When querying unstructured data, the ability to use whatever structure is known about the data can have significant impact on performance. Examples abound in optimizations for generalized path expression (see [CACS94, CCM96], among others). We have explored a new notion of a graph schema appropriate for edge-labeled graph databases. Since the known structure of graph databases may be weaker than that of a traditional database, we use unary formulas instead of constants for edge labels. We describe how a graph database conforms to a schema and observe that a graph database may conform to multiple schemas. Since there is a natural ordering on graph schemas, it is possible to take the least upper bound of a set of schemas and combine into a single schema all their constraints. We then describe a "deterministic" subclass of schemas that uniquely classifies nodes of (tree) databases. When optimizing queries for distributed graph databases, node classification allows us to decompose and specialize the query for a target site [Suc96].

In current work, we are using schemas for query optimization and query decomposition. Consider the following UnQL query Q [Suc96], which selects all papers in the Computer Science Department in Fig. 1:

$$\text{select } \textit{"Papers".t} \text{ where } \_*.\textit{"CS-Department".}\_*.\textit{"Papers".t} \leftarrow DB$$

Without any knowledge about the data's structure, one has to search the entire database. We can exploit knowledge about the structure of the data in order to prune the search. For example, if we know that the data conforms to the the schema in Fig. 4(d), we can prune the search after every department edge that is not a Computer Science Department. This can be described by another query, Q_{opt}. An interesting question is what happens if the database DB fails to conform to the schema S, which is likely in unpredictable data sources like the Web. As discussed in Subsection 4.3, one can still describe the precise semantics of $Q_{opt}(DB)$, namely as $Q(DB_0)$, where DB_0 is the canonical fragment of DB conforming to S (Subsection 4.3). Similarly, we plan to address query decomposition. [Suc96] describes a query decomposition technique that ignores any information about the structure of the data, or how it is distributed. Assuming the database DB is distributed on two sites, the technique in [Suc96] poses three different queries on each site. We plan to use deterministic schemas to describe data in a distributed environment. For example, we could use the schema in Fig. 4(d) to describe how the nodes in the database are located on the two sites and reduce the queries posed at each site from three to one. Maximizing the benefits of these techniques for query decomposition and optimization is an area of future work.

The definition of a graph schema we have given is extremely general. For example, it cannot constrain a graph to be an instance of a relation in the sense that Fig. 2(a) describes a relation, because multiple edges with the same attribute name are allowed in the graph instance. Furthermore, our schemas only place outer bounds on what edges may emanate from a node. In future work, we may consider a dual notion of schema that places inner bounds on edges by requiring certain edges to exist. One could consider further constraints that restrict the number of edges that emanate from a node, as is done in [TMD92] to model variants.

References

[Abi97]   Serge Abiteboul. Querying semi-structured data. In *ICDT*, 1997.

[BDFS96]   Peter Buneman, Susan Davidson, Mary Fernandez, and Dan Suciu. Adding structure to unstructured data. Technical Report MS-CIS-96-21, University of Pennsylvania, Computer and Information Science Department, 1996.

[BDHS96a]   Peter Buneman, Susan Davidson, Gerd Hillebrand, and Dan Suciu. A query language and optimization techniques for unstructured data. In *SIGMOD*, 1996.

[BDHS96b]   Peter Buneman, Susan Davidson, Gerd Hillebrand, and Dan Suciu. A query language and optimization techniques for unstructured data. Technical Report 96-09, University of Pennsylvania, Computer and Information Science Department, February 1996.

[BDS95]   Peter Buneman, Susan Davidson, and Dan Suciu. Programming constructs for unstructured data. In *Proceedings of DBPL'95*, Gubbio, Italy, September 1995.

[CACS94]   V. Christophides, S. Abiteboul, S. Cluet, and M. Scholl. From structured documents to novel query facilities. In Richard Snodgrass and Marianne Winslett, editors, *Proceedings of 1994 ACM SIGMOD International Conference on Management of Data*, Minneapolis, Minnesota, May 1994.

[CCM96]   V. Christophides, S. Cluet, and G. Moerkotte. Evaluating queries with generalized path expressions. In *Proceedings of 1996 ACM SIGMOD International Conference on Management of Data*, Montreal, Canada, June 1996.

[CM90]   M. P. Consens and A. O. Mendelzon. Graphlog: A visual formalism for real life recursion. In *Proc. ACM SIGACT-SIGMOD-SIGART Symp. on Principles of Database Sys.*, Nashville, TN, April 1990.

[Gun92]   Carl A. Gunter. *Semantics of Programming Languages: Structures and Techniques*. Foundations of Computing. MIT Press, 1992.

[HHK95]   Monika Henzinger, Thomas Henzinger, and Peter Kopke. Computing simulations on finite and infinite graphs. In *Proceedings of 20th Symposium on Foundations of Computer Science*, pages 453–462, 1995.

[KS95]   David Konopnicki and Oded Shmueli. Draft of W3QS: a query system for the World-Wide Web. In *Proc. of VLDB*, 1995.

[MMM96]   SuA. Mendelzon, G. Mihaila, and T. Milo. Querying the world wide web. Manuscript, available from http://www.cs.toronto.edu/ georgem/WebSQL.html, 1996.

[Per90]   D. Perrin. Finite automata. In *Formal Models and Semantics*, volume B of *Handbook of Theoretical Computer Science*, chapter 1, pages 1–57. Elsevier, Amsterdam, 1990.

[PGMW95]   Y. Papakonstantinou, H. Garcia-Molina, and J. Widom. Object exchange across heterogeneous information sources. In *IEEE International Conference on Data Engineering*, March 1995.

[PT87]   Robert Paige and Robert Tarjan. Three partition refinement algorithms. *SIAM Journal of Computing*, 16:973–988, 1987.

[QRS+95]   D. Quass, A. Rajaraman, Y. Sagiv, J. Ullman, and J. Widom. Querying semistructure heterogeneous information. In *International Conference on Deductive and Object Oriented Databases*, 1995.

[Suc96]   Dan Suciu. Query decomposition for unstructured query languages. In *VLDB*, September 1996.

[TMD92]   J. Thierry-Mieg and R. Durbin. Syntactic Definitions for the ACEDB Data Base Manager. Technical Report MRC-LMB xx.92, MRC Laboratory for Molecular Biology, Cambridge, CB2 2QH, UK, 1992.

Correspondence and Translation for Heterogeneous Data*

Serge Abiteboul[1] and Sophie Cluet[2] and Tova Milo[3]

[1] Stanford University, Standford, CA 94402[†]
[2] INRIA, Domaine de Voluceau, 78153 Le Chesnay, France
[3] Tel Aviv University,Tel Aviv, Israel

1 Introduction

A primary motivation for new database technology is to provide support for the broad spectrum of multimedia data available notably through the network. These data are stored under different formats: SQL or ODMG (in databases), SGML or LaTex (documents), DX formats (scientific data), Step (CAD/CAM data), etc. Their integration is a very active field of research and development (see for instance, for a very small sample, [10, 6, 7, 9, 8, 12, 19, 20]). In this paper, we provide a formal foundation to facilitate the integration of such heterogeneous data and the maintenance of heterogeneous replicated data.

A sound solution for a data integration task requires a clean abstraction of the different formats in which data are stored, and means for specifying the correspondences/relationships between data in different worlds and for translating data from one world to another. For that we introduce a *middleware* data model that serves as a basis for the integration task, and *declarative rules* for specifying the integration.

The choice of the *middleware* data model is clearly essential. One common trend in data integration over heterogeneous models has always been to use an integrating model that encompasses the source models. We take an opposite approach here, i.e., our model is minimalist. The data structure we use consists of ordered labeled trees. We claim that this simple model is general enough to capture the essence of formats we are interested in. Even though a mapping from a richer data model to this model may loose some of the original semantics, the data itself is preserved and the integration with other data models is facilitated. Our model is similar to the one used in [7] and to the OEM model for unstructured data (see, e.g., [21, 20]). This is not surprising since the data formats that motivated these works are part of the formats that our framework intends to support. A difference with the OEM model is that we view the children of each vertex as ordered. This is crucial to describe lists, an essential component of DX formats. Also, [13] introduces BNF generated trees to unify hierarchical data models. However, due to the fixed number of sons of a rule, collections are represented by left or right deep trees not suitable for the casual users.

A main contribution of the paper is in the declarative specification of correspondences between data in different worlds. For this we use datalog-style rules, enriched with, as a novel feature, *merge* and *cons* term constructors. The semantics of the rules takes into consideration the fact that some internal nodes represent collections with specific properties (e.g., sets are insensitive to order and duplicates). We show that correspondences between data elements can be computed in polynomial time in many cases, and may require exponential time only when insensitivity to order or duplicates are considered.

Deriving correspondences within existing data is only one issue in a heterogeneous context. One would also want to translate data from one representation to another. Interestingly, we show that

---

[†] This author's permanent position is INRIA-Rocquencourt, France. His work was supported by the Air Force Wright Laboratory Aeronautical Systems Center under ARPA Contract F33615-93-1-1339, and by the Air Force Rome Laboratories under ARPA Contract F30602-95-C-0119.

* This work was partially supported by EC Projects GoodStep and Opal and by the Israeli Ministry of Science

in most practical cases, translation rules can be automatically be derived from the correspondence rules. Thus, a complete integration task (derivation of correspondences, transformation of data from one world to the other, incremental integration of a new bulk of data, etc.) can be specified using a single declarative set of rules. This is an important result. It saves in writing different specifications for each sub-component of the integration task, and also helps in avoiding inconsistent specifications.

It should be noted that the language we use to define correspondence rules is very simple. Similar correspondences could be easily derived using more powerful languages previously proposed (e.g., LDL [5] or IQL [4]). But in these languages it would be much more difficult (sometimes impossible) to derive translation rules from given correspondence rules. Nevertheless, our language is expressive enough to describe many desired correspondences/translations, and in particular can express all the powerful document-OODB mappings supported by the *structuring schemas* mechanism of [2, 3].

As will be seen, correspondence rules have a very simple and intuitive graphical representation. Indeed, the present work serves as the basis for a system, currently being implemented, where a specification of integration of heterogeneous data proceeds in two phases. In a first phase, data is abstracted to yield a tree-like representation that is hiding details unnecessary to the restructuring (e.g., tags or parsing information). In a second phase, available data is displayed in a graphical window and starting from that representation, the user can specify correspondences or derive data.

The paper is organized as follows. Section 2 introduces a core data model and Section 3 a core language for specifying correspondences. In Section 4, we extend the framework to better deal with collections. Section 5 deals with the translation problem. The last section is a conclusion. More examples and figures are given in two appendixes.

2 The Data Model

Our goal is to provide a data model that allows declarative specifications of the correspondence between data stored in different worlds (DX, ODMG, SGML, etc.). We first introduce the model, then the concept of correspondence. To illustrate things we use below an example. A simple instance of an SGML document is given in Figure 1. A tree representation of the document in our middleware model, together with correspondences between this tree and a forest representation of a reference in a bibliographical OODB is given in Figure 2.

2.1 Data Forest

We assume the existence of some infinite sets: (i) **name** of names; (ii) **vertex** of vertexes; (iii) **dom** of data values. A *data forest* is a forest of *ordered labeled trees*. An *ordered labeled tree* is a tree with a labeling of vertexes and for each vertex, an ordering of its children. The internal vertexes of the trees have labels from **name** whereas the leaves have labels from **name** ∪ **dom** ∪ **vertex**. The only constraint is that if a vertex occurs as a leaf label, it should also occur as a vertex in the forest. Observe that this is a rather conventional tree structure. This is a data model in the spirit of complex value model [17, 1, 11] and many others, it is particularly influenced by models for unstructured data [21, 20] and the tree model of [7]. A particularity is the ordering of vertexes that is important to model data formats essentially described by files obeying a certain grammar (e.g., SGML).

Definition 1. A *data forest* F is a triple (E, G, L), where (E, G) is a finite *ordered* forest (the ordering is implicit); E is the set of vertexes; G the set of edges; L (the *labeling function*) maps some leaves in E to $E \cup$ **dom**; and all other vertexes to **name**.

For each vertex v in E, the maximal subtree of root v is called the *object v*. The set of vertexes E of a forest F is denoted $vertex(F)$ and the set of data values appearing in F is denoted $dom(F)$.

Remark. Observe that by definition, we allow a leaf to be mapped to a name. For all purposes, we may think of such leaves as internal vertexes without children. This will turn useful to represent for instance the empty set or the empty list. In the following, we refer by the word *leaf* only to vertexes v such that $L(v)$ is a vertex or is in **dom**.

We illustrate this notion as well as syntactic representations we use in an example. Consider the graphical representation of the forest describing the OODB, shown in the lower part of Figure 2. A tabular representation of part of the same forest is given in Figure 3. Finally, below is the equivalent textual representation:

$$\&2 \; reference \; \{ \; \&21 \; key \; \{ \; \&211 \; \text{``}ACM96\text{''} \; \{ \; \} \; \},$$
$$\&22 \; title \; \{ \; \&221 \; \text{``}Correspondence...\text{''} \; \{ \; \} \; \},$$
$$\&23 \; authors \; \{ \; \&231 \; \&3 \; \{ \; \}, \; \&232 \; \&4 \; \{ \; \}, \; \&233 \; \&5 \; \{ \; \} \; \},$$
$$\&24 \; abstract \; \{ \; \&241 \text{``}...\text{''} \; \{ \; \} \; \} \; \}$$

...

To get a more compact representation, we omit brackets when a vertex has a single or no children, and omit vertex identifiers when they are irrelevant for the discussion. For example the above reference tree may be represented by

$$\&2 \; reference \; \{ \; key \; \text{``}ACM96\text{''},$$
$$\&22 \; title \; \text{``}Correspondence...\text{''},$$
$$authors\{ \; \&3, \&4, \&5 \; \},$$
$$\&24 \; abstract \; \text{``}...\text{''} \; \}$$

Let us now see how various common data sources can be mapped into our middleware model.

We consider here three different types of mappings. The first concerns relational databases, but also all simple table formats. The second is used for object-oriented databases, but a similar one will fit most graph formats. Finally, the last will fit any format having a BNF (or similar) grammar description. Note that the three mappings are invertible and can easily be implemented.

Relations can be represented by a tree whose root label is the relation name and which has as many children as rows in the relation. At depth 2, nodes represent rows and are labeled by the label "tuple". At depth 3, 4 and 5, nodes are labeled respectively by attribute names, types and values.

An object oriented database is usually a cyclic graph. However, using object identifier one may easily represents a cyclic graph as a tree [4].

We pick one possible representation but many other ones can be proposed. A class extent is represented by a tree whose root node is labeled with the class name. This node has as many children as there are objects in the extent, each of which is labeled by the object type. We assume that objects appear in the class extent of their most specific class. We now describe the representation of subtrees according to types.

- A node labeled by an atomic type has a unique child whose label is the appropriate atomic value.
- A node labeled "tuple" has one child for each attribute. The children are labeled with the attribute names and each has one child labeled by the appropriate type and having the relevant structure.
- A node labeled "set" (or "list", "bag", ...) has as many children as elements in the collection, one for each collection member. (For lists the order of elements is preserved). Each child is labeled by the appropriate type, and has the relevant structure.
- A node labeled by an object type has a unique child labeled by the identifier of the node that representing the object in the tree of the class extent to which it belongs.

A document can be described by a simplified representation of its parsing tree. The labels of the internal nodes (resp. leaves) represent the grammar non-terminal symbols (resp. tokens).

SGML and HTML, among other formats, allow references to internal and external data. Parsers do not interpret these references. They usually consider them as strings. In our context, these references should be interpreted when possible. As for object databases, the reference can be replaced by the identifier of the node containing the referred data.

Note that the only identification of data in the middleware model is given by the nodes identifiers. This means that it is the responsability of the data sources to keep relationships between the exported data and the node identifiers. This relationship is not always needed (e.g., for a translation process), and may be of a fine or large grain according to the application needs and the data source capacities.

The identification of data in the data sources can take various forms. It can be the key of a row or some internal address in relational databases. For object databases, it can be the internal oid (for objects), a query leading to the object/value, or similar ideas as in the relational case. For files it can be an offset in the file, node in the parse tree, etc.

2.2 Correspondence

We are concerned with establishing/maintaining correspondences between objects. Some objects may come from one data source with particular forest F_1, and others from another forest, say F_2. To simplify, we consider here that we have a single forest (that can be viewed as the union of the two forests) and look for correspondences *within* the forest. (If we feel it is essential to distinguish between the sources, we may assume that the nodes of each tree from a particular data source have the name of that source, e.g., F_1, F_2, as part of the label.) We describe correspondences between objects using predicates.

Example 1. Consider the following forest with the SGML and OODB trees of Figure 2.

> &1 *article* {..., &12 *title "Correspondence...",* &13 *author "S.Abiteboul",*
> &14 *author "S.Cluet",* &15 *author "T.Milo",* &16 *abstract "...", ... }*
> &2 *reference { key "ACM96",* &22 *title "Correspondence...", authors{* &3, &4, &5 } ,
> &24 *abstract "..." }*
> &3 *author { fn "S.", ln "Abiteboul" }*
> &4 *author { fn "S.", ln "Cluet" }*
> &5 *author { fn "T.", ln "Milo" }*

We may want to have the following correspondences:

> { *is*(&1, &2), *is*(&12, &22), *is*(&13, &3), *is*(&14, &4), *is*(&15, &5), *is*(&16, &24)
> *concat*("S.Abiteboul", "S.", "Abiteboul"), *concat*("S.Cluet", "S.", "Cluet"),
> *concat*("T.Milo", "T.", "Milo") }.

Note that there is an essential difference between the two predicates above: *is* relates objects that represent the same real world entity, whereas *concat* is a standard concatenation predicate/function that is defined externally. The *is*-relationship is represented on Figure 2.

Definition 2. Let **R** be a relational schema. An **R**-*correspondence* is a pair (F, I) where F is a data forest and I a relational instance over **R** with values in $vertex(F) \cup dom(F)$.

For instance, consider Example 1. Let **R** consists of binary relation *is* and a ternary one *concat*. For the forest F and correspondences I as in the example, (F, I) is an **R**-correspondence. Note that we do not restrict our attention to 1-1 correspondences. The correspondence predicates may have arbitrary arity, and also, because of data duplication, some n-m correspondences may be introduced.

3 The Core Language

In this section, we develop the core language. This is in the style of rule-based languages for objects, e.g., IQL [4], LDL [5], F-logic [15] and more precisely, of MedMaker [19]. The language we present in this section is tailored to correspondence derivation, and thus in some sense more limited. However, we will consider in a next section a powerful new feature.

We assume the existence of two infinite sorts: a sort **data-var** of data variables, and **vertex-var** of vertex variables. Data variables start with capitals (to distinguish them from names); and vertex variables start with the character & followed by a capital letter.

Rules are built from correspondence literals and tree terms. Correspondence literals have the form $R(x_1, x_2, ..., x_n)$ where R is a relation name and $x_1, x_2, .., x_n$ are data/vertex variables/constants. Tree terms are of the form $\&X\ L$, $\&X\ L\ t_1$, and $\&X\ L\ \{t_1, t_2, ..., t_n\}$ where $\&X$ is a vertex variable/constant, L is a label and $t_1, t_2, ..., t_n$ are tree terms. The $\&X$ and Ls can also be omitted. A rule is obtained by distinguishing some correspondence literals and tree terms to be in the body, and some to be in the head. Semantics of rules is given in the sequel. As an example, consider the following rule that we name r_{so}. Note again the distinction between *concat* which is a predicate on data values and can be thought of as given by extension or computed externally, and the derived *is* correspondence predicate.

$$
\begin{array}{ll}
& \&X_0 \; article \; \{ \; \&X_1, \\
& \qquad\qquad \&X_2 \; title \; X_3, \\
& \qquad\qquad \&X_4 \; author \; X_5, \; \&X_6 \; author \; X_7, \; \&X_8 \; author \; X_9, \\
& \qquad\qquad \&X_{10} \; abstract \; X_{11}, \\
& \qquad\qquad \&X_{12} \; \} \\
is(\&X_0, \&X_{13}) & \&X_{13} \; reference \; \{ \; \&X_{14}, \\
is(\&X_2, \&X_{15}) & \qquad\qquad \&X_{15} \; title \; X_3, \\
is(\&X_{10}, \&X_{19}) \; \leftarrow & \qquad\qquad authors\{ \; \&Y_{16}, \&X_{17}, \&X_{18} \; \} \; , \\
is(\&X_4, \&X_{16}) & \qquad\qquad \&X_{19} \; abstract \; X_{11} \; \} \\
is(\&X_6, \&X_{17}) & \&X_{16} \; author \; \{ \; fn \; X_{20}, \; ln \; X_{21} \; \} \\
is(\&X_8, \&X_{18}) & \&X_{17} \; author \; \{ \; fn \; X_{22}, \; ln \; X_{23} \; \} \\
& \&X_{18} \; author \; \{ \; fn \; X_{24}, \; ln \; X_{25} \; \} \\
\\
& concat(X_5, X_{20}, X_{21}) \\
& concat(X_7, X_{22}, X_{23}) \\
& concat(X_9, X_{24}, X_{25})
\end{array}
$$

A *rule* consists of a body and a head. When a rule has only literals in its head, it is said to be a *correspondence rule*. We assume that all variables in the head of a correspondence rule also occur in the body. We now define the semantics of correspondence rules.

Definition 3. Given an instance (F, I) and some correspondence rule r, a *valuation* ν over (F, I) is a mapping over variables in r such that

1. ν maps data variables to $dom(F)$ and object variables to $vertex(F)$.
2. For each term H in the body of r
   (a) H is a correspondence literal and $\nu(H)$ is true in I; or
   (b) H is a tree term and $\nu(H)$ is an object[5] of F.

We say that a correspondence $C(\&U, \&V)$ is *derived from* (F, I) *using* r if $C(\&U, \&V) = \nu(H)$ for some term H in the head of r, and some valuation ν over (F, I).

Let $\mathcal{P}$ be a set of rules. Let $I' = \{ H' \mid H'$ derived from (F, I) using some r in $\mathcal{P} \}$. Then, $(F, I \cup I')$ is denoted $T_{\mathcal{P}}(F, I)$. If $\mathcal{P}$ is recursive, we may be able to apply $T_{\mathcal{P}}$ to $T_{\mathcal{P}}(F, I)$ to derive new correspondences. The limit $T_{\mathcal{P}}^{\omega}(F, I)$, when it exists, of the application of $T_{\mathcal{P}}$ is denoted, $\mathcal{P}(F, I)$.

Theorem 4. *For each (possibly recursive) finite set $\mathcal{P}$ of correspondence-rules and each data forest (F, I), $\mathcal{P}(F, I)$ is well-defined (in particular, the sequence of applications of $T_{\mathcal{P}}$ converges in a finite number of stages). Furthermore, $\mathcal{P}(F, I)$ can be computed in* PTIME.

Sketch: We represent data forests using a relational database. A relation *succ* gives a portion of the successor function over the integers. The number of facts that can be derived is polynomial. Each step can be computed with a first-order formula, so it is in PTIME. □

The above rule r_{so} is an example of a non-recursive correspondence rule. (We assume that the extension of *concat* is given in I.) To see an example of a recursive rule, we consider the correspondence between "left-deep" and "right-deep" trees. For instance, we would like to derive a correspondence between the right and left deep trees shown in Figure 4. This is achieved using the program $r2l$ which consists of the following rules:

---

[5] Recall that an object of a forest F is a maximal subtree of F rooted in some vertex of F.

$$r2l: \dfrac{R2L(\&U, \&V) \leftarrow \begin{array}{l} \&U \; right\{\} \\ \&V \; left\{\} \end{array}}{\begin{array}{l} \&U \; right\{X, \; \&Y\} \\ R2L(\&U, \&V) \leftarrow \&V \; left\{\&Z, \; X\} \\ R2L(\&Y, \&Z) \end{array}}$$

Suppose that we start with $I = \emptyset$, and the forest F shown on Figure 4. Then we derive the correspondences $R2L(\&3, \&3')$, $R2L(\&2, \&2')$, $R2L(\&1, \&1')$. The computation is:

$$T^1_{r2l}(F, \emptyset) = F \cup R2L(\&3, \&3') \qquad T^2_{r2l}(F, \emptyset) = T^1_{r2l}(F, \emptyset) \cup R2L(\&2, \&2')$$
$$T^3_{r2l}(F, \emptyset) = T^2_{r2l}(F, \emptyset) \cup R2L(\&1, \&1') \qquad r2l(F, \emptyset) = T^3_{r2l}(F, \emptyset)$$

This kind of deep trees is frequent in data exchange formats and it is important to be able to handle them. However, what we have seen above is not quite powerful enough. It will have to be extended with particular operations on trees and to handle data collections. This is described next.

4 Dealing with Collections

When data sources are mapped into the middleware model, some forest vertexes may represent data collections. Observe that, in the above rules, the tree describes vertexes with a bounded number of children, (where the number depends on the term structure). Data collections may have an arbitrary number of members, and thus we need to extend our language to deal with vertexes having arbitrary number of children. Also observe that ordered trees are perfect to represent ordered data collections such as lists or arrays. However, if we want to model database constructs such as sets or bags, we have to consider properties such as insensitivity to order or duplicates. The rules that we developed so far do not support this. In this section, we address these two issues by extending our framework to incorporate (i) operators on trees and (ii) special collection properties.

4.1 Tree Constructors

We consider two binary operations on trees. The first, $cons(T_1, T_2)$, takes two objects as input. The first one is interpreted as an element and the second as the collection of its children vertexes. The operation adds the element to the collection. The second operator, $merge$, allows to merge two data collections into one. (The $cons$ operator can be defined using a merge with a singleton collection.) For example

$$mylist\{1, 2, 3, 4\} \equiv cons(1, mylist\{2, 3, 4\}) \equiv$$
$$merge(mylist\{1\}, mylist\{2, 3, 4\}) \equiv merge(mylist\{1, 2\}, mylist\{3, 4\})$$

More formally, let T, T', T'' be some trees where the roots of T' and T'' have the same label l and children $S'_1, ..., S'_n$ and $S''_1, ..., S''_m$ respectively. Then

- $cons(T, T')$ is a tree with root labeled by l and children $T, S'_1, ..., S'_n$, in that order.
- $merge(T', T'')$ is a tree with root labeled by l and children $S'_1, ..., S'_n, S''_1, ..., S''_m$, in that order.

The $cons$ and $merge$ operators provide alternative representations for collections that are essential to describe restructuring. The data trees in the forests we consider are all reduced in the sense that they will not include $cons$ or $merge$ vertexes. But, when using the rules, we are allowed to consider alternative representations of the forest trees. The vertexes/objects of the trees with $cons$ and $merge$ are regarded as implicit. So, for instance if we have the data tree $\&1 \; mylist\{\&2, \&3\}$, we can view it as $\&1 \; cons(\&2, \&v)$ where the object $\&v$ is implicit and has the structure $mylist\{\&3\}$. Indeed, we will denote this object $\&v$ by $mylist(\&1, \&3)$ to specify that it is an object with label $mylist$, that it is a subcollection of $\&1$, and that it has a single child $\&3$. This motivates the following definition:

Definition 5. Given a forest F, a vertex $\&v$ in F with children $\&v_1, ..., \&v_n$ (for $0 \leq n$) and label l, the expression $l(\&v, \&v_i, \&v_{i+1}, ..., \&v_j)$ is called an *implicit object* of F for each subsequence[6] $\&v_i, \&v_{i+1}..., \&v_j$ of $\&v_1, ..., \&v_n$. The set of all implicit objects of F is denoted $impl(F)$.

---

[6] A *subsequence* $\&v_i, \&v_{i+1}..., \&v_j$ of $\&v_1, ..., \&v_n$ is obtained by removing 0 or more elements from the head and the tail of $\&v_1, ..., \&v_n$.

Observe that $vertex(F)$ can be viewed as a subset of $impl(F)$ if we identify the object $l(\&v, \&v_1, ..., \&v_n)$ of the definition, with $\&v$. Observe also that the cardinality of $impl(F)$ is polynomial in the size of F.

We can now use *cons* and *merge* in rules. The following example uses *cons* to define a correspondence between a list structured as a right-deep tree and a list structured as a tree of depth one (Observe that in the example *mylist* is not a keyword but only a name with no particular semantics; *cons* is a keyword with semantics, the cons operation on trees):

$$tl: \frac{TreeList(\&U, \&V) \leftarrow \begin{array}{l} \&U\ R\{\} \\ \&V\ mylist\{\} \end{array}}{\begin{array}{l} \&U\ R\{Z, \&X\} \\ TreeList(\&U, \&V) \leftarrow \&V\ cons(Z, \&Y) \\ TreeList(\&X, \&Y) \end{array}}$$

Of course, to use such rules, we have to extend the notion of valuation to allow terms containing *cons*. The new valuation may now assign implicit objects to object variables.

The fixpoint $T_P^\omega(F, I)$ is computed as before using the new definition of valuation. Observe that $T_P^i(F, I)$ may now contain correspondences involving vertexes in $impl(F)$ and not only F. Since we are interested only in correspondences between vertexes in F, we ultimately ignore all other correspondences. So, $\mathcal{P}(F, I)$ is the restriction of $T_P^\omega(F, I)$ to objects in F. For instance, consider rule tl and $F = \{ \&1\ R\{a, \&2\ R\{b, \&3\ R\{\}\}\}\ ,\ \&1'\ mylist\{a, b\} \}$. Then:

$$impl(F) = F \cup \{mylist(\&1',), mylist(\&1', a), mylist(\&1', b), R(\&1), R(\&1, a), etc.\}$$
$$T_{tl}^1(F, \emptyset) = TreeList(\&3, mylist(\&1',))$$
$$T_{tl}^2(F, \emptyset) = T_{tl}^1(F, \emptyset) \cup TreeList(\&2, mylist(\&1', b))$$
$$T_{tl}^\omega(F, \emptyset) = T_{tl}^2(F, \emptyset) \cup TreeList(\&1, mylist(\&1', a, b)) = T_{tl}^2(F, \emptyset) \cup TreeList(\&1, \&1')$$
$$tl(F, \emptyset) = (F, TreeList(\&1, \&1'))$$

In the sequel, we call the problem of computing $\mathcal{P}(F, I)$, the *matching problem*.

Theorem 6. *The matching problem is in* PTIME *even in the presence of* cons *and* merge.

Sketch: The number of facts that can be derived is polynomial and each step can be computed with a first-order formula, so is polynomial. $\square$

4.2 Special Properties

Data models of interest include collections with specific properties: e.g., sets that are insensitive to order or duplicates, bags that are insensitive to order. In our context this translates to properties of vertexes with particular labels. We consider here two cases, namely insensitivity to order (called bag property), and insensitivity to both order and duplicates (called set property). For instance, we may decide that a particular label, say *mybag* (resp. *myset*) denotes a bag (resp. a set). Then, the system should not distinguish between:

$$cons(a, cons(a, mybag\ \{b\})) \equiv cons(a, cons(b, mybag\ \{a\}))$$
$$cons(a, cons(a, myset\ \{b\})) \equiv cons(a, myset\ \{b\})$$

The fact that these should be the same implicit objects is fundamental. (Otherwise the same set would potentially have an infinite number of representations and computing correspondences would become undecidable.) In the context of set/bag properties, the definition of implicit objects becomes a little bit more intricate.

Definition 7. Given a forest F, a vertex $\&v$ in F with children $\&v_1, ..., \&v_n$ (for $0 \le n$) and label l, implicit objects of vertexes with bag/set properties are obtained as follows:

l has *set* property: $l(\&v, \&v_{i_1}, ..., \&v_{i_j})$ for each subset $\{\&v_{i_1}, ..., \&v_{i_j}\}$ of $\{\&v_1, ..., \&v_n\}$.

l has *bag* property: $l(\&v, \&v_{i_1}, ..., \&v_{i_j})$ for each subbag $\{\{\&v_{i_1}, ..., \&v_{i_j}\}\}$ of $\{\{\&v_1, ..., \&v_n\}\}$.

The notion of valuation is extended in a straightforward manner to use the above implicit objects and take into consideration tree equivalence due to insensitivity to order and duplicates, (details omitted for lack of space). It is important to observe at this point that the number of implicit objects is now exponential in the size of F.

The next example shows how *cons*, and the set property can be used to define a correspondence between a list and a set containing one copy for each distinct list member:

$$
ls : \dfrac{ListSet(\&U, \&V) \leftarrow \begin{array}{l} \text{label } myset \quad : \text{ set} \\ \&U \ mylist \ \{\} \\ \&V \ myset \ \{\} \end{array}}{ListSet(\&U, \&V) \leftarrow \begin{array}{l} \&U \ cons(Z, \ \&X) \\ \&V \ cons(Z, \ \&Y) \\ ListSet(\&X, \&Y) \end{array}}
$$

Observe the symmetry of the rules between set and list. The only distinction is in the specification of label *myset*. Using essentially the same proof as in Theorem 6 and a reduction to 3-sat, one can prove:

Theorem 8. *In the presence of* cons, merge, *and collections that are insensitive to order/duplicates, the matching problem can be solved in* EXPTIME. *Even with insensitivity to order and cons only, the matching problem becomes* NP-hard.

Remark. The complexity is data complexity. This may seem a negative result (that should have been expected because of the matching of commutative collections). But in practice, merging is rarely achieved based on collections. It is most often key-based and, in some rare cases, based on the matching of "small collections", e.g., sets of authors.

To conclude the discussion of correspondence rules, and demonstrate the usage of *cons* and *merge*, let us consider the following example where a correspondence between articles and OO references is defined. Observe that while the correspondence rule r_{so} presented at the beginning of the paper handles articles with exactly three authors, articles/references here deal with arbitrary number of authors. They are required to have the same title and abstract and the same author list (i.e., the authors appear in the same order). The definition uses an auxiliary predicate *same_list*.

The first rule defines correspondence between authors. The second and third rules define an auxiliary correspondence between sequences from both world. It is used in rule R_4 that defines correspondence between articles and references. It also defines correspondence between titles and abstracts from both worlds.

$$
r_1 : is(\&X_0, \&X_2) \quad \leftarrow \begin{array}{l} \&X_0 \ author \ X_1 \\ \&X_2 \ author \ \{ \ fn \ X_3, \ ln \ X_4 \ \} \\ concat(X_1, X_3, X_4) \end{array}
$$

$$
r_2 : same\_list(\&X_0, \&X_2) \leftarrow \begin{array}{l} \&X_0 \ cons(\&X_1, \ \&X_2) \\ \&X_3 \ cons(\&X_4, \ \&X_5) \\ is(\&X_1, \&X_4) \\ same\_list(\&X_2, \&X_5) \end{array}
$$

$$
r_3 : same\_list(\&X_0, \&X_3) \leftarrow \begin{array}{l} \&X_0 \ \{\} \\ \&X_3 \ \{\} \end{array}
$$

$$
\begin{aligned}
&\&X_0 \; merge(\; \{\; \&X_1, \&X_2 \; title \; X_3\},\\
&\qquad\qquad\quad merge(\&X_4,\\
&\qquad\qquad\qquad\qquad article\{\&X_5 \; abstract \; X_6, \&X_7\;\}\;)\;)
\end{aligned}
$$

$$
r_4 : \begin{aligned}
&is(\&X_0, \&X_8)\\
&is(\&X_2, \&X_{10})\\
&is(\&X_5, \&X_{12})
\end{aligned} \quad \leftarrow \quad
\begin{aligned}
&\&X_8 \; reference \; \{\; \&X_9,\\
&\qquad\qquad\qquad \&X_{10} \; title \; X_3,\\
&\qquad\qquad\qquad \&X_{11},\\
&\qquad\qquad\qquad \&X_{12} \; abstract \; X_6 \;\}
\end{aligned}
$$

$$
same\_list(\&X_4, \&X_{11})
$$

We illustrated the language using rather simple examples. Nevertheless, it is quite powerful and can describe many desired correspondences, and in particular all the document-OODB mappings supported by the *structuring schemas* mechanism of [2, 3] (Omitted).

5 Data Translation

Correspondence rules are used to derive relationships between vertexes. We next consider the problem of translating data. We first state the general translation problem (that is undecidable). We then introduce a decidable subcase that captures the practical applications we are interested in. This is based on *translation rules* obtained by moving tree terms from the body of correspondence rules to the head.

We start with a data forest and a set of correspondence rules. For a particular forest object $\&v$ and a correspondence predicate C, we want to know if the forest can be extended in such a way that $\&v$ is in correspondence to some vertex $\&v'$. In some sense, $\&v'$ could be seen as the "translation" of $\&v$. This is what we call the *data translation problem*.

input: an R-correspondence (F, I), a set $\mathcal{P}$ of correspondence rules, a vertex $\&v$ of F, and a binary predicate C.

output: an extension F' of F such that $C(\&v, \&v')$ holds in $\mathcal{P}(F', I)$ for some $\&v'$; or *no* if no such extension exists.

For example consider a forest F with the right deep tree $\&1 \{1, \{2, \{3, \{\}\}\}\}$. Assume we want to translate it into a left deep tree format. Recall that the *r2l* correspondence rules define correspondences between right deep trees and left deep trees. So, we can give the translation problem the R-correspondence (F, I), the root vertex $\&1$, and the correspondence predicate $R2L$. The output will be a forest F' with some vertex $\&v'$ s.t. $R2L(\&1, \&v')$ holds. The tree rooted at $\&v'$ is exactly the left deep tree we are looking for.

Remark. In the general case: (i) we would like to translate an entire collection of objects; and (ii) the correspondence may be a predicate of arbitrary arity. To simplify the presentation, we consider the more restricted problem defined above. The same techniques work for the general case with minor modifications.

It turns out that data translation is in general very difficult. (The proof is by reduction of the acceptance problem of Turing machines.)

Proposition 5.1 *The translation problem is undecidable, even in absence of cons, merge, and labels with set/bag properties.*

Although the problem is undecidable in general, we show next that translation is still possible in many practical cases and can often be performed efficiently. To do this, we impose two restrictions:

1. The first restriction we impose is that we separate data into two categories, input vertexes and output vertexes. Vertex variables and labels are similarly separated[7]. We assume that the presence of an output object depends solely on the presence of some input object(s) and possibly some correspondence conditions. It allows us to focus on essentially one kind of recursion: that found in the source data structure.
2. The second restriction is more technical and based on a property called *body restriction* that is defined in the sequel. It prevents pathological behavior and mostly prevent correspondences that relate "inside" of tree terms.

---

[7] Note that vertexes can easily be distinguished using their label.

These restrictions typically apply when considering data translation or integration, and in particular we will see that all the examples above have the appropriate properties.

The basic idea is to use correspondence rules and transform them into translation rules by moving data tree terms containing output variables from the body of rules to their head. For example, consider the $r2l$ correspondence rules. To translate a right deep tree into a left deep tree, we move the terms of the left deep trees to the head of rules, and obtain the following translation rules. (Variables with prime are used to stress the separation between the two worlds.)

$$r2l' : \frac{r : \begin{array}{l} \&U'\ L\{\} \\ R2L(\&U, \&U') \end{array} \leftarrow \&U\ R\{\}}{r' : \begin{array}{l} \&U'\ L\{\&Y',\ X\} \\ R2L(\&U, \&U') \end{array} \leftarrow \begin{array}{l} \&U\ R\{X,\ \&Y\} \\ R2L(\&Y, \&Y') \end{array}}$$

Of course we need to extend the semantics of rules. The tree terms in the head, and in particular those containing variables that do not appear in the body, are used to create new objects. (This essentially will do the data translation). We use Skolem functions in the style of [9, 14, 16, 18] to denote new object ids. There are some difficulties in doing so. Consider a valuation ν of the second rule above. One may be tempted to use the Skolem term $r'(\nu(\&U), \nu(X), \nu(\&Y), \nu(\&Y'))$ to denote the new object. But since $\&Y'$ is itself a created object, this may lead to a potentially non-terminating loop of object creation. To avoid this we choose to create objects only as a function of **input** objects and not of new output created objects. (Thus in the above case the created object is denoted $r'\&U'(\nu(\&U), \nu(X), \nu(\&Y))$.)

Now, the price for this is that (i) we may be excluding some object creation that could be of interest; and (ii) this may result in inconsistencies (e.g., the same object with two distinct values). We accept (i), although we will give a class of programs such that (i) never occurs. For (ii), we rely on non determinism to choose one value to be assigned to one object. Note that we need some form of nondeterminism for instance to construct a list representation from a set.

For lack of space we do not give here the refined semantics for rules, (it is given in the full paper,) but only state that:

Proposition 9. *For each finite set $\mathcal{P}$ of translation-rules and each R-correspondence (F, I), each of the possible sequences of application of $T_{\mathcal{P}}$ converges in a finite number of stages. Furthermore, for rules with no set/bag labels each sequence converges in* PTIME, *and otherwise in* EXPTIME.

So far, a program computation can be viewed as purely syntactic. We are guaranteed to terminate, but we don't know the semantic properties of the constructed new objects and derived correspondences.

It turns out this evaluation of translation rules allows to solve the translation problem for a large class of correspondence rules. (Clearly not all since the problem is unsolvable in general.) In particular it covers all rules we presented in the previous section, and the translations specified by the structuring schemas mechanisms of [3] (proof omitted). We next present conditions under which the technique can be used.

Definition 10. A correspondence rule r is said to be *body restricted* if in its body (1) all the variables in correspondence literals are leaves of tree terms, and each such variable has at most one occurrence in a correspondence literal, and (2) non-leaf variables have at most one occurrence (as non leafs) in tree terms, and (3) the only variables that input and output tree terms share are leaf variables.

We are considering correspondences specified with input/output data forests.

Proposition 5.2 *Consider an input/output context. Let $\mathcal{P}$ be a set of body restricted correspondence rules where correspondence literals always relate input to output objects. Let (F, I) be an R-correspondence where F is an input data forest, $\&v$ a vertex in F, and C a binary correspondence predicate. Let $\mathcal{P}'$ be the translation rules obtained from $\mathcal{P}$ by moving all output tree terms to the head of rules. Then,*

- *If the translation problem has a solution on input (F, I) $\mathcal{P}$, $\&v$, C that leaves the input forest unchanged, then each possible computations of $\mathcal{P}'(F, I)$ derives $C(\&v, \&v')$ for some output object $\&v'$.*

– *if some computation of $\mathcal{P}'$ derives $C(\&v, \&v')$ for some object $\&v'$, then the forest F' computed by this computation is a correct solution to the translation problem.*

By Proposition 5.2, to solve the translation problem (with unmodified input) for body restricted rules, we only need to compute nondeterministically one of the possible outputs of $\mathcal{P}$, and test if $C(\&v, \&v')$ holds for some $\&v'$.

6 Conclusion

We presented a specification of the integration of heterogeneous data based on correspondence rules. We showed how a unique specification can served many purposes (including two-way translation) assuming some reasonable restrictions. We claim that the framework and restrictions are acceptable in practice, and in particular one can show that all the document-OODB correspondences/translations of [2, 3] are covered. We are currently working on further substantiating this by more experimentation.

When applying the work presented here a number of issues arise such as the specification of default values when some information is missing in the translation. A more complex one is the introduction of some simple constraints in the model, e.g., keys.

Another important implementation issue is to choose between keeping one of the representations virtual vs. materializing both. In particular, it is conceivable to apply in this larger setting the optimization techniques developed in a OODB/SGML context for queries [2] and updates [3].

Acknowledgment: We thank Catriel Beeri for his comments on a first draft of the paper.

References

1. S. Abiteboul and C. Beeri. On the power of languages for the manipulation of complex objects. Technical report, INRIA and the department of computer science of the Hebrew University of Israel, 1987.
2. S. Abiteboul, S. Cluet, and T. Milo. Querying and updating the file. In *Proc. VLDB*, 1993.
3. S. Abiteboul, S. Cluet, and T. Milo. A database interface for files update. In *Proc. of the ACM SIGMOD Conf. on Management of Data*, San Jose, California, 1995.
4. S. Abiteboul and P. C. Kanellakis. Object identity as a query language primitive. In *Proc. of the ACM SIGMOD Conf. on Management of Data*, pages 159–173, 1989. to appear in *J. ACM*.
5. C. Beeri, S. Naqvi, R. Ramakrishnan, O. Shmueli, and S. Tsur. Sets and negation in a logic database language (LDL1). In *Proc. ACM SIGMOD/SIGACT Conf. on Princ. of Database Syst. (PODS)*, pages 21–37, 1987.
6. P. Buneman, S. Davidson, K. Hart, C. Overton, and L. Wong. A data transformation system for biological data sources. In *Proc. Int. Conf. on Very Large Data Bases (VLDB)*, pages 158–169, Zurich, Switzerland, 1995.
7. P. Buneman, S. Davidson, and D. Suciu. Programming constructs for unstructured data, May 1996.
8. M.J. Carey et al. Towards heterogeneous multimedia information systems: The Garlic approach. Technical Report RJ 9911, IBM Almaden Research Center, 1994.
9. T.-P. Chang and R. Hull. Using witness generators to support bi-directional update between object-based databases. In *Proc. ACM SIGMOD/SIGACT Conf. on Princ. of Database Syst. (PODS)*, San Jose, California, May 1995.
10. V. Christophides, S. Abiteboul, S. Cluet, and M. Scholl. From structured documents to novel query facilities. In *Proc. ACM Sigmod, Minneapolis*, 1994.
11. O. Deux. The story of O_2. *IEEE Trans. on Data and Knowledge Eng.*, 2(1):91–108, March 1990.
12. J.C. Franchitti and R. King. Amalgame: a tool for creating interoperating persistent, heterogeneous components. *Advanced Database Systems*, pages 313–36, 1993.
13. M. Gyssens, J.Paredaens, and D. V. Gucht. A grammar based approach towards unifying hierarchical data models. In *Proc. of the ACM SIGMOD Conf. on Management of Data*, 1989.
14. R. Hull and M. Yoshikawa. ILOG: Declarative creation and manipulation of object-identifiers. In *Proc. Int. Conf. on Very Large Data Bases (VLDB)*, Brisbane, Australia, Aug 1990.
15. M. Kifer and G. Lausen. F-logic: A higher-order language for reasoning about objects. In *sigmod*, 1989.
16. M. Kifer, G. Lausen, and Wu James. Logical foundations of object-oriented and frame-based languages. *Journal of ACM*, MAY 1995.

17. G. M. Kuper and M. Y. Vardi. The logical data model. *ACM Trans. on Database Systems*, 18(3):379–413, Sept 1993.

18. D. Maier. A logic for objects. Technical Report TR CS/E-86-012, Oregon Graduate Center, Nov 1986.

19. Y. Papakonstantinou, H. Garcia-Molina, and J. Ullman. Medmaker: A mediation system based on declarative specifications. Available by anonymous ftp at db.stanford.edu as the file /pub/papakonstantinou/1995/medmaker.ps.

20. Y. Papakonstantinou, H. Garcia-Molina, and J. Widom. Object exchange across heterogeneous information sources. In *International Conference on Data Engineering*, 1995.

21. D. Quass, A. Rajaraman, Y. Sagiv, J. Ullman, and J. Widom. Querying semistructured heterogeneous information. Technical report, Stanford University, 1995. Available by anonymous ftp from db.stanford.edu.

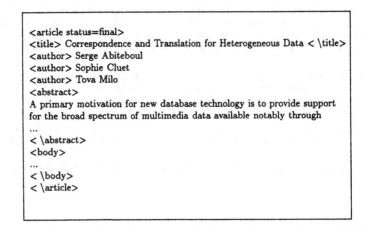

Fig. 1. An instance of an SGML document

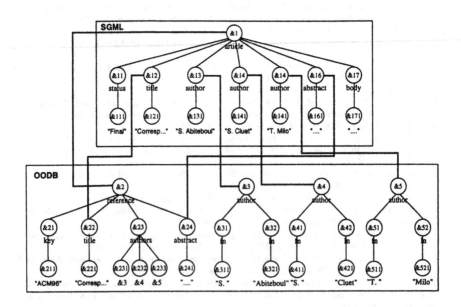

Fig. 2. Correspondence between SGML file and an OODB

vertex label		children
&2	reference	{&21, &22, &23}
&21	key	{&211}
&211	"ACM96"	{ }
&22	title	{&221}
&221	"Correspondence..."	{ }
&23	authors	{&231, &232, &233}
&231	&3	{ }
&232	&4	{ }
&233	&5	{ }
&24	abstract	{&241}
&241	"..."	{ }
&3	author	{&31, &32}
&31	fn	{&311}
&311	"S."	{ }
&32	ln	{&321}
&321	"Abiteboul"	{ }
...		

Fig. 3. A Data Forest

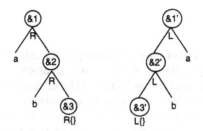

Fig. 4. Right- and Left-Deep Trees

Type-Consistency Problems for Queries in Object-Oriented Databases

Yasunori ISHIHARA   Hiroyuki SEKI   Minoru ITO

Graduate School of Information Science
Nara Institute of Science and Technology
E-mail: {ishihara, seki, ito}@is.aist-nara.ac.jp

Abstract Method invocation mechanism is one of the essential features in object-oriented programming languages. This mechanism contributes to data encapsulation and code reuse, but there is a risk of run-time type errors. In the case of object-oriented databases (OODBs), a run-time error causes rollback. Therefore, it is desirable to ensure that a given OODB schema is consistent, i.e., no run-time type error occurs during the execution of queries under any database instance of the OODB schema.

This paper discusses the computational complexity of type-consistency problems. As a model of OODB schemas, we adopt update schemas introduced by Hull et al., which have all of the basic features of OODBs such as class hierarchy, inheritance, complex objects, and so on. For some subclasses of update schemas, the complexity of a type-consistency problem is presented. Importantly, it turns out that non-flatness of the class hierarchy, nontermination of queries, and update operations in queries each make the problem difficult.

1 Introduction

Among the many features of object-oriented programming languages (OOPLs), method invocation (or message passing) mechanism is an essential one. It is based on method name overloading and late binding by method inheritance along the class hierarchy. For a method name m, different classes may have different definitions (codes, implementations) of m. When m is applied to an object o, one of its definitions is selected depending on the class to which o belongs, and is bound to m in run-time (late binding or dynamic binding). This mechanism is important for data encapsulation and code reuse, but there is a risk of run-time type errors. For example, when a method m is invoked, the definition of m to be bound may not be uniquely determined. Particularly with queries in object-oriented databases (OODBs), a run-time error causes rollback, i.e., all the modification up to the error must be cancelled.

In this paper, we discuss the computational complexity of type-consistency problems for queries in OODBs. A database schema **S** is said to be *consistent* if no type error occurs during the execution of any method under any database instance, i.e.,

1. for every method invocation m, the definition of m to be bound is uniquely determined by using the class hierarchy with inheritance; and
2. no attribute-value update violates any type declaration given by **S**.

It is quite advantageous for a given database schema to be consistent. First, since it is ensured at compile-time that no type error occurs under any database instance, run-time type check can be omitted. Another advantage is an application to method-based authorization checking [4], [5], [13].

As a model of OODB schemas, we adopt *update schemas* [9] introduced by Hull et al. Update schemas have all of the basic features of OODBs, such as class hierarchy, inheritance, complex objects, and so on. Method implementations are based on a procedural OOPL model. Therefore, updating database instances is simply modeled as assignment of objects or basic values to attributes of objects. In Ref. [9], it is shown that the type-consistency problem for update schemas is undecidable. In Ref. [13], a subclass of update schemas, called *non-branching update schemas*, is introduced. And, it is shown that consistency for a given non-branching update schema is solvable in polynomial time provided that all the database instances are acyclic.

The aim of this paper is to investigate the computational complexity of the type-consistency problem. We focus on the following three factors and show that each of them creates difficulty in the problem (see also Fig. 1):

1. *Non-flatness of the class hierarchy* (Sect. 3.1). Define the *height* of the class hierarchy as the maximum length of a path in the hierarchy. If the height is zero, then all classes are completely separated and there is no superclass-subclass relation at all. For such a "flat" database schema, consistency is in P. However, consistency for a non-flat schema is undecidable even if the height of the class hierarchy is bounded by one.

2. *Nontermination* (Sect. 3.2). A database schema S is said to be *terminating* if the execution of every method terminates under every database instance of S. Consistency for a terminating retrieval (see below) schema is in P, while consistency for a very restricted but nonterminating retrieval schema is coNP-hard. Although termination property is undecidable for an arbitrary schema [9], there are decidable sufficient conditions such as recursion-freeness.

3. *Update operations* (Sect. 3.3). A database schema S is said to be *retrieval* if no method definition in S contains any update operation. As stated above, consistency for a terminating retrieval schema is in P. On the other hand, consistency for a recursion-free (thus terminating) update schema is coNEXPTIME-complete even if the height of the class hierarchy is bounded by one.

The model adopted in this paper requires the following three conditions. First, every method should be monadic (i.e., every method should have exactly one argument). From the result in [2], it is easily shown that if the number of arguments is not bounded, then the consistency problem becomes undecidable even for retrieval schemas. Secondly, there should be no program constructs such as conditional branch and while statement. Actually, by using update operations, if-then statements can be simulated (see Example 3). Thirdly, the class hierarchy should be a forest (i.e., multiple inheritance is excluded). However, the results in this paper remain valid if an appropriate mechanism for multiple inheritance is incorporated into the model. That is, the third condition is merely for simplicity.

There has been much research on type-consistency problems for OOPLs. For example, Abiteboul et al. [2] introduced *method schemas* and studied the complexity of the type-consistency problems for many subclasses of them. In method schemas, each method is allowed to have more than one arguments. However, method schemas cannot represent updates of database instance since their method implementations are based on a functional OOPL model. The followings are some of the main results of Ref. [2]:

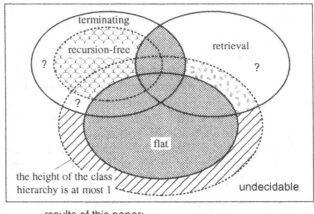

results of this paper:

▦ : solvable in polynomial time
▨ : coNP-hard
▨ : coNEXPTIME-complete
▨ : undecidable

Fig. 1. Complexity of Type-Consistency Problems.

1. consistency for a method schema is undecidable,
2. coNP-complete for a recursion-free method schema, and
3. solvable in polynomial time for a monadic method schema (that belongs to a proper subclass of retrieval schemas of ours).

Moreover, for a recursion-free method schema, an optimal incremental algorithm for the consistency checking is presented in Ref. [14]. In Ref. [1], the complexity of type-consistency (and also the expressive power) for both update and method schemas is summarized.

In Ref. [11], a type inference algorithm for a procedural OOPL is proposed. For each expression e of a program, a type variable $[\![e]\!]$ that denotes the type of e is introduced, and type-consistency is analyzed by computing the least solution of the equations that denote the relations among these type variables (also see Refs. [10] and [12]). In Refs. [3] and [6], another kind of type-consistency is discussed. It is assumed that we know in advance the class to which the returned objects should belong for every method implementation body. Then the consistency problem is simply to determine whether for each method name m, the already-known classes of the returned objects of all the implementation bodies of m satisfy a condition such as contravariance. Therefore, no analysis of method implementation bodies are necessary. Type systems for OOPLs have also been extensively studied [7], [8]. However, computational complexity of the type-consistency problem has scarcely been studied in these articles.

The remainder of the paper is organized as follows. In Sect. 2, we define database schemas and their instances, and show some examples. In Sect. 3, we show the computational complexity of the type-consistency problems for several subclasses of database schemas mentioned above. Lastly, in Sect. 4, we summarize the paper.

2 Database Schemas

2.1 Syntax

Definition 1. A *database schema* is a 6-tuple $S = (C, \leq, Attr, Ad, Meth, Impl)$ where:

1. C is a finite set of *class names*.
2. $\leq$ is a partial order on C representing a *class hierarchy*. If $c' \leq c$, then we say that c' is a *subclass* of c and c is a *superclass* of c'. For simplicity, we assume that the class hierarchy is a forest on C, that is, for all $c_1, c_2, c \in C$, either $c_1 \leq c_2$ or $c_2 \leq c_1$ whenever $c \leq c_1$ and $c \leq c_2$.
3. *Attr* is a finite set of *attribute names*.
4. $Ad : C \times Attr \rightarrow C$ is a partial function representing *attribute declarations*. By $Ad(c, a) = c'$, we mean that the value of attribute a of an object of c must be an object of c' or its subclass.
5. *Meth* is a finite set of *method names*.
6. $Impl : C \times Meth \rightarrow WFS$ is a partial function representing *method implementations*, where *WFS* is the set of *well-formed sequences of sentences* defined below.

A sentence is an expression which has one of the following forms:

1. $y := y'$,	4. $y := m(y')$,
2. $y := \text{self}$,	5. $\text{self}.a := y'$,
3. $y := \text{self}.a$,	6. $\text{return}(y')$,

where y, y' are *variables*, a is an attribute name, m is a method name, and self is a reserved word that denotes the object on which a method is invoked (or, to which a message is sent). Let $s_1; s_2; \cdots; s_n \ (= \alpha)$ be a sequence of sentences. We say that α is *well-formed* when no undefined variable is referred to and only the last sentence s_n has the form $\text{return}(y')$ for some variable y' (thus the other sentences $s_1, s_2, \ldots, s_{n-1}$ must be one of types 1 to 5). □

Example 1. Consider the following three sequences of sentences:

$s_{11} : y := \text{self}.a;$	$s_{21} : y' := \text{self}.a;$	$s_{31} : y := \text{self}.a;$
$s_{12} : \text{self}.a' := y;$	$s_{22} : \text{self}.a' := y';$	$s_{32} : \text{self}.a' := y;$
$s_{13} : y' := m(y);$	$s_{23} : y' := m(y);$	$s_{33} : \text{return}(y);$
$s_{14} : \text{return}(y').$	$s_{24} : \text{return}(y').$	$s_{34} : y' := m(y).$
(a)	(b)	(c)

Sequence (a) is well-formed while (b) is not, since sentence s_{23} refers to variable y but no value is assigned to y in any of the preceding sentences s_{21} and s_{22}. Neither is sequence (c) since the last sentence s_{34} is not in the form of $\text{return}(y')$. □

Without loss of generality, we often omit temporary variables for readability. For example, we write "$y := m(\text{self}.a)$" instead of "$y' := \text{self}.a; \ y := m(y')$," where y' is a temporary variable.

Definition 2. The *description size* of S, denoted $\|S\|$, is defined as follows:

$$\|S\| = \ |C| + |Attr| + |Meth|$$
$$+ \text{(the number of attribute declarations given by } Ad)$$
$$+ \text{(the total number of sentences given by } Impl),$$

where $|X|$ is the cardinality of a set X. □

2.2 Semantics

The *inherited implementation* of method m at class c, denoted $Impl^*(c, m)$, is defined as $Impl(c', m)$ such that c' is the smallest superclass of c (with respect to the partial order $\leq$) at which an implementation of m exists, that is, if $Impl(c'', m)$ is defined and $c \leq c''$, then it must hold that $c' \leq c''$. If such an implementation does not exist, then $Impl^*(c, m)$ is undefined. Similarly, the *inherited attribute declaration* of attribute a at class c, denoted $Ad^*(c, a)$, is defined as $Ad(c', a)$ such that c' is the smallest superclass of c at which an attribute declaration of a exists. If such an attribute declaration does not exist, then $Ad^*(c, a)$ is undefined.

A *database instance* of $\mathbf{S}$ is a pair $\mathbf{I} = (\nu, \mu)$, where:

1. To each class $c \in C$, ν assigns a disjoint, finite set, denoted $\nu(c)$, as *object identifiers* for c. Each $o \in \nu(c)$ is called an *object* of class c. Let $O_{\mathbf{S},\mathbf{I}} = \cup_{c \in C} \nu(c)$. Let $cl(o)$ denote the class c such that $o \in \nu(c)$.
2. To each object $o \in \nu(c)$ and each attribute $a \in Attr$ such that $Ad^*(c, a)$ is defined, μ assigns an object, denoted $\mu(o, a)$, that is the *value* of attribute a (or simply a-value) of o. If $Ad^*(c, a) = c'$, then $\mu(o, a)$ must belong to $\nu(c'')$ for some c'' ($c'' \leq c'$). Hereafter, we often denote $\mu(o, a)$ by $o.a$.

The *operational semantics* of $\mathbf{S}$ is originally defined by using a *method execution tree* [9]. In this paper, we give a simpler definition, in which the execution of a method is defined by rewriting rules on configurations of an interpreter for method implementations.

Definition 3. A *configuration* is one of the expressions

$$\langle \mu, o \rangle, \quad active(\mu, o, m, i, \sigma), \quad CF \circ await(o, m, i, \sigma),$$

where μ is an assignment denoting attribute values, o is an object, m is a method name, i is an integer, σ is an assignment of objects to variables appearing in $Impl$, and CF is a configuration. An *initial configuration* is $active(\mu, o, m, 1, \sigma_\perp)$ such that $Impl^*(cl(o), m)$ is defined, where $\sigma_\perp$ is an assignment undefined everywhere. $\qquad \square$

Although the formal semantics of configurations is presented in the next definition, we give an informal explanation here. $active(\mu, o, m, i, \sigma)$ means that the interpreter is executing the i-th sentence of $Impl^*(cl(o), m)$, where self in $Impl^*(cl(o), m)$ is interpreted as o, the current variable assignment is given by σ, and the current database instance is given by μ. $CF \circ await(o, m, i, \sigma)$ represents that another method has been invoked at the i-th sentence of $Impl^*(cl(o), m)$. $\langle \mu, o \rangle$ is the pair of the resulting database instance and the returned value after an execution of a method.

Definition 4. Let $s(c, m, i)$ denote the i-th sentence of $Impl^*(c, m)$. Let $f[a/b]$ denote the function f' such that $f'(a) = b$ and $f'(x) = f(x)$ for all $x \neq a$. The *one-step execution relation* $\rightarrow$ on configurations is defined as shown in Table 1. Note that the execution is deterministic, that is, for every configuration CF, there is at most one CF' such that $CF \rightarrow CF'$. $\qquad \square$

Definition 5. Let $o \in O_{\mathbf{S},\mathbf{I}}$. A *partial execution* of method m for object o under instance $\mathbf{I}$ is a (possibly infinite) sequence $EX = \langle CF_0, CF_1, \ldots \rangle$ of configurations such that $CF_0 = active(\mu, o, m, 1, \sigma_\perp)$ is the initial configuration and $CF_i \rightarrow CF_{i+1}$ for all i.

Table 1. One-Step Execution Relation.

(R1) If $s(cl(o), m, i) = $ "$y := y'$,"

$$active(\mu, o, m, i, \sigma) \rightarrow active(\mu, o, m, i + 1, \sigma[y/\sigma(y')]).$$

(R2) If $s(cl(o), m, i) = $ "$y := $ self,"

$$active(\mu, o, m, i, \sigma) \rightarrow active(\mu, o, m, i + 1, \sigma[y/o]).$$

(R3) If $s(cl(o), m, i) = $ "$y := $ self.a,"

$$active(\mu, o, m, i, \sigma) \rightarrow active(\mu, o, m, i + 1, \sigma[y/\mu(o, a)]).$$

(R4) If $s(cl(o), m, i) = $ "$y := m'(y')$" and $Impl^*(cl(\sigma(y')), m')$ is defined,

$$active(\mu, o, m, i, \sigma) \rightarrow active(\mu, \sigma(y'), m', 1, \sigma_\perp) \circ await(o, m, i, \sigma).$$

(R5) If $s(cl(o), m, i) = $ "self.$a := y'$" and $cl(\sigma(y')) \leq Ad^*(cl(o), a)$,

$$active(\mu, o, m, i, \sigma) \rightarrow active(\mu[(o, a)/\sigma(y')], o, m, i + 1, \sigma).$$

(R6) If $s(cl(o), m, i) = $ "return(y'),"

$$active(\mu, o, m, i, \sigma) \rightarrow \langle \mu, \sigma(y') \rangle.$$

(R7) If $s(cl(o), m, i) = $ "$y := m'(y')$,"

$$\langle \mu, o' \rangle \circ await(o, m, i, \sigma) \rightarrow active(\mu, o, m, i + 1, \sigma[y/o']).$$

A partial execution EX is said to be *terminating* if $EX = \langle CF_0, \ldots, CF_n \rangle$ is a finite sequence and there is no CF_{n+1} such that $CF_n \rightarrow CF_{n+1}$. If on the other hand EX is an infinite sequence, then EX is said to be *nonterminating*. Furthermore, EX is said to be *complete* if it is either terminating or nonterminating. □

Definition 6. A terminating execution $EX = \langle CF_0, \ldots, CF_n \rangle$ is *successful* if $CF_n = \langle \mu', o' \rangle$ for some μ' and o', and *aborted* otherwise. □

Aborted executions are caused by two types of sentences "$y := m'(y')$" and "self.$a := y'$." By the rewriting rule (R4), an execution is aborted if method m' is undefined for the class of the object assigned to y'. By (R5), an execution is aborted if the class of the object assigned to y' violates the attribute declaration given by Ad. Both cases are viewed as *type errors*. Now we are ready for defining the notions of consistency and termination.

Definition 7. **S** is *consistent* if every terminating execution is successful under every instance of **S**, and **S** is *terminating* if every complete execution is terminating under every instance of **S**. □

Example 2. Consider a database schema $\mathbf{S}_1 = (C_1, \leq_1, Attr_1, Ad_1, Meth_1, Impl_1)$, where

- $C_1 = \{$director, manager, employee$\}$ and director $\leq_1$ manager $\leq_1$ employee;
- $Attr_1 = \{$boss, supervisor, secretary$\}$ and Ad_1 is shown in Fig. 2; and
- $Meth_1 = \{$get_secretary, query1$\}$ and $Impl_1$ is shown in Fig. 3.

Class employee
boss, supervisor : employee

Class manager
boss, supervisor : director

Class director
secretary : employee

(director, get_secretary) :
return(self.secretary).

(employee, query1) :
y := get_secretary(self.supervisor);
return(y).

Fig. 2. Definition of Ad_1.

Fig. 3. Definition of $Impl_1$.

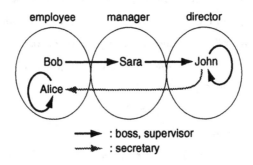

Fig. 4. A Database Instance $\mathbf{I}_1$.

Fig. 4 illustrates a database instance $\mathbf{I}_1 = (\nu_1, \mu_1)$ of $\mathbf{S}_1$, where Bob, Sara,... are objects and Bob $\rightarrow$ Sara means $\mu_1(\text{Bob, boss}) = \mu_1(\text{Bob, supervisor}) = \text{Sara}$. Consider the execution of query1 on Bob. Since $\mu_1(\text{Bob, supervisor}) = \text{Sara} \in \nu_1(\text{manager})$ and $Impl_1^*(\text{manager, get\_secretary})$ is undefined, the execution is aborted. And it is easily checked that $\mathbf{S}_1$ is terminating.

Let $\mathbf{S}_1' = (C_1, \leq_1, Attr_1, Ad_1, Meth_1', Impl_1')$, where $Meth_1' = \{\text{calc\_supervisor}, \text{get\_secretary, query2}\}$ and $Impl_1'$ is shown in Fig. 5. $\mathbf{I}_1$ is also an instance of $\mathbf{S}_1'$. The execution of calc_supervisor for Bob is successful and the last configuration is $\langle \mu_1, \text{John} \rangle$, i.e., the returned value of the execution is John. On the other hand, the execution of calc_supervisor for Alice is nonterminating. It can be shown that calc_supervisor returns an object of class director when it terminates. Then consider the execution of query2 on Bob. When control reaches the second sentence of (employee, query2) in Fig. 5, Bob.supervisor has been set to John $\in \nu_1(\text{director})$. Therefore the execution is successful. Consequently, it can be proved that $\mathbf{S}_1'$ is consistent. $\qquad \square$

Example 3. Consider a database schema $\mathbf{S}_2 = (C_2, \leq_2, Attr_2, Ad_2, Meth_2, Impl_2)$, where

- $C_2 = \{c, c_t, c_f\}$ such that $c_t \leq_2 c$ and $c_f \leq_2 c$ (i.e., c is a superclass of both c_t and c_f, see Fig. 6(a)); and
- Ad_2 is shown in Fig. 6(b).

We adopt the following Boolean-value representation: Let o be an object of class c_t. Each attribute $a \in \{a_1, a_2, a', a_f\}$ of o represents true if $o.a = o$, and false otherwise. Note that $o.a_f$ always represents false because of the declaration $Ad_2(c_t, a_f) = c_f$.

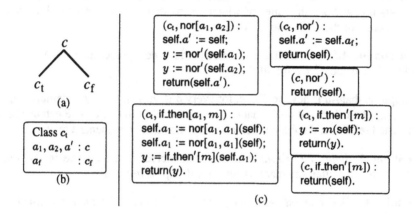

Fig. 5. Definition of $Impl'_1$.

Fig. 6. Definition of S_2.

Then, we define two methods $nor[a_1, a_2]$ and $if\_then[a_1, m]$ as shown in Fig. 6(c). $nor[a_1, a_2]$ calculates NOR of $o.a_1$ and $o.a_2$. Since every Boolean operator can be represented by NORs, we can construct a method which calculates every given Boolean formula by using $nor[a_1, a_2]$. On the other hand, $if\_then[a_1, m]$ simulates if-then statements: m is invoked on o if and only if $o.a_1 = o$. By the first two lines of $(c_t, if\_then[a_1, m])$, $o.a_1$ is "normalized" so that $o.a_1 = o.a_f$ whenever $o.a_1$ represents false. □

2.3 Subclasses of the Database Schema

In the last part of this section, we define some notions to define subclasses of the database schema.

Definition 8. The *height* of $\leq$ is defined as the maximal integer n such that there exist distinct $c_0, c_1, \ldots, c_n \in C$ satisfying $c_0 \leq c_1 \leq \cdots \leq c_n$. □

If the height of $\leq$ is zero, then the class hierarchy is *flat*. That is, all classes are completely separated and there is no superclass-subclass relation at all. We often say that **S** is *flat* if $\leq$ is flat.

Definition 9. *Ad* is *covariant* if $c_1 \leq c_2$ implies $Ad^*(c_1, a) \leq Ad^*(c_2, a)$ for all $c_1, c_2 \in C$ and $a \in Attr$. □

Usually, covariance is defined as a property of method signatures. For example, in Ref. [2], a schema is said to be covariant if for each built-in method m (assumed to be monadic for simplicity) and for each pair $(m : c_1 \rightarrow c_1')$, $(m : c_2 \rightarrow c_2')$ of signatures of m, we have that $c_1' \leq c_2'$ whenever $c_1 \leq c_2$. In our model, an attribute a can be regarded as a built-in method m_a such that the signatures of m_a are given by Ad and the interpretation of m_a is given by a database instance.

There are many situations in which it is natural to assume the covariance. For example, technical_paper $\leq$ literature and Ad^*(technical_paper, author) $\leq$ Ad^*(literature, author), the latter of which means that the authors of technical-papers are a subclass of those of general literatures.

Definition 10. *Ad* is *acyclic* if there exists a partial order $\sqsubseteq$ on C such that $Ad^*(c, a) = c'$ implies $c'' \sqsubseteq c$ and $c'' \neq c$ for all $c'' \leq c'$. □

Suppose that Ad is acyclic. Then, for every $o \in \nu(c)$ and every nonempty sequence $a_1, \ldots, a_n$ of attributes, it holds that $o.a_1.\ldots.a_n \notin \nu(c)$. In this case, **S** can be regarded as a nested relational database schema, where each class represents a relation.

Definition 11. *Impl* is *retrieval* if it does not include any sentence in the form of "self.$a := y$." We often say that **S** is *retrieval* if *Impl* is retrieval. □

Definition 12. The *method dependency graph* $G = (V, E)$ of *Impl* is defined as follows [2]:

- $V = Meth$; and
- An edge from m to m' is in E if and only if there is a class c such that m appears in *Impl*(c, m').

If the method dependency graph of *Impl* is acyclic, then *Impl* is *recursion-free*. We often say that **S** is *recursion-free* if *Impl* is recursion-free. Note that **S** is terminating whenever it is recursion-free. □

3 Complexity of the Type-Consistency Problem

3.1 Non-Flatness of the Class Hierarchy

In this section, we show how non-flatness of the class hierarchy affects the complexity of the type-consistency problem. First, the following theorem says that consistency for a flat schema is solvable in polynomial time.

Theorem 13. *Let* $\mathbf{S} = (C, \leq, Attr, Ad, Meth, Impl)$ *be a database schema. If* **S** *is flat, then consistency for* **S** *is in P.*

Proof. Define an instance $\tilde{\mathbf{I}} = (\tilde{\nu}, \tilde{\mu})$ of **S** as follows:

- $\tilde{\nu}(c) = \{o_c\}$ for each $c \in C$; and
- $\tilde{\mu}(o_c, a) = o_{c'}$ if $Ad^*(c, a) = c'$.

First, we show that there is an aborted execution under $\tilde{\mathbf{I}}$ if and only if $\mathbf{S}$ is inconsistent. It is clear that there is an aborted execution under $\tilde{\mathbf{I}}$ only if $\mathbf{S}$ is inconsistent. Conversely, let $\mathbf{I}$ $(= (\nu, \mu))$ be an arbitrary instance of $\mathbf{S}$ and $h : O_{\mathbf{S},\mathbf{I}} \rightarrow O_{\mathbf{S},\tilde{\mathbf{I}}}$ be a homomorphism such that $h(o) = o_c$ for any $o \in \nu(c)$. It can be shown that for every (partial) execution EX under $\mathbf{I}$, $h(EX)$ is a (partial) execution under $\tilde{\mathbf{I}}$ by induction on the length of EX. Then, it can be easily proved that $h(EX)$ is aborted whenever EX is aborted.

To check whether there is an aborted execution under $\tilde{\mathbf{I}}$, compute the last configuration of the execution of each m for each $o \in O_{\mathbf{S},\tilde{\mathbf{I}}}$, not the entire execution, since computing the entire executions takes exponential time in general. We use a table T, where $T(o_c, m, i)$ represents the last configuration of the partial execution from the first sentence up to the i-th sentence in $Impl^*(c, m)$. Define $T(o_c, m, 0)$ as $active(\tilde{\mu}, o_c, m, 1, \sigma_\perp)$. If $s(c, m, i)$ is not $y := m'(y')$, compute $T(o_c, m, i + 1)$ from $T(o_c, m, i)$ by using the corresponding rewriting rule. Suppose that $s(c, m, i + 1) = $ "$y := m'(y')$." Also suppose that $T(o_c, m, i) = active(\mu, o, m, i, \sigma)$. Compute $T(o_c, m, i + 1)$ from $T(\sigma(y'), m', n)$ and (R7), where n is the number of sentences in $Impl^*(cl(\sigma(y')), m')$. For all c and m such that $Impl^*(c, m)$ is defined, compute $T(o_c, m, i)$ in a depth-first manner. Since each $T(o_c, m, i)$ is computed at most once, this algorithm terminates in a linear time of the size of T. And T has a linear size of the total number of sentences given by $Impl$ since flatness implies $Impl = Impl^*$. □

However, consistency for a non-flat schema becomes undecidable as follows:

Theorem 14. Let $\mathbf{S} = (C, \leq, Attr, Ad, Meth, Impl)$ be a non-flat database schema. Consistency for $\mathbf{S}$ is undecidable, even if the height of $\leq$ is one and Ad is covariant. □

To prove Theorem 14, for a given input string x of a fixed deterministic Turing machine M, we construct a schema $\mathbf{S}_{M,x}$ satisfying the condition in the theorem. Then we show that $\mathbf{S}_{M,x}$ is inconsistent if and only if M accepts x. First, we define a Turing machine and an instantaneous description.

Definition 15. A *deterministic Turing machine* M is a triple (Q, Σ, δ), where

- Q is a finite set of states. Q contains three special states: the initial state q_0, the accepting state q_{yes}, and the rejecting state q_{no};
- Σ is a finite set of symbols. Σ contains two special symbols: the *blank symbol* B and the *first symbol* $\triangleright$. The first symbol is always placed at the leftmost cell of the tape;
- δ is a function which maps $(Q - \{q_{yes}, q_{no}\}) \times \Sigma$ to $Q \times \Sigma \times \{\leftarrow, \rightarrow, -\}$. We assume that if $\delta(q, \triangleright) = (q', \sigma, d)$, then $\sigma = \triangleright$ and $d = \rightarrow$. Therefore, the tape head never falls off the left end of the tape. □

Definition 16. An *instantaneous description* (ID) I of M is a finite sequence $\langle q_1, \sigma_1 \rangle, \ldots, \langle q_k, \sigma_k \rangle$, where $q_i \in Q \cup \{\perp\}$ and $\sigma_i \in \Sigma$. It is required that exactly one q_i is in Q (i denotes the head position). The i-th pair $\langle q_i, \sigma_i \rangle$ of an ID I is denoted by $I[i]$. The transition relation $\vdash_{M}$ over the set of IDs is defined as usual. Let I_j denote the ID after j transitions of M on x. □

Because of the space limitation, we only describe the idea of simulating M by $\mathbf{S}_{M,x}$. Consider a database instance shown in Fig. 7(a), where c_t is defined in Example 3 and $a_\Rightarrow$ is a new attribute (attribute a_{cont} is explained later). An element of an ID is stored in

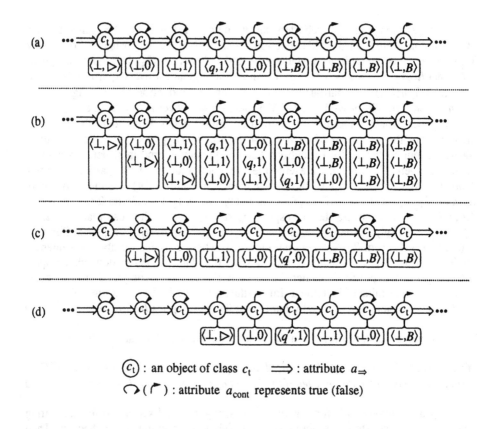

(a)

(b)

(c)

(d)

$\bigcirc_{c_t}$: an object of class c_t $\Longrightarrow$: attribute $a_\Rightarrow$

$\curvearrowright$ ($\curvearrowleft$) : attribute a_{cont} represents true (false)

Fig. 7. Working Space to Simulate M.

an object in the "$a_\Rightarrow$-chain" by the binary encoding method stated in Example 3. Then, let us compute the next ID. Note that $I_j[i]$ can be computed from $I_{j-1}[i-1]$, $I_{j-1}[i]$, and $I_{j-1}[i+1]$. Therefore, if three adjacent elements are stored in one object, we can compute the element of the next ID by using nor[∗, ∗] stated in Example 3. To do this, for every object o in the $a_\Rightarrow$-chain, we copy the element in o to $o.a_\Rightarrow$ and $o.a_\Rightarrow.a_\Rightarrow$ as shown in Fig. 7(b). (It seems impossible to copy the data in $o.a_\Rightarrow$ to o, although we do not know its formal proof.) Method copy[a_1, a_2] defined in Fig. 8 copies the Boolean-value represented by $o.a_1$ to $o.a_\Rightarrow.a_2$ when it is invoked on o. Thus we can obtain the next ID, and the place where the ID is stored is "shifted to right" (see Fig. 7(c)). Next, we explain the new attribute a_{cont}. This attribute indicates whether the next step should be simulated or not. Let o be the object in which the first element of the ID is stored. If $o.a_{\text{cont}}$ represents true, we recursively continue simulating M. Otherwise, we stop the simulation. For example, in the case of Fig. 7(c), we stop the simulation after two steps (Fig. 7(d)). After the simulation, we invoke a method, say test, which causes a type error if and only if q_{yes} is in the last ID.

Suppose that M accepts x. Then, M halts after finite steps. Therefore, a type error occurs under a database instance such that both the length of $a_\Rightarrow$-chain and the number of steps indicated by a_{cont}'s are enough large. Conversely, suppose that M does not accept

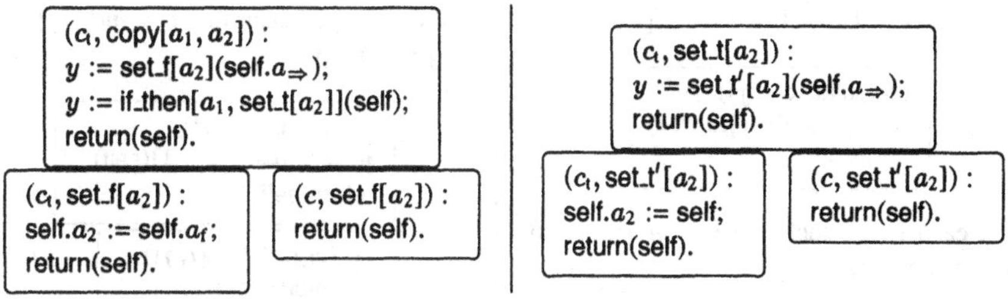

$(c_t, \text{copy}[a_1, a_2])$:
$y := \text{set\_f}[a_2](\text{self}.a_{\Rightarrow});$
$y := \text{if\_then}[a_1, \text{set\_t}[a_2]](\text{self});$
$\text{return(self)}.$

$(c_t, \text{set\_f}[a_2])$:
$\text{self}.a_2 := \text{self}.a_f;$
$\text{return(self)}.$

$(c, \text{set\_f}[a_2])$:
$\text{return(self)}.$

$(c_t, \text{set\_t}[a_2])$:
$y := \text{set\_t}'[a_2](\text{self}.a_{\Rightarrow});$
$\text{return(self)}.$

$(c_t, \text{set\_t}'[a_2])$:
$\text{self}.a_2 := \text{self};$
$\text{return(self)}.$

$(c, \text{set\_t}'[a_2])$:
$\text{return(self)}.$

Fig. 8. Definition of Method $\text{copy}[a_1, a_2]$.

x. Since q_{yes} never appears in the $a_{\Rightarrow}$-chain, invocation of test causes no type error. Note that we can easily ensure that all the methods except test cause no type error: If $Impl^*(c, m)$ is undefined for some c and m, we give a dummy definition of m at c.

3.2 Nontermination

The following theorem can be obtained from Theorem 2 of Ref. [13].

Theorem 17. *Let* $S = (C, \leq, Attr, Ad, Meth, Impl)$ *be a retrieval schema. If* S *is terminating, then consistency for* S *is in P.* □

On the other hand, consistency for a nonterminating retrieval schema is coNP-hard.

Theorem 18. *Let* $S = (C, \leq, Attr, Ad, Meth, Impl)$ *be a retrieval schema. If* S *is nonterminating, then consistency for* S *is coNP-hard, even if all of the following conditions are satisfied:*

1. *the height of* $\leq$ *is one;*
2. *every class has at most one direct subclass, i.e., if* $c_1 \leq c$ *and* $c_2 \leq c$, *then* $c_1 \leq c_2$ *or* $c_2 \leq c_1$;
3. *Ad is covariant;*
4. *Ad is acyclic; and*
5. *every class* c *has at most one attribute, i.e., there is at most one* $a \in Attr$ *such that* $Ad^*(c, a)$ *is defined.*

Proof. We show a reduction from 3-CNF. Let $F = C_1 \wedge \cdots \wedge C_n$ be a Boolean formula in 3-CNF with k variables $x_1, \ldots, x_k$. Let $L_{i,j}$ $(1 \leq i \leq n, 1 \leq j \leq 3)$ denote the j-th literal of the i-th clause C_i. Let $ind[i, j]$ $(1 \leq i \leq n, 1 \leq j \leq 3)$ denote the index of the variable appearing in $L_{i,j}$. Without loss of generality, we assume that $ind[i, j] \leq ind[i, j']$ if $j \leq j'$.

In what follows, we construct a database schema S such that there is an aborted execution under an instance of S if and only if F is satisfiable. First, define $C, \leq, Attr$, and Ad as follows:

- $C = \{c_{t,1}, \ldots, c_{t,k}, c_{t,k+1}, c_{f,1}, \ldots, c_{f,k}\}$;
- $c_{f,l} \leq c_{t,l}$ for each l $(1 \leq l \leq k)$;

For each i, j, l such that $l < ind[i,j]$,

> $(c_{t,l}, \text{clause}[i,j])$:
> $y := \text{clause}[i,j](\text{self}.a)$;
> return(self).

For each i, j, l such that $l = ind[i,j]$ and $L_{i,j}$ is positive,

> $(c_{t,l}, \text{clause}[i,j])$:
> return(self).

> $(c_{f,l}, \text{clause}[i,j])$:
> $y := \text{clause}[i,j+1](\text{self})$;
> return(self).

For each i, j, l such that $l = ind[i,j]$ and $L_{i,j}$ is negative,

> $(c_{t,l}, \text{clause}[i,j])$:
> $y := \text{clause}[i,j+1](\text{self})$;
> return(self).

> $(c_{f,l}, \text{clause}[i,j])$:
> return(self).

For each i and l,

> $(c_{t,l}, \text{clause}[i,4])$:
> $y := \text{clause}[i,4](\text{self})$;
> return(self).

Fig. 9. Definition of Method $\text{clause}[i,j]$.

- $Attr = \{a\}$; and
- $Ad(c_{t,l}, a) = c_{t,l+1}$ for each l ($1 \leq l \leq k$).

Since a is the only attribute and the a-value of an object of class $c_{t,l}$ or $c_{f,l}$ is an object of class $c_{t,l+1}$ or $c_{f,l+1}$, it suffices to consider a database instance of **S** which consists of $k + 1$ objects $o_1, \ldots, o_{k+1}$, where

- $o_l \in \nu(c_{t,l}) \cup \nu(c_{f,l})$ ($1 \leq l \leq k$), $o_{k+1} \in \nu(c_{t,k+1})$, and
- $o_l.a = o_{l+1}$ ($1 \leq l \leq k$).

In this reduction, a database instance is considered as an interpretation for F, i.e., X_l is true if $o_l \in \nu(c_{t,l})$, and false otherwise. Note that we adopt a different Boolean-value representation from the one stated in Example 3 since we cannot use any update operations here.

Now define method 3-CNF as follows:

> $(c_{t,1}, \text{3-CNF})$:
> $y := \text{clause}[1,1](\text{self})$;
> $\vdots$
> $y := \text{clause}[n,1](\text{self})$;
> $y := \text{test}(\text{self})$;
> return(self).

Also define method $\text{clause}[i,j]$ as shown in Fig. 9 (method test is undefined for all classes). It is easily checked that a type error is possible only at the line "$y := \text{test}(\text{self})$" in the definition of 3-CNF. Therefore, it suffices to show that test is executed during the execution of 3-CNF if and only if F is satisfiable.

Method $\text{clause}[i,j]$ checks whether $L_{i,j}$ is true under the given interpretation. If $L_{i,j}$ is true, it just executes return to evaluate $L_{i+1,1}$. Otherwise, it invokes $\text{clause}[i,j+1]$

to check whether $L_{i,j+1}$ is true. Thus, invocation of clause$[i,4]$ means that C_i is false (therefore F is false) under the given interpretation. In this case, the method execution is nonterminating (i.e., no type error occurs). When all the clauses are true, method test is invoked and a type error occurs. Thus, there is an aborted execution under an instance of S if and only if F is satisfiable. ☐

3.3 Update Operations

By Theorem 17, consistency for a terminating retrieval schema is in P. And by the following theorem, consistency for a recursion-free (thus terminating) schema with updates is in coNEXPTIME.

Theorem 19. *Let* $S = (C, \leq, Attr, Ad, Meth, Impl)$ *be a recursion-free schema with updates. Then, consistency for* S *is in coNEXPTIME.*

Proof. Since S is recursion-free, the length of any execution under any instance of S is bounded by $||S||^{||S||}$. Therefore, to solve inconsistency for S, nondeterministically guess an instance of size $||S||^{||S||} = 2^{||S|| \log ||S||}$ which causes a type error. That is, consistency for S is in coNEXPTIME. ☐

The following theorem gives a tight lower bound for recursion-free schemas.

Theorem 20. *Let* $S = (C, \leq, Attr, Ad, Meth, Impl)$ *be a recursion-free schema with updates. Consistency for* S *is coNEXPTIME-hard, even if the height of* $\leq$ *is one and Ad is covariant.*

Sketch of Proof. Let M be a fixed $2^{p(n)}$-time bounded nondeterministic Turing machine for a polynomial p, and x an input string for M with length n. For x, we construct, in polynomial time $p'(n)$ of n, a recursion-free schema $S'_{M,x}$ that is inconsistent if and only if M accepts x.

The idea of simulating M is similar to Theorem 14. However, two problems still remain. First, we have to simulate the nondeterministic transitions of M. To do this, we introduce new attributes into each object in the $a_\Rightarrow$-chain. The j-th nondeterministic choice ch_j is represented by the new attributes of object o in which the first element of the $(j-1)$-th ID I_{j-1} is stored. Then we can compute $I_j[i]$ from $I_{j-1}[i-1]$, $I_{j-1}[i]$, $I_{j-1}[i+1]$, and ch_j.

The other problem is how to simulate $2^{p(n)}$ steps of M with a recursion-free schema containing at most $p'(n)$ methods. To solve this problem, we use methods m_i ($0 \leq i \leq p(n)$) defined as follows:

(c_1, m_i) $(1 \leq i \leq p(n))$:	(c_1, m_0) :
$y := m_{i-1}(\text{self});$	$\vdots$
$y := m_{i-1}(y);$	
$\text{return}(y).$	$\text{return}(\text{self}.a_\Rightarrow).$

It is easily verified that if $m_{p(n)}$ is invoked on an object o, then m_0 is sequentially invoked on the first $2^{p(n)}$ objects in the $a_\Rightarrow$-chain from o. ☐

4 Conclusions

We have discussed the complexity of the type-consistency problems for some subclasses of queries in OODBs. Moreover, by comparing the results, we have shown how the complexity is affected by non-flatness, nontermination, and updates.

Some problems remain open; for example, it is a future study to give a tight upper bound of the complexity for retrieval schemas. It is also important to develop an incremental algorithm for type-consistency checking.

References

1. S. Abiteboul, R. Hull and V. Vianu, "Foundations of Databases," Addison-Wesley, 1995.
2. S. Abiteboul, P. Kanellakis, S. Ramaswamy and E. Waller, "Method Schemas," Journal of Computer and System Sciences, Vol. 51, No. 3, pp. 433–455, Dec. 1995.
3. R. Agrawal, L. DeMichiel and B. Lindsay, "Static Type Checking of Multi-Methods," Proc. OOPSLA'91, pp. 113–128, Oct. 1991.
4. R. Ahad, J. Davis, S. Gower, P. Lyngbaek, A. Marynowski and E. Onuegbe, "Supporting Access Control in an Object-Oriented Database Language," Proc. EDBT'92, LNCS 580, pp. 184–200, Mar. 1992.
5. E. Bertino, "Data Hiding and Security in Object-Oriented Databases," Proc. 8th IEEE Int'l Conf. on Data Engineering, pp. 338–247, Feb. 1992.
6. C. Chambers and G. T. Leavens, "Typechecking and Modules for Multimethods," ACM Trans. on Programming Languages and Systems, Vol. 17, No. 6, pp. 805–843, Nov. 1995.
7. J. Eifrig, S. Smith, V. Trifonov and A. Zwarico, "Application of OOP Type Theory: State, Decidability, Integration," Proc. OOPSLA'94, pp. 16–30, Oct. 1994.
8. G. Ghelli, "A Static Type System for Message Passing," Proc. OOPSLA'91, pp. 129–145, Oct. 1991.
9. R. Hull, K. Tanaka and M. Yoshikawa, "Behavior Analysis of Object-Oriented Databases: Method Structure, Execution Trees, and Reachability," Proc. 3rd Int'l Conf. on Foundations of Data Organization and Algorithms, pp. 372–388, June 1989.
10. N. Oxhøj, J. Palsberg and M. I. Schwartzbach, "Making Type Inference Practical," Proc. ECOOP, LNCS 615, pp. 329–349, June 1992.
11. J. Palsberg and M. I. Schwartzbach, "Object-Oriented Type Inference," Proc. OOPSLA'91, pp. 146–161, Oct. 1991.
12. J. Palsberg and M. I. Schwartzbach, "Object-Oriented Type Systems," John Wiley & Sons, 1994.
13. H. Seki, Y. Ishihara and M. Ito, "Authorization Analysis of Queries in Object-Oriented Databases," Proc. DOOD'95, LNCS 1013, pp. 521–538, Dec. 1995.
14. E. Waller, "Schema Updates and Consistency," Proc. DOOD'91, LNCS 566, pp. 167–188, Dec. 1991.

Object-Oriented Database Evolution

Jean-Bernard Lagorce, Arūnas Stočkus, Emmanuel Waller

{lagorce, stockus, waller, }@lri.fr
LRI, Université d'Orsay
91405 Orsay cedex, France

Abstract. An *evolution language* is composed of an instance update language, a schema update language, and a mechanism to combine them. We present a formal evolution language for object-oriented database management systems. This language allows to write programs to update simultaneously both the schema and the instance. Static checking of these programs insures that the resulting database is consistent.

We propose an autonomous *instance update language*, based on an adequate specific query language and a pure instance update language. The main features of the query language are a formal type inference system including disjunctive types, and the decidability of the satisfiability problem, despite a negation operator. The pure instance update language allows objects migration, and objects and references creation and deletion; its semantics is declarative, and an algorithm to compute it is presented.

We propose an *evolution mechanism* for combining this instance update language with a classical schema update language, and use it to obtain an evolution language. *Decidability of consistency* is shown for a fragment of this language, by reduction to first-order logic with two variables.

1 Introduction

In object-oriented databases, objects have an existence independent of their value and are grouped into classes that capture their commonalities. The class definitions model the schema and the objects are the instance of the database.

In general, modifying the schema of a database leads to an inconsistent instance. One must then adapt this instance without knowing if the resulting instance will be consistent or not.

The general problem we consider here is to define a mechanism which allows to modify the schema and the instance at the same time in order for the updated instance to fit to the updated schema. We do not consider automatic adaptation as in [BKKK87].

The specific problem we consider is: How to provide the user with an update language allowing static consistency checking? By consistency, we mean that every typing constraint of the updated schema must be valid in the updated instance. Moreover, in correct instances, objects belong to only one class, single-valued attributes have only one value, etc.

For example, "The owner of a car must be a Person". When updating the schema this typing constraint may change, "The owner of a car must be an Employee". The cars owned by students will then not validate the typing constraints. The programmer must adapt the instance immediately, by deleting these objects or migrating them in a new class. But, if he deletes them without setting the references pointing on them, the database will be inconsistent. Because some objects will continue to refer the deleted objects. If the programmer migrates them, new typing problems may arise in the new class.

We want to be able to tell the user that the adaptation program he proposes will be sure for every instance of the schema. The problems we will then encounter are related to attribute redefinition and object identity. When considering cars, what specific class do cars owners belong to? Do they work as students in a university or as employees in a company? If we migrate them, will other objects continue to refer to them through now ill-typed references? How to get these objects?

The contributions of this paper are: an instance update programming language with static consistency checking, a typable paths query language allowing to denote objects and their types, and a mechanism to combine instance update languages and schema update languages.

Next section presents the problem and the approach we use for instance update through an example. Section 3 describes the data model. Section 4 presents the path expression query language and results of satisfiability for this language. Section 5 gives the formal definitions of the instance update language and uses some results of section 4 for decidability of consistency. Section 6 details the database evolution mechanism allowing to combine schema update languages and instance update languages.

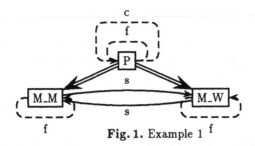

Fig. 1. Example 1 ᶠ

2 An Example

In this section, we only consider instance update to give an intuition of our instance update and path languages. The update programming language we introduce features five primitives. A program over this language is a set of primitive calls. Intuitively, assuming that x and x' are formal parameters denoting object or sets of objects and c a class name, the syntax and semantics of the primitive calls are the following:

• *move x c* migrates all the objects in x into class c without changing their identity and their references.

• *cut x a x'* delete all attribute links labeled with a between objects in x and objects in x'.

• *set x a x'* establishes references labeled with a between objects in x and objects in x'.

• *new x c* creates a new object into the population of class c.

• *delete x* deletes the objects in x. Let us consider the schema of Figure 1 representing persons (P), married men and women $(M\_M$ and $M\_W)$ which inherit from P. We want to write an instance update program allowing to marry any two persons belonging to class P, denoted by formal parameters x and x'. To design this kind of update, the user can simply move one object in class M_M, the other one in class M_W and set their spouse (s) attributes. This can be done by writing the following program:

$\{move\ x\ M\_W, move\ x'\ M\_M,$
$set\ x\ s\ x', set\ x'\ s\ x\}$

But, as the friends (f) attribute is redefined in classes (M_M) and (M_W), some references will then become ill-typed because the migrated objects will continue to refer to objects specifically in class P through attribute f. This checking is performed statically and tells that the program is not consistent because it can generate ill-typed instances. As a consequence, One can not move the object in x to class M_M without treating its references to objects not in class M_M.

To reach these objects, we use a path query language the main constructs of which are: Given path z the semantics of which is a set of objects, we can get all the objects referenced via attribute a from the objects in z with the path expression $z.a$. Similarly, we can get all objects that refer to objects in z via attribute a with the $z.a^{-1}$ expression. We can also select objects in z that are specifically in class c with the $z : c$ expression. Union, intersection and difference of paths are also provided.

The path expression $(x.f) - (x.f : M\_M)$ denotes exactly the objects causing ill-typed references after migration. So we just have to cut the references from x to these objects and repeat the process for x' to obtain a well-typed instance. If the programmer adds the two following primitive calls, the new program is consistent.

$cut\ x\ f\ (x.f - (x.f : M\_W)), cut\ x'\ f\ (x'.f - (x'.f : M\_M))$

This modification is of course not mandatory, the programmer could have migrated the objects into another class. Our aim is just to decide whether a program is consistent or not.

3   Preliminaries—Data Model

We recall briefly the model defined in [AKW90], without methods, and that we extend with sets.

We assume the existence of the following disjoint countable sets of *class names* $\{c_1, c_2, ..\}$ and *attribute names* $\{a_1, a_2, ..\}$ (simply called classes and attributes in the following). A *signature* is an expression $c \to c'$ or $c \to \{c'\}$, where c and c' are classes. An *attribute definition* of a at c is a pair $(a, c \to c')$ or $(a, c \to \{c'\})$ (also denoted $a : c \to c'$, resp. $a : c \to \{c'\}$) where a is an attribute, and $c \to c'$ and $c \to \{c'\}$ are signatures.

A *schema* is a triple $(C, \leq, \Sigma)$ where
1. C is a finite set of classes and $\leq$ is (the transitive closure of) a forest on C (the root of a tree is a maximum for $\leq$); (if $c' \leq c$, c' is a *subclass* of c and c the *superclass* of c'; for each c, we denote $c^* = \{c' \mid c' \leq c\}$);
2. Σ is a set of attribute definitions with classes in C;
3. each attribute has at most one definition at c for each c;
4. if $a : c_1 \to t_1$, $a : c_2 \to t_2$ are in Σ, and $c_1 \leq c_2$, then both $t_1 = c_1'$ and $t_2 = c_2'$, or $t_1 = \{c_1'\}$ and $t_2 = \{c_2'\}$, for some c_1', c_2'.

In a schema $(C, \leq, \Sigma)$, attribute definitions in Σ are called *explicit*. Moreover, if an attribute a is explicitly defined at c, its definition d is *implicitly* defined in each $c' \leq c$; we say that d is *inherited* in c'. We say that attribute name a is *overloaded* if there is more than one definition of a in Σ. As a consequence of overloading and inheritance, for some given c there may be several definitions of a at c (at most one explicit one). The *resolution of* (*overloading on attribute name*) a at c is the explicit definition of a in the smallest $c' \geq c$ in which a has an explicit definition. If such a c' exists, a is *(well) defined* at c, otherwise a is *undefined* at c.

We assume the existence of a countable set of *object identifiers* $\{o_1, o_2, ...\}$ (simply called objects in the following), disjoint from classes and attributes. Given a schema $(C, \leq, \Sigma)$, a *disjoint object assignment* ν for C is a total function from C to finite sets of objects, such that $c \neq c' \Rightarrow \nu(c) \cap \nu(c') = \emptyset$. For each c, we denote $\nu(c^*) = \bigcup_{c' \leq c} \nu(c')$. We will refer to $\bigcup_{c \in C} \nu(c)$ as the set of objects in ν (denoted ν).

An *instance* of a schema $S = (C, \leq, \Sigma)$ is a pair $I = (\nu, \mu)$ where ν is a disjoint object assignment for C and μ is a total function from the attribute names in S to partial functions such that:
1. if a is undefined at c, then $\mu(a)$ is undefined everywhere in $\nu(c)$; and
2. if the resolution of a at c is $a : c_1 \to c'$ (resp. $a : c_1 \to \{c'\}$) for some $c_1 \geq c$, then $\mu(a) \mid_{\nu(c)}$ is a total function into $\nu(c'^*)$ (resp. into the subsets of $\nu(c'^*)$).

We will need in the following to manipulate pairs (ν, μ) before knowing whether they are instances or not. The following definition is weaker than that of an instance, and independant of any schema. A *pre-instance* is a pair (ν, μ) such that: (1) ν is a partial function from classes into finite sets of objects (defined only for a finite number of classes); and (2) μ is a partial function from attributes into finite binary relations of objects (defined only for a finite number of attributes). For a pre-instance (ν, μ) we will simply write $(o, c) \in \nu$ if $o \in \nu(c)$, and $o \xrightarrow{a} o' \in \mu$ if $(o, o') \in \mu(a)$ (or $o \in c$ and $o \xrightarrow{a} o'$ when no ambiguity arise); and allow to consider ν and μ as sets, with usual set operations.

Given a pre-instance I and a schema S, if the classes and attributes for which I is defined are in S (regardless of any other constraint), we say that I is a *pre-instance of* S. An instance of S is clearly a pre-instance of S. Given a pre-instance I and a schema S, practically checking whether I is an instance of S is immediate.

4 Objects Designation

4.1 Types

A *type* is an expression $c_1 \vee ... \vee c_n$ or $\{c_1 \vee ... \vee c_n\}$ or $s_1 \vee ... \vee s_n$, where $n \geq 1$, the c_i's, $1 \leq i \leq n$, are distinct classes, and each s_i, $1 \leq i \leq n$, is a type $\{c_{i,1} \vee ... \vee c_{i,n_i}\}$ where the $c_{i,j}$'s, $1 \leq j \leq n_i$, are distinct classes. It is a *type of schema* S if its classes are in S. Given S and an instance I of S, the *semantics* of type $c_1 \vee ... \vee c_n$ of S in I is $[c_1 \vee ... \vee c_n]_I = \bigcup_{1 \leq i \leq n} \nu(c_i)$, resp. $[\{c_1 \vee ... \vee c_n\}]_I = 2^{[c_1 \vee ... \vee c_n]_I}$, and $[s_1 \vee ... \vee s_n]_I = \bigcup_{1 \leq i \leq n} 2^{[s_i]_I}$ (where 2^E denotes the subsets of any set E).

4.2 Paths—Syntax and Typing

We assume the existence of a countable set of *typed variables* $\{x, y, ...\}$ disjoint from classes, attributes and objects; each variable x has an associated type, and for each type there are countably many variables of this type. To simplify the presentation, only types of the form c or $\{c\}$, for some class c, are considered here; corresponding variables may be explicitly written x^c (resp. $x^{\{c\}}$).

Definition 4.1 A *path* is one of the following recursively defined expressions, where c is a class, x a variable, a an attribute, and l and l' paths (and $.,^{-1},:$ $,\cap,\cup,-$ are auxiliary symbols): x, $l.a$, $l.a^{-1}$, $l:c$, $l \cap l'$, $l \cup l'$, $l - l'$. $\square$

Given a schema $S = (C, \leq, \Sigma)$, we define the following *typing rules* (Figure 2), where the axioms are rules 1. (For $E \subseteq C$ we denote $a(E) = \{c'^* \mid c \in E$ and the resolution of a at c is $a : c'' \to c'$ or $a : c'' \to \{c'\}\}$, and simply write $a(c)$ if $E = \{c\}$; and $a^{-1}(E) = \{c \mid a(c) \cap E \neq \emptyset\}$. Attribute definition $a : c \to c'$ is said *single-valued* and $a : c \to \{c'\}$ *set-valued*.)

The design of a type system is traditionally done as follows (see e.g. [Mit90]). First, the set of queries that are considered by the designer as intuitively "correct" is chosen, together with its complement: the set of queries that are considered intuitively not interesting. Second, the type system (the set of rules) is designed so as to capture exactly this set of "correct" query expressions, and reject the others. Finally, the result of a query is expected to be an element of the type of the query. This is the way we proceed here.

The design of the set of "correct" queries was done here based on our programming experience with a restricted maquette, and complementary examples.

1. $\dfrac{}{x^c \,:\, c'_1 \vee \dots \vee c'_m}$ (resp. $\dfrac{}{x^{(c)} \,:\, \{c'_1 \vee \dots \vee c'_m\}}$) if the c'_j's, $1 \leq j \leq m$, are the subclasses of c

2. $\dfrac{l \,:\, c_1 \vee \dots \vee c_n}{l.a \,:\, c'_1 \vee \dots \vee c'_m}$ if for each c_i, $1 \leq i \leq n$, a at c_i is (defined and) single-valued; and where $a(\{c_1, \dots, c_n\}) = \{c'_1, \dots, c'_m\}$

3. $\dfrac{l \,:\, c_1 \vee \dots \vee c_n}{l.a \,:\, \{c'_{1,1} \vee \dots \vee c'_{1,m_1}\} \vee \dots \vee \{c'_{n,1} \vee \dots \vee c'_{n,m_n}\}}$ if for each c_i, $1 \leq i \leq n$, a at c_i is set-valued; and $a(c_i) = \{c'_{i,1}, \dots, c'_{i,m_i}\}$

4. $\dfrac{l \,:\, \{c_{1,1} \vee \dots \vee c_{1,k_1}\} \vee \dots \vee \{c_{n,1} \vee \dots \vee c_{n,k_n}\}}{l.a \,:\, \{c'_{1,1} \vee \dots \vee c'_{1,m_1}\} \vee \dots \vee \{c'_{n,1} \vee \dots \vee c'_{n,m_n}\}}$ if for each $c_{i,j}$, $1 \leq i \leq n$, $1 \leq j \leq k_i$, a is defined at $c_{i,j}$; and where for each i, $1 \leq i \leq n$, we have $a(\{c_{i,1}, \dots, c_{i,k_i}\}) = \{c'_{i,1}, \dots, c'_{i,m_i}\}$

5. $\dfrac{l \,:\, c_1 \vee \dots \vee c_n}{l.a^{-1} \,:\, \{c'_{1,1} \vee \dots \vee c'_{1,m_1}\} \vee \dots \vee \{c'_{n,1} \vee \dots \vee c'_{n,m_n}\}}$ if for each c_i, $1 \leq i \leq n$, $a^{-1}(c_i) = \{c'_{i,1}, \dots, c'_{i,m_i}\} \neq \emptyset$

6. $\dfrac{l \,:\, \{c_{1,1} \vee \dots \vee c_{1,k_1}\} \vee \dots \vee \{c_{n,1} \vee \dots \vee c_{n,k_n}\}}{l.a^{-1} \,:\, \{c'_{1,1} \vee \dots \vee c'_{1,m_1}\} \vee \dots \vee \{c'_{n,1} \vee \dots \vee c'_{n,m_n}\}}$ if for each $c_{i,j}$, $1 \leq i \leq n$, $1 \leq j \leq k_i$, there exists c' such that $c_{i,j} \in a(c')$; and where for each i, $1 \leq i \leq n$, we have $a^{-1}(\{c_{i,1}, \dots, c_{i,k_i}\}) = \{c'_{i,1}, \dots, c'_{i,m_i}\}$

7. $\dfrac{l \,:\, c_1 \vee \dots \vee c_n}{(l \colon c) \,:\, c_{i_1} \vee \dots \vee c_{i_k}}$ (resp. $\dfrac{l \,:\, \{c_1 \vee \dots \vee c_n\}}{(l \colon c) \,:\, \{c_{i_1} \vee \dots \vee c_{i_k}\}}$) if $c^* \cap \{c_1, \dots, c_n\} = \{c_{i_1}, \dots, c_{i_k}\} \neq \emptyset$

In the following rules, each t_i, t'_j, t''_i, or $t''_{i,j}$ is of the form $\{c_1 \vee \dots \vee c_n\}$. (For the sake of presentation, such a type $t = \{c_1 \vee \dots \vee c_n\}$ will be denoted below as the set $\{c_1, \dots, c_n\}$, and we will allow to simply write $t \cap t'$ and $t \cup t'$ for such types.)

8. $\dfrac{l \,:\, t_1 \vee \dots \vee t_n}{(l \colon c) \,:\, t''_1 \vee \dots \vee t''_n}$
   if there exists i, $1 \leq i \leq n$, such that $c^* \cap t_i \neq \emptyset$; and where for each i, $1 \leq i \leq n$, $t''_i = c^* \cap t_i$ if $c^* \cap t_i \neq \emptyset$, and t''_i doesn't appear otherwise

9. $\dfrac{l \,:\, t_1 \vee \dots \vee t_n \qquad l' \,:\, t'_1 \vee \dots \vee t'_{n'}}{l \cap l' \,:\, t''_{1,1} \vee \dots \vee t''_{n,n'}}$ if there exists i, j, $1 \leq i \leq n$, $1 \leq j \leq n'$, such that $t_i \cap t'_j \neq \emptyset$; and where for each i, j, $1 \leq i \leq n$, $1 \leq j \leq n'$, we have $t''_{i,j} = t_i \cap t'_j$ if $t_i \cap t'_j \neq \emptyset$, and $t''_{i,j}$ doesn't appear otherwise

10. $\dfrac{l \colon t_1 \vee \dots \vee t_n \qquad l' \,:\, t'_1 \vee \dots \vee t'_{n'}}{l \cup l' \,:\, t''_{1,1} \vee \dots \vee t''_{n,n'}}$ where for each i, j, $1 \leq i \leq n$, $1 \leq j \leq n'$, $t''_{i,j} = t_i \cup t'_j$

11. $\dfrac{l \,:\, t_1 \vee \dots \vee t_n \qquad l' \,:\, t'_1 \vee \dots \vee t'_{n'}}{l - l' \,:\, t_1 \vee \dots \vee t_n}$ if there exists i, j, $1 \leq i \leq n$, $1 \leq j \leq n'$, such that $t_i \cap t'_j \neq \emptyset$

Fig. 2. Typing Rules

It is thus motivated but arbitrary: If a different set of "correct" queries were to be considered, it is easy to modify the rules, while keeping the same properties. For instance, the idea of Rule 4 is to flatten sets roughly, provided attribute a is defined on each $c_{i,j}$, but possibly mono-valued for one $c_{i,j}$ and set-valued for another. It is easy to modify this rule, for instance by making the *if* clause more restrictive as follows: For each i, $1 \leq i \leq n$, attribute a should be either mono-valued for all $c_{i,j}$'s, $1 \leq j \leq k_i$, either set-valued for all. In a second variant of this rule, it should be for instance either mono-valued for all $c_{i,j}$'s, $1 \leq i \leq n$, $1 \leq j \leq k_i$, either set-valued for all.

We say that l *is typable (in S) of type t* (denoted $l : t$), if $l : t$ is derivable using the rules defined above. (That is, there exists a (finite) derivation tree, the root of which is $l:t$, the leaves axioms, and the internal nodes related by rules.)

Proposition 4.2 Given a schema S and a path l, it is decidable whether l is typable in S. If so, there is a unique type t of S such that $l:t$, which is inferred by the natural algorithm. $\square$

For example, in Example 1 $z.c.f.c^{-1}:M\_W$ which denotes the married mothers of the friends of the children of z has type: set of M_W, where z is in P or M_M or M_W. If the variable z is of type P, then the path: $z.c.f.c^{-1}$ has type heterogenous set of objects in classes P, M_M and M_W.

4.3 Paths—Semantics

Given a finite set X of variables, a *valuation* v over X is a mapping from X into objects and sets of objects such that for each x^c or $x^{\{c\}}$ in X, $v(x^c)$ is an object and $v(x^{\{c\}})$ a set of objects. Given a schema S and a pre-instance $I=(\nu,\mu)$ of S, a valuation v over X is said to be *in* I, if for each class c in S and variable x^c (resp. $x^{\{c\}}$) in X, we have $v(x^c)\in\nu(c^*)$, (resp. $v(x^{\{c\}})\subseteq\nu(c^*)$). (The general case, i.e., variables of any type, follows naturally from the semantics of types.) (For function f with domain A and range B, for $E\subseteq A$ and $F\subseteq B$ we denote $f(E)=\{f(o)\mid o\in E\}$ if $f|_E$ is total, and $f^{-1}(F)=\{o\in A\mid f(o)\in F\}$ if f is single-valued, resp. $f(o)\subseteq F$ if f is set-valued, and simply write $f^{-1}(o')$ if $F=\{o'\}$.)

Definition 4.3 Given a schema S, an instance $I=(\nu,\mu)$ of S, a typable path l of S and a valuation v over the variables of l in I, the *semantics* of l in I under v (denoted $[\,l\,]_{I,v}$) is recursively defined as follows.

1. $[\,x\,]_{I,v}=v(x)$
2. $[\,l.a\,]_{I,v}=\mu(a)([\,l\,]_{I,v})$
3. $[\,l.a^{-1}\,]_{I,v}=\mu(a)^{-1}([\,l\,]_{I,v})$
4. $[\,l:c\,]_{I,v}=[\,l\,]_{I,v}\cap\nu(c^*)$ (resp. $\{[\,l\,]_{I,v}\}\cap\nu(c^*)$ if $l:c_1\vee\ldots\vee c_n$ for some $c_1,\ldots,c_n$)
5. $[\,l\cap l'\,]_{I,v}=[\,l\,]_{I,v}\cap[\,l'\,]_{I,v}$
   $[\,l\cup l'\,]_{I,v}=[\,l\,]_{I,v}\cup[\,l'\,]_{I,v}$
   $[\,l-l'\,]_{I,v}=[\,l\,]_{I,v}-[\,l'\,]_{I,v}$ $\square$

Proposition 4.4 Given a schema S, a path l and a type t, if $l:t$ in S, then for each instance I of S and valuation v over the variable of l in I, we have $[\,l\,]_{I,v}\subseteq[\,t\,]_I$. $\square$

Theorem 4.5 Satisfiability of paths queries is decidable (if the construct $l.a$ with a mono-valued is not considered). $\square$

Proof (Sketch) In other words, given a path l in schema S, we can tell whether there exists an instance and a valuation such that the evaluation of l yields a non-empty result. We consider here the fragment of first-order logic called first-order logic with two variables, and denoted FO2 [Mor75]. The syntax is the usual one of first-order logic without function symbols, except that only two variable symbols are allowed (instead of countably many), here z and z'. We reduce satisfiability of paths queries to satisfiability of FO2. Given a schema $S = (C, \leq, \Sigma)$ and a path l typable in S, an FO2 formula φ_l is associated to l such that φ_l is satisfiable iff there exists an instance I and a valuation v such that $[l]_{I,v} \neq \emptyset$. As satisfiability of an FO2 formula is decidable, the satisfiability of our paths language is decidable. The first-order language is the same as that used to build formulas to design the semantics of the pure instance update language in Section 5.1. Intuitively, to each path l, a formula with one free variable $\varphi_l(z)$ is associated as follows: $\varphi_{l.a}(z) = \exists z'(a(z', z) \wedge \varphi_l(z'))$; $\varphi_{l.a^{-1}}(z) = \exists z'(a(z, z') \wedge \varphi_l(z'))$; $\varphi_{l::c}(z) = \varphi_l(z) \wedge (\bigvee_{c' \leq c} c'(z))$; $\varphi_{l \cup l'}(z) = \varphi_l(z) \vee \varphi_{l'}(z)$; $\varphi_{l \cap l'}(z) = \varphi_l(z) \wedge \varphi_{l'}(z)$; $\varphi_{l-l'}(z) = \varphi_l(z) \wedge \neg \varphi_{l'}(z)$. Examples: $\varphi_{x.a.b} = \exists z \exists z'(b(z', z) \wedge \exists z(a(z, z') \wedge x(z)))$; $\varphi_{x.a-y.b^{-1}} = \exists z((\exists z'(a(z', z) \wedge x(z'))) \wedge (\exists z'(b(z, z') \wedge y(z'))))$. To see that l is satisfiable iff φ_l is satisfiable, we need to define the semantics of our first-order language. This semantics is the set of structures defined in Section 5.1 for the satisfiability of $\psi_{S,P}$. $\square$

5 Instance Update

5.1 Pure Instance Update

We assume the existence of five *instance update primitive* symbols: *new, delete, move, set* and *cut,* distinct from classes, attributes, objects and variables. An *instance update instruction* is one of the following expressions (strictly speaking a pair, triple or 4-tuple), where c is a class, a an attribute, and x and x' variables.

1. *new x c* — called *object creation* (in class c)
2. *delete x* — *object(s) deletion* (of object(s) denoted by variable x)
3. *move x c* — *object(s) migration* (of x to c)
4. *set x a x'* — *reference(s) creation* (from x to x' for attribute a)
5. *cut x a x'* — *reference(s) deletion* (from x to x' for a)

Definition 5.1 A *pure instance update program* is a finite set of instance update instructions. $\square$

A program is *well-formed* if for each instruction *new x c* the type of x is c, and no variable in a *new* instruction also occurs in a *delete, move* or *cut* instruction. Its *formal parameters* are its variables but the ones in a *new* instruction.

A program is *legal for designation* upon a schema S if the classes of its formal parameters are in S; and for each *cut x a x'*, if the type of x is c or $\{c\}$ and that of x' is c' or $\{c'\}$, then a is defined at c and $c' \in a(c)$. It is *legal for specification* upon S if for each *new x c* or *move x c*, c is in S; and for *set x a x'*, a is in S. It is simply said *legal* when it is legal for both. We will consider in the following only well-formed programs, legal upon the schemas considered.

Given a schema $S = (C, \leq, \Sigma)$ and a program P upon S, we consider the following language. The usual variables $(\{z, z', ...\})$, connectives and auxiliary symbols of first-order logic; and the predicate symbols are the classes in S and the variables in P (unary), and the attributes in S (binary). We consider the usual semantics of first-order logic [Bar77], and denote $\mathcal{M} \models \psi$ when structure $\mathcal{M}$ for this language satisfies formula ψ over this language.

A formula (over this language) is associated to each instruction in P (regardless of the others) as follows.

1. *new x_1 c or move x_1 c :* $\quad \forall z \ (x_1(z) \rightarrow (c(z) \wedge \bigwedge_{c' \in C-\{c\}} \neg c'(z)))$

2. *delete x_1 :* $\qquad\qquad\qquad \forall z \ (x_1(z) \rightarrow (\bigwedge_{c \in C} \neg c(z)))$

3. *set x_1 a x_2 :* $\quad \forall z \ (x_1(z) \rightarrow [(\bigvee_{c \in C} c(z)) \wedge \forall z' \ (x_2(z') \leftrightarrow [(\bigvee_{c \in C} c(z')) \wedge a(z, z')])])$

4. *cut x_1 a x_2 :* $\qquad\quad \forall z \ (x_1(z) \rightarrow \forall z' \ (x_2(z') \rightarrow \neg a(z, z')))$

The (first-order) *formula associated to P (upon S)* (denoted $\psi_{S,P}$, or ψ when no ambiguity arises) is the conjunction of all these formulas. We will consider in the following only such formulas (and not general formulas of this first-order language).

Given a schema S, a program P upon S, and a pre-instance $I = (\nu, \mu)$ of S, let X be the set of variables in P and $Y \subseteq X$ the variables occuring in an instruction *new*. We will consider in the following only valuations v over X that are both: *in I except for Y*, that is, v is in I for $X - Y$, and $y \in Y \Rightarrow v(y) \cap \nu = \emptyset$; and *disjoint for Y*, that is, $x, y \in Y, y \neq x \Rightarrow v(y) \cap v(x) = \emptyset$.

Given S, P upon S, $I = (\nu, \mu)$ pre-instance of S and v over (the variables of) P in I, we simply write (I, v) for the following structure for the language considered above. The domain is the union of the objects in v and those in ν; the predicate symbols are mapped to relations over the domain as follows: for each variable x in P, $x \mapsto v(x)$; for each class c in S, $c \mapsto \nu(c)$; and for each attribute a in S, $a \mapsto \mu(a)$ (when a is set-valued, there is a tuple for each $o \stackrel{a}{\mapsto} o'$). We will consider in the following only such structures.

Given S, P upon S, and v over P, the formula $\psi_{S,P}$ is *satisfiable w.r.t. v* if there exists a pre-instance I of S such that v is in I and $(I, v) \models \psi_{S,P}$; otherwise it is *unsatisfiable w.r.t. v*.

Proposition 5.2 Let be given S, P upon S, v over P, and ψ associated to P upon S. ψ is unsatisfiable w.r.t. v if, and only if, there are variables x and y of P such that $v(x) \cap v(y) \neq \emptyset$ (strictly speaking $v(x) = v(y)$ if they are not sets), and one of the following holds.

1. *delete x, move y c* are instructions in P
2. *delete x, set y a x'*
3. *delete x, set x' a y*
4. *move x c, move y c'* (with $c \neq c'$)
5. *set x a x', set y a y'* are in P, and $v(x') \neq v(y')$
6. *set x a x', cut y a y'* are in P, and $v(x') \cap v(y') \neq \emptyset$ $\square$

Given S and P upon S, the pairs of variables (x, y) in cases 1, 2, 3, 4 above are said *conflictual*. Valuation v over P is *conflictual* if it is such that: for some pair (x, y) in cases 1, 2, 3 or 4 above, $v(x) \cap v(y) \neq \emptyset$; in case 5, both $v(x) \cap v(y) \neq \emptyset$ and $v(x') \neq v(y')$; and in case 6, both $v(x) \cap v(y) \neq \emptyset$ and $v(x') \cap v(y') \neq \emptyset$. In other words, Proposition 5.2 says that ψ is unsatisfiable w.r.t. v iff v is conflictual. If there exists such a v, P is said *contradictory*.

Proposition 5.3 Given S, it is decidable whether P is non contradictory. $\square$

Proof (Sketch) First, use Proposition 5.2 to look whether there are conflictual variables in P. If not, then no v is conflictual, and by Proposition 5.2 ψ is satisfiable w.r.t. v. If there are conflictual variables (x, y), check whether there exists a valuation v conflictual for (x, y), that is, $v(x) \cap v(y) \neq \emptyset$ (resp. $v(x') \neq v(y')$). But the answer is immediate, and positive; thus P is contradictory. $\square$

Given S, we consider the following partial ordering (denoted $\subseteq$) over the pre-instances of S. Let $I = (\nu, \mu)$ and $I' = (\nu', \mu')$; $I \subseteq I'$ if $\nu \subseteq \nu'$ and $\mu \subseteq \mu'$ (see Section 3 for notations).

Theorem 5.4 Let be given S, P upon S, I instance of S, v over P in I, and ψ associated to P upon S.

1. If ψ is satisfiable w.r.t. v, then the set $\{I' \mid I' \subseteq I$ and $\exists I'' \supseteq I'$ s. t. $(I'', v) \models \psi\}$ is not empty and has a unique maximum, denoted *invariant*(I).
2. In this case, the set $\{I' \mid invariant(I) \subseteq I'$ and $(I', v) \models \psi\}$ is not empty and has a unique minimum, denoted $decl_{S,P,v}(I)$. $\square$

Proof (Sketch) Roughly speaking, the proof is constructive and corresponds to the following algorithm. Let $P = \{\alpha_1, ..., \alpha_m\}$. To each instruction α_i in P, $1 \leq i \leq m$, we associate a 4-tuple $(\nu_i^+, \nu_i^-, \mu_i^+, \mu_i^-)$ as follows.
1. To *new* x c we associate: $(\{(c, o)\}, \emptyset, \emptyset, \emptyset)$, for some o not in ν, and different from each other object created by such an instruction;
2. *delete* x : $(\emptyset, \{(c, o) \mid c \in S, o \in v(x)\}, \emptyset, \emptyset)$;
3. *move* $x^{c'}$ c : $(\{(c, o) \mid o \in v(x)\}, \{(c', o) \mid o \in v(x)\}, \emptyset, \emptyset)$;
4. *set* x a x' : $(\emptyset, \emptyset, \{(o \xrightarrow{a} o') \mid o \in v(x), o' \in v(x')\}, \emptyset)$;
5. *cut* x a x' : $(\emptyset, \emptyset, \emptyset, \{(o \xrightarrow{a} o') \mid o \in v(x), o' \in v(x')\})$.

Then we check whether this set of operations involves some contradiction, namely if there exist $1 \leq i \neq j \leq m$, such that one of the following holds.
1. $\{o \mid (o, c') \in \nu_i^-\} \cap \{o \mid (o, c'') \in \nu_j^+\} \neq \emptyset$;
2. $\{(o, a) \mid (o \xrightarrow{a} o') \in \mu_i^+\} \cap \{(o, a) \mid (o \xrightarrow{a} o'') \in \mu_j^+\} \neq \emptyset$;
3. $\mu_i^- \cap \mu_j^+ \neq \emptyset$.

If no such contradiction arises, we define:
$$[P]_{I,v}^S = ((\nu - \bigcup_{1 \leq i \leq m} \nu_i^-) \cup (\bigcup_{1 \leq i \leq m} \nu_i^+), (\mu - \bigcup_{1 \leq i \leq m} \mu_i^-) \cup (\bigcup_{1 \leq i \leq m} \mu_i^+)). \square$$

Definition 5.5 Let be given S, P upon S non contradictory, I instance of S, and v over P in I non conflictual. The *semantics* of P upon S on I under v is $[P]_{I,v}^S = decl_{S,P,v}(I)$. $\square$

Theorem 5.6 Given S and P, it is decidable whether for each I and v, $[P]_{I,v}^S$ is an instance. $\square$

5.2 Concrete Instance Update Programs

A *concrete instance update program* is a triple (L, α, P) where L is a finite set of paths, P a pure instance update program, and α a mapping from the formal parameters of P onto L; moreover, the set of variables of L and P are disjoint.

It is *legal* upon a schema S, if the paths in L are typable, P is legal upon S, and the type of each formal parameter of P is equal to that of its image by α.[1] Only legal programs will be considered in the following.

A valuation for such a program (L, α, P) is over the set of variables of L union the set Y of the variables occuring in a *new* instruction in P. Given an instance I, we consider only valuations that are in I except for Y. To each such valuation v is associated a valuation $\tilde{v}$ over P, as follows. Over Y, $\tilde{v} = v$; and for each formal parameter x of P, let $\alpha(x)$ be the path in L associated to x; then $\tilde{v}(x) = [\alpha(x)]_{I,v}$. Note that $\tilde{v}$ is itself in I except for Y.

Proposition 5.7 Given S, it is decidable whether Q is non contradictory, that is, if ψ is satisfable w.r.t. $\tilde{v}$. $\square$

Proof (Sketch) We generalize the proof of Proposition 5.3. Given (x, y) conflictual, we have to decide whether $\tilde{v}$ is conflictual, that is, whether $\tilde{v}(x) \cap \tilde{v}(y) \neq \emptyset$ and $\tilde{v}(x) \neq \tilde{v}(y)$ (considering the latter, $l \neq l'$ iff $l - l' \neq \emptyset$ or $l' - l \neq \emptyset$). But $\tilde{v}(x) = [\alpha(x)]_{I,v}$. That is, decide whether $\alpha(x) \cap \alpha(y)$ and $(\alpha(x) - \alpha(y)) \cup (\alpha(x) - \alpha(y))$ are satisfiable, which is the case by Theorem 4.5. $\square$

Given S, $Q = (L, \alpha, P)$, I and v, the *semantics* of Q upon S on I under v is $[Q]_{I,v}^S = [P]_{I,\tilde{v}}^S$.

Definition 5.8 A concrete instance update program Q upon a schema S is *consistent* if for each instance I and valuation v, $[Q]_{I,v}^S$ is an instance. $\square$

Theorem 5.9 Given S and Q, it is decidable whether Q upon S is consistent. $\square$

Proof (Sketch) As for Proposition 5.6, we only show here how to decide whether $[Q]_{I,v}^S$ has no ill-typed references. We generalize the case analysis of the proof for pure instance update programs. We treat the *move* instruction. Given $Q = (L, \alpha, P)$, let $x_1, ..., x_n$ be the parameters of P. Assume there is an instruction *move* $x_1\ c_1'$, with $x_1 : c_1$, $a : c_1 \rightarrow c_2$, and $a : c_1' \rightarrow c_2'$, with $c_2 \not\leq c_2'$. Then $[Q]_{I,v}$ has ill-typed references except if (that is, is well typed iff) there is an instruction (1) *move* $x_i\ c_2'$, or (2) *cut* $x_j\ a\ x_i$, with $[\alpha(x_1).a]_{I,v} \subseteq [\alpha(x_i)]_{I,v}$ and $[\alpha(x_1)]_{I,v} \subseteq [\alpha(x_j)]_{I,v}$ for each I and v. But this is true iff $[\alpha(x_1).a - \alpha(x_i)]_{I,v} = \emptyset$ and $[\alpha(x_1) - \alpha(x_j)]_{I,v} = \emptyset$ for each I, v; iff $\alpha(x_1).a - \alpha(x_i)$ and $\alpha(x_1) - \alpha(x_j)$ are unsatisfiable, which, as satisfiability, is decidable. $\square$

---

[1] From a practical point of view, the user only declares the types of the paths variables; the system infers the types of the paths (general types as presented in Section 4.1) and declares the formal parameters of the pure instance update program from these types.

5.3 Pure *versus* Concrete Instance Updates

Providing the paths language makes more programs consistent:

Proposition 5.10 Given S and $Q = (L, \alpha, P)$, if the pure instance update program P is consistent, then Q is consistent. □

Proof Immediate: $[P]_{I,v}$ is an instance for each v, and $\tilde{v}$ is simply a particular valuation. □

The intuition here is simply the following. In the pure instance update language, P has to be checked against the set $\mathcal{V}(I)$ of all valuations. In the concrete instance update language, L specifies a subset of $\mathcal{V}(I)$; P needs only to be checked against this subset.

The programs made consistent by the introduction of the paths language are useful:

Theorem 5.11 The concrete instance update language is more expressive than the pure instance update language. □

Proof We show that given S, there exists a function f from the instances of S to the instances of S, such that (1) no pure instance update program expresses f, and (2) f is expressed by a concrete instance update program. Let $S = (\{c_1, c_2, c_3, c_4\}, \emptyset, \{a : c_1 \to c_2, a : c_3 \to c_4\})$, let A be any set of objects, and let f be defined as follows. For each $I = (v, \mu)$, if $A \subseteq v$, then $f(I) = (v', \mu')$, where $v' = v$, except that $A \subseteq v(c_3)$ and $A.a \subseteq v(c_4)$; and $\mu' = \mu$. Assume P implements f; then P has to have two *move* instructions, namely *move* x c_3 and *move* x' c_4 (one is not enough, because both c_3 and c_4 have to be augmented). But then, there exists a non-empty valuation v such that $v(x) \cap v(x') \neq \emptyset$ (e.g. $v(x) = v(x') = \{o\}$), which is conflictual. The following program implements f. $L = \{y, y.a\}$; $\alpha : x \mapsto y, x' \mapsto y.a$; $P = \{move\ x\ c_3, move\ x'\ c_4\}$. □

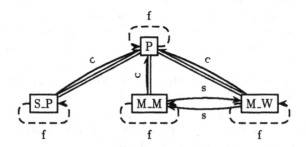

Fig. 3. Example 2

6 Database Evolution

In this section, we present the mechanism allowing to perform a well-typed database evolution by simultaneously updating the schema and the instance. The purpose of this mechanism is to be independant from the schema update language and the instance update language and to allow static typechecking. We will use the language presented in section 5 to illustrate the database evolution process.

Definition 6.1 An *evolution program* is a pair (R, Q) where R is a schema update program and Q a concrete instance update program. □

Given schemas $S = (C, \leq, \Sigma)$ and $S' = (C', \leq', \Sigma')$, we denote $S \oplus S'$ the schema $(C \uplus C', \leq \uplus \leq', \Sigma \uplus \Sigma')$, where $\uplus$ is the usual disjoint union over sets. If c (resp. a) appears in both S and S', the c in S' is denoted $\tilde{c}$ (resp. $\tilde{a}$).

Let be given a schema S and an evolution program $E = (R, Q)$ such that: R is non contradictory, and legal and consistent upon S; and $Q = (L, \alpha, P)$ is legal for designation upon S, and legal for specification upon $[R]_S$. The *concrete instance update program associated to* (R, Q) *and* S, $\overline{Q} = (L, \alpha, \overline{P})$, is upon $S \oplus [R]_S$, and is defined as follows.

1. Each *delete* or *cut* instruction in P is in $\overline{P}$;
2. for each *new x c* (resp. *move x c, set x a x'*) in P, we have *new x $\tilde{c}$* (resp. *move x $\tilde{c}$, set x $\tilde{a}$ x'*) in $\overline{P}$;
3. for each class c in S such that $-c \notin R$, there is an instruction *move x_c $\tilde{c}$* in $\overline{P}$, where x_c is a variable (of type $\{c\}$) appearing only in this instruction.

Note that $\overline{Q}$ is legal. E is said *legal* upon S if $\overline{Q}$ is non contradictory upon $S \oplus [R]_S$.

For each class c in S, let $var(c)$ denote the set of variables appearing in a *move* or *delete* instruction in Q, and in the type of which c appears. Let I be an instance of S, and v a valuation over the variables of Q in I. We define the valuation $\overline{v}$ as extending v to each variable x_c introduced in item 3 above, as: $\overline{v}(x_c) = \nu(c) - \bigcup_{x \in var(c)} v(x)$; $\overline{v}$ is said *empty for c* if $\overline{v}(x_c) = \emptyset$.

Definition 6.2 Let be given S, $E = (R, Q)$ legal upon S, I instance of S and v over Q in I non conflictual; let $\overline{Q}$ be associated to E and S, and $\overline{v}$ extending v. Let v be such that $\overline{v}$ is empty for each deleted class. The *semantics* of E upon S on I under v is the pair (S', I'), where $S' = [R]_S$, and $I' = [\overline{Q}]_{I, \overline{v}}^{S \oplus S'}$. □

Given S, an evolution program is *consistent*, if for each I and v, its semantics is an instance.

Proposition 6.3 Given S and R, it is decidable whether $\overline{Q}$ is contradictory. □

Proof (Sketch) It is an extension of the proof of Proposition 5.7. □

Theorem 6.4 Given S, it is decidable whether E is consistent (for path queries without the *l.a* construct for *a* mono-valued). □

Proof (Sketch) It is a careful extension of the proof of Theorem 5.9 taking into account the changes in the schema. □

To illustrate our topic, we consider the schema of Example 3 derived from the one in Example 1. This modification of the schema from example 1 consists in creating a class S_P which represents the single parents, which inherits from P and which has an attribute c. The attribute c has to be deleted in class P.

The following schema update program is designed to perform this modification of the schema:

$+_c\ S\_P,\ +_a\ c : S\_P \rightarrow P,\ +_a\ c : M\_W \rightarrow P,\ +_a\ c : M\_M \rightarrow P,\ +_a\ f : S\_P \rightarrow S\_P,\ +_h\ S\_P\ P,\ -_a\ c\ P \rightarrow P$

It is obvious that if the instance stay unchanged, it will be non-consistent w.r.t. the schema. The reason is that some objects in class P will have an attribute c which is now undefined in this class.

It is clear that the schema update and the instance update can not be performed sequentially. Because the class S_P does not exists to allow the instance update program to run first. And because running the schema update program first will lead to a non-consistent instance. We could cut the instance update program and the schema update program to interlace their instructions, but the system would then not be able to detect errors that would lead to a non consistent database. To maintain consistency, we can cut the links for attribute c of objects in class P but it seems better to migrate the objects from class P, which have an attribute c different from the empty set, into class S_P. Furthermore, we will have to cut all the attribute links f from these objects to objects which are not single parents.

The only necessary parameter for the instance update program that will perform this update is the whole population of the class P and its subclasses M_M and M_W. This parameter will be denoted as z.

Using the path query language, we can define the objects that are single parents. These objects are defined by the path expression: $z.c^{-1} - (z.c^{-1} : M\_W \cup z.c^{-1} : M\_M)$

In the following this expression will be denoted as the formal parameter z_1. The instance update program performing the desired adaptation is then:

$\{move\ z_1\ S\_P,\ cut\ z_1\ f\ (z - z_1)\}$

7   Conclusion

In this paper, we first presented a declarative instance update language using typed parameters. The way of designating these parameters is based on attribute paths existing in the schema. Some typing results have been exposed for this instance update language. Then, we have defined a database evolution mechanism. This mechanism relies on the combination of two languages. The first one is a basic schema update language featuring the addition and removal of classes, inheritance links and attribute definition. The syntax of this language is close from the one in [BKKK87]. The second language is the instance update language presented in section 5. This work is different from the ones defined in [FMZ+95],

[BKKK87] in the fact that the mechanism is independant from the schema and instance update languages and that there is no automatic reorganization of the instance consecutive to the schema update. The task of the system is only to tell whether the resulting database will be a consistent database (consistent schema and instance of this schema) or not.

References

[AKW90] S. Abiteboul, P. Kanellakis, and E. Waller. Method schemas. In *PODS*, pages 16–27, 1990.

[ALP91] J. Andany, M. Leonard, and C. Palisser. Management of schema evolution in databases. In *VLDB*, 1991.

[Bar77] J. Barwise. Chapter: An introduction to first-order logic. In *Handbook of Mathematical Logic*, 1977.

[BKKK87] J. Banerjee, W. Kim, H.-J. Kim, and H. F. Korth. Semantics and implementation of schema evolution in object-oriented databases. In *SIGMOD*, 1987.

[FMZ+95] F. Ferrandina, T. Meyer, R. Zicari, G. Ferran, and J. Madec. Schema and database evolution in the o2 object database system. In *VLDB*, pages 170–181, 1995.

[Lag]   J.B. Lagorce. Aspects of updates in databases. PhD thesis in preparation.

[LSW]   J.B. Lagorce, A. Stočkus, and E. Waller. Object-oriented databases evolution. Technical Report in preparation, Orsay.

[Mit90] J. C. Mitchell. Chapter: Type systems for programming languages. In *Handbook of Theoretical Computer Science*, 1990.

[MMW94] A. Mendelzon, T. Milo, and E. Waller. Object migration. In *PODS*, 1994.

[Mor75] M. Mortimer. On languages with two variables. In *Zeitschr. f. mat. Logik und Grunlagen d. Math, Bd. 21*, pages 135–140, 1975.

[NR89]   G.T. NGuyen and D. Rieu. Schema evolution in object-oriented database systems. In *Data and Knowledge Engineering*, 1989.

[PS87]   D. J. Penney and J. Stein. Class modification in the gemstone object-oriented dbms. In *OOPSLA*, 1987.

[Sto95] A. Stockus. Migration dans les bases de données orientées objet. DEA report, Orsay, 1995.

[Su91]   J. Su. Dynamic constraints and object migration. In *VLDB*, pages 233–242, 1991.

[Wal91] E. Waller. Schema updates and consistency. In *DOOD*, 1991.

[Zdo87] S. Zdonik. Can objects change types, can types change objects? In *Workshop on OODBS*, 1987.

[Zic92] R. Zicari. A framework for schema updates in an object-oriented database system. In *The O2 Book*, 1992.

Performance of Nearest Neighbor Queries in R-trees *

Apostolos Papadopoulos   Yannis Manolopoulos

Department of Informatics
Aristotle University
54006 Thessaloniki, Greece
email : { *apapadop,manolopo* } *@athena.auth.gr*

Abstract. Nearest neighbor (NN) queries are posed very frequently in spatial applications. Recently a branch-and-bound algorithm based on R-trees has been developed in order to answer efficiently NN queries. In this paper, we combine techniques that were inherently used for the analysis of range and spatial join queries, in order to derive measures regarding the performance of NN queries. We try to estimate the number of disk accesses introduced due to the processing of an NN query. Lower and upper bounds are defined estimating the performance of NN queries very closely. The theoretical analysis is verified with experimental results, under uniform and non-uniform distributions of queries and data, in the 2-dimensional address space.

1 Introduction

Spatial data management is an active area of research over the past ten years [Same90a, Same90b, Laur92, Guti94]. Research interests focused mainly on the design of robust and efficient spatial data structures [Gutt84, Henr89, Guen89, Beck90, Kame94], the invention of new spatial data models [Laur92], the construction of effective query languages [Egen94] and the query processing and optimization of spatial queries [Oren86, Aref93, Papa95].

A very important research direction is the estimation of the performance and the selectivity of a query. Given a query, the problem is to estimate the response time (performance) and the fraction of the objects that fulfils the query versus the database population (selectivity). Evidently, we want this information available prior to query processing, in order for the query optimizer to determine an efficient access plan.

Nearest Neighbor (NN) queries are very important in Geographic Information Systems [Same90b, Rous95], in Image Databases [Arya93, Nibl93] as weel as in Multimedia Applications [Fagi96]. However, researchers working on spatial accesses methods focused mainly on range queries [Page93, Kame93, Fal94, Theo96] and spatial join queries [Brin93, LoRa94, Belu95]. In the past the problem of NN query processing has been addressed by examining access methods

---

* Work supported by European Union's TMR program and by national PENED and EPET programs.

based on k-d trees [Frie77] and quadtrees [Same90b]. Only recently a branch-and-bound algorithm based on R-trees has been developed, in order to answer efficiently NN queries [Rous95]. In this paper we combine techniques that were inherently used for the analysis of range and spatial join queries, in order to derive effective measures regarding the performance of NN queries. We give average lower and upper bounds for the number of leaf pages retrieved during NN query processing. Evidently, CPU time is also important for computationally intensive queries, but in general the I/O subsystem overhead dominates, specifically in large spatial databases.

The rest of the article is organized as follows. In the next section we present the appropriate background on the R-tree family of spatial data structures and describe shortly the branch-and-bound algorithm of [Rous95]. Section 3 contains the derivation of the formulae for the upper and lower bounds towards the prediction of NN query performance. In Section 4 we give the experimental results, and finally in Section 5 we conclude the paper, and motivate for future research in the area.

2 Background

2.1 R-trees

The R-tree [Gutt84] is a hierarchical, height balanced data structure (all leaf nodes appear at the same level), designed for use in secondary storage, and it is a generalization of the B^+-tree for multidimensional spaces. A sample 2-d dataspace with a corresponding R-tree is presented in Figure 1 below. The

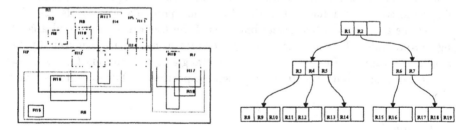

Fig. 1. R-tree example.

structure handles objects by means of their conservative approximation. The most simple and frequently used conservative approximation of an object's shape is the rectilinear Minimum Bounding Rectangle (MBR). Each node of the tree corresponds to exactly one disk page. Internal nodes contain entries of the form *(R,child-ptr)*, where R is the MBR that encloses all the MBRs of its descendants and *child-ptr* is the pointer to the specific child node. Leaf nodes contain entries of the form *(R,object-ptr)* where R is the MBR of the object and *object-ptr* is the pointer to the objects detailed description. Since MBRs of internal nodes are allowed to overlap, we may have to follow multiple paths from root to leaves when answering a range query. This inefficiency triggered the design of the R^+-tree [Sell87] which does not permit overlapping MBRs of the nodes.

One of the most important factors affecting the overall structure performance is the node split strategy used. In [Gutt84] three split policies have been reported, namely exponential, quadratic and linear. However, more sophisticated policies reducing the overlap of MBRs have been reported in [Beck90] (the R^*-tree) and in [Kame94] (the Hilbert R-tree).

Finally, some R-tree variants have been reported to support a static or a nearly static database. If the objects composing the dataspace are known in advance, we can apply several packing techniques, with respect to the spatial proximity of the objects, in order to design a more efficient data structure, with increased initial overhead. Packing techniques have been reported in [Rous85, Kame93].

In this paper, we base our work on the packed R-tree of Kamel and Faloutsos [Kame93]. In this variant, the Hilbert value of each data object is calculated and then the whole dataset is sorted. Next, the leaf level of the tree is formulated by taking consecutive objects (with respect to the Hilbert order) and storing them in one data page. The same process is repeated for the upper levels of the structure. The derived R-tree has little overlap and square-like MBRs, both being reasonable properties of a "good" R-tree [Kame93, Fal94, Theo96].

2.2   The Branch-and-Bound Algorithm

In [Rous95] an efficient branch-and-bound R-tree traversal algorithm is reported, that answers NN and k-NN queries. It is a modification of the algorithm reported in [Frie77] for k-d-trees. In order to find the nearest neighbor of a point, the algorithm starts form the root of the R-tree and proceeds downwards. The key idea of the algorithm is that many branches of the tree can be discarded according to some rules. Two basic distances are defined in $n-$d space, between a point P with co-ordinates $(p_1, p_2, ..., p_n)$ and a rectangle R with corners $(s_1, s_2, ..., s_n)$ and $(t_1, t_2, ..., t_n)$ (bottom-left and top-right respectively). Two definitions follow [Rous95]:

Definition 1
The distance $MINDIST(P, R)$ of a point P from a rectangle R, is defined as follows:

$$MINDIST(P, R) = \sqrt{\sum_{j=1}^{n} |p_j - r_j|^2}$$

where:

$$r_j = \begin{cases} s_j, & p_j < s_j \\ t_j, & p_j > t_j \\ p_j, & \text{otherwise} \end{cases}$$

□

Definition 2

The distance $MINMAXDIST(P, R)$ of a point P from a rectangle R, is defined as follows:

$$MINMAXDIST(P,R) = \sqrt{\min_{1 \le k \le n}\left(|p_k - rm_k|^2 + \sum_{1 \le j \le n, j \ne k}|p_j - rM_j|^2\right)}$$

where:

$$rm_k = \begin{cases} s_k, & p_k \le \frac{s_k + t_k}{2} \\ t_k, & \text{otherwise} \end{cases}$$

$$rM_j = \begin{cases} s_j, & p_j \ge \frac{s_j + t_j}{2} \\ t_j, & \text{otherwise} \end{cases}$$

□

Clearly the $MINDIST$ is the optimistic metric, since it is the minimum possible distance that the NN of the query point P can reside in the corresponding data page. On the other hand, $MINMAXDIST$ is the pessimistic metric since it is the furthest possible distance where the NN of P can reside in the current data page. Therefore, the latter metric guarantees that the NN of P lies in a distance $\le MINMAXDIST$. The above definitions are shown graphically in Figure 2.

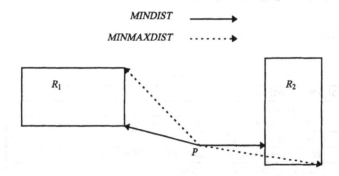

Fig. 2. *MINDIST* and *MINMAXDIST* between a point P and two rectangles R_1 and R_2.

The three basic rules used for pruning the search in the R-tree during traversal follow. Notice that these rules are applied only if one nearest neighbor is required.

Rule 1

If an MBR R has $MINDIST(P, R)$ greater than the $MINMAXDIST(P, R')$ of another MBR R', then it is discarded because it cannot enclose the nearest neighbor of P.

□

Rule 2
If an actual distance d from P to a given object, is greater than the $MINMAX$-
$DIST(P, R)$ of P to an MBR R, **then** d is replaced with $MINMAXDIST(P, R)$
because R contains an object which is closer to P.   □

Rule 3
If d is the current minimum distance, **then** all MBRs R_j with $MINDIST(P, R_j)$
> d are discarded, because they cannot enclose the nearest neighbor of P.   □

Upon visiting an internal node of the tree, Rules (1) and (2) are used in
order to discard irrelevant branches. Then, a branch is selected according to a
priority order. Roussopoulos et al. suggest that when the overlap is small, the
$MINDIST$ order should be used since it would discard more candidates. This
is also verified in the experimental results of their work. Therefore, the branch
which correspond to the minimum $MINDIST$ among all node entries is chosen.
Upon returning from the processing of the subtree, Rule (3) is applied in order to
discard other candidates (if there are any). Due to limited space, we are not going
into more details of the branch-and-bound algorithm. The reader is prompted
to reference [Rous95].

3 Analytical Considerations

3.1 Preliminaries

Symbol	Description
S	a set of 2-d points
N	population of the indexed dataset
n	space dimensionality
σ	side of the square-like data page MBR
D_0	*Hausdorff* fractal dimension
D_2	*correlation* fractal dimension
C_{max}	maximum number of objects per node
C_{avg}	average number of objects per node
U_{avg}	average space utilization
d_{nn}	distance between a query point and its NN point
d_m	distance from a query point to the $MINMAXDIST$ vertex of the first retrieved data page
q	query window side
$L(q)$	number of leaf accesses for a window query of side q
L_{bound}	lower bound for the number of leaf accesses
U_{bound}	upper bound for the number of leaf accesses

Table 1. Basic notations used throughout the analysis.

In this section, we derive lower and upper bounds for the performance of the branch-and-bound algorithm. We are interested in the estimation of the number of disk accesses to R-tree leaf pages, because in general the upper levels occupy small space in comparison to the leaf level, and therefore can fit in main memory. The basic notations are presented in Table 1.

Assume the dataspace is composed of a set of points S in the 2-d space. The problem is, given a point $P(p_1, p_2) \in S$, to find its NN point $Q(q_1, q_2)$. Let d_{nn} be the actual Euclidean distance between the points P and Q. The following propositions hold:

Proposition 1
The minimum number of leaf pages touched is the number of leaf pages intersected by the circle C_1 with center P and radius d_{nn}.

Proof
The distance d_{nn} is not known in advance. Therefore, even if the nearest neighbor of the query point is found, the algorithm does not stop until all candidates are examined. As a consequence, all data pages X_i with $MINDIST(P, X_i) \leq d_{nn}$ must be searched. □

Before stating Proposition 2, we introduce the following basic assumption which is a reasonable property of the algorithm, when the tree nodes have no or very little empty space:

Basic Assumption
The first data page that the algorithm visits, is the data page with the minimum $MINDIST$ among all data pages. □

Proposition 2
The maximum number of leaf pages touched is the number of leaf pages that the circle C_2 with center P and radius d_m intersects, where d_m is the $MINMAXDIST$ between P and the first touched leaf page.

Proof
Let R denote the first visited data page MBR. Clearly, the distance $MINMAXDIST(P, R)$ is the maximum possible "safe" distance where a nearest neighbor can be found in this data page. Moreover, it is possible that all data pages X_i with $MINDIST(P, X_i) \leq MINMAXDIST(P, R)$ will be visited, if a particular visiting sequence occurs. □

In Figure 3a an example is illustrated for Proposition 1. The arrow points to the NN of the query point P. Even if the algorithm reaches this point, it is not known that this is the NN of P, until data pages 1 and 2 are examined. In Figure 3b Proposition 2 is explained. Page 1 is the first visited data page. In the worst case the NN of P, in this page, resides in $MINMAXDIST(P, 1)$ from P.

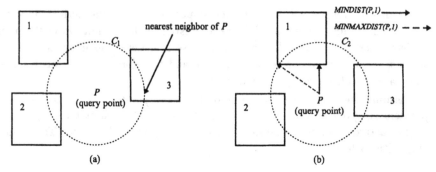

Fig. 3. (a): example of Proposition 1, (b): example of Proposition 2

However, it is not guaranteed that pages 2 and 3 will be visited. This will occur in the worst case only, and depends on the visiting sequence and the location of the "temporary" NN point in each data page.

The above propositions give a lower bound (Proposition 1) and an upper bound (Proposition 2) for the number of leaf nodes touched by the algorithm, on the average. We note the importance of the distance d_{nn}, which is the expected distance from P to its nearest neighbor. Therefore, if we had an estimation for d_{nn}, we could provide estimations for the best and worst performance of NN queries. The following subsection deals with the estimation of d_{nn} and d_m.

3.2 Estimation of d_{nn} and d_m

We are interested in the estimation of d_{nn} for arbitrary object distributions. Real datasets show a clear divergence from the uniformity and independence assumption [Fal94] and, therefore, it is better to consider uniformity as a special case. In [Belu95] a formula has been reported that estimates the average number of neighbors $nb(\epsilon, shape)$ of a point P within distance ϵ from P, using the concept of the *correlation* fractal dimension of the point set:

$$nb(\epsilon, shape) = \left(\frac{volume(\epsilon, shape)}{volume(\epsilon, rect)} \right)^{D_2/n} \cdot (N - 1) \cdot 2^{D_2} \cdot \epsilon^{D_2} \qquad (1)$$

where N is the population of the dataset, D_2 is the correlation fractal dimension, n is the dimensionality of the dataspace (2 in our case), and *shape* is the shape that has its center of gravity on a point P of the dataset. Since we are interested in NN queries with respect to the Euclidean distance, it is sufficient to set *shape* = *circle*. Making the appropriate modifications in Equation (1) we get:

$$nb(\epsilon, circle) = \left(\frac{\pi \epsilon^2}{4\epsilon^2} \right)^{D_2/2} \cdot (N - 1) \cdot 2^{D_2} \cdot \epsilon^{D_2}$$

By simplifying we get:

$$nb(\epsilon, circle) = (\sqrt{\pi})^{D_2} \cdot (N - 1) \cdot \epsilon^{D_2} \qquad (2)$$

We can use Equation (2) to estimate the average distance (d_{nn}) of a point P to its nearest neighbor. We are searching for an ϵ such that $nb(\epsilon, circle) = 1$. After substitution in Equation (2) and algebraic manipulations we reach:

$$d_{nn} = \epsilon = \frac{1}{\sqrt{\pi} \cdot {}^{D_2}\!\!\sqrt{(N-1)}} \qquad (3)$$

The above equation holds for an arbitrary dataset, when we allow queries to land only on data points. The uniformity case is derived by setting $D_2 = 2$.

Let us now try to estimate the distance d_m, which is the minimum $MIN-MAXDIST$ between the query point P and the first visited data page. We assume that the MBRs of the data pages are squares with side σ. The following proposition holds:

Proposition 3
The maximum possible difference between $MINMAXDIST(P, R)$ and $MIN-DIST(P, R)$ from a query point P to an MBR R is σ.

Proof
This happens when the query point P coincides with a vertex of the MBR R. This is demonstrated in Figure 4. As we can see, when the query point P approaches the bottom-right vertex of the MBR, the difference between $MINMAXDIST$ and $MINDIST$ increases. $\qquad\qquad\qquad\qquad\qquad\qquad\qquad\qquad\square$

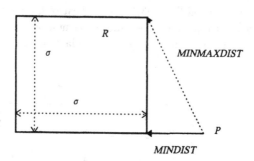

Fig. 4. When the query point P coincides with a vertex of the MBR, then the maximum difference (σ) between $MINDIST$ and $MINMAXDIST$ is obtained.

Assuming that the NN of a query point lies in the half distance (on the average) between the difference of $MINDIST$ and $MINMAXDIST$, we need only to augment d_{nn} by $\sigma/2$ in order to reach the $MINMAXDIST$. Therefore, we conclude that the distance d_m which gives the upper bound of Proposition 2 is calculated by the following Equation:

$$d_m = \frac{1}{\sqrt{\pi} \cdot \sqrt[D_2]{(N-1)}} + \frac{\sigma}{2} \tag{4}$$

3.3 Performance Estimation

Let S be a set of N data points distributed in the unit square address space. We are interested in estimating the number of data pages retrieved, when the NN is requested for any point $P \in S$. Given a query window $q \times q$ the number of leaf nodes $L(q)$ retrieved is given by a formula reported in [Fal94], which assumes that queries are distributed uniformly on the address space i.e. each portion of the dataspace has the same probability to be requested:

$$L(q) = \frac{N}{C_{avg}} \cdot (\sigma + q)^2 \tag{5}$$

$$\sigma = \left(\frac{C_{avg}}{N}\right)^{1/D_0}$$

$$C_{avg} = C_{max} \cdot U_{avg}$$

where N is the population of the dataset, D_0 is the *Hausdorff* (box counting) fractal dimension of the underlying point dataset, C_{max} is the maximum node capacity and U_{avg} is the average space utilization of the R-tree nodes.

However, in our case we cannot use Equation (5). This is because, the queries can land only on (existing) data points and therefore at least one leaf access will occur. In other words, in our case the query model assumes that the query distribution follows the data distribution (i.e. each data object has the same probability of retrieval [Page93]). To the best of the authors' knowledge no closed formula has been reported to estimate the number of leaf accesses in this query model. Therefore, we must derive a formula that obeys the latter query model.

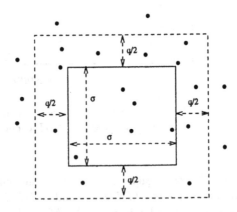

Fig. 5. Example of an enlarged data page.

Assume we have a $q \times q$ window and we have to perform a range query Q over the underlying address space. We know that the average size of each data page MBR is $\sigma \times \sigma$. We are interested in calculating the probability P_{fetch} that a data page will be fetched due to the execution of Q. A data page will be fetched only if the centroid of the window $q \times q$ falls in the area surrounded by the dashed line of Figure 5. Note however, that the centroid of the query window can only coincide with an existing data point (according to the query model considered in this paper). Therefore, the probability P_{fetch} can be defined as:

$$P_{fetch} = \frac{GoodPoints}{AllPoints} \qquad (6)$$

where $GoodPoints$ is the number of points enclosed by the enlarged $(\sigma + q) \times (\sigma + q)$ window, and $AllPoints$ is the population, N, of the indexed dataset. However, we have the appropriate mathematical tools to calculate $GoodPoints$. We can use Equation (1) setting[1] $shape = rect$ and $\epsilon = \frac{\sigma+q}{2}$. Therefore, we have:

$$GoodPoints = (N - 1) \cdot (\sigma + q)^{D_2} \qquad (7)$$

From Equations (6) and (7) we get:

$$P_{fetch} = \frac{N - 1}{N} \cdot (\sigma + q)^{D_2} \qquad (8)$$

Our next step is to calculate the average number of data page accesses. We know that the total number of data pages is $\frac{N}{C_{avg}}$. Therefore:

$$L(q) = \frac{N}{C_{avg}} \cdot P_{fetch} \Rightarrow L(q) = \frac{N - 1}{C_{avg}} \cdot (\sigma + q)^{D_2} \qquad (9)$$

In order to get the lower and upper bounds for the number of leaf accesses, we must substitute q in Equation (9), with $2 \cdot d_{nn}$ from Equation (3), and $2 \cdot d_m$ from Equation (4), respectively. Therefore, we have:

$$L_{bound} = \frac{N - 1}{C_{avg}} \cdot (\sigma + 2 \cdot d_{nn})^{D_2} \qquad (10)$$

$$U_{bound} = \frac{N - 1}{C_{avg}} \cdot (\sigma + 2 \cdot d_m)^{D_2} \qquad (11)$$

Equations (10) and (11) include uniformity as a special case. Clearly, for uniform point sets $D_0 \approx 2$ and $D_2 \approx 2$, so we can use the above equations for any kind of point set. Also, we note that L_{bound} and U_{bound} are bounds on the average case and not absolute ones. This means that during NN query processing, the lower bound may be higher than the leaf pages touched. However, we are interested on the average case, and exceptional cases do not harm the generality.

---

[1] This requires an optimistic assumption that we can always find a data point on the centroid of the data page MBR.

4 Experimental Results

4.1 Preliminaries

We implemented the branch-and-bound algorithm [Rous95] and the Hilbert-packed R-tree [Kame93] in the C programming language under UNIX, and ran the experiments on a DEC Alpha 3000 workstation. We used randomly (almost uniform) generated as well as real-life points, in order to verify the theoretical aspects. The datasets used are depicted in Figure 6. The real-life points are 9,552 road intersections of the Montgomery County, Maryland. For uniform point sets we have $D_0 \approx 2$ and $D_2 \approx 2$, whereas for the MG points $D_0 \approx 1.719$ and $D_2 \approx 1.518$ [Belu95].

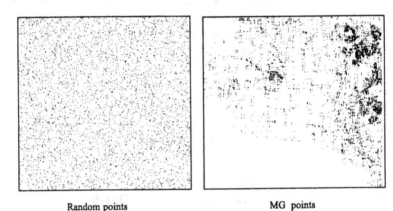

Random points   MG points

Fig. 6. Datasets used in the experiments.

4.2 Experimentation

In all experimental series, for each dataset, the average number of leaf accesses was determined by issuing an NN query for each existing data point. Also, the lower and upper bounds for the average number of leaf accesses were calculated. The measured average number of leaf accesses is shown in the last column of each subsequent table.

Experiment 1

The dataset is composed of a number of uniformly distributed points. The maximum R-tree node capacity was set to 50 objects. In Table 2 we present the results for uniform data of various populations.

Experiment 2

The dataset is composed of uniformly distributed points. Here we keep the population of the dataset constant at 50,000 and vary the maximum fanout of the tree from 10 to 200. The results are shown in Table 3.

Experiment 3

The dataset is composed of the $\approx 9,000$ MG points. Again, we vary the fanout of the tree from 10 to 200 as in Experiment 2. The results are presented in Table 4.

Population	Lower	Upper	Measured
1,000	1.34	4.66	1.63
2,000	1.34	4.66	1.58
10,000	1.34	4.66	1.70
20,000	1.34	4.66	1.80
50,000	1.34	4.66	2.04
100,000	1.34	4.66	1.88
200,000	1.34	4.66	2.28
500,000	1.34	4.66	1.97

Table 2. Leaf accesses versus data population. Data=Uniform, Fanout=50.

Fanout	Lower	Upper	Measured
5	2.26	6.27	3.02
10	1.84	5.55	2.68
20	1.56	5.07	2.19
50	1.34	4.66	2.03
100	1.23	4.46	1.90
200	1.16	4.32	1.82

Table 3. Leaf accesses versus fanout. Data=Uniform, Population=50,000.

Fanout	Lower	Upper	Measured
5	3.22	7.99	4.13
10	2.70	7.01	3.06
20	2.33	6.24	2.36
50	1.98	5.44	2.27
100	1.77	4.94	1.89
200	1.61	4.52	1.81

Table 4. Leaf accesses versus fanout. Data=MG points, Population $\approx$ 9,000.

4.3 Result Interpretation

From these tables it is evident that the lower and upper bounds enclose very well the measured average number of leaf accesses. Therefore, one could use the simple Formulae (10) and (11) in order to estimate the performance of an NN query. We observe that the measured number of leaf accesses is generally closer to the lower bound than the upper bound. This gives us a strong indication that the branch-and-bound algorithm with the $MINDIST$ criterion exploits the "goodness" property of the packed R-tree very effectively. Lower bound gives an optimistic metric and upper bound a pessimistic metric and are both valuable in query processing and optimization. Another observation is that when the data (and hence the query) distribution is uniform, the bounds do not depend on the population of the dataset. This can be verified by substituting the appropriate values for σ, d_{nn} and d_m in Equations (10) and (11), and is illustrated in Table 2.

5 Conclusions and Future Work

In this paper we have focused on the performance estimation of NN queries in spatial data structures and particularly in R-trees. The only known algorithm for NN queries in R-trees is the branch-and-bound algorithm of Roussopoulos et al. [Rous95], to the best of the authors' knowledge. We have shown that the actual distance between a point and its NN plays a very important role for the performance estimation of NN queries. Experiments based on synthetic and real-life data have shown that the derived bounds enclose very closely the number of leaf accesses introduced during the processing of an NN query. In fact, the performance of the branch-and-bound algorithm is closer to the lower bound, and therefore is very efficient. This estimation could be exploited by a query optimizer, to derive an efficient query processing plan. However, more work is needed, since this field is yet unexplored. Future work in the area may include:

- modification of the Formulae (10) and (11), in order to estimate the performance of arbitrary k-NN queries,
- derivation of a formula for the exact performance prediction of NN query processing (not just lower and upper bounds),
- the relaxation of the basic assumption (Section 3),
- generalization for non-point objects,
- consideration of complex queries with several constraints (e.g. find the NN of the point P, such that the distance is $\geq d$).
- consideration of the case where we request the NN for a point P that does not belong to the data set.
- examination of the case where the R-tree is not that "good" as the packed R-tree (e.g. Guttman's R-tree).

We are currently working on the performance estimation of general k-NN queries ($k > 1$) in high dimensional address spaces ($d > 2$). Also, we consider more real datasets in order to justify the usefulness of the analytical results in the prediction of NN query performance.

Acknowledgements

The authors would like to thank Alberto Belussi (at Politecnico di Milano) for providing the MG point dataset and also, the anonymous referees for their helpful comments and suggestions regarding this article.

References

[Aref93] W. Aref: "Query Processing and Optimization in Spatial Databases", *Technical Report CS-TR-3097, Department of Computer Science*, University of Maryland at College Park, MD, 1993.

[Arya93] M. Arya, W. Cody, C. Faloutsos, J. Richardson and A. Toga: "QBISM: a Prototype 3-d Medical Image Database System", *IEEE Data Engineering Bulletin*, 16(1), pp.38-42, March 1993.

[Beck90] N. Beckmann, H.P. Kriegel and B. Seeger: "The R*-tree: an Efficient and Robust Method for Points and Rectangles", *Proceedings of the 1990 ACM SIGMOD Conference*, pp.322-331, Atlantic City, NJ, 1990.

[Belu95] A. Belussi and C. Faloutsos: "Estimating the Selectivity of Spatial Queries Using the 'Correlation' Fractal Dimension", *Proceedings of the 21th VLDB Conference*, pp.299-310, Zurich, Switzerland, 1995.

[Brin93] T. Brinkhoff, H.P. Kriegel and B. Seeger: "Efficient Processing of Spatial Join Using R-trees", *Proceedings of the 1990 ACM SIGMOD Conference*, pp.237-246, Washington DC, 1993.

[Egen94] M. Egenhofer: "Spatial SQL: a Query and Presentation Language", *IEEE Transactions on Knowledge and Data Engineering*, vol.6, no.1, pp.86-95, 1994.

[Fagi96] R. Fagin: "Combining Fuzzy Information from Multiple Systems", *Proceedings of the 15th ACM SIGACT-SIGMOD-SIGART Symposium on Principles of Database Systems (PODS '96)*, pp.216-226, Montreal, Canada, 1996.

[Fal94] C. Faloutsos and I. Kamel: "Beyond Uniformity and Independence, Analysis of R-trees Using the Concept of Fractal Dimension", *Proceedings of the 13th ACM SIGACT-SIGMOD-SIGART Symposium on Principles of Database Systems (PODS '94)*, pp.4-13, Minneapolis, MN, 1994.

[Frie77] J.H. Friedman, J.L. Bentley and R.A. Finkel: "An Algorithm for Finding the Best Matches in Logarithmic Expected Time", *ACM Transactions on Math. Software*, vol.3, pp.209-226, 1977.

[Guen89] O. Guenther: "The Design of the Cell Tree: an Object-Oriented Index Structure for Geometric Databases", *Proceedings of the 5th IEEE Conference on Data Engineering*, pp.598-615, Los Angeles, CA, 1989.

[Guti94] R.H. Guting: "An Introduction to Spatial Database Systems", *The VLDB Journal*, vol.3, no.4, pp.357-399, 1994.

[Gutt84] A. Guttman: "R-trees: a Dynamic Index Structure for Spatial Searching", *Proceedings of the 1984 ACM SIGMOD Conference*, pp.47-57, Boston, MA, 1984.

[Henr89] A. Henrich, H.W. Six and P. Widmayer: "The LSD-tree: Spatial Access to Multidimensional Point and non-Point Objects", *Proceedings of the 15th VLDB Conference*, pp.45-53, Amsterdam, Netherlands, 1989.

[Kame93] I. Kamel and C. Faloutsos: "On Packing R-trees", *Proceedings of the 2nd Conference on Information and Knowledge Management (CIKM)*, Washington DC, 1993.

[Kame94] I. Kamel and C. Faloutsos: "Hilbert R-tree: an Improved R-tree Using Fractals", *Proceedings of the 20th VLDB Conference*, pp.500-509, Santiago, Chile, 1994.

[Laur92] R. Laurini and D. Thompson: *"Fundamentals of Spatial Information Systems"*, Academic Press, London, 1992.

[LoRa94] M.L. Lo and C.V. Ravishankar: "Spatial Joins Using Seeded Trees", *Proceedings of the 1994 ACM SIGMOD Conference*, pp.209-220, Minneapolis, MN, 1994.

[Nibl93] W. Niblack, R. Barber, W. Equitz, M. Flickner, E. Glasman, D. Petkovic and P. Yanker: "The QBIC Project: Querying Images by Content Using Color, Texture and Shape", *Proceedings of the SPIE Conference on Storage and Retrieval for Image and Video Databases*, vol.1908, pp.173-187, 1993.

[Oren86] J. Orenstein: "Spatial Query Processing in an Object-Oriented Database System", *Proceedings of the 1986 ACM SIGMOD Conference*, pp.326-336, Washington DC, 1986.

[Page93] B.U. Pagel, H.W. Six, H. Toben and P. Widmayer: "Towards an Analysis of Range Query Performance in Spatial Data Structures", *Proceedings of the 12th ACM SIGACT-SIGMOD-SIGART Symposium on Principles of Database Systems (PODS '93)*, pp.214-221, Washington DC, 1993.

[Papa95] A. Papadopoulos and Y. Manolopoulos: "Multiple Range Query Optimization in Spatial Databases", *Information Systems*, submitted.

[Rous85] N. Roussopoulos and D. Leifker: "Direct Spatial Search on Pictorial Databases Using Packed R-trees", *Proceedings of the 1985 ACM SIGMOD Conference*, pp.17-31, Austin, TX, 1985.

[Rous95] N. Roussopoulos, S. Kelley and F. Vincent: "Nearest Neighbor Queries", *Proceedings of the 1995 ACM SIGMOD Conference*, pp.71-79, San Jose, CA, 1995.

[Same90a] H. Samet: *"The Design and Analysis of Spatial Data Structures"*, Addison-Wesley, MA, 1990.

[Same90b] H. Samet: *"Applications of Spatial Data Structures: Computer Graphics, Image Processing and GIS"*, Addison-Wesley, MA, 1990.

[Sell87] T. Sellis, N. Roussopoulos and C. Faloutsos: "The R^{+}-tree: a Dynamic Index for Multidimensional Objects", *Proceedings of the 13th VLDB Conference*, pp.507-518, Brighton, UK, 1987.

[Theo96] Y. Theodoridis and T. Sellis: "A Model for the Prediction of R-tree Performance", *Proceedings of the 15th ACM SIGACT-SIGMOD-SIGART Symposium on Principles of Database Systems (PODS '96)*, Montreal, Canada, 1996.

Optimal Allocation of Two-Dimensional Data (Extended Abstract)

Khaled A. S. Abdel-Ghaffar*[1] and Amr El Abbadi**[2]

[1] Department of Electrical and Computer Engineering, University of California, Davis, CA 95616, USA
[2] Department of Computer Science, University of California, Santa Barbara, CA 93106, USA

Abstract. Efficient browsing and retrieval of geographically referenced information requires the allocation of data on different storage devices for concurrent retrieval. By dividing a two dimensional space into tiles, a system can allow users to specify regions of interest using a query rectangle and then retrieving all information related to tiles overlapping with the query. In this paper, we derive the necessary and sufficient conditions for strictly optimal allocations of two-dimensional data. These methods, when they exist, guarantee that for any query, the minimum number of tiles are assigned the same storage device, and hence ensures maximal retrieval concurrency.

1 Introduction

Information displayed on a two dimensional screen is often used as a tool for supporting the retrieval of more detailed data that is associated with a specific part of the screen. A common example in geographic applications is to display a schematic or low resolution map of the world on a screen. A user may then specify a region of the map (via a two dimensional rectangle) and request the displaying of a higher resolution satellite image of that region. Alternatively, the user may request that pictures of famous historical monuments located in cities in the selected region be displayed. Efficient support of such queries is quite important for image databases in particular, and for browsing geographically referenced information in general. In the Alexandria Digital Library project [Smi96], a large satellite image is often divided into tiles and each tile is decomposed using wavelet decomposition [VH92]. A wavelet decomposition of an image results in a lower resolution image of the original image, in addition to higher order coefficients that can be used to retrieve higher resolution versions of the same image. Similar approaches are common in other systems for browsing large image

---

* This author was supported in part by the National Science Foundation under grant NCR-9115423.

** This author was supported in part by the National Science Foundation under grant IRI-9411330.

databases [FBF+94,OS95]. A user would usually browse the lower resolution images fast and then specify regions to be expanded to display at a higher resolution. Such reconstruction requires the retrieval of the higher resolution coefficients (or, in general, components) for the various tiles that overlap with the specified region.

In this paper we address the problem of efficiently retrieving data that is associated with a rectilinearly oriented rectangle defined on a two dimensional grid. Since the data associated with individual tiles of the grid can be quite large, we would like to store them on parallel I/O devices in such a way that for a given query, retrieval from these parallel devices can occur concurrently. Ideally, the information related to each tile would be stored on a distinct I/O device and for any query all tile information would be retrieved concurrently. However, in general, the number of I/O devices is much less than the number of tiles. In this paper, we first define an optimality criterion for the allocation of two dimensional data and then provide both necessary and sufficient conditions for optimal allocation methods. In the cases where an optimal allocation method exists, we provide simple allocation methods that can be easily implemented. Previous research concentrated on efficient retrieval of images for circular queries [CR93] and, more generally, on the disk allocation of relational databases for range queries [Fal88,LSR92,CC92], as well as the organization of raster-graphics memory [CLRS86]. We discuss their relationship to our work as well as future extensions in the conclusion of the paper.

2 Problem Statement

Consider the domain of discourse, an $n_1 \times n_2$ array whose elements (i,j), where $0 \le i \le n_1 - 1$ and $0 \le j \le n_2 - 1$, are called *tiles*. Each tile can be viewed as containing more detailed information about the area it covers. For example, if the array is a low resolution image of a geographic region, the higher resolution wavelet coefficients may be associated with the individual tiles. Alternatively, pictures of famous monuments may be associated with the tiles where they are geographically located. Given two tiles (i_1,j_1) and (i_2,j_2), where $i_1 \le i_2$ and $j_1 \le j_2$, we define the two dimensional query

$$R[(i_1,j_1),(i_2,j_2)] = \{(i,j) : i_1 \le i \le i_2 \text{ and } j_1 \le j \le j_2\}.$$

This represents the $(i_2 - i_1 + 1) \times (j_2 - j_1 + 1)$ rectangle with (i_1,j_1) and (i_2,j_2) as opposite corner tiles. The area of this rectangle is $(i_2 - i_1 + 1)(j_2 - j_1 + 1)$, which equals the number of tiles in the rectangle.

Each tile (i,j) in the $n_1 \times n_2$ array is assigned a number $f(i,j)$ in the set $\{0, 1, \ldots, M - 1\}$. For efficient retrieval, this set of numbers refer to M I/O storage devices on which the tile-related information can be stored. We say that f is an M-assignment for the $n_1 \times n_2$ array. Clearly, any rectangle of area A has at least $\lceil A/M \rceil$ tiles that are assigned the same number. We say that the M-assignment f is *strictly optimal* if no rectangle of area A has more than $\lceil A/M \rceil$

tiles that are assigned the same number. In particular, in a strictly optimal M-assignment, the numbers assigned to the tiles in any rectangle of area at most M are distinct. Hence, given a grid with a strictly optimal M-assignment, all tiles of any rectangle query of size M will reside on different I/O devices and hence can be retrieved in parallel, ensuring minimal retrieval time.

We may identify the assignment f by an $n_1 \times n_2$ array where entry (i,j) is given by $f(i,j)$. For example, the 5-assignment

0	1	2	3	4	0	1	2
2	3	4	0	1	2	3	4
4	0	1	2	3	4	0	1
1	2	3	4	0	1	2	3
3	4	0	1	2	3	4	0
0	1	2	3	4	0	1	2

is strictly optimal for the 6×8 array, while the 5-assignment shown below is not.

0	1	2	0	1	2	0	1
3	4	0	3	4	0	3	4
0	1	2	0	1	2	0	1
3	4	0	3	4	0	3	4
0	1	2	0	1	2	0	1
3	4	0	3	4	0	3	4

Theorem 1 is the main result of this paper. It gives necessary and sufficient conditions for the existence of strictly optimal M-assignments for $n_1 \times n_2$ arrays in terms of M, n_1, and n_2.

Theorem 1. *A strictly optimal M-assignment exists for an $n_1 \times n_2$ array if and only if any of the following conditions holds:*

- $\min\{n_1, n_2\} \leq 2$,
- $M \in \{1, 2, 3, 5\}$,
- $M \geq n_1 n_2 - 2$,
- $M = n_1 n_2 - 4$ *and* $\min\{n_1, n_2\} = 3$,
- $M = 8$ *and* $n_1 = n_2 = 4$.

The proof of this result is presented in the following two sections. In the next section, we describe strictly optimal M-assignments if any of the conditions stated in Theorem 1 is satisfied. In Section 4, we complete the proof of the theorem by showing that no strictly optimal assignments exist for other choices of M, n_1, and n_2.

3 Strictly Optimal Assignments

We start by establishing strictly optimal assignments when one of the two dimensions of the array is less than or equal to two or when M is restricted to one, two, three, or five.

Lemma 2. *Suppose that $n_1 \leq 2$ or $M \in \{1, 2, 3, 5\}$. Consider the assignment f given by $f(i, j) = \lfloor M/2 \rfloor i + j \bmod M$. Then, any rectangle of area A has no more than $\lceil A/M \rceil$ tiles that are assigned the same number. In particular, the assignment f is strictly optimal.*

Proof. We consider different cases.

- $n_1 = 1$: In this case, the tiles in the array are $(0, 0), (0, 1), \ldots, (0, n_2 - 1)$ and any rectangle of area A is a $1 \times A$ rectangle. Since $f(i, j) = j \bmod M$, and the numbers $t, t + 1, \ldots, t + M - 1$ are distinct modulo M, for any integer t, it follows that the lemma holds.
- $n_1 = 2$: In this case, any rectangle of area A is either a $1 \times A$ or $2 \times \lfloor A/2 \rfloor$ rectangle. Using the same argument used in case $n_1 = 1$, it can be shown that the lemma holds for $1 \times A$ rectangles. If M is even, then the numbers $(M/2)i + j$, where $0 \leq i \leq 1$ and $t \leq j \leq t + M/2 - 1$, are distinct modulo M for any integer t. Hence the lemma holds for $2 \times \lfloor A/2 \rfloor$ rectangles. If M is odd, then the numbers $((M - 1)/2)i + j$, where $0 \leq i \leq 1$ and $t \leq j \leq t + M - 1$, assume each value modulo M exactly twice for any integer t. Hence, it suffices to consider $2 \times \lfloor A/2 \rfloor$ rectangles where $\lfloor A/2 \rfloor \leq M - 1$. On the other hand, the numbers $((M - 1)/2)i + j$, where $0 \leq i \leq 1$ and $t \leq j \leq t + (M - 3)/2$, are distinct modulo M for any integer t. Hence, we may assume that $(M + 1)/2 \leq \lfloor A/2 \rfloor \leq M - 1$. From the above, it follows that the rectangle $R[(0, t), (1, t + \lfloor A/2 \rfloor - 1)]$ has at most one tile (i', j'), where $t \leq j' \leq t + (M - 3)/2$, and at most one tile (i'', j''), where $t + (M - 1)/2 \leq j'' \leq t + \lfloor A/2 \rfloor - 1 \leq t + M - 2$, that are assigned the same number. Hence, there are at most two distinct tiles that are assigned the same number in any $2 \times \lfloor A/2 \rfloor$ rectangle, where $\lfloor A/2 \rfloor \geq (M + 1)/2$. This proves the lemma.
- $M = 1$: In this case, all tiles are assigned the same number and the lemma holds trivially.
- $M \in \{2, 3, 5\}$: In this case M is a prime and the M numbers $\lfloor M/2 \rfloor i + j$, where i is fixed and j runs over M consecutive integers, or vice versa, are distinct modulo M. Hence, it suffices to consider $a_1 \times a_2$ rectangles, where $a_1, a_2 \leq M - 1$. If $a_1 \leq 2$ or $a_2 \leq 2$, then the argument used in case $n_1 = 2$ shows that the lemma holds for such rectangles. Therefore, the lemma holds if $M \in \{2, 3\}$. If $M = 5$, it is easy to check that any $a_1 \times a_2$ rectangle where $3 \leq a_1, a_2 \leq 4$ has at most $\lceil a_1 a_2 / 5 \rceil$ tiles assigned the same number. This proves the lemma. □

Next, we establish strictly optimal assignments for the remaining cases listed in Theorem 1.

Lemma 3. *Consider the following M-assignments f for an $n_1 \times n_2$ array depending on the values of n_1, n_2, and M, where $n_2 \geq n_1 \geq 3$, $0 \leq i \leq n_1 - 1$, and $0 \leq j \leq n_2 - 1$:*

- $M \geq n_1 n_2$: $f(i,j) = n_2 i + j$.
- $M = n_1 n_2 - 1$: $f(i,j) = \begin{cases} 0 & \text{if } (i,j) = (n_1 - 1, n_2 - 1), \\ n_2 i + j & \text{otherwise.} \end{cases}$
- $M = n_1 n_2 - 2$:

$$f(i,j) = \begin{cases} 0 & \text{if } (i,j) = (n_1 - 1, n_2 - 1), \\ n_2 - 1 & \text{if } (i,j) = (n_1 - 1, 0), \\ n_2(n_1 - 1) + j - 1 & \text{if } i = n_1 - 1 \text{ and } j = 1, \ldots, n_2 - 2, \\ n_2 i + j & \text{if } i = 0, \ldots, n_1 - 2. \end{cases}$$

- $M = n_1 n_2 - 4$ and $n_2 > n_1 = 3$:

$$f(i,j) = \begin{cases} 0 & \text{if } (i,j) = (n_1 - 1, n_2 - 2), \\ 1 & \text{if } (i,j) = (n_1 - 1, n_2 - 1), \\ n_2 - 2 & \text{if } (i,j) = (n_1 - 1, 0), \\ n_2 - 1 & \text{if } (i,j) = (n_1 - 1, 1), \\ n_2(n_1 - 1) + j - 2 & \text{if } i = n_1 - 1 \text{ and } j = 2, \ldots, n_2 - 3, \\ n_2 i + j & \text{if } i = 0, \ldots, n_1 - 2. \end{cases}$$

- $M = 8$ and $n_1 = n_2 = 4$: $f = \begin{array}{|c|c|c|c|} \hline 0 & 1 & 2 & 3 \\ \hline 4 & 5 & 6 & 7 \\ \hline 2 & 3 & 0 & 1 \\ \hline 6 & 7 & 4 & 5 \\ \hline \end{array}$

Then, any rectangle of area A has no more than $\lceil A/M \rceil$ tiles that are assigned the same number. In particular, the assignment f is strictly optimal.

Proof. In each case, we list all pairs of tiles that are assigned the same number.

- $M \geq n_1 n_2$: none.
- $M = n_1 n_2 - 1$: $((0,0), (n_1 - 1, n_2 - 1))$.
- $M = n_1 n_2 - 2$: $((0,0), (n_1 - 1, n_2 - 1)), ((0, n_2 - 1), (n_1 - 1, 0))$.
- $M = n_1 n_2 - 4$ and $n_2 > n_1 = 3$: $((0,0),(n_1-1,n_2-2)), ((0,1),(n_1-1,n_2-1)), ((0, n_2 - 2),(n_1 - 1, 0)), ((0, n_2 - 1),(n_1 - 1, 1))$.
- $M = 8$, $n_1 = n_2 = 4$: $((0,0),(2,2)), ((0,1),(2,3)), ((0,2),(2,0)), ((0,3),(2,1)), ((1,0),(3,2)), ((1,1),(3,3)), ((1,2),(3,0)), ((1,3),(3,1))$.

It is easy to check that no rectangle of area at most M contains any of the above pairs. Furthermore, since no three tiles are assigned the same number, the lemma holds. $\square$

4 Necessary Conditions for Strict Optimality

In this section, we conclude the proof of Theorem 1 by showing that no strictly optimal assignments exist if none of the conditions stated in the theorem is satisfied.

Lemma 4. *Consider an $n_1 \times n_2$ array where $n_2 \geq n_1 \geq 3$. If $M \leq 2n_2 - 1$ and $M \notin \{1, 2, 3, 5\}$, then there is no strictly optimal M-assignment for this array.*

Proof. Suppose that f is a strictly optimal assignment. Then, the tiles in the rectangle $R[(0,0),(1,\lfloor M/2 \rfloor - 1)]$ are assigned distinct numbers. We may assume that $f(i,j) = \lfloor M/2 \rfloor i + j$, where $0 \le i \le 1$ and $0 \le j \le \lfloor M/2 \rfloor - 1$. Then, the numbers $0, 1, \ldots, 2\lfloor M/2 \rfloor - 1$ are assigned to distinct tiles in the rectangle. The tiles in each of the three rectangles $R[(0,0),(0,\lfloor M/2 \rfloor)]$, $R[(1,0),(1,\lfloor M/2 \rfloor)]$, and $R[(0,1),(1,\lfloor M/2 \rfloor)]$ are assigned distinct numbers. If M is even, this implies that $f(0,0) = f(1,M/2)$ and $f(1,0) = f(0,M/2)$. A similar argument yields $f(2,0) = f(1,M/2)$. Hence, $f(0,0) = f(2,0)$. Since the tiles $(0,0)$ and $(2,0)$ are in a rectangle of area equal to 3 and $M \ge 4$, we get a contradiction. On the other hand, if M is odd, then $f(1,(M-1)/2) \in \{f(0,0), M-1\}$ and $f(0,(M-1)/2) \in \{f(1,0), M-1\}$. Clearly, $f(0,(M-1)/2) \ne f(1,(M-1)/2)$ since the tiles $(0,(M-1)/2)$ and $(1,(M-1)/2)$ are in a rectangle of area equal to 2. Therefore, we may assume, without loss of generality, that $f(1,(M-1)/2) = f(0,0) = 0$. The tiles in each of the rectangles $R[(1,1),(2,(M-1)/2)]$ and $R[(0,0),(2,0)]$ are assigned distinct numbers. Hence, for $0 \le a_2 \le (M-3)/2$, $f(2,a_2) \ne 0$, and $f(2,a_2) \ne f(1,a_2')$, where $a_2' = 0, 1, \ldots (M-3)/2$. In particular, the $(M-1)/2$ tiles $(2,a_2)$, where $a_2 = 0, 1, \ldots (M-3)/2$, are assigned distinct numbers in the set $\{1, \ldots, (M-3)/2, M-1\}$ of $(M-1)/2$ numbers. Since $M \ge 7$ (as M is odd and M not in $\{1,2,3,5\}$), each of the rectangles $R[(0,0),(2,\lfloor (M-1)/4 \rfloor)]$ and $R[(0,\lfloor (M-1)/4 \rfloor),(2,(M-3)/2)]$ has an area of at most M. Hence, for $a_2 = 0, 1, \ldots, (M-3)/2$, $f(2,a_2) \ne f(0,\lfloor (M-1)/4 \rfloor) = \lfloor (M-1)/4 \rfloor$. This implies that the a_2's cannot be assigned distinct values in the set $\{1, \ldots, (M-3)/2, M-1\}$. This contradiction shows that no strictly optimal assignment exists. $\quad\square$

Lemma 5. *Suppose that an $n_1 \times n_2$ array has a strictly optimal M-assignment. Then, for any integer $t \le n_1$,*

$$\sum_{k=\lfloor M/n_2 \rfloor + 1}^{t} (2\lfloor M/k \rfloor - n_2) \le M - n_2 \lfloor M/n_2 \rfloor.$$

Proof. Clearly, the lemma holds in case $\lfloor M/n_2 \rfloor = 0$, i.e., $n_2 \ge M + 1$. So, assume in the following that $\lfloor M/n_2 \rfloor \ge 1$. The $n_2 \lfloor M/n_2 \rfloor$ tiles (i,j), where $0 \le i \le \lfloor M/n_2 \rfloor - 1$ and $0 \le j \le n_2 - 1$, are assigned different numbers since they are contained in a rectangle of area at most M. Similarly, if $\lfloor M/n_2 \rfloor + 1 \le k \le n_1$, then the tiles (i,j), where $0 \le i \le k - 1$ and $0 \le j \le \lfloor M/k \rfloor - 1$, are assigned different numbers and the tiles (i,j), where $0 \le i \le k - 1$ and $n_2 - \lfloor M/k \rfloor \le j \le n_2 - 1$, are also assigned different numbers. Hence, the $\max\{0, 2\lfloor M/k \rfloor - n_2\}$ tiles $(k-1,j)$, where $n_2 - \lfloor M/k \rfloor \le j \le \lfloor M/k \rfloor - 1$, are assigned distinct numbers that differ from the numbers assigned to the tiles (i,j) where $i \le k - 2$. Therefore, for any integer $t \le n_1$, the tiles $(k-1,j)$, where $\lfloor M/n_2 \rfloor + 1 \le k \le t$ and $n_2 - \lfloor M/k \rfloor \le j \le \lfloor M/k \rfloor - 1$, are assigned distinct numbers that differ from the $n_2 \lfloor M/n_2 \rfloor$ numbers assigned to the tiles (i,j), where $0 \le i \le \lfloor M/n_2 \rfloor - 1$ and $0 \le j \le n_2 - 1$. Hence,

$$\sum_{k=\lfloor M/n_2 \rfloor + 1}^{t} (2\lfloor M/k \rfloor - n_2) \le \sum_{k=\lfloor M/n_2 \rfloor + 1}^{t} \max\{0, 2\lfloor M/k \rfloor - n_2\} \le M - n_2 \lfloor M/n_2 \rfloor.$$
$\quad\square$

Using the above lemmas, we can complete the proof of Theorem 1.

Proof of Theorem 1.

Without loss of generality, we may assume that $n_1 \leq n_2$. If any of the conditions is satisfied, then the result follows from Lemmas 2 and 3. So, assume in the following that none of the conditions holds and, to obtain a contradiction, that a strictly optimal M-assignment exists. If $n_2 = 3$, then $n_1 n_2 = 9$. Since $M < n_1 n_2 - 2$, we have $M = 4$ or 6. By Lemma 4, $M = 6$. However, it is easy to check that there is no strictly optimal 6-assignment for a 3×3 array. Hence, $n_2 \geq 4$. Lemma 4 implies that $M \geq 2n_2$, i.e., $\lfloor M/n_2 \rfloor \geq 2$. Since $M < n_1 n_2$, $\lfloor M/n_2 \rfloor \leq n_1 - 1$. Taking $t = \lfloor M/n_2 \rfloor + 1$ in Lemma 5, we obtain

$$n_2(\lfloor M/n_2 \rfloor + 1) - M \leq 2 \left\lceil \frac{n_2(\lfloor M/n_2 \rfloor + 1) - M}{\lfloor M/n_2 \rfloor + 1} \right\rceil.$$

This implies one of the following conditions:

1. $n_2(\lfloor M/n_2 \rfloor + 1) - M = 1$.
2. $n_2(\lfloor M/n_2 \rfloor + 1) - M = 2$.
3. $n_2(\lfloor M/n_2 \rfloor + 1) - M = 4$ where $\lfloor M/n_2 \rfloor = 2$.

If $\lfloor M/n_2 \rfloor = n_1 - 1$, then each of these conditions implies a condition stated in the theorem. Hence, $\lfloor M/n_2 \rfloor \leq n_1 - 2$. Taking $t = \lfloor M/n_2 \rfloor + 2$ in Lemma 5, we obtain the following for conditions 1, 2, and 3, respectively.

- Condition 1: $n_2(\lfloor M/n_2 \rfloor + 1) - M = 1$ gives $n_2 \leq 2\lceil (n_2 + 1)/(\lfloor M/n_2 \rfloor + 2) \rceil + 1$. Since $n_2 \geq 4$ and $\lfloor M/n_2 \rfloor \geq 2$, it follows that either $n_2 = 4$ and $\lfloor M/n_2 \rfloor = 2$ or $n_2 = 5$ and $2 \leq \lfloor M/n_2 \rfloor \leq 3$. If $n_2 = 4$ and $\lfloor M/n_2 \rfloor = 2$, then $M = 11$ and $4 = \lfloor M/n_2 \rfloor + 2 \leq n_1 \leq n_2 = 4$, i.e., $n_1 = 4$. However, it is easy to check that no strictly optimal 11-assignment exists for a 4×4 array. If $n_2 = 5$ and $\lfloor M/n_2 \rfloor = 2$, then $M = 14$ and $n_1 = 4$ or 5. Again, it is easy to check that no strictly optimal 14-assignment exits for 4×5 or 5×5 arrays. If $n_2 = 5$, and $\lfloor M/n_2 \rfloor = 3$, then $M = 19$ and $n_1 = 5$. Again, no strictly optimal 19-assignment exits for 5×5 arrays.
- Condition 2: $n_2(\lfloor M/n_2 \rfloor + 1) - M = 2$ gives $n_2 \leq 2\lceil (n_2 + 2)/(\lfloor M/n_2 \rfloor + 2) \rceil$. Since $n_2 \geq 4$ and $\lfloor M/n_2 \rfloor \geq 2$, it follows that $n_2 = 4$ and $2 \leq \lfloor M/n_2 \rfloor \leq 3$. If $\lfloor M/n_2 \rfloor = 2$, then $M = 10$ and $n_1 = 4$. However, it is easy to check that no strictly optimal 10-assignment exists for a 4×4 array. If $\lfloor M/n_2 \rfloor = 3$, then $n_1 \geq 5$, which contradicts the assumption $n_1 \leq n_2$.
- Condition 3: $n_2(\lfloor M/n_2 \rfloor + 1) - M = 4$ where $\lfloor M/n_2 \rfloor = 2$ gives $n_2 \leq 2\lceil n_2/4 \rceil + 2$, i.e., $n_2 = 4, 5$, or 6. If $n_2 = 4$, then $M = 8$ and $n_1 = 4$, which implies a condition stated in the theorem. If $n_2 = 5$, then $M = 11$ and $n_1 = 4$ or 5. However, it is easy to check that no strictly optimal 11-assignment exists for 4×5 or 5×5 arrays. If $n_2 = 6$, then $M = 14$ and $n_1 = 4, 5$, or 6. Again, no strictly optimal 14-assignment exits for 4×6, 5×6, or 6×6 arrays. □

5 Discussion

In this paper, we derived the necessary and sufficient conditions for the existence of strictly optimal M-assignments of two-dimensional data. We show that except for a few cases, solutions cannot be strictly optimal. However, the results are important in that they have several ramifications from the practical point of view, as well as implications on future research. In terms of allocating tiled images on multiple I/O storage devices, a direct implication of Theorem 1 is that unless the system under consideration has the exact number of I/O devices specified in Theorem 1, the best tiling of a two dimensional grid is one that divides the space into strips (n_1 or $n_2 = 1$) or first into stripes and then each stripe is divided in two (n_1 or $n_2 = 2$).

Alternatively, Theorem 1 states that strict optimality can be achieved if the number of parallel devices is 1, 2, 3 or 5. Although this may seem quite limited, in fact, for some applications such as wavelet decomposition that require recursive decompositions, multiples of these numbers of storage devices would also result in optimal allocation methods. In particular, each tile in the lower resolution image grid can be expanded into the next higher resolution image using three coefficients [VH92]. Hence, assuming we have 15 parallel I/O devices, we cluster them into 5 groups, each with 3 disks. Theorem 1 is first used to partition the tiles among the 5 groups (there is a strictly optimal solution for this case). Subsequently, within each group, the 3 coefficients are distributed to 3 different devices. In fact, if r levels of decomposition are used, as many as $m * 3^r$, where $m = 1, 2, 3, 5$, I/O devices can be used for any tiling of an image.

A closely related problem to the M-assignment of two dimensional data arises in graphical interfaces where clustered pixels are stored on different memory chips for simultaneous access. Chor, Leiserson, Rivest, and Shearer [CLRS86] present an almost optimal technique based on a Fibonacci lattice to accomplish this task. However, their approach is different in that the memory organization guarantees that given a fixed number M of memory chips, if any rectangle contains less than $M/\sqrt{5}$ pixels (or tiles in our context), then all pixels will reside on different memory chips. In our problem, we are concerned with strict optimality for any rectangle, and not ones whose sizes are a function of the number of memory chips (or in general I/O devices).

In general, the problem of allocating a two dimensional grid on multiple I/O devices can be viewed as an important instance of range queries for multi-dimensional files. Two types of queries have been considered: partial match queries and range queries [AU79,Du86,Sun87,KP88,FM91,AE93]. The problem discussed in this paper can be viewed as a special case of range queries that are limited to two attributes on a relation with n attributes (the two attributes are the x and y axes, and the rest of the attributes correspond to the data associated with each unique combination of x and y). Optimality results for partial match queries have been derived [AE93]. However, for range queries, only a few allocation methods have been proposed [Fal88,GD90,GDQ92,CC92,LSR92,CR93]. Ghandeharizadeh, DeWitt and Qureshi [GD90,GDQ92] demonstrated, using simulation, that declustering data on multiple disks results in significant improvements in response time for range queries. In [Fal88], Faloutsos uses gray code techniques and in [FB93], Faloutsos and Bhagwat use fractals for declustering multi-dimensional files for range queries. Experiments show that declustering using these techniques provide further improvements in response time. The CMD method proposed by Li *et al.* [LSR92] also uses a modulo approach for allocating data on disks, however no optimality conditions have been derived. In [CR93], a declustering algorithm is proposed for images and maps where queries are defined by a circle around a point of interest rather than a rectangle. For a given number of storage devices, the algorithm searches for an allocation method that maximizes the query radius such that no two tiles are on the same device. However, the search is restricted to a certain class of allocation methods called vector based declustering and no closed form solution is presented. Chen and Chang in [CC92] study the disk modulo allocation method for range queries and give sufficient (but not necessary) conditions for strict optimality. This method was originally developed by Du and Sobolewski for partial match queries [DS82]. For two-dimensions, and using the language of our paper, the allocation method assigns the number $x + y \bmod M$ to the tile represented by (x, y). It is shown in [CC92] that the method is strictly optimal if $M = 2$ or 3. This result, in two-dimensions, follows from Lemma 1 which states that the assignment $\lfloor M/2 \rfloor x + y \bmod M$ is strictly optimal if $M \in \{1, 2, 3, 5\}$.

In conclusion, the contributions of this paper are twofold. For the efficient retrieval and displaying of geographically referenced data based on a two dimensional image or map, we derived strictly optimal assignments to multiple I/O devices and showed that these assignments satisfy the necessary and sufficient conditions for optimality. In the more general context of allocating multi-attributed data, our results give a complete solution for the important case of queries with arbitrary range on two attributes, and represent a significant step towards a general solution of the entire problem.

References

[AE93] K. A. S. Abdel-Ghaffar and A. El Abbadi. Optimal disk allocation for partial match inquiries. *ACM Transactions on Database Systems*, 18(1):132–156, March 1993.

[AU79] A. V. Aho and J. D. Ullman. Optimal partial-match retrieval when fields are independently specified. *ACM Trans. Database Syst.*, 4(2):168–179, 1979.

[CC92] C. Y. Chen and C. C. Chang. On GDM allocation method for partial range queries. *Information Systems*, 17(5):381–394, 1992.

[CLRS86] B. Chor, C. E. Leiserson, R. L. Rivest, and J. B. Shearer. An application of number theory to the organization of raster-graphics memory. *Journal of ACM*, 33(1):86–104, 1986.

[CR93] L. T. Chen and D. Rotem. Declustering objects for visualization. In *Proceedings of the 19th VLDB conference*, pages 85–96, August 1993.

[DS82] H. C. Du and J. S. Sobolewski. Disk allocation for cartesian product files on multiple-disk systems. *ACM Trans. Database Syst.*, 7(1):82–101, 1982.

[Du86] H. C. Du. Disk allocation method for binary cartesian product files. *BIT*, 26(2):138–147, 1986.

[Fal88]   C. Faloutsos. Gray codes for partial match and range queries. *IEEE Transactions on Software Engineering*, 14(10):1381–1393, October 1988.

[FB93]   C. Faloutsos and P. Bhagwat. Declustering using fractals. In *Proceedings of the Second International Conference on Parallel and Distributed Information Systems*, pages 18–25, January 1993.

[FBF⁺94]   C. Faloutsos, R. Barber, M. Flickner, J. Hafner, W. Niblack, D. Petkovic, and W. Equitz. Efficient and effective querying by image content. *Journal of Intelligent Information Systems*, 3:231–262, 1994.

[FM91]   C. Faloutsos and D. Metaxas. Disk allocation methods using error correcting codes. *IEEE Transactions on Computers*, 40(8):907–914, August 1991.

[GD90]   S. Ghandeharizadeh and D. J. DeWitt. Hybrid-range partitioning strategy: A new declustering strategy for multiprocessor database machines. In *Proceedings of 16th International Conference on Very Large Data Bases*, pages 481–492, August 1990.

[GDQ92]   S. Ghandeharizadeh, D. J. DeWitt, and W. Qureshi. A performance analysis of alternative multi-attribute declustering strategies. In *Proceedings of the ACM SIGMOD International Conference on Management of Data*, pages 29–38, June 1992.

[KP88]   M. H. Kim and S. Pramanik. Optimal file distribution for partial match retrieval. In *Proceedings of the ACM SIGMOD International Conference on Management of Data*, pages 173–182, June 1988.

[LSR92]   J. Li, J. Srivastava, and D. Rotem. CMD: A multidimensional declustering method for parallel database systems. In *Proceedings of the 18th VLDB Conference*, pages 3–14, August 1992.

[OS95]   V. E. Ogle and M. Stonebraker. Chabot: Retrieval from a relational database of images. *Computer*, 28(9):40–48, September 1995.

[Smi96]   T. R. Smith. A digital library for geographically referenced materials. *Computer*, 29(5):54–60, May 1996.

[Sun87]   Y. Y. Sung. Performance analysis of disk modulo allocation method for cartesian product files. *IEEE Transactions on Software Engineering*, 13(9):1018–1026, September 1987.

[VH92]   M. Vitterli and C. Herley. Wavelets and filter banks: Theory and design. *IEEE Transactions on Signal Processing*, 40(9):2207–2232, September 1992.

Efficient Indexing for Constraint and Temporal Databases

Sridhar Ramaswamy*

Bell Labs, Room 2D144, 600 Mountain Ave, Murray Hill, NJ 07974, USA.
Email: sridhar@bell-labs.com

Abstract. We examine new I/O-efficient techniques for indexing problems in constraint and temporal data models. We present algorithms for these problems that are considerably simpler than previous solutions. Our solutions are unique in the sense that they only use B^+-trees rather than special-purpose data structures. Indexing for many general constraint data models can be reduced to interval intersection. We present a new algorithm for this problem using a query-time/space tradeoff, which achieves the optimal query time $O(\log_B n + t/B)$ I/O's in linear space $O(n/B)$ using B^+-trees. (Here, n is the number of intervals, t the number of intervals in the output of a query, and B the disk block size.) It is easy to update this data structure, but small worst-case bounds do not seem possible. Previous approaches have achieved these bounds but are fairly complex and rely mostly on reducing the interval intersection problem to special cases of two-dimensional search. Some of them can also handle updates in $O(\log_B n)$ I/O's amortized. Indexing in many temporal models becomes a generalization of interval management, where each temporal object is characterized by an interval *and a key*. There are many different ways of querying these objects, and we achieve optimal bounds for many of these queries. These bounds are achieved using a modification of the technique used for the constraint indexing problem. Our technique is much simpler than other techniques that have been used for achieving similar bounds.

1   Introduction

The successful realization of any data model in a large-scale database requires supporting its language features with efficient secondary storage manipulation. Consider the relational data model of [5]. While the declarative programming features (relational calculus and algebra) of the model are important, it is crucial to support these features by data structures for searching and updating that make optimal use of secondary storage. B-trees and their variants B^+-trees [2, 6] are examples of such data structures. They have been an unqualified success in supporting external dynamic 1-dimensional range searching in relational database systems.

---

* This work was done while the author was at Bell Communications Research, Morristown, NJ 07960, USA.

In this paper, we study indexing in the context of constraint and temporal data models. We do not better previously known worst-case bounds for these problems (many of them were optimal to begin with!), but using a query-time/space tradeoff, we present algorithms that are considerably simpler than previously known algorithms. Since the algorithms we present use only B^+-trees, which are standard on all database systems, we believe that our algorithms are also of practical significance.

We first introduce our model for secondary storage algorithms and then look at the performance of B-trees for 1-dimensional range searching, since we will use B^+-trees as our "benchmark". We make the standard assumption that each secondary memory access transmits one page or B units of data, and we count this as one I/O. The efficiency of our algorithms is measured in terms of the number of I/O operations that they perform. Let R be a relation with n tuples and let the output of a query on R have t tuples. Our I/O bounds are expressed in terms of n, t and B and all constants are independent of these three parameters. We will also use the symbol n to indicate the number of intervals to be indexed in the constraint indexing problem, and the number of temporal objects to be indexed in the temporal indexing problem. A B^+-tree on attribute x of the n-tuple relation R uses $O(n/B)$ pages of secondary storage. The following operations define the problem of *external dynamic 1-dimensional range searching* on relational database attribute x, with the corresponding I/O time performance bounds using the B^+-tree on x: (1) Find all tuples such that for their x attribute $(a_1 \leq x \leq a_2)$. If the output size is t tuples, then this range searching is in worst-case $O(\log_B n + t/B)$ secondary memory accesses. If $a_1 = a_2$ and x is a key, i.e., it uniquely identifies the tuple, then this is key-based searching. (2) Insert or delete a given tuple are in worst-case $O(\log_B n)$ secondary memory accesses. In this paper, we will be concerned with indexing for constraint and temporal data models. We will aim for algorithms with provably good worst-case I/O bounds.

Indexing Constraints: Constraint programming paradigms are inherently "declarative", since they describe computations by specifying how these computations are constrained. A general constraint programming framework for database query languages called Constraint Query Languages or CQLs was presented in [11]. This framework adapts ideas of Constraint Logic Programming, e.g., from [10], to databases, provides a calculus and algebra, guarantees low data complexity, and is applicable to managing spatial data.

It is, of course, important to index constraints and thus support these new language features with efficient secondary storage manipulation Fortunately, it is possible to do this by reducing the problem of indexing constraints, for a fairly general class of constraints, to dynamic interval management on secondary storage. Given a set of input intervals, dynamic interval management involves being able to perform the following operations efficiently: (1) Answer interval intersection queries. That is, to report all the input intervals that intersect a query interval. (2) Delete or insert intervals from the interval collection.

Previous approaches [1,12,14,17] are fairly complex and rely mostly on reducing the interval intersection problem to special cases of two-dimensional range searching. Typically, these approaches achieve the optimal query time of $O(\log_B n + t/B)$ I/O's using optimal $O(n/B)$ disk blocks of storage. Update processing seems much harder to do and some of these methods achieve $O(\log_B n)$ I/O's for updates, typically amortized. In this paper, we present a new algorithm for this problem based on a radically different approach using a query-time/space tradeoff. Our approach is based on an algorithm developed by Chazelle in [4] for interval intersection in main memory. Our approach uses only B$^+$-trees, achieves the optimal query time of $O(\log_B n)$ I/O's using linear space $O(n/B)$. It can handle updates, but it does not seem possible to obtain non-trivial bounds for update processing.

Indexing Temporal Objects: The temporal model we use is a tuple-versioning model [15,18]. ([15] is a comprehensive survey of the field of temporal indexing.) In our model of the temporal indexing problem, each record to be indexed is assumed to have three fields: (1) a time invariant *key* attribute, (2) a time variant *interval* attribute, where each interval consists of a *start-time* and an *end-time*, and (3) an object *id*. Further, we also assume that the underlying database system only supports the notion of *transaction time* [15,18]. Essentially, this means the following:

- When an object is *added* to the database at time e_1, its time interval is (e_1, now) where *now* is a reference to the "current" time. The intuition is that this object is activated at time e_1 and will continue to exist until it is deleted.
- When a previously inserted object is *deleted* at time instant e_2, its time interval, which was originally (e_1, now) is changed to (e_1, e_2).
- No other operations are allowed on objects that already exist in the database. For example, it is illegal to change the time interval of an object from (e_1, e_2) to (e_1', e_2') or add an object that references time in the "past".

Essentially, these conditions make the temporal indexing problem an *append only* problem. We will use a derivative of the constraint index for the temporal indexing problem. Even though the constraint indexing technique cannot give reasonable bounds for arbitrary updates, it can be made to give good amortized bounds for the append only case and that will be the crucial property that we will use for the temporal index.

It is possible to arrive at a number of different ways to query a temporal index. The three main problems that we will be concerned with are:

- Given a time instant e, find every object whose time interval contains the query instant. This is called the *pure-timeslice* query in [15].
- Given a time instant and a key range, find each object whose time interval contains the query instant, and whose key value falls in the query key range. This is called the *range-timeslice* query in [15].
- Given a time instant and a key value, find the object whose time interval contains the query instant, and whose key value equals the query key value. We will call this the *pure-key-timeslice* query.

We believe that these are good representatives of temporal indexing problems. Some more general problems are also considered by [15]. E.g., a generalization of the range-timeslice query, where a time interval is used instead of a time instant. Clearly, this problem is a generalization of two dimensional search which is known to be hard to solve with good worst-case bounds [17]. (It is known, for example, that any algorithm that achieves poly-log query bounds has to use almost logarithmic storage replication.) Some simpler problems are also considered by [15]. For example, given a key range, find the history of the keys in the range. This can be easily be solved by using a secondary B$^+$-tree index on the key value.

The data structure in [13] achieves the optimal bound of $O(\log_B n + t/B)$ I/O's for pure-timeslice queries, the sub-optimal bound of $O(\log_B n + s/B)$ I/O's for range-timeslice queries (s is the number of objects that belong in the output of the pure-timeslice query corresponding to the range-timeslice query), and the optimal bound of $O(\log_B n)$ I/O's for pure-key-timeslice queries. This data structure is fairly involved. We present a solution based on the constraint indexing technique that achieves the same bounds using a single B$^+$-tree. Updates can be made to this structure, but the optimal bound obtained ($O(\log_B n)$) is amortized.

Orthogonal to these approaches, constraint indexing can be performed using members from the R-tree family [3,9,16]. These data structures do not guarantee good worst-case bounds, but have been empirically determined to provide good average performance for interval indexing and other problems.

In summary, we present solutions for constraint and temporal indexing that are considerably simpler than previous solutions. Their practical significance lies in the fact that they use only B$^+$-trees, raising the possibility that these data models can be implemented on top of existing relational and object-oriented backends.

2 An Optimal Solution to the Interval Intersection Problem on Disk

In this section, we present a new, simple solution to the interval intersection problem. It is shown in [11,12] that indexing for a large class of constraint data models reduces to this problem. Our solution is adapted from Chazelle's algorithm for interval overlap in main memory [4].

We first consider the slightly simpler case of what has been referred to as the "stabbing" query in [12]. It has been shown in [12] that interval intersection can easily be reduced to this problem. In the stabbing query problem, the input is a set of n intervals $[a_i, b_i]$, $1 \leq i \leq n$. (The a_i's and b_i's can come from any ordered domain.) Given a query point q, we are asked to find all the input intervals that intersect this point.

A straightforward method to handle this problem is to identify the set of all unique endpoints[2] in the input, and for each such endpoint, associate the set

---

[2] We will use the term *endpoint* to generically refer to both the starting and ending points of input intervals. Where necessary, we will use the phrase "ending point" explicitly.

of all intervals that intersect that endpoint. We then index these sets, using a B^+-tree, with each set keyed by the endpoint that it is associated with. In order to answer a stabbing query, we find the endpoint nearest to the query point, on the right, and examine the intervals in the set corresponding to the endpoint, and report the intervals that intersect with the query point as the answer to the query. (Only those intervals that actually begin at that nearest endpoint will not belong in the answer to the query.) In fact, what has been described here is the essence behind the Time Index of [7,8]. It can easily be seen that this method is fairly wasteful of space, storing upto $O(n^2)$ intervals in the worst case in the B^+-tree. (Inserting and deleting intervals is also fairly hard, taking upto $O(n)$ insertions/deletions to/from the B^+-tree.) Let us call this solution the *all-points* method for easy reference.

The key intuition behind obtaining a more efficient data structure is: *On the average, adjacent sets in the* all-points *method do not differ greatly from each other.* By choosing the sets that we decide to index carefully, it is possible to reduce the storage needed from $O(\frac{n^2}{B})$ to $O(n/B)$.

First, let us sort the input endpoints, $a_1, a_2, \ldots, a_n$ and $b_1, b_2, \ldots, b_n$, to give $e_1, e_2, \ldots, e_{2n}$. Instead of choosing the set of all endpoints and indexing them, we will choose a set of *windows*, $W_1, W_2, \ldots, W_p$, (The algorithm that we devise will choose this $p < 2n$ appropriately.) over endpoints $w_1, w_2, \ldots, w_{p+1}$. These endpoints are chosen from the input set of endpoints such that $w_1 = e_1$, $w_{p+1} = e_{2n}$, $w_j \leq w_{j+1}$ and $W_j = [w_j, w_{j+1}]$. In words, the windows represent a partition of the interval between e_1 and e_{2n} into p contiguous intervals. Associated with each window, is its *window-list*, the set of all input intervals that intersect the window's interval W_j. We will use $|W_j|$ to indicate the number of elements in window W_j's window-list.

We store the window-lists in a B^+-tree, indexing them by the starting point of the corresponding window. In order to answer a stabbing query, we perform a search for the query point and retrieve the window-list of the window that it falls into. (If it falls exactly on the boundary of two windows, we look at both the window-lists in the B^+-tree .) We then examine every interval in the window-list(s) and report all the intervals that intersect with the query interval.

We enforce two key conditions on the windows to make search efficient and space needed to store the window-lists low:

1. For each query point q that intersects with a window W_j, the number of input intervals that belong in the output set O_q satisfies the condition $0 < |W_j| \leq \delta \max(1, |O_q|)$, where $\delta > 1$ is a slack parameter that provides a tradeoff between space and query time, and $|O_q|$ the size of the output O_q. Essentially, we guarantee that searching a window-list to answer a query that intersects with its window is never inefficient.

2. $\sum_{1 \leq j \leq p} |W_j| < \frac{2\delta}{\delta-1} n$ That is, the window-lists need only linear storage.

Once these two conditions are satisfied, it is easy to show that stabbing queries can be answered efficiently. Searching for the appropriate window clearly only takes $O(\log_B n)$ disk accesses. If the window-list contains t intervals, Condition 1 guarantees that at least t/δ of them belong in the query. Therefore, the query time is $O(\log_B n + t/B)$ disk accesses, which is optimal. Figure 1 presents an algorithm for creating the data structure. (The algorithm first creates a window-list and then inserts the whole list into the B^+-tree. This is to make the proof easier. In a more practical setting, one would insert intervals as they were processed. That is, operations that manipulate the *intervals* member of the W_{win} structure in Figure 1 would directly insert intervals into the B^+-tree.)

Procedure *construct-wlist* in Figure 1 takes as input the sorted set of endpoints, with ties broken arbitrarily. It keeps adding intervals to the "current" window as long as the total number of intervals in the window does not exceed $\delta \times low$, where *low* is the minimum number of intervals that any query falling in the current window will intersect with. When this condition is no longer satisfied, the current window is inserted into the B^+-tree, and a new window started with those intervals in the current set whose ending points are greater than the current endpoint. If we have many intervals with coincident endpoints, it is possible that *construct-wlist* will produce windows with zero width. The simplest way to handle that problem is to discard all windows of zero width and store only the first and last windows produced at the coincident endpoint. Since these two windows will list all intervals at the coincident endpoints, we will not miss any endpoints. See Figure 2 for an example of windows produced by procedure *construct-wlist*.

Lemma 2.1 *There exists an algorithm for answering stabbing queries optimally in $O(\log_B n + t/B)$ disk accesses, using $O(n/B)$ blocks on disk. It can be constructed in $O((\frac{n}{B})\log_B n)$ I/O's.*

Proof. We will prove this lemma in three parts. We will first prove that the window lists produced by Procedure *construct-wlist* in Figure 1 use only linear space. That done, we will show how to use a B^+-tree to index the window lists and answer stabbing queries optimally. Finally, we will show that the data structure takes only $O((\frac{n}{B})\log_B n)$ I/O's to build. To show the first part, we will prove the following inequality:

$$\sum_{1 \le j \le p} |W_j| < \frac{2\delta}{\delta - 1} n \qquad (1)$$

Initially, we will make the assumption that input intervals do not share endpoints. We will show how to remove this restriction later.

In order to prove the inequality above, we observe that an input interval $[a_i, b_i]$ can be situated in many windows. In order to establish an upper bound on the space we use for the window lists, we need to count the total number of times input intervals are stored in different windows. In order to do that, we divide an input interval into A-parts and B-parts. Parts of an interval that

/* *Input to this routine is a sorted list of* (endpoint, interval) *pairs. This routine inserts p window-lists into a* B^+-tree. *Each window-list has two components, a key that identifies the beginning of its interval, and a list of intervals associated with it.*/

Procedure *construct-wlist*

Initialize an empty B^+-tree BT

win = 1; W_{win}.key = e_1;/* win is the number of the "current" window */

total = 0; /* total is the total number of intervals in the current window */

low = 1; /* low is the *minimum* number of intervals that *any* stabbing query in the current window would intersect */

cur = 0; /* cur is the number of intervals that a stabbing query at the *current* point would intersect with */

for (i=1; i <= 2n; i++)

    if (e_i is a starting endpoint)

        cur++;

        total++;

        if ($\delta \times low < total$) then /* current window is finished */

            Insert W_{win} into BT

            win++;

            W_{win}.intervals = {Intervals in W_{win-1} whose ending point > e_i} $\bigcup$ current interval

            W_{win}.key = e_i;

            low = total = cur;

        else /* add interval to current window */

            Add current interval to W_{win}.intervals

    else /* e_i is an ending point */

        cur = cur - 1;

        low = min(low, cur);

        if ($\delta \times low < total$) then /* current window is finished */

            Insert W_{win} into BT

            win++;

            W_{win}.intervals = {Intervals in W_{win-1} whose ending point > e_i}

            W_{win}.key = e_i;

            low = max(cur,1); total = cur;

Fig. 1. Procedure *construct-wlist* (adapted from [4]) used in the construction of the window lists used to prove Theorem 2.2

fully coincide with a window's W_j aperture (or width) $[w_j, w_{j+1}]$ are called its A-parts, and those parts that partially coincide with a window are called its B-parts. Let A_j (B_j resp.) represent the total number of A-parts (B-parts resp.) in window W_j. Our non-coinciding endpoint assumption assures us now that $A_p \leq 1$.

Let us use O_x to indicate the set of intervals that intersect with query point x and $|O_x|$ to indicate the cardinality of O_x. Let low_j stand for $\min_{x \in [w_j, w_{j+1}]}(|O_x|)$, the minimum number of intervals that intersect *any* point in window W_j.

A new window W_{j+1}, for $j < p$ is started only under the following two conditions:

1. We are scanning the starting point of an interval and $\delta \times low_j < |W_j| + 1$.

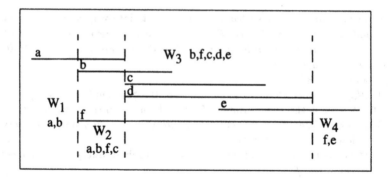

Fig. 2. Windows produced by procedure *construct-wlist* on a set of intervals. In this example, $\delta = 2$

2. We are scanning the ending point of an interval and $\delta \times (\text{low}_j - 1) < |W_j|$.

In either case, for $\delta > 1$, $\delta \times \text{low}_j < |W_j| + \delta$, or, $\delta \times \text{low}_j < A_j + B_j + \delta$. It is also clear that for all $j < p$, $\delta A_j \le \delta \times \text{low}_j$. Therefore, for $j < p$, $\delta A_j < A_j + B_j + \delta$ or $A_j < \frac{B_j + \delta}{\delta - 1}$. This implies that

$$\sum_{1 \le j \le p} (A_j + B_j) < \sum_{1 \le j < p} \left(\frac{B_j + \delta}{\delta - 1} + B_j \right) + A_p + B_p$$

$$= \sum_{1 \le j < p} \left(\frac{\delta B_j}{\delta - 1} + \frac{\delta}{\delta - 1} \right) + A_p + B_p \qquad (2)$$

Each endpoint of an input interval (totally, there are $2n$ of them) can give rise to exactly one B-part. In addition, $p+1$ of the endpoints cannot give rise to any B-parts because they fall on window boundaries. Hence, $\sum_{1 \le j \le p} B_j \le (2n - p - 1)$. Substituting this into Inequality 2, we get

$$\sum_{1 \le j \le p} (A_j + B_j) < \frac{\delta(2n - p - 1 - B_p) + \delta(p - 1) + (\delta - 1)B_p}{\delta - 1} + A_p$$

$$< \frac{2\delta}{\delta - 1} n \qquad (3)$$

Combining $\sum_{1 \le j \le p} |W_j| = \sum_{1 \le j \le p} (A_j + B_j)$ with Inequality 3, we get Inequality 1. In order to prove the same inequality without the assumption of non-coincident endpoints, we simply observe that exactly the same window-lists are produced by Procedure *construct-wlist* if the endpoints are replaced by their rankings.

The second part of the proof is easy. We will index every window-list using its key, which is the endpoint at which it was started. The construction of the window lists using Procedure *construct-wlist* guarantees that in any window, the inequality $|W_j| < \delta \times \text{low}$ is always true. This means that if t intervals are contained in a window list, at least t/δ of them will belong in the output. Given a stabbing query, we can locate the window into which it falls by looking for the window list whose key is immediately to the left of the stabbing query. Clearly, this can be done in $O(\log_B n)$ disk accesses. Therefore the whole output can be reported in $O(\log_B n + t/B)$ I/O's.

The final part is also easy. The major portion of the time to build the data structure comes from sorting the $2n$ endpoints, which takes $O((\frac{n}{B}) \log_B n)$ I/O's. Once that is done, we insert no more than $O(n)$ entries into a B^+-tree, which can also be done in $O((\frac{n}{B}) \log_B n)$ I/O's. The lemma then follows.□

Using the result from [12] (Proposition 2.2) that reduces interval management to stabbing queries, we get an optimal static solution for the interval management problem. (This reduction divides interval management into the problems of answering stabbing queries and performing range searches on B^+-trees.)

Theorem 2.2 *There exists an optimal algorithm for the interval management problem that can answer interval intersection queries in optimal $O(\log_B n + t/B)$ I/O's, using optimal storage $O(n/B)$. Here, n is the number of input intervals, B the block size on disk and t, the number of intervals in the output to the query.*

Unfortunately, it does not seem easy to get good worst-case bounds on the update performance of this data structure. It is easy to add (delete) intervals into (from) the data structure (one simply adds/deletes the interval to/from all the windows that intersect it), but the amount of I/O that needs to be performed does not seem to have non-trivial upper bounds. Adding and deleting arbitrary intervals can also ruin the querying efficiency of this data structure.

In spite of this disadvantage, we believe that this is a practical data structure for the problem of constraint indexing. Occasional reorganizations can take care of imbalances introduced by insertions and deletions. Furthermore, the fact that the data structure only standard B^+-trees opens the possibility that constraint databases can be implemented on top of relational and object-oriented backends. The backends can provide the physical layer support and the concurrency control and recovery support, while the other desirable constraint linguistic features are implemented on top.

3 Efficient Temporal Indexing

In this section, we will modify the constraint indexing technique from the previous section to obtain an efficient index for many temporal indexing problems. The bounds we get are similar to the ones obtained in [13], but the resulting data structure is extremely simple and uses only a single B^+-tree. We will first consider the static version of the problem, where all the temporal objects are available and then consider the dynamic version, where objects are added in increasing time order.

Recall that in our temporal indexing model, each object has associated with it, a key, a time interval and on oid. In order to index these objects, we first

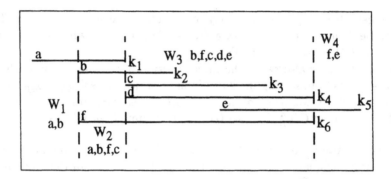

Fig. 3. Indexing a set of temporal objects: Each object is identified by a time interval and a key value. In this example also, $\delta = 2$.

construct window-lists based on objects' time intervals. Now, these window-lists will contain temporal objects instead of intervals.

While indexing constraints, we indexed each window-list as a whole based on starting point of the window's interval. For temporal indexing, we index each temporal object in the window-lists separately. The key for each object in a window-list is the pair *(starting-point-of-window, key-of-temporal-object)*. That is, we use a composite key consisting of the window's starting point and the temporal object's key. In this fashion, we insert all the objects in all the window-lists into a B^+-tree.

Example 3.1 *Consider the temporal objects represented in Figure 3. The time intervals corresponding to these objects are the same as the intervals in Figure 2. Each object, in addition, is also identified with a key value. Object a is associated with key k_1, b with key k_2, etc.*

As in the constraint indexing case, window-lists are created using the interval endpoints. Let x_1 denote the starting point of the time interval of object x, and x_2 its ending point. From window W_1, we insert (a_1, k_1, a), and (a_1, k_2, b) into the temporal index, where (a_1, k_1) is the composite key for object a, and (a_1, k_2) is the composite key for object b. We then insert (b_1, k_1, a), (b_1, k_2, b), (b_1, k_6, f) and (b_1, k_3, c) from window W_2 into the B^+-tree , and so on for all the windows. (Objects can be inserted multiple times in the index.)□

Answering a pure-timeslice query in this environment is no different from answering a stabbing query in the constraint environment. Given a timeslice query at time e, we take the following steps:

- Locate the window into which time instant e falls. (We look for the first object whose key value is less than $(e, -\infty)$ in the index. Using this, we can identify the window.) Let that window's key be w.
- Perform a range query to retrieve all objects in the range $[(w, -\infty), (w, +\infty)]$.

It is easy to show that this search is optimal because at least $1/\delta$ fraction of the objects in w's window will belong in the output.

The real power of the composite index is used for answering range-timeslice and pure-key-timeslice queries. In order to answer a range-timeslice query, say on a temporal key range (k_1, k_2), at time instant e, we first identify w, the starting point of the window into which e falls as before. We then perform a range query to retrieve all objects in the range $[(w, k_1), (w, k_2)]$. However, the size of the output of this query can be as large as the number of objects in w's window, which is not optimal.

The pure-key-timeslice query at temporal key value k and time instant e, which is a special case of the range-timeslice query can be answered by retrieving all objects whose composite key equals (w, k), where w is the starting point of the window into which e falls.

Let us now consider the dynamic version of the problem. The key observation behind making the data structure dynamic is that Procedure *construct-wlist* needs only the values of the variables *total*, *low*, and *cur* to process intervals in an online fashion. The crucial assumption is, of course, that endpoints are given to Procedure *construct-wlist* in sorted order. If endpoints represent time instants, this is clearly true. We can get a dynamic procedure for processing endpoints by replacing the idea of adding an object to a window-list by adding the object (with its composite key of *(starting-point-of-window, temporal-key)*) into a B+-tree.

The one catch is that the endpoints of freshly inserted temporal objects are not known in advance. (The algorithm assumes that both the endpoints are known even when a starting point is processed.) It is possible to handle this, however, by marking each object's ending point as "open" when it is first inserted into the B+-tree. When an object is "deleted", we change the ending point of the object in the current window to the correct endpoint. *Note that it is crucial that we only modify an object in the current window.* An object can be present in an unbounded number of windows. In every window that it is present in except the last one, its ending point will be marked as "open", which simply implies that it covers the whole width from the starting point to the end of that window.

Finally, the transition from one window to another in *construct-wlist* is not smooth. (W_{j+1} is constructed from W_j by taking all intervals in W_j that are "open".) This implies, unfortunately, that our bounds for updating have to be amortized. It is clear that inserting n objects into a temporal index results in no more $\frac{2\delta}{\delta-1}n$ additions to the B+-tree, but individual operations don't have nontrivial bounds. We put everything together in the following theorem:

Theorem 3.2 *There exists a data structure that uses only B+-trees and occupies $O(n/B)$ disk blocks, that can:*

- *answer pure-timeslice queries in optimal $O(\log_B n + t/B)$ I/O's;*
- *answer range-timeslice queries in sub-optimal $O(\log_B n + s/B)$ I/O's;*
- *answer pure-key-timeslice queries in optimal $O(\log_B n)$ I/O's;*

Here, n is the number of objects in the data structure, t, the number of objects that belong in the output of the timeslice query, s the number of objects that belong *in the output of the pure-timeslice query corresponding to the range-timeslice query, and B is the disk blocksize.*

Temporal objects can be "inserted" into or "deleted" from this data structure in $O(\log_B n)$ I/O's amortized.

Even though we do not explore the idea here, we believe that it is possible to migrate "older" parts of the temporal data structure to tertiary storage without re-organizing the entire index. Also, as was the case with constraint indexing, it is possible to chase down individual temporal objects and completely delete them from the temporal index or add arbitrary temporal objects (thus implementing what are called "valid time" temporal indexes). As in constraint indexing, those operations are unbounded and can also affect the query performance of the data structure.

4   Conclusions and Open Problems

We have presented new algorithms for constraint and temporal indexing using B^+-trees. The constraint indexing solution is optimal for querying, but does not have good worst-case bounds for updating. Therefore, the search for a good, simple data structure for interval intersection that can also handle updates in optimal worst-case time continues.

We believe that both algorithms that we have suggested in this paper are of practical significance. Both the algorithms have very small constants, which we believe will make them suitable for implementation. We are currently exploring the empirical performance of these data structures. In particular, we are comparing their average case performance against the R^*-tree [3], the efficient data structure from the R-tree family.

Acknowledgments: This paper is dedicated to the memory of my beloved advisor Prof. Paris Kanellakis.

Jan Chomicki read initial drafts of this paper and suggested many improvements. The comments of the anonymous referees significantly improved the presentation of the paper and also helped fix some bugs. Their help is gratefully acknowledged.

References

[1] L. Arge & J. S. Vitter, "Optimal Interval Management in External Memory," 1995, Private Communication.

[2] R. Bayer & E. McCreight, "Organization of Large Ordered Indexes," *Acta Informatica* 1 (1972), 173–189.

[3] N. Beckmann, H. Kriegel, R. Schneider & B. Seeger, "The R^*-tree: An Efficient and Robust Access Method for Points and Rectangles," *Proc. 1990 ACM-SIGMOD Conference on Management of Data* (1990).

[4] B. Chazelle, "Filtering Search: A New Approach to Query-Answering," *Siam J. of Computing* 15(3) (1986), 703–724.

[5] E. F. Codd, "A Relational Model for Large Shared Data Banks," *CACM* 13(6) (1970), 377–387.

[6] D. Comer, "The Ubiquitous B-tree," *Computing Surveys* 11(2) (1979), 121–137.

[7] R. Elmasri, Y. Kim & G. Wuu, "Efficient Implementation Techniques for the Time Index," *Proc. of the 7th IEEE Intl. Data Engineering Conference* (1991).

[8] R. Elmasri, G. Wuu & Y. Kim, "The Time Index: An Access Structure for Temporal Data," *Proc. 16th Conference on Very Large Databases* (1990).

[9] Antonin Guttman, "R-Trees: A Dynamic Index Structure for Spatial Searching," *Proc. 1984 ACM-SIGMOD Conference on Management of Data* (1985).

[10] J. Jaffar & J. L. Lassez, "Constraint Logic Programming," *Proc. 14th ACM POPL* (1987).

[11] P. C. Kanellakis, G. M. Kuper & P. Z. Revesz, "Constraint Query Languages," *Proc. 9th ACM PODS* (1990), invited to the special issue of *JCSS* on Principles of Database Systems (to appear). A complete version of the paper appears as Technical Report TR-CS-90-31, Brown University.

[12] P. C. Kanellakis, S. Ramaswamy, D. E. Vengroff & J. S. Vitter, "Indexing for Data Models with Constraints and Classes," *Proc. 12th ACM PODS* (1993), invited to the special issue of *JCSS* on Principles of Database Systems (to appear). A complete version of the paper appears as Technical Report TR-CS-93-21, Brown University.

[13] N. Kangelaris & V. J. Tsotras, "The Snapshot Index, an I/O-Optimal Access Method for Timeslice Queries," CATT-Tech. Report 93-68, Polytechnic University, Dec. 1993. Accepted for publication, Information Systems, An International Journal, 1994.

[14] S. Ramaswamy & S. Subramanian, "Path Caching: A Technique for Optimal External Searching," *Proc. 13th ACM PODS* (1994).

[15] B. Salzberg & V. J. Tsotras, "A Comparison of Access Methods for Time Evolving Data," To appear in the ACM Computing Surveys. Available as Technical Report CATT-TR-94-81, Polytechnic Univ. or NU-CCS-94-21, Northeastern Univ.

[16] T. Sellis, N. Roussopoulos & C. Faloutsos, "The R+-Tree: A Dynamic Index for Multi-Dimensional Objects," *Proc. 13th VLDB Conference* (1987).

[17] S. Subramanian & S. Ramaswamy, "The P-range tree: A new data structure for range searching in secondary memory," *Proceedings of the Sixth Annual ACM-SIAM Symposium on Discrete Algorithms* (1995).

[18] A. U. Tanzel, J. Clifford, S. Gadia, S. Jajodia, A. Segev & R. Snodgrass, eds., *Temporal Databases: Theory, Design and Implementation*, The Benjamin/Cummings Publishing Company Inc., 1993.

On Topological Elementary Equivalence
of Spatial Databases

Bart Kuijpers[1], Jan Paredaens[1] and Jan Van den Bussche[2]

[1] University of Antwerp (UIA), Dept. Math. & Computer Sci.,
Universiteitsplein 1, B-2610 Antwerp, Belgium
Email: {kuijpers, pareda}@uia.ua.ac.be
[2] University of Limburg (LUC), Dept. WNI
B-3590 Diepenbeek, Belgium
Email: vdbuss@luc.ac.be

Abstract. We consider spatial databases and queries definable using first-order logic and real polynomial inequalities. We are interested in topological queries: queries whose result only depends on the topological aspects of the spatial data. Two spatial databases are called topologically elementary equivalent if they cannot be distinguished by such topological first-order queries. Our contribution is a natural and effective characterization of topological elementary equivalence of closed databases in the real plane. As far as topological elementary equivalence is concerned, it does not matter whether we use first-order logic with full polynomial inequalities, or first-order logic with simple order comparisons only.

1 Introduction and summary

Spatial database systems [5, 12, 1, 9] are concerned with the representation and manipulation of data that have a geometrical or topological interpretation. In this paper, we are interested in *planar* spatial databases; the conceptual view of such a database is that of a possibly infinite set of points in the real plane.

Of course one needs a spatial data model that describes exactly which kinds of sets of points can be handled by the system, and how they can be queried. A rather general spatial data model is the *semi-algebraic* one. A semi-algebraic set is defined by a finite union of systems of polynomial equations and inequalities. This semi-algebraic model is an instance of the framework of constraint databases [14] (see also [17]).

By viewing the spatial database, a set of points in the real plane, as a binary relation over the real numbers, we can use the relational calculus, augmented with polynomial comparisons, as a spatial query language. For example, to verify whether the database S is contained within a straight line, one would write

$$(\exists a)(\exists b)(\exists c)(\forall x)(\forall y)(S(x, y) \to ax + by + c = 0), \qquad (*)$$

or to verify whether the database contains a disk as a subset, one would write

$$(\exists x_0)(\exists y_0)(\exists r \neq 0)(\forall x)(\forall y)((x - x_0)^2 + (y - y_0)^2 < r^2 \to S(x, y)). \qquad (\dagger)$$

Naturally, quantifiers range over the real numbers. Such *spatial calculus queries* can be effectively answered on semi-algebraic databases [14], but a discussion of how this is done is outside the scope of the present paper. In this paper, we focus on Boolean queries (returning true or false) only.

Some queries are concerned with the topological properties of the spatial data only. Query (†) above is an example of such a query; a database contains a disk if and only if its topological interior is non-empty, and this is a purely topological property of the database. In contrast, query (∗) is not a topological query; from a purely topological point of view, a straight line is no different from a curved line. Technically, two databases are considered topologically the same if one can be mapped into the other by a topological transformation of the real plane (mathematically, a *homeomorphism* of $\mathbf{R}^2$). A query is then called *topological* if it has the same result on databases that are topologically the same.

There is not much understanding yet of the class of spatial calculus queries that are topological in the above sense. One of the natural questions that arise in this respect is that of understanding *topological elementary equivalence*. In mathematical logic, two structures are called elementary equivalent if they cannot be distinguished logically, i.e., if every first-order formula has the same truth value on them. We study the corresponding notion in the spatial context: two spatial databases A and B are called topologically elementary equivalent if for every topological spatial calculus query Q, $Q(A)$ is true if and only if $Q(B)$ is.

We have been able to find a natural characterization of topological elementary equivalence in the case of *closed* databases. A spatial database is called closed if it is a closed subset of the real plane in the ordinary topological sense. This simply means that there are no points lying infinitely close to the database without actually lying in the database. Spatial databases occurring in practical applications, such as geographic information systems, are closed almost by default.

In the course of proving our result, we will also deal with a more relaxed notion of topological query, interesting in itself, which considers two databases to be the same topologically if one can be mapped into another by an *isotopy* rather than a general homeomorphism. Isotopies are homeomorphisms that preserve orientation.

Our characterization is based on a known topological property of semi-algebraic sets [7], namely that locally around each point they are "conical". We partition the points in the database according to the types of their cones. Roughly, our characterization then says that two databases are topologically elementary equivalent if and only if the cardinalities of the equivalence classes of their partitions match. A corollary of our characterization is that topological elementary equivalence of spatial databases is decidable. Another corollary is that as far as topological elementary equivalence is concerned, it does not matter whether we use first-order logic with full polynomial inequalities, or first-order logic with simple order comparisons only.

Our proof of the characterization involves various techniques. For the if-direction we show that it is expressible in the spatial calculus that the cone around a point has some specific type. For the only-if direction we show that two databases with matching equivalence classes can be transformed into topologically one and the same database. The transformation rules used in this transformation are shown to produce topologically elementary equivalent databases. The proof of the latter uses a recent collapse theorem on the expressiveness of first-order logic with polynomial inequalities by Benedikt, Dong, Libkin and Wong [3], and involves reduction techniques inspired by those introduced by Grumbach and Su [11].

A variation of topological queries was studied extensively by Egenhofer and his collaborators under the term "topological spatial relationships" (e.g., [8]). Their work is concerned with the topological relationships that can exist between two given individual spatial objects. Papadimitriou, Suciu and Vianu [16] significantly extended this work to collections of named spatial objects. As explained above, our work is different in scope, being concerned with the intrinsic topological properties of single spatial databases. In fact, our work is more in the spirit of topological model theory (e.g., [13, 10, 18]).

This paper is organized as follows. Definitions are given in Section 2. The partition of a database according to the cone types of its points is described in Section 3. The main results are formulated in Section 4. The main proof is sketched in Section 5. Concluding remarks are presented in Section 6.

2 Preliminaries

In this section we give the basic definitions we will be using concerning spatial databases and topological queries.

Spatial databases. We denote the real numbers by $\mathbf{R}$, so $\mathbf{R}^2$ denotes the real plane. A semi-algebraic set in $\mathbf{R}^2$ is a set of points that can be defined as

$$\{(x,y) \in \mathbf{R}^2 \mid \varphi(x,y)\},$$

where $\varphi(x,y)$ is a formula built using the Boolean connectives $\wedge$, $\vee$, and $\neg$, from atoms of the form $p(x,y) > 0$, where $p(x,y)$ is a polynomial in the variables x and y with integer coefficients. Observe that $p = 0$ is equivalent to $\neg(p > 0) \wedge \neg(-p > 0)$, so equations can be used as well as inequalities.

A *closed semi-algebraic database in the real plane* (or simply *database*) is a semi-algebraic set in $\mathbf{R}^2$ that is closed in the ordinary topological sense. It is known [4] that these are precisely the finite unions of sets of points that can be defined as

$$\{(x,y) \in \mathbf{R}^2 \mid p_1(x,y) \geq 0 \wedge \ldots \wedge p_m(x,y) \geq 0\}.$$

In other words, we disallow the essential use of strict inequalities in the definition of a database.

Queries. A *spatial calculus formula* is a first-order logic formula built using the logical connectives and quantifiers from two kinds of atomic formulas: $S(x,y)$ and $p(x_1,\ldots,x_k) > 0$, where S is the binary relation name representing the spatial database and $p(x_1,\ldots,x_k)$ is a polynomial in the variables $x_1, \ldots, x_k$ with integer coefficients.

A *spatial calculus query* (or simply *query*) is a spatial calculus formula without free variables. A query Q can be evaluated on a database A, yielding true or false, by letting variables range over $\mathbf{R}$ and by interpreting $S(x,y)$ to mean that the point (x,y) is in A. That Q evaluates to true on A would be denoted in model-theoretic notation as $(\mathbf{R}, A) \models Q(S)$, but we will simply write $A \models Q$.

Homeomorphism-invariance and -equivalence. Two databases A and B are called *homeomorphic* if there is a homeomorphism h of $\mathbf{R}^2$ such that $h(A) = B$.[3] A query Q is called *invariant under homeomorphisms* (abbreviated as $\mathcal{H}$-*invariant*) if whenever databases A and B are homeomorphic, then $A \models Q$ if and only if $B \models Q$. Finally, two databases A and B are called $\mathcal{H}$-*equivalent* if for each $\mathcal{H}$-invariant query Q, $A \models Q$ if and only if $B \models Q$.

Of course, databases that are homeomorphic are also $\mathcal{H}$-equivalent, but the converse does not hold. For example, we will see later that if A consists of a single disk, and B consists of two separate disks, then A and B are $\mathcal{H}$-equivalent.

Isotopy-invariance and -equivalence. An *isotopy* is a homeomorphism that is isotopic to the identity.[4] Two databases A and B are called *isotopic* if there is an isotopy h such that $h(A) = B$. Intuitively, this means that A can be continuously deformed into B without leaving the plane. The prototypical example of a homeomorphism that is not an isotopy is a reflection. As a matter of fact, it is known [15] that every homeomorphism either is an isotopy, or is isotopic to a reflection. Hence, when two databases A and B are homeomorphic, either A is actually isotopic to B, or A is isotopic to the mirror image of B. For example, Figure 1 shows two databases that are mirror-images of each other but that are not isotopic. They can be thought of as a left hand and a right hand, where the arm and the thumb have thickness and the wrist and the other fingers have no thickness.

A query Q is called *invariant under isotopies* (abbreviated as $\mathcal{I}$-*invariant*) if whenever databases A and B are isotopic, then $A \models Q$ if and only if $B \models Q$. Finally, two databases A and B are called $\mathcal{I}$-*equivalent* if for each $\mathcal{I}$-invariant query Q, $A \models Q$ if and only if $B \models Q$.

---

[3] A homeomorphism of $\mathbf{R}^2$ is a continuous bijection from $\mathbf{R}^2$ to itself whose inverse is also continuous.

[4] Two homeomorphisms f and g are *isotopic* if there is a function $F : \mathbf{R}^2 \times [0,1] \to \mathbf{R}^2$ such that

1. for each $t \in [0,1]$, the function $F_t : \mathbf{R}^2 \to \mathbf{R}^2 : p \mapsto F(p,t)$ is a homeomorphism;
2. F_0 is f and F_1 is g; and
3. $F(p,t)$ is continuous in t.

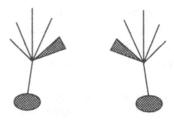

Fig. 1. Two homeomorphic, but not isotopic databases.

Clearly, $\mathcal{H}$-invariance implies $\mathcal{I}$-invariance and $\mathcal{I}$-equivalence implies $\mathcal{H}$-equivalence.

Examples. The query $(*)$ mentioned in the Introduction is a typical example of a query that is neither $\mathcal{I}$-invariant nor $\mathcal{H}$-invariant. The following queries are all $\mathcal{H}$-invariant (and hence also $\mathcal{I}$-invariant):

- The query $(\dagger)$ mentioned in the Introduction. In other words this query expresses that the database contains 2-dimensional parts.
- The query

$$(\exists r)(\forall x)(\forall y)(S(x,y) \to x^2 + y^2 \leq r^2)$$

  expresses that the database is bounded.
- The query

$$(\exists x)(\exists y)(S(x,y) \wedge (\exists \varepsilon \neq 0)$$
$$(\forall x')(\forall y')((x-x')^2 + (y-y')^2 < \varepsilon^2 \wedge S(x',y')) \to (x' = x \wedge y' = y))$$

  expresses that the database contains isolated points.
- The query expressing that the database consists exclusively of lines that do not intersect. (We omit the formula; informally, this formula states that for each point p in the database all sufficiently small circles around p intersect the database either in one or in two points.)

Another natural topological property of databases one might want to test for, is topological connectivity; however, this is not expressible in the spatial calculus [3, 11] and therefore outside the scope of the discussion in the present paper.

3   Point-structures

In this section, we define the "point-structure" of a database. This definition is based on a known topological property of semi-algebraic sets [7], namely that locally around each point they are conical. This is illustrated in Figure 2. More precisely, for every non-isolated point p of a semi-algebraic set A there exists an $\varepsilon > 0$ such that $D(p,\varepsilon) \cap A$ is isotopic to the planar cone with top p and base

$C(p, \varepsilon) \cap A$.[5] More precisely, $D(p, \varepsilon) \cap A$ is isotopic to $\{\lambda \cdot (x, y) + (1 - \lambda) \cdot (x', y') \mid (x', y') \in C(p, \varepsilon) \cap A \wedge 0 \leq \lambda \leq 1\}$, where $p = (x, y)$.

For every isolated point p of a database, there exists an $\varepsilon > 0$ such that $D(p, \varepsilon) \cap A = \{p\}$, so in this case we could say we have a cone with an empty base. We can thus refer in both cases to *the cone of p in A*; this cone is defined up to isotopy.

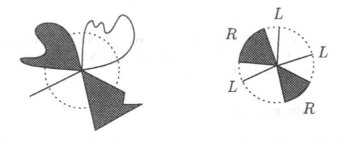

Fig. 2. A database and the cone of one of its points.

A database is also conical around the point at infinity.[6] More precisely, there exists an $\varepsilon > 0$ such that $\{(x, y) \mid x^2 + y^2 \geq \varepsilon^2\} \cap A$ is isotopic to $\{\lambda \cdot (x, y) \mid (x, y) \in C((0, 0), \varepsilon) \cap A \wedge \lambda \geq 1\}$. We can indeed view the latter set as the cone with top ∞ and base $C((0, 0), \varepsilon) \cap A$, and call it *the cone of ∞ in A* (again defined up to isotopy).

We use the following finite representation for cones. The cone having a full circle as its base is represented by the letter F (for "full"). Any other cone can be represented by a circular list of L's and R's (for "line" and "region" resp.) which describes the cone in a complete clockwise turn around the top. For example, the cone of Figure 2 is represented by $(LLRLR)$. The cone with empty base is represented by the empty circular list $(\ )$.

Let $\mathcal{C}$ be the set of cones represented in this way. We define:

Definition 1. Let A be a database. The *point-structure of A* is the function Π_A from $A \cup \{\infty\}$ to $\mathcal{C}$ that maps each point to its cone.

It can be shown that $\Pi_A^{-1}(c)$ is empty on all but a finite number of cones c. Moreover, as illustrated in Figure 3, there are only three cones c where $\Pi_A^{-1}(c)$ can be infinite: (R), (LL), and F. It can indeed be shown that in each database, the points with a cone different from these three are finite in number. We will refer to these points as the *singular* points of the database. Non-singular points are also called *regular* points.

---

[5] $D(p, \varepsilon)$ is the closed disk with center p and radius ε, $C(p, \varepsilon)$ is its bordering circle.

[6] If we project $\mathbf{R}^2$ stereographically onto a sphere, the point at infinity corresponds to the missing point on the sphere.

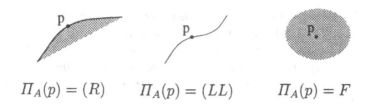

$$\Pi_A(p) = (R) \qquad \Pi_A(p) = (LL) \qquad \Pi_A(p) = F$$

Fig. 3. Regular points.

Definition 2. Let A and B be databases. We say that Π_A is *isomorphic* to Π_B (denoted by $\Pi_A \cong \Pi_B$) if there is a bijection f from $A \cup \{\infty\}$ to $B \cup \{\infty\}$ with $f(\infty) = \infty$, such that $\Pi_A = \Pi_B \circ f$.

4 The main results

Our main technical result is a characterization of $\mathcal{I}$-equivalence in terms of point-structure isomorphism:

Theorem 3. *Two databases A and B are $\mathcal{I}$-equivalent if and only if $\Pi_A \cong \Pi_B$.*

The proof will be sketched in the next section. A corollary of the theorem is a similar characterization of $\mathcal{H}$-equivalence:

Theorem 4. *Let σ be some fixed reflection of $\mathbf{R}^2$. Two databases A and B are $\mathcal{H}$-equivalent if and only if $\Pi_A \cong \Pi_B$ or $\Pi_A \cong \Pi_{\sigma(B)}$.*

Proof. Assuming Theorem 3, we have to prove that A and B are $\mathcal{H}$-equivalent if and only if A and B are $\mathcal{I}$-equivalent or A and $\sigma(B)$ are $\mathcal{I}$-equivalent. The if-implication follows from the fact, already mentioned in the Introduction, that every homeomorphism is either an isotopy or is isotopic to σ. For the only-if-implication, assume on the contrary that A and B are $\mathcal{H}$-equivalent and that there exist $\mathcal{I}$-invariant queries Q and Q' such that $A \models Q$, $B \not\models Q$, $A \models Q'$, and $\sigma(B) \not\models Q'$. Then the query $\bar{Q}$ defined by

$$\bar{Q}(S) = (Q(S) \vee Q'(\sigma(S))) \wedge (Q'(S) \vee Q(\sigma(S))),$$

is $\mathcal{H}$-invariant, and $A \models \bar{Q}$ but $B \not\models \bar{Q}$. This contradicts the assumption. $\square$

Examples. One disk and two separate disks have isomorphic point-structures: the points on the border have (R) as cone, and the points in the interior have F as cone. As a consequence of Theorem 3, they are $\mathcal{I}$-equivalent, hence also $\mathcal{H}$-equivalent.

Although all points on the unit circle and all points on the x-axis have the same cone (namely, (LL)), these databases do not have isomorphic point-structures. Indeed, in the former database the cone of ∞ is ( ) (in other words, this database is bounded), while in the latter database the cone of ∞ is (LL).

Figure 4 shows two databases that are not $\mathcal{I}$-equivalent. Indeed, the cone of the center point in the database on the left is $(LLLRLLRLR)$, while that on the right is $(LRLLRLLLR)$, which is a different circular list. The two database are of course $\mathcal{H}$-equivalent since they are mirror images of each other. We point out that it is possible that two mirror images are still $\mathcal{I}$-equivalent; for instance, the two databases shown in Figure 1 have isomorphic point-structures.

Fig. 4. Two databases that are $\mathcal{H}$-equivalent but not $\mathcal{I}$-equivalent.

Remark: In classical logic, if A and A' are elementary equivalent and B and B' are elementary equivalent, then the disjoint union of A and B and the disjoint union of A' and B' are also elementary equivalent. Theorem 3 implies that this is also true for $\mathcal{I}$-equivalence. However, it is not true for $\mathcal{H}$-equivalence; for instance, take A, A', and B to be the database on the left of Figure 4, and take B' to be the one on the right.

5 The proof

In this section we sketch the proof of Theorem 3.

Transformation rules. The crucial tool in our proof consists of the following three transformations rules that locally change databases:

Strip-cut: The *strip-cut* transformation, shown by the left-to-right arrow in Figure 5(a), locally cuts a strip in the database in two.

Strip-paste: The *strip-paste* transformation, shown by the right-to-left arrow in Figure 5(a), is the inverse of strip-cut.

Line-cut&paste: The *line-cut&paste* transformation, shown in Figure 5(b), locally cuts two parallel lines in the database and connects the corresponding loose ends. An isolated part D of the database may be present between the lines, which will come free after the line-cut&paste.

Note that the line-cut&paste transformation is its own inverse.

A fundamental property of the transformation rules is:

Proposition 5. *If a database B is obtained from a database A by a strip-cut, a strip-paste, or a line-cut&paste transformation, then A and B are $\mathcal{I}$-equivalent.*

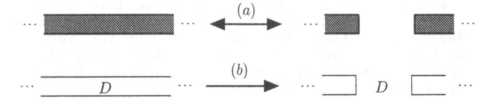

Fig. 5. The transformation rules: (a) strip-cut and strip-paste, (b) line-cut&paste.

Proposition 5 is proven in a number of steps:

1. First, a variation of the proposition is proven for weak versions of the three transformation rules (Lemma 6). These are illustrated in Figure 6. Line-cut&paste is split in a weak line-cut (arrow (b) from left to right) and a weak line-paste (arrow (b) from right to left).
2. The gap between the weak and the original rules is then closed via the notions of *2-regular* and *1-regular* database (Lemmas 8 and 9).

Due to space limitations, the proofs of the Lemmas have been omitted.

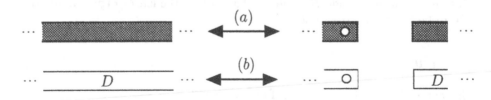

Fig. 6. Weak forms of the three transformation rules.

Lemma 6. *If a database B is obtained from a database A by a weak transformation rule, then A and B are $\mathcal{I}$-equivalent.*

Definition 7. A database is called *2-regular* if is not empty and all of its points have either F or (R) as cone. A database is called *1-regular* if it is not empty and all of its points have (LL) as cone.

Lemma 8. *Let A be a database and O be an open disk in $\mathbf{R}^2$.*

1. *If $A \cap O$ is a 2-regular database, then replacing $A \cap O$ by any other 2-regular database, yields a database that is $\mathcal{I}$-equivalent to A.*
2. *The same holds for 1-regular databases.*

Lemma 9. *Let A be a database and O be an open disk in* $\mathbf{R}^2$. *If* $A \cap O$ *consists of a part D surrounded by a circle, then replacing* $A \cap O$ *by a circle and D outside this circle, yields a database that is* $\mathcal{I}$-*equivalent to A.*

Proof of Proposition 5. (Sketch) We only sketch the proof for the line-cut&paste transformation. It is illustrated in Figure 7. First, the database is isotopically deformed. Second, weak line-cut&past is applied. Third, Lemma 9 is applied. Fourth, Lemma 8 is applied. The last arrow in the figure comprises three applications of weak line-cut&paste. □

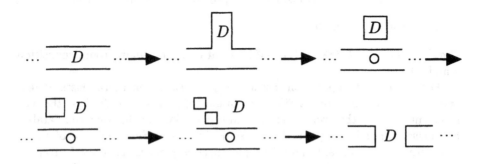

Fig. 7. The proof of the line-cut&paste transformation.

The transformation process. Having our tools, as furnished by Proposition 5, in place, we now show:

Proposition 10. *Let A and B be databases such that* $\Pi_A \cong \Pi_B$. *Then A and B can be transformed, by a finite sequence of strip-cut, strip-paste and line-cut&paste transformations and isotopies, into one and the same database.*

Proof. (Sketch) Since $\Pi_A \cong \Pi_B$, the singular points in A and B can be put in a one-one correspondence, with matching cones. For each singular point p in A and its corresponding point q in B, as well as for the point at infinity, we proceed as follows. From each region in the cone of p we cut out a bounded lobe coming out of p, using strip-cut. We do the same for q. Then, we choose a line l in the cone of p and then use line-cut&paste to connect l and the next line (in the clockwise order around p) into a loop starting and ending in p. We continue this process in the clockwise order around p until all lines, or all lines but one, form loops. We hereby make sure that no isolated parts of the database become trapped in these loops. Similarly, we cut loops in q starting from a line corresponding to l. If the number of lines in the point p is even, we obtain a "flower" around p. If the number is odd, we obtain a "flower with a stem". This stem is necessarily connected to another flower. Note that a flower can just be a single point.

After this process, all connected components are situated in the same area of $\mathbf{R}^2$. As "residual material" of the process we get isolated, bounded, regular parts, that are isotopic to circles, disks, or disks with holes. This material can be transformed to a single closed disk, a single circle, or the disjoint union of a closed disk and a circle. If a flower with points of type (LL) (resp. (R)) is present, the circle (resp. the disk) can even be absorbed by this flower.

The only way in which the resulting databases can still differ is that stems can connect different flowers. We can interchange stems by isotopically bringing them into a parallel position (this is possible since all stems are in the same area) and by then using a line-cut&paste transformation. This finally yields isotopic databases.

An illustration of the transformation process is given in Figure 8. □

We are finally ready for:

Proof of Theorem 3. (Sketch) The if-implication is immediate from Propositions 5 and 10.

For the only-if implication, assume $\Pi_A \not\cong \Pi_B$. Then there exists at least one cone for which A has a different number of points than B. It is therefore sufficient to show that we can express in the spatial calculus that the database has a certain number of points having some fixed cone. Since the cone of a point in a database is invariant under isotopies, such a query is certainly $\mathcal{I}$-invariant. Query (†) in the Introduction is a trivial example of such a query; it expresses that there is a point whose cone is F.

The expressibility of such queries is based on the following refinement of the property that databases are locally conical around each point, including ∞ (proof omitted):

Lemma 11. *Let p be a point in a database A. There exists an $\varepsilon_0 > 0$ such that for every ε, with $0 < \varepsilon < \varepsilon_0$, $C(p,\varepsilon) \cap A$ is isotopic to $C(p,\varepsilon_0) \cap A$. There also exists an $\varepsilon_0 > 0$ such that for every ε, with $\varepsilon > \varepsilon_0$, $C((0,0),\varepsilon) \cap A$ is isotopic to $C((0,0),\varepsilon_0) \cap A$.*

By this lemma, it is sufficient to show that we can describe the intersection of such circles with the database by means of a spatial calculus formula. The points on such an intersection are of three types: interior points of the database, border-points of the interior of the database, and border-points of the database that are not on the border of the interior. The latter being points on lines. All three types of points can be described by a spatial calculus formula. There is also a spatial calculus formula that expresses that a point is between an ordered pair of points on a fixed circle in clockwise order. This completes the proof. □

6 Concluding remarks

Theorems 3 and 4 have two interesting corollaries. The first one is:

Corollary 12. *$\mathcal{I}$- and $\mathcal{H}$-equivalence are decidable.*

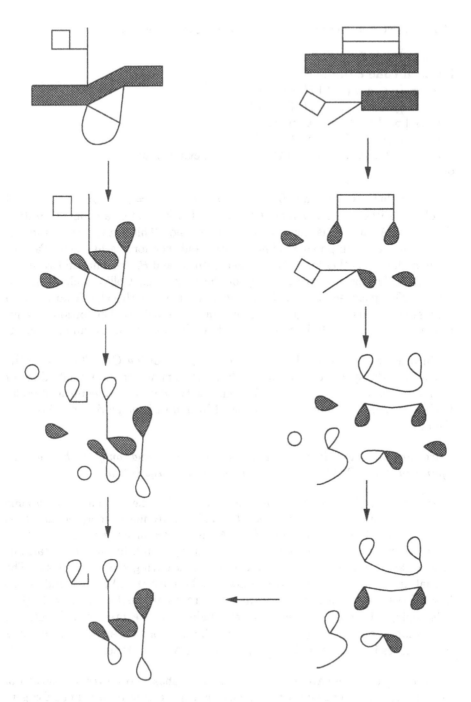

Fig. 8. Two databases with isomorphic point-structures and their transformation into the same database. After the first step, lobes have been cut out. After the second step, loops have been formed. After the third step, the residue has been absorbed. In the fourth step, stems are interchanged in the bottom-right database to obtain a database isotopic to the bottom-left database.

Proof. A decision algorithm for $\mathcal{I}$-equivalence is as follows:

$V_A := \emptyset; V_B := \emptyset;$
for each cone c do
$\quad A_c := \{p \in A \cup \{\infty\} \mid \Pi_A(p) = c\};$
$\quad B_c := \{p \in B \cup \{\infty\} \mid \Pi_B(p) = c\};$
$\quad$**if** $|A_c| \neq |B_c|$ **then return** *false*;
$\quad V_A := V_A \cup A_c; V_B := V_B \cup B_c;$
$\quad$**if** $V_A = A \cup \{\infty\} \wedge V_B = B \cup \{\infty\}$ **then return** *true*
od.

The algorithm tests whether $\Pi_A \cong \Pi_B$. The test $|A_c| \neq |B_c|$ can be performed as follows. Either c is F, (R), or (LL), in which case the test amounts to testing that one of A_c and B_c is empty and the other is not. This is a test expressible in first-order logic with polynomial inequalities and therefore decidable by Tarski's theorem. If c is another kind of cone, then both A_c and B_c are finite and symbolic algorithms for the first-order theory of the reals (e.g., Collins's algorithm [6, 2]) can effectively enumerate them. All other steps in the algorithm are also expressible in first-order logic with polynomial inequalities. The for-loop always terminates since in each database only a finite number of cones can appear. $\quad\Box$

In order to formulate the second corollary, we define CALC($<$) to be the fragment of the spatial calculus in which as polynomial inequalities only those of the form $x - y > 0$ (i.e., $x > y$) are allowed. Call two databases $\mathcal{I}$-equivalent *under* CALC($<$) if they cannot be distinguished by $\mathcal{I}$-invariant queries of CALC($<$). We have:

Corollary 13. *Two databases are $\mathcal{I}$-equivalent if and only if they are $\mathcal{I}$-equivalent under* CALC($<$). *The same holds for $\mathcal{H}$-equivalence.*

Proof. (Sketch) The only-if implication is trivial. For the if-implication, assume A and B are not $\mathcal{I}$-equivalent. Then Π_A and Π_B are not isomorphic, and thus there exists at least one cone for which A has a different number of points than B. In the proof of Theorem 3 we saw that it is expressible in the spatial calculus that a database has a certain number of points having some fixed cone. The crucial observation is that this can actually be done in CALC($<$). Indeed, as base of the cone of a point we can take a rectangle instead of a circle (this is isotopic). All needed properties of rectangles can be expressed in CALC($<$). Also, that a point is an interior point (or a border point) is expressible in terms of rectangles instead of circles as well. Hence, CALC($<$) is sufficient. $\quad\Box$

In this paper, we have focused on *closed* databases. However, the notion of point-structure, fundamental to our development, can also be defined for general semi-algebraic sets in $\mathbf{R}^2$. Unfortunately, due to the possible presence of components of the interior of semi-algebraic sets with mixed borders (open and closed), our transformation-based proof (in particular Proposition 10) does not carry over to this more general setting in a straightforward way.

We are also looking at other dimensions. In dimension one, the notions of $\mathcal{I}$-equivalence and $\mathcal{H}$-equivalence coincide with isotopic and homeomorphic. Generalizations to higher dimensions seem feasible. Indeed, the local cone structure around points in a semi-algebraic set, which provided the main inspiration for our work, also holds there. It remains to be investigated how the cut and paste transformations can be generalized.

References

1. D. Abel and B.C. Ooi, editors. *Advances in spatial databases—3rd Symposium SSD'93*, volume 692 of *Lecture Notes in Computer Science*. Springer-Verlag, 1993.
2. D.S. Arnon. Geometric reasoning with logic and algebra. *Artificial Intelligence*, 37:37–60, 1988.
3. M. Benedikt, G. Dong, L. Libkin, and L. Wong. Relational expressive power of constraint query languages. In *Proceedings 15th ACM Symposium on Principles of Database Systems*, pages 5–16. ACM Press, 1996.
4. J. Bochnak, M. Coste, and M.-F. Roy. *Géométrie algébrique réelle*. Springer-Verlag, 1987.
5. A. Buchmann, editor. *Design and implementation of large spatial databases—First Symposium SSD'89*, volume 409 of *Lecture Notes in Computer Science*. Springer-Verlag, 1989.
6. G.E. Collins. Quantifier elimination for real closed fields by cylindrical algebraic decomposition. *Lecture Notes in Computer Science*, 33:134–183, 1975.
7. M. Coste. Ensembles semi-algébriques. In *Géometrie algébrique réelle et formes quadratiques*, volume 959 of *Lecture Notes in Mathematics*, pages 109–138. Springer, 1982.
8. M.J. Egenhofer and R.D. Franzosa. Point-set topological spatial relations. *Int. J. Geographical Information Systems*, 5(2):161–174, 1991.
9. M.J. Egenhofer and J.R. Herring, editors. *Advances in Spatial Databases*, volume 951 of *Lecture Notes in Computer Science*. Springer, 1995.
10. J. Flum and M. Ziegler. *Topological Model Theory*, volume 769 of *Lecture Notes in Mathematics*. Springer-Verlag, 1980.
11. S. Grumbach and J. Su. First-order definability over constraint databases. In U. Montanari and F. Rossi, editors, *Principles and practice of constraint programming*, volume 976 of *Lecture Notes in Computer Science*, pages 121–136. Springer, 1995.
12. O. Gunther and H.-J. Schek, editors. *Advances in spatial databases—2nd Symposium SSD'91*, volume 525 of *Lecture Notes in Computer Science*. Springer-Verlag, 1991.
13. C.W. Henson, C.G. Jockusch, Jr., L.A. Rubel, and G. Takeuti. *First order topology*, volume CXLIII of *Dissertationes Mathematicae*. 1977.
14. P.C. Kanellakis, G.M. Kuper, and P.Z. Revesz. Constraint query languages. *Journal of Computer and System Sciences*, 51(1):26–52, August 1995.
15. E.E. Moise. *Geometric topology in dimensions 2 and 3*, volume 47 of *Graduate Texts in Mathematics*. Springer, 1977.
16. C.H. Papadimitriou, D. Suciu, and V. Vianu. Topological queries in spatial databases. In *Proceedings 15th ACM Symposium on Principles of Database Systems*, pages 81–92. ACM Press, 1996.

17. J. Paredaens, J. Van den Bussche, and D. Van Gucht. Towards a theory of spatial database queries. In *Proceedings 13th ACM Symposium on Principles of Database Systems*, pages 279–288. ACM Press, 1994.
18. A. Pillay. First order topological structures and theories. *Journal of Symbolic Logic*, 52(3), September 1987.

Model-Theoretic Minimal Change
Operators for Constraint Databases*

Peter Z. Revesz

Department of Computer Science and Engineering
University of Nebraska, Lincoln, NE 68588
revesz@cse.unl.edu, (402) 472-3488

Abstract: Database systems should allow users to insert new information (described by a first-order sentence) into a database without specifying exactly how. The database systems should be able to figure out what tuples to add or delete from the current database to satisfy fully the user's request. The guiding principle of accomplishing such insertions is the concept of model-theoretic minimal change. This paper shows that this concept can be applied to constraint databases. In particular, any constraint database change operator that satisfies the axioms for revision [AGM85], update [KM92], or arbitration [Rev96] accomplishes a model-theoretic minimal change in a well-defined sense. The paper also presents concrete operators for revision, update, and arbitration for constraint databases with real polynomial inequality constraints.

1 Introduction

Most change operators in current database systems require the users to know the exact contents of the database. Users are expected to know what tuples are in the database and specifically command to delete, modify or add specific tuples. However, it is very difficult to know exactly what is in a complex database and database users should be freed from that burden. This is especially true in constraint databases [KKR95]. Users should be able to change a database by simply telling the database system what new information to incorporate into it. The database system should be able to figure out by itself how to incorporate the new information.

The idea of automatic change requires a solution to the well-known frame problem of artificial intelligence: if some things are known to change, what other things must change with them and what things must stay the same? A nice solution to this problem is the principle of model-theoretic minimal change. Let's call the set of models of the world that are currently thought possible the database. Each new information, described in some logical form, allows several models of the world. The principle of minimal change states that the result of adding the new information to a database should be the set of models of the new information that are closest to some possible models in the current database. Hence the database change problem can be largely reduced to finding good measures for distance between models of the world.

---

* This work was supported by NSF grants IRI-9625055 and IRI-9632871.

While the principle of minimal change is agreed upon by most people, to say precisely what are good operators and distance measures between models is difficult. Katsuno and Mendelzon [KM91, KM92] pointed out that there are in fact two very different contexts for database change. They divided change operators into two broad classes: revision and update. They characterized these two classes of change operators by a set of axioms that they have to satisfy and proved that members in each class accomplish a model-theoretic minimal change, in different ways. To these classes, [Rev96] added a third class of change operators: arbitration, which is also defined by a set of axioms. [Rev96] proved that members in this class also accomplish a model-theoretic minimal change, in a way distinct from both revision and update. Arbitration is motivated by heterogeneous database systems which often require combining information from various sources before answering queries (see also [BKMS92, BNR95, TSIMMIS, LS95, Sub94, Wie92]).

The model-theoretic characterizations in [KM91, KM92, Rev96] were shown only for propositional knowledgebases. It seems much more difficult to define operators for first-order knowledgebases that can be similarly characterized. Fagin et al. [FKUV86] present a revision operator for first-order logical databases but it violates an important axiom in [AGM85] on which the characterization depends, namely it violates the Principle of Irrelevance of Syntax. Grahne et al. [GMR92] present an update operator but it uses the active domain semantics, which may be unnatural for constraint databases.

In this paper we present for a simple type of first-order database, namely constraint (or generalized) databases with rational order constraints [KKR95], revision, update, and arbitration operators that satisfy appropriate generalizations of the axioms in [KM91, KM92] and [Rev96]. We also show that all operators satisfying the relevant axioms have a model-theoretic characterization.

Potential applications of the paper occur mainly in manipulating spatial data described by constraint databases. For example, a Geographic Information System (GIS) for agriculture would need update after overflooding of a river, or a new crop being planted. Revision may be needed in light of new data, e.g. this is a corn field, not wheat, and arbitration would solve many sensor fusion problems, e.g., merge of two different soil maps derived from two different satellite measurements.

This paper is organized as follows. Section 2 reviews basic concepts in constraint databases and database change operators. Section 3 presents a syntax independent way of measuring the size of constraint databases. Section 4 presents a syntax independent way of measuring distance. Sections 5-7 give model-theoretic characterizations of revision, update, and arbitration. Section 8 considers the case when the new information is a first-order sentence. Section 9 gives a conclusion and mentions open problems.

2   Basic Concepts

The following are basic definitions adopted from [KKR95].

Definition 2.1 Let Φ be the set of atomic constraints of some constraint theory. A *generalized k-tuple* over variables $x_1, \ldots, x_k$ is of the form: $r(x_1, \ldots, x_k) :\!-\!$ $\phi_1 \wedge \ldots \wedge \phi_n$ where r is a relation symbol, and $\phi_i \in \Phi$ for $1 \leq i \leq n$ and uses only the variables $x_1, \ldots, x_k$.

A *generalized relation r with arity k* is a finite set of generalized k-tuples with symbol r on left hand side.

A *generalized database* is a finite set of generalized relations.

A *generalized knowledgebase* is a finite set of generalized databases. $\Box$

Definition 2.2 Let D be the domain over which variables are interpreted. Then the *model of a generalized k-tuple t* with variables $x_1, \ldots, x_k$ is the unrestricted k-ary relation $\{(a_1, \ldots, a_k) : (a_1, \ldots, a_k) \in D^k$ and the substitution of a_i for x_i satisfies the right hand side$\}$.

The *model of a generalized relation* is the union of the models of its generalized tuples.

The *model of a generalized database* is the set of the models of its generalized relations.

The *model of a generalized knowledgebase* is the set of the models of its generalized databases. $\Box$

In this paper we will denote the models of a A by $Mod(A)$ where A is a generalized relation, database, or knowledgebase.

Katsuno and Mendelzon studied propositional knowledgebases. Each propositional knowledgebase is described by a single propositional formula. The models of the formula are interpretations (truth assignments to propositional variables) that make the formula true. Contrast that with our definition of a generalized knowledgebase: instead of a set of interpretations we have a set of generalized databases. This change is important because a crucial issue for [KM91] is to define the distance between pairs of interpretations. For us an important task will be to define distances between pairs of generalized databases.

Let $\mathcal{M}$ be the set of all possible generalized databases. (In [KM91] $\mathcal{M}$ is the set of interpretations.) A *pre-order* $\leq$ over $\mathcal{M}$ is a reflexive and transitive relation on $\mathcal{M}$. A pre-order is *total* if for every pair $I, J \in \mathcal{M}$, either $I \leq J$ or $J \leq I$ holds. We define the relation $<$ as $I < J$ if and only if $I \leq J$ and $J \not\leq I$. The set of *minimal elements* of a subset S of $\mathcal{M}$ with respect to a pre-order $\leq_\psi$ is defined as:

$$Min(S, \leq_\psi) = \{I \in S : \nexists I' \in S \text{ where } I' <_\psi I\}$$

Katsuno and Mendelzon gave the following model-theoretic characterization of revision and update when the knowledge base is represented by a single propositional formula. Let the symbol $\circ$ denote revision and the symbol $\diamond$ denote update operators.

Suppose we have for each knowledge base ψ a total pre-ordering $\leq_\psi$ of interpretations for closeness to ψ, where the pre-order $\leq_\psi$ satisfies certain conditions [KM91]. Revision operators that satisfy the AGM postulates are exactly those that select from the models of the new information ϕ the closest models to the propositional knowledge base ψ. That is,

$$Mod(\psi \circ \phi) = Min(Mod(\phi), \leq_\psi)$$

For updates assume for each interpretation I some partial pre-ordering $\leq_I$ of interpretations for closeness to I. Update operators select for each model I in $Mod(\psi)$ the set of models from $Mod(\phi)$ that are closest to I. The new theory is the union of all such models. That is,

$$Mod(\psi \diamond \phi) = \bigcup_{I \in Mod(\psi)} Min(Mod(\phi), \leq_I)$$

A third type of theory change that is axiomatically defined in [Rev96] is called arbitration. Let $\triangleright$ denote arbitration. Then arbitration operators will be characterized similarly to revision above, but the pre-order $\leq_\psi$ has to satisfy a different set of conditions.

3   A Multi-Measure for Real Polynomial Constraint Relations

In the context of aggregate operators, Kuper [Kup93] suggested area to measure generalized databases, and Chomicki and Kuper [ChK95] suggested as a measure the asymptotic probability that an arbitrary point belongs to the model of the generalized database. This section presents another measure for the area of constraint databases assuming that the atomic constraints are real polynomial inequalities.

The reason for introducing a multi-measure is that even a very large difference between two regions in dimension i is unimportant compared to the smallest difference in dimension $i + 1$. For example, if two drawings in the $\mathcal{R}^2$ plane differ in any small line segment, then it should be considered more important than that they also differ on any finite number of points. However, in case they agree on all line segments, then the number of point differences can be very useful to know. Hence we need a multi-measure that records all dimensional volumes simultaneously, i.e. some vector of dimension $k + 1$ for measuring k dimensional regions.

Definition 3.1 A region is *elementary* if and only if it is one of (a) a point (b) a line without endpoints or (c) an open region. $\square$

Definition 3.2 A *partition* of a region R is a disjoint set of elementary regions $P_1, \ldots, P_n$ such that $Mod(R) = Mod(P_1 \cup \ldots \cup P_n)$. $\square$

Since the elements of a partition are disjoint, no two lines may cross each other and no region may contain other elements in the partition. We call a point *extensional* if it is within the partition but is not within any line or region of the partition. We also call the number of line elements incident on a point within a partition the *degree* of the point.

In 3-dimensional space the degree of each edge is two, nd the degree of each corner is three. For any higher dimension we take the degree of a line (hyperplane facet) to be the number of surfaces (higher dimensional hyperplane facets) that have the whole line (hyperplane facet) as a boundary.

Definition 3.3 Let P be any partition of k-dimensional region R. For each $1 \leq i \leq n$, the *multi-measure* of P_i, denoted $m(P_i)$ is the following $(a_0, \ldots, a_k)$ form vector:

(1) $(0, \ldots, 0, 1)$ if P_i is an extensional point.

(2) $(0, \ldots, 0, degree(P_i) \times length(P_i), -(a+b))$ if P_i is a line without endpoints where P_i is incident upon points A and B and $a = 1/degree(A)$ if A is extensional otherwise $a = 0$, and $b = 1/degree(B)$ if B is extensional otherwise $b = 0$.

(3) $(0, \ldots, a_{k-j}, a_{k-(j+1)}, \ldots, 0)$ where $a_{k-j} = degree(P_i) \times volume(P_i)$ and $a_{k-(j+1)} = -boundary(P_i)$ if P_i is any $j \geq 2$ dimensional open region.

The multi-measure of P is the sum of the vectors $m(P_i)$ for $1 \leq i \leq n$. □

There are certain balances built into the above definition to make it partition independent. For example, if we have a square region in the plane and cut it diagonally by a line, then we introduced a new line segment (the diagonal). This would increase the sum of measures considered under condition (2) above in a positive direction, and those considered under (3) above in a negative direction by the same amount. In general, we can prove the following.

Theorem 3.1 Let R be any region, then all partitions of R have the same multi-measure. □

Definition 3.4 The multi-measure of a region R is $m(P)$ where P is any partition of R. □

Example 3.1 Let R be a region defined as follows: $A(x,y) :- 3 < x \wedge x < 12 \wedge 3 < y \wedge y < 12$

Note that R is elementary because it is an open square region. Hence a trivial partition of R is just itself. The measure of R is $m(R) = (162, -36, 0)$ applying the definition. Another partition of R is shown in the figure below. Hence another way of finding the measure of R is to sum up the measure of the disjoint regions in the figure.

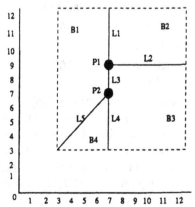

Here B1-B4 are open regions and L1-L5 are lines without endpoints and $P1, P2$ are extensional points. We find that $m(B_1) = (56, -(16\sqrt{2} + 18), 0)$, $m(B_2) = (30, -16, 0)$, $m(B_3) = (60, -22, 0)$, $m(B_4) = (16, -(16\sqrt{2} + 8), 0)$, $m(L_1) = (0, 6, -1/3)$, $m(L_2) = (0, 10, -1/3)$, $m(L_3) = (0, 4, -2/3)$, $m(L_4) = (0, 8, -1/3)$, $m(L_5) = (0, 32\sqrt{2}, -1/3)$, $m(P_1) = (0, 0, 1)$, $m(P_2) = (0, 0, 1)$, The sum of these measures is $(162, -36, 0)$ matching the value we found using the other partition. □

Next, let's see an example in 3-dimension.

Example 3.2 The open cube with opposite corners $(0, 0, 0)$ and $(9, 9, 9)$ has multi-measure $(729, 0, 0, 0)$. Suppose that the cube is partitioned into an open cube with opposite corners $(3, 3, 3)$ and $(6, 6, 6)$, a volume surrounding the cube, and the sides, edges, and corners of the little cube. The surrounding region will have multi-measure $(702, -54, 0, 0)$, little cube will have $(27, -54, 0, 0)$, each of its six sides will have $(0, 2 \times 9, -12, 0)$, each of its twelve edges will have $(0, 0, 2 \times 3, -2/3)$ and its eight corners will have $(0, 0, 0, 1)$. The sum of the multi-measures of the partition is still $(729, 0, 0, 0)$. □

4 A Distance Measure between Relations

The *distance measure* between two regions R_1 and R_2, denoted $dist(R_1, R_2)$, is $m((R_1 \cup R_2) \setminus (R_1 \cap R_2))$. It follows from Theorem 3.1 that for any two regions R_1 and R_2, $dist(R_1, R_2)$ is a unique multi-measure. The distance between two constraint relations with the same relation symbol is the distance between regions associated with them. The distance between two constraint databases is the sum of the distances between the corresponding constraint relations in them, and the measure of the constraint relations whose symbol occurs in only one of them.

Example 4.1 Suppose that we are given two constraint databases I_1 and I_2 describing land areas. I_1 is the constraint database:

$Wood(x, y) :- 3 < x \wedge x < 10 \wedge 3 < y \wedge y < 15$

and I_2 is the constraint database:

$Wood(x, y) :- 3 < x \wedge x < 10 \wedge 3 < y \wedge y < 10$
$Wood(x, y) :- x = 15 \wedge y = 15$

Let's call ϕ_1, and ϕ_2 respectively the (disjunction) of the formulas on the right hand side of I_1 and I_2. Let us use the partition shown in the figure below, where r_1, r_3, r_5 are open regions, r_2, r_4 are lines without endpoints, and r_6 is a point. Clearly, it is possible to express each r_i as a conjunction of atomic constraints and ϕ_1 as $r_1 \vee r_2 \vee r_3 \vee r_4 \vee r_5$ and ϕ_2 as $r_1 \vee r_2 \vee r_3 \vee r_6$. Now we can calculate the distance between the two regions as $dist(I_1, I_2) = m((I_1 \cup I_2) \setminus (I_1 \cap I_2)) = m(r_4 \cup r_5 \cup r_6) = (0, 14, 0) + (70, -24, 0) + (0, 0, 1) = (70, -10, 1)$. □

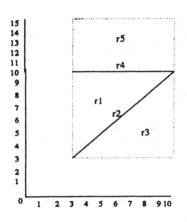
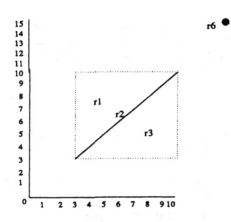

Jagadish [Jag91] considered as a distance measure between two-dimensional regions composed of a set of rectangles the difference in their areas. This measure cannot distinguish between the picture of a rectangle and the picture of the same rectangle with a dot on top of it. Nor can it distinguish between an open and a closed rectangle. In contrast, the distance measure introduced in this paper does distinguish in the above cases.

5 Revision

Katsuno and Mendelzon [KM91] translated the AGM [AGM85] postulates into six equivalent axioms on propositional knowledgebases. Since we use generalized knowledgebases, we translate the AGM axioms into a slightly different set of axioms. We say that ∘ is a revision operator on generalized knowledgebases if for each generalized knowledgebase ψ, μ and ϕ the following hold:

(R1) $Mod(\psi \circ \mu) \subseteq Mod(\mu)$.
(R2) If $\psi \sqcap \mu$ is nonempty then $Mod(\psi \circ \mu) = Mod(\psi \sqcap \mu)$.
(R3) If μ is nonempty then $\psi \circ \mu$ is nonempty.
(R4) If $Mod(\psi_1) = Mod(\psi_2)$ and $Mod(\mu_1) = Mod(\mu_2)$ then $Mod(\psi_1 \circ \mu_1) = Mod(\psi_2 \circ \mu_2)$.
(R5) $Mod((\psi \circ \mu)) \sqcap \phi) \subseteq Mod(\psi \circ (\mu \sqcap \phi))$.
(R6) If $(\psi \circ \mu) \sqcap \phi$ is nonempty then $Mod(\psi \circ (\mu \sqcap \phi)) \subseteq Mod((\psi \circ \mu) \sqcap \phi)$.

In the above $\mu \sqcap \phi = \{I \in \mu : \exists J \in \phi \text{ such that } Mod(I) = Mod(J)\}$. Note that $Mod(\mu \sqcap \phi) = Mod(\mu) \cap Mod(\phi)$. Next we define a concrete revision operator based on the distance measure in Section 4. We define the distance between a generalized knowledgebase ψ and a generalized database I as follows:

$$dist(\psi, I) = \min_{J \in \psi} dist(I, J)$$

In comparing multi-measures, we consider the elements from left to right to be the most to least significant. Hence for example, $(1, 0, 5) \le (2, 1, 6)$ and

$(5, -8, 7) \leq (5, -7, 2)$. Next we define with respect to any generalized knowledge-base ψ a total pre-order $\leq_\psi$ as follows. For each pair of generalized databases I and J let $I \leq_\psi J$ if and only if $dist(\psi, I) \leq dist(\psi, J)$. Now the revision operator $\circ$ can be defined as:

$$\psi \circ \mu = Min(\mu, \leq_\psi)$$

Example 5.1 Suppose that there are two options for landscaping an empty area I_1. (Note that I_1 is described by an empty database.) The first option J_1 is:
$Wood(x, y) :\!- 0 < x \wedge x < 1 \wedge -10 < y \wedge y < 0$
$Wood(x, y) :\!- 1 < x \wedge x < 10 \wedge -1 < y \wedge y < 0.$
   The second option J_2 is:
$Wood(x, y) :\!- 0 < x \wedge x < 1 \wedge -10 < y \wedge y < 0$
$Wood(x, y) :\!- 10 < x \wedge x < 11 \wedge -10 < y \wedge y < 0.$
   Which landscape option is better to choose assuming that we want to do minimal work, i.e. to forest a minimal area? In this example let $\mu = \{J_1, J_2\}$. We need to find out which options in μ are closest to I_1. That is, we need to find $\{I_1\} \circ \mu$. Let ϕ_1 and ϕ_2 be the disjunctions of the right hand sides in J_1 and J_2. Let us use in this example the partition shown in the figure below. Here $\phi_1 = r_1 \vee r_2 \vee r_3 \vee r_4 \vee r_5$ and $\phi_2 = r_1 \vee r_2 \vee r_3 \vee r_6 \vee r_7 \vee r_8$.

Since the partition of I_1 is empty $dist(I_1, J_1) = m((I_1 \cup J_1) \setminus (I_1 \cap J_1)) = m(J_1) = m(r_1 \cup r_2 \cup r_3 \cup r_4 \cup r_5) = (2, -4, 0) + (0, 2, 0) + (18, -20, 0) + (0, 2, 0) + (18, -20, 0) = (38, -40, 0)$. Similarly, we calculate that $dist(I_1, J_2) = (40, -44, 0)$. Note that $dist(I_1, J_1) < dist(I_1, J_2)$, hence $J_1 <_{\{I_1\}} J_2$. Therefore $\{I_1\} \circ \mu = \{J_1\}$. That means that we should choose the first landscape option, because it will require less work to realize. $\square$
   Our next example is more complex in that the knowledgebase to be revised contains several possible databases.

Example 5.2 Suppose that we have the option of purchasing the land either completely cleared I_1 or with a patch of wooded area remaining I_2. The price of the two options is the same. Here the second purchase option can be described as:

$Wood(x, y) :- 10 < x \land x < 11 \land -10 < y, y < 0$

What is the best landscape option to choose in this case? Let $\psi = \{I_1, I_2\}$. To answer the question we need to do revision.

Calculating distances we find that $dist(I_2, J_1) = m(\cup_{1 \leq i \leq 8} r_i) = (58, -62, 0)$ and $dist(I_2, J_2) = (20, -22, 0)$. We see that the minimum distance among pairs of I's and J's is between I_2 and J_2. Hence $\psi \circ \mu = \{J_2\}$, that is, in this case we should choose the second landscape option (and implicitly buy the lot with the wooded patch in it.). $\square$

A generalized *faithful* assignment is a function that assigns for each generalized knowledgebase ψ a pre-order $\leq_\psi$ such that the following conditions hold. For each $I, J \in \mathcal{M}$ and generalized knowledgebases ψ, ψ_1, ψ_2:

(1) If $Mod(I), Mod(J) \in Mod(\psi)$ then $I <_\psi J$ does not hold.
(2) If $Mod(I) \in Mod(\psi)$ and $Mod(J) \notin Mod(\psi)$ then $I <_\psi J$.
(3) If $Mod(\psi_1) = Mod(\psi_2)$ then $\leq_{\psi_1} = \leq_{\psi_2}$.

The revision operator defined above is faithful. It is also possible to show that it satisfies the axioms (R1-R6). In general, we can extend the characterization theorem of Katsuno and Mendelzon as follows.

Theorem 5.1 A revision operator satisfies axioms (R1-R6) if and only if there exists a generalized faithful assignment that maps each generalized knowledgebase ψ to a total pre-order $\leq_\psi$ such that for every other generalized knowledgebase μ, $Mod(\psi \circ \mu) = Mod(Min(\mu, \leq_\psi))$. $\square$

6 Update

We say that $\diamond$ is an update operator on generalized knowledgebases if for each generalized knowledgebase ψ and μ and generalized database I the following hold:

(U1) $Mod(\psi \diamond \mu) \subseteq Mod(\mu)$.
(U2) If $Mod(\psi) \subseteq Mod(\mu)$ then $Mod(\psi \diamond \mu) = Mod(\psi)$.
(U3) If ψ and μ nonempty, then $\psi \diamond \mu$ is nonempty.
(U4) If $Mod(\psi_1) = Mod(\psi_2)$ and $Mod(\mu_1) = Mod(\mu_2)$ then $Mod(\psi_1 \diamond \mu_1) = Mod(\psi_2 \diamond \mu_2)$.
(U5) $Mod((\psi \diamond \mu) \sqcap I) \subseteq Mod(\psi \diamond (\mu \sqcap I))$.
(U6) If $Mod(\psi \diamond \mu_1) \subseteq Mod(\mu_2)$ and $Mod(\psi \diamond \mu_2) \subseteq Mod(\mu_1)$ then $Mod(\psi \diamond \mu_1) = Mod(\psi \diamond \mu_2)$.
(U7) $(Mod((\{I\} \diamond \mu_1) \sqcap (\{I\} \diamond \mu_2))) \subseteq Mod(\{I\} \diamond (\mu_1 \cup \mu_2))$.
(U8) $Mod((\psi_1 \cup \psi_2) \diamond \mu) = Mod((\psi_1 \diamond \mu) \cup (\psi_2 \diamond \mu))$.

Note that axioms (U1) and (U4-U5) are the same as axioms (R1) and (R4-R5). Axiom (U2) is a weakening of axiom (R2) in the case when ψ is satisfiable. Axiom (U3) is a weakening of axiom (R3) that is needed to avoid defining the update of an empty knowledgebase. Axioms (U6-U7) replace axiom (R6). They generalize (R6) slightly by admitting orderings where some pair of models of the new information are not comparable as to closeness to the knowledgebase. Axiom (U8) guarantees that each model in the knowledgebase is updated independently.

Next we define with respect to any generalized database I a pre-order $\leq_I$ as follows. For each pair of generalized databases J and K let $J \leq_I K$ if and only if $dist(I,J) \leq dist(I,K)$. Next we define a concrete update operator $\diamond$ as follows:

$$\psi \diamond \mu = \bigcup_{I \in \psi} Min(\mu, \leq_I)$$

Example 6.1 Let us return to Example 5.2. Suppose the neighbor tries to figure out what the new land will be like. The neighbor knows both the landscape options and the two ways of purchasing the land. However, suppose that the neighbor does not know that the price of the two purchase options is the same. What can the neighbor conclude?

This would require calculating $\psi \diamond \mu$, which turns out to be μ. This is because to I_1 the closest is J_1 and to I_2 the closest is J_2. Hence the neighbor can expect that if I_1 is purchased then J_1 and if I_2 is purchased then J_2 will be the landscape chosen. However, even though $dist(I_2, J_2) \leq dist(I_1, J_1)$ as far as the neighbor knows the price of I_1 may be much lower than the price of I_2 to offset the extra landscaping work required. Therefore, the neighbor can conclude only that one of the two landscape options will be chosen, but cannot say for sure which one. □

A generalized *faithful* assignment for updates satisfies the following condition: For any generalized database I if $I \neq J$ then $I <_I J$.

The update operator $\diamond$ defined above is faithful for updates and satisfies the axioms (U1-U8). In general, we have that:

Theorem 6.1 An update operator satisfies axioms (U1-U8) if and only if there exists a generalized faithful assignment that maps each generalized database I to a pre-order $\leq_I$ such that for every generalized knowledgebases ψ, μ, $Mod(\psi \diamond \mu) = \bigcup_{I \in Mod(\psi)} Mod(Min(\mu, \leq_I))$. □

7 Arbitration

We call generalized arbitration operators, denoted by $\triangleright$, those operators that satisfy axioms (R1) and (R3-R6) and axioms (A2) and (A7) below:

(A2) If ψ is empty, then $\psi \triangleright \mu$ is empty.

(A7) $Mod((\psi_1 \triangleright \mu) \sqcap (\psi_2 \triangleright \mu)) \subseteq Mod((\psi_1 \cup \psi_2) \triangleright \mu)$.

Axiom (A7) asserts that any generalized database that is closest to both ψ_1 in μ and to ψ_2 in μ must also be a closest generalized database to $\psi_1 \cup \psi_2$ in μ. This is sometimes called the overall distance requirement. We define the *overall distance* between a generalized knowledgebase ψ and a generalized database I as follows:

$$odist(\psi, I) = \max_{J \in \psi} dist(I, J)$$

Note the change to max from min in the corresponding definition for revisions. Similarly to the previous cases, we define with respect to any generalized knowledgebase ψ a total pre-order $\leq_\psi$ as follows. For each pair of generalized databases I and J let $I \leq_\psi J$ if and only if $odist(\psi, I) \leq odist(\psi, J)$. Then a concrete arbitration operator is the following:

$$\psi \triangleright \mu = Min(\mu, \leq_\psi)$$

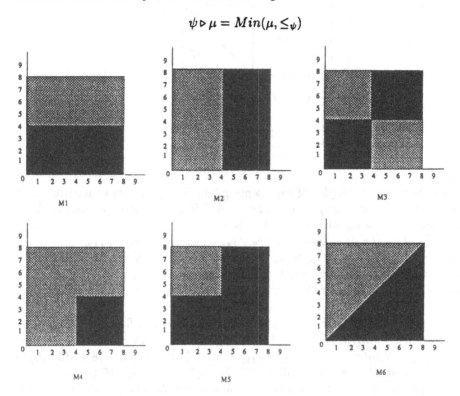

Example 7.1 You are chosen to design the flag of a newly independent country that has two factious parties each suggesting a different flag, namely flags M1 and M2 shown in the figure above. Upon some consideration of the materials available, sewing techniques, dyes, aspect ratios and other esthetic reasons, you limited the choices to M1 and M2 and four other flags shown above. At this point you receive death threats from supporters of both parties "in case you don't choose the right flag". Which flag would you choose?

In this case we need to find out which one of the six possible flags would irk least both parties, i.e., be closest to their flag proposals. That of course we can find out using arbitration. We will calculate $\psi \triangleright \mu$ where $\psi = \{M1, M2\}$ and $\mu = \{M1, M2, M3, M4, M5, M6\}$.

We can represent each flag by a relation $Flag(x, y, z)$ where the x and y will be points in the area of the flag and z its color. Let $z = 10$ be gray and $z = 20$ be black. Since we use x, y, z coordinates we have a 3-dimensional problem. Each flag can be represented as the union of the elementary regions r_i in the gray and r_{ib} in the black plane for $1 \leq i \leq 12$, where the regions in the gray plane are shown below. The elementary regions in the black plane are like the ones in the gray plane but shifted up 10 units.

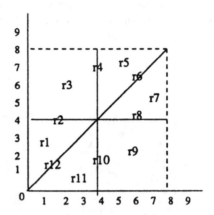

We give some examples of representing flags using the above partition. We assume that the boundary between any two differently colored regions is black, i.e., they are sewn together by black stitches.

$M1 = r_{1b} \lor r_{2b} \lor r_3 \lor r_4 \lor r_5 \lor r_6 \lor r_7 \lor r_{8b} \lor r_{9b} \lor r_{10b} \lor r_{11b} \lor r_{12b}$

$M2 = r_1 \lor r_2 \lor r_3 \lor r_{4b} \lor r_{5b} \lor r_{6b} \lor r_{7b} \lor r_{8b} \lor r_{9b} \lor r_{10b} \lor r_{11} \lor r_{12}$

$M4 = r_1 \lor r_2 \lor r_3 \lor r_4 \lor r_5 \lor r_6 \lor r_7 \lor r_{8b} \lor r_{9b} \lor r_{10b} \lor r_{11} \lor r_{12}$

$M6 = r_1 \lor r_2 \lor r_3 \lor r_4 \lor r_5 \lor r_{6b} \lor r_{7b} \lor r_{8b} \lor r_{9b} \lor r_{10b} \lor r_{11b} \lor r_{12b}$

Next, let's calculate the distance between some pair of flags.

$dist(M1, M4) = m((M1 \cup M4) \setminus (M1 \cap M4)) = m(r_1 \lor r_{1b} \lor r_2 \lor r_{2b} \lor r_{11} \lor r_{11b} \lor r_{12} \lor r_{12b}) = 2(m(r_1) + m(r_2) + m(r_{11}) + m(r_{12})) = 2((0, 16, -(8 + \sqrt{32}), 0) + (0, 0, 8, 0) + (0, 16, -(8 + \sqrt{32}), 0) + (0, 0, 2\sqrt{32}, 0)) = (0, 64, -16, 0)$

Similarly we can calculate that $dist(M2, M4) = dist(M1, M5) = dist(M2, M5) = (0, 64, -16, 0)$. Also, $dist(M1, M6) = dist(M2, M6) = (0, 64, -16\sqrt{2}, 0)$. After calculating the other distances, it is easy to see that the flags $M4$ and $M5$ give the smallest maximum distances to the two original proposals. Hence after arbitration the new knowledge base will contain these two flags, i.e., $\psi \triangleright \mu = \{M4, M5\}$. (Note that $M6$ will not be in the solution because although its area distance from $M1$ and $M2$ is as good as that of $M4$ and $M5$, its line distance is less than optimal.) $\square$

A generalized assignment is *loyal* if it satisfies the following:
(1) If $Mod(\psi_1) = Mod(\psi_2)$ then $\leq_{\psi_1} = \leq_{\psi_2}$. (2) If $I \leq_{\psi_1} J$ and $I \leq_{\psi_2} J$ then $I \leq_{\psi_1 \cup \psi_2} J$.
The above arbitration operator $\triangleright$ is loyal and satisfies axioms (R1,A2,R3-R6,A7). In general:

Theorem 7.1 A knowledgebase operator satisfies axioms (R1,A2,R3-R6,A7) if and only if there exists a loyal assignment that maps each knowledge base ψ to a total pre-order $\leq_\psi$ such that $Mod(\psi \triangleright \mu) = Mod(Min(\mu, \leq_\psi))$. $\square$

8 Changing a Knowledgebase by First-Order Sentences

The previous sections described revision, update, and arbitration when the new information is a set of models. Grahne et al [GMR92] described a method of updating knowledgebases composed of a set of relational databases by a first-order sentence. [BNR95, Rev96] described similar methods for revision and arbitration by first-order sentences. We can extend these ideas to generalized knowledgebases.

The idea is to allow new informations that are describable in a constraint-query language. For example, if the new information is described in the language of Datalog with dense order constraints, then it describes a query that is evaluable in closed-form on any dense-order constraint database. Hence the new information can be applied to any knowledgebase composed of a set of dense order constraint databases. For example, the updated knowledgebase will be the union of the constraint database outputs obtained when applying the new information to the constraint database inputs.

9 Conclusions and Further Work

It would be interesting to test the above operators for real data sets that have a fractal dimension [FK94]. It would be also interesting to compare the operators with other measures, (for example Hausdorff distance [Dou92]) and also to test how well people's assessments correlate with the proposed distance measure and operators.

References

[AGM85] C. E. Alchourrón, P. Gärdenfors & D. Makinson. On the logic of theory change: Partial meet contraction and revision functions. *Journal of Symbolic Logic*, (50), pages 510–530, 1985.

[BKMS92] C. Baral, S. Kraus, J. Minker & V.S. Subrahmanian. Combining knowledge bases consisting of first-order theories. *Computational Intelligence*, vol. 8, no. 1, pages 45–71, 1992.

[BNR95] A. Benczur, A.B. Novak, & P.Z. Revesz. On Weighted Knowledgebase Transformations. *Proc. Fourth Symposium on Programming Languages and Software Tools*, pp. 404–415, Visegrad, Hungary, June 1995.

[TSIMMIS] S. Chawathe, H. Garcia-Molina, J. Hammer, K. Ireland, Y. Papakonstantinou, J. Ullman, & J. Widom. The TSIMMIS Project: Integration of Heterogeneous Information Sources, *Proc. IPSJ Conf.*, Tokyo, Japan, Oct 1994.

[ChK95] J. Chomicki & G. Kuper. Measuring Infinite Relations. *Fourteenth ACM Symposium on Principles of Database Systems*, pages 246–260, 1995.

[Dou92] E.R. Dougherty. An Introduction to Morphological Image Processing. *SPIE Press*, 1992.

[FKUV86] R. Fagin, G. Kuper, J. D. Ullman & M. Y. Vardi. Updating logical databases. In: *Advances in Computing Research*, Vol. 3, P. C. Kanellakis and F. Preparata eds., pages 1–18, JAI Press, 1986.

[FK94]   C. Faloutsos & I. Kamel. Beyond Uniformity and Independence: Analysis of R-tree Using the Concept of Fractal Dimension. *Proc. 13th ACM Symposium on Principles of Database Systems*, pages 4–13, 1994.

[GMR92]   G. Grahne, A. O. Mendelzon, & P. Z. Revesz. Knowledgebase transformations. *Journal of Computer and System Sciences*, to appear. (Preliminary version in *Proc. 11th ACM PODS*, 1992.)

[Jag91]   H. V. Jagadish. A retrieval technique for similar shapes. *ACM SIGMOD Symposium on the Management of Data*, pages 208–217, 1991.

[KKR95]   P. C. Kanellakis, G. M. Kuper, & P. Z. Revesz. Constraint Query Languages, *Journal of Computer and System Sciences*, vol. 51, pages 26–52, 1995. (Preliminary version in *Proc. 9th ACM PODS*, 1990.)

[KM91]   H. Katsuno & A. O. Mendelzon. Propositional knowledge base revision and minimal change. *Artificial Intelligence*, 52, pages 263–294, 1991.

[KM92]   H. Katsuno & A. O. Mendelzon. On the difference between updating a knowledge base and revising it. In: *Belief Revision*, Gärdenfors, ed., pages 183–203, Cambridge University Press, 1992.

[Kup93]   G. Kuper. Aggregation in constraint databases. *First Workshop on Principles and Practice of Constraint Programming*, p. 176–183, 1993.

[LS95]   P. Liberatore & M. Schaerf. Arbitration: A commutative operator for belief revision. *World Conference on the Fundamentals of Artificial Intelligence*, 1995.

[Rev96]   P. Z. Revesz. On the semantics of arbitration. *International Journal of Algebra and Computation*, to appear. (Preliminary version in *Proc. 12th ACM PODS*, 1993.)

[Sub94]   V.S. Subrahmanian. Amalgamating Knowledge bases. *ACM Transactions on Database Systems*, Vol 19, no. 2, p. 291–331, 1994.

[Wie92]   G. Wiederhold. Mediators in the Architecture of Future Information Systems. *IEEE Computers*, Vol. 25, p. 38–49, 1992.

Tractable Iteration Mechanisms for Bag Languages

Preliminary Report

Latha S. Colby   Leonid Libkin

Bell Laboratories/Lucent Technologies
600 Mountain Avenue
Murray Hill, NJ 07974, USA
Email: {|colby, libkin|} @research.bell-labs.com

Abstract. The goal of this paper is to study tractable iteration mechanisms for bags. The presence of duplicates in bags prevents iteration mechanisms developed in the context of sets to be directly applied to bags without losing tractability. We study two constructs for controlling tractability of iteration over bags. The deflationary fixpoint construct keeps removing elements from a bag until a fixpoint is reached. The bounded fixpoint construct is an inflationary iteration mechanism that never exceeds some predefined bounding bag. We study these constructs in the context of a standard (nested) bag algebra. We show that the deflationary and bounded inflationary fixpoint constructs are equally expressive and strictly more expressive than their set-based counterparts. We also show that, unlike in the set case, the bag algebra with bounded fixpoint fails to capture all PTIME queries over databases with ordered domains. We then show that adding just one construct, which can be used to assign unique tags to duplicates, captures the class of all polynomial time queries over bags when a total ordering on the domain of atomic elements is available. Finally, we compare the expressive powers of the bag algebra and the nested relational algebra with aggregate functions in the presence of these fixpoint operators.

1 Introduction

While much of database theory is based on the theory of sets, in recent years, there has been a growing trend towards research on other collection data types such as bags and lists. An important goal in the design of query languages is to strike a reasonable balance between expressiveness and tractability. We use the term tractability to mean polynomial-time computable. The focus of this paper is on studying *tractable* iteration mechanisms for bags.

Such mechanisms have been developed in the context of set languages [11, 12, 14, 19, 21]. Most typically, an inflationary fixpoint construct is used for flat relations (sets of tuples). It was shown by Vardi [21] and by Immerman [14] that the relational algebra, when augmented with the inflationary fixpoint construct, can express all polynomial time queries over sets in the presence of a total ordering on the domain of elements. For nested relations, this causes intractability, as too many sets at a different level of nesting can be constructed. For instance, the powerset operator is definable via an inflationary fixpoint operator. Thus, several techniques have been developed in order to restrict the fixpoint operator. In [12], no operation creating additional levels of nesting can be iterated over; and in [19] a bound for the result of the fixpoint operator is precomputed. Both approaches give us precisely the PTIME queries over nested sets when a total order on the domain of atomic elements is available (this follows from the results in the papers cited above and in [13]).

It is shown in [10] that tractability may be obtained, in the context of complex-object languages, by a combination of restrictions and assumptions about the input database. They considered families of calculi with restrictions on set nesting and showed that if the input database is dense[1] with respect to its types, then the inflationary and partial fixpoint extensions of the corresponding calculus, express exactly the PTIME and PSPACE queries, respectively. They obtained similar expressiveness results by considering range-restricted versions of the calculi.

In the case of bags, the presence of duplicates prevents us from directly extending the results from the set-oriented framework. For instance, finite convergence for the inflationary fixpoint is not guaranteed because one can keep adding elements to a bag indefinitely. Iteration schemes with a predetermined finite number of iteration steps (such as, for example, loops in [16]) are also prone to intractability problems. For example, the function $\lambda x.(x\ bag-union\ x)$, when applied repeatedly, will result in an exponential blow-up due to repeated doubling [5]. Techniques for controlling recursion in the presence of duplicates were presented in [5] in the context of nested lists and in [9] in the context of partially-ordered flat multisets. Tractability was achieved in [5] by controlling the number of recursion steps and the operations within the recursion steps, and in [9] by using a size-bounded structural recursion scheme.

As pointed out in [3, 8, 16], most real-life database systems provide query languages based on bag semantics and it is therefore natural to investigate expressiveness and tractability issues in the bag framework. We look at various ways of increasing expressiveness while maintaining tractability in a pure bag-oriented setting. In particular, we consider adding various tractable fixpoint operators to the standard nested bag algebra developed in [8, 7, 16, 17].

We first introduce a *deflationary fixpoint operator*, *dfp* which repeatedly *removes* elements from a bag, as opposed to inflationary fixpoint which adds elements. Thus, we avoid both nontermination and exponential blowup. We then introduce a (bag) *bounded fixpoint operator*, *bfp*, based on the one introduced by Buneman and studied in [19] in the context of nested relations. The main idea of this operator is that before the iteration starts, a bounding set or bag is computed, and after each step the intersection of the current result and the

---

[1] Density is measured in terms of the ratio of the cardinality of the database to the cardinality of the set of all objects of a type that are constructible from the set of atomic elements in the database.

bound is taken. Thus, the result of the fixpoint never exceeds this precomputed bound, and this avoids exponential blowup in the size of the result. It should be noted that the bounding is based on an element-wise comparison as opposed to a global size bound such as in the one used for controlling intractability in [9].

There are two ways of introducing the fixpoint operators. We can define a *set*- or *bag*-based fixpoint, depending on whether duplicates are or are not eliminated at each iteration step. We then consider these operators in the context of the standard (nested) bag algebra from [16], which we denote by $\mathcal{BQL}$ here. We prove that the set-based (bounded inflationary and deflationary) fixpoints are strictly weaker than the bag-based fixpoints, and that the bounded inflationary fixpoints are equivalent to their corresponding deflationary fixpoints.

In the case of sets, the (nested) relational algebra with the (bounded) fixpoint operator captures the class of all polynomial-time queries on (nested) relations over ordered domains. Does an equivalent result hold in the case of the bag algebra? We answer this question in the negative by showing that the bounded fixpoint language fails to capture PTIME. However, the solution to this problem is remarkably simple. Only one extra primitive is required to capture all PTIME queries. We show that the *gen* primitive, introduced in [17], when added to the bounded fixpoint bag algebra gives us a language that captures all PTIME queries (in the presence of an order on the domain). This operator was originally defined in the context of $\mathcal{NRL}^{\mathrm{nat}}$ which is the nested algebra with aggregates. It takes a number n and generates a sequence of numbers from 0 to n. By definition, this is a non-polynomial operation since it takes a number whose binary representation is of size $\log n$ and generates output that is of size $O(n \log n)$. However, in a bag setting, the corresponding operation is polynomial, since the numbers are coded in unary, that is, n is represented as a bag of n empty tuples.

It should be pointed out that the PTIME characterization presented in this paper is different from those of [5] and [9] for lists where a total ordering of *all* elements (including duplicates) is available (as opposed to an order relation on the domain). Also, unlike [9], we do not consider exponential primitives such as powerset when dealing with bags of nesting depth greater than one, and thus our PTIME characterization is not restricted to flat inputs and outputs. We believe that a similar PTIME result can be obtained by replacing the bounded (or deflationary) fixpoint constructs with a bounded structural recursion construct where the structural recursion is based on the insert presentation of bags (see [17]) and the bounding is similar to those used for the fixpoint constructs in this paper. Structural recursion with a size-based bound as in [9] would yield a similar characterization and would not require the *gen* operation since it would be expressible using such a recursion scheme.

The intuition behind the use of *gen* is rather simple. The order relation on the domain is needed for capturing polynomial-time queries over sets so that the order in which elements appear on a Turing machine tape can be modeled. Now assume that we have a bag $\{\!| a, a, a |\!\}$. This can be encoded on a Turing machine tape as $\{\!| enc(a) \# enc(a) \# enc(a) |\!\}$, assuming that $\{\!|, |\!\}, \#$ are in the alphabet and $enc(a)$ is the encoding of a. Thus, from the point of view of a polynomial-time

TM there is the first a, the second a and the third a, whereas the bag algebra, even with the order relation, cannot distinguish between these a's! To eliminate this mismatch, we can use the *gen* operator as a tagging primitive. Note that *gen* does *not* force bag-based objects into set-based objects, because it uses bags in an essential way, as will be seen later.

Another interesting consequence of adding the *gen* operator is that the difference in expressive powers between the bag-based and set-based bounded fixpoints disappears. In other words, the set-based fixpoint algebras are equivalent to the bag-based fixpoint algebras in the presence of the *gen* operator.

We investigate the relationship between the bag languages and languages with aggregates in the presence of fixpoint operators. In [17], it was shown that the bag algebra $\mathcal{BQL}$ has the same expressive power as a nested relational language with aggregate functions $\mathcal{NRL}^{\text{nat}}$. We show that adding the equivalent of the *gen* operation to $\mathcal{NRL}^{\text{nat}}$ results in a language that is extremely powerful. In the presence of certain additional operators and set-based bounded fixpoint, it expresses all polynomial-time computable functions on natural numbers, but it can also express many EXPTIME computable functions.

Organization The next section introduces the basic bag algebra $\mathcal{BQL}$, and the (deflationary and bounded inflationary) bag-based and set-based fixpoint operators. In Section 3, we study the relationship between these fixpoint constructs. The characterization of the PTIME queries over bags is given in Section 4. In Section 5, we study the connections between bag languages and set languages with aggregates and fixpoints. Some open problems are listed in Section 6.

2 Bag algebra and fixpoint operators

In this section, we give an overview of the bag language $\mathcal{BQL}$, and introduce the different fixpoint operators.

2.1 Bag algebra

Figure 1 contains the expressions of the language $\mathcal{BQL}$ (Bag Query Language) [16, 17]. The design of this language is based on a general framework for the design of query languages over collection types [2]. It must be noted that languages like $\mathcal{BQL}$ normally have three equally expressive components: the algebra, the calculus, and the comprehension language, cf. [2]. In this preliminary report we use only the algebra; the calculus is very helpful in doing some inductive proofs and will be used, together with the algebra, in the full version.

The types of $\mathcal{BQL}$ are given by the grammar

$$s, t ::= b \mid unit \mid s \times t \mid \{\!\!\{s\}\!\!\},$$

where b is a base type whose domain is an unspecified infinite set, type *unit* has the unique element denoted by (), elements of type $s \times t$ are pairs (x, y) where x

$$
\frac{}{id^s : s \to s} \quad \frac{h : r \to s \quad g : s \to t}{g \circ h : r \to t} \quad \frac{g : r \to s \quad h : r \to t}{\langle g, h \rangle : r \to s \times t}
$$

$$
\frac{}{\pi_1^{s,t} : s \times t \to s} \quad \frac{}{\pi_2^{s,t} : s \times t \to t} \quad \frac{}{!^s : s \to unit}
$$

$$
\frac{}{b\_\eta^s : s \to \{\!|s|\!\}} \quad \frac{}{b\_\mu^s : \{\!|\{\!|s|\!\}|\!\} \to \{\!|s|\!\}} \quad \frac{f : s \to t}{b\_map(f) : \{\!|s|\!\} \to \{\!|t|\!\}}
$$

$$
\frac{}{K\{\!||\!\}^s : unit \to \{\!|s|\!\}} \quad \frac{}{\uplus^s : \{\!|s|\!\} \times \{\!|s|\!\} \to \{\!|s|\!\}} \quad \frac{}{b\_\rho_2^{s,t} : s \times \{\!|t|\!\} \to \{\!|s \times t|\!\}}
$$

$$
\frac{}{\dot- ^s : \{\!|s|\!\} \times \{\!|s|\!\} \to \{\!|s|\!\}} \quad \frac{}{\varepsilon^s : \{\!|s|\!\} \to \{\!|s|\!\}}
$$

Fig. 1. Expressions of $\mathcal{BQL}$

is of type s and y is of type t, and elements of type $\{\!|s|\!\}$ are finite bags containing elements of type s.

Let us briefly review the semantics, cf. [17]. id is the identity function. $g \circ h$ is the composition of functions g and h; that is, $(g \circ h)(x) = g(h(x))$. The bang ! produces () on all inputs. π_1 and π_2 are the two projections on pairs. $\langle g, h \rangle$ is pair formation; that is, $\langle g, h \rangle(x) = (g(x), h(x))$. $K\{\!||\!\}$ produces the empty bag. $\uplus$ is additive bag union; for example, $\uplus(\{\!|1, 2, 3|\!\}, \{\!|2, 2, 4|\!\})$ returns $\{\!|1, 2, 3, 2, 2, 4|\!\}$. b_η forms singleton bags; for example, $b\_\eta(3)$ evaluates to the singleton bag $\{\!|3|\!\}$. b_μ flattens a bag of bags; for example, $b\_\mu(\{\!|\{\!|1, 2|\!\}, \{\!|1, 3|\!\}, \{\!|2, 4|\!\}|\!\})$ evaluates to $\{\!|1, 1, 2, 2, 3, 4|\!\}$. $b\_map(f)$ applies f to every item in the input bag; for example, $b\_map(\lambda x.1 + x) \{\!|1, 2, 1, 6|\!\}$ evaluates to $\{\!|2, 3, 2, 7|\!\}$ and $b\_map(\lambda x.1) \{\!|1, 2, 1, 6|\!\}$ evaluates to $\{\!|1, 1, 1, 1|\!\}$. $b\_\rho_2(x, y)$ pairs x with every item in the bag y; for example, $b\_\rho_2(3, \{\!|1, 2, 3, 1|\!\})$ returns $\{\!|(3, 1), (3, 2), (3, 3), (3, 1)|\!\}$. We use $\dot-$ to denote bag difference; for example, $\dot-\ (\{\!|1, 1, 2, 3, 3|\!\}, \{\!|1, 2, 2|\!\}) = \{\!|1, 3, 3|\!\}$. Finally, ε eliminates duplicates: $\varepsilon(\{\!|1, 1, 2, 2, 2|\!\}) = \{\!|1, 2|\!\}$.

We shall always omit the type superscripts as the most general types can be inferred. We shall also occasionally use the infix notation for operations like $\dot-$ and $\uplus$, that is, we will write $B \dot- B'$, $B \uplus B'$, etc.

The language $\mathcal{BQL}$ as presented here was introduced in [16]; it is also equivalent to the polynomial fragment of the BALG algebra of [8]. The operations max, min, eq, $member$, $subbag$ and many others are also definable in it [16] (max and min are maximal and minimal bag intersections, and eq, $member$ and $subbag$ test for equality, membership and containment). Following [17], for notational convenience we add booleans (truth value represented by $\{\!|()|\!\}$ and false by $\{\!||\!\}$) and the conditional construct if-$then$-$else$. We also use the λ-notation, i.e. we write $\lambda x.f(x)$ provided x is of object type (that is, no higher-order functions are allowed). For syntactic convenience, we define functions Π, σ and $\times$ to denote projection, selection and cartesian product on bags. These constructs do not add expressive power. For example, Π_i can be defined as $b\_map(\pi_i)$.

In what follows, $\mathcal{L}(p_1, \ldots, p_n)$ is the notation for a language $\mathcal{L}$ augmented with primitives $p_1, \ldots, p_n$. We shall often use the language $\mathcal{BQL}(\leq)$, where the function $\leq: b \times b \rightarrow \{|unit|\}$ testing a linear order on the elements of base types is available.

The following is from [2, 17]:

Proposition 1. *Every function expressible in $\mathcal{BQL}(\leq)$ has polynomial-time complexity with respect to the size of the input.* □

2.2 Fixpoint operators

As we mentioned before, we must define fixpoint operators over bags that do not lead to nontermination and maintain tractability. To this end, we look at two possibilities for controlling the fixpoint computation. Both use the idea of bounds. The first construct, *the deflationary fixpoint*, removes elements from some initial bag at each step of the iteration. In contrast, the *bounded fixpoint*, keeps adding elements as long as they are within some precomputed bound. The iteration terminates when there is no change in the result of two successive iteration steps.

Let us give the formal definitions. Both deflationary and bounded fixpoints have the following typing rule:

$$\frac{f : s \times \{|t|\} \rightarrow \{|t|\} \qquad g : s \rightarrow \{|t|\}}{dfp_{f,g} : s \rightarrow \{|t|\}} \qquad \frac{f : s \times \{|t|\} \rightarrow \{|t|\} \qquad g : s \rightarrow \{|t|\}}{bfp_{f,g} : s \rightarrow \{|t|\}}$$

To define the semantics of these operations, assume that we are given an input object x of type s. Let $B = g(x)$. This is the "bound" for the computation. We define two families of bags:

- $Y_0 = \{||\}$, $Y_{i+1} = (Y_i \uplus f(x, Y_i))$ min B;
- $Z_0 = B$, $Z_{i+1} = Z_i \dotdiv f(x, Z_i)$.

Now $bfp_{f,g}(x)$ is defined to be Y_i where $Y_i = Y_{i+1}$ and i is the smallest such. We define $dfp_{f,g}(x)$ to be Z_i where $Z_i = Z_{i+1}$ and i is the smallest such. It is easy to see that in both cases the i at which the computation stops is at most the cardinality of the bounding (or initial) bag B.

It should be noted that the definition in [19] allows types of the form $\{|t_1|\} \times \{|t_2|\} \times \ldots \times \{|t_m|\}$ to be used in place of $\{|t|\}$ in the definition of the bounded fixpoint for set languages. The operations $\cup$ and $\cap$ are performed componentwise. It is then shown in [19] that this is only a matter of convenience, that is, no expressiveness is gained. Similar results can be shown in the bag setting.

To simulate the more general fixpoint, we encode each tuple $(B_1, \ldots, B_m)$ of type $\{|t_1|\} \times \{|t_2|\} \times \ldots \times \{|t_m|\}$ by a bag B of type $\{|\{|t_1|\} \times \{|t_2|\} \times \ldots \times \{|t_m|\}|\}$, where for each $x \in B_i$, there exists a tuple of the form $(\{||\}, \ldots, \{|x|\}, \ldots, \{||\})$ in B

($\{|x|\}$ occurs in the ith position). For example, $(\{|a, b|\}, \{||\}, \{|c|\})$ is represented by $\{|(\{|a|\}, \{||\}, \{||\}), (\{|b|\}, \{||\}, \{||\}), (\{||\}, \{||\}, \{|c|\})|\}$. Each Y_i (or Z_i) is represented using this encoding and is decoded into the original representation before the fixpoint operation f is applied. The bounding bag $g(x)$ is represented using the same encoding. The encode and decode steps are easily expressible in $\mathcal{BQL}$ and are simpler[2] than those used in [19]. Thus, for the sake of simplicity we use fixpoints as they are defined above in this report.

Recursive queries such as the transitive closure of a graph can be expressed using *bfp* by translating the corresponding solutions from the set case in [19] verbatim to the bag case. For transitive closure, one uses $B = \varepsilon((\Pi_1(R) \uplus \Pi_2(R)) \times (\Pi_1(R) \uplus \Pi_2(R)))$ as the bound, where R is the binary relation representing the set of edges. That is, B is the complete graph on the set of nodes. Then the composition of relations is iterated until the transitive closure is constructed.

As another example, we show how to define the parity of the cardinality of a bag using the deflationary fixpoint construct. Let

$g = b\_map(!)$ and

$f = \lambda(x, y).if\ eq(y, b\_\eta(!(y)))\ then\ K\{||\}(!(y))\ else\ b\_\eta(!(y)) \uplus b\_\eta(!(y))$

In other words, for each n-element bag x, $g(x)$ returns the bag of n units (), and f returns the empty bag if its input is $\{|()|\}$ and it returns $\{|(), ()|\}$ otherwise. Then $dfp_{f,g}(x)$ is $\{|()|\}$ if n is odd, and $\{||\}$ if n is even, thus giving us the parity test. Note that we did not use the order relation in this example.

Finally, we define the *set-based bounded fixpoint bfp*^{set} and the *set-based deflationary fixpoint dfp*^{set}. Their typing rules are exactly the same as those for *bfp* and *dfp*. The semantics of *bfp*^{set} is defined similar to the semantics of *bfp* except that B is defined as $\varepsilon(g(x))$, not as $g(x)$. That is, the result produced at each iteration step has no duplicates. This corresponds precisely to the bounded fixpoint for set languages that was studied in [19]. The semantics of *dfp*^{set} is defined analogously.

Proposition 2. *Every function definable in* $\mathcal{BQL}(\leq, dfp)$, *or* $\mathcal{BQL}(\leq, bfp)$, *or* $\mathcal{BQL}(\leq, bfp^{set})$, *or* $\mathcal{BQL}(\leq, dfp^{set})$ *has polynomial-time complexity with respect to the size of the input.*

Proof sketch: The proof is by a simple induction argument. All functions expressible in $\mathcal{BQL}(\leq)$ are polynomial-time computable. Suppose that y is an input to $bfp_{f,g}$. The size of $g(y)$ (and hence the size of the result of $bfp_{f,g}$) is bounded by a polynomial p on the size of y. From the definition of bounded fixpoint, we see that the number of iteration steps in the computation of $bfp_{f,g}$ is no greater than the cardinality of $g(y)$, and each iteration step is polynomial-time computable, from which polynomial-time computability of $bfp_{f,g}(y)$ follows. The proofs for dfp, bfp^{set} and dfp^{set} are similar. □

---

[2] In [19], the encodings are chosen so that there is no increase in set height. This is necessary for the proof of the conservativity result presented in that paper.

3 Relative expressive power of fixpoint operators

In this section, we study the relationship between the various fixpoint operators from the previous section. Our first result is this:

Theorem 3. *(a) $\mathcal{BQL}(dfp)$ and $\mathcal{BQL}(bfp)$ have the same expressive power, and (b) $\mathcal{BQL}(dfp^{set})$ and $\mathcal{BQL}(bfp^{set})$ have the same expressive power.*

Proof sketch: We show that dfp is expressible in $\mathcal{BQL}(bfp)$ and, vice versa, that bfp is expressible in $\mathcal{BQL}(dfp)$. The main idea behind the simulation of dfp in terms of bfp is to use bfp to compute the complement of the result of the deflationary fixpoint, and similarly for the converse simulation.

Lemma 4. *Let f be a function of type $s \times \{\!|t|\!\} \to \{\!|t|\!\}$ and g be of type $s \to \{\!|t|\!\}$. Let $f' = \lambda(y,z).f(y,(g(y) \div z))$. Then $dfp_{f,g}(o) = g(o) \div bfp_{f',g}(o)$ for any object o of type s.*

Proof: Fix o of type s and let $Y_i : \{\!|t|\!\}$ denote the ith iteration of $bfp_{f',g}(o)$, and Z_i denote the ith step of $dfp_{f,g}(o)$. We show by induction on i, that $g(o) \div Y_i = Z_i$. The lemma will follow from this. If $i = 0$, then this follows from $Z_0 = g(o)$ and $Y_0 = \{\!||\!\}$. Assume $g(o) \div Y_i = Z_i$ and prove $g(o) \div Y_{i+1} = Z_{i+1}$:

$$
\begin{aligned}
&g(o) \div Y_{i+1} \\
&= g(o) \div ((Y_i \uplus f(o,(g(o) \div Y_i))) \ min \ g(o)) &&\text{by definition of } bfp \text{ and } f' \\
&= g(o) \div ((Y_i \uplus f(o, Z_i)) \ min \ g(o)) &&\text{by the hypothesis} \\
&= g(o) \div (Y_i \uplus f(o, Z_i)) &&\text{since } A \div (B \ min \ A) \equiv A \div B \\
&= (g(o) \div Y_i) \div f(o, Z_i) &&\text{since } (A \div B) \div C = A \div (B \uplus C) \\
&= Z_i \div f(o, Z_i) &&\text{by the hypothesis} \\
&= Z_{i+1} &&\text{by definition of } dfp
\end{aligned}
$$

The converse is established in the following lemma.

Lemma 5. *Let f be a function of type $s \times \{\!|t|\!\} \to \{\!|t|\!\}$ and g be of type $s \to \{\!|t|\!\}$. Let $f' = \lambda(y,z).f(y,(g(y) \div z))$. Then $bfp_{f,g}(o) = g(o) \div dfp_{f',g}(o)$, for any object o of type s.*

Proof: As before, fix $o : s$ and let Y_i and Z_i denote ith stage of the computation of $bfp_{f,g}(o)$ and $dfp_{f',g}(o)$, resp. Again, it suffices to show that $g(o) \div Z_i = Y_i$ for all i. The base case is the same as in Lemma 4. Now assume $g(o) \div Z_i = Y_i$ and prove $g(o) \div Z_{i+1} = Y_{i+1}$.

First note that all Z_js are subbags of $g(o)$. From this, using the equations for reasoning about the equivalence of bag expressions from [6], calculate

$$
\begin{aligned}
&g(o) \div Z_{i+1} \\
&= g(o) \div (Z_i \div f'(o, Z_i)) &&\text{by definition of } dfp \\
&= g(o) \div (Z_i \div f(o,(g(o) \div Z_i))) &&\text{by definition of } f' \\
&= g(o) \div (Z_i \div f(o, Y_i)) &&\text{by the hypothesis} \\
&= (g(o) \div Z_i) \uplus ((Z_i \ min \ f(o, Y_i)) \div (Z_i \div g(o))) &&\text{by (P8) of [6, p. 333]} \\
&= (g(o) \div Z_i) \uplus (Z_i \ min \ f(o, Y_i)) &&\text{since } Z_i \subseteq g(o)
\end{aligned}
$$

On the other hand,

$$
\begin{aligned}
Y_{i+1} &= (Y_i \uplus f(o, Y_i)) \min g(o) && \text{by definition of } bfp \\
&= ((g(o) \mathbin{\dot-} Z_i) \uplus f(o, Y_i)) \min g(o) && \text{by the hypothesis} \\
&= [(g(o) \mathbin{\dot-} Z_i) \min g(o)] \uplus [f(o, Y_i) \min(g(o) \mathbin{\dot-} (g(o) \mathbin{\dot-} Z_i))] && \text{by (P12) of [6]} \\
&= (g(o) \mathbin{\dot-} Z_i) \uplus (Z_i \min f(o, Y_i)) && \text{since } Z_i \subseteq g(o)
\end{aligned}
$$

which proves the lemma.

Using these lemmas, one can show by a straightforward induction argument, that bfp is expressible in $\mathcal{BQL}(dfp)$ and vice versa, thus proving Theorem 3(a).

We now sketch the proof of Theorem 3(b). Let $dfp^{\text{set}}_{f,g}$ be an expression in $\mathcal{B}(dfp^{\text{set}})$, and let f' be constructed as in the proofs of Lemmas 4 and 5. Then, for any object o,

$$
dfp^{\text{set}}_{f,g}(o) = dfp_{f,(\varepsilon \circ g)}(o) = \varepsilon(g(o)) \mathbin{\dot-} bfp_{f',(\varepsilon \circ g)}(o) = \varepsilon(g(o)) \mathbin{\dot-} bfp^{\text{set}}_{f',g}(o)
$$

Using this equation and its symmetric analog, one can easily conclude that dfp^{set} and bfp^{set} are interdefinable, from which Theorem 3(b) follows. $\quad\Box$

Next, we compare the expressive powers of the set- and bag-based fixpoints.

Theorem 6. $\mathcal{BQL}(bfp)$ *is strictly more expressive than* $\mathcal{BQL}(bfp^{\text{set}})$. *Also,* $\mathcal{BQL}(\leq, bfp)$ *is strictly more expressive than* $\mathcal{BQL}(\leq, bfp^{\text{set}})$. *Similar results hold for* dfp *and* dfp^{set}.

Proof sketch: The inclusion is obvious as bfp^{set} can be simulated with bfp: $bfp^{\text{set}}_{f,g} = bfp_{f,\varepsilon \circ g}$. To prove strictness, let a be an object of base type b, and let M_a be the collection of all bags of the form $\{\!|a, \ldots, a|\!\}$. For any function $f : \{\!|b|\!\} \to \{\!|unit|\!\}$, let $\text{TRUE}(f, a) = \{card(x) \mid x \in M_a, f(x) = \{\!|()|\!\}\}$.

To prove separation, we need the following proposition.

Proposition 7. *For every* $\mathcal{BQL}(\leq, bfp^{\text{set}})$ *function* $f : \{\!|b|\!\} \to \{\!|unit|\!\}$, *and every object* a *of type* b, *the set* $\text{TRUE}(f, a)$ *is either finite or co-finite. In particular, the parity test is inexpressible in* $\mathcal{BQL}(\leq, bfp^{\text{set}})$.

This proposition and the observation made above that the parity test is definable in $\mathcal{BQL}(bfp)$ prove the theorem.

To sketch the proof of Proposition 7, we need a definition first. Given a number $k > 0$, define the class OBJ_k of k-*objects* as follows. First, every object of the base type and the object () of type $unit$ belong to OBJ_k. A pair (x, y) is a k-object if both its components are. Finally, a bag is a k-object if it has at most k distinct elements and each of them is a k-object. Now, we prove the following lemma.

Lemma 8. *Let* $f : s \to t$ *be a* $\mathcal{BQL}(\leq, bfp)$ *function, and let* $k > 0$. *Then there exists a number* $c > 0$, *that depends only on* k *and* f, *such that for any* x *of type* s *in* OBJ_k, *it is the case that* $f(x) \in \text{OBJ}_c$.

We prove this lemma by induction on the $\mathcal{BQL}(\leq, bfp)$ expressions. Let us give a few cases for illustration. If $f = b\_\mu$ and $x \in \text{OBJ}_k$, then $f(x) \in \text{OBJ}_{k^2}$. Indeed, if $x = \{\!\{B_1, \ldots, B_n\}\!\}$ with at most k of B_is being distinct, and each B_i having at most k distinct elements, then $B_1 \uplus \ldots \uplus B_n$ has at most k^2 distinct elements. Assume that $f = b\_map(g)$ and $x \in \text{OBJ}_k$. By induction hypothesis, find c_0 such that $g(y) \in \text{OBJ}_{c_0}$ for y in OBJ_k. Then we can take c to be $\max(c_0, k)$: indeed, $f(x)$ contains at most k distinct objects, each being a c_0-object. Finally, if $f = bfp_{g,h}$, then for each k, the constant c is determined by h, since if a bag $B \in \text{OBJ}_c$ and B' is a subbag of B, then $B' \in \text{OBJ}_c$.

Given the lemma (which applies to every $\mathcal{BQL}(\leq, bfp^{\text{set}})$ function as well), we fix k and consider an expression of the form $bfp^{\text{set}}_{f,g}$. When applied to a k-object x, it first computes a bound, $\varepsilon(g(x))$. Since $g(x) \in \text{OBJ}_c$ for some fixed c, the bound has at most c elements and thus the fixpoint computation can be simulated directly in $\mathcal{BQL}(\leq)$. Applying this argument inductively, we obtain that for every $k > 0$ and every $\mathcal{BQL}(\leq, bfp^{\text{set}})$ expression f, there is a $\mathcal{BQL}(\leq)$ expression f' such that $f(x) = f'(x)$ whenever $x \in \text{OBJ}_k$. In particular, every $f : \{\!\{b\}\!\} \to \{\!\{unit\}\!\}$ coincides with some $\mathcal{BQL}(\leq)$ function f' on bags from M_a. It follows from the results of [16, 17] that $\mathcal{BQL}(\leq)$ can test only finite or co-finite cardinalities of bags from M_a, which completes the proof of Theorem 6. $\qquad\square$

In particular, the theorem above shows that the set-based bounded fixpoint we defined is different from $\varepsilon \circ bfp$, since the parity test is definable using $\varepsilon \circ bfp$, but is not definable using bfp^{set}.

The question arises: what does one have to add to $\mathcal{BQL}(bfp^{\text{set}})$ in order to express bfp? It turns out that we only need to add one extra primitive that will play the crucial role in the next section.

4 Capturing all PTIME queries on nested bags

It was shown in [19] that adding the bounded fixpoint to a nested *set* language is sufficient to capture all PTIME queries over nested *sets*, if a linear order is available on the base type. One may ask if a similar result holds for bags. Somewhat surprisingly, the answer is no.

Let us first recall the operator *gen*, introduced in [16]. Its type is $\{\!\{unit\}\!\} \to \{\!\{\{\!\{unit\}\!\}\}\!\}$. We denote the bag of n units, $\{\!\{(), \ldots, ()\}\!\}$, by $\underline{n}$. On the input $\underline{n}$, *gen* produces $\{\!\{\underline{0}, \ldots, \underline{n}\}\!\}$. For example,

$$gen(\{\!\{(), (), ()\}\!\}) = \{\!\{\{\!\{\}\!\}, \{\!\{()\}\!\}, \{\!\{(), ()\}\!\}, \{\!\{(), (), ()\}\!\}\}\!\}.$$

Note that *gen* is polynomial-time computable. In contrast, the analogous operation gen^{nat} on natural numbers defined as $gen^{\text{nat}}(n) = \{0, \ldots, n\}$, is not a polynomial operation.

This operator is quite powerful and can compute some queries that are not definable in $\mathcal{BQL}$, for example, the parity test, see [16]. The theorem below demonstrates that $\mathcal{BQL}(\leq, bfp)$ fails to capture all PTIME queries over bags, in particular, *gen*.

Theorem 9. *The function gen is not definable in $\mathcal{BQL}(\leq, bfp)$.*

Proof. Recall the definition of k-*objects* from the proof of Proposition 7. Assume that f is a function of $\mathcal{BQL}(\leq, bfp)$ that implements *gen*. Then, by Lemma 8, there exists a number c such that $f(x) \in \mathrm{OBJ}_c$ for any input x to *gen*, since $x \in \mathrm{OBJ}_1$. However, $gen(\underline{c}) \in \mathrm{OBJ}_{c+1} - \mathrm{OBJ}_c$. Thus, *gen* is not $\mathcal{BQL}(\leq, bfp)$-definable. □

Now we define the class $\mathrm{PTIME}^{\mathrm{bag}}$ of polynomial-time queries over nested bags. In what follows, we restrict ourselves to *product-of-bag* types, that is, types of the form $\{\!|t_1|\!\} \times \ldots \times \{\!|t_m|\!\}$, where t_is are arbitrary types. In other words, we are interested in queries that take a tuple of bags as an input and produce outputs that are tuples of bags. This restriction is often made when one captures a complexity class over relations or complex objects, cf. [19, 20]. Extension to scalar types can be achieved rather straightforwardly, for example, by using a function extracting an element from a singleton set.

We use the standard encoding scheme such as the one in [1]. Given a set of values $A = \{a_1, \ldots, a_n\}$ of the base type b such that $a_1 < \ldots < a_n$, we encode a_i as the binary representation of i. We use 0 to encode the unique element of type *unit*. Next, using the brackets $\{\!|, |\!\}, (,)$ and the separator # we encode complex objects, relative to the set A. By the standard encoding of an object we now mean the one relative to the *active domain* of the object.

Consider two types s and t. We say that a function f from objects of type s to objects of type t that does not extend the active domain of its input, belongs to $\mathrm{PTIME}^{\mathrm{bag}}_{s,t}$ if there exists a polynomial-time Turing machine M such that: (1) when the input tape does not have the standard encoding of an object of type s, it prints a special symbol meaning "error" on its tape and stops, and (2) when the input tape contains the standard encoding of an object of type s (that is, the encoding relative to A, the active domain), it returns the encoding of $f(x)$, relative to A.

Finally, we define $\mathrm{PTIME}^{\mathrm{bag}}$, the class of polynomial-time queries over nested bags, to be the union of $\mathrm{PTIME}^{\mathrm{bag}}_{s,t}$ for all pairs of (product-of-bags) types s and t. The following can be seen from Theorem 9.

Corollary 10. $\mathcal{BQL}(\leq, bfp) \subset \mathrm{PTIME}^{\mathrm{bag}}$. □

The main result of this section characterizes the class $\mathrm{PTIME}^{\mathrm{bag}}$.

Theorem 11. *The language $\mathcal{BQL}(\leq, bfp, gen)$ expresses precisely the class of queries in $\mathrm{PTIME}^{\mathrm{bag}}$: $\mathcal{BQL}(\leq, bfp, gen) = \mathrm{PTIME}^{\mathrm{bag}}$.*

Proof sketch: The inclusion $\mathcal{BQL}(\leq, bfp, gen) \subseteq \mathrm{PTIME}^{\mathrm{bag}}$ follows from Proposition 2 and the polynomiality of *gen*. For the reverse inclusion, assume that a query f of type $s \to t$ is computable by a PTIME machine M, whose number of steps is bounded by a polynomial $p(n)$, where n is the length of the input. It is not hard to construct an expression g that, given an object x whose encoding takes n cells, produces $\underline{m}$, where $p(n) \leq m$. This gives us the required count. Applying *gen* to $\underline{m}$, we obtain a representation of the tape (i.e., each cell is now identified by its unique label). The rest of the proof follows the standard idea: an input is encoded, then the machine M's actions are simulated on it, and the result is decoded back into an object. Since we use the bounded fixpoint in our language, let us just give an idea of how the bound is computed and the work of M is simulated. Assume for simplicity that each cell is either 0 or 1 (i.e., there are no other symbols in the alphabet; in fact, one needs three bits to encode the alphabet that contains all appropriate delimiters). It can change its value at most m times. The idea of the simulation is that when the ith cell changes its value, we look at all pairs $(\underline{i}, \underline{l})$ in the working bag (which is of type $\{\{\{unit\} \times \{unit\}\}\}$), find the maximum such l and add $(\underline{i}, \underline{l+1})$ to the bag. Thus, we can use $gen(\underline{m}) \times gen(\underline{m})$ as the bound for the fixpoint computation on the working bag that simulates M. When the simulation is done, a bag B is computed. One can use B to get the contents of the tape as follows: look at the initial value of the ith cell and the parity of the bag $\sigma_{\pi_1(x)=\underline{i}}(B)$. This determines if the value of the cell has changed during the computation. Since this parity test can be computed using either the fixpoint operation or gen, we get the encoding of the result which can then be decoded into the corresponding object. More details and the routine encoding and decoding schemes will be given in the full version. □

Since the primitive gen assigns unique tags to duplicates, it is sufficient to simulate bfp with bfp^{set}. That is,

Proposition 12. $\mathcal{BQL}(bfp^{set}, gen)$ *can express* bfp. □

From this we conclude:

Corollary 13. $\mathcal{BQL}(\leq, bfp^{set}, gen) = \text{PTIME}^{bag}$. □

5 Aggregation and fixpoint operators

In this section, we study the relationship between bag languages and languages with aggregation in the presence of fixpoint operators. In [17], it is shown that $\mathcal{BQL}$ has the same expressive power as the nested relational language with aggregate functions over the natural numbers, denoted by $\mathcal{NRL}^{nat}$. It is known how to capture PTIME over the nested relations [10, 13, 19], and it is also known how to capture many complexity classes for arithmetic functions [4, 15]. Thus, one might ask if the correspondence between $\mathcal{BQL}$ and $\mathcal{NRL}^{nat}$ allows us to enrich the latter to capture PTIME in both worlds: relational and arithmetical. We shall prove a few initial results indicating that it is hard to find a natural extension like this.

First, let us review how the language $\mathcal{NRL}^{nat}$ is obtained. Take $\mathcal{BQL}$ and replace each bag operator with its set analog. For example, replace ⊎ with union and $\dot{-}$ with set difference. Then add the type of natural numbers $\mathbb{N}$ with the usual arithmetic operations $+, *, \dot{-}$ and 1 as a constant (that is, $K1 : unit \to \mathbb{N}$), and the summation construct $\sum(f) : \{s\} \to \mathbb{N}$, provided f is of type $s \to \mathbb{N}$. When applied to a set $\{x_1, \ldots, x_n\}$, the summation construct yields $\sum_{i=1}^{n} f(x_i)$. For instance, if $f = K1o!$ (that is, $f(x) = 1$ for any x), then $\sum(f)$ is the cardinality function.

In the proof of equivalence of expressive power, each natural number n is translated into $\underline{n}$, that is, $\{()，\ldots, ()\}$, n times. Correspondingly, gen is translated into $gen^{nat} : \mathbb{N} \to \{\mathbb{N}\}$, $gen^{nat}(n) = \{0, 1, \ldots, n\}$. Note that unlike gen, gen^{nat} is *not* a polynomial-time operation.

Our first result shows that adding gen^{nat} to $\mathcal{NRL}^{nat}$ makes the language already very powerful. Recall that a rudimentary set is a set of tuples of natural numbers definable by a formula of bounded arithmetic in the language L_{PA} of Peano arithmetic [15]. Equivalently, it is the class of the linear time hierarchy languages over the natural numbers. A function is *rudimentary* if it is majorized by a polynomial and its graph is a rudimentary set.

Proposition 14. *All rudimentary functions are definable in $\mathcal{NRL}^{nat}(gen^{nat})$.* $\square$

Thus, $\mathcal{NRL}^{nat}(gen^{nat})$ is very powerful; for example, there are NP-complete rudimentary sets that are definable in this language. However, not all polynomial-time computable functions are definable in $\mathcal{NRL}^{nat}(gen^{nat})$. For example, the function $d(x, y) = 2^{|x| \cdot |y|}$, where $|x|$ is the length of the binary representation of x, is in PTIME [15], but every function in $\mathcal{NRL}^{nat}(gen^{nat})$ is majorized by a polynomial. We do not know if adding the function $d(x, y)$ to $\mathcal{NRL}^{nat}(gen^{nat})$ suffices to capture all PTIME functions on natural numbers, but we can show the following, using Cobham's characterization of PTIME, cf. [18].

Proposition 15. *Every polynomial-time computable function on natural numbers is definable in $\mathcal{NRL}^{nat}(gen^{nat})$ augmented with $d(x, y)$ and the set bounded fixpoint construct.* $\square$

One might ask why the function $|x|$ is not mentioned in Proposition 15. It turns out that this function is definable as the cardinality of the set $S_x = \{y \mid y \le x, y = 2^w \text{ for some } w\}$. Notice that the following first-order formula (cf. [15]) $\phi(y) \equiv \forall v \le y \, \forall u < y. \, (v \ne 1 \wedge u \cdot v = y) \to (\exists z < v. \, 2 \cdot z = v)$ holds iff y is a power of 2, and thus this test can be expressed in $\mathcal{NRL}^{nat}(gen^{nat})$ since all the quantification is bounded.

However, the language of Proposition 15 is very powerful. We can use some of the results from [4] to show the following.

Proposition 16. *Let f be a EXPTIME-complexity function on natural numbers such that f is majorized by a polynomial. Then f is definable in $\mathcal{NRL}^{nat}(gen^{nat})$ augmented with $d(x, y)$ and the set bounded fixpoint construct.* $\square$

Thus, it is hard to find a reasonable balance between equally expressive and tractable languages over bags, and languages over sets with aggregate functions.

6 Conclusions and open problems

We presented preliminary results on increasing the expressive power of languages for bag-based complex objects without losing tractability. We defined deflationary and bounded inflationary fixpoint operators and showed that they are equally expressive and strictly more expressive than their set-based counterparts. We showed that these fixpoint operators are not sufficient to capture the class of all PTIME queries over bags and that the *gen* operator fills the gap. Finally, we studied the effects of adding the fixpoint operators and the *gen* primitive to languages with aggregate functions.

We now discuss some of the problems currently under investigation. The use of nesting is a key technique in achieving the characterization of PTIME over bags. We would like to find a language that captures PTIME over *flat* bags. Of course, one can just use $\mathcal{BQL}$ restricted to queries from flat inputs to flat outputs, but it would be desirable to find a natural flat language. Note that the conservative extension property [17] does not help us here, because $\mathcal{BQL}$ only possesses this property beyond the first level of nesting.

We know that the class of queries $\text{PTIME}^{\text{bag}}$ is captured by $\mathcal{BQL}(\leq, bfp, gen)$. Can we obtain similar characterizations for other complexity classes, for example, L^{bag}, NL^{bag} and NC^{bag}? For example, a characterization of NC queries over nested relations that uses divide-and-conquer recursion was given in [20]. Does a similar recursion mechanism (essentially the structural recursion on the union presentation, cf. [2]), when added to $\mathcal{BQL}(\leq, gen)$, capture NC^{bag}? More generally, let $\mathcal{C}$ be a complexity class, and $\mathcal{L}$ a set language of the form $\mathcal{NRA}(\mathbf{p}, \leq)$ that captures all $\mathcal{C}$ queries over sets. Here $\mathcal{NRA}$ is the nested relational algebra and $\mathbf{p}$ is some family of primitives. Is there a systematic way of deriving a new family of bag primitives $\mathbf{p}_b$ such that $\mathcal{BQL}(\leq, \mathbf{p}_b, gen)$ captures $\mathcal{C}^{\text{bag}}$? Note that *gen* has to be included for any class above L, unless it is definable with $\mathbf{p}_b$.

We are continuing to investigate the relationship between $\mathcal{BQL}$ and $\mathcal{NRL}^{\text{nat}}$ in the presence of *gen* and fixpoints. The power of gen^{nat} seems to be essential to express many arithmetic operations (e.g., minimization or various primitive recursion schemas), but makes it hard to find a tractable language with aggregates that would be equally expressive as some tractable bag language. However, a related operator that takes an n-element set and returns $\{0, \ldots, n\}$ *is* expressible in $\mathcal{NRL}^{\text{nat}}$ in the presence of order. We believe that this observation may help us model more arithmetic in $\mathcal{NRL}^{\text{nat}}$ without gen^{nat} and thus find a reasonable balance between tractable bag languages and set languages with aggregates.

Acknowledgements We thank Limsoon Wong and Tim Griffin for their comments. The first author would also like to thank Dirk Van Gucht for several insightful discussions during the early stages of this work.

References

1. S. Abiteboul, R. Hull and V. Vianu. *Foundations of Databases*. Addison Wesley, 1995.
2. P. Buneman, S. Naqvi, V. Tannen, L. Wong. Principles of programming with complex objects and collection types. *Theoretical Computer Science*, 149(1):3–48, September 1995.
3. S. Chaudhuri and M. Vardi. Optimization of *real* conjunctive queries. In *Proceedings of the 12th Symposium on Principles of Database Systems*, Washington DC, 1994.
4. P. Clote. Computation models and function algebras. *Proc. Logic and Computational Complexity*, Springer LNCS 960, 1994, pages 98–130.
5. L. S. Colby, E. L. Robertson, L. V. Saxton, and D. Van Gucht. A query language for list-based complex objects. In *Proceedings of the 13th Symposium on Principles of Database Systems*, pages 179–189, Minneapolis, MN, 1994.
6. T. Griffin and L. Libkin. Incremental maintenance of views with duplicates. In *Proceedings ACM SIGMOD*, 1995, pages 328–339.
7. S. Grumbach, L. Libkin, T. Milo and L. Wong. Query languages for bags: expressive power and complexity. *SIGACT News* 27(2): 30–37, 1996.
8. S. Grumbach and T. Milo. Towards tractable algebras for bags. In *Proceedings of the 12th -SIGART Symposium on Principles of Database Systems*, pages 49–58, Washington, DC, May 1993.
9. S. Grumbach and T. Milo. An algebra for pomsets. In *Proceedings of the International Conference on Database Theory*, Prague, 1995, pages 191–207, 1994.
10. S. Grumbach and V. Vianu. Tractable query languages for complex object databases. *J. Comput. and Syst. Sci.* 51(2): 149–167, 1995.
11. Y. Gurevich and S. Shelah. Fixed-point extensions of first-order logic. *Annals of Pure and Applied Logic* 32 (1986), 265–280.
12. M. Gyssens and D. Van Gucht. A comparison between algebraic query languages for flat and nested databases. *Theoretical Computer Science* 87 (1991), 263–286.
13. M. Gyssens, D. Van Gucht and D. Suciu. On polynomially bounded fixpoint construct for nested relations. In *Proceedings of 5th Workshop on Database Programming Languages*, Gubbio, Italy, 1995. Available as Springer Electronic WiC publication.
14. N. Immerman. Relational queries computable in polynomial time. *Information and Control*, 68:86–104, 1986.
15. J. Krajíček. *Bounded Arithmetic, Propositional Logic, and Complexity Theory*. Cambridge University Press, 1995.
16. L. Libkin and L. Wong. Some properties of query languages for bags. In *Proceedings of the 4th Workshop on Database Programming Languages*, Springer Verlag, 1994.
17. L. Libkin and L. Wong. Query languages for bags and aggregate functions. *J. Comput. and Syst. Sci.*, to appear. Extended abstract in *PODS'94*.
18. H. Rose. *Subrecursion: Functions and Hierarchies*. Oxford, 1984.
19. D. Suciu. Fixpoints and bounded fixpoints for complex objects. In *Proceedings of the 4th Workshop on Database Programming Languages*, Springer Verlag, 1994.
20. D. Suciu and V. Tannen. A query language for NC. In *Proceedings of the 13th Symposium on Principles of Database Systems*, Minneapolis, MN, 1994.
21. M. Vardi. The complexity of relational query languages. In *Proceedings of the 14th ACM Symposium on Theory of Computing*, pages 137–146, 1982.

Author Index

Springer
and the
environment

At Springer we firmly believe that an international science publisher has a special obligation to the environment, and our corporate policies consistently reflect this conviction.

We also expect our business partners – paper mills, printers, packaging manufacturers, etc. – to commit themselves to using materials and production processes that do not harm the environment. The paper in this book is made from low- or no-chlorine pulp and is acid free, in conformance with international standards for paper permanency.

 Springer

Lecture Notes in Computer Science

For information about Vols. 1–1107

please contact your bookseller or Springer-Verlag